The United States and
Inter-American Security,
1889-1960

J. Lloyd Mecham

The United States and Inter-American Security, 1889-1960

Published for the Institute
of Latin American Studies,
The University of Texas

AUSTIN · UNIVERSITY OF TEXAS PRESS

Other books by the author

Francisco de Ibarra and Nueva Vizcaya

(DUKE UNIVERSITY PRESS)

Church and State in Latin America

(UNIVERSITY OF NORTH CAROLINA PRESS)

Fifth printing 1967

Library of Congress Catalog Card No. 61-10426
Copyright © 1961 by the University of Texas Press
All Rights Reserved
Manufactured in the United States of America by
The University of Texas Printing Division

To my wife

MABEL OLIVE MECHAM

whose assistance, counsel, and inspiration are
inadequately measured by the content of this
volume.

Preface

When the San Francisco United Nations Conference drafted the Charter of the United Nations containing an entire chapter recognizing the validity of regional-security arrangements, there were in existence at that time only two such formal associations: the time-tested inter-American system and the Arab League, which antedated the Conference by but a few days. Since the adoption of the Charter several other regional-defense compacts have come into existence, all claiming status as regional arrangements under the nominal aegis of the United Nations. As a matter of fact these regional understandings, despite the fact that the United Nations presumably possesses the primary responsibility for the organization and preservation of world peace, are fully autonomous security systems.

This trend toward regionalism within the context of the United Nations Charter points up the necessity of our understanding more clearly the meaning and nature of this present-day feature of international-security organization. Accordingly there is here presented a comprehensive case study of regional organization for international security, using as a model the world's oldest, best-organized, and most effective of all existent regional arrangements: the Organization of American States. Following an introductory description of other regional-security systems, all aspects of Western Hemisphere security cooperation are examined: the historical origins and development of the inter-American system; the formalizing and perfecting of the security structure applicable both to inter-American disputes and to extracontinental aggression; and the system under test, not only by numerous inter-American disputes but also by two world wars, the Korean war, and the aggressive threats of international Communism.

The literature on Pan Americanism is voluminous, for the subject of inter-American cooperation has long struck the fancy of Anglo-American and Latin-American authors. Yet, hardly one of them has fulfilled the essential and primary purpose of presenting a realistic description of the inter-American security system. Almost without exception they have failed to grasp, or at least have refrained from describing, the inter-American system as it really is.

The Western Hemisphere security arrangement is, it is true, a regional system comprised of twenty-one sovereign, equal, American republics; but it is also, and more particularly, a security arrangement between the United States and the twenty Latin-American republics.

The association of one Great Power with twenty weak, and for the most part underdeveloped, states is the fact of paramount importance which distinguishes this particular regional arrangement.

I believe this to be the first work which frankly and realistically recognizes and describes the position of the United States in the Organization of American States. Legalistic equality is by no means fictional in the inter-American system, but it is unquestioned that the preponderant power, wealth, and influence of this country are reflected in the leadership it enjoys. The inter-American system exists because of United States membership. The fact that the Latin-American countries enjoy exceptional advantages through their formal association with the United States—an arrangement without parallel in the history of Great Power and small-states relations—is the cement of the alliance.

Given the true role of the United States in the inter-American system, it follows that the strength and effectiveness of that system are conditioned by the degree of solidarity that exists between this country and its Latin-American associates. For this reason I undertook an exhaustive inquiry into the problems of United States–Latin-American relationships which are threatening to undermine cooperation and understanding. Also, because the recent disturbing utterances and manifestations of anti-United States sentiment are indicative of a weakening of United States–Latin-American unity, they have been analyzed and remedies are suggested.

For generous financial assistance in making possible the publication of this volume the writer is obligated to the Institute of Latin American Studies of the University of Texas. I wish particularly to thank Dr. Eastin Nelson, acting director of the Institute, for his sympathetic interest in this project. Research assistance received from the Graduate School of the University of Texas is also gratefully acknowledged.

J. Lloyd Mecham

Austin, Texas

Table of Contents

threat in Guatemala, 436; The Caracas Conference, 440; The over-throw of Communism in Guatemala, 445; The issue before the UN and the OAS, 447; The aftermath in Guatemala, 451; Communist activities heightened, 453; The Cuban situation, 455; Conclusion, 462.

Charts and Tables

The United States and

Inter-American Security

1889-1960

I Regionalism and Regional Arrangements

No one in the Americas has given up hope for a world community of nations. We have merely thought the transition from nationalism to universalism could best be accomplished by strengthening first the regional agencies.

CARLOS DÁVILA, 1954

SINCE ANCIENT TIMES states within limited geographical areas have banded together to better attain commonly-desired objectives. The characteristics, purposes, and successes of such regional groupings have varied widely; but the validity of the principle that similar aims in international affairs may be more fully realized through joint action by a group of states comprising or having an interest in some geographical areas has fostered the idea of regionalism throughout the ages. It is very much alive today, for the present trend is toward, rather than away from, such groupings.

Within the last forty years, however, a new concept of international collective security based on the principle of universality of interest among all nations has found acceptance and practical application in the League of Nations and the United Nations. These world organizations for collective security sprang from the strong desire of states to find peace following costly global wars.

The universalists say that political, economic, and strategic interests cannot be divided into regions, but, like peace itself, are indivisible. Geographical association, they say, does not necessarily correspond to the actual interests of neighbors, for neighboring nations are not always logical and actual cooperators, whereas distant nations often are, since the seas no longer separate them. While reasonable universalists do not argue the impossible—that is, the abolition of regionalism— they do point out that regional association without the possibility of resort to strong universal control would hold grave danger of internal friction and little hope of security. A quite possible result of any

COLLECTIVE DEFENSE ARRANGEMENTS

NORTH ATLANTIC TREATY

1 United States
2 Canada
3 Iceland
4 Norway
5 United Kingdom
6 Netherlands
7 Denmark
8 Belgium
9 Luxembourg
10 Portugal
11 France
12 Italy
13 Greece
14 Turkey
15 Federal Republic
   of Germany

RIO TREATY

1 United States
16 Mexico
17 Cuba
18 Haiti
19 Dominican
   Republic
20 Honduras
21 Guatemala
22 El Salvador
23 Nicaragua
24 Costa Rica
25 Panama
26 Colombia
27 Venezuela
28 Ecuador
29 Peru
30 Brazil
31 Bolivia
32 Paraguay
33 Chile
34 Argentina
35 Uruguay

SOUTHEAST ASIA TREATY

1 United States
5 United Kingdom
11 France
36 New Zealand
37 Australia
38 Philippines
39 Thailand
40 Pakistan

CENTRAL TREATY ORGANIZATION

5 United Kingdom
40 Pakistan
41 Iran
14 Turkey

ARAB LEAGUE

42 Egypt
43 Iraq
44 Jordan
45 Lebanon
46 Libya
47 Morocco
48 Saudi Arabia
49 Syria
50 Tunis
51 Yemen
52 Sudan

WARSAW PACT

53 Soviet Union
54 Poland
55 Czechoslovakia
56 Bulgaria
57 Rumania
58 Hungary
59 East Germany
60 Albania

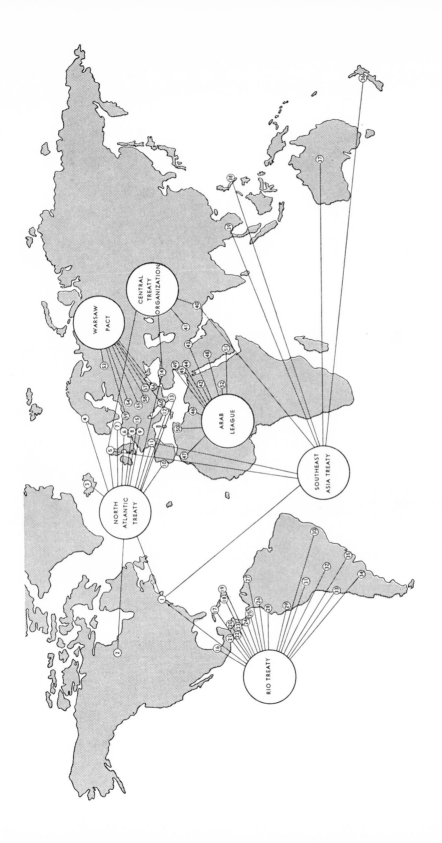

strong application of regionalism would be the setting up of large blocs of nations against one another, and even of continents and hemispheres one against the other.

Although the forces of nationalism are still significant, the modern world has come to realize that the national state is too small a political unit and the old-style balance of power too precarious a means to ensure security in the twentieth century. The creation of the recent two great experiments in world organization for collective security has by no means meant the disappearance of regional association of nations for security purposes. On the contrary regionalism flourished during the short life of the League of Nations, and, in the drafting of the United Nations Charter, the principle of universalism was compromised to the extent of providing for the accommodation of autonomous regional-security arrangements. The meaning of regionalism and the nature of regional-security arrangements compatible with UN principles and objectives are here discussed briefly as background for an extended consideration of the classic example of all regional arrangements: the inter-American system.

The meaning of regionalism. "Regionalism" as a concept of international collaboration and organization for security purposes has no precise and generally-accepted meaning. Neither individuals nor nations have agreed on a definition. In fact the committee on regional arrangements at the San Francisco United Nations Conference studiously avoided attempting a definition because of the obvious impossibility of reconciling divergent views. It was decided that since the situations to which the term "regional arrangement" might apply are so diverse, and since attempts to formulate a precise definition would be impossible, the wisest course would be to provide unlimited latitude for a generally-understood and accepted meaning of the term to develop through experience. As will be noted, the history of regional arrangements under the United Nations has proved the wisdom of this decision, for although regionalism assumed unexpected forms, a clearer understanding of the concept has developed.

For example, in defining a regional arrangement it would normally be expected that an essential element would be geographical contiguity of a group of states. In fact the Egyptian delegation at San Francisco proposed to limit the term "regional arrangement" to

organizations of a permanent nature, grouping in *a given geographical area,* several countries which, by reason of their proximity, community of interests or cultural, linguistic, historical, or spiritual affinities, make themselves jointly responsible for the peaceful settlement of any disputes which may arise between them and for the maintenance of peace and security in their region, as well as for the safeguarding of their interests and the development of their economic and cultural relations [Italics mine].[1]

The decision to reject this definition as too restrictive allowed for the development of a concept of regionalism as in NATO, in which the land area does not have to be adjacent. The Soviet government protested this extension of the meaning of regionalism, but to no avail. According to Kelsen it is not required that the parties to the regional agreement be geographical neighbors. It is essential only that the actions of the organization established by the regional arrangement be restricted to a certain area which is determined by the agreement.[2] This requisite has been met by our contemporary regional-security pacts.

A regional-security arrangement is generally regarded as a voluntary association of a group of sovereign states either within a certain area or having common interests in that area for a joint defense purpose. Cooperation must be based on consent rather than force, and this consent can be obtained only when there is coherence in the group.

What about the number and the status of the component elements constituting a regional arrangement? There must obviously be more than a single political unit, and to be genuinely "regional" there should be more than two states. Also, they must be independent. The consensus[3] seems to be that a regional arrangement is a voluntary association of sovereign states. This requisite would eliminate as genuine

---

[1] Leland H. Goodrich and Evard Hambro, *Charter of the United Nations: Commentary and Documents* (Boston, 1949), 310–311.

[2] Hans Kelsen, "Is the North Atlantic Treaty a Regional Arrangement?" *American Journal of International Law*, XLV, No. 1 (Jan. 1951), 163. See also E. N. van Kleffens, "Regionalism and Political Pacts," *ibid.*, XVIII (Oct. 1949), 669.

[3] On the general subject of regionalism see: Ward P. Allen, "Regional Arrangements and the United Nations," U.S. Dept. of State, *Bulletin*, XIV (June 2, 1946), 923–928; Edgar S. Furniss, Jr., "A Reexamination of Regional Arrangements," *Journal of International Affairs*, IX (May 1955); Ernst B. Haas and Allen S. Whiting, *Dynamics of International Relations* (New York, 1956), 491–533; Norman J. Padelford and George A. Lincoln, *International Politics* (New York, 1954), 609–646; Norman D. Palmer and Howard C. Perkins, *International Relations* (2d ed., Boston, 1957), 608–645; "Regional Organizations: Their Role in the World Community," *Columbia Journal of International Affairs*, III (Spring, 1949); Pitman B. Potter, "Universalism versus Regionalism in International Organization," *American Political Science Review*, XXXVII (Oct. 1943), 850–862; American Council on Public Affairs, *Regionalism and World Organization* (Washington, 1944).

regional arrangements the Warsaw Treaty Organization and the East European bloc within the Soviet "orbit." By no stretch of the imagination can the satellite states be regarded as sovereign and independent, and in reality the security action of this group is that of one state only.

It is held by many writers that a *real* regional arrangement cannot exist without a fairly elaborate organization. Also, that a regional "understanding" is quite different from a regional "arrangement," for the former may be entirely without machinery to implement common policies. The understanding suggests only a common attitude, whereas the arrangement is an integrated or concerted action which is consonant with "organization" or "orderly conditions." Although it is quite true that the real regional arrangement should provide fairly elaborate organization—and on this basis ordinary military defensive alliances would not qualify—who is to gainsay the protests of those military allies that theirs is a regional arrangement "consistent with the purposes and principles of the United Nations"?

With respect to objectives, what are the criteria of a regional-security arrangement? It is held that a regional arrangement must be multipurpose, that is, it may be primarily a military defensive alliance, but it must be more than that. It must provide for cooperation in other respects, as for example, that the partners in a regional-security arrangement seek common defense not only in a pooling of military resources but also in strengthening these resources through a program of economic and cultural cooperation. Although it may be highly advisable that associates in a regional-security system extend their cooperation to these non-political areas, it might also be argued that it is no less a regional arrangement if confined to the purely military aspects of defense cooperation. Thus, there seems to be no valid reason to disqualify as a regional arrangement an association of nations grouped for the sole and exclusive purpose of the military defense of a geographical area.

The term "security" allows for a wide range of procedures to enforce peace in the region and/or provide for its defense against external aggression. The degree and extent to which the pacts provide for these obligations determine whether the security system is "limited" or "inclusive," and whether it is weak or effective. For example, a group of nations concerned with the preservation of peace in a region may negotiate a series of treaties providing that disputes be submitted to the peaceful procedures of mediation, inquiry, conciliation, and arbitration. They also may enter into various agreements regulating their international conduct in matters relating to the preservation of peaceful relations in the area. This is a "limited" security arrangement since it does not provide for common defense against aggression from outside the bloc. It may be strong or weak, within its restricted area, depending on the nature of the instruments for peaceful settlement and how dedicated the members are in meeting their obligations.

On the other hand, a group of nations resident in, or having interests in, a geographical area, and threatened by outside aggression, combine for their common defense. This is primarily, even exclusively, a military defense alliance, with no provision for the amicable settlement of disputes among its members. It is also a "limited" regional-security arrangement, and it may be weak or strong, according to the nature of the mutual commitments. When a regional arrangement has as its objective not only the preservation of peace within a given region, but also common defense against attack from an external source, it becomes "inclusive," that is, a full-fledged regional-security system. Prior to 1936 the inter-American system was a limited security arrangement in that its peace procedures applied only to controversies among the American countries themselves. After 1936, when the procedure of consultation was applied to situations of extracontinental aggression, the inter-American system became an inclusive regional-security arrangement. Since NATO and other similar military alliances employ the phraseology of the Rio de Janeiro Inter-American Treaty of Reciprocal Assistance (1947) that an armed attack from *any* source against one or more of the parties to the treaty shall be considered an attack against them all, these are all inclusive security arrangements.

In sum, regional arrangements may apply to as few as two or three sovereign states, or as many as a score or more; they do not have to include all the states within the area immediately affected, for a state may be excluded for political or ideological reasons, or it may choose to stay out; states may be geographically contiguous in a corner of a continent, or they may extend across broad oceans from the western Atlantic to the eastern Mediterranean; and the arrangements may be integrated and implemented by an elaborate organization or by a very simple one. As for the nature and degree of collaboration for security objectives, regional arrangements range from limited commitments for applying peaceful procedures within the area, or for military defense alone, to comprehensive pledges of collaboration in the political, military, economic, social, and cultural spheres. The meaning of regionalism will be further clarified by the following discussion of regional arrangements before and after World War II.

Regional arrangements: pre-World War II. The history of the Western world during the century preceding World War I presented several possible examples of regional-security arrangements. These included, in Europe, the Holy Alliance, which was a famous mutual-aid pact, and the Germanic Confederation of thirty-eight Central European states and free cities, established by the Congress of Vienna in 1815. Although, prior to 1914, regional policies were expressed by customs unions and other systems of economic preference, and these in some instances preceded the coming of political unity, they are not listed here, for they were not security arrangements. In the Western Hemisphere the great example of regionalism was the Pan American movement. Starting in 1826, the cooperative association of American republics had become by 1914 an encouraging manifestation of inter-American solidarity. Although up to that time it was only a limited regional arrangement, in that it did not formally provide for collective security, it did afford numerous examples during World War I of cooperation for common defense. However, despite these and other possible examples of security regionalism, it is a mere statement of fact that, when the League of Nations Covenant was drafted, effective regional arrangements were nonexistent, and so the principle had few advocates at the Paris Conference.

It is significant that the original draft of the Covenant of the League of Nations contained no reference whatever to the subject of regional arrangements. It is known that Woodrow Wilson wanted the League to supersede and be incompatible with any form of partial alliance or union.[4] Yet President Wilson was forced to do the most damage to this idea by consenting to insert Article 21 in the Covenant to safeguard the Monroe Doctrine.

Article 21 provided that: "Nothing in this Covenant shall be deemed to affect the validity of international engagements, such as treaties of arbitration or regional understandings like the Monroe Doctrine, for securing the maintenance of peace." Thus, wide latitude was provided for establishing almost any type of regional arrangement, although the phrase "regional understanding" was coined merely in an effort to define the Monroe Doctrine. Most certainly it did not re-

[4] E. Howard Ellis, *Origin, Structure, and Working of the League of Nations* (London, 1928), 157–158.

sult from the belief that the principle of universalism *must* be tempered with regionalism. This, however, is exactly what took place.

Within Europe, the first attempt to create a regional-security system supplementary to the League of Nations was the Draft Treaty of Mutual Assistance (1922/23). This draft treaty, which reflected the influence of the regional idea in providing for the possibility of defensive agreements in addition to League obligations, was defeated largely because the British Labour government feared that an agreement between two states to take precautions against a third state might easily degenerate into little more than a military alliance of the old style. Prime Minister MacDonald condemned the proposed defense blocs as being contrary to the collective principles of the League.

With a change of government in 1924, Great Britain reversed its stand and became a leader of those who advocated the regional approach. First, Sir Austen Chamberlain, foreign secretary in Baldwin's Conservative government, rejected the Geneva Protocol for the Pacific Settlement of International Disputes (1924), which in its fundamental bases represented a return to the theory of general and universal security and the rejection of the principle of special regional pacts. Then, on March 12, 1925, the Baldwin government submitted the Balfour Memorandum to the League Council, advocating a security system based upon regional arrangements. The memorandum frankly declared that

the best solution would be to supplement the Covenant, with the cooperation of the League, by making special arrangements in order to meet special needs. That these arrangements should be purely defensive in character, that they should be framed in the spirit of the Covenant, working in close harmony with the League and under its guidance, is manifest.[5]

Following an extended period of negotiation, the Locarno Pact was signed on October 16, 1925. The pact, signed by Germany, Belgium, France, Great Britain, and Italy, provided for mutual guarantees of the frontiers of Western Germany and perpetual demilitarization of the Rhineland. It was the embodiment of the Baldwin government's formula for peace and security through regional arrangements. And it was the direct result of the unwillingness of two great Western powers to take a positive stand for international security on a universal basis. Thus, although the League had been established to guarantee collec-

[5] H. Arthur Steiner, *Principles and Problems of International Relations* (New York, 1940), 530–533; League of Nations, *Ten Years of Cooperation* (Secretariat of the League of Nations, 1930), 58–63, 75–76.

tive security, the Locarno Pact replaced universal responsibility with regional responsibility.

Following the Locarno Pact, other regional agreements were entered into. First, a system of bilateral mutual-assistance treaties, negotiated shortly after World War I, among Czechoslovakia, Rumania, and Yugoslavia "gradually developed into a broader political organization, and, after 1933, came to approximate a close diplomatic confederation with definite organizational structure."[6] This was the Little Entente, one of the outstanding examples of regionalism following World War I. The Organic Pact of February 16, 1933, provided for a complete unification of their general policies and the establishment of an organization by which this common policy should be directed. It was composed of a permanent secretariat at Geneva, and an economic council. Although the attempt at economic cooperation was not successful, politically the Little Entente showed a great deal of international cooperation for a number of years, and played a significant role in helping to stabilize conditions in Central Europe. It collapsed when Hitler went on the march.

There was also the Balkan Entente (Yugoslavia, Rumania, Greece, and Turkey), created by the pact of 1934, which was an effort at regional cooperation to maintain the security *status quo* in the Balkan area. This union had been preceded by conferences between representatives of these four states, which showed significant tendencies toward collaboration and political understanding as bases for the formation of a regional system. The Balkan Pact provided for a permanent council for discussing common problems. Also, in 1934, Latvia, Lithuania, and Estonia placed their hopes for peace and security in a Baltic Pact. This regional cooperation was designed to enable these countries to meet the troubled situation in Europe created by the rise of Hitler. The three countries agreed that their foreign policies were matters of common concern and therefore their foreign ministers should meet together twice a year.

These, and other regional arrangements attempted within Europe during the interwar period, failed because they required a stable continental community. Moreover, these smaller associations could not be entirely independent of the balance-of-power struggle among the Great Powers. They collapsed at the first shock of conflict. It was a different story in the Western Hemisphere, for after World War I, the inter-American system expanded steadily both in purpose and in

[6] Allen, 923.

organization until, on the eve of World War II, it had achieved the status of being the outstanding example of regional arrangement. The shock of the war, instead of weakening the security aspects, stimulated far-reaching changes in strengthening them, so that when the San Francisco United Nations Conference convened from April to June of 1945, the inter-American system was without doubt the world's best example of international regionalism in its most advanced form.

Regionalism under the United Nations. In contrast to the Covenant of the League of Nations, regional arrangements were given positive and detailed endorsement in the Charter of the United Nations. Although there seemed to be little dissent at San Francisco concerning the need for regional-security agreements, there was great disagreement concerning the proper relation between such compacts and the new world organization. The question at issue was the nature and extent of autonomy that could be safely accorded regional arrangements within the context of a universal-security system. The stipulation in the Dumbarton Oaks Proposals that a regional organization could not take enforcement action without being expressly authorized to do so by the Security Council of the United Nations aroused strong objection, particularly among the Latin Americans. They envisaged a single permanent member of the Security Council blocking regional-security action with its veto. They came to San Francisco, therefore, determined to defend the autonomy of the inter-American system.

Fortunately, the Latin Americans were not without support, for there were other countries with special interests that also favored varying degrees of autonomy for regional or limited arrangements within the general framework of the United Nations. These were: the Arab states, which desired that the status of the newly-created Arab League be preserved; the U.S.S.R., which wished to except from any restrictive control under the Charter the system of bilateral mutual-assistance pacts; France, whose concern over possible renewal of German aggression led her to seek freedom of action against former enemy states without the necessity of awaiting prior action by the Security Council; and the small states, which were generally uneasy over the power granted the Security Council in the light of the Yalta voting formula.[7]

The critical problem of finding a formula that would recognize the paramount authority of the United Nations in all enforcement action, and yet permit regional action independently in case of undue delay or ineffectiveness, precipitated a stalemate which for a time

[7] *Ibid.*, 925.

threatened the entire efforts of the Conference. The impasse was broken by a compromise formula which stated that the right of self-defense is inherent in every nation-state, individually or collectively. Thus, in the event of an attack against any one of a group of countries associated for mutual assistance these states could take concerted defensive action. This does not deny to the Security Council the right to take any action it deems necessary to maintain international peace and security. This formula became the substance of Article 51 of the Charter of the United Nations, and, it was hoped, protected the autonomy of regional arrangements without destroying the authority of the Security Council to intervene. With the integration of regional-security arrangements into the United Nations accounted for, it is now in order to indicate briefly the nature, extent, and significance of the Charter provisions on this subject.

The United Nations Charter devotes an entire chapter (Chap. VIII, Art. 52–54) to the subject "Regional Arrangements." Articles 33 and 51 also relate to the matter. In general, nothing in the Charter

precludes the existence of regional arrangements or agencies for dealing with such matters relating to the maintenance of international peace and security as are appropriate for regional action, provided that such arrangements or agencies and their activities are consistent with the purposes and principles of the United Nations [Art. 52, par. 1].

The Charter imposes upon the members of regional arrangements or agencies the obligation to "make every effort to achieve pacific settlement of local disputes" before referring them to the Security Council (Art. 52, par. 2). This is reinforced by additional similar injunctions in the Charter: "The parties to any dispute, the continuance of which is likely to endanger the maintenance of international peace and security, shall first of all seek a solution" by peaceful means of their own choice including "resort to regional agencies or arrangements" (Art. 33, par. 1); the Security Council is obligated to "encourage the development of pacific settlement of local disputes through such regional arrangements or by such regional agencies either on the initiative of the states concerned or by reference from the Security Council" (Art. 52, par. 3); and "the Security Council shall, when it deems it necessary, call upon the parties to settle their dispute" by peaceful means of their own choice, including regional arrangements (Art. 33, par. 2).

In case of threats to, or breaches of, the peace or acts of aggression, the Security Council is directed to utilize regional arrangements or agencies for carrying out enforcement measures. But no enforcement action shall be taken under regional arrangements or by regional agencies without the authorization of the Security Council (Art. 53, par. 1). There is, however, an important exception to this rule: if the breach of the peace or act of aggression takes the form of "an armed attack," Article 51 provides that nothing in the Charter "shall impair the inherent right of individual or collective self-defense . . . until the Security Council has taken the measures necessary to maintain international peace and security."

To preserve the supremacy of the United Nations' system of collective security, the Charter makes it clear that while the regional arrangement may be expected to be the normal medium for the settlement of local disputes, and while Security Council authorization is not always necessary for enforcement action, the rights of the Security Council to take action at any time regarding any dispute remain unimpaired. Also, the Security Council must "be kept fully informed of activities undertaken or in contemplation under regional arrangements or by regional agencies for the maintenance of international peace and security" (Art. 54). In sum, the Security Council retains the right to step in at any stage of a dispute to determine whether the regional approach is desirable, or to recommend other appropriate procedures or methods of adjustment (Art. 36).

Despite these foregoing "precautionary provisions" in support of the principle of universalism, the effect of Article 51 has been to open the way for a proliferation of regional arrangements outside the effective control of the United Nations. The failure of the Charter to define "regional arrangements or agencies" and the looseness of the term itself have enabled nations to make, with great facility, regional arrangements "little more than a series of treaty structures creating bilaterally-assumed obligations within a context limited as to area or as to function."[8] Most of these countries have been actuated by a feeling of insecurity in the face of aggressive Soviet threats and acts, and the concurrent inability of the United Nations to cope with the menace effectively. Thus, because of the impasse in the Security Council resulting from the Great

---

[8] Furniss, 213. There is no provision for the formal recognition of regional arrangements by the United Nations. Nor has either the Security Council or the General Assembly expressly decided that a given regional arrangement or agency did or did not fulfill the requirements stated in Article 52 (par. 1). Neither of these two organs has on any occasion taken a decision intended to define the scope of the relevant provisions on regional arrangements in the Charter.

Powers veto and the impotence of the General Assembly as an instrument for maintaining and enforcing peace, the major non-Communist countries have been forced to rely more and more upon regional-security arrangements.

Although there is justifiable reason for these regional-security media as alternatives to ineffective universal collective security, the trend has placed the United Nations "in a position of inferiority, so that now the links between the regional arrangements and the world organization exist at the practical pleasure of the former."[9] Moreover, there is danger that these arrangements will degenerate into military alliances against certain nations which will retaliate in kind. Thus the United Nations is certainly not going to be strengthened by the multiplication of these regional-security arrangements, and it cannot reach maximum effectiveness until they decline in importance and their operation is subordinate to the responsible organs of the world organization. But in the meantime, and in the foreseeable future, regional-security arrangements, real and pseudo, all claiming compatibility with the principles and objectives of the United Nations, will attempt to preside over the peace of the regions—and of the world. We turn now to a brief consideration of the leading contemporary security arrangements outside the Western Hemisphere.

Western European Union. As Eastern Europe succumbed to the Red Plague, Western Europe began the task of uniting for the security that the Security Council of the United Nations could not provide. Winston Churchill, though he had been relieved of his responsibilities as prime minister by the British electorate and thus could not speak officially for His Majesty's government, sounded the keynote of unity in September 1946. Speaking at Zurich he warned "Under and within that world concept [United Nations] we must recreate the European family in a regional structure, called, it may be, the United States of Europe, and the first practical step would be to form a Council of Europe."[10]

Belgium, the Netherlands, and Luxembourg made the first move toward a formal union of Western Europe when they established the Benelux tariff union late in 1947. The impetus behind this regional arrangement was primarily the desire to create an economic unit sufficiently large, in terms of its foreign trade, to compete successfully in the postwar world market. Unity for economic collaboration was soon followed by an arrangement for security cooperation. Since it was becoming quite evident that the United Nations was unable to deter possible Russian aggression, on January 22, 1948, British Foreign Minister Ernest Bevin, in an address to the House of Commons, called for a consolidation of Western Europe. In detailing his plan he said, "All the steps I have mentioned are in keeping with the Charter of the United Nations. . . . They are all designed upon a regional basis to fit in with the Charter."[11] Following this initiative, the Brussels Pact, establishing the Western Union, was signed on March 17, 1948, by France, Belgium, Luxembourg, the Netherlands, and the United Kingdom to achieve closer collaboration in economic, social, and cultural matters, and of course, for collective self-defense. The heart of the Brussels Pact was found in Article IV, which provided: "If any of the High Contracting Parties should be the object of an armed attack in Europe, the other High Contracting Parties will, in accordance with the provisions of Article 51 of the Charter of the United Nations, afford the party so attacked all military and other aid and assistance in their power."[12]

The major significance of the Western Union lay in the fact that its establishment reflected official recognition of the need for collective self-defense and the consolidation of Western Europe. Its primary function was to provide permanent consultative machinery for joint defense against armed aggression in Europe. The organizational framework of the pact included: a consultation council, the supreme authority of the Western Union organization, composed of the foreign ministers of the five member nations; a permanent commission to act on behalf of the council between sessions as a coordinating and consultation organ; a secretariat to assist both the consultative council and the permanent commission; and several subordinate committees, boards, and subcommittees of ministers or experts on military, economic, social, and cultural questions.

Since the Brussels Pact powers did not have the strength by themselves to defend Western Europe, the Western Union was virtually absorbed by the North Atlantic Treaty Organization, which was pursuing generally the same purposes, but on a broader basis. Thus along with the activities of the Supreme Headquarters Allied Powers, Europe (SHAPE), the military functions of the Western Union were absorbed

11 *Ibid.*, 126.
12 U.S. Dept. of State, *Bulletin*, XVIII (May 9, 1948), 601. For the Western European Union, see M. Margaret Ball, *NATO and the European Union Movement* (London, 1959), 356–401.

by the North Atlantic Treaty Organization (NATO). Also because the Organization for European Economic Cooperation (OEEC), which included all of the Brussels Pact powers, was formed only one month after the signature of the Brussels Pact, economic cooperation never became a major concern of the Western Union. Finally, the social and cultural activities of the organization were transferred to the Council of Europe.

Just when the Brussels treaty organization seemed to be on the verge of extinction, it was given a new lease on life. In October 1954 measures were taken to devise an alternative for the European Defense Community (EDC) treaty, which provided for, among other things, German rearmament and which had been killed by the French National Assembly. France had refused to ratify EDC because the United Kingdom had declined to participate, and without British participation the French feared a German resurgence once West Germany was rearmed. To meet both the German government's desire for rearmament and the French demand for guarantees against a revival of German militarism, a Western European Union (WEU) treaty was negotiated which provided that: West Germany and Italy should be invited to join the Brussels Pact; troops and armaments ceilings were fixed for all members, with a special prohibition on certain types of weapons to Germany; an Armaments Control Agency was to inspect and report on the levels of troops and armaments maintained by the members; and Great Britain was pledged to maintain military forces on the Continent. The contributions of each WEU member in armaments and in men were to be determined by special agreements. Militarily, WEU became the continental European sector of NATO, and in operational matters was subject to NATO orders. Numerous references have already been made to the North Atlantic Treaty Organization. We turn now to an examination of this, the most important of all the regional alliances contracted since 1945.

NATO. As the pressure of Russian-inspired world Communism continued to grow, the Western nations, despairing of collective security under the auspices of the United Nations, sought still further safeguards among themselves. This time there was no attempt to disguise the fear of Soviet expansion under the cloak of a possible new threat by Germany. In the United States the way was prepared for the negotiation of the North Atlantic Treaty[13] when the Senate adopted,

---

[13] For the North Atlantic Treaty and NATO, see Ball, *op. cit., passim*; U.S. Dept. of State, *NATO, North Atlantic Treaty Organization*, General Foreign Policy Ser., No. 75 (Aug. 1952).

on June 11, 1948, Senator Arthur Vandenberg's resolution favoring the development of regional and other collective arrangements for individual and collective self-defense. The resolution called for the "association of the United States, by constitutional process, with such regional and other collective arrangements as are based on continuous and effective self-help and mutual aid, and as affect its national security." The passage of this resolution (sixty-four to four) was a formal announcement by the United States that it was relinquishing its traditional isolation policy and adopting a collective-security policy. It is an interesting fact that, within a few years after the Vandenberg resolution was passed, the United States became the key member, or "switching center," for several of the regional arrangements of the free world.

In the summer of 1948 conversations were initiated in Washington between the United States, Canada, and the Western Union Treaty signatories (Belgium, France, Luxembourg, the Netherlands, and the United Kingdom) on a treaty of mutual assistance for the North Atlantic area within the framework of Article 51 of the United Nations Charter. At the time of the North Atlantic Treaty's signature, on April 4, 1949, these seven powers were joined by Denmark, Iceland, Italy, Norway, and Portugal. To the original membership of twelve countries, three more—Greece, Turkey, and West Germany—were added later.

Following the model set by the Inter-American Treaty of Reciprocal Assistance (Rio de Janeiro, 1947), the North Atlantic pact contains an article which reconciles it with United Nations obligations by referring to the fact that in cases of armed attack against one or more of the parties to the pact in Europe or North America, the right to exercise individual or collective self-defense is recognized by Article 51 of the Charter. Any such attack and all measures taken as a result thereof shall immediately be reported to the Security Council. There are several more express references to the United Nations Charter, but none to the regional-arrangements clause. It apparently was deemed preferable to place the pact exclusively under Article 51, under which more freedom of action was allowed, and thus avoid misunderstandings that might arise if it were planned as a regional arrangement.[14]

Yet inevitably the new alliance came to be regarded as a regional agreement, and its members have not denied that it was so intended. The Soviet Union saw the North Atlantic pact as such, but denied its

[14] Clyde Eagleton, "The North Atlantic Defense Pact," *Columbia Journal of International Affairs*, III (Spring, 1949), 29–30.

validity as being truly regional in a geographical sense, and as being directed against Russia, a fellow member of the United Nations. To the Soviet Union one of the most irritating features of the pact was the fact that her neighbor, Norway, had the boldness to become a signatory. Following an unsuccessful attempt by Norway, Sweden, and Denmark to form a Scandinavian regional arrangement, the Soviet government addressed a note to Oslo asking the Norwegian government to express its attitude concerning the proposed North Atlantic pact. In its reply, Norway declared that, in view of the fact that the United Nations had not become strong enough to maintain peace and security,

it is necessary to seek increased security through regional cooperation in the field of defense. Regional pacts of this kind are expressly provided for in the United Nations Charter and are, in the opinion of the Norwegian government, in accordance with the aims of the Charter as far as the prevention of aggression is concerned.[15]

Although Norway assured the Soviet Union that she would never agree to provide bases for the military forces of other powers so long as Norway was not attacked, the Kremlin was not satisfied. In its reply, Moscow summarized its opinion of the proposed Atlantic pact. It contended that the Atlantic Union was not aimed at uniting all peaceful states but was "directed toward setting one group of countries against other states," and that it was in reality "being created outside of and in circumvention of the United Nations to serve the interests and aggressive policy of certain great powers."[16] The Soviet objections did not deter Norway from signing, for she regarded the alliance as purely defensive in character since the pact required an overt act by an outside nation to bring its potential force into operation.

The North Atlantic Treaty Organization (NATO) was established in November 1949, in accordance with provisions of the North Atlantic Treaty, which had become effective in August 1949. No attempt was made to set up in advance an elaborate organizational structure. Article 9 merely provided for the establishment of a council to implement the treaty, and left it to the council to set up whatever machinery might be necessary. For this reason the structure has gone through several stages of organization, and is constantly being changed in response to new international developments. As of recent date the basic structure was as follows:

1. North Atlantic Council. The apex of the somewhat complicated organization for the exercise of NATO civil and military functions is the council,

[15] *New York Times*, Feb. 2, 1949.   [16] *Ibid.*, Feb. 6, 1949.

which may consist of either ministers or permanent representatives of the member states who are at ambassadorial level. When the council meets at the ministerial level, normally twice a year, the members may be foreign ministers, defense ministers, or finance ministers, depending on the nature of the problems to be discussed at any particular meeting. When the ministers are not meeting in council, that body, consisting of the permanent representatives, meets regularly throughout the year in Paris. The chairmanship of the council is vested in the secretary-general of NATO. The decisions of the council are by unanimous consent. The individual members can register the positions of their governments on various subjects and in this way reach agreement, but the council and its dependent bodies have no power to take decisions binding on governments. NATO is not a supergovernment or supranational body having powers to dictate to the participating states.

2. Military Organization. On the military side of NATO, under the council is the Military Committee, which supervises the work of the military organization. This committee consists of the chiefs of staff of all member states except Iceland, which is represented by a civilian since it has no army. As it is not possible for the chiefs of staff to be always available, the Military Representatives of the Chiefs of Staff, a committee at deputy level, meets in Washington in permanent session. Decisions of the Military Committee are implemented by a key unit of the whole system, the Standing Group, also located in Washington, and consisting of the chiefs of staff, or their representatives, of Britain, France, and the United States. The Standing Group coordinates military planning, actually directs the command structure, and supervises agencies dealing with aspects of defense activity. Liaison between the Standing Group in Washington and the North Atlantic Council in Paris is maintained through the Standing Group Representative.

The major military commands under NATO are subordinate to the Standing Group. These are: Supreme Allied Commander Europe (SACEUR), heading the Supreme Headquarters Allied Powers, Europe (SHAPE) in Paris; Supreme Allied Commander Atlantic (SACLANT), with headquarters at Norfolk, Virginia; the Channel Committee and Channel Command (CHANCOM) in London and Portsmouth; and the Canada–United States Regional Planning group in Washington.

The European commands set up under SHAPE are: Commander-in-Chief Allied Forces Northern Europe, with headquarters at Oslo, Norway; Commander-in-Chief Allied Forces Central Europe, with headquarters at Fontainebleau, France; Commander-in-Chief Allied Forces Southern Europe, with headquarters at Naples, Italy, and Commander-in-Chief Allied Forces Mediterranean, with headquarters at Malta. Forces are assigned only to SHAPE in time of peace. There are three types of forces in the NATO membership: those assigned to NATO, those marked for assignment in time of emergency, and the regular national forces.

The Atlantic Command has set up two subcommands: Commander-in-Chief Western Atlantic Area, with headquarters at Norfolk, Virginia, and Commander-in-Chief Eastern Atlantic Area, with headquarters at Northwood, United Kingdom. Northwood is also the headquarters for the Air Commander-in-Chief Eastern Atlantic Area. The Atlantic Command has no assigned forces, but eight nations (Canada, Denmark, France, Netherlands, Norway, Portugal, the United Kingdom, and the United States) have marked for assignment forces to be used in time of war.

3. Civil Organization. On the same level as the Military Committee, and also responsible to the North Atlantic Council, are other organs which may be classified as civil. From a considerable number of such committees which have been set up by the council, an illustrative selection includes the following: Defense Production Committee, Food and Agriculture Planning Committee, Manpower Planning Committee, Coal and Steel Planning Committee, Science Committee, and Committee on Information and Cultural Relations.

4. Permanent Secretariat. The work of the secretariat, with headquarters in Paris, is divided into the following three divisions: Political Affairs, Economics and Finance, and Logistics.

In recent years greater attention has been given to ways and means to improve and extend NATO cooperation in nonmilitary fields. In consideration of the fact that the Soviet threat had become, by 1956, at least as much political and economic as military, members of NATO began to advocate the desirability of expanding their cooperation in the social and economic areas. John Foster Dulles contributed the idea that the free world should give more emphasis to cooperation *for* something rather than *against* something. The time had come, he said, to consider whether NATO did not "need to be further developed if it is adequately to serve the needs of this and coming generations."[17] As a result of this initiative the NATO council made a study of the matter but, while agreeing in principle, was distracted from undertaking any radical changes in the economic, social, or cultural activities of NATO by serious new divergences of policy within its membership.

Recent events have demonstrated that it is more difficult by far to reconcile conflicting economic interests than those confined strictly to military security. This is not to deny, however, that NATO has developed the outlines of a true multipurpose regional arrangement, for although the commitments and machinery for military defense are dominant, there are various organs which constitute the machinery

[17] U.S. Dept. of State, *Bulletin,* XXXIV (April 30, 1956), 710; (May 21, 1956), 836–837; Ball, 49.

through which the members may coordinate their political, economic, and military policies for the purpose of developing their individual and collective potential and of "promoting conditions of stability and well-being." NATO was the model for SEATO, a defensive alliance of free states in Southeast Asia.

SEATO. The Southeast Asia Collective Defense Treaty, also known as the Manila Pact, was signed at Manila on September 8, 1954, by the representatives of Australia, France, New Zealand, Pakistan, the Philippines, Thailand, the United Kingdom, and the United States. The treaty came into force on February 19, 1955, and four days later the Council of Ministers met in Bangkok to create the framework of the Southeast Asia Treaty Organization (SEATO).[18]

In the Manila Pact, the eight signatory governments, alarmed by the developing Communist threat, agreed to maintain and develop their individual and collective capacities to resist armed aggression and subversion directed from without. They also stressed their intention to build up better understanding between their peoples and to promote economic and social progress. The signatory governments agreed that, in the event of aggression against any of the parties in the "treaty area," each would take action to meet the common danger *in accordance with its own constitutional processes.* This treaty makes no reference, as does the North Atlantic Treaty, to the fact that exercising the right of self-defense is recognized by Article 51 of the UN Charter, nor is there any reference to "regional arrangements." The pact makes provisions for consultation between the signatory governments in the event of a threat to any member state. Since the eight countries are all members of the United Nations, the treaty declares that it does not in any way "affect the rights and obligations of any of the Parties under the Charter of the United Nations or the responsibilities of the United Nations for the maintenance of international peace and security."

In the "self-help and mutual-aid" articles of the treaty, the members of SEATO pledged themselves to take steps individually to develop their capacity to meet an armed attack and to help one another to do so, and to counter attempts at subversion. They also undertook to strengthen their free institutions and to cooperate with one another for the economic progress and social well-being of their peoples.

[18] U.S. Dept. of State, *SEATO, Southeast Asia Treaty Organization*, Far Eastern Ser., No. 72 (March 1956); U.S. Dept. of State, *Bulletin*, "Report on SEATO, 1958–1959," XL (April 27, 1959), 605–614.

Like NATO, SEATO has developed a quite elaborate organization. Its structure is as follows:

1. The Council of Ministers. The over-all controlling body of SEATO is the council, consisting of ministerial representatives from member countries who meet at least once a year to make policy decisions for the organization, to state general objectives, and to assess progress toward those objectives. There have been seven meetings of the Council of Ministers: Bangkok (1955); Karachi (1956); Canberra (1957); Manila (1958); Wellington (New Zealand) (1959); Washington (1960); and Bangkok (1961).

   The Council Representatives, consisting of the heads of the diplomatic missions of member countries, meets at SEATO headquarters in Bangkok to maintain continuing consultation on matters relating to the treaty and to supervise the work of the organization.

2. Military Organization. The military activities of the organization are directed by the Military Advisers, a group consisting of one senior military representative of each member country. They meet normally twice a year. Under their direction is the Military Planning Office in Bangkok, which carries on the work of developing detailed defensive plans. An important part of the Military Advisers' work is to ensure that the armed forces of the member countries learn to work together. With this in mind, combined military and naval exercises have been held in accord with annual training schedules. Considerable progress has been made in training and coordinating the armed forces of the member nations. Through mutual assistance in training and by providing equipment it has been possible for member countries to build up far more effective forces than they would individually have been able to do. Unlike NATO, SEATO has no assigned troops and no unified command.

3. Civil Organization. The growing scope and usefulness of the civil side of the organization is reflected by the SEATO bodies working in that area. The Council Representatives direct the nonmilitary work of the organization when the council is not in session. The organization has three civil-expert committees: the Committee of Economic Experts, the Committee of Security Experts, and the Committee on Information, Cultural, Educational and Labor Activities. Economic assistance to SEATO countries is given largely on a bilateral basis. Certain projects have, however, justified collective study and action. It is the function of the Committee of Economic Experts to study economic problems of certain areas of the Asian member countries and try to find suitable remedies. It is the function of the Committee of Security Experts to deal with the problem of Communist subversion in the area. Although the responsibility for action in countering Communist subversion rests primarily with the member governments, this committee has supplied valuable guidance in countering

subversion in their territories. The activities of the Committee on Information, Cultural, Educational and Labor Activities are reflected by the development and extension of cultural programs and public-information activities. While not neglecting the military aspects of a collective defense system, it is realized that a prime objective of SEATO must be to improve the social and economic lot of the peoples of the member nations and to strengthen the internal structure of the respective countries.

Although not the equal of NATO in complexity of organization and in firm commitment, SEATO is nevertheless a regional arrangement in the modern connotation of the term. It has been held that "the evolution of a regional community in the case of SEATO is all but made impossible by the fact that only three of the members are 'indigenous' to the area, and that most Asian states oppose the Pact."[19] Nonetheless, born in the determination of its members to preserve their freedom and their right to choose their independent path into the future, the free and equal partnership of SEATO has created a bond between the nations of East and West, with widely-separated peoples of different races, cultures, and religions.

The Baghdad Pact and CENTO. The vulnerability of the Middle East to Soviet aggression led to British and United States efforts to organize the area and strengthen it as a barrier against Communism. These efforts finally culminated in 1955 in the negotiation of the Baghdad Pact, but initially there was a pact of mutual defense signed on February 24, 1955, between Turkey and Iraq. By November they had been joined in a multipartite alliance by Great Britain, Pakistan, and Iran, thus forming a "northern tier" defense bulwark against the U.S.S.R.

The general purpose of the Baghdad Pact was declared to be the promotion of the peace and prosperity of its members. It sought the peaceful economic development of the region through cooperative efforts. The main clause of the pact contains the familiar declaration that, consistent with Article 51 of the United Nations Charter, the high contracting parties will "cooperate" for their security and defense. Such measures as they may agree to take to make their cooperation effective will become the subject of special agreements with each other. The pact contains no firm obligation and is little more than a mutual agreement to consult. A Permanent Council of Representatives was set up to function within the framework of the purposes of the pact. The headquarters, under a secretary-general, was transferred from Baghdad

---

[19] Ernst B. Haas, *Regional Integration and National Policy*, International Conciliation, No. 513 (May 1957), 411.

to Ankara in October 1958. As in SEATO, there are committees of experts in economic, military, and antisubversive fields, but their existence has not led to the growth of centrally-directed policies in these matters. Again like SEATO, there has been a shift of emphasis toward economic development.[20]

Iraq ceased to participate in the activities of the pact after the revolution in July 1958 and formally withdrew on March 24, 1959. The United States, though not a full member, has permanent military liaison with the organization and is represented on certain of its committees. It has pledged its support in the event of Soviet aggression. With the withdrawal of Iraq an important link in the northern tier defense system was lost, and the alliance lost most of its meaning as a regional-security arrangement. One of the obstacles which the Baghdad arrangement was unable to surmount was the Arab League, which had opposed Arab alliances with the West. The Baghdad Pact's successor is the Central Treaty Organization, or CENTO.

The Arab League. Another example of regionalism in Asia is the Arab League, which in several respects stands in marked contrast to the Southeast Asia and Baghdad regional arrangements. In fact it is one of our clearest and most valid examples of regional organization, albeit it has been notable for its impotence.

The Arab League[21] was created by the Pact of the Arab League, signed at Cairo on March 22, 1945, by the delegates of Egypt, Iraq, Lebanon, Saudi Arabia, Syria, Transjordan, and Yemen. This was the culmination of a movement of long standing, stemming from an Arab cultural revival which later acquired an increasingly-political emphasis. After World War I it was British policy to build up an Arab empire, but the project failed because of many divisive factors among the Arabs themselves and among the Western powers. As a result, the Arab world, instead of becoming a united country, was fragmented. During World War II the British once more supported unification, but again the project failed because of bitter divisions among the Arabs. Failing union, they finally decided on a loose association, based on a pact signed only a month before the San Francisco United Nations Conference. Thus, the Arab League antedated, if only by a few

---

[20] *Ibid.*

[21] For the Arab League, see B. Y. Boutros-Chali, *The Arab League, 1945–1955,* International Conciliation, No. 498 (May 1954); T. R. Little, "The Arab League: A Reassessment," *Middle East Journal,* X, No. 2 (Spring, 1956); Halford L. Hoskins, *The Middle East: Problem Area in World Politics* (New York, 1954), Chap. 8; Majid Khadduri, "The Arab League as a Regional Arrangement," *American Journal of International Law* (Oct. 1946), 756–777.

days, the United Nations Charter and its provision for regional arrangements.

From its inception, the league has met the requisite of a regional-security arrangement both as to purpose and functions as well as to structure. Its purposes are, on the one hand, to strengthen relations between member states and coordinate their policies to safeguard their independence and sovereignty—i.e., security—and, on the other hand, to promote cooperation of the member states in economic, cultural, and social matters. In the security sphere the pact provides for procedures of peaceful settlement and collective defense. Recourse to force for the settlement of disputes between members is not allowed, and the council assumes the mediatory role. In the event of aggression or threat of aggression by a state against a member state, the aggrieved party may request a meeting of the council, which shall by unanimous vote determine the necessary measures to repel the aggression. In 1950 the Arab states adopted the Collective Security Pact, which reinforced the security features of the original league pact. It provides for an automatic collective-security system, that is to say, in case of aggression the member states will come to the aid of the victim and take all available measures, including the use of armed force, to repel the aggression. In sum, the league's powers in security matters are severely limited, for the decisions of the council are not binding unless unanimous, and the league cannot enforce decisions which involve "the independence, sovereignty, or territorial integrity" of a member state. A state which, in the opinion of the council, is not fulfilling its obligations under the pact, may be expelled by unanimous vote.

In its other sphere of activity the original league pact spelled out the fields in which collaboration should be pursued: economics; communications; cultural matters; matters relating to nationality, passports, and visas; social welfare; and health. The pact specified that a special committee should be formed for each of these six categories.

The General Assembly, on November 1, 1950, adopted a resolution requesting the secretary-general of the United Nations to extend an invitation to the secretary-general of the Arab League to attend sessions of the General Assembly. It may or may not be a matter of significance that the Organization of American States was the only other regional arrangement that was invited (October 16, 1948) to be represented at the sessions of the General Assembly.[22]

[22] *Repertory of Practice of United Nations Organs* (New York, 1955), II, 443–448.

Regionalism and Regional Arrangements

The organizational structure of the Arab League is as follows:

1. Council (*Majlis*). The council, composed of the prime ministers or their representatives of all member states, is the chief organ of the league. It meets regularly twice a year, but can be called into extraordinary sessions. It discusses matters of common concern, and by unanimous agreement makes recommendations. Membership is open to any independent Arab state. Thus, with the recent extension of independence to other Arab states, whose cause the league had supported, the membership of the league council includes Iraq, Jordan, Lebanon, Libya, Morocco, Saudi Arabia, Tunis, United Arab Republics, and Yemen. Nonmember Arab countries are not entitled to representation on the council, but are urged to participate in league committees. Tunis has broken off relations with the United Arab Republics and has not taken part in league affairs.
2. Economic Council. The treaty of 1950 created an economic council, composed of the ministers of economic affairs, to organize and coordinate inter-Arab economics.
3. Permanent Secretariat-General. The seat of the league is Cairo, and because of this fact, and also because the secretary-general has always been an Egyptian, the league instruments have usually manifested a pro-Egyptian bias. The major divisions of the secretariat are the Political, Economic, Social, Legal, Cultural, Press and Publicity, Administrative and Financial, and Palestine Departments. Most of these departments have their counterparts in council committees.
4. Security Structure. The treaty of 1950 provided for the establishment of the Joint Defense Council, composed of the foreign and defense ministers of the member states, and the Permanent Military Commission, representing the general staffs of the armies of the member states. The treaty has remained largely a dead letter because of the difficulties of implementation. In fact, the Arab League has been aptly described as "an ambitious institutional structure which nevertheless has facilitated the survival of only a small residuum of common aims."

A prime characteristic of the Arab League has been its futility. Militarily, in hostilities with the Israelis, it proved to be far weaker than had been imagined. As regards proposals and plans for economic, social, and cultural cooperation, the league has been long on resolutions and short on implementation.

It has been impossible to develop any effective machinery for carrying out common policy because of inter-Arab feuds, dynastic rivalries, schisms between Moslem sects, and jealousy over Egypt's claim to leadership. The league has remained weak economically, politically, and militarily. In spite of many divisive factors within, the survival of the Arab League is said to be due to "resistance to Israel, to colonialism, and to Western economic exploitation.''[23] These furnish continuing common interests that ensure at least a loose alliance, and the looseness may, in fact, be an asset instead of a liability, for a rigid confederation would have broken down under the stresses and strains of inter-Arab dissensions and disputes. However, as a regional-security arrangement, the Arab League has failed to contribute to the peace and stability of the Near East.

The Warsaw Pact. On May 14, 1955, the Soviet and the satellite states signed, at Warsaw, a Treaty of Friendship, Cooperation, and Mutual Assistance. To some extent it was modeled after the North Atlantic Treaty, and it was the Soviet answer to NATO. Like the various regional-security pacts of the free nations, the Warsaw Pact declared its compatibility with United Nations obligations under the dispensations of Article 51, and proclaimed the usual formula of collective security that an attack on one member of the alliance shall be regarded as an attack on all, who in that event will cooperate in defense.

The Warsaw Treaty Organization (WTO) has also been modeled after NATO. The main organ is the Political Consultative Committee, which has the power to set up any auxiliary organs it may consider necessary. There is also the Council for Mutual Economic Assistance, which directs and supervises the member countries' armaments production. Since the military establishments of Poland, Czechoslovakia, Albania, Bulgaria, Rumania, Hungary, and East Germany have been virtually merged, the headquarters of the unified command are in Moscow, where each member state maintains permanent representatives on the general staff.

The Warsaw security system seems to meet the requisite of a regional arrangement in that it is multipurpose, is applicable to a definite area, and has an organizational structure. The one serious deficiency is that all of the Soviet's partners in the alliance are dependent states; therefore, WTO is not a true regional arrangement.

Conclusion. The development of regional-security arrangements under the guise of compatibility with the obligations of United Nations membership has gone much further than was obviously contemplated by the framers of the Charter. This trend was inevitable, since the nations lacked conviction that the United Nations could maintain peace and security. Thus, it was plausible that they would organize for peace on a regional basis, and try to ensure the maximum possible freedom of action for those agencies by keeping them outside the UN

[23] Haas, 401.

system. There can be no denying the fact that this is damaging to the prestige of the world organization and retards its development. However, the divisive influence of regionalism will rule so long as collective security cannot be ensured by a world organization. But it follows that the advent of an effective world-security organization will be obstructed by the existence of these same autonomous regional arrangements. It is a vicious circle.

There are, nonetheless, certain encouraging aspects in the development of postwar regional-security systems. They have eschewed the role of being simply military alliances, and have aspired to the cultivation and development of common interests in addition to the purely defensive. Of course it is expected that the mutual development of resources and the strengthening of solidarity will be reflected in a more effective security organization. It is interesting that the regional arrangements which we have examined and the inter-American system, which we are about to examine, are giving increasing attention to the nonpolitical and nonmilitary aspects of regional cooperation. This broadening of base of regional arrangements among the member states, this cultivation and identification of common interests over and above the purely defensive, should be excellent preparation for nations in international cooperation, to be applied eventually, we hope, on a world-wide scale.

Whether there shall be regionalism is not the question; there always has been and probably always will be. The question is whether regionalism shall take the form of separate spheres of influence and conflicting blocs under Great Power domination, or whether regional agencies, in matters of concern to extraregional states or to the world at large shall be supervised by a universal organization. After all, there is no inherent contradiction between universalism and regionalism, for neither is an exclusive principle. Both have a role to play in the modern world, for upon the steadying influence of regional cooperation may be built a stronger world organization. If international regionalism is properly developed and is closely integrated into a universal framework such as is provided by the United Nations, it can contribute much to the more effective organization of international society.

II The "Old" Pan Americanism
(1826–1888)

It is time the interests and relations uniting the American Republics, formerly Spanish colonies, should have a fundamental basis that shall perpetuate, if possible, those Governments.

SIMÓN BOLÍVAR, 1824

OF THE SEVERAL CONTEMPORARY "regional arrangements" which have been gathered under the accommodating canopy of the United Nations, the one superior to all others in maturity and in elaborateness of organizational and functional features is the Organization of American States—the OAS. In fact it was primarily because of the existence and importance of the inter-American system that it was necessary, when the Charter of the United Nations was drafted, to contrive a reconciliation between regionalism and global-security organization. By recourse to statesmanship, this difficult task of reconciling the seemingly irreconcilable was accomplished. There will be more about this later at a logical juncture of the discussion.[1] At the outset it seems appropriate to recount the evolving nature of the Pan American association of nations, with particular emphasis, of course, on its security[2] aspects. It is only by such historical background that the unique, but substantial, components of the inter-American security system can be properly understood.

The inter-American cooperative movement, once known as Pan Americanism, has evolved through three chronological phases, and is

[1] See Chap. IX.

[2] The term "security," in international usage, cannot be reduced to precise definition. Some would restrict it to the political and military guarantees of safety and adequate protection. But there are others who would include also juridical and economic guarantees. The present discussion inclines to the broader interpretation, particularly as applicable to the more recent periods of inter-American cooperation.

now in its fourth. The first extends from the time the Spanish American states won their independence until about 1888, and is called in this volume the "old" Pan Americanism. This phase was marked by the participation of only Spanish American states—and these on a numerically-limited scale. The primary purpose of their cooperation was security, i.e., defense of their newly-won independence. The second phase, called "new" Pan Americanism, embraced the years from 1889 to 1932. The two characteristic features of this second period were the all-inclusive membership of the American republics, and the virtual elimination of politico-security matters from cooperative consideration. This approach was the will of the United States, which dominated the movement. The third phase, which began about 1933 and continued to 1945, is known as the "Good Neighbor" era and is marked by the significant expansion of the security aspects of inter-American cooperation and their implementation in World War II. And finally, for want of a better name, we shall call the contemporary phase, which was inaugurated about the end of World War II, the "Impatient Neighbors" one, although it has also been called the "Equal Partner" phase. The politico-military aspects of hemispheric security having been perfected, the Latin-American members now argue that the security structure will be weak so long as their economic needs are neglected. The salient features of these several phases, as they relate to the security aspects of inter-American cooperation, will be the subjects of the ensuing discussions.

Bolívar's initiative. Simón Bolívar, the great Liberator, is regarded as the father of the "old" Pan American movement. It is true that he was the greatest exponent of close cooperation of the former Spanish colonies for their mutual development and protection, yet he was no more the originator of the idea of inter-American cooperation than were Washington and Monroe the originators of the principles of "no entangling alliances" and the "doctrine of the two spheres." Many other Latin Americans had also realized the necessity and advantages of cooperation and confederation.[3] According to Zeballos, the leaders for Spanish American independence, actuated by a common feeling of continental brotherhood, "recognized the necessity of organizing sufficient strength to inspire respect and resist any attempt on the part

[3] San Martín, Martínez de Rojas, Juan Egaña, Bernardo O'Higgins, Rodrigo Pinto Argueda, and Bernardo Monteagudo supported the cause of American cooperation. Their proposals ranged from organization of the colonies in a single state to a loose confederation.—Enrique V. Corominas, *Historia de las Conferencias Interamericanas* (Buenos Aires, 1959), 29–31.

of Europe to restore the old regime."[4] Yet it remained for Bolívar to attempt to convert this idea into a reality. In his famous "Jamaica Letter," dated September 6, 1815, he said:

It is a grand conception to consolidate the New World into a single nation with a single bond uniting all its parts. Since the different parts have the same origin, language, customs, and religion, they ought to be confederated into a single state; but this is not possible because differences of climate, diverse conditions, opposing interests and dissimilar characteristics divide America. How grand it would be if the Isthmus of Panama should become for us what the Isthmus of Corinth was for the Greeks! God grant that we may have the fortune some day to install there an august congress of representatives of the republics, kingdoms, and empires to deliberate upon the high interests of peace and of war with the nations of the other three-quarters of the world.[5]

In this, his first definite utterance on the idea of a union of the American nations, Bolívar had in mind a league of the former Spanish colonies, now sovereign states, and dedicated to confederation for their common defense. This political objective always remained the true Bolivarian conception of inter-American cooperation, and today, with certain modifications, it has been converted into a reality.

In a letter to Pueyrredón, supreme director of the United Provinces of Río de la Plata, Bolívar wrote, on June 12, 1818, that when Venezuela's independence should be achieved he would hasten to negotiate an American compact to constitute all of the republics into a single body politic which would "present America to the world in an aspect of majesty and grandeur unexampled among the nations of antiquity."[6] The war with Spain delayed for several years the practical application of Bolívar's idea. However, by 1822, as a result of improved prospects for independence, the government of Colombia, at the instance of the Liberator, took the lead in inviting the other Spanish American republics to enter into treaties of union, association, and confederation.

Treaties were negotiated by Colombia with Chile (October 21,

[4] E. S. Zeballos, *Conferencias Internacionales Americanas, 1797–1910* (Valencia, 1914), 8.

[5] Vicente Lecuna, *Cartas del Libertador* (New York, 1948), XI, 55; see also J. M. Torres Caicedo (ed.), *Union latino-americana; pensamiento de Bolívar para formar una liga americana; su origen y sus desarrollos* (Paris, 1865).

[6] Vicente Lecuna and Harold A. Bierck, Jr. (eds.), *Selected Writings of Bolívar* (New York, 1951), I, 160.

1822), Peru (July 6, 1822), Buenos Aires (March 8, 1823),[7] Mexico (October 3, 1823), and Central America (March 15, 1825). By these treaties the parties, with the exception of Argentina, pledged themselves to

> unite, league, and confederate, from this time forward forevermore, in peace and war, to sustain with their influence, and forces by sea and land, as far as circumstances may permit, their independence of the Spanish nation, and of every other foreign dominion; and to secure, after the recognition of their independence, mutual prosperity, perfect harmony, and good understanding between their peoples, subjects, and citizens, as well as with such other powers as may enter into relations with them.[8]

The contracting parties undertook to induce the other Spanish American states to enter into a treaty of confederation. It was further agreed that, as soon as "this grand and important object" was accomplished, their plenipotentiaries would meet at Panama for the purpose of cementing closer relations. This Panama assembly was to serve as a council in serious crises, as an authentic interpreter of their public treaties, and as judge-arbitrator and conciliator of their misunderstandings and differences. The Colombian treaties, which were ratified by all of the contracting governments with the exception of Chile, were the first definite steps that led eventually to the Pan American conference held at Panama in 1826.

United States reaction. The United States government watched these diplomatic overtures with considerable interest. Through its special agents in South America the Department of State was informed of the negotiations being conducted by Joaquín Mosquera. From Santiago, Chile, Special Agent John B. Prevost, after describing the general objectives of the proposed confederation, optimistically endorsed the plan for a congress of plenipotentiaries at Panama. He reported on November 15, 1822, that the United States would be invited and he

---

[7] The treaty with Buenos Aires was merely a pact of friendship. It omitted all reference to the assembly of plenipotentiaries. The great Argentine statesman Rivadavia was skeptical of treaties of alliance in general and of Bolívar's project in particular.—Víctor Andrés Belaunde, *Bolívar and the Political Thought of the Spanish American Revolution* (Baltimore, 1938), 261–262.

[8] Full texts of these treaties are to be found in Antonio José Uribe (ed.), *Anales Diplomaticos y Consulares de Colombia* (Bogotá, 1920), Tomo Sexto, "Tratados Publicos," cited hereinafter as *Anales*. Extracts from *British and Foreign State Papers* are printed in Alejandro Álvarez, *The Monroe Doctrine* (New York, 1924), 135–141.

urged acceptance.[9] Charles Todd, confidential agent of the United States at Bogotá, reported to Secretary of State John Quincy Adams, in a letter dated March 6, 1823, that Dr. Gual, Colombian minister for foreign affairs, had informed him that

the Treaties with Peru and Chile . . . were Alliances . . . that they were of a political character and would not embarrass the negotiations for commercial arrangements with the United States, nor preclude our commerce from the advantages of the most favored nation; that these Treaties developed the Continental policy of America, and when published, would produce much discussion in the United States as to the course we should adopt; that the different Governments in Spanish America (Colombia, Peru, Chile, and Buenos Aires), had agreed to meet and confer together on their General Interests, somewhat on the plan of the Holy Alliance, and it would be a question with the United States to unite or not as she may see proper.[10]

Dr. Gual also told Todd that the Portuguese government had made proposals to Colombia for a general confederacy of all America, North and South, together with the constitutional governments of Portugal and Spain, as a counterpoise to the European Holy Alliance, but that the proposals had been rejected because of their European aspect. According to Secretary of State John Quincy Adams the Portuguese had presented a similar proposal to the United States, but it had not been considered worthy of deliberation.

The early policy of Secretary Adams toward Latin-American confederation and the proposed conference was first set forth in his general instructions, dated May 27, 1823, to Richard C. Anderson, newly-appointed minister to Colombia. With respect to confederation, Secretary Adams bestowed upon it the unqualified blessings of the United States, regardless of whether its object should be to form a defensive alliance against Europe or to create a real confederation. Yet, regarding United States participation in the proposed congress of plenipotentiaries, the policy of this country was (in 1823) noncommittal. Adams pointed out that if a meeting was desired in which the United States should participate, a study of the objectives and methods must necessarily precede our decision to accept or decline the invitation.[11] He was not prepared to abandon his idea that a continental American system was ridiculous.

[9] William R. Manning (ed.), *Diplomatic Correspondence of the United States Concerning the Independence of the Latin American Nations* (3 vols., New York, 1925), I, 1071.

[10] *Ibid.*, II, 1245.   [11] *Ibid.*, I, 205.

Shortly thereafter, however, Secretary Adams indicated his acceptance of the concept of the American system as the basis for the national policy which was declared by President Monroe in 1823. But
the implication from the Monroe Doctrine that the peoples of the
Western Hemisphere stood in a special relation one to another which
set them apart from the rest of the world, having seemingly served an
immediate purpose, was allowed to recede into the indistinct and
almost forgotten background. Although the affirmative response of
the Adams-Clay Administration to the invitations to a conference
of American states at Panama struck a weak but harmonious note of
inter-American cooperation, several decades were to elapse before the
United States would indicate a desire to develop the positive implications of the American system. In short, it is difficult, if not impossible,
to trace the roots of inter-American security cooperation, so far as the
United States is concerned, into the period known as the "old" Pan
Americanism. Nevertheless it will be helpful to see the early expressions of views on the subject by American statesmen.

Invitations to the Congress of Panama. General political developments in South America prevented immediate action on Colombia's
initiative for a congress of plenipotentiaries. However, toward the
close of 1824, Bolívar, then president of Peru, revived the project
which had long been the object of his solicitude. In a circular letter,
December 7, 1824, he inivited "the American republics, formerly
Spanish colonies," to send plenipotentiaries to Panama to meet with
Peru in a congress. The object of the conference was declared to be
"the establishment of certain fixed principles for securing the preservation of peace between the nations of America, and the concurrence
of all those nations to defend their common cause, each contributing
thereto upon the basis of its population."[12]

Bolívar also extended an invitation to Great Britain, for he believed
that the presence of that power was vital to the success of the conference. He said, "If we bind ourselves to England, we shall exist; if
we do not bind ourselves we shall be lost without fail." In brief, it
was Bolívar's hope that an American amphictyonic union might be
erected under the direction and with the protection of England.

It is to be noted that the Liberator's invitation did not include the
United States and Brazil. He felt that the Spanish colonies had a com-

[12] Daniel Florencio O'Leary (ed.), *Memorias del General O'Leary publicadas
por su hijo, Simón B. O'Leary* (32 vols., Caracas, 1879–1888), XXIV, 250–
253.

mon enemy, Spain, and that it was vital for them to band together in defense of their independence, whereas the United States and Brazil, as neutrals, could not feel the same interest in this enterprise. He feared also that federation with the United States would compromise the new Spanish American states with England, for, he said, "the Americans of the United States are the only rivals of England in respect of America."[13] A minor objection was Bolívar's thought that the existence of slavery in the United States would be an obstacle to free discussion of the abolition of the African slave trade. Later the United States and Brazil were invited to participate in the Panama conference—the United States by the governments of Colombia, Mexico, and Central America, and Brazil by Colombia. Bolívar acquiesced in these actions without demur.

In extending their invitations to the United States, the governments of Colombia, Mexico, and Central America each gave assurance that this country would not be embarrassed by being called upon to depart from its policy of neutrality with respect to the war between Spain and her former colonies. However, the Colombian invitation pointed out that the Panama meeting offered the United States a wonderful opportunity "to fix some principles of international law, the unsettled state of which has caused much evil to humanity." It also made reference to a possible implementation of the newly-enunciated Monroe Doctrine, and declared that "the manner in which all colonization of European powers in the American Continent shall be resisted, and their interference in the present contest between Spain and her former colonies prevented, are other points of great interest." It was proposed that an eventual alliance might be considered.[14]

Determining of policy by the United States. Secretary of State Henry Clay, a long-time advocate of closer relations with Latin America, did not delay long in indicating the Administration's willingness to accept the invitations to the conference at Panama. Clay had expressed his view on continental unity many years before. On March 25, 1818, he had said: "There can be no doubt that [in] Spanish America, once independent, whatever might be the form of the governments established in its several parts, those governments would be animated by an American feeling and guided by an American policy. They would obey the laws of the system of the New

13 *Ibid.*, 260.
14 Pedro A. Zubieta, *Apuntaciones sobre las Primeras Misiones Diplomaticas de Colombia* (Bogotá, 1924), 103–105.

World, of which they form a part, in contradistinction to that of Europe."[15]

In identical notes of acknowledgment to the Colombian and Mexican ministers, dated November 30, 1825, the Secretary of State briefly indicated the decision of President Adams, subject to approval by the Senate, to send commissioners to the conference. Although these delegates were to be fully empowered and instructed upon all questions in which the nations of America had a common interest, they would not be authorized to enter into any deliberation or decision inconsistent with the neutral position of the United States.

In a special message to Congress on December 26, 1825, President Adams made a full statement of policy. First, he assured Congress that the United States neither intended, nor was expected, to take part in any deliberations of a belligerent character. Also, that our attendance was neither to contract alliances nor to engage in any undertaking or project importing hostility to any other nation. Next, and quite significantly, the President invited the attention of the Congress to the desirability of meeting with the representatives of the Latin-American nations, to urge "with disinterested and friendly persuasion" the adoption of "principles of a liberal commercial intercourse." In this connection the President alluded to a tendency in the Latin-American states to establish duties and imposts unfavorable to the United States and advantageous to European powers. Another proposed subject for discussion in the conference, said the President, concerned principles of maritime neutrality. As for the recently-enunciated Monroe Doctrine, Adams said, "It [the Monroe Doctrine] may be so developed to the new southern nations that they will all feel it as an essential appendage to their independence." Another proper subject for discussion, said the President, would be the advancement of religious liberty.[16]

It is impossible to detect anything in the President's message which is indicative of the Western Hemisphere idea, certainly not to the point of favoring any kind of security or political commitment. The reasons advocated by President Adams for participation in the Congress of Panama were generally removed from considerations of regional-security interests.

United States participation in the Panama conference was opposed

[15] Quoted by J. B. Lockey, *Pan Americanism: Its Beginnings* (New York, 1920), 282.

[16] J. D. Richardson (ed.), *A Compilation of the Messages and Papers of the Presidents, 1789–1897* (10 vols., Washington, 1899), II, 318–320.

in the U.S. Congress as being an unwise departure from the nonintervention policy advised by President Washington. It was feared by some that the plan of inter-American cooperation would commit this country to a more hazardous connection with the fortunes of other countries than was desirable. More particularly, participation was opposed by representatives of the slave states because the subject of abolishing the African slave trade was on the conference agenda. However, partisan politics was the real reason for opposition and although participation was approved in the end, so much time had been lost in reaching the decision that it was impossible for the United States to be represented in the conference.

The instructions of Secretary Clay[17] (May 8, 1826) to our delegates to the conference reveal how far the Administration was willing to go at that time in participating in an inter-American cooperative movement. First, the Secretary emphasized that the congress was to be regarded as a diplomatic body without powers of ordinary legislation; nor was it "an amphictyonic council invested with power finally to decide controversies between the American states or to regulate in any respect their conduct." It was merely to afford opportunities for free and friendly conference and to facilitate the concluding of treaties.

After this preliminary admonition, our delegates were instructed not to enter into discussions relating to the war with Spain. They were to confine themselves strictly to subjects in which all American nations, belligerent or neutral, might have an interest, particularly the maintenance of peace, "the greatest want of America." Since the policy of the United States was declared to be "peace and neutrality," one matter of great importance was maritime neutrality. The delegates accordingly were to advocate security for private property upon the high seas, a restricted definition of "contraband," and the principle that free ships make free goods and enemy ships make enemy goods.

With respect to commercial intercourse, the United States representatives were not to seek exclusive privilege, even against European states, but should accept the most-favored-nation principle.

As for the Monroe Doctrine, our delegates were to propose a joint declaration that each American state, acting for and binding only itself, would allow no European colonies to be established within its territory. Thus, the Doctrine was to be preserved as a unilateral policy.

[17] John Bassett Moore, *The Principles of American Diplomacy* (New York, 1918), 370–375.

Regarding an interoceanic canal (for Bolívar included a Panama Canal on the agenda), the United States demanded merely that the benefits of the canal ought not to be exclusively appropriated to any one nation.

Since the Congress of Panama was scheduled to consider the question of the liberation of Cuba, our delegates were authorized to state that the United States could not view with indifference a war for the liberation of the island. It comported with American policy that Cuba should remain in Spanish hands, for it was feared that a weak independent Cuba would attract the intervention of strong European powers.

As for forms of government and free institutions, it was the declared United States policy, while preferring republican institutions, to refrain from any interference in matters concerning the original structure or subsequent internal changes in the governments of other independent nations.

President Adams' message to Congress and Secretary Clay's instructions to our delegates indicated clearly and adequately the conditions under which the United States was willing to participate in a Pan American conference. These earliest evidences of an official United States policy toward a cooperative movement with the other American republics reveal that this country wished to scrupulously avoid political commitments and involvements. While there was willingness, and even desire, to enter into agreements that might be conducive to enlarged trade relationships with Latin America, and also to enlist those countries in support of the United States' conception of neutral rights, *there was a distinct distaste for anything that savored of security commitments.* In these matters the United States government preferred to go its way alone. Thus the newly-declared Monroe Doctrine was to remain a unilateral policy; and, although the Latin-American states were to be encouraged to espouse its principles, this was to be done entirely on their own and without having the United States assume any obligations. Although the maintenance of peace was declared to be the policy of the United States, nothing was said about arbitration or other methods of peaceful settlement of international disputes. Notwithstanding this omission, it may be assumed that this government would not have imposed serious objections to such agreements, provided the pledges of peaceful and friendly recourse were entirely disassociated from anything savoring of a league, confederation, or alliance. It is significant that, with respect to fundamentals, the earliest Pan American policy of the United States, as devised by the

Adams-Clay Administration, was not substantially different from the one supported by the United States for some years after 1889—the fostering of trade relationships but the shunning of political commitments. The United States was not interested in security cooperation.

The Congress of Panama. The Congress of Panama, the first of a series of Spanish American conferences, met on June 22 and adjourned July 15, 1826. Although only four American states—Peru, Colombia, Central America, and Mexico—were represented, they embraced an area now occupied by eleven of the twenty Latin-American states. The United Provinces of Río de la Plata and Paraguay declined to take part. Brazil accepted an invitation, but because of the impending conflict with Buenos Aires, did not send her plenipotentiary. The governments of Bolivia, Chile, and the United States all appointed delegates too late for them to be able to participate in the congress. The British and the Dutch were unofficially represented by agents. The British agent, Edward J. Dawkins, had been instructed by Canning to "oppose any project for putting the United States of North America at the head of any American Confederacy," and to discourage the conference from taking any action concerning Cuba which might end in United States occupation of the island. The British consistently opposed the extension of American influence in the Caribbean.[18] Had the British been aware of the instructions to our delegates to the congress, they certainly would have felt no such anxieties.

The acts of the congress included: (1) the Treaty of Perpetual Union, League, and Confederation, (2) a convention providing for future meetings of the congress, and (3) two conventions concerning the contingents of armed forces and money subsidies that the member states should contribute to the projected confederation. Although the Treaty of Perpetual Union, League, and Confederation was ratified by but one state, Colombia, and thus never became effective, it represents, nevertheless, a definite landmark in the evolution of the inter-American security system and for this reason warrants brief analysis.[19]

The object of this treaty was declared to be

to support in common defense, or offense if necessary, the sovereignty and independence of each and every one of the confederated powers of America against all foreign domination, and to assure now and forever the blessings of unalterable peace, and to promote greater harmony and good understand-

[18] John P. Humphrey, *The Inter-American System: A Canadian View* (Toronto, 1942), 25.

[19] For texts of treaties, see *International American Conferences, 1889–1890* (Washington, 1890), IV, 189–190.

ing both among the people, citizens, and respective subjects, as well as with the other powers with whom they ought to maintain or enter into friendly relations.

The treaty, together with the supplementary conventions, set forth provisions relating to the common defense, particularly to the danger of Spanish reconquest. A number of the articles dealt with the obligation to employ armed force against the enemies of any or all of the confederated powers. To strengthen their front against external enemies, and to contribute to the maintenance of peace and friendship among the confederate powers, there should be a meeting of a general assembly every year while the war with Spain lasted, and every two years thereafter.

The treaty then provided several means of recourse to the general assembly for the preservation of peace. All differences between the contracting parties that could not be amicably compromised should be mediated by the general assembly. No matter what the injury or provocation, the contracting parties should not declare war or resort to reprisals without first submitting their grievances to the conciliatory decision of the general assembly. No party should go to war against an outsider without first soliciting the good offices, interposition, and mediation of its allies.

Probably to give effect to the declaration of President Monroe regarding noncolonization, the contracting parties pledged themselves to cooperate, with force if necessary, to prevent colonial settlements within their borders. They also agreed mutually to guarantee, as soon as their boundaries should be determined, the integrity of their respective territories. Finally, the treaty provided for abolishing the African slave trade and the mutual extension of the rights of citizenship.

This first essay at an inter-American league was at best a loose confederation. The general assembly was little more than a diplomatic congress made up of plenipotentiary delegates of equal states that retained the complete exercise of their sovereignty.

Because of unsatisfactory health conditions on the Isthmus, the congress agreed to transfer its activities to Tacubaya, near Mexico City, where it would continue to meet periodically.[20] But the plan to renew the sessions of the congress in Mexican territory never materialized.

---

[20] Bolívar opposed moving the assembly to Tacubaya. He said, "The transfer of the Assembly to Mexico is going to put it under the immediate influence of that power, already preponderant, and also under the influence of the United States of the North."—Belaunde, 346.

As has been noted, the agreements negotiated at Panama failed of ratification by all of the signatory states except Colombia.

It is disillusioning that Bolívar's interest in the Panama conference had cooled to the point of his actually opposing the ratification of the treaties by both Colombia and Peru. The Liberator, who once supported the idea of an amphictyony based on the principles of sovereignty and equality, had become convinced, even before the Panama meeting, of the failure of confederation. The policies of individual countries, notably Buenos Aires and Mexico, caused him to doubt any cordial concurrence on their part. Reversing his earlier views regarding the dangers of overlarge nations erected on the ruins of the Spanish empire, by 1826 Bolívar had turned to the idea of a federation of the Andes. This grandiose project envisaged a cohesive federal union composed of Great Colombia, Peru, and Bolivia, headed by a life-term president (Simón Bolívar). There is little doubt that personal ambition played a large part in influencing the Liberator's ideas concerning Spanish American federations. It is somewhat ironic that the man who is honored as the "father of Pan Americanism" disavowed his brain child in its infancy.[21]

With respect to tangible achievements, the Panama conference was a failure. Yet, in the realm of the intangibles it was not without significance, for it gave stimulus to the idea of inter-American conference for the discussion of mutual problems affecting the American republics. It was the germ from which evolved the Pan American security system. However, for a number of years, interest in the movement was confined to only a few of the Spanish American republics.

The progress of Pan Hispano-Americanism. Five years after the congress at Panama, the Mexican government, in pursuance of the Panama agreement, issued a call for another conference to consider the three following subjects: the promotion of union of the Spanish American states for defense against foreign invasion; encouragement of mediation in international disputes; and the formulation of a code of public law to determine international obligations.[22] The Mexican invitation, issued in 1831 and repeated in 1838, 1839, and 1840, never materialized in a meeting. Indeed, the next meeting of Latin-American states did not take place until twenty-one years after the Panama conference.

[21] Francisco Cuevas Cancino, *Del Congreso de Panamá a la Conferencia de Caracas, 1826–1954* (2 vols., Caracas, 1955), I, 159–162.
[22] Samuel Guy Inman, *Problems in Pan Americanism* (New York, 1925), 112.

The second conference of the "old" Pan American movement met in Lima, on invitation of the Peruvian government, from December 11, 1847, to March 1, 1848. Bolivia, Chile, Ecuador, New Granada (Colombia), and Peru were represented at this conference, which, like the Congress of Panama, was occasioned primarily by fear of Spain. It seems that a former president of Ecuador, General Juan José Flores, was attempting to raise an armed force in Spain for an invasion of Ecuador in order to establish a Spanish prince there. For his projected expedition he bought some ships and raised some troops in Great Britain. The news of these activities caused great excitement and apprehension in Spanish America and led to the calling of the conference at Lima.

According to our consular representative at Lima, the United States was invited to send a representative to this conference in order to convince the governments of Europe "that all America, North and South, will unite to oppose and put down any attempt at conquest or subversion of American institutions."[23] It has also been suggested that the invitation to the United States was probably intended as a pointed reminder to this country, then engaged in a war with Mexico, of the prime object of the conference—respect for territorial integrity.[24]

The Polk Administration did not send an envoy, for it did not regard the meeting seriously, perhaps because the danger from Flores' plan had already largely disappeared with the British government's forbidding the sailing of the ships that had been bought in England. United States influence was not entirely absent from the conference, however, for at the instance of American Chargé d'Affaires J. Randolph Clay, the Congress of Lima adopted resolutions reaffirming the noncolonization principle and denying the right of European powers to intervene in the affairs of the New World. "I am pleased to find," wrote Clay, "that the declaration concerning colonization and non-interference has been made, for I consider them important principles and belonging to the true policy of America, both North and South."[25]

[23] Stanhope Prevost, United States Consul at Lima, to James Buchanan, Secretary of State of the United States, Lima, February 1, 1847.—William R. Manning (ed.), *Diplomatic Correspondence of the United States: Inter-American Affairs, 1831–1860* (12 vols., Washington, 1938), I, 551, cited hereinafter as *Inter-American Affairs.*

[24] Moore, 381.

[25] John Randolph Clay, United States Chargé d'Affaires at Lima, to James Buchanan, Secretary of State of the United States, Lima, January 12, 1849.—Manning, *Inter-American Affairs*, X, 561–562.

One New Granadine delegate proposed—the idea was not accepted —that a protocol be drafted pledging all the confederated nations to maintain legations at Washington so that "in this great American center there might be formed a diplomatic gathering of America to facilitate means of communication and accord for emergencies and other extraordinary circumstances."[26] It appears that the desire to include the United States in an association of American states was much stronger in Latin America than in the United States.

In the Lima congress two treaties—one of confederation and the other of commerce—and two conventions—one consular and the other postal—were signed. The Treaty of Confederation,[27] signed at Lima on February 8, 1848, pledged the signatory *Spanish American Republics* to "forsake the state of isolation," and devise effective means to "strengthen their union, in order to maintain their independence, sovereignty, institutions, dignity, and interests, and settle always through peaceful and free channels such differences as may arise among them." To these ends the treaty provided that the contracting parties should help each other with land and naval forces in the manner and under the terms stipulated in the treaty. In the event any of the confederated republics should be the object of attack, offense, or insult by any foreign power, the Congress of Plenipotentiaries should determine without delay whether a *casus foederis* had arisen, and, on the basis of its decision, appropriate measures were to be taken. Neither this treaty nor the other instruments drafted at Lima were ratified by the participating governments, and although the other American governments, including the United States, were invited to subscribe to the several conventions, the response was unanimously negative. There appeared to be little disposition, even among the Spanish American states, to transform the ideal of inter-American security cooperation into a reality, for evidently the feeling of insecurity was neither immediate nor compelling.

Nevertheless, animated by the same considerations that influenced the convening of the 1847 congress, a third international meeting of a limited number of West coast South American states met in Santiago (Chile) in September 1856. This conference, attended by representatives of Peru, Chile, and Ecuador, was also inspired largely by fear, both of the United States, which had shown an alarming appetite for Latin-American territory in 1848, and of further aggression by fili-

---

[26] *Ibid.*, 155. Alejandro Álvarez (*The Monroe Doctrine*, 16) sees in this proposal the beginning of the Pan American Union.

[27] For text of the treaty, see Álvarez, *The Monroe Doctrine*, 170–175.

bustering expeditions such as that of William Walker in Central America.[28] United States Minister Clay at Lima wrote on November 10, 1856:

Indeed, I have no doubt that the Governments of Chile and Peru are aiming to form a kind of Continental alliance, among the nations of South America, against what they are pleased to call the ambition and incursions of the United States. . . . They think to attain this object by exciting the prejudices of the inhabitants throughout South America, by representing us as foreign to them "in blood and religion."[29]

On September 15, 1856, the delegates signed at Santiago another treaty of alliance and confederation, the so-called "Continental Treaty."[30] Although this treaty followed rather closely the terms of the Lima convention, in some particulars it was more comprehensive. For example, it contained (1) a pledge "not to cede or alienate in any form to another state or government, any part of its territory"; (2) several provisions designed to prevent the organizing of hostile expeditions by political emigrees within any of the allied states; and (3) a provision that the Congress of Plenipotentiaries should have the right to offer mediation in case of dispute between the contracting states, "and none of them shall refuse to accept the said mediation."

The other Spanish American states, and Brazil, "after the exchange of ratifications," were to be invited to join a union. However, it was the same old story: the Continental Treaty was never ratified.

In Washington, in the same year that the Santiago conference met, the ministers of Costa Rica, Guatemala, Mexico, New Granada, Peru, El Salvador, and Venezuela signed on November 9, 1856, a Treaty of Alliance and Confederation. Indicative undoubtedly of the concern of the treaty framers, the signatory states pledged themselves to prevent the organizing of expeditions by political exiles against an allied government.[31] It is to be recalled that in 1856 filibustering was at its height. Other articles provided for mutual assistance, with force if necessary, whenever an allied state should be invaded or threatened

---

[28] For justification of this fear, see John Bassett Moore (*op. cit.*, 381–383), who believes that, fortunately for Latin-American relations, the Civil War cured the expansionistic tendencies of the United States.

[29] Manning, *Inter-American Affairs*, X, 776.

[30] For portions of the text of the treaty, see Álvarez, *The Monroe Doctrine*, 176–178; Gustave A. Nuernberger, "The Continental Treaties of 1856: An American Union Exclusive of the United States," *Hispanic American Historical Review*, XX (Feb. 1940), 32–55.

[31] For text of the Treaty of Washington, see Uribe, *Anales*, VI, 619, 622.

with invasion by a foreign enemy. To convert this pact of alliance and confederation into a universal "Confederation of the Hispanic-American States," a conference was to convene at Lima in December of the following year. Needless to say, neither was the pact ratified nor the conference convened.

The next conference of Spanish American states convened in Lima from November 14, 1864, to March 13, 1865. The real occasion prompting this meeting was a new European threat proceeding from the interventions by Spain in the Dominican Republic and by France in Mexico. On the initiative of Peru, "the republics which at one time belonged to Spain" were invited to the conference for the purpose of "organizing into one family." It was attended by Bolivia, Chile, Colombia, Ecuador, Guatemala, Peru, and Venezuela. Treaties negotiated, but, alas, never ratified, were the following: Treaty of Union and Defensive Alliance, Treaty for the Preservation of Peace between the Contracting American States, Treaty of Commerce and Navigation, and the Postal Treaty.

The first-named, like the earlier treaties of confederation, pledged the contracting parties "to unite and ally themselves and mutually guarantee the independence, sovereignty, and integrity of their respective territories," and to defend each other against all aggression from any source.

The most significant feature of the Treaty for the Preservation of Peace was the agreement of the signatories never to have recourse to arms as a means of settling their differences, but to submit them to the unappealable decision of an arbitrator in case they could not settle them otherwise. Other articles of this treaty contained the familiar guarantees against organizing hostile expeditions in neighboring territory, particularly by political refugees. These latter measures reflected the dominant concern of the republics—a concern greater by far than any fear of overseas aggression.

The Lima conference of 1865 was the last Spanish American congress dedicated to political objectives consonant with the Bolivarian ideal of inter-American cooperation. There were other meetings prior to 1889, but these related to juridical and nonpolitical questions. There were two juridical conferences. The first met at Lima in December 1877, "to write the tables of the new American Decalogue." This conference, to which the United States was invited,[32] was attended by

[32] Since the purpose of the conference was to simplify the principles of private international law applicable in the countries of America, the United States declined the invitation for two reasons: first, because of the fundamental differ-

representatives of Argentina, Bolivia, Chile, Costa Rica, Ecuador, Guatemala, Peru, Uruguay, and Venezuela. Two treaties signed, but not ratified, concerned uniform rules of private international law and extradition. A second juridical conference convened in Montevideo in 1888/89. This so-called "South American International Conference," attended by delegates from Argentina, Bolivia, Brazil, Chile, Paraguay, Peru, and Uruguay, resulted in a series of treaties respecting civil law, property, trade-marks, patents, and the exercise of the liberal professions.[33] Other conferences of Latin-American states held before 1889 whose deliberations were restricted to specialized subjects were: The Pedagogical Congress of South America, 1882; a congress commemorating the Bolívar centenary, 1883; the Sanitary Congress of the Río Plata countries and Brazil, 1887; and the American Sanitary Conference of Lima, 1888. The meetings of these technical conferences terminated the "old" Pan Americanism.

An appraisement of the "old" Pan Americanism. It is clear from the foregoing that the chief purpose of these early multipartite efforts at union and confederation was to bring about closer political relations among the states of Spanish origin, customs, and institutions, with the view of making their independent status secure. It is significant that the immediate occasion for the calling of every one of the conferences of the "old" Pan American movement was the fear, real or imagined, of foreign aggression. According to a leading authority on this subject, "All those congresses were conceived at times when a Spanish reconquest was feared; once the danger which had brought them into being had passed, no one gave a second thought to the necessity of convoking them until a new threat again united the American nations in the organization of their common defense."[34]

Beginning in 1822 the Spanish American nations began to develop a cooperative policy whose primary objects were defense and the preservation of peace. The system of treaties negotiated by Great Colombia between 1822 and 1825 initiated this policy. At the Congress of Panama, and in the subsequent conferences, a series of treaties containing notable progressive features relating to mutual defense, mediation, conciliation, arbitration, and war renunciation were negotiated.

ence in the common law as compared with the civil law, and second, because of the dual nature of the legislative system in the United States, divided as it is between the federal government and state governments.

[33] For texts, see Uribe, *Anales*, VI, 632–681.

[34] Jesús María Yepes, *El Panamericanismo y el Derecho Internacional* (Bogotá, 1930), 51.

Unfortunately these treaties were not ratified. The ideals they embodied were apparently too advanced for the time.

Although these efforts at multilateral action failed, nevertheless the individual states did negotiate among themselves, between 1826 and 1889, no fewer than fifty general bipartite conventions pledging to apply amicable methods to the settlement of international disputes, the obligations ranging all the way from a vague promise "to maturely consider" whether it would not be better to resort to arbitration, to binding agreements for obligatory arbitration. It is significant that many of these latter treaties provided for submitting to arbitration virtually all disputes that might arise between the contracting parties. The American nations were making real progress in establishing arbitration as "a principle of American international law."[35]

Although these early conferences failed to realize their major objectives, they nevertheless demonstrated that the Latin-American states had a certain capacity to join together in the face of a threat to their national security. They were manifestations of solidarity in moments of crisis. Also, the treaties negotiated, even though not ratified, were important in that they incorporated fundamental rules of national behavior destined later to become basic features of inter-American cooperation: nonintervention, territorial integrity, arbitration, and the renunciation of war. This same idea has been well expressed by a distinguished Colombian statesman and diplomat:

The congresses and conferences . . . as well as the pacts which were signed at them (even though the latter may not have been ratified), were undeniably beneficial, inasmuch as they contributed powerfully to the development and the final orientation of the foreign policy of the American States; they tightened remarkably the bonds between these states; and they inaugurated a series of traditions and precedents of the highest value in the political and juridical realm. Thus, when the first Pan American conference met on October 2, 1889, the members recognized that the principles which were to guide them in their mutual relations as well as their relations with other states throughout the world, had long been part of the conscience of the American nations.[36]

Yet, in the realm of tangible achievement the "old" Pan Americanism was a failure. The conferences were poorly attended, and their acts were never consummated. For this there were several reasons.

[35] See William R. Manning (ed.), *Arbitration Treaties Among The American Nations To The Close Of The Year 1910* (New York, 1924), 1–188.

[36] Francisco José Urrutia, *Le Continent Américain et le Droit International* (Paris, 1928), 46–47.

First and foremost, "being born in a common prejudice of fear," the Spanish American states became less and less disposed to cooperate as the foreign menace to their independence became less and less real. Second, the development of a spirit of nationalism made increasingly repugnant the rigid unity envisaged by Bolívar. Jealousy of their sovereignty caused the new states to be suspicious of entangling alliance, and particularly of confederation. In this respect Argentina was the archexample. Following the advice of her revolutionary hero, Mariano Moreno, Argentina adhered to a strict isolationist policy and avoided all federationist pacts as being dangerous to national autonomy. After the menace of European aggression had passed, Argentina felt that there existed for the Spanish American republics more ties, more interests, more harmony with Europe than with each other. Third, an inability to cooperate and compromise is a Latin-American trait which has been inherited from the individualistic Spaniards, but not, of course, to such an accentuated degree. Cooperative military efforts, such as those of Bolívar and San Martín in the wars for independence, were exceptional, and were not likely to be repeated except under stress of similar circumstances. Finally, the movement was a failure because of inertia and lack of leadership. With the passing of Bolívar (and even the Liberator's motives had been viewed with suspicion), the movement lacked aggressive direction. While accepting the proposition that the erstwhile members of the Spanish empire constituted one family in origin, language, religion, and customs, and that cooperation should be a natural consequence, no one was disposed to do much about it. There was need of new leadership directed toward less rigid unity and with freer course of action for each country. This need was supplied by the United States in 1889, and thus was inaugurated the second phase of the Pan American movement.

III The "New" Pan Americanism: I
(1889–1913)

> We believe that hearty cooperation . . . will save all American states from
> the burdens and evils which have long and cruelly afflicted the older nations
> of the world.
>
> JAMES G. BLAINE, 1889

THE SECOND PHASE of the Pan American movement, inaugurated
in 1889, was, at least in its earlier years, so different from the
original concept of inter-American cooperation as envisaged by Simón
Bolívar that the two policies appeared to be completely independent
of, and unrelated to, each other. The old Pan American movement
was exclusively Spanish American in membership (with meager participation at that), and with objectives mostly political in nature. Attempts had been made on several occasions between 1826 and 1865 to
form a closely-integrated confederation of states, leagued for common
defense and pledged to applying peaceful procedures for the settlement of their interstate disputes.

In contrast, the new movement sponsored by the United States became all-inclusive in membership, a truly "pan" affair;[1] all the American states—the United States, Brazil, and Haiti, as well as all the
Spanish American states—became participating members. The objectives, too, were significantly different. No longer was security the
raison d'être of inter-American cooperation. Not one of the first six
conferences was called because of peril to American peace and security.
As a matter of fact the conferences met by the calendar, at times
neither critical nor urgent but merely convenient for considering
measures to promote the common welfare of the Americas. Organiz-

---

[1] J. B. Lockey (Pan Americanism: Its Beginnings, 2) attributes the origin of
the term "Pan Americanism" to the New York Evening Post, which first employed the term on June 27, 1882.

ing cooperative action to confront any immediate or future aggression from a non-American source never appeared on the agenda of any of these conferences. There was concern, however, over the maintenance of peace among the American nations themselves, and the scrupulous observance of regard for their respective sovereignties. Consideration of these matters was about the extent of the security aspects of the "new" Pan Americanism.

It was the policy of the United States, effectively imposed for a number of years, to limit the consideration of "political" questions,[2] and to confine the discussions at the Pan American conferences to those subjects in the realms of economic, educational, scientific, and social relations which afforded the best prospects for friendly agreement. Quite truly, therefore, the inter-American movement as sponsored by the United States bore only slight resemblance to the one inaugurated by Simón Bolívar. This is not to say, however, that security aspects of inter-American cooperation were ignored, for as will be revealed in the following discussion, it was during the course of the new Pan Americanism that the foundation was laid for the inter-American security structure.

Blaine's initiative. The new Pan Americanism was called into being by James G. Blaine, whose study of the speeches of Henry Clay is supposed to have inspired his belief in the Western Hemisphere idea, that is, the idea that the peoples of this hemisphere stand in a special relationship to one another, and accordingly, their common interests should be promoted by cooperation. Blaine's Americanism has been described as a curious blend of nationalism and continentalism. At any rate the "Plumed Knight" contributed much to the revival of the hemisphere idea which had remained moribund since the days of Adams and Clay.[3]

When Blaine was secretary of state in the Garfield Administration he seized on the War of the Pacific in South America, waged by Chile against Bolivia and Peru, as the occasion which called the United

[2] Political questions pertain or relate to the public policy of a state. In inter-American relations, political questions are those which concern the juridical equality, territorial integrity, national independence, international obligations, and rights of American states. This includes such matters as the codification of international law, an American league of nations and court of justice, the pacific settlement of international conflicts, and the maintenance of peace in the continent.

[3] W. S. Robertson, *Hispanic-American Relations* (New York, 1923), 391; A. P. Whitaker, *The Western Hemisphere Idea: Its Rise and Decline* (Ithaca, 1954), 76.

States to leadership in the quest for continental security and solidarity. In the background was Blaine's concern that Latin-American conflicts should not invite European intervention and thus threaten the Monroe Doctrine. Accordingly, on November 29, 1881, the Secretary invited the independent states of North and South America to participate at Washington in a general conference "for the purpose of considering and discussing the methods of preventing war between the nations of America." In his circular letter of invitation he stated that President Garfield desired that the attention of the conference be "strictly confined to this one great object." The Latin-American states were assured that the United States was not preparing to assume the place of counselor for the other states, but rather a place of equality with them.[4]

If the conference had met as originally scheduled and had limited its discussions to "the methods of preventing war between the nations of America," it would have remained within the stream of earlier security developments. However, the assassination of President Garfield and the appointment of a new secretary of state by President Arthur resulted in a change of policy and withdrawal of the invitations.

Mr. Blaine, disappointed, undertook to explain his projected conference in a magazine article entitled "The Foreign Policy of the Garfield Administration." He stated frankly that he had had two objects in view: to promote peace in the Americas, and to cultivate friendly commercial relations. "To attain the second object, the first must be accomplished," he said. He revealed that he had intended to follow up the peace conference with a commercial conference. Blaine, one of the most farsighted of our secretaries of state, felt that the United States, on the verge of launching into overseas economic expansion, was becoming strong enough to cherish ambitions of supplanting the European nations in the trade of Latin America. He entertained hopes of securing special advantages in Latin-American markets through reciprocity equivalent to the establishment of an American customs union or *Zollverein*. But prerequisite to trade was the maintenance of peace and stability in Latin America, which happy condition, incidentally, would make it unnecessary to defend the Monroe Doctrine.[5] Significantly, "peace and commerce," as urged by Blaine, were to be-

---

[4] First International Conference of American States, *Report of Committee*, Sen. Exec. Doc. No. 232, 51st Cong., 1st Sess. (Washington, 1890), 225–258, cited hereinafter as First Int. Conf. of Am. States, *Report of Committee*.

[5] Robertson, 391.

come the dual objectives of the Pan American policy of the United States for many years.

Although the Arthur and Cleveland administrations were unfriendly to the idea of an inter-American conference, it found strong support in the Congress, which, after several futile attempts, finally succeeded on May 24, 1888, in adopting a resolution authorizing President Cleveland to arrange an international conference "for the purpose of discussing and recommending for adoption to their respective governments, some plan of arbitration for the settlement of disagreements and disputes that may hereafter arise between them, and for considering questions relating to the improvement of business intercourse and means of direct communication between said countries, and to encourage such reciprocal commercial relations as will be beneficial to all, and secure more extensive markets for the products of each of said countries."[6]

The President, acquiescing in the manifest desire of the Congress, allowed the resolution to become law without his signature, and instructed Secretary of State Bayard to extend invitations. In the invitations the President set forth the identical agenda provided by the Congressional resolution:

1. Measures that shall tend to preserve the peace and provide for the prosperity of the several American states.
2. Measures toward the formation of an American customs union, under which the trade of the American nations with each other shall, as far as possible and profitable, be promoted.
3. The establishment of regular and frequent communication between the governments of the several American states.
4. The establishment of a uniform system of custom regulations in each of the independent American states to govern the mode of importation and exportation of merchandise in the ports of each country, and a uniform system of invoices, and the subject of the sanitation of ships and quarantine.
5. The adoption of a uniform system of weights and measures, and laws to protect the patent rights, copyrights, and trade-marks of citizens of either country in the other, and for the extradition of criminals.
6. The adoption of a common silver coin, to be issued by each government, the same to be legal tender in all commercial transactions between the citizens of all the American states.

[6] First International Conference of American States, *Minutes*. Sen. Exec. Doc. No. 231, 51st Cong., 1st Sess. (Washington, 1890), 1, cited hereinafter as First Int. Conf. of Am. States, *Minutes*.

7. An agreement upon the recommendation for adoption to their respective governments of a definite plan of arbitration of all questions, disputes, and difficulties that may now or hereafter exist between them to the end that all difficulties and disputes between such nations may be peacefully settled and wars prevented.

8. And to consider such other subjects relating to the welfare of the several states represented as may be presented by any of the said states which are hereby invited to participate in the said conference.[7]

Reassured by the United States that the conference was to be merely consultative, was not to be an agency for compelling the adjustment of particular disputes, was not designed to affect existing treaty relations, and that all states were to meet as equals, the Latin-American republics, with only one exception (the Dominican Republic), accepted the invitations. This near-unanimity augured favorably for future all-American participation in the international conferences of American states. It should be noted here that the Congressional resolution made no provision for inviting Canada, although this had originally been suggested. There was no objection to Canada's attending merely on the grounds that she did not possess a republican form of government —Brazil when invited was still an empire—but Canada's relationship to Great Britain seemed to constitute an insurmountable obstacle. The fact is that Canada was not interested in joining the incipient inter-American system, nor did this attitude change later after there was no longer any question concerning the Dominion's independence.

The Washington Conference. The conference met in Washington on October 2, 1889. Mr. Blaine, who by a stroke of poetic justice was again secretary of state in the new Harrison administration, presided. In his welcoming address the Secretary declared that this was to be "a peaceful conference of seventeen independent American Powers, in which all shall meet together on terms of absolute equality. . . . a conference which will tolerate no spirit of conquest, but will aim to cultivate an American sympathy as broad as both Continents; . . . a conference, in fine, which will seek nothing, propose nothing, endure nothing that is not, in the general sense of all the delegates, timely, and wise, and peaceful."[8]

The conferees did not get down to serious business immediately, for at the end of the first session and until November 18, they made an official tour of the industrial centers of the United States as guests of the government. It obviously was the intention of Mr. Blaine to

[7] *Ibid.*, 1–3.   [8] *Ibid.*, 11.

impress the Latin-American delegates with the fact that American industry had the potentialities to supply their import needs should they be willing to give this country preference over European nations.

These propaganda efforts on the part of Mr. Blaine proved unavailing, for his startling proposal of a Pan American customs union, i.e., "commercial reciprocity approaching free trade on a vast scale," failed to elicit a favorable response from the Latin Americans. They objected that in return for slight, if any, concession by the United States—most of our imports from Latin America were already on the free list—they would be asked to give the United States preference over European nations in their markets. The Argentine delegation was particularly emphatic in its objections. Sr. Sáenz Peña argued that the system of "belligerent tariffs" would precipitate "the war of one continent against another, eighteen sovereignties allied to exclude from the life of commerce that same Europe which extends to us her hand, sends us her strong arms, and complements our economic existence, after having apportioned us her civilization and culture, her sciences and her arts, industries and customs that have complemented our sociologic evolution." According to Sr. Peña, Argentina opposed any action, economic or political, which would weaken traditional ties with Europe. "I do not lack affection or love for America," he said, "but I lack ingratitude or distrust towards Europe."[9] The Blaine proposal for a customs union was voted down in favor of a recommendation for bilateral reciprocity treaties.

Despite the cold reception given the idea of an American *Zollverein,* some slight progress was made by the adoption of recommendations designed to promote economic intercourse. There were resolutions recommending that all the American states adopt the metric decimal system of weights and measures, that steps be taken to construct an intercontinental railway, that inter-American steamship communications be improved,[10] and that a common system for the nomenclature of merchandise be adopted. There were other recommendations relating to an international monetary union and inter-American bank, consular fees, port dues, sanitary regulations, patents, and trade-marks. A resolution on the navigation of rivers, which provided that international rivers be "open to the free navigation of the merchant marine or ships

[9] *Ibid.,* 323; T. F. McGann, *Argentina, the United States, and the Inter-American System, 1880–1914* (Cambridge, Mass., 1957), 130–165.

[10] So occasional were the direct steamship sailings between the United States and Latin America that normally travelers found it more convenient to make their connections in Britain.

of war of the riparian nations," was adopted but with the United States voting in the negative. The American delegation was doubtful concerning how far the rights of navigation belonged to the world as against the riparian sovereignty.[11]

It was not economic but political problems that had attracted our southern neighbors to the conference. They were quick to see in the United States-sponsored inter-American meeting an excellent opportunity to press their demands for equal respect for the sovereignty of small and backward states. Consequently a resolution was proposed which provided that "a nation has not, nor recognizes in favor of foreigners, any other obligation or responsibilities than those which in favor of the natives are established, in like cases, by the constitution and the laws." Thus, in this first Pan American conference the Latin Americans took their stand in support of the Calvo Doctrine of absolute sovereignty, a position from which they never deviated in all the subsequent conferences. Their traditional policy with respect to resident aliens has been that under no condition does the alien enjoy the right to have his own government interpose in his behalf. They rejected the rather generally-accepted principle of international law which requires states to maintain a minimum standard of treatment of foreigners irrespective of how they treat their own nationals. Following Calvo, they contended that this makes foreigners privileged above the citizens of their own country.

The United States, eager to maintain high standards of international conduct, was the only state that voted against the resolution. William H. Trescot, the American delegate, said that the United States "cannot concur in any opinions which diminish the right or reduce the power of a nation by diplomatic reclamation, which is the manifestation of moral strength and vitality, to protect the rights and interests of its citizens."[12] In subsequent conferences the United States consistently opposed this proposal which the Latin Americans were trying to inject into international law, but it finally capitulated at the Montevideo conference of 1933.

 Another resolution, indicative of Latin America's quest for security not only against non-American states but against American states as well, declared territorial conquest in defiance of arbitration to be contrary to American public law. The resolution provided that: (1) "all cessions of territory made during the continuance of the treaty of arbi-

[11] First Int. Conf. of Am. States, *Minutes*, 813–814.
[12] *Ibid.*, 810–811, 832–833.

tration shall be void if made under threats of war or the presence of armed force," and (2) "any nation, from which such cessions shall be exacted, may demand that the validity of the cessions so made shall be submitted to arbitration." The resolution carried unanimously, but with Chile abstaining from voting. That power, the despoiler of Bolivia and Peru in the recent War of the Pacific, felt self-consciously that the resolution was aimed too directly at her. However, the United States—the despoiler of Mexico in 1848 but feeling no like restraint —registered approval of the resolution.[13] Since the contemplated arbitration treaty never materialized, the principle of the illegality of conquest was not established.

The proposition on the agenda of the Washington conference which aroused the greatest interest was the plan for an international compulsory-arbitration treaty. This subject revealed such great divergence of opinion among the delegations as to threaten stalemate. The Mexican government objected to compulsory arbitration, and indeed had instructed its delegation in advance to oppose such a project. Chile, while favoring limited arbitration, was anxious to prevent any outside interference in her recent territorial conquests, and objected to any plan which applied to existing disputes or disagreements that might arise from difficulties of the past or of the present. The Chilean delegate declared his conviction that to conclude such a treaty would produce "more difficulties, and more pernicious results, than those which it proposes to obviate or avoid." Chile contended that no system of absolute obligatory arbitration could be effective without a superstate to enforce the arbitral awards. And as for the creation of a superstate, Chile was emphatically opposed.[14]

On the other hand, the United States and the other states seemed to be prepared to accept obligatory arbitration. But here again the range of opinion concerning the extent of the obligatory clause was wide. Colombia and Guatemala were willing to sign a treaty with no exceptions. Argentina and the United States wished to except cases involving the independence of a state. Mexico desired to add to the exceptions those cases involving the dignity and honor of either party in a dispute. Chile demanded that pending questions be excepted. Allow these exceptions and obviously the treaty would lose its compulsory character.[15]

---

[13] *Ibid.*, 802–806.   [14] *Ibid.*, 706–718.
[15] Clifford B. Casey, "The Disposition of Political Proposals of the Various Pan American Conferences, 1889–1928" (Ph.D. dissertation, University of Texas, Austin, Texas, June 1931), 177.

After protracted debate, on April 8, 1890, a committee reported a plan for a so-called "general" compulsory-arbitration treaty, since it excepted only those cases which might endanger the independence of either party involved in a dispute. More specifically the project of an arbitration treaty provided that: (1) arbitration should be adopted as a principle of American international law for the settlement of disputes between the American republics; (2) arbitration should be obligatory in all cases, including disputes arising out of conditions antedating the treaty, and excepting only those disputes which, in the judgment of one of the states involved in the controversy, might imperil its independence; (3) the court of arbitration should consist of one or more persons selected by the disputants, but if the court should consist of an even number of arbitrators, an umpire should be appointed who should decide all questions upon which the arbitrators might disagree; and (4) decisions of a majority of the arbitrators should be final except in cases where unanimity was expressly provided.[16]

The committee report, imperceptibly modified by the plenary conference, was finally approved on April 19, 1890, by the affirmative vote of fifteen of the delegations, with Mexico and Chile not voting. In order to give special form to the project of a treaty of arbitration it was agreed that it should be signed by the delegations approving it.[17] Eleven of the states signed. However, certain of the delegations, notably those of Argentina, Brazil, and Peru, did not sign, evidently fearing that signature might be equivalent to making the project a binding treaty.[18]

Article XIX of the project provided that to become effective as a treaty it should be ratified by all the states approving it (fifteen) before May 1, 1891. By that date not one had ratified. Thus the Washington plan of arbitration remained merely a model available but never utilized. Perhaps the loss was not serious, for the project was nothing more than an agreement to agree to arbitrate, since there was no provision for resorting to arbitration except through the cooperation and consent of both parties to a dispute.[19] It might be added that reaction

[16] First Int. Conf. of Am. States, *Report of Committee*, 690.

[17] *Ibid.*, 1075. Having approved the resolution recommending arbitration for the settlement of all disputes among the American republics, the conference adopted another resolution "to express the wish that all controversies between them and the nations of Europe may be settled in the same friendly manner." —*Ibid.*, 800.

[18] Casey, 174.

[19] John P. Humphrey, *The Inter-American System: A Canadian View* (Toronto, 1942), 48.

against the extreme claims made by proponents of obligatory and unlimited arbitration treaties seems to have been such a prime factor in
building up opposition during the following decades that reservation
clauses became commonplace even in bipartite treaties.[20] It is to be
recalled that the early bilateral arbitration treaties negotiated by the
Latin-American nations were remarkably devoid of subjects excluded
from arbitration.

We are forced to the conclusion that, although arbitration was paid
lip service at the Washington conference as "a principle of American
international law," there seemed to be little disposition to convert the
abstraction into a reality. It would not be fair to point an accusing
finger at any particular nation or nations, for reluctance to take the
radical step of effective obligatory arbitration was rather general. It is
also true that the opinions expressed and the actions taken by national
delegations in this and in subsequent conferences were not always ac-
curate reflections of official policy. The approval of a resolution or the
signing of a treaty in a conference carried no assurance that the delegation's government would later implement or ratify it. For example,
although the American delegation signed the plan of arbitration, and
although President Benjamin Harrison strongly recommended its ratification by the United States Senate, that body failed to act. Thus, the
lofty declarations of the American delegates in support of arbitration
did not reflect governmental policy. They were merely opinions which
the Executive hoped the government would incorporate into policy.
This is an important fact which must never be overlooked in appraising the work of this and subsequent conferences.

The principal and almost sole tangible achievement of the Washington conference was the establishment of the International Union
of American Republics, which was to be represented in Washington
by the Commercial Bureau of the American Republics. The functions
of the bureau, later called the Pan American Union and becoming a
permanent secretariat of the conferences, were originally confined to
commercial matters. Significantly, it was the Committee on Customs
Regulations which reported the resolution that there should be established in Washington, under the supervision of the secretary of state
of the United States, an inter-American agency devoted to the "prompt
collection and distribution of commercial information," its financial
support to be apportioned to each country in proportion to its popula-

[20] Robert R. Wilson, "A New American Venture in Obligatory Arbitration,"
Southwestern Political and Social Science Quarterly, IX, No. 2 (Sept. 1928),
121.

tion.[21] The conference by unanimous vote on April 14, 1890, approved the establishment of the International Union of American Republics. It is to commemorate this action that April 14 is celebrated as Pan American Day.

The United States Congress soon appropriated money for the support of the bureau, and the other American governments did likewise. Thus there came into existence in Washington such visible evidence of inter-American cooperation that although the conference made no provision for calling subsequent ones, it was clearly implied that conferences would be held from time to time.

The Washington conference proved to be the first of a series of regular and special Pan American conferences which have attested to the broadening sense of inter-American cooperation and solidarity. This is not to say, however, that spectacular or even notable achievements, particularly in the political and security realms, were accomplished in the early decades of the movement. In fact, prior to the fifth conference at Santiago, Chile, in 1923, remarkably little progress was made in fabricating a Pan American peace structure. The political actions of the second, third, and fourth international American conferences, held at Mexico City (1901/02), Rio de Janeiro (1906), and Buenos Aires (1910), can be told briefly.

The Mexico City Conference. The initiative for the Second International Conference of American States, like that for the First, came from the government of the United States, whose leadership of the Pan American movement through the first four conferences was virtually unchallenged. Growing out of a suggestion by President McKinley in his Message to Congress on December 5, 1899, a consultation of diplomatic representatives of the American republics in Washington designated Mexico City as the site of the second international conference. This decision, coupled with the recent invitation to Mexico as the only Latin-American power to participate in the First Hague Peace Conference, was significant recognition of the lofty status that Mexico had attained in international opinion during the regime of Porfirio Díaz.

 Accordingly, in the ancient capital of the Aztec emperors, delegates from all the American republics convened on October 22, 1901. The conference agenda, drafted by the Commercial Bureau of the American Republics, contained the following subjects:

1. The reconsideration, if deemed advisable, of any agreement reached at the first conference.

[21] First Int. Conf. of Am. States, *Minutes*, 683–688.

2. A plan of international arbitration.
3. An international court of claims.
4. Measures tending to the promotion of economic relationships among the American nations.
5. Reorganization of the Commercial Bureau of American Republics.

At the Mexico conference, as at Washington, the subject of arbitration commanded the greatest attention. It also disclosed certain significant changes of viewpoint, particularly on the part of the United States. It appears that the experiences of the American Executive, in futile efforts to convince the United States Senate of the virtues of obligatory arbitration, had been quite self-educative for this branch of the government. It had now become clear to the President, as a result of the Senate debates on the Olney-Pauncefote arbitration treaty with Great Britain, that obligatory arbitration was out of the question. Consequently the American delegation arrived in Mexico City with specific instructions that all arbitration should be on a voluntary basis.[22] William I. Buchanan, chairman of the United States delegation, in explaining the American position said that obligatory arbitration was ideal but illusory because of the impracticability of enforcing its observance. An obligatory clause had force only to the extent that the signatory states were willing to carry it out. Moreover, said Mr. Buchanan, since Chile's opposition to compulsory arbitration, because of her troubles with Peru over Tacna and Arica, was well known, President Roosevelt had instructed the delegation "to assume a more conservative stand on the question," i.e., to promote the cause of arbitration, but not at the sacrifice of a greater cause, namely, American unity and cooperation.[23] The President, also aware of the sensitiveness of the Latin Americans and that their suspicions of the United States had been rekindled by a number of incidents as well as by the Spanish-American War, cautioned the delegates against assuming a too prominent role in the conference, or taking sides upon issues between Latin-American states. With respect to "political questions," President Roosevelt said that the delegates should "proceed with great caution" and that "the general principle should be to enter as little as possible into these questions."[24]

[22] Second International Conference of American States, *Report of Delegates of the United States, with Accompanying Papers.* Sen. Exec. Doc. No. 330, 57th Cong., 1st Sess. (Washington, 1902), 35, cited hereinafter as Second Int. Conf. of Am. States, *Report of Delegates.*

[23] William I. Buchanan, "Latin America and the Mexican Conference," *Annals* of American Academy of Political and Social Science, XXIII (1903), 45–55.

[24] Second Int. Conf. of Am. States, *Report of Delegates,* 32.

As at Washington, Chile was adamant against the compulsory arbitration of past or pending disputes. When the agenda for the conference was being decided upon, Chile held out against the inclusion of arbitration and consented only when it was agreed that her wishes would be respected. But notwithstanding this guarantee an inclusive plan of obligatory arbitration was brought before the Mexico City conference. Chile protested this alleged breach of faith and threatened to withdraw. Thanks to the unremitting efforts of the United States delegation the Chileans were dissuaded and the conference was saved. Brazil, because of boundary questions pending with her western neighbors, also was strongly opposed to the discussion of obligatory arbitration.

The great divergence of views concerning the scope of obligatory arbitration made it very difficult to get any form of statement that would satisfy all the delegates. After much wrangling and surviving several near-fatal crises, they agreed upon a plan that was in the nature of a compromise: (1) the adherence of the American states that were not already members (as were Mexico and the United States) to The Hague conventions, which provided for voluntary arbitration; and (2) a treaty of compulsory arbitration to be signed by those republics advocating it.[25]

In pursuance of this agreement a protocol, signed by the delegations of sixteen of the nineteen countries represented at the conference,[26] provided that all the republics that had not already subscribed to The Hague conventions should adhere to them and recognize as a part of American international law the principles set forth therein. The Convention for the Pacific Settlement of International Disputes provided a system of purely voluntary arbitration. Although loudly acclaimed, it was looked upon by many as being meaningless and without force. Since it was a closed convention and could be adhered to by non-signatory states only with the consent of the signatory powers, the United States and Mexico—the two signatory states—were asked to negotiate for the adherence of the other American republics. This was done, and eventually, at the Second Hague Peace Conference in 1907, a protocol of adherence was opened for signature by the American republics. Seventeen Latin-American States signed.[27]

A treaty of compulsory arbitration was drafted at the Mexico City conference by those delegations that could be satisfied with nothing

[25] *Ibid.*, 47–55.   [26] *Ibid.*, 36–39.
[27] The other two Hague conventions, which dealt with the laws of war, were adhered to by sixteen of the Latin-American republics.

‡·less than obligatory recourse to the arbitral procedure. Despite its alleged compulsory character, the treaty was burdened with exceptions which greatly vitiated it as an obligatory instrument. All cases in controversy should be submitted to the Permanent Court of Arbitration at The Hague, unless one of the parties to the dispute preferred a special *ad hoc* tribunal. In addition to its arbitral provisions, the treaty provided for the use of good offices, mediation, inquiry, and conciliation. It was signed by nine of the Latin-American delegations but was subsequently ratified by only six of the states.

While opposing general obligatory arbitration, the United States believed that the principle could more profitably be applied to restricted subjects—pecuniary claims,[28] for example. It felt that if any type of dispute was susceptible of arbitral settlement it would be claims for damages by individual citizens of one state against the government of another, since these controversies are usually free of the emotional factor which makes recourse to arbitral procedure so difficult in the settlement of political questions. Moreover, it was felt that a multilateral treaty on the compulsory arbitration of pecuniary claims not only would give the American states opportunity to prove their attachment to the principle but would be valuable preparation for extending the scope of compulsory arbitration.

On their part, most of the Latin-American states, having suffered infractions of their national sovereignty at the hands of powerful states acting on behalf of the claims of their nationals, and pending the general adoption of the Calvo Doctrine, were disposed to favor a scheme for adjusting international claims on a legal basis which would render justice regardless of the size and strength of the respective parties. For this reason there was included on the agenda of the Mexico City conference the establishment of an international court of claims, from which eventuated the Treaty of Arbitration for Pecuniary Claims, which was signed by all of the delegations present.

The principal features of the pecuniary-claims treaty were as follows: (1) the contracting parties should submit to arbitration by the Permanent Court at The Hague all claims for pecuniary damages presented by their respective citizens which it was not possible to settle through diplomacy; (2) if both parties preferred, a special arbitral court should be constituted; (3) the treaty was not to be obligatory except upon those states that should ratify the protocol of adherence to

---

[28] The term "pecuniary claims" refers to all controversies between states founded upon private claims for monetary damages on the part of the nationals of one state against the government of another.

The Hague conventions; and (4) the treaty should be binding when ratified by five states, and it should endure for a period of five years.[29]

Like the so-called "compulsory-arbitration" treaty, also drafted at the Mexico City conference, the pecuniary-claims convention was in reality little more than an agreement to agree to arbitrate, for while the parties undertook to submit their disputes to the Permanent Court of Arbitration at The Hague (which was neither permanent nor a court, but merely a panel of names), any one of them could insist on the creation of an *ad hoc* tribunal, the organization of which required the state's previous cooperation as did, of course, the organization of a tribunal under The Hague treaty.[30] A virtue of the pecuniary-claims convention was that there was no exemption in favor of disputes affecting independence or national honor. The convention was ratified by ten states.

At Mexico City, as at the Washington conference, it was not to be expected that the Latin Americans would forgo an opportunity to press their demands for equal respect of the sovereignty of small and backward states. Accordingly, a resolution dealing with the rights of aliens—substantially the same as the one adopted by the Washington conference—was signed, but again not by the United States. Its three significant features were that states owe to foreigners no obligations or responsibilities not guaranteed to their own citizens; states are not responsible for damages sustained by aliens in civil war; and claims of aliens shall be made to a competent court of the country, and not through diplomatic channels. It was patent that the principles of this resolution were incompatible with the pecuniary-claims convention. Little wonder, then, that the latter never became an effective feature of the Pan American peace set-up.

Finally, the conference reorganized the Commercial Bureau of the American Republics, which now became the International Bureau of American Republics. Its functions were enlarged, making it a sort of permanent secretariat of the "Union of American Republics." To answer the criticism that the bureau was too much an agency of the United States government, its administration was transferred from the secretary of state to the Governing Board, consisting of the secretary of state, who was to act as chairman, and the chiefs of Latin-American diplomatic missions at Washington.

The Rio de Janeiro Conference. Latin-American suspicions and fears

---

[29] Second Int. Conf. of Am. States, *Minutes*, 853–855.
[30] Humphrey, 53.

of the United States, not yet fully manifest at the Mexico City conference in 1901, burst into full bloom soon after, thanks to actions by
President Theodore Roosevelt. The "taking" of the Panama Canal,
the establishment of protectorates over Cuba and Panama, the exercise
with "the big stick" of a self-appointed international police-power in
the Caribbean, and the assuming of customs control in the Dominican
Republic—all these evidences of the new Yankee imperialism created
a profound distrust of the United States. Obviously, given this unfriendly atmosphere, it would have been foolhardy for the United
States to allow the pending third Pan American conference at Rio de
Janeiro to be used as a forum for the denunciation of Yankee imperialism and for the formulation of anti-United States policies.

Consequently the United States exercised its influence to exclude
controversial political subjects from the conference agenda. The discussions were to be confined, as much as possible, to the "safe and
sane" economic, social, and cultural topics. The four political items
which remained after very careful culling were the reorganization of
the International Bureau of American Republics; the adherence of the
American republics to the principle of arbitration; consideration of the
extension of the treaty on pecuniary claims; and a proposal to recommend the question of the collection of public debts for the consideration of the Second Hague Peace Conference. Two legal, or juridical,
items on the program were a proposal to create a commission of jurists
to prepare a draft of a code of public and private international law; and
the consideration of questions concerning aliens and naturalization.

In his instructions to the United States delegates to the conference
at Rio de Janeiro in 1906, Secretary of State Elihu Root reiterated the
words of President Roosevelt in 1901 that, with respect to political
questions, they should "proceed with great caution" and enter into
them as little as possible.[31] Mr. Root's concern regarding the dangerous
possibilities of bringing up political questions was further revealed by
an address which he delivered, as an honored guest, to the conference
on July 31, 1906. He commented on the possibilities for fruitful
achievement by the conference since it would not be distracted by political questions, the settlement of claims, or the passing of judgment
on the conduct of any state.[32]

In an effort to conciliate the Latin-American delegates, so fearful

[31] Third International Conference of American States, *Report of Delegates.*
Sen. Exec. Doc. No. 365, 59th Cong., 2d Sess., 39, cited hereinafter as Third
Int. Conf. of Am. States, *Report of Delegates.*

[32] *Ibid.,* 63.

and suspicious of the United States, Mr. Root made to the conference this famous statement of reassurance:

We wish for no victories but those of peace; for no territory except our own; for no sovereignty except the sovereignty over ourselves. We deem the independence and equal rights of the smallest and weakest member of the family of nations entitled to as much respect as those of the greatest empire, and we deem the observance of that respect the chief guaranty of the weak against the strong. We neither claim nor desire any rights, or privileges, or powers that we do not freely concede to every American Republic.[33]

Although the cynic must have found it difficult to reconcile Mr. Root's reassurances with the unfolding of American policy in the Caribbean area, the Secretary's sincerity and persuasiveness elicited a favorable response both in the conference and throughout Latin America. For this reason, and also because the program had been carefully culled of all topics which might cause disagreement, the Third International Conference of American States was much more harmonious than might have been expected.

On the subject of arbitration, a topic of acrimonious debate in the preceding conferences, a proposal by Bolivia and Peru for an iron-clad statement in favor of compulsory arbitration was rejected, and the conference adopted instead on August 7, 1906, a resolution

to ratify adherence to the principle of arbitration; and to the end that so high a purpose may be rendered practicable, to recommend to the Nations represented at this conference that instructions be given to their Delegates to the Second Conference to be held at The Hague, to endeavor to secure by that said assembly, of world-wide character, the celebration of a general arbitration convention, so effective and definite that, meriting the approval of the civilized world, it shall be accepted and put into force by every nation.[34]

Any possible inclination by the United States to consider a general arbitration treaty had been completely suppressed because of the indifferent reception given the Treaty of Arbitration for Pecuniary

[33] Third International Conference of American States, *Minutes, Resolutions, and Documents* (Rio de Janeiro, 1907), 131–132, cited hereinafter as Third Int. Conf. of Am. States, *Minutes*.

[34] *Ibid.*, 569–590. The Second Hague Conference of 1907 adopted a general convention for the pacific settlement of international disputes. This provided for the use of good offices, mediation, commissions of inquiry, and voluntary arbitration. A project of unrestricted obligatory arbitration, introduced at The Hague by the Dominican Republic, was put aside by the conference as being premature.

Claims. According to Secretary of State Root, since so many of the states had not ratified that treaty—"the very simplest and narrowest form of a general agreement to arbitrate"—it was useless to discuss arbitration on a wider scope. He therefore instructed the American delegates to seek a five-year extension of the treaty and the adherence of the other American states (only nine had ratified).[35]

The conference Committee on Arbitration, in reporting to the plenary body a recommendation that the pecuniary-claims convention be continued for another five-year period, undertook to rally the non-ratifying states to its support by assuring them that the arbitral arrangement did not make it easier for aliens to avoid internal jurisdiction. According to the committee, "the treaty embraced only those cases which could not be adjusted amicably through diplomatic channels, and . . . it was reasonable to presume that this would include only cases in which diplomatic intervention was justified and in which local remedies had been exhausted."[36] The conference approved the extension of the convention to December 31, 1912, but the expected ratifications were not forthcoming.

Most of the interest at the Rio conference was focused on the fourth topic of the agenda: "a resolution recommending that the Second Peace Conference at The Hague be requested to consider whether, and if at all, to what extent, the use of force for the collection of public debts is admissible."[37] This topic inaugurated in inter-American discussions a new aspect of the problem of international claims. The issue, a direct repercussion of the Anglo-German-Italian intervention in Venezuela in 1902, was whether a state had the right to resort to force for the collection of contract claims. Although international law was not clear on the subject, it was nevertheless a not infrequent practice for strong states to embark upon debt-collecting expeditions. Since many of the weaker republics of Latin America had been the victims of such interventions, with consequent great violence to their national sovereignties, there developed vigorous agitation, inspired by the writings (about the middle of the nineteenth century) of the great Argentine international lawyer Carlos Calvo to outlaw the practice of intervention. Seizing on the Venezuelan crisis, Luis María Drago, Argentine minister of foreign affairs, proposed to Secretary of State John

---

[35] Third Int. Conf. of Am. States, *Report of Delegates,* 41–42.

[36] Casey, 297.

[37] The public debt of a state, more generally called a "contract debt," embraces governmental bonds, note issues, and other obligations. "Contract claims" are those arising from the default by a state on its contract debt.

Drago Doctrine

Hay on December 29, 1902, "that the public debt cannot occasion armed intervention nor even the actual occupation of the territory of American nations by a European Power." Drago's proposal, to become known as the Drago Doctrine, was a restatement, but in a somewhat restricted sense, of the Calvo Doctrine. He argued that since public debts are contracted by the sovereign power of a state, they constitute a special kind of obligation and are therefore not subject to forcible collection.[38]

Drago sought to influence United States support of his doctrine by demonstrating its correlation to the Monroe Doctrine. "The collection of debts by military means," he pointed out, "implies territorial occupation to make them effective, and territorial occupation signifies the suppression or subordination of the governments of the countries on which it is imposed." According to Drago, such a situation was clearly at variance with the principles of the Monroe Doctrine—"a doctrine to which the Argentine Republic has heretofore solemnly adhered."[39] A few years later Drago explained that his doctrine was "an American thesis" maintained "by solidarity with the nations of this continent, with scope and purposes purely American. . . . We enunciated it as a result of the Venezuelan conflict, because Venezuela is a sister republic. We could not have spoken had the country compelled by force to pay its debts been Turkey or Greece."[40]

Although the United States had on a number of occasions given tacit recognition to the right of European governments to use force for the collection of contractual claims, President Theodore Roosevelt recognized the threat of this practice to the Monroe Doctrine. But while accepting within limits the validity of Drago's argument, the President was not willing to forgo the right of the United States government to protect its citizens' investments abroad. The dilemma was resolved by the "Roosevelt corollary" of the Monroe Doctrine. In his annual message of December 6, 1904, the President made the following statement:

Chronic wrongdoing, or an impotence which results in a general loosening of the ties of civilized society, may in America, as elsewhere, ultimately

[38] U.S. Dept. of State, *Foreign Relations of the United States, 1903*, 3.
[39] *Ibid.*
[40] "Letter of Dr. Drago to the Minister of Foreign Affairs of the Argentine Republic, May 9, 1906," in Alejandro Álvarez, *The Monroe Doctrine*, 254. According to Whitaker (*The Western Hemisphere Idea*, 88), it was unfortunate that the United States did not accept Drago's proposal, for if it had, the whole future history of United States–Argentine relations might have been changed for the better.

require intervention by some civilized nations, and in the Western Hemisphere the adherence of the United States to the Monroe Doctrine may force the United States, however reluctantly, in flagrant cases of such wrongdoing or impotence, to the exercise of an international police power. . . . We would interfere with them [our southern neighbors] only in the last resort, and then only if it became evident that their inability or unwillingness to do justice at home and abroad had violated the rights of the United States or had invited foreign aggression to the detriment of the entire body of American nations.[41]

The policy adopted by the United States government to anticipate the development of situations in Latin America which might eventuate in debt-collecting expeditions was regarded by the southern neighbors as a remedy possibly even more dangerous than the malady itself. In their view the United States, by assuming responsibility for their good behavior, now held over them a vastly extended right of intervention.

In an effort to diminish this danger, the Argentine government insisted that the Drago Doctrine be included on the program of the Rio conference. The great majority of the states represented indicated their willingness to vote solemn sanction of the principles of the Doctrine. All eyes were then turned on the United States. Its delegation suggested that the conference avoid "taking definite action on the question of the forcible collection of contract debts on the grounds that any action in this respect would arouse distrust on the part of European capitalists, and thus would harm the credit of certain of the American states."[42] However, the United States had no objection to the problem's being recommended for discussion at The Hague. The United States view prevailed. So, on August 22, 1906, the conference adopted a resolution "to recommend to the governments represented therein that they consider the point of inviting the Second Peace Conference, at The Hague, to examine the question of the compulsory collection of public debts, and, in general, means tending to diminish between nations conflicts having an exclusively pecuniary origin."[43]

It is to be noted that the conference action, instead of being a direct, collective recommendation to The Hague, was merely a recommendation to the individual American governments to instruct their delegates to bring up the matter at The Hague conference. What action was

[41] James D. Richardson (ed.), *Messages and Papers of the Presidents* (20 vols., Washington, 1917), XVI, 7053–7054.
[42] Casey, 309.
[43] Third Int. Conf. of Am. States, *Minutes*, 218.

taken at The Hague in 1907 is worthy of more than a footnote. In deference to the resolution adopted at Rio de Janeiro, the United States delegation went to The Hague under instructions to support the principle that contract claims cannot occasion armed intervention. This was not, however, an unqualified acceptance of the Drago Doctrine, for the United States proposal, presented to The Hague conference by delegate General Horace Porter, forbade the use of force for the collection of contract debts *provided* the debtor state accepted arbitration and the arbitral award. This so-called Porter Doctrine, which was approved by the nations assembled at The Hague on October 18, 1907, meant that the right to use force was not outlawed unconditionally, as demanded by the Latin Americans, but that its renunciation was made contingent on the acceptance of arbitration. This was a bitter disappointment to our southern neighbors, and it was only because they recognized that the Porter convention was better than nothing at all that they all agreed, with only one exception, to sign it. It was never ratified, however, by more than six of them. Nevertheless the Porter Doctrine, by virtue of its general acceptance by the nations of the world at The Hague, became a part of international law. Drago's effort to curb the right of intervention had boomeranged.

Now to return to the remaining acts of the Rio conference relating in any way to the problem of security. Beyond enlarging somewhat the functions of the International Bureau of American Republics, and providing for an International Commission of Jurists to draft codes of international law,[44] which would clearly define the status, rights, and duties of aliens so as to limit the right of intervention (presumably by the United States), the conference contributed little more that was illustrative of the slowly developing trend toward inter-American security cooperation. But, almost coincidental with the Rio de Janeiro meeting, this concept was being implemented, on a limited scale, by the Central American republics.

. *The Central American Conference in Washington.* One of the resolutions of the Rio conference had been an acknowledgment of the mediation of Presidents Roosevelt and Porfirio Díaz in a Central

---

[44] A convention signed at the Mexico City conference of 1902 provided for the creation of a commission of five Americans and two Europeans to draft a code of international law. The convention was not ratified and thus did not become effective. The Rio convention was ratified and became effective, subject, however, to amendment by a subsequent protocol which allowed each American state to appoint two representatives to the commission instead of one. The International Commission of Jurists finally met in Rio de Janeiro in 1912, but its work was interrupted by the outbreak of World War I.

American conflict. As a result of this mediation a conference of all the Central American states, under the sponsorship of the United States and Mexico, met in Washington in 1907 to discuss the problems of their mutual relationships. Several conventions were signed providing for, among other things: the Central American Court of Justice; the neutralization of Honduras, whose geographical position made her a cockpit for her neighbors north and south; prohibiting revolutionary chieftains from residing in regions adjacent to a country whose peace they might disturb; the promotion of constitutional reforms prohibiting presidential re-election; agreement not to recognize any government that came into existence by revolution until it should have been legitimized by a free vote of the people; and no intervention in favor of either of the parties contending in a civil war. It is to be noted that these security measures were the result of, and were designed to meet, problems characteristic of Central America. They did not confront threats from any non-Central American source.

Undoubtedly the most significant action of this conference was the convention providing for the Permanent Court of Justice, composed of one judge each for the five Central American states. The contracting states bound themselves to submit to this tribunal all disputes and controversies, *without exception,* which might arise between them and which they were unable to settle through diplomatic channels. The jurisdiction of the court was not limited to disputes between states, for it could take cognizance of cases between a citizen of a Central American state and the government of another state. It also could consider controversies submitted by special agreement between a Central American state and a foreign government. Decisions of the court were to be by a majority of three, and the contracting states bound themselves to submit to its judgments and "lend all moral support that may be necessary in order that they may be properly fulfilled."[45] Conforming to the standards set by arbitration jurists, the treaty was well-nigh perfect. Nevertheless the Central American court failed.

In its very first case the judges, who were supposed to be free of any national or partisan bias, clearly voted as the interests of their own governments dictated. Then, shortly thereafter, one of the judges was replaced by his government for purely partisan reasons.[46] Consequently

[45] "Convention Establishing the Central American Court of Justice," in William R. Manning (ed.), *Arbitration Treaties Among The American Nations To The Close Of The Year 1910* (New York, 1924), 394–401.
[46] Dana G. Munro, *The United States and the Caribbean Area* (Boston, 1934), 202.

the court failed to command respect as a truly impartial international tribunal, and nothing that it did prior to 1916 helped to improve the opinion in which it was held. In that year the court entertained the case which brought about its downfall.

Costa Rica and El Salvador complained to the court that their rights had been violated by the Bryan-Chamorro treaty entered into by Nicaragua with the United States in 1916. Under the terms of this treaty Nicaragua granted to the United States perpetual proprietary canal right across the country and a leasehold for a naval base on the Gulf of Fonseca. Costa Rica objected on the ground that Nicaragua was bound by a prior treaty between the two countries never to make a grant for a canal without the other's consent. El Salvador held that the waters of the Gulf of Fonseca constitute a condominium, and consequently Nicaragua had no right to cede a portion of the gulf to a foreign power.

Although Nicaragua refused to admit the jurisdiction of the court, both suits were decided against that country. Nicaragua, with the backing of the United States, disregarded the decision and gave the necessary one year's notice of its intention to abrogate the treaty which had established the court. One year later, on March 12, 1918, the Central American Permanent Court of Justice went out of existence. The noble experiment which had been widely acclaimed by peace leaders proved to be unworkable when put to the test, for, quite independent of United States involvement, the five Central American republics merely presented in miniature the identical prejudices, fears, emotions, jealousies, suspicions, and national sensitiveness that have always been barriers to the effective operation of any international peace organization.

The Buenos Aires Conference. The lessons of the Central American peace fiasco came too late for the architects of an inter-American peace structure to apply them before World War I. Nevertheless it was to the credit of the United States government that a calm, circumspect, and gradual approach to the goal of inter-American security was recognized as the only sound policy. The basis of true unity and solidarity had to be established first by demonstrations of cooperative action in those many areas— economic, social, cultural—that lent themselves to this end, meanwhile postponing to the indeterminate future consideration of more difficult, contentious, and vital political subjects. For this reason the United States exercised extreme caution in approving the agenda for the Fourth International Conference of American States scheduled to meet in Buenos Aires in 1910. Only two of the subjects given sanction bore a political semblance. One had to do with extending the time the pecuniary-claims treaty would remain in effect, and the other related to the reorganization of the International Bureau of American Republics.

General arbitration, for the first time since the "new" Pan Americanism began, was not on the conference agenda. Moreover, the United States delegation was instructed to oppose any effort of the conference to conclude a general obligatory-arbitration convention. Their instructions pointed to The Hague convention and existing bipartite treaties as indicating the extent to which it was advisable to go for the time being in the matter of obligatory arbitration. The Root treaties of 1908/09, which excepted from arbitration disputes affecting the vital interests, independence, or honor of the contracting parties, and the interests of third states, were undoubtedly the model bipartite treaties to which these instructions referred. Such treaties had recently been negotiated by the United States with Mexico, Peru, El Salvador, Costa Rica, Ecuador, and Haiti. Also the Convention for the Pacific Settlement of International Disputes, adopted at the second Hague conference in 1907, provided for good offices, mediation, commissions of inquiry, and arbitration. Article 38 provided that "in questions of a legal nature, and especially in the interpretation or application of international conventions, arbitration is recognized by the contracting Powers as the most effective means of settling disputes which diplomacy has failed to settle." The Hague convention, therefore, merely *recommended* the arbitral procedure.

As anticipated, the discussions at Buenos Aires were remarkably harmonious, though there was some debate in committee on pecuniary claims. Some of the Latin-American delegations wanted to make more restrictive the treaty clause which determined the right of a state to require another state to arbitrate a claim. They were of the opinion that there should not be recourse to obligatory arbitration except in case of a denial of justice; furthermore it was proposed that the propriety of diplomatic action to invoke the arbitration of claims should itself be made the subject of obligatory arbitration. Both of these attempted evasions were defeated by the United States delegation. On August 11, 1910, the conference voted to continue the Treaty of Arbitration for Pecuniary Claims in force for an indefinite period. It thus became a permanent feature of the inter-American security system, though it was never ratified by more than eleven countries. Its contributions to the settlement of inter-American disputes have been indiscernible.

The other quasi-political action of the Buenos Aires conference was the adoption of a resolution providing for a reorganization of the International Bureau of American Republics. The title of the bureau was changed to "The Pan American Union," and its functions were somewhat enlarged so that it could operate more effectively "as a permanent committee of the International American Conferences." Administered by a director-general, the control of the Union was vested in a governing board composed of the diplomatic representatives of the American republics accredited to the government of the United States, with the secretary of state as the permanent chairman. In answer to the objection that a state having no diplomatic representative at Washington would be denied representation on the Governing Board, it was agreed that such a state might designate a member of the Governing Board to represent it. However, the proposal that the chairmanship of the board be made elective was suffocated a-borning. Not only was the Pan American Union—shortly to be housed in a million-dollar palace, thanks to the generosity of Andrew Carnegie— visual evidence of the developing realization of inter-American unity, but also, because of its adjacency to the State Department and the White House, it symbolized the dominance of the United States over this cooperative movement.

An appraisement of Pan American development. The success of the United States in blocking consideration of political subjects in the conferences, at the very time when our motives and methods in the Caribbean were the subjects of bitter criticism, virtually killed all enthusiasm in Latin America for Pan Americanism. Dr. Naón, Argentine ambassador to the United States, said in 1913, "There is no Pan Americanism in South America; it exists only in Washington."

The very term "Pan Americanism" was associated with "Yankee imperialism," and was represented as a "Made in the U.S.A." antidote to counteract the Monroe Doctrine poison. According to the Latin-American view, the United States ministered Pan American good-will in order to allay the ill-will engendered by its practices of intervention. Thus, it was not surprising that when Brazil tried, at the Buenos Aires conference, to secure general acknowledgment of the benefits of the Monroe Doctrine, her efforts were frustrated. The other Latin Americans insisted that before putting on record their approval of the Doctrine it should be redefined in such a way as to remove the features that were an impairment of the sovereignty of their countries. "We reject Pan Americanism," cried *La Época* of Buenos Aires," which is but a hollow mockery for us South Americans."

Fortunately this view was not reflected in official governmental policy, for there was no significant deviation from the accustomed support of the movement. Although the failure to measure up to the Latin-American, or Bolivarian, ideal of inter-American cooperation was very disappointing to the *Latinos,* the manifest evidences of progress in converting the idea of unity and solidarity into a reality made the "new" Pan Americanism—even though dominated by the United States—too valuable to be abandoned. World War I soon presented an occasion to test the attachment of the American republics to the ideals of cooperation and solidarity.

But before taking note of how Pan Americanism confronted the problems of a great world conflict, it is desirable at this point to take stock of the inter-American peace structure as it existed at that date. To what extent had the American states adopted security measures to meet the dangers of a foreign war? The simple truth is that in the deliberations of the first four international American conferences, no consideration whatever had been given to the problems of security created by a foreign war or by the attack of an overseas aggressor. Beyond certain vague and general commitments to submit controversies with non-American states to procedures of peaceful settlement, the inter-American peace structure was designed solely for the settlement of inter-American disputes.

The failure of the conferences held after 1889 to reckon with European threats to the peace and security of the Americas contrasts sharply with the major concern of the "old" Pan Americanism. The early conferences, as has been noted, drafted treaties of alliance and confederation in order to present a common front to a foreign enemy. Why, then, did the "new" Pan Americanism fail to reckon with possible threats from beyond American shores? In the first place, the European threat to the peace and security of the Americas was felt to be so remote as not to warrant serious consideration. The rise of Germany and her threat to British naval supremacy did not shake this confidence. And in the second place, the United States, while more aware of latent dangers in the European situation than her southern neighbors, did not see fit to favor defense commitments with them. This reluctance was due not only to the national tradition of avoiding alliances but also to a belief that the Latin-American nations could offer nothing to us, militarily speaking. Because of their great weakness and instability it was feared that defense arrangements with them would be liabilities rather than assets. Perhaps it was also the thought of United States policy-makers that if we were uncommitted, our contributions to the establishment of orderly and peaceful conditions in and among the Latin-American nations would pay richer dividends in the event of war.

Notwithstanding the foregoing, by 1914 the inter-American peace structure had attained no mean proportions. Numerous inter-American bilateral arbitration treaties, varying in scope, were in effect.[47] For example, eleven treaties excepted no disputes whatsoever from arbitration. There were seventeen treaties which excepted from arbitration disputes affecting vital interests, independence, sovereignty, national honor, or the interests of third states. The United States was a party to six of these, known as the Root treaties. Five treaties excepted from arbitration disputes affecting territorial integrity. Latin Americans were very chary about submitting to arbitration disputes affecting constitutional principles or provisions; twenty of their arbitration treaties contained such exceptions. Three others excepted cases of denial of justice. Of all the arbitration treaties listed, the only ones to which the United States was a party were the six Root treaties.[48]

Numerous bilateral treaties, providing for commissions of conciliation or commissions of inquiry, were in force in 1914 between the American republics. The United States had recently entered into such pacts—known as the Bryan "cooling off" treaties—with eleven Latin-American countries. They provided for submitting all disputes of whatever character to an international commission for investigation and report. These commissions were permanent in membership, ensuring that questions might be referred to them without the necessity of constituting *ad hoc* commissions when a dispute occurred. When the commission was making its inquiry—it was allowed as long as a year—the parties to the dispute were bound to withhold resort to arms; this constituted the "cooling off" feature. Although Secretary of State Bryan regarded his formula as a great contribution to the peace movement, the writer knows of not a single instance in which a Bryan treaty was invoked. Moreover several of the signatories were lax in setting up and maintaining the permanent commissions required by the convention.[49]

[47] For a list of all treaties of arbitration, see Sexta Conferencia Internacional Americana, *Comentarios sobre los temas del Programa* (Havana, 1927), 39–42. Treaties concluded to 1910 are found in Manning, *Arbitration Treaties Among The American Nations.*

[48] The above data are taken from *Arbitration on the American Continent*, Foreign Policy Association, *Information Service*, IV, No. 17, Appendix.

[49] *Ibid.*, 341. The Bryan "cooling-off" formula was inspiration later for the Gondra treaty.

In 1914, there also existed among the American nations certain multilateral treaties for the pacific settlement of disputes of a purely American character. The Mexico City conference in 1902 had negotiated the Treaty on Compulsory Arbitration, which pledged its adherents to submit to arbitration by the Permanent Court of The Hague, or to a special tribunal, all questions pending, or that might arise in the future, which did not affect independence or national honor. This treaty was signed by nine states and ratified by six. The United States did not ratify; since the Washington conference in 1889, it had been opposed to the system of compulsory arbitration. As a creditor nation the United States was more disposed to favor the arbitration of pecuniary claims. Although the debtor Latin-American states feared that arbitration of claims might be resorted to in cases which should properly be decided by the national courts, they were pressured by the United States to enter into a multilateral convention for the arbitration of pecuniary claims. This treaty was ratified by only eleven countries. Among the inter-American multilateral arbitration treaties existent in 1914, there should also be included the convention drafted by the Central American Conference in Washington, which provided for the Permanent Court of Justice to act as a court of arbitration.

From the foregoing it can be fairly concluded that, by 1914, the framework for the settlement of purely inter-American controversies was rather extensive. However, it was a topsy-like structure, thrown together without design or plan. Moreover there were many gaps which weakened the entire edifice and afforded slight protection against the elements of international discord in an emergency. Besides the failure to reckon with foreign aggression, its principal deficiency was the lack of a multilateral agreement for obligatory arbitration with a minimum of escape clauses. Bilateral treaties excepting no disputes from arbitration existed among nine states in eleven treaties. The negotiation of similar treaties by the remaining states would have greatly improved the situation; yet even more effective as a preserver of peace would have been a multilateral compulsory arbitration treaty, for it would have given each signatory state a vital interest in every dispute. A second defect in the peace structure was the absence of a multilateral convention on conciliation, including the use of good offices, mediation, investigation, and report. Virtually the only practicable means of ensuring resort to conciliation is to give third states an interest, as signatory members, in the observance of the contractual obligation. The multilateral convention, whether it be for arbitration or conciliation, is vastly superior to the bilateral treaty because it brings to bear upon reluctant states the powerful sanction of public opinion.

With respect to the pacific settlement of international disputes, it can be said, therefore, that the first four Pan American conferences explored the possibilities of multipartite agreement. The essential problems had been carefully analyzed and the necessary spadework done. It was possible now for the subsequent conferences to undertake the construction of a more or less schematic system of multilateral treaties.

It would be a great mistake, however, to predicate the efficacy of a security system merely on the purely technical perfection of the peace machinery, for the machinery is merely the means to an end. The essence of the problem is the will of the member states to peace. Two states, sincerely, honestly, and unselfishly seeking to find a peaceful solution of their difficulty, will not be deflected from the goal by a so-called inadequate peace pact. Usually the inadequacy is found not in the pact but in the will to peace.

The first four conferences of the "new" Pan American phase may not apparently have contributed much to the American security structure. It is conceded that, from a short-range view, the progress and achievements were very modest, to say the least. However, as pointed out by the great Brazilian statesman Joaquim Nabuco, the conferences cannot proceed faster than the individual states are prepared to go, for the rule of unanimity obtains. But, the discussions, by reflecting continental opinion, do influence subsequent conduct and policies of individual states. Thus the action of a later conference on a particular subject either constitutes a step in advance of that taken previously on the same subject, or it represents an attempt to find a formula acceptable to all of the states. Nabuco said, "This method may appear slow, but I believe it to be the only efficacious one." In the same vein Elihu Root said, "Not by a single conference nor by a single effort can very much be done. You labor more for the future than for the present."[50] The foundations were laid in these early conferences for more significant achievement in the later ones.

[50] *Report of the Delegates of the United States to the Third International Conference of American States* (Washington, 1907), 64.

IV The "New" Pan Americanism: II (1914–1928)

Pan Americanism implies the equality of all sovereignties, large and small, the assurance that no country will attempt to diminish the territory of others. . . . It is, in short, an exponent of deep brotherly sentiment, and a just aspiration for material and moral aggrandizement of all the peoples of America.

BALTASAR BRUM, 1920

THE OUTBREAK OF WORLD WAR I not only forced a postponement of the Fifth International Conference of American States, scheduled to meet at Santiago, Chile, in 1914, but also posed for the American republics problems which tested as never before the validity of their protestations of unity and solidarity. These were the problems of neutrality (1914–17) and belligerency (1917/18). Since the four preceding Pan American conferences had given no consideration to the advantages of collaboration to preserve neutrality in the event of a foreign war, or to defend against possible belligerent aggression, the outbreak of war in 1914 found the nations of America without any agreed-upon plan of action. Consequently the measures of cooperation that were undertaken were on a completely *ad hoc* basis.

The problems of neutrality. The eruption of war in Europe was viewed in the Americas as a strictly non-American affair, and so the republics individually and independently declared their neutrality. Their only joint actions during the first two and one-half years (i.e., prior to April 1917) were confined to proposals to safeguard neutrality, and measures to meet the economic problems created by the war.

The Governing Board of the Pan American Union, acting on the initiative of Peru, created early in the war the Special Neutrality Commission, with the secretary of state of the United States as *ex officio* chairman, to study problems affecting American neutrality growing out of the European war, and to submit suggestions for their solution. The commission first met on December 8, 1914. Peru made the novel proposal that the American republics adopt the principle that their commerce be immune from belligerent interference in the waters surrounding the Americas and extending to lines equidistant from Europe and from Asia.[1] Venezuela and Uruguay proposed calling a conference of neutrals. Chile, troubled by the presence of belligerents' ships in her waters, recommended that the American nations agree to restrict the amount of coal a ship could obtain to the amount necessary to reach the nearest coaling station of a neighboring country. The commission itself made a number of recommendations defining and protecting the rights of neutrals, notably that belligerent warships should not be supplied with coal in American ports and that the property of a neutral or of an enemy on board neutral vessels should be inviolable on the high seas. These recommendations were forwarded to the member states by the Governing Board of the Pan American Union. It cannot be recorded that any action was taken.[2]

There was more effective cooperation to meet the economic problems created by the war. Owing to the initiative of Secretary of the Treasury William McAdoo, the financial ministers of the American republics met in Washington in May 1915, in the First Pan American Financial Conference, "to study the measures," said the Secretary, "which should be taken in order to protect their own interests against the consequences of the colossal European conflict." Revealing that the purpose of the United States in sponsoring the conference went beyond immediate economic and financial objectives, Secretary McAdoo recommended that the conference initiate those measures that would place the countries of the Western Hemisphere in a safe and independent position from the disastrous consequences growing out of future coalitions among the nations of Europe. "It seems to be the opportune time," he said, "to develop the spirit at least of continental solidarity." Secretary of State Bryan also spoke on the same theme. In addressing the conference he said that the United States

---

[1] When the Declaration of Panama was drafted years later (1939), this proposal was referred to as precedent for the announcement of the famous "Neutrality Belt."

[2] James H. McCrocklin, "Latin American Attitude with Respect to World War I" (Master's thesis, University of Texas, Austin, Texas, 1949), 2–5.

wanted not one foot of land from any other country; what it wanted was to have hemispheric solidarity.[3]

Since the acts of the Financial Conference belong to the categories of finance, commerce, and transportation, and hence were only semi-political in character, there is no occasion to elaborate on its functions and activities here, except to note its creation of a continuing agency, the International High Commission. This body, composed of as many as nine members from each country, was to devote itself to the study of pressing problems exclusively commercial and financial. Although this commission preserved the spark of life until 1933, it was remarkably unproductive of significant achievement.

There also met in Washington, from December 1915 to January 1916, the Second Pan American Scientific Congress. Its agenda was strictly nonpolitical, and so contributed nothing to security action with reference to the war. The conference nevertheless made its slight contribution to conditioning the public mind of the Americas to the virtues of unity, solidarity, and cooperation. It was this Pan American gathering which President Wilson used as a sounding board for his famous proposal to "Pan Americanize" the Monroe Doctrine.[4]

The record of Pan American cooperation during the period of neutrality (August 1914–April 1917) was, as set forth in the foregoing paragraphs, most disappointing. Joint action looking toward the defense of neutral rights and insulation against the hazards of involvement in the world conflict was feeble and completely devoid of any tangible consequence. It was only in the economic realm that, largely through the instrumentality of the Financial Conference and its creature the International High Commission, a measure of cooperation was effected.

Why this failure, in face of the menace of the European war, to make any needed repair or addition to the inter-American security structure? In the first place, the nature of the threat was not fully comprehended in Latin America. Only vaguely did our southern neighbors realize what a German victory would mean. The belief persisted that the issues of the war were non-American, hence the whole business was none of America's affair. Therefore, since there was insufficient apprehension of danger, the essential compulsion for security

[3] *Actas del Primer Congreso Financiero Pan Americano* (Washington, 1915), 116–117.

[4] *Foreign Relations of the United States, The Lansing Papers, 1914–1920* (2 vols., Washington, 1940), II, 471–502.

action was absent. And in the second place, the United States, though more aware than the other American republics, of the dangerous potentialities inherent in the world conflict, as evidenced by the preparedness agitation of 1916, neglected to promote a joint-security program with them. Since the initiative had to come from the only country in the Americas with the power capable of implementing security measures, this neglect by the United States was a betrayal of its responsibilities of leadership. Despite the ill-will and suspicions stirred up by Wilsonian interventions, the possibilities of achievement must have been considerable had vigorous and intelligent leadership been forthcoming. For this reason the negative record of Pan American security cooperation during the period of neutrality was not only unfortunate, it was inexcusable.

The problems of belligerency. If the failure of the American republics to adopt a continental policy of neutrality raised serious doubts concerning the validity of their protestations of solidarity, these were partially eradicated by clear evidences of inter-American unity following the German declaration of unrestricted submarine warfare on February 1, 1917. When the United States severed diplomatic relations with Germany three days later, President Wilson sent notes to all neutral countries urging them to do likewise. Although the President's appeal was a summons to all neutrals to defend their common rights, it carried for the Latin Americans an additional appeal to validate the principle of continental solidarity. Their response, though marred by certain defections, was generally encouraging, for most of them, faced now by the realities of war, proved their willingness to implement the principle of American unity. More specifically, how well did the inter-American system measure up to its greatest test?

Eight of the Latin-American republics eventually declared war on Germany. Five ruptured diplomatic relations. Seven remained neutral. Thus, thirteen of the twenty Latin-American states manifested their solidarity with the United States either by declaring war on Germany or severing relations with her. Superficially, this would appear to be a remarkable demonstration of American unity, and to a certain extent this was a fact. However, before giving any evaluating judgment on the nature and extent of continental solidarity in 1917/18, it seems advisable to account first for actual evidence of security cooperation.

The eight states that declared war were Brazil, Cuba, Costa Rica, Guatemala, Haiti, Honduras, Nicaragua, and Panama. It is to be noted that all but one of these—Brazil—were Caribbean and Central American states, and because they occupied the geographical zone of greatest strategical importance to the United States, had been the objects, for good or ill, of American imperialistic pressures. The paradox that those Latin-American states that had experienced United States intervention were the very ones that became the war partners of their powerful neighbor at the time of her greatest danger calls for a bit of explaining.

Cuba and Panama declared war on Germany on April 7, 1917, one day after the United States declaration. Both countries had come into existence under the aegis of the United States, and for this reason felt tied by the bonds of gratitude and brotherhood. Equally important, the United States enjoyed special treaty-relations with both countries which they interpreted as obligating them to enter the war on the side of their great patron. For example, President Menocal, when asking the Cuban Congress for a declaration of war, referred to "the explicit and implicit obligation of the treaty of political relations of May 22 of 1903."[5] And President Valdez of Panama, in reply to President Wilson's note of February 3, 1917, declared that if force became unavoidable, Panama would "faithfully carry out the engagements it has contracted with the nation [the United States] and will cooperate in the most efficacious manner for the defense of the canal."[6] Thus, the war policies of Cuba and Panama were so considerably dictated by special political, economic, and sentimental relations with the United States that it is very difficult to separate these from the considerations of continental solidarity. But that solidarity was at least partially influential cannot be denied.

Both Haiti and Nicaragua were also United States protectorates of a sort, and under the circumstances it would be rather difficult to conceive of their having pursued independent foreign policies. In Haiti it was the sharp prodding by the U.S. State Department which produced, on June 17, 1917, the severance of diplomatic relations with Germany. But the opposition to a declaration of war was so great in the National Assembly that it was only after that body had been dissolved, and a Council of State had been appointed, that a state of war was declared on July 12, 1918.[7] In Nicaragua there was no opposition, for the government of President Chamorro supinely acquiesced in the indicated desires of Secretary of State Lansing, first, by severing relations (May 18, 1917), and giving the United States port facilities for the prosecution of the war; and second (March 8, 1918), by declaring

[5] *New York Times*, April 7, 1917.
[6] *Foreign Relations of the United States, 1917*, Supp. 1, I, 225.
[7] *Ibid.*, 275–276, 279, 301.

war on the Central Powers.[8] The fact that neither Haiti nor Nicaragua was free of United States pressure in their decisions to enter the war makes it impossible, as with Cuba and Panama, to determine to what extent they were motivated by attachment to the principle of continental unity.

But as for the remaining four Latin-American belligerents, their decisions were made on their own initiative and without United States pressure. In fact, one of them, Costa Rica, declared war in opposition to President Wilson's wishes (May 23, 1919), in order to secure recognition for the Tinoco government. However, this stratagem did not alter the attitude of the United States, for until the end of the war Tinoco remained unrecognized.

Guatemala referred to "continental solidarity" when declaring war on April 23, 1918. And when the government of Honduras declared war on July 19, 1919, it announced that "continental solidarity imposes upon the states of America the duty of contributing according to the measure of their abilities towards the triumph of the cause of civilization and of right which, with the Allied Nations, the United States of America defends."[9] The cynic might add that Guatemala and Honduras, and several other countries as well, saw in belligerency or a suspension of diplomatic relations both an opportunity to increase the friendship of the United States, with consequent advantages in trade and protection, and an opportunity to confiscate large German holdings.

Of all the Latin-American countries, the war policy of Brazil was probably the most truly reflective of the Pan American ideals of unity and cooperation. On April 25, 1917, the President of Brazil referred to the fact that "one of the belligerents [the United States] forms an integral part of the American continent" and that Brazil was bound to this belligerent by traditional friendship and by a similarity of political opinion in the defense of the vital interests of America. Later, on June 2, 1917, the Brazilian government announced that "in the critical moment of the world's history" it would continue to give to its foreign policy "a practical form of continental solidarity." Brazil went further —much further—than any other Latin-American country in implementing the logical implication of continental solidarity, namely, that an attack on one member of the American community was tantamount to an attack on all the rest, and thus called for common defense.[10]

Of the Latin-American belligerents, only Brazil can be said to have taken anything like an active part in the war, its contributions being

[8] *Ibid.*, 228–229.   [9] *Ibid., 1918*, Supp. 1, I, 710.
[10] McCrocklin, 24–25.

principally naval aid in combatting the submarine menace. Insofar as military cooperation was effected by the American belligerents it was all on an *ad hoc* bilateral basis. In other words, there was nothing accomplished resembling multilateral inter-American security cooperation. All of the defense agreements were bilateral, and they were principally with the United States. This was true not only of the eight countries that declared their belligerency but also of the five that severed diplomatic relations with the Central Powers.

The Latin-American states that broke relations with Germany were Bolivia, the Dominican Republic,[11] Ecuador, Peru, and Uruguay. It is noteworthy that, although the countries of this category were not technically belligerents, their status of nonbelligerency or "friendly neutralists" toward the United States incurred risks equal to those assumed by the nonactive belligerents. It is also significant that these countries were motivated by an attachment to the ideal of American unity quite as real and strong as that which influenced the belligerents themselves. For example, when on December 7, 1917, Ecuador broke off diplomatic relations with Germany, it declared that the rupture "signifies that Ecuador, whose doctrine has always been that of American solidarity, is united in heart and thought with her sister Republics of the Continent."[12]

Of these five nations, Uruguay was without doubt the most staunch and loyal supporter of the principle of solidarity. On June 18, 1917, some four months before rupturing diplomatic relations with Germany, and while presumably a neutral, the Uruguayan President issued the following decree: "No American country, which in defense of its own rights should find itself in a state of war with nations of other continents will be treated as a belligerent." Bolivia and Peru almost immediately expressed unqualified approval of this position. The Peruvian government declared that because of its attachment to the principle of solidarity it had refrained from declaring neutrality after the United States' declaration of war, and for this reason it endorsed the Uruguayan policy as a natural supplement to its own.

Nor did any of the countries that remained neutral (Argentina, Chile, Colombia, Mexico, Paraguay, El Salvador, and Venezuela) fail

[11] In 1917 the United States, which was in occupation of the Dominican Republic, canceled the exequaturs of the German consuls in the Republic. This act is generally considered a severance of diplomatic relations. Actually, Dominican independence had temporarily lapsed (1916–24).

[12] Warren H. Kelchner, *Latin American Relations with the League of Nations* (Boston, 1929), 29.

by word or deed to give support to the principle of solidarity. Although El Salvador remained technically a neutral, she declared herself a "friendly neutral" toward the United States. This meant, said her President, that United States naval and merchant vessels could come, remain, and leave at will without let or hindrance. This benevolent neutrality surely reflected a realization of community interest.[13]

Although Chile remained neutral, her nitrates became so indispensable to the success of the Allies that Chileans began to regard themselves as more valuable as neutrals than as belligerents. It is quite true that, with the exception of the two active belligerents, Cuba and Brazil, the neutrals did contribute in raw materials quite as much to the cause of the Allies as did the so-called belligerents. However, this significant fact should be noted: the nitrates, copper, wheat, beef, sugar, cotton, etc. were available to all purchasers. We cannot be certain that, without the Anglo-American naval blockade German buyers would not have been received in the exchanges of the Latin-American neutrals.

It is a matter of record, not to the credit of American continentalism, that the Pan American states failed in the face of a great world crisis to consult or act cooperatively on a multilateral basis. There were a number of suggestions but no action. For example, when Germany announced unrestricted submarine warfare, and President Wilson made his appeal to the neutrals, the Bolivian government proposed some kind of collective protest by the American republics. Failing in this, Bolivia then tried to get her neighbors to make a declaration of solidarity embodying the principle that an attack by submarine upon neutral merchant vessels, even within blockaded zones, was illegal, and should be dealt with in accordance with international precedent.[14]

Peru felt that the whole continent should give concerted ratification to President Wilson's proposal. The Ecuadorean government suggested "some form of joint American action, looking toward the legitimate defense of the rights of neutrals."[15]

On June 15, 1917, the Uruguayan government, in a note to Brazil, made an earnest plea for an inter-American congress that "should give expression once and for all in juridical formulae or practical actions to the fertile aspiration of continental solidarity." It was the view of President Viera of Uruguay, expressed at a later date, that had the

[13] Ibid., 209.
[14] P. A. Martin, Latin America and the War (Baltimore, 1925), 477–478.
[15] Ibid., 392; Foreign Relations of the United States, 1917, Supp. 1, I, 231–232.

American governments agreed promptly, through the medium of a conference or by means of direct negotiations, to implement the principle of continental solidarity, Uruguay would not only have severed relations but even declared war.[16]

The President of Paraguay also expressed disappointment that the American states had failed to collaborate and make a reality of the continental ideal. In an address to the Congress of Paraguay, on April 2, 1918, he said:

The Paraguayan government has felt from the very beginning, in view of the imminent intervention of America, that a continental conference ought to be convoked in order to determine upon a line of conduct which would be uniform and if possible identical. It is to be regretted that under circumstances which are so grave for the future of America, this spirit of fraternity and cooperation could not be manifested in a collective declaration of purpose, an expression of the sentiments and aspirations of the new world.[17]

However unfortunate the failure of the American republics to implement by collective action the principles of continental solidarity, the several official pleas to that end, which have been noted, are not without significance.

The pseudo-cooperative proposals of the noncooperators—Argentina and Mexico—must not be overlooked. Following the declaration of war by the United States, President Irigoyen of Argentina invited the Latin-American states to a conference "to obtain a uniformity of opinion on the war and to bring closer together the American Republics and strengthen their position in the concert of nations." Although most of the invitations had been accepted by the middle of May 1917, there was little enthusiasm for a conference with such an indefinite program and without the presence of the United States. Opposition mounted and the plan had to be abandoned. But a few months later it was revived; in October Argentina again sent invitations to all the Latin-American states to attend a congress. Mexico and El Salvador accepted. The other states either declined outright or awaited an indication of the attitude of the United States. The U.S. State Department soon declared that it felt that the congress should not be held unless it conformed to a recent Peruvian proposal which read as follows:

The Government of Peru considers that the policy on this continent should be one with the policies of the United States; that in consequence of the

---

[16] McCrocklin, 87, 91.
[17] *Foreign Relations of the United States, 1918*, Supp. 1, I, 681.

attitude of the United States in this war, the Monroe Doctrine must necessarily become firmer and ampler; and that the defense of the United States and all other American nations against German imperialism requires, as an essential condition, a uniform policy throughout the entire continent. The Government of Peru is willing to cooperate most decidedly for the attainment of such a purpose.[18]

A Mexican delegation arrived in Buenos Aires in January 1918, only to find that the congress had been indefinitely postponed. Thus the Argentine attempt to take advantage of United States involvement in the war in order to seize the leadership of the Latin-American nations failed miserably.

In keeping with his anti-United States and suspect pro-German attitude, President Carranza of Mexico also came forward with a phony cooperative proposal for neutrals. He proposed that all neutrals, particularly those of America, offer their mediatory services to the belligerents in seeking an end to the war. If within a reasonable time peace could not be restored by this means, they should refuse any kind of supplies to the belligerents and suspend all commercial relations with them.[19] The plan, of course, would have harmed Germany not at all, but would have done irreparable damage to the Allies. Whether intentional or not, Carranza's proposal at the time smelled like pro-German bait, and there were no takers among the American neutrals.

Despite the failure of the Pan American states to agree collectively on common policies to confront the problems of neutrality and belligerency, they measured up surprisingly well to the test of World War I by their demonstrations of solidarity. This considered judgment runs counter to the usual view that the war proved the insubstantiality of inter-American unity. It is quite true that seven of the republics (including Argentina, Chile, and Mexico) remained neutral throughout the conflict, and their abstention did detract greatly from the ideal of "American solidarity"; but of greater significance is the fact that no fewer than thirteen others saw fit to take action favorable to the United States after it entered the conflict. The spontaneity with which most of these states supported the United States, in spite of the rash of interventionism during the Wilson administration, and without benefit of appeasement, concessions, and subsidies of the later "good neighborliness," proved the reality of American solidarity and continental unity. In fact, ten of the thirteen states that either declared war or severed diplomatic relations with the

18 *Ibid.*, *1917*, 368, 382, 388–389.   19 *Ibid.*, 45–46.

Central Powers specifically stated that they were animated in doing so because they appreciated the importance of maintaining a community of interests.

By 1917 the idea of continentalism had developed in the Americas to the point where a majority of the American republics realized that an attack on one of them jeopardized all the rest. This marked a great advance in the development of the concept of American security and demonstrated a great truth: that the inter-American security system was comprised, in 1917 as in 1941, not only of formal pacts and concrete evidence of preparation for common defense but also of a realization of interdependence and mutuality of interests which in times of great danger prevails over the divisive forces of petty national jealousies and sensitiveness of sovereignty. At a time of crisis most of the American nations demonstrated their ability to identify their national interests.

The inter-American system vis-à-vis the League of Nations. All the Latin-American nations that had declared war upon Germany or severed relations with her, except Costa Rica and the Dominican Republic,[20] were represented at the peace conference which assembled in Paris on January 18, 1919. They were little more than onlookers, however, for the Great Powers arrogated to themselves the exclusive roles of peace-makers. So, being denied a voice in arranging the peace settlement (which role in fact they did not seek), the Latin Americans turned their attention to measures that might prevent the recurrence of another world conflict.

It was quite in line with the American tradition of conciliation, arbitration, and judicial settlement of international disputes that the Latin-American representatives at Paris should throw their support behind President Wilson's grand project. And when the neutral nations were invited to meet with a subcommittee of the League of Nations Commission, Argentina, Chile, and El Salvador were among those present. All three endorsed the project, although the enthusiasm of Chile and El Salvador was tempered by certain doubts. Chile expressed concern that the League of Nations "maintain a scrupulous respect for existing treaties." In other words, it was Chile's view that the Treaty of Ancón, out of which developed the Tacna-Arica con-

[20] As stated already, the United States had refused to recognize the Tinoco government and so opposed the admission of Costa Rica to the peace conference. Although the Dominican Republic had severed diplomatic relations with Germany, this occurred while the United States was in occupation. Technically, Dominican independence had lapsed from 1916 until 1924. See note 11, above.

troversy (discussed in a later chapter), should not be subject to review by the new world organization. El Salvador, after expressing to the subcommittee the hope that the League would guarantee the integrity and autonomy of small nations, declared its reluctance to become a member so long as Article 21 retained an unclear reference to the Monroe Doctrine.[21] This objection, and a similar one voiced by the Honduran delegate, failed to receive much attention at the conference, for no change was made in the phraseology of Article 21.[22]

Nine of the Latin-American nations—Bolivia, Brazil, Cuba, Guatemala, Haiti, Honduras, Panama, Peru, and Uruguay—became original members of the League of Nations by virtue of their ratification of the Treaty of Versailles. Six others—Argentina, Chile, Colombia, Paraguay, El Salvador, and Venezuela—also became original members because of their adherence to the Covenant (detached from the Treaty of Versailles) within two months of the date it became effective (January 10, 1920). Thus fifteen of the American republics became charter members of the League of Nations. Nicaragua and Costa Rica became members some months later so that when the first meeting of the League of Nations Assembly took place in November 1920, all the Latin-American republics except the Dominican Republic, Ecuador, and Mexico were represented.[23]

Factors which influenced the Latin-American republics to become members of the League of Nations were varied. "Idealism and considerations of prestige," says Dr. Warren Kelchner, "played a relatively larger part in acceptance of the League by the American re-

[21] Article 21 provided that "nothing in the Covenant shall be deemed to affect the validity of international engagements, such as treaties of arbitration or regional understandings like the Monroe Doctrine, for securing the maintenance of peace."

[22] For this reason when the government of El Salvador was later considering adherence to the Covenant of the League of Nations, it requested the United States, on December 14, 1919, for an interpretation of the Monroe Doctrine. Acting Secretary of State F. L. Polk replied that "the opinion of this government with regard to the Monroe Doctrine" was expressed in the speech by President Wilson before the Pan American Scientific Conference at Washington in January 1917. Although this was at best a very inadequate interpretation of the Monroe Doctrine, the Salvadorean government seemed to be satisfied, for it shortly thereafter adhered to the Covenant.

[23] The Dominican Republic was admitted to membership in 1924, following the termination of United States occupation. Later, Mexico and Ecuador became members. Of all the American republics, the United States was the only one that never became a member of the League of Nations.

publics than was true of most other countries."[24] Given their fervent desire to promote peace and security by peaceful settlement of international disputes, a process which to the Latin Americans had become a traditional policy, it was natural that they would want to collaborate with a world organization dedicated to these ends. According to Kelchner, the concept of an international law binding upon the governments of the world was an idea which naturally appealed to the idealism of the Latins, for to them a world in which the cooperation of men and nations rather than the rivalry and the aggrandizement of one at the expense of another was worthy of support.[25] Then, too, the prestige redounding from the fact that in the League of Nations— in the Assembly, the Council, and the committees—the representatives of the small nations participated on a basis of equality with the Great Powers encouraged Latin-American membership. Here was a unique opportunity, heretofore unknown outside the Western Hemisphere, for the representatives of the small states to speak up, on the basis of equality, in an international assemblage.[26]

Another factor which influenced the Latin Americans to join the League was their obvious expectation of protection against aggression, not only external aggression, but also further encroachment by the United States itself. There can hardly be any doubt, wrote Duggan, "that one of the motives which animated a considerable number of Latin American nations in joining the League was the belief that it would act as a counterpoise to the United States."[27] Article X, which guaranteed political independence and territorial integrity of League members—and the article which was largely responsible for the United States' rejection—made a strong appeal to the Latins.

The enthusiastic affiliation of the Latin-American nations with the League of Nations has been represented as manifesting their desire to abandon Pan Americanism in favor of a world organization which seemed to offer better prospects of guaranteeing their security. This

---

[24] Kelchner, 6. [25] *Ibid.*, 14–15.

[26] "This was in sharp contrast," says Stephen P. Duggan, "to the Pan American conference where the United States dominated and the Latin American states felt that they occupied a place of inferiority."—"Latin America, the League, and the United States," *Foreign Affairs* (January 1943), 283. The contrast was purely imaginary, for in the inter-American system, as in the League of Nations, all members were legally and technically equal, but inequalities did in fact exist as a natural and obvious consequence of the great inequalities in the size, wealth, and power of the members.

[27] Duggan, 283.

raises an important question: What effect did the establishment of the League of Nations have on the American system as a security arrangement?

The Covenant of the League did not prohibit regional-security arrangements nor did it declare them to be incompatible with League membership. On the contrary, Article 21 recognized the validity of regional understandings for the maintenance of peace, although this sole allusion to regionalism in the Covenant occurred merely by chance. The draft of the Covenant published on February 15, 1919, contained no mention of regional arrangements or understandings, nor of the Monroe Doctrine either, for that matter. Because of the latter omission great pressure was put on President Wilson to incorporate in the League draft an article obviating any doubt that the Monroe Doctrine was unaffected by the League's jurisdiction. The President acquiesced, and in order to make way for this exception, the original contents of Article 21 were deleted.[28] The phrase "regional understanding" was coined only as a consequence of the effort to define the Monroe Doctrine,[29] and most certainly did not result from a belief that provision should be made in the Covenant to coordinate the League with regional arrangements. It is a fair inference that, had it not been for American insistence on safeguarding the Monroe Doctrine, the Covenant would have remained silent on the subject of regional-security arrangements. This would not have meant necessarily, however, that regionalism was regarded as incompatible with the League.

The reason that the framers of the League Covenant did not mention regionalism in the original draft was perhaps the fact that in 1919 there existed no regional-security system worthy of serious consideration. The only regional arrangement of any consequence was the Pan American system, and it was regarded as "a vague, diplomatic, and timid ideal" which, largely because of the policy of the United States, was alleged never to have resolutely confronted any problem of real political concern to all of the Americas. The grandiose network of

[28] The original Article 21 related to freedom of transit and equitable treatment of commerce.—*New York Times*, Feb. 15, 1919.

[29] The British members of the League of Nations Commission "objected to the attempt to define the Monroe Doctrine, contending that any attempt to define it might limit or extend its application. Their real motive being probably to protect similar understandings of their own, they proposed a different statement which was finally written into the Covenant as Article 21."—D. F. Fleming, *The United States and the League of Nations* (New York and London 1932), 185.

peace procedures, which later became a significant feature of the American security system, was yet to be constructed. Therefore, the inter-American system of 1919, because of its impotence, failed to impress on the framers of the Covenant the advantages of integrating into the League regional organizations whose primary responsibility would be the maintenance of peace within their respective regions. It was not that regionalism was opposed, but rather that there seemed to be no good reason why it should be mentioned.

The adoption of the new Article 21 obviated any doubts regarding the compatibility of regional-security arrangements with the Covenant. It stated clearly that regional understandings for securing the maintenance of peace remained valid, and implied that they were not to be affected by obligations assumed under the other League articles. This duality assuredly could make for numerous exceptions to League jurisdiction in security matters.

The Second League Assembly, which met in September 1921, contributed some clarification of Article 21. In pursuance of action taken at the First Assembly various proposed amendments to the Covenant were submitted for consideration by the Committee on Amendments for the Council, two of them dealing with Article 21. China sought to limit to the Monroe Doctrine, alone, international engagements regarded as compatible with the Covenant, and would omit the words "treaties of arbitration or regional understandings." Czechoslovakia, on the other hand, wanted to encourage regional conferences or treaties.[30]

On the basis of the Czech proposal, the Committee on Amendments agreed to recommend to the Second Assembly an addition to Article 21 whereby the League would not only approve but would also promote agreements tending to assure peace and encourage cooperation. The Assembly, however, felt that the existent text of Article 21 did not exclude the application of the ideas contained in the proposed amendment and so rejected it as unnecessary. "At the same time, it drew attention to the fact that agreements tending to define or complete the engagements contained in the Covenant for the maintenance of peace or the promotion of international cooperation, may be regarded as of a nature likely to contribute to the progress of the League on the path of practical realization."[31] Thus it was clear that Article 21 did not make it impossible for the inter-American security system to develop

[30] *Monthly Summary of the League of Nations* (April 1921), I, 3–4.
[31] *Ibid.* (Oct. 1921), 114.

and operate autonomously without infringing upon the responsibilities of its members to the League of Nations.

There is no evidence that the membership of Latin-American countries in the League of Nations lessened their interest in Pan Americanism or visibly retarded the gradual fabrication of an inter-American peace structure. On the contrary, it was soon evident that their attachment to the new universal organization was somewhat less than abiding. First, Argentina, after the rejection of her demands for certain modifications of the League Covenant, withdrew from the First Assembly and refrained from further participation until 1933. Then Bolivia and Peru, failing in their efforts to invoke Article 19 of the Covenant for a revision of the treaties of 1883 and 1904 with Chile, abstained after the Second Assembly from further attendance until 1929. Even Brazil, which state had been honored by notable appointments on League bodies, including a nonpermanent seat on the Council from 1920 to 1926, withdrew from membership in 1926 because her demand for a permanent Council seat was rejected. Brazil was the second nation to definitely withdraw from the League, the first being another Latin-American country, Costa Rica. On December 25, 1924, that Central American republic gave notice of withdrawal because of budgetary reasons.[32]

Further evidence of waning interest in the League of Nations was the very irregular attendance of the Latin-American delegations at the annual Assembly meetings. Frequently, only a bare majority of the so-called "participating" members was present. An explanation offered for this lack of interest was that questions of immediate concern to the Americas were not on the agenda. The problems of Europe and the Eastern Hemisphere, relating as they usually did to the liquidation of World War I, understandably held no special interest for Latin-

[32] When the Council urged Costa Rica to reconsider her decision to withdraw, the Costa Rican government replied that before deciding to accept the invitation to remain, it wished "to know the interpretation placed by the League of Nations on the Monroe Doctrine and the scope given to that doctrine when it was included in Article 21 in the Covenant." The astute reply of Council President Hjalmar Procopé of Finland was that while Article 21 gave "the states parties to international engagements the guaranty that the validity of such of these engagements as secure the maintenance of peace would not be affected by accession to the Covenant of the League of Nations," it referred "only to the relations of the Covenant with such engagements; it neither weakens nor limits any of the safeguards provided in the Covenant." As to the scope given to the Monroe Doctrine by its inclusion in the article, Procopé declared that it was not given a sanction or validity which it did not previously possess.—League of Nations, *Official Journal*, IV, 1608–1609.

American delegates. Therefore, they felt that they lost nothing and risked nothing by their absence, for the critical problems of Europe were far away. There seemed to be no compelling reason for their constant attention to the work of the League.

This indifference was also illustrated by a woeful indisposition to ratify the international agreements negotiated under League auspices. Of the 80 conventions, agreements, and protocols drafted up to 1934, there were 1,545 ratifications; of these only 164 were Latin-American. Also, by 1934 only nine member states of the League of Nations had failed to ratify the Protocol of the Permanent Court of International Justice, and of them five were Latin-American.[33] This dilatoriness and shirking of responsibility caused the other members of the League considerable irritation, particularly since the Latin-American bloc exercised preponderant voting strength.

While the Latin-American nations did not modify their original view that the League of Nations should confront the broader and more general issues of international cooperation, they did incline more and more to the opinion that purely American problems belonged to their own regional organization. In fact, they upheld the inter-American system as a model and repeatedly referred to inter-American cooperation at League meetings.[34]

The failure of the United States to join the League of Nations, generally regarded in Latin America as betrayal, was a decisive factor in determining the future course of Pan Americanism. It meant that the United States concentrated its interest on the regional organization, whereas if it had become a League member it most likely would have done everything possible to ensure the success and prestige of the League even at the sacrifice of regional association. Since no great progress had been made by 1920 in setting up a formal security system in the Americas, there would have been much less restraint than existed in 1945 to make sacrifices in favor of universalism at the expense of regionalism. There would not have been much to lose through sacrifice. For about a decade, therefore, after the establishment of the League of Nations, the United States was suspicious of League activity in the region covered by the Monroe Doctrine. The infant world organization, aware of its own weakness and the imprudence of provoking the United States by interfering in American disputes, adopted a hands-

---

[33] Duggan, 289. Latin America's nonratification of Pan American treaties has been equally deplorable, as will be noted later.
[34] Kelchner, 5, n. 3.

off policy, notably evident with respect to the Tacna-Arica controversy and the boundary dispute between Costa Rica and Panama.

Because of this situation, the Latin-American states, in balancing American regionalism against Geneva universalism, found the latter wanting. The inevitable result was the strengthening of the regional concept.

Central American security. Just before the meeting of the fifth Pan American conference, the Second Conference on Central American Affairs met in Washington from December 4, 1922, to February 7, 1923. Although limited in geographic scope, it nevertheless contributed certain additions to the formal inter-American pattern of cooperation and security. Among these were the International Central American Tribunal and the International Commissions of Inquiry. The tribunal, unlike the court created by the first Central American conference, was not intended to be either permanent or compulsory, but, on the plan of The Hague Court, was merely a panel from which judges could be selected. Disputes affecting sovereignty and independence could not be the objects of arbitration. The United States was not a party to the convention setting up the tribunal, but it was a party to another convention whose main object was to unify and recast the Bryan treaties of inquiry which the United States had concluded individually with several of the Central American republics in 1913/14. This convention provided that disputes originating in some divergence of opinion regarding questions of fact be submitted to a commission of inquiry. Questions affecting sovereignty, independence, honor, and vital interests were specifically excluded.[35] This multilateral treaty, signed and ratified by the United States and all five Central American states, is known to have influenced the drafting of the famous Gondra treaty at the Santiago conference.

The Santiago Conference. The Fifth International Conference of American States, originally scheduled to meet in Santiago in 1914 but postponed because of the war, finally convened in the Chilean capital in March 1923. All the American republics were represented except Mexico, Bolivia, and Peru—Mexico because its government had not been recognized by the United States, and so was not represented in the Pan American Union, and the latter two because of the critical nature of their relations with Chile attending the Tacna-Arica controversy.

The following political subjects, an exceptional number, appeared

[35] *Conference on Central American Affairs* (Washington, 1923), 339–342, 392.

on the conference program: (1) organization of the Pan American Union; (2) consideration of the work accomplished by the Rio de Janeiro Commission of Jurists; (3) consideration of measures tending toward closer association, with the view of promoting common interests; (4) consideration of the best means to give wider application to the principle of judicial and arbitral settlement of disputes; (5) reduction and limitation of armaments; (6) consideration of questions arising out of an encroachment by a non-American power on the rights of an American nation; and (7) consideration of the rights of aliens resident within the jurisdiction of any of the American republics.[36]

The inclusion of so many political subjects on a conference agenda indicated that the Latin Americans were unwilling to accept the Anglo-American concept of inter-American association. They refused to confine their discussions, as in the past, to innocuous subjects on which unanimous agreement could be reached. Their experiences during World War I, at the Paris Conference, and as members of the League of Nations caused them to feel more strongly than ever the full import of their position as independent American states. They had become more conscious, somewhat as a result of President Wilson's declarations, of the rights of small states, and were determined to assert them against the United States itself, whose economic and political policies meanwhile continued to cause grave apprehension. This agenda surely represented the most serious attack to date on the United States' conception of Pan Americanism.

Under these circumstances, the U. S. State Department believed it the very best strategy not to oppose too strenuously having topics so close to the hearts of the Latin-American members introduced into the discussions, but, later, as unobtrusively as possible, to put the brakes on tangential excursions. Also it should be noted that, following the Allied victory in World War I, the United States no longer needed to condition its relations with the Latin-American nations in terms of fear of overseas aggression or interference. It was now in position to indulge the Latins in their protestations of "sovereign" prerogatives. This was the beginning of relaxed controls on Latin America, the so-called "liquidation of American imperialism."[37]

In reviewing the actions taken by the Santiago conference on the above-mentioned political topics, we note first the problem of re-

[36] Fifth International Conference of American States, *Special Handbook for the Use of the Delegates* (Pan American Union, Washington, 1922), 30–32.

[37] Samuel F. Bemis, *The Latin American Policy of the United States* (New York, 1943), 202.

organization of the Pan American Union. There was widespread dissatisfaction with the Union because of the preponderant position occupied by the United States, as follows: the seat of the Union was in Washington; membership on the Governing Board was confined to diplomatic representatives to the United States government in Washington; the United States was represented by its secretary of state, who outranked diplomatically all other members; the secretary of state was the permanent chairman of the board; and the director-general of the Union was an Anglo-American.

The absence of Mexico at the conference because nonrecognition of her government by the United States denied her representation on the Governing Board of the Pan American Union accented the demand for reform. The Latin Americans wanted the privilege to name whomsoever they desired as their representatives. The United States objected on the ground that the prestige of the Governing Board required diplomatic representation. Finally a compromise was reached which provided that any government not having a diplomatic representative at Washington might designate a special representative to serve as a member. Also, instead of designating the secretary of state as *ex officio* chairman, it was agreed that the chairman and vice-chairman should be elected by the board.[38]

There was also dissatisfaction because limitations imposed on the activities of the Union seemed to condemn it to the role of a bureaucratic commercial organization. It was felt that its scope should be enlarged so that it could become an inclusive international organization, qualified to treat all inter-American questions. In line with this view a resolution was adopted which called for creating four permanent committees to assist the Pan American Union in studying economic and commercial relations, international organization of labor, hygiene, and intellectual cooperation. This was far short of the hopes of many that a closer association of American states could be created in the form of an American league.[39]

A Uruguayan proposal, the Brum plan for an American League of Nations, came up for discussion. After the United States Senate had for the second time rejected the Treaty of Versailles, and it was assumed that this country would not become a member of the League of Na-

[38] Fifth International Conference of American States, *Declaration Record of the Plenary Sessions* (Santiago, 1923), II, 166–174.

[39] Samuel Guy Inman, "Pan American Conferences and their Results," *Southwestern Political and Social Science Quarterly*, IV, No. 4 (March 1924), 353.

tions, President Baltasar Brum of Uruguay proposed an American League of Nations, based upon the Monroe Doctrine. He suggested that each American nation make a declaration similar to that of Monroe, and bind itself to intervene in favor of any one of them in event of attack by a non-American country. He held that such a declaration would place all the American nations on a plane of equality with the United States. Moreover, since Article 21 of the League Covenant seemed to imply a limitation on League jurisdiction in the Americas, the area was open for an American League composed of all the republics, including the United States.[40] Here was a proposal, unique up to that date, to provide for inter-American security against non-American aggression.

Although the Brum plan was quite in line with President Wilson's proposal of 1916 to "Pan Americanize" the Monroe Doctrine, the Republican administration of 1923 was unfavorable to leagues of nations, either universal or regional. Accordingly several times in the course of committee debates the United States delegates announced that their government was not favorable to any kind of a league that would take up political questions. But in spite of this forewarning the Brum proposal came before the conference, and thus afforded some of the delegates opportunity to direct sharp shafts at the Monroe Doctrine. Since the plan called for a continentalization of the Monroe Doctrine, Ambassador Henry Fletcher, head of the United States delegation, terminated the discussion by informing the delegates that the Monroe Doctrine had been and would continue to be a unilateral policy. The project was killed, but to disguise this fact it was ordered sent to the Governing Board of the Pan American Union for "further study."[41]

The discussions on the subject of arbitration were equally fruitless. A number of projects were sent to the juridical committee of the conference. The United States, apparently believing that existing peace instruments were adequate, expressed the hope that the American republics would find it possible to utilize appropriate agencies for the juridical and arbitral settlement of disputes.[42] The discussions terminated with the adoption of a general resolution which noted with pleasure "the extension which has taken place in recent years in the

[40] Dexter Perkins, *Hands Off: A History of the Monroe Doctrine* (Boston, 1941), 330–331. For a summarization of the Brum plan for an American league of nations, see *Foreign Relations of the United States, 1923*, I, 293–294.

[41] Inman, 354–355.

[42] Fifth International Conference of American States, *Verbatim Record* (Santiago, 1923), I, 616–625.

application of conciliation, judicial settlement, and arbitration as a means of deciding controversies," and expressed the hope "that the progress of these methods of settlement may continue and that their application in the near future may be as general and as broad as possible."[43]

It is noteworthy that the most important contribution of the Santiago conference—the Gondra treaty—issued from the Disarmament Committee, which technically had no jurisdiction in the matter. Its province was "the reduction and limitation of military and naval expenditures." Since there was no disposition to examine military expenditures, the question was virtually limited to Argentina, Brazil, and Chile, for the other Latin-American countries had no navies and the United States considered that she was not affected because she had recently entered into naval commitments at the Washington Disarmament Conference. The secret sessions of the Disarmament Committee resulted in complete failure to agree, for, although there was no thought of reducing the practically irreducible navies of the three countries, it was hoped that future expenditures might be limited. On this there were opposing points of view which it was impossible to reconcile.

At this juncture Dr. Manuel Gondra, former president of Paraguay and head of the Paraguayan delegation, came forward with a proposal to attack the problem of military and naval strength by facing up to the question of limiting the use of these forces. He proposed that all the American countries "sign together, as a continental pact, that which they all signed individually with the United States in 1914, known as the Bryan formula," i.e., commissions of inquiry. "If all the American countries would sign together such a pact," he said, "whatever might be the amount of military force each had, a war between these countries would be very difficult."[44]

The Gondra proposal was, of course, no solution for the disarmament problem; in fact it was an evasion, for the way was still open for unrestricted armaments expenditures, with all the attendant dangers. Nevertheless the conference, eager to break the disarmament deadlock, hastily approved. To assert that they believed a treaty of inquiry would cancel out the dangers and evils of excessive armaments expenditures would be to attribute to the conferees an unbelievable naïveté. They were merely approving a face-saving device which, interestingly

---

[43] Fifth International Conference of American States, *Report of the Delegates of the United States* (Washington, 1924), 133.

[44] Inman, 358–359; Francisco Cuevas Cancino, *Del Congreso de Panamá a la Conferencia de Caracas, 1826–1954* (Caracas, 1955), II, 69–71.

enough, became extremely important as one of the basic component features of the inter-American security system.

The Treaty to Avoid or Prevent Conflicts Between the American States, popularly known as the Gondra treaty, provides for submitting to a commission of inquiry all controversies not settled through diplomatic channels and not submitted to arbitration in accordance with existing treaties. Important exceptions are made of disputes involving questions arising out of national constitutions, and of disputes relating to questions already settled by treaty. To put the machinery of inquiry into motion, the treaty provides for two permanent commissions or facilitating agencies, composed of the three American diplomatic representatives longest accredited in Washington and Montevideo. Upon request for inquiry, by either party to a dispute, the commission will notify the other party. Steps will then be taken to constitute a special commission of inquiry to consist of five members, chosen in the following way: each disputant is to name two, only one of whom shall be a national of the appointing country, and these four name the fifth, who shall not be of the same nationality as any of the others. The special commission of inquiry is allowed one year to investigate the dispute and make its report. The disputants agree not to make war preparations from the time the commission is convened until six months after the report. Gondra frankly acknowledged the Bryan "cooling off" treaties as the inspiration for his proposal.

The principal defect of the Gondra treaty was that inquiry could be instituted only by the cooperative action of both parties to a dispute. As a first step, one of the two permanent diplomatic commissions had to be appealed to by a disputant; the diplomatic commission could not act of its own initiative. The second step, therefore, is to transmit the request to the other party to the dispute. If the second party is agreeable, the third step is to constitute an *ad hoc* commission of inquiry. Thus cooperation of the disputants is required. The lack of a permanent commission of inquiry was a serious weakness, and in this respect the Gondra treaty was inferior to the Bryan treaties, which provided for permanent commissions.[45] The original Gondra treaty was little more than an agreement to consider submission to an investigation. Some of these deficiencies were ironed out later.

With respect to the several political topics on the agenda of the Santiago conference, the net achievements, with the exception of the

---

[45] *Report of the Delegates of the United States to the Fifth International Conference of American States* (Washington, 1923), 22–23.

Gondra treaty, were almost nil. The United States, owing to its great influence and control over many of the small states, and owing to disunity and nationalistic suspicions between the Latin-American states themselves, successfully warded off the attack on its conception of Pan Americanism.

The reaction was very bad. *La Prensa* of Buenos Aires, in an editorial dated June 2, 1923, declared that at least fifteen of the Latin-American countries were openly antagonistic toward the United States as evidenced by proposals, counterproposals, and debates in the committees. "The other delegates manifested a strong bias against the United States and its proposals—a sullen suspicion of Pan Americanism and a hostile attitude not shown in any previous Congress." Press comments on the conference throughout Latin America were generally unfriendly.

Why the United States, in view of the lessons of inter-American cooperation—or lack of cooperation—during World War I, and its own repudiation of the League of Nations, indicated not the slightest interest in transforming the association of American nations into an effective regional-security system is astounding and reflects how little vision there was on the part of those who directed American policy in the early postwar years. If not the Brum plan, then some other kind of cooperative defense arrangements against a non-American aggressor would probably have been acceptable to the Latin-American nations. The lack of interest shown by the United States may have been due not only to resurgent isolationism and opposition to so-called "entangling alliances," but also to the shortsighted view that the crushing of the German menace eliminated all threats to the Western Hemisphere. Therefore, believing that there was no need for a regional defensive arrangement, the Republican administrations of the 1920's felt that Pan Americanism approached the ideal of regional association in ratio to the elimination of security considerations.

The Havana Conference. The Sixth International Conference of American States met in Havana in 1928 under the most unfavorable circumstances conceivable, that is, from the viewpoint of the United States, because of the current criticism of our Latin-American policies, particularly in Mexico and Nicaragua. Also, following the frustrations of Latin-American hopes at the Santiago conference, discontent with United States-managed Pan Americanism continued to mount to the inevitable crisis. At Havana the United States took its final stand for the "new" Pan Americanism.

Fully aware of the seriousness which the situation portended, the

Coolidge Administration sent to Havana an exceptionally strong delegation headed by Charles E. Hughes. President Coolidge himself went to Havana to address the conference. However, the American government was not disposed to abandon its policy of opposing the inclusion of controversial political questions in the conference. Only two political questions—reorganization of the Pan American Union (with a view to limiting United States control) and the report of the Rio Commission of Jurists—were on the agenda. But despite the precautions of the United States, the second topic afforded the Latins ample opportunity to give vent to their grievances and assail Pan Americanism "Made in the U.S.A."

The perennial question of an improved organization of the Pan American Union was presented to the conference, the predominance of the United States having been only slightly disturbed at Santiago. In an effort to reduce the influence of the United States and make the Union more democratic, the Mexican government took the lead at Havana in offering a plan for reorganization. Features of the Mexican proposal were: (1) the American republics need not necessarily be represented on the Governing Board by their diplomatic representatives at Washington; (2) the offices of chairman and vice-chairman of the Governing Board should rotate annually among the members in alphabetical order; (3) the director-general should be appointed annually, the position rotating in alphabetical order; (4) the director-general should not accept from the government of any country offices or commissions other than those of a purely educational nature; (5) in no case should the Pan American Union be given political functions.[46] There were other proposals for Union reform presented by other delegations, but those of Mexico seemed to hit more directly at the heart of the problem.

The proposal that the Latin-American nations have the fullest liberty in appointing their members on the Governing Board was approved, but with the understanding that diplomatic representatives might continue to be appointed. Although Mr. Hughes declared that the United States had no desire to be accorded special privileges in the organization of the Union, and that any plan of reorganization approved by the other states would be entirely acceptable to the United States, the proposal to rotate the office of chairman was rejected in favor of retaining the principle of free election. The proposal to rotate annually

[46] Sexta Conferencia Internacional Americana, *Diario de Sesiones* (Havana, 1928), 194–195.

the office of director-general was also rejected as being incompatible with good administration. It was agreed, however, that the director-general should not serve on the delegation of any country but should attend the conferences in an advisory capacity and at the expense of the Union.[47]

Of particular significance was the conference approval of the Mexican proposal that the Union should not exercise functions of a political character. In view of the general tendency to assign to the Union a key role in plans for American international organization or the perfecting of instruments for the peaceful settlement of disputes, the Mexican government feared that a strengthened Union might mean increased control by the United States.[48] Evidently a majority of the Latin Americans shared this view, for the Mexican proposal was embodied in a resolution.[49] This action was tantamount to a public declaration that, since it had been impossible to curb United States control of the Union, the powers of the Union were to be strictly circumscribed. Of course the United States joined in approving the resolution, but for entirely different reasons.

Conforming to a resolution adopted by the Santiago conference, the Governing Board presented a draft convention on the organization of the Pan American Union. Hitherto the Union had rested solely on resolutions adopted by the successive conferences. Since it was felt that a formal treaty would give it a more firm juridical base, the Governing Board had been ordered to draft such a convention. The draft followed closely the acts of the previous conferences, with a few elaborations. A condition of signature was that the convention should not become operative until ratified by all the twenty-one states, and that no subsequent amendment could be made except by unanimous consent.[50] Since only sixteen states subsequently ratified the convention, the Union continued on a resolution basis. This was not un-

[47] Dr. Leo S. Rowe, the director-general, went to Havana as a member of the United States delegation. Mr. Hughes explained that Rowe had been appointed to the delegation because there was no appropriation available by which he could represent the Union.— Foreign Policy Association, "The Sixth Pan American Conference," *Information Service*, IV, No. 4 (April 27, 1928), 54.

[48] *Ibid.*, 55.

[49] Sixth International Conference of American States, *Final Act; Motions, Agreements, Resolutions, and Conventions* (Havana, 1928), 113, cited hereinafter as Sixth Int. Conf. of Am. States, *Final Act*.

[50] *Report of the Delegates of the United States to the Sixth International Conference of American States* (Washington, 1928), 231–238.

fortunate, for approval of the convention would assuredly have put the Union in a strait jacket, since the amendment concerning the unanimity rule would have made change next to impossible.

The debates on the preamble to the proposed Pan American Union convention precipitated one of the crises of the conference. To the statement that the moral union of the American republics "rests on the juridical equality of the Republics of the Continent and in the mutual respect of the right inherent in their complete independence," Dr. Honorio Pueyrredón, head of the Argentine delegation, insisted that there be added a declaration against barriers to inter-American trade. Concerned because of the excessively high tariff wall which obstructed the entry of Argentine products into the United States, Pueyrredón argued that Pan American unity was impossible without economic harmony. Recalling the proposal of James G. Blaine, the Argentine statesman proposed nothing less than an American *Zollverein*, such as his own country had rejected in 1890. Now in 1928, to make the reversal complete, the American government rejected the suggestion of free trade. It was not the United States alone that defeated the proposal, however, for most of the Latin-American delegates were by no means unaware of the importance of customs revenues in their national economies.

Pueyrredón had threatened to resign unless his proposals were accepted, and he did withdraw from the conference, even as he had withdrawn from the First League of Nations Assembly when that body rejected an Argentine ultimatum. As a partial concession to the Argentines a clause was added to the preamble stating that the Pan American Union desired to "promote effectively the harmonious development of the economic interests of the American Republics."[51] The issue proved to be fruitless, for as has been noted, the convention failed to receive unanimous ratification. The sum result, therefore, was the opportunity afforded Argentina and several other states to attack the tariff policy of the United States.

It was the debate on intervention, however, which released the greatest barrage against the United States. One of a number of projects that had been prepared for the conference by the Rio Commission of Jurists[52] was a draft treaty entitled "States: Existence, Equality, Recog-

[51] Foreign Policy Association, *Information Service*, IV, 57–60.

[52] The projects of public international law recommended by the commission and approved by the conference were: (1) Fundamental Bases of International Law; (2) States: Existence, Equality, Recognition; (3) Status of Aliens; (4) Treaties; (5) Exchange of Publications; (6) Interchange of Professors and

nition," which contained the clause "no state may intervene in the internal affairs of another." The American delegates, at the meeting of the Pan American Commission of Jurists in Rio de Janeiro, in April 1927, had insisted on a limiting interpretation of this general phraseology to mean that intervention might still take place for reasons of humanity or self-defense.[53] It was possible for Mr. Hughes at Havana to approve the draft treaty with this limited interpretation of the term "intervention," but he did not choose to do so, for it was the policy of the United States in the 1920's to hold aloof from any commitments restrictive of liberty of action.

In a classic defense of American intervention policy, Hughes told the conference:

> We want no aggression. . . . We desire to respect the rights of every country and to have the rights of our country equally respected. We do not wish the territory of any American Republic. We do not wish to govern any American Republic. We do not wish to intervene in the affairs of any American Republic. We simply wish peace and order and stability and recognition of honest rights properly acquired so that this hemisphere may not only be the hemisphere of peace but the hemisphere of international justice. . . . Now what is the real difficulty? Let us face the facts. The difficulty, if there is any, in any one of the American Republics, is not of any external aggression. It is an internal difficulty, if it exists at all. From time to time there arises a situation most deplorable and regrettable in which sovereignty is not at work, in which for a time in certain areas there is no government at all—in which for a time and within a limited sphere there is no possibility of performing the functions of sovereignty and independence. Those are the conditions that create the difficulty with which at times we find ourselves confronted. What are we to do when government breaks down and American citizens are in danger of their lives? Are we to stand by and see them killed because a government in circumstances which it cannot control and for which it may not be responsible can no longer afford reasonable protection? . . . Now it is the principle of international law that in such a case a government is fully justified in taking action—I would call it interposition of a temporary character—for the purpose of protecting the lives and property of its nationals. I could say that that is not intervention. . . . Of course the United States cannot forgo its right to protect its citizens. International law cannot be changed by the resolutions of this conference.[54]

Students; (7) Diplomatic Agents; (8) Consuls; (9) Maritime Neutrality; (10) Asylum; (11) Obligations of States in Event of Civil War; (12) Pacific Settlement of International Conflicts. The commission also drafted a code of private international law.

[53] Foreign Policy Association, *Information Service*, IV, 66.

[54] *New York Times*, Feb. 19, 1928.

Although most of the Latin-American delegations had made strong declarations in favor of the principle of nonintervention, it was realized that a resolution without the concurrence of the United States would be meaningless. It was agreed, therefore, to postpone further consideration of the problem until the next conference, scheduled at that time to meet in Montevideo in 1932. A Colombian delegate bespoke the attitude of all Latin America when he declared that the hope for a true Pan Americanism was futile as long as the right of intervention was asserted.

Since Mr. Hughes did not regard intervention, even by force, as an act of aggression, he saw no contradiction in giving his approval to a resolution which prohibited acts of aggression. The resolution provided that all aggression is considered illicit and as such is prohibited; and that the American states would employ all pacific means to settle conflicts which might arise between them.[55]

Various proposals to strengthen the inter-American peace machinery were presented to the Havana conference, but they were either rejected or held for later consideration. A proposal by Costa Rica and Colombia to establish a court of American justice was rejected. A Cuban proposal to establish a conciliation section in the Pan American Union had to be dropped because of the decision not to vest the Union with political functions. Dr. Guerrero of El Salvador proposed an American conciliation commission, composed of five states, to "look after the maintenance of peace and order in America."[56] The most important of these proposals was the project for a treaty of pacific settlement, presented by the Rio Commission of Jurists. It provided for good offices, mediation, and conciliation. Since the conference felt that more time was needed to draft a Pan American arbitration convention, it merely resolved to adopt in principle obligatory arbitration for the settlement of justiciable disputes, and decided to convene in Washington, within a year, a special conference on conciliation and arbitration "to give conventional form to the realization of this principle."[57]

Thus the Havana conference prohibited the exercise of political functions by the Pan American Union, rejected the efforts of Argentina to bring important economic matters such as tariffs within its purview, and failed to reach agreement in regard to intervention. On the other hand, it adopted resolutions declaring against aggression and providing for an arbitration conference to be held in Washington.

[55] Sixth Int. Conf. of Am. States, *Final Act*, 179.
[56] Foreign Policy Association, *Information Service*, IV, 74.
[57] Sixth Int. Conf. of Am. States, *Final Act*, 175.

In general it can be said that the United States delegation, headed by Mr. Hughes, succeeded in preventing any serious deviation from the usual path of "safe" discussions, and a decided victory was won by that school which, headed by the United States, sought to exclude major political issues and tried to keep the conference and the Pan American Union in a rut of cumulative, bureaucratic operations. Havana represented the final stand by the United States for the "new" Pan Americanism, for by the time of the next general conference, a new view of our Latin-American relations obtained in Washington.

The Washington arbitration and conciliation treaties. It was reserved for the final meeting of the "new" Pan American phase, the Conference of American States on Conciliation and Arbitration, which met in Washington from December 10, 1928, to January 5, 1929, to make two significant contributions to the inter-American security structure.[58] It produced a general treaty of arbitration, with an annexed protocol on progressive arbitration, and a general convention on conciliation. These two instruments became the central part of the inter-American system of pacific settlement of international disputes.[59]

The General Convention of Inter-American Conciliation was designed to supplement, not supplant, the Gondra treaty, for the conference recognized both the difficulty of securing universal adoption of a multilateral treaty and the value of many features of the existing treaty.[60] Thus, the Washington convention accepted the permanent diplomatic commissions and the *ad hoc* special commissions of inquiry, as provided by the Gondra treaty, but invested both types of commissions with conciliatory functions. The diplomatic commissions were privileged to exercise such functions either at the request of a party to a dispute or on their own initiative, but their competence was limited to the interim period before the parties had created the *ad hoc* commission, which should then assume the function of conciliation in addition to that of inquiry. The conciliation convention makes no exception whatever concerning types of disputes to be submitted to the procedure of conciliation.[61]

Although the Washington conciliation convention was an improve-

[58] Argentina was the only American state not represented at the conference. President Irigoyen was not interested.

[59] Manley O. Hudson, "The Inter-American Treaties of Pacific Settlement," *Foreign Affairs*, XV, No. 1 (Oct. 1936), 170.

[60] William T. Stone, "The Pan American Arbitration Treaty," Foreign Policy Association, *Information Service*, V, No. 18, 316.

[61] International Conference of American States on Conciliation and Arbitration, *Proceedings* (Washington, 1929).

ment over the Gondra treaty in that it conferred conciliatory functions on the permanent diplomatic and special *ad hoc* commissions, and enabled the diplomatic commissions to act without first being requested to do so by one of the parties to a dispute, still it could hardly be called satisfactory. A fundamental objection is the continued reliance placed on *ad hoc* agencies which can be created only by cooperative action of both parties—a very unlikely possibility when passions are at fever heat. However, the conciliatory function vested in the permanent diplomatic commissions was a gain. The conference committee which reported this project declared that the draft takes "into account that between the closing of diplomatic channels and the constitution of a commission of inquiry a more or less long period of time might transpire, which is, perhaps, the most dangerous period for grave conflicts to arise between the parties in dispute. At that opportune moment, therefore, its conciliatory action will be carried out."[62] All of the states present at the conference signed the convention. Argentina was not represented and thus she neither signed nor ratified. Although both Bolivia and Paraguay signed, neither ratified for fear of compromising their positions in the Chaco territorial dispute.

A second general convention for the pacific settlement of international disputes signed at the Washington conference was the General Treaty of Inter-American Arbitration, said to be one of the most advanced multilateral arbitration pacts ever concluded. The contracting parties were bound to submit to arbitration all international disputes of a justifiable nature. Among the questions falling in that category were: the interpretation of a treaty; any question of international law; the existence of any fact which, if established, would constitute a breach of any international obligation; and the nature and extent of the reparation to be made for the breach of an international obligation.[63] Only two subjects were excluded: domestic questions and questions concerning third states.

Regarding the agency to conduct the arbitration, the treaty permits the parties to agree upon the designation of any type of tribunal. If they fail to agree on an existent tribunal, provision is made for selecting a special court; each disputant selects two arbitrators and these four select a fifth, who acts as president of the tribunal.

The phrasing of the question to be arbitrated is to be established by

[62] *Ibid.*, 290–291.
[63] This specific indication of the types of questions suitable for arbitration was borrowed from Article 26 of the Statutes of the Permanent Court of International Justice.

108

THE UNITED STATES AND INTER-AMERICAN SECURITY

special agreement. The treaty further provides that if this agreement is not reached within three months, "reckoned from the date of the installation of the court," it shall be formulated by the court itself. Manley Hudson calls this "an artificial provision," and adds, "It is rather fantastic to imagine that two states would be able to create an arbitral tribunal without being able to agree upon the precise question to be arbitrated."[64]

A majority of the American nations signed and ratified the Washington arbitration treaty, but with reservations. Ten of them excepted disputes arising from cases in which the national courts are competent, except where there has been a denial of justice. Six countries excepted all cases arising out of events or acts which took place prior to the date of the treaty. This reservation seriously weakened the treaty, for the great majority of international disputes have their roots in the past. Although neither Paraguay nor Bolivia ratified the treaty, their reservations inserted at the time of signature could have effectively prevented its being applied to the Chaco dispute even if they had ratified. Paraguay excepted all questions affecting the integrity of its national territory, and Bolivia reserved to the effect that "for the submission to arbitration of a territorial controversy or dispute, the zone to which the said arbitration is to apply must be previously determined in the arbitral agreement."[65]

When the United States Senate consented to the ratification of the arbitration treaty it did so with its customary reservation that "no special agreement would be made on behalf of the United States except with the advice and consent of the Senate." This reservation vitiates the obligatory character of the arbitral pact. It means that the United States merely obligates itself, when a dispute arises, to consider whether it wishes to arbitrate. Indeed, this deficiency is implicit in the whole treaty, for since each party has kept control of the reference of its disputes, it is the master of its own role in the cooperation required to set up a tribunal.

The unique Protocol of Progressive Arbitration was also drafted at the Washington conference. It established a method by which parties

[64] Hudson, 171.

[65] For the reservations, see Pan American Union, *Improvement and Coordination of Inter-American Peace Instruments* (5 vols., Washington, 1941–43), II, 37–39; Volume III, *Existing Inter-American Peace Instruments and Other General Peace Treaties Signed by the American States* (1941), contains the texts of the treaties and other documents comprising the inter-American peace structure.

might formally abandon all or part of the reservations or exceptions that they may previously have formulated to the arbitration treaty, thus progressively extending the scope of arbitral jurisdiction.

The adoption of the Gondra treaty and the Washington arbitration and conciliation treaties were important contributions to the formal inter-American peace structure. They not only met the demand that multilateral instruments of peaceful settlement supplement the numerous bilateral treaties, but intrinsically they were about as advanced as any treaties negotiated to that date. True, the procedures provided were not actually obligatory, but history has demonstrated that the effectiveness of such treaties is based in good will, confidence, and loyalty to principle rather than in the theoretical compulsion of a formal engagement.

The inter-American peace treaties under test. How did these general peace treaties measure up in the face of actual tests? Since the Washington treaties of arbitration and conciliation were of too recent date to be applicable to inter-American controversies during the period under discussion, our attention must of necessity be confined to the Gondra treaty.

One of the most explosive controversies in the history of inter-American relations was the Tacna-Arica controversy, the so-called "Alsace-Lorraine question" of South America. This dispute, a residue of the War of the Pacific and the Treaty of Ancón, dragged on for years, defying all efforts at settlement by direct negotiation; and, in order to escape any legal compulsion to settle by arbitration or conciliation, the disputants studiously avoided adherence to any Pan American pact of peaceful settlement. Therefore the refusal of both Chile and Peru to ratify the Gondra treaty rendered that pact inapplicable to the Tacna-Arica controversy. It is rather significant that Peruvian ratification was withheld until December 26, 1928,[66] shortly after the resumption of diplomatic relations with Chile. The final settlement of the Tacna-Arica question (July 28, 1929) was the result of direct negotiation facilitated by the good offices of President Hoover. Thus, the formal inter-American peace procedures were ineffective for the settlement of this long-standing dispute.

Nor was it possible to apply the Gondra treaty to the Chaco controversy between Bolivia and Paraguay. When that dispute flared into armed conflict on December 8, 1928, Paraguay attempted to invoke the

[66] Pan American Union, *Improvement and Coordination of Inter-American Peace Instruments*, III, 126. Chile ratified the Gondra treaty on September 23, 1925. Bolivia adhered on July 31, 1928, but never ratified.

Gondra treaty, which that country had ratified in 1925. Bolivia refused her cooperation in setting up a commission of inquiry, claiming that her recent adherence to the Santiago pact had yet to be ratified by the Bolivian legislature. Thus the Gondra treaty was inapplicable to this controversy also since the two countries were not common parties to it.

Both nations were, however, members of the League of Nations, and this should have afforded the mutual commitment necessary to compel a peaceful settlement. The League Council was in session in December 1928 when armed clashes occurred in the Chaco between Bolivian and Paraguayan troops. The Council requested its acting president, Aristide Briand, to telegraph both governments reminding them of their obligations under the Covenant. On the basis of their replies Briand announced to the Council that, since Bolivia and Paraguay had accepted the good offices of the International Conference of American States on Conciliation and Arbitration, then meeting at Washington, no extraordinary session of the Council would be necessary.

The mediatory effort of the Washington conference resulted in the creation of a special commission of investigation and conciliation, composed of two delegates each from Bolivia and Paraguay, and one delegate each from the United States, Mexico, Colombia, Uruguay, and Cuba. The commission succeeded in obtaining a renewal of diplomatic relations between the two disputants, and the restoration of the *status quo ante* on December 5, 1928. But its failure to settle the boundary issue left the way open for an early and even more violent revival of the controversy.[67]

The history of the Gondra treaty vis-à-vis the Tacna-Arica and Chaco controversies did not reveal any ineffectiveness inherent in the treaty itself, for it had not been invoked in either dispute, but it did reveal a glaring weakness of the entire inter-American peace structure: the failure to ratify. One of the paradoxes of the inter-American cooperative movement has been the failure of states to ratify treaties and conventions which their delegates so laboriously drafted in conferences to the accompaniment of ardent lip service paid to the principles of peaceful settlement.

The failure of the inter-American peace pacts to take account of the possibility of an overseas attack has already been noted. The three multilateral treaties negotiated after World War I provided exclusively for the settlement of inter-American controversies. The lessons of

[67] Gordon Ireland, *Boundaries, Possessions, and Conflicts in South America* (Cambridge, Mass., 1938), 66–95.

World War I in demonstrating the need for cooperative action for mutual defense were all forgotten. The American nations were preoccupied, in fabricating their security structure, only with the means of preserving peace among themselves, and of containing or restraining the United States. Had not the defeat of Germany removed all threat of foreign attack? Why bother about security measures to combat a nonexistent or highly improbable danger?

V The Good Neighbor (1929–1939)

The faith of the Americas lies in the spirit. The system, the sisterhood, of the Americas is impregnable so long as her nations maintain that spirit.

FRANKLIN D. ROOSEVELT, 1936

THE DECADE FOLLOWING the Havana and Washington conferences, and particularly after 1933, was marked by the most significant developments in the history of the Pan American movement up to that time. Not only were extremely important agreements adopted providing for innovations in the procedures of peaceful settlement and the extension of security to include overseas threats, but, equally important, the psychological bases of inter-American cooperation were greatly strengthened. Long-standing fears, suspicions, and distrust of the motives of the dominant member of the inter-American system had obscured the view of the twenty other members concerning the true mutuality of continental interests. Because of the United States' interventionism and imperialism it was really expecting too much of weak and backward states, excessively sensitive of their national sovereignties, to subscribe to the security principle "all for one, one for all." Yet, this became a reality by the end of the decade after the atmosphere had been cleared by the enunciation of the Good Neighbor policy, the essence of which was United States recognition, by word and action, of the sovereignty and territorial integrity of the Western Hemisphere nations. Then the American states, for the first time, were able to see their mutual interests clearly.

Enunciation of the policy of the Good Neighbor. The debates at Havana in 1928 had made it more apparent than ever that the incompatibilities latent in United States–Latin-American relations could never be resolved except by a reorientation of policy. This being the case, that conference served the dual purpose of reinforcing a conviction and stimulating a decision. The United States had become convinced that it was no longer necessary to premise its Latin-American

The Good Neighbor

policy on an assertive hegemony in the Caribbean area. Thanks to its great strength following World War I, and the nonexistence of any overseas threat, it could now afford to be indulgent about those comic-opera political demonstrations in the banana republics which in the past had provoked an energetic wielding of the "Big Stick." Thus, the wise and opportune decision was to salvage the Pan American movement by compromising with the Latin-American, or Bolivarian, ideal of inter-American cooperation.

The Good Neighbor phase of Pan Americanism—the main feature of which was the decision of the United States to abandon imperialism in Latin America and to make concessions in the interest of confidence and good will—though carried to its much-publicized heights by the New Deal, really started when President Coolidge reversed United States policy by sending Henry Stimson to Nicaragua and Dwight Morrow to Mexico to clean up imperialistic messes created by the United States. But more significant reversals of policy occurred during the Hoover Administration. The following acts of President Hoover and Secretary Stimson indicate that they intended to pursue a new course in our Latin-American relations: (1) repudiation of the Roosevelt corollary of the Monroe Doctrine, and the declaration that the Doctrine is opposed solely to Europe and not to Latin America;[1] (2) abandonment of the Wilson *de jure* recognition policy, which was regarded in Latin America as a form of intervention, and the return to the traditional Jeffersonian *de facto* recognition policy; (3) withdrawal of United States Marines from Nicaragua, and preparations for their withdrawal from Haiti; (4) notification to American investors in certain Latin-American countries that they must exhaust local remedies before appealing for diplomatic protection; and (5) refusal of the U.S. State Department to press for full and punctual settlement of financial obligations due American citizens. Moreover, to dispel fears current in Latin America that the United States might claim the right to dictate peace in the Americas, League of Nations cooperation in the settlement of the Leticia dispute between Colombia and Peru was accepted.[2]

The foregoing policy changes during the administration of Presi-

[1] The *Memorandum on the Monroe Doctrine*, which repudiated the Roosevelt corollary, had been prepared for Secretary of State Kellogg in December 1928 by Undersecretary of State J. Reuben Clark, but it had been kept secret. Its publication in 1930 by the State Department was equivalent to a public announcement that the Roosevelt corollary was being abandoned.

[2] See pp. 163–165.

dent Hoover were considerably accelerated and broadened, both in the political and in the economic fields, after 1933. President Roosevelt and Secretary of State Cordell Hull made the new policy vital and dynamic. In the Inaugural Address on March 4, 1933, President Roosevelt set forth the principle that was to govern the foreign policy of his administration: "In the field of world policy I would dedicate this nation to the policy of the good neighbor—the neighbor who resolutely respects himself, and, because he does so, respects the rights of others—the neighbor who respects his obligations and respects the sanctity of his agreements in and with a world of neighbors."

In his Pan American Day address on April 12, 1933, the President specifically applied his good neighbor principles to the American republics:

The essential qualities of a true Pan Americanism must be the same as those which constitute a good neighbor, namely, mutual understanding, and through such understanding, a sympathetic appreciation of the others' point of view. It is only in this manner that we can hope to build up a system of which confidence, friendship, and good will are the cornerstones.

Only a month later, on May 16, when President Roosevelt proposed that the nations of the world agree not to send troops across the frontiers of another state except in accordance with treaties, he indicated his willingness to forgo the practice of armed intervention in the countries of the Caribbean and elsewhere. Thus the stage was set for the grand renunciation at Montevideo.[3]

The Montevideo Conference. The Good Neighbor policy bore rich fruit in friendly good will at the Seventh International Conference of American States, which met at Montevideo in December 1933. There the old feelings of suspicion and resentment vanished in view of the willingness of the United States to allow free and open discussion of any topic of general interest, and to concede all demands concerning the troublesome old questions of the rights and duties of states.

Secretary of State Hull, head of the United States delegation, set the tone of the conference when he expounded the policy of the New Deal as "that application of the Golden Rule by which we mean the good will of the true good neighbor." "Let us," he urged, "in the broad spirit of this revitalized policy make this the beginning of a great new era of a great renaissance in American cooperative effort to

[3] New York *Herald Tribune*, May 17, 1933. In 1928, Franklin D. Roosevelt wrote in an article in *Foreign Affairs*, "Single-handed intervention by us in the internal affairs of other nations must end."

promote our entire material, moral, and spiritual affairs and to erect an edifice of peace that will forever endure."

Mr. Hull's statement evoked an enthusiastic response, particularly from those countries that had felt the weight of American imperialism. For example, the delegate from Haiti said, "We applaud the lofty ideal of which Mr. Hull's address is a most eloquent expression. We therefore entertain the hope that, putting the word into action, he will promptly give to the Republic of Haiti the things she is legitimately entitled to." Of the same tenor was the speech of Portell Vilá of Cuba: "Those statements honor Secretary Hull personally and Cuba hopes that those assertions shall concrete themselves in deeds which may banish suspicions and avoid differences between both peoples."[4]

Since the formal Convention on the Rights and Duties of States, signed and later ratified by the United States, embodied most of the political objectives toward which the Latin Americans had been striving since the very inception of the Pan American movement, the pertinent articles are presented herewith:

ARTICLE IV. States are juridically equal, enjoy the same rights, and have equal capacity in their exercise. The rights of each one do not depend upon the power which it possesses to assure its exercise, but upon the simple fact of its existence as a person under international law.

ARTICLE VI. The recognition of a state merely signifies that the state which recognizes it accepts the personality of the other with all the rights and duties determined by international law. Recognition is unconditional and irrevocable.

ARTICLE VIII. No state has the right to intervene in the internal or external affairs of another.

ARTICLE IX. The jurisdiction of states within the limits of national territory applies to all the inhabitants.

Nationals and foreigners are under the same protection of the law and the national authorities, and the foreigners may not claim rights other or more extensive than those of the nationals.

ARTICLE X. The primary interest of states is the conservation of peace. Differences of any nature which arise between them should be settled by recognized pacific methods.

ARTICLE XI. The contracting states definitely establish as the rule of their conduct the precise obligation not to recognize territorial acquisitions or special advantages which have been obtained by force whether this consists in the employment of arms, in threatening diplomatic representations, or in

---

[4] Seventh International Conference of American States, *Minutes of the First, Second and Eighth Committees* (Montevideo, 1933), 24–26, cited hereinafter as Seventh Int. Conf. of Am. States, *Minutes, First Committee.*

any other effective coercive measure. The territory of a state is inviolable and may not be the object of military occupation nor of other measures of force imposed by another state directly or indirectly or for any motive whatever, even temporarily.

The convention was, as expected, enthusiastically endorsed by all the Latin-American delegations. When Mr. Hull observed this unanimity, he abandoned his original demand that the project should first incorporate interpretations and definitions and he signed also, but with the reservation that the nonintervention pledge applied only for the duration of the Roosevelt Administration and that the United States reserved its rights "by the law of nations as generally recognized."[5]

If the Hull reservation created any doubts concerning the meaning of American renunciation of the right of intervention, they were soon removed by President Roosevelt. On December 28, 1933, he said:

The definite policy of the United States from now on is one opposed to armed intervention. The maintenance of constitutional government in other nations is not, after all, a sacred obligation devolving upon the United States alone. The maintenance of law and the orderly processes of government in this hemisphere is the concern of each individual nation within its borders first of all. It is only if and when the failure of orderly processes affects the other nations of the continent that it becomes their concern, and the point to stress is that in such an event it becomes the joint concern of the whole continent in which we are all neighbors.[6]

Thus the Latin Americans had at long last won their fight to outlaw intervention, albeit the meaning of the term remained susceptible of various interpretations. Another substantial victory for them was the virtual acceptance of the Calvo Doctrine, for inviolable sovereignty was the true meaning of Article IX. The articles dealing with recognition approximated an acceptance of the Estrada Doctrine, so named after the Mexican foreign minister who argued that conditional recog-

[5] Pan American Union, *Improvement and Coordination of Inter-American Peace Instruments* (5 vols., Washington, 1941–43), III (1941), 59–63. At Havana, Mr. Hughes had pointed out the dangers of accepting a formula in general terms: "If I should subscribe to a formula which others thought might prevent the action which a nation is entitled to take in these circumstances, there might come later the charge of bad faith because of acceptance of a formula with one interpretation in my mind while another interpretation of it is in the minds of those proposing the formula."—Foreign Policy Association, *Information Service*, IV, No. 4, 66, n. 86.

[6] *New York Times*, Dec. 29, 1933.

nition is a form of intervention, and that recognition should not be used as an instrument of policy. The other articles also represented triumphs for the traditional Latin-American position on such subjects as equality of states, inviolability of territory, and nonrecognition of the fruits of force.[7]

With the removal of intervention as a corrosive element in United States–Latin-American relations, and the acceptance of the other guarantees of the juridical equality of states, it was now possible to stimulate the good will and friendship so indispensable to the functioning of a regional-security arrangement.

The Montevideo conference was concerned with the problems of security, both in the abstract and in the acute reality of the Chaco War. With respect to the former, the conference was aware of deficiencies in the peace pacts, limited though they were to inter-American disputes. Since it was realized that the system of conciliation as provided by the Gondra and Washington treaties was weak in that it depended upon the action of *ad hoc* agencies, the conference drafted an Additional Protocol to the General Convention of Inter-American Conciliation, giving permanent character to the commissions of investigation and conciliation. Each signatory country was to name as soon as possible, by means of bilateral agreements, the two members of the commission provided for in Article 4 of the Gondra treaty. It was probably contemplated that the same persons would represent each state on its various commissions. It was left to the Governing Board of the Pan American Union "to initiate measures for bringing about the nomination of the fifth member of each Commission of Investigation and Conciliation in accordance with the stipulation established in Article IV of the Convention of Santiago, Chile."[8]

It was felt that it would be an additional safeguard to the peace of the Americas if these commissions were organized in advance and were always ready to take cognizance of controversies. This attempt to strengthen the conciliation pacts ended in failure, however, for few of the states ratified and even fewer took steps to appoint the permanent commissions.[9]

[7] Samuel F. Bemis (*The Latin American Policy of the United States* [New York, 1943], 273) remarks that the name of the Montevideo convention is a misnomer, for it stresses only *rights* and ignores the *duties* of states. Most weak and backward nations incline to be remiss in this respect.

[8] Seventh International Conference of American States, *Plenary Sessions, Minutes and Antecedents* (Montevideo, 1933), 121–122, cited hereinafter as Seventh Int. Conf. of Am. States, *Plenary Sessions.*

[9] No more than twelve states have ratified the Additional Protocol.

Another weakness of the peace machinery of which the conference took note was the chronic failure of so many states to ratify the treaties and conventions. To expedite the study, approval, and ratification of inter-American treaties and conventions, and to stimulate the fulfillment of the resolutions and recommendations of the conferences, the Pan American Union was instructed to send one or more representatives of diplomatic standing to the American countries to promote this work. The Union was also ordered to publish semiannually a chart showing the status of Pan American treaties.

To encourage mediation, the conference approved a "Declaration on Good Offices and Mediation," proposed by J. Reuben Clark of the American delegation, which read: "It shall never be deemed an unfriendly act for any state or states to offer good offices or mediation to other states engaged in a controversy threatening or rupturing their peaceful relations."[10]

An interesting addition to the formal peace structure was the Anti-War Treaty of Non-Aggression and Conciliation. This treaty, drafted by Argentine Minister of Foreign Relations Carlos Saavedra Lamas, had been signed at Rio de Janeiro on October 10, 1933, by six Latin-American republics: Argentina, Brazil, Chile, Mexico, Paraguay, and Uruguay. The treaty was then thrown open to general signatures, and so was not intended to be an exclusive Western Hemisphere pact.[11] One of the last official acts of Stimson as Secretary of State in the Hoover Administration had been to reject the Argentine invitation to sign Saavedra Lamas' pact on the ground that it impaired the vigor of the Kellogg-Briand war renunciation treaty, signed in Paris in 1928. Incidentally, Argentina had refused to sign the Kellogg pact.[12]

Saavedra Lamas, succumbing to Mr. Hull's flattery, put his treaty before the Montevideo conference for acceptance by the other American countries. To facilitate adherence, Saavedra Lamas proposed a resolution urging those countries that had not already done so to sign and ratify "a number of peace instruments that would be an ample and sufficient guarantee of the high purposes asserted," viz., the Gondra treaty, the two Washington treaties of 1929, the pact of Paris, and his

[10] Seventh Int. Conf. of Am. States, *Plenary Sessions*, 84.

[11] It eventually received the ratification of the following non-American countries: Bulgaria, Czechoslovakia, Finland, Greece, Italy, Norway, Portugal, Roumania, Spain, Turkey, and Yugoslavia.

[12] Cordell Hull, *The Memoirs of Cordell Hull* (2 vols., New York, 1948), I, 309, cited hereinafter as *Memoirs*.

own antiwar treaty.[13] Mr. Hull could readily affix his signature to the last-named treaty since it was really quite innocuous, despite the fact that it was destined to win for the Argentine statesman the coveted Nobel Peace Prize.

Saavedra Lamas had borrowed the dominating theme of his pact from the Kellogg-Briand treaty, but with some departures. There was a condemnation of wars of aggression, but not a renunciation of war as an instrument of policy. It also borrowed from the Stimson doctrine by creating an obligation to refrain from recognizing any territorial arrangement brought about by force of arms.

The sanctions which provided for the observance of the above-mentioned obligations were, in the words of Judge Manley Hudson, "adumbrated but feebly." The signatories were to endeavor to maintain peace by adopting "in their character as neutrals, a common and solidary attitude; they will exercise the political, juridical, or economic means authorized by international law, [and] they will bring the influence of public opinion to bear, but will in no case resort to intervention, either diplomatic or armed." Instead of facilitating the enforcement of the treaty by offering effective sanctions, the pact made enforcement doubly difficult by prohibiting diplomatic intervention. It would have been better had it remained silent on the subject of sanctions.

Considerable attention was given to conciliation by Saavedra Lamas. The treaty contemplated the functioning of *ad hoc* conciliation commissions and thus added little to the Santiago and Washington conventions in this respect. The pact prescribed compulsory conciliation for all disputes except four categories of questions which any state might reject in whole or in part at the time of signature or ratification.[14] Undoubtedly great thought had been given to the framing of these exceptions, but it is surprising and illuminating that the Argentine statesman thought it necessary to elaborate safeguards against a procedure

[13] Seventh Int. Conf. of Am. States, *Plenary Sessions,* 39. According to Bemis (*op. cit.,* 271), Mr. Hull secured an Argentine pledge to ratify the enumerated treaties in return for the United States' signature of the Saavedra Lamas pact. The Argentine government did not make good on its Minister's promise. At the least Saavedra Lamas formally announced at the conference that his government would sign the Gondra pact and the two Washington agreements of 1929.—Seventh Int. Conf. of Am. States, *Minutes, First Committee,* 21.

[14] Pan American Union, *Improvement and Coordination of Inter-American Peace Instruments,* III, 19–30. Several of the countries took full advantage of the opportunity afforded by Article 5 to reserve on all four categories of questions.

designed merely to lead to a report and a proposed settlement having no compulsory or binding character.

Although the Argentine antiwar treaty was of some potential value it quite unnecessarily complicated the inter-American system of pacific settlement. Perhaps the best that can be said for the treaty is that, in view of Argentina's failure to ratify the other peace pacts, her ratification of this her own pact provided the only mutual commitment, however inadequate, upon which to seek peaceful settlement of disputes involving that country. The Saavedra Lamas pact has been ratified or adhered to by every American nation, perhaps because it is so ineffectual. The United States Senate without much delay approved ratification but with the reservation that "in adhering to the treaty the United States does not thereby waive any rights it may have under other treaties or conventions or under international law."

Before taking leave of the Montevideo conference there should be mention of Secretary Hull's liberal-trade resolution and the resolution for the codification of international law. On motion by Mr. Hull a resolution was adopted which recommended that the American republics reduce the barriers to trade, particularly excessive tariffs. Of this practice the United States was the most guilty party with its recent enactment (1930) of the Smoot-Hawley Tariff Act. Latin-American resentment over that act tended to obscure an otherwise bright dawn of United States–Latin-American good neighborliness. Hull, reversing the position taken by Hughes at Havana in 1928, introduced discussion of the tariff into the realm of international diplomacy by proposing the negotiation of bilateral reciprocity agreements based upon mutual concessions. The Secretary of State was proposing economic disarmament not only because of the economic objective *per se* but also because he believed that the elimination of economic conflict was essential to world peace. In 1931 he had said, "There can be no real progress towards confidence or peace nor permanent trade recovery while retaliations and bitter controversies arise."[15] The liberal-trade resolution was, therefore, a peace proposal and for that reason is here considered with the other security proposals.

In this same category belongs the resolution concerning the codification of international law. Recognizing the necessity for continuing the work of gradual and progressive codification of American international law, the conference adopted a resolution providing for the permanent maintenance of the International Commission of Jurists which, since its meeting in Rio in 1927, had ceased to function. To

[15] Harold B. Hinton, *Cordell Hull* (New York, 1942), 210.

facilitate the work of the international commission, the resolution provided that each government should create a national commission for the codification of international law, composed of both official and lay specialists, and also that there should be created a Commission of Experts, composed of such jurists selected from those nominated by the member states. The national commissions were to assist the Commission of Experts, which, as a subcommittee of the International Commission of Jurists, was to submit projects to that body after thorough screening and study.[16]

The mechanism for codifying the public law of the Americas was a component part of the regional-security system. The codification commissions served a twofold purpose. First, their existence made it easier to avoid international disputes and facilitated the settlement of such disputes when they did arise. Since so many international controversies arise because the disputants adhere to conflicting legal principles, a clear, systematic, and authoritative statement of what constitutes accepted international practice not only helps to prevent the development of serious international disputes, but also is of service to arbitral and juridical bodies applying the principles of uniform law.

A second purpose served by the codification commissions was to inject new principles into the public law of the Americas. Instead of being confined solely to the codification of *existent* law, the commissions were used by the Latin-American members as convenient media for injecting into American international law their own concepts of the rights and duties of states.

The Montevideo conference, having given consideration to the various abstract problems of security, could not ignore the embarrassing fact that a fierce war was raging in the not too distant Chaco. To disregard the Chaco crisis, as some of the members advocated, would be to admit complete futility. However, sad to relate, the sum total of the mediatory efforts of the conference was a three weeks' truce. The familiar affirmations at Montevideo about how deeply attached the American nations were to the process of peaceful settlement were thrown off key by the reverberations of gunfire in the Chaco. It is a commentary on the impotence of the inter-American peace machinery that the Chaco war continued its dreary and bloody course until the belligerents, exhausted, were no longer able to carry on the conflict. It was only then, on June 14, 1935, that the Buenos Aires mediators were able to secure a definitive termination of the hostilities.

[16] Seventh Int. Conf. of Am. States, *Plenary Sessions*, 112–113.

The Buenos Aires Peace Conference. The termination of hostilities in the Chaco afforded President Roosevelt the occasion to propose an inter-American peace conference to take stock of the security system. In personal letters sent to the presidents of all the American republics on January 30, 1936, the President of the United States suggested an extraordinary conference at Buenos Aires

to determine how the maintenance of peace among the American republics may best be safeguarded—whether perhaps through the prompt ratification of all of the inter-American peace instruments already negotiated;[17] whether through the amendment of existing peace instruments in such manner as experience has demonstrated to be most necessary; or perhaps through the creation, by common accord, of new instruments of peace, additional to those already formulated.[18]

The fiasco of the Chaco peace-makers had indeed demonstrated the need for revamping the inter-American peace machinery. But in calling the conference, President Roosevelt had another objective which can only be inferred from his letter: he stated that such steps as he proposed might "supplement and reinforce the efforts of the League ... in seeking to prevent war." Thus the President had in mind something more world-wide than safeguarding security from inter-American wars alone. The developing crisis in Europe, marked by the aggrandizement of Nazi power in Germany, the outbreak of the Italo-Ethiopian War, and the Japanese attack on China raised the specter of another general war, with all the attendant dangers of American involvement. The Neutrality Act of 1935, pacifist- and isolationist-inspired, was the Roosevelt-Hull Administration's reaction to the danger. It became clear, in the course of the following months before the convening of the conference in December, that the United States government wanted the American nations to organize a common neutrality front in the event of a non-American war. Considering the menacing prospect of a general European war, this was, in the view

[17] At that moment the ratification status of the principal peace instruments was as follows: Gondra treaty, nineteen; Washington conciliation convention, seventeen; Washington arbitration treaty, fifteen; and Argentine antiwar treaty, ten.

[18] "Letter of Franklin Delano Roosevelt to the Presidents of the Latin American Republics," in A. Curtis Wilgus (ed.), *Readings in Latin American Civilization* (New York, 1946), 394. For the text of President Roosevelt's letter to the President of Argentina, see Inter-American Conference for the Maintenance of Peace, *Special Handbook for the Use of the Delegates* (Pan American Union, Washington, 1936), 1.

of President Roosevelt and Secretary Hull, the most important problem to be met by the conference. Secretary Hull felt that they dared not wait until the scheduled Lima conference in 1938, for events were moving too swiftly beyond the Atlantic and the Pacific. He said in retrospect, "The newborn friendship among the American Republics required solidifying."[19]

Considering that a Pan American conference was scheduled to be called upon—for the first time since the inception of the movement at Washington in 1889—to consider a cooperative defense policy against an overseas danger, it will be illuminating to see how the Buenos Aires Peace Conference met the challenge. Up to 1936, the security interests of the various conferences had been confined exclusively to the problems of inter-American relations. Also, prior to 1936, there apparently was no direct connection between the developing world crisis and the reorientation of the United States' relations with Latin America. The fact that the United States renounced intervention and assumed certain political commitments was *not caused* by any fear concerning the situation in Europe. These actions were the result of an upsurge of public opinion *in the United States* which condemned our previous Latin-American policy. Although the Good Neighbor had not been enunciated with the idea of winning allies against non-American aggressors, this nevertheless was a happy by-product of the new policy. The two factors which contributed greatly to the increase of inter-American solidarity in the pre-World War II days were the Good Neighbor policy and Hitler's rise to power.

One Latin-American government that was in the van of its sister states in recognizing the dangers of a world conflict was Guatemala. In 1935, President Ubico Castañeda drafted a project of a general treaty of solidarity and cooperation among the nations of the hemisphere. The treaty provided that any extracontinental aggression or intervention would be considered as an offense to all, a danger to their integrity and independence, and in view of their solidarity all should take measures of common defense.[20]

The early application of the principle of the Good Neighbor to our relations with the other American republics left no doubt concerning the good faith and sincerity of the Roosevelt-Hull Administration. Military occupation of Haiti was terminated in August 1934. With reference to politically and economically distressed Cuba, the United

[19] Hull, *Memoirs*, II, 493.
[20] *Aporte de Guatemala a la Solidaridad y Cooperación Interamericanas.* Publicación de la Secretaría de Relaciones Exteriores (Guatemala, Sept. 1942).

124

States refrained from armed intervention and assisted the Cuban people to rehabilitate their nation by negotiating a new reciprocity agreement, and by giving them a fair quota in the American market for their sugar. Also, a new treaty of relations was negotiated eliminating the Platt Amendment, which had granted us the right to intervene in Cuban affairs. With Panama, likewise, a new treaty was made which eliminated sources of friction between the two countries, particularly the right of intervention and guarantees of Panamanian independence. All this, and more that could be mentioned, proved to our neighbors that the Good Neighbor Policy was more than merely a paper program. The winning of Latin-American confidence and good will was productive of harmonious discussion and constructive achievement in the Buenos Aires conference.

The Inter-American Conference for the Maintenance of Peace met in Buenos Aires, December 1–23, 1936. Argentine Foreign Minister Carlos Saavedra Lamas, whose antiwar pact had recently won for him the Nobel Peace Prize, presided. Just returned from Geneva where he had presided over the League Assembly, the able but egotistical diplomat apparently had his eyes more on the dying League than on the living Pan American ideal. After the exceptional show of cooperation at Montevideo he reverted to an attitude of inflexible opposition. This was quite in line with traditional Argentine policy, as described by Mr. Hull, "to remain aloof from any movements of leadership in the hemisphere unless they themselves were furnishing the chief leadership and policies."[21]

President Roosevelt, honored guest of the Argentine nation, addressed the conference at its opening session. Revealing his desire for a strengthening of the inter-American security system by erecting bulwarks against aggression from abroad, he said:

In the determination to live at peace among ourselves we in the Americas make it at the same time clear that we stand shoulder to shoulder in our final determination that others who, driven by war madness or land hunger, might seek to commit acts of aggression against us, will find a hemisphere wholly prepared to consult together for our mutual safety and our mutual good. I repeat what I said in speaking before the Congress and the Supreme Court of Brazil: "Each of us has learned the glories of independence. Let each one of us learn the glories of interdependence."[22]

[21] Hull, *Memoirs*, I, 609.
[22] *New York Times,* Dec. 2, 1936. The text of President Roosevelt's speech is found also in *Report of Delegates of the United States to the Inter-American Conference for the Maintenance of Peace* (Washington, 1937).

Mr. Hull, in his opening speech before the conference, also endeavored to arouse the delegates to the dangerous realities of the world situation:

The Western Hemisphere must now face squarely certain hard realities. For the purpose of our undertaking, we must frankly recognize that for some time the forces of militarism have been in the ascendant in a large part of the world; those of peace have been correspondingly on the decline. We should be lacking in common sense if we ignored the plain fact that the effects of these forces will unavoidably have direct impact upon all of us. We should be lacking in ordinary caution if we fail to counsel together for our common safety and welfare.[23]

For the first time in a Pan American conference, at least since the inauguration of the "new" Pan Americanism, the delegates were being urged to consider security measures against a non-American aggressor. It is primarily for this reason that the Buenos Aires conference is an important landmark in the history of the inter-American security system.

If the number of formal agreements negotiated is indicative of the success of a conference, the Buenos Aires meeting was a huge success. Eight conventions, two treaties, one protocol, and a number of resolutions and declarations emerged from the three weeks' deliberations, most of them to be added to the already top-heavy peace structure. A magic formula featuring the most important of these agreements was the principle of consultation, which had been alluded to by both President Roosevelt and Mr. Hull in their opening speeches, and which was incorporated in a draft convention proposed by Mr. Hull. It was seized upon avidly by the conference as a practical procedure which offered possibilities for cooperative action yet made it possible at the same time to avoid compromising commitments.

The draft convention, containing the consultation formula proposed by Mr. Hull, was called a "Convention Coordinating the Existing Treaties between the American States and Extending Them in Certain Respects."[24] It was intended to serve the twofold purpose of providing machinery for coordinating existing peace instruments, and of providing common measures of neutrality. With respect to the first objective, the draft convention roughly summarized the provisions and renewed pledges to the five important treaties already entered into by most of the American republics—the Gondra treaty, the Kellogg-

---

[23] *New York Times,* Dec. 6, 1936.
[24] For text, see *ibid.,* Dec. 7, 1936.

Briand pact of 1928, the Washington conciliation convention, the Washington arbitration treaty, and the Argentine antiwar pact. It was the belief of the United States government that these pacts, if invoked, amply provided the means of peaceful settlement of inter-American disputes. Therefore, a primary purpose of the draft convention was to coordinate and make more effective by means of consultation these five peace instruments calculated to compose inter-American disputes by peaceful procedures. The problem was to set in motion the machinery provided by these peace treaties. To meet this need, the Hull "coordinating convention" provided for the creation of a permanent inter-American consultation committee, composed of the ministers of foreign affairs of each contracting country. The committee was charged with arranging efficient methods of consultation in order to act with dispatch in an emergency.

A second purpose of the Hull draft was to agree on a common neutral policy in the event of war between any of the signatories. When the permanent committee should find that hostilities between nations constituted a state of war, then those countries remaining neutral were pledged to impose embargoes on arms shipments and loans to the belligerents. This provision took into account the recent neutrality legislation of the United States by requiring that such prohibitions and restrictions applied *equally* to all belligerents except in instances where any of the parties were bound to take other action by virtue of multilateral treaties to which they were parties. This exception referred to obligations under the League of Nations.

The United States draft seemed to be concerned solely with inter-American disputes and wars. However, the possibility of a concerted, united American front against an overseas threat was suggested by the statement in the Preamble that a purpose of the permanent consultative committee was "to provide a means whereby the American republics, with the full recognition of their juridical equality as sovereign and independent states and their general right to individual liberty of action, may nevertheless, in every way consistent therewith, take counsel together whenever emergencies arise which affect their common interests."

A spokesman for the United States delegation explained that the intent of this statement was only to cover threats of catastrophic wars that would inevitably involve the Americas one way or another. Whether or not this was the sum total of United States intent, the statement was phrased in terms sufficiently general to provide for consultation in the event of *any kind* of overseas threat to the security of the Americas.

It was not because of this feature, however, that the Hull project had to be abandoned. Although the idea of coordinating the five peace treaties through consultation was generally acceptable, it was the provision for a permanent inter-American consultative committee composed of the foreign ministers that was vigorously objected to by Argentina. Saavedra Lamas seemed to feel that a highly formalized American peace organization would tend to remove the Western Hemisphere from the jurisdiction of the League of Nations and would thus weaken the world organization. Probably the truth of the matter was not that Saavedra Lamas loved the League of Nations more but that he cared less for an inter-American political agency with potentialities for effective development. Other delegations, however, members of the League of Nations, also counseled against any kind of agreement which might lead to conflict with their obligations under the Covenant. Undoubtedly the latent fears of interventionism strongly influenced this attitude.

Basically, the argument that a strengthened regional-security arrangement was incompatible with a virile universal organization was fallacious. Any improvement or development of the machinery for international cooperation in the Americas reinforced the same fundamental purposes for which the League of Nations itself had been established. That the conference recognized this fact is reflected by the provision in the agenda which specifically called for consideration of "measures of cooperation with other international entities."

It was the neutrality provisions of the Hull project which aroused the greatest dissent. The Latin Americans were unconvinced that a rigid outlining of procedure in advance of the outbreak of war, without knowledge of the peculiar conditions which might surround any given conflict, was the answer to the problem. Preferring to retain a measure of freedom, they argued that a neutrality policy such as that proposed by the United States might easily drag them into a war which it was intended to avoid. Also they argued that, granting the propriety of neutrals collaborating to impose arms embargoes on belligerents, it was inconceivable that no distinction should be made between the aggressor and the victim of aggression. Fortunately, Mr. Hull's effort to "continentalize" the blind, selfish, and inane neutrality policy of the United States found little support among the Latin-American delegations. Many of them interpreted his project as isolationist and anti-

League of Nations.[25] Thanks to this opposition, the United States was saved from the egregious error of foisting its own mistaken policy upon its Latin-American associates.

Carlos Saavedra Lamas had also drafted for the consideration of the conference a coordinating treaty called "General Treaty to Re-enforce the Means for the Maintenance of Peace."[26] To supplement the moral sanctions of the Kellogg pact and to assure the effectiveness of the sanctions provided for in the Saavedra Lamas pact, the Argentine project proposed (1) the nonrecognition of territorial adjustments obtained by other than pacific means, and (2) the adoption of a joint and solidary attitude by the neutral signatories. This neutral action by negotiation through diplomatic channels or in a conference of neutrals might, if conciliation failed, take the form of an embargo upon armaments as well as upon coal, petroleum, or any other material which might be directly used in war. In his proposed pact, Saavedra Lamas also stipulated that force be abolished as a means of settling controversies between states; that intervention, including "excessive diplomatic protection of nationals residing in foreign countries," be outlawed; that recognition be obligatory in their mutual relations of "the principle that the civil equality of the foreigner and of the national constitutes the maximum limit to which a foreigner may aspire in the positive legislation of the states"; and that economic intercommunications be freed by checking "the incessant increase of tariff rates" and by revising "the unjustified prohibitions of a sanitary order."[27] Dr. Saavedra Lamas overlooked precious little that might have been incorporated in his draft project except, significantly, any provisions to protect the common interest of the Americas against overseas emergencies. This omission was corrected all too handsomely by a project submitted by the head of the Brazilian delegation, Foreign Minister José Carlos Macedo Soares, who undertook to break the stalemate created by the United States and Argentine draft conventions.

The Brazilian project was nothing less than a combination of the Monroe Doctrine and the principle of nonintervention. It declared that each and every one of the contracting parties would regard as an

25 *Ibid.*, Dec. 8, 1936.

26 *Draft of a Convention for the Maintenance of Peace. A contribution to the labors of the forthcoming Inter-American Peace Conference by His Excellency the Minister of Foreign Affairs of the Argentine Republic, Dr. Carlos Saavedra Lamas* (Washington, May 1936).

27 *Ibid.*, 11–13. Argentina was touchy on the subject of sanitary restrictions because the United States quarantine had adverse effects on the importation of Argentine beef.

unfriendly act any interposition by a non-American power in any American country, provided such intervention threatened the national security and territorial integrity of that country. In such an event the contracting parties were pledged to consult at once with one another "for the common defense and protection of all." Thus would the Monroe Doctrine be made the common doctrine of all the American republics—and the prime objective of the Hull draft be achieved.

Since absolute nonintervention was the principal aim of the Saavedra Lamas project, Dr. Macedo Soares proposed to conciliate the Argentine Foreign Minister by including in his project the declaration that intervention by any one of the parties in the internal affairs of another would be considered an unfriendly act.

Saavedra Lamas was opposed to the Monroe Doctrine and to any generalization of it. Moreover, he was opposed to any direct or implied challenge to Europe, so in deference to his wishes the phrase "noncontinental country" (i.e., European) was dropped in favor of a generalization of the source from which the threat might come. And so it went with the various draft proposals. They were drained of their very essence, and thus the conference, operating under a constricting unanimity rule, produced a number of wordy and generally ineffectual pacts to be added to the already overburdened inter-American peace structure. These additions will now be briefly described.

Foremost—and with this the conference might have rested—was the Convention for the Maintenance, Preservation and Re-establishment of Peace, popularly known as the Consultation Pact. Declaring in its preamble that war anywhere concerns all states everywhere, the pact provides for consultation among the governments of the American republics for the purpose of finding and adopting methods of cooperation in three sets of contingencies: (1) in the event that the peace of the Americas is menaced from any source; (2) in the event of war or virtual state of war between American states; and (3) in the event of a war outside America which might menace the peace of the American republics. Although in no one of the three contingencies is there any obligation to do more than consult, it is noteworthy that in only the third case is the cooperation not limited to *peaceful* collaboration. The Consultation Pact provided no machinery for consultation, a defect remedied two years later at Lima.

The mere obligation to consult was the great achievement of the Buenos Aires conference. It expressed the collective concern and common interest of each of the American republics in the security of all. Also, it implied that the contracting parties did accept a degree of collective responsibility for a situation created by a threat to the peace —at least to the extent of finding and adopting a method of peaceful cooperation. It was a demonstration of American solidarity in a world where war threats were only too abundant. The subsequent history of inter-American consultation has not nullified Mr. Hull's enthusiastic declaration that the Consultation Pact represented "the strongest assurance of peace which this continent has ever had."[28]

But to claim that this convention "Pan Americanized" the Monroe Doctrine is to miss the meaning of the venerable American policy. The Monroe Doctrine is a warning by the United States to any foreign nation against any action taken in the Americas by it which, in the opinion of the United States, menaces our peace or national safety. The inhibition of the policy is not on the Latin-American nations but on overseas nations that threaten by force to introduce changes in the political or territorial conditions in the Western Hemisphere disturbing to the welfare of the United States. It is an essentially unilateral policy and does not lend itself to multilateral agreement with other nations because the United States alone determines for itself and at its own discretion when it shall be invoked, and what action if any should be taken to enforce it. The Monroe Doctrine by its very nature can never entail contractual obligations between nations. This does not deny the right of other states to adopt similar policies.

In contrast to this thumbnail description of the Monroe Doctrine, we discover in the Consultation Pact a declaration that "in the event the peace of the American Republics is menaced," they will consult together "for the purpose of finding and adopting methods of *peaceful cooperation.*" Contrast the Monroe Doctrine warning with the "peaceful cooperation" of the Consultation Pact. The Monroe Doctrine, supported by our military strength, shielded the Latin Americas from non-American aggression. How effective would the Monroe Doctrine have been as a shield if the United States had put other nations on notice that their interpositions would be *peacefully* opposed? The Monroe Doctrine, like all true policy, includes not only a commitment but also the means of supporting it—in this instance the military strength of the United States. Force is absent from the Consultation Pact and this deprives it of even a slight resemblance to the Monroe Doctrine.

Saavedra Lamas saw no resemblance. In an article which appeared in the January 4, 1937, issue of the Baltimore *Sun,* he wrote:

[28] *New York Times,* Dec. 13, 1936.

When going over the text of the agreements of recommendations no hypotheses of a European attack will be found, inasmuch as this would imply a taint of Monroeism. . . . Those of us who know the antecedents of these facts know that, in order to adopt the two main agreements [the Consultative Pact and the coordination convention] of the Conference, we expressly indicated the need of eliminating all reference to this imaginative hypothesis, and that was done.

Of the treaties and conventions signed at Buenos Aires, second in importance to the Consultation Pact was the Convention to Coordinate, Extend and Assure the Fulfillment of the Existing Treaties Between the American States, in short, the Convention on Treaty Coordination and Neutrality. This combination peace-and-neutrality pact contained the residue of the Hull coordinating convention after deletions had satisfied the objections of Argentina and other states. Like the Hull original, it summarized and reaffirmed the obligations assumed by adherence to the five important peace treaties (Gondra treaty, Washington conciliation treaty and the arbitration treaty, Kellogg pact, and Saavedra Lamas pact). Then followed a stipulation that consultation, as provided by the recently concluded Consultation Pact, should be invoked to assist "through the tender of friendly good offices and of mediation, the fulfillment by the American Republics of existing obligations for pacific settlement, *and to take counsel together . . . when an emergency arises which affects their common interest in the maintenance of peace.*"[29] Had not the Consultation Pact already provided for consultation "in the event that the peace of the Americas is menaced from any source," the provision italicized would have made the coordinating convention notable. But as it turned out, it was a rather unnecessary repetition.

Like the Hull proposal, the coordinating convention looked to the adoption of a common policy of neutrality in the event that the peace machinery should fail. However, the proposed extension of the United States' "pseudo neutrality" legislation as a Pan American policy was thrown out of the neutrality plan. It merely provided that "in the case of an outbreak of hostilities or threat of an outbreak of hostilities between two or more of them, they shall, through consultation, immediately endeavor to adopt in their character as neutrals a common and solidary attitude in order to discourage or prevent the spread or prolongation of hostilities." As for sanctions, with well-understandable

[29] The italicized words were taken with only slight change, but with identical meaning, from the Hull draft which read: "take counsel together whenever emergencies arise which affect their common interests."

caution they agreed that "they may consider the imposition of prohibi-tions or restrictions on the sale or shipment of arms, munitions and implements of war, loans or other financial help to the states in conflict."[30]

In sum, the coordinating convention merely proposed a common neutrality policy as a general objective, and left to the various nations the liberty to act in accordance with their treaty commitments and domestic legislation, including obligations to other peace agencies (the League of Nations). It is to be noted that the consultation-embargo feature applied only to hostilities between American states signatories to this treaty. It is indeed doubtful whether the coordinat-ing convention made any contribution whatsoever either to the im-provement of peace procedures by the so-called "coordinating" of the peace pacts, or to the formulation of a common neutrality policy for the Americas, for as a matter of fact everything that it proposed could have been accomplished quite as well under the general terms of the Consultation Pact. If there is virtue in reiteration, then the coordinat-ing convention was justified; otherwise not.

The consultation formula was also attached to the nonintervention agreement which had been signed at Montevideo in 1933. An Addi-tional Protocol Relative to Nonintervention declared "inadmissible the intervention of any of them [the High Contracting Parties], directly or indirectly, and for whatever reason, in the internal or external affairs of any other of the Parties," and in cases of violation there should be "mutual consultation, with the object of exchanging views and seeking methods of peaceful adjustment." The Additional Protocol was also excess, for any act of intervention violative of the Treaty on the Rights and Duties of States (Montevideo, 1933) would menace the peace of the American republics, and so become the subject of consultation under the terms of the Consultation Pact. Unlike the Montevideo renunciation of intervention, the United States' ratifica-tion of the Additional Protocol was without reservation.

The Buenos Aires conference of 1936 added conventions other than the consultation pacts to the peace structure. One of these, the Treaty on Good Offices and Mediation, provided a procedure whereby a list of eminent citizens, two from each contracting state, is main-tained at the Pan American Union. From this list disputants may select a mediator. This treaty is practically worthless, since the countries

[30] Important reservations by Argentina and Paraguay exempted from the scope of the pact foodstuffs and raw materials intended for the civilian popu-lation, and loans for their purchase.

in controversy must first agree to have recourse to good offices, and then must agree on the person to be selected as mediator.

Then there was the Treaty on the Prevention of Controversies. It pledged the contracting parties to establish permanent bilateral mixed commissions to study and submit to the governments recommendations on the best methods of dealing satisfactorily with conditions that might lead to dispute. It is difficult to imagine how such commissions could be effective in eliminating the potential causes of international controversies, but their appointment would at least have been concrete evidence of the sincere desire of the contracting parties to preserve peaceful relations. The signatories of the treaty did not bother to set up the commissions. Let the reader draw whatever implications he may wish.

In a summation of the principles of American freedom and collective security, already accepted in various treaties and resolutions, the Buenos Aires conference adopted a Declaration of Principles of Inter-American Solidarity and Cooperation, which, though it contained little that was new, was nevertheless important to the future development of American international law. After considering a community of spiritual and political ideals and common interests among the American republics, the declaration states:

1. The American Nations, true to their Republican institutions, proclaim their absolute juridical liberty, their unrestricted respect for their individual sovereignties, and the existence of a common democracy throughout America.

2. Every act susceptible of disturbing the peace of America affects each and every one of them, and justifies the initiation of the procedure of consultation provided for in the Convention for the Maintenance, Preservation and Re-establishment of Peace signed at this Conference.[31]

3. The following principles are accepted by the international American Community:

[31] This article originally read: "All of the American nations will consider as an attack upon themselves individually an attack which may be made by any nation upon the rights of another, and such a situation shall give rise to an agreement or consultation between the foreign offices with the object of determining what position is to be taken or, it may be, the rules of a concerted neutrality." Argentina objected that the language of this article went beyond the terms of the treaties already contracted. Consequently the phrases relating to an "attack" and "concerted neutrality" were omitted.—Charles G. Fenwick, "The Buenos Aires Conference, 1936," Foreign Policy Association, *Report*, XIII, No. 8 (July 1, 1937), 94.

a) Proscription of territorial conquest, and in consequence, no acquisition made through violence shall be recognized;
b) Intervention by one State in the internal or external affairs of another State is condemned;
c) Forcible collection of pecuniary debts is illegal; and
d) Any difference or dispute between the American nations, whatever its nature or origin, shall be settled by the methods of conciliation, or full arbitration, or through operation of international justice.

Among the numerous resolutions adopted by the conference was one entitled Coordination of Pacific Instruments with the Covenant of the League of Nations. The United States abstained from voting on this. A number of projects which the conference was either unable or unwilling to consider were disposed of by resorting to the convenient device of referring them either to the Governing Board of the Pan American Union or to the Commission of Experts on the Codification of International Law.[32]

By resolution the conference reaffirmed approval of Secretary Hull's liberal-trade principles. That this resolution was meaningless was supported by the fact that, after the approval of a similar resolution at Montevideo, there had been no abatement of restrictive and discriminatory trade practices except for the few reciprocal trade agreements negotiated by Mr. Hull. Moreover, Argentina—an ardent supporter of the Hull resolution at Montevideo—renewed her Roca-Runciman pact with Great Britain, which provided for exclusive preferential import and foreign exchange quotas. This action, taken on November 26, 1936, focused rather unfavorable light on the effectiveness of conference resolutions.

Was the special peace conference at Buenos Aires a success? Yes, undoubtedly. The adoption of consultation was the greatest contribution yet made to American security. Simple but effective, it strengthened the machinery of continental peace and laid the basis for defense against overseas threats. Applied to inter-American controversies, it might be expected to diminish the prospect of recurring tragedies such as Chaco. The adoption of the procedure of consultation

[32] A project for an American court of international justice was referred to the Governing Board for report to the eighth conference. A project for an American league of nations was ordered included in the agenda of the eighth conference. Projects referred to the Commission of Experts were: a Mexican project on a code of peace, a Bolivian project defining an "aggressor" and applying sanctions, a Brazilian project on the prevention of war, and a project on the coordination of arbitration and conciliation treaties.

The Good Neighbor

also represented an initial defense measure against the dangers presented by foreign wars or threats to American security from abroad. Based as it was in the frankly expressed principle of American security interdependence (the corollary of solidarity), consultation provided the inter-American system, at a most opportune moment, with the means of organizing defensive measures against developing threats by the fascist aggressors. It might be expected to diminish the likelihood of an attack on an American state because it enabled the American community to organize a united front against the foreign aggressor. The Buenos Aires Consultation Pact represented a move toward greater responsibility for security by all the American nations. Opposition to any aggression from overseas was now recognized as a *collective* right and responsibility.

With due respect to the obvious virtues of consultation, the acts of the Buenos Aires conference fell short of the kind of positive measures which President Roosevelt and Mr. Hull were seeking. The fears of the United States regarding the deteriorating European situation still were not shared by the Latin Americans. Saavedra Lamas probably reflected the majority view when he scoffed at the suggestion of a European attack as an "imaginative hypothesis." The Latin-American press openly accused the United States of "crying wolf" in order to garner economic advantage in Latin America.

External dangers. Throughout the next two years the political security of the world suffered from successive shocks at the hands of aggressive totalitarianism. By the time the delegates of the American nations gathered once more in general conference at Lima in December 1938, Austria, Czechoslovakia, Spain, and China had fallen victims to the irresponsible might of the aggressors. The League of Nations did nothing to halt the deterioration of the international situation, and the democratic powers were faced by the alternatives of war or the surrender of their liberties through successive appeasements of fascist powers.

The "cold war" was not confined to Europe; the struggle had already extended to Latin America. There, by the use of typical totalitarian practices (trade manipulation, the organization of national minorities and fifth columns, antidemocratic propaganda, and press subsidization), the Axis powers hoped to "soften up" and "condition" the American states for eventual political domination.

President Roosevelt was among the first to realize the mounting dangers to world peace, for it was some time before Munich that he began to urge the necessity of cooperative defense by the prospective victims of the aggressors. In his famous "Quarantine Speech," delivered in Chicago on October 5, 1937, the President declared:

The moral consciousness of the world . . . must be aroused to the cardinal necessity of honoring sanctity of treaties, of respecting the rights and liberties of others, and of putting an end to all acts of international aggression. It seems to be unfortunately true that the epidemic of world lawlessness is spreading. When an epidemic of physical disease starts to spread, the community approves and joins in a quarantine of the patients in order to protect the health of the community against the spread of the disease.[33]

Later, on the occasion of Pan American Day (April 14, 1938), President Roosevelt urged upon the Good Neighbors the necessity of strengthening the collective will if their "good fortune was to continue."

In view of the Administration's awareness of developing dangers, and consequently the necessity of continental solidarity, an intensification of the tone of good neighborliness was beamed on Latin America. The final vestiges of any right of intervention, or of any control by the United States over a Latin-American country, were liquidated,[34] the United States thereby giving evidence of its complete acceptance of the nonintervention protocol of Buenos Aires. The Bolivian and Mexican oil expropriations put the new policy to a severe test, but the United States government resisted pressures, and there were no interventions. Little wonder, therefore, that the Good Neighbor policy paid off in rich dividends of Latin-American good will at Lima, where, for the first time at a Pan American conference, there were no longer any fears of the "Colossus of the North." Cooperation and unity supplanted suspicion and division.

It was the Munich crisis which caused President Roosevelt to propose on November 15, 1938, on the eve of the Lima conference, a defensive alliance of the American nations against external aggression. The declared objective of the United States defense program was to maintain continental security from Canada to Tierra del Fuego. "We must have," he said, "a sufficiently large air force in being to deter anyone from landing in either North or South America." Asked whether the problem of national defense had now become a problem of *continental* defense, the President answered, "Yes, but continental defense that does not rest solely on our shoulders."[35]

[33] U.S. Dept. of State, *Press Release*, Oct. 9, 1937, p. 279.
[34] The countries affected were Haiti, Panama, and the Dominican Republic.
[35] *New York Times*, Nov. 16, 1938.

The Good Neighbor

Writing of the Lima conference in retrospect, Mr. Hull said that to him the danger to the Western Hemisphere was real and imminent. Beyond the possibility of military invasion, it was more acute in its indirect form of propaganda, penetration, organizing of political parties, buying some adherents, and blackmailing others.[36]

Like the United States, the Latin-American nations were beginning to realize that their own interests were affected by what was happening in Europe and Asia. Even the blindest were developing some vision. All the Latin-American states, in terms of modern warfare, were weak, and they could not avoid noting what was happening to "weak states" in an anarchic world. Fear is the cement of international defense unions, and here was a spectacle capable of arousing their most profound apprehension. With awareness of common danger, a solid Pan American front was for the first time possible. Hitherto the virtual absence, since the days of Bolívar, of any overseas threats to their security had enabled the American republics to concentrate on internal problems. Circumstances had allowed them to indulge an overweening jealously of their political liberty of action. Consequently they tended to pull apart, and precious little was achieved, prior to 1936, to confront overseas threats. It was not until the darkening of the European horizons that defense cooperation became compulsive.

Yet, unfortunately, in 1938 as in 1936, all too many were still insisting that the United States was "crying wolf." The Latin-American press, particularly in Argentina, Chile, and Mexico, was very suspicious of the program which the United States was taking to Lima and which embodied the following points: (1) an effective cooperative agreement to block Nazi and Fascist economic and ideological penetration of Latin America, and (2) a formal convention on continental defense. According to President Roosevelt, the United States aspired to mutual solidarity backed by sufficient arms to defend the political independence of the American republics.

Leading Latin-American newspapers scoffed at "the existence of aggressive perils" and insisted that the real purpose of the United States, in proposing a continual defense organization, was to arouse Latin-American opposition to Nazi trade methods and ideological propaganda in order to monopolize the trade of the Americas.

El Imparcial of Santiago (Chile) opposed bringing the President's project before the conference at Lima, declaring:

It is destined to create deep differences between the participating countries, many of whom are averse to the promotion of an arms race, just to prepare

[36] Hull, *Memoirs,* I, 602.

themselves on the grand scale to repel hypothetical agression from European and Asiatic nations with whom they are living in absolute peace and with commercial interchange growing daily more important.[37]

La Prensa (Buenos Aires) commented as follows:

The existence of aggressive perils must be proved, and it is essential not to confuse the defense conveniences of the United States with the defense of the American continent. Will that country increase its armaments because it considers this necessary for itself or only to take charge of American peace?

And from *El Universal*, a leading Mexico City daily:

Armaments at all times have been the instruments of domination and imposition. Monroe protested against European intervention in Latin America, and Roosevelt pretends to make holy the intervention of the United States in the right of Latin American countries to trade with whom they please—a right Washington proconsuls have nothing to do with.[38]

Dr. José María Cantilo, foreign minister of Argentina, was spokesman for the opposition to an armed alliance. He said:

Such an alliance is already made in our history and does not require pacts of any sort which would bring to America a regime of armaments under unacceptable conditions. America will defend herself; the nations forming this continent will defend themselves if the case arises, as they did during their independence war battling for one common ideal with absolute disregard of boundaries.[39]

Thanks in no small measure to Axis encouragement, the belief gained wide currency that the real purpose of the United States in trying to arouse Latin-American opposition to Nazi trade methods and ideological propaganda was to monopolize the trade of the Americas. The Chilean press reported that the United States was jealous because Germany had made a success of her new economic policy. The general complaint in Argentina and Chile was that the United States looked to Latin America only as a market for exports, and they warned that if we wished to sell we must also buy. *El Mercurio* of Santiago suggested that part of the U.S. State Department's million-dollar appropriation for propaganda be used to study how the United States could buy more from Latin America. *El Universal* (Mexico City), in its

---

[37] This quotation and the one following are taken from the *Christian Science Monitor*, Dec. 15, 1938.

[38] *El Universal*, Dec. 3, 1938.

[39] *Christian Science Monitor*, Dec. 7, 1938.

The Good Neighbor

November 18, 1938, issue, openly charged that the meaning of President Roosevelt's appeal for continental solidarity was simply a "desire to have and to hold American markets without participation of non-American nations." The other Mexico City newspaper, *Excelsior*, editorialized in the following vein:

Is it by chance that the United States seeks closer relations in order to preserve and better its Latin American markets before the danger—for the United States—that Germany, Italy and Japan will invade them? There is not a remote possibility that the doctrine of America for the Americans will be revived in these days of intranquility.[40]

Despite the antagonistic press which chose to harbor old-time suspicions of the United States' motives, most of the Latin-American delegations went to Lima aware of the dangers from a new Holy Alliance in Europe and willing to stand beside the United States in its defense of the Monroe Doctrine. Indeed, Brazil and several Caribbean countries whose exposed positions or adjacency to the Panama Canal convinced them that they would be the first objects of an overseas attack, were eager to enter into defensive commitments even exceeding those desired by the United States.

The Lima Conference. The Eighth International Conference of American States, which met in Lima, Peru, December 9–27, 1938, was unique in several respects: (1) it was the shortest in the history of the Pan American movement; (2) it negotiated not a single treaty or convention, although it approved 112 declarations, resolutions, recommendations, and agreements; (3) this assemblage of delegates, which paid repeated lip service to democratic principles, met in the Peruvian Legislative Chamber from which the national deputies had been ejected by the Peruvian dictator; and (4) among the national banners displayed along the flag-bedecked streets of Lima—meeting place of an exclusively American conference—those most in evidence, next to the flag of Peru, were the banners of Germany, Italy, and Japan.[41] Such a display of the symbols of the Axis powers in an exclusively American conference was peculiarly unseemly in that the prin-

[40] Quoted in *New York Times,* Dec. 4, 1938.
[41] "Among the flags that line every street, forming an arch of brilliance that undulates beneath Spanish balconies and modern business facades, German swastikas predominate, next to the red, white, and red vertical bars of Peru. Italian and Japanese flags are plentiful. Only occasionally is an American, British or French flag seen."—*Christian Science Monitor,* Dec. 21, 1938. At the conference the agents of the totalitarian states resorted to every device possible to create division.

cipal and almost exclusive concern of the conference, meeting in the shadow of Munich, was to develop more effective inter-American cooperation against political and cultural penetration and possible armed aggression by the totalitarian states.

It was not easy for the assembled American delegations to demonstrate enough solidarity to give pause to potential foreign aggressors when a group of the South American nations, headed by Argentina, did not share the alarm of the United States concerning the immediacy of the Nazi-Fascist menace. The opposing points of view were presented to the conference in addresses by Minister of Foreign Affairs Cantilo and Secretary of State Hull. The Argentine Minister, who had come to Lima ostentatiously in a battleship, and not as a delegate to the conference but as a guest of the Peruvian nation, said:

American solidarity is a fact, which no one doubts, and which no one could doubt. Each and all of us are ready to maintain and prove this solidarity in the face of any danger regardless of whence it comes, regardless of which state in this part of the world it is whose independence is threatened. For this we do not need any special pacts. A pact is already made in our history.[42]

Argentina remained unalterably opposed to a formal pact of any kind because of her attachment to a traditional policy of no entangling engagements. "Continental solidarity, but individual policy," said Sr. Cantilo. "Argentina believes that each American country, with its own unmistakable identity, should develop its own policy without forgetting, however, the great continental solidarity and the natural influence of reciprocal interests which group them geographically." From Sr. Cantilo's address there could be inferred a pledge of general willingness to oppose aggression but refusal to be bound by specific commitments.

Paradoxically it was the behavior of his own country during World War II which contradicted the calm assurance of the Argentine Foreign Minister concerning the readiness of the American countries, without formal pact, to prove their solidarity in the face of any danger. Declaring in an interview that he could detect no present danger in the European situation, Sr. Cantilo said:

When a nation from the outside really threatens us, then is the time when we are to take decisive and united action to defend ourselves. . . . What I

[42] *New York Times,* Dec. 11, 1938.

do think is that America ought to stand solidly together for its own development. Our program ought to be drawn not because we fear an outside enemy, but because we want to make a strong America.[43]

In spite of overwhelming concerted opinion among the delegates for unification of ideals and efforts, Cantilo reminded that European markets were important to River Plate countries, and that those interests necessarily must be considered in their international policies; that European immigration and capital had developed their resources; that Spanish blood and religion, French culture, and even Italy and Germany had contributed to important aspects of America's evolution. The Argentine Minister declared, however, that his concept of necessary individual policy was not irreconcilable with continental solidarity.

Mr. Hull was neither so complacent nor so blind. After warning the conference of the developing dangers abroad, and referring to the attachment of the American nations to the processes of law and peace, he declared, "There should not be a shadow of a doubt anywhere as to the determination of the American nations not to permit the invasion of this hemisphere by activities contrary or inimical to this basis [mutual respect, fair dealing, and noninterference] of relations among nations."[44]

The American delegation had originally favored an outright mutual-defense pact, but when Mr. Hull realized that there was too much opposition to put this through, he hastened to sponsor a strong resolution proclaiming the common disposition of the American republics to defend their liberties and independence on all fronts against non-American aggressors. He cited the United States' defense program, but affirmed the right of each American nation to determine its own defense measures. Mr. Hull later denied that he had ever favored a political or military alliance at Lima, although a military alliance was desired, he said, by some of the Latin-American delegations.[45]

Argentina objected that the proposed declaration pointed too directly at the totalitarian states and she was fearful that it would give them offense. Sr. Cantilo, professing poor health, had left Lima for the Chilean lake country, thereby necessitating negotiations by remote contact (probably not distasteful to his ego). He proposed an affirmation of common allegiance to American ideals and a determination to

[43] Samuel Guy Inman, "Lima Conference and the Totalitarian Issue," *Annals* of the American Academy of Political and Social Science, 204 (July 1939), 10.

[44] U.S. Department of State, *Press Release*, Dec. 10, 1938, 426.

[45] *Ibid.*, Dec. 24, 1938; Jan. 9, 1939.

consult at the threat of menace *from any source* (which would include the United States). Since Argentina stood adamant, and since the conference could not afford to split over the issue and thus exhibit a lack of solidarity before the Axis, twenty nations bowed to the demands of one. Argentina's devitalized proposal, called the "Declaration of Lima," was adopted.

The Declaration of Lima, the most significant achievement of the conference, can be divided into two parts: an affirmation of solidarity, and a declaration of purpose for supporting it. In somewhat extravagant terms the principles upon which American solidarity is established are enumerated: spiritual unity through republican institutions, unshakable will for peace, sentiments of humanity and tolerance, absolute adherence to international law, equal sovereignty of states, and individual liberty without religious or racial prejudices. The enumeration and affirmation of these principles—many of them honored more in the breach than in actual observance—might be construed as a challenge to the totalitarian regimes. Having reaffirmed continental solidarity, the American states then declared their intention to support these principles, as follows:

First, that they reaffirm their continental solidarity and their purpose to collaborate for the maintenance of principles upon which said solidarity is based.

Second, that faithful to the above-mentioned principles and to their absolute sovereignty they reaffirm them against all foreign intervention or activity that may threaten them.

Third, that in case the peace, security or territorial integrity of any American Republic is thus threatened by acts of any nature that may impair them, they proclaim their common concern and their determination to make effective their solidarity, coordinating their respective sovereign wills by means of the procedure of consultation established by the conventions in force and by declarations of inter-American conferences, using measures that in each case circumstances may make advisable. It is understood that the governments of the American Republics will act independently in their individual capacities, recognizing fully their juridical equality as sovereign states.

Fourth, that in order to facilitate consultations established in this and other American peace instruments, the Ministers of Foreign Affairs of the American Republics, when deemed desirable and at the initiative of any one of them, will meet in their several capitals by rotation and without protocolary character. Each government may, under special circumstances or for special reasons, designate a representative as a substitute for its Minister of Foreign Affairs.

The Declaration of Lima repeated, in slightly stronger though only slightly less abstruse terms, the identical pledges to consult contained in the Declaration of Inter-American Solidarity and the Consultation Pact, both negotiated at the Buenos Aires conference of 1936. The Buenos Aires declaration stated that every act susceptible of disturbing the peace of an American state affects each and every one of them and justifies the initiation of consulation as provided by the Consultation Pact, which on its part pledged consultation to find methods of peaceful cooperation in the event of threat to the peace of the American republics. The Lima declaration differed in that: (1) defensive cooperation was not limited to *peaceful* measures; (2) it seemed to be aimed only at non-American threats;[46] (3) the scope of the consultation procedure was enlarged to include, in addition to "threats to the peace," "the security and territorial integrity of any American Republic"; (4) it forecast common action against subversive activities; and (5) in the meetings of the foreign ministers, it provided machinery to implement the procedure of consultation. This last provision was the only significant one in the Declaration of Lima. It was what the United States had argued for at Buenos Aires but what Saavedra Lamas had objected to on the ground that it might lead to a regional American association with *political* functions. At Lima, the Argentine government changed its position on this point, and it is an interesting fact that it was an Argentine-proposed formula for consultation by the foreign ministers which was accepted by the conference.[47]

Mr. Hull appraised the Declaration of Lima as a great advance over previous Pan American agreements, for according to the Secretary it provided for joint action not only against a military assault but also against the underground infiltration methods pursued by the Axis.

[46] Argentina had objected to the use, as originally proposed, of the term "non-American" and forced the substitution of "foreign," which could mean, within the context, a threat from any source. However, according to Fenwick (*Annals* of the American Academy of Political and Social Science [July 1939], 121), the declaration did not apply among the American republics themselves. If trouble should break out between them, he says, there is no obligation to protect either party. It was believed that adequate machinery already existed to take care of such a dispute; therefore it was not necessary to set up a system of mutual protection among the American states, but only against foreign aggression and attack.

[47] Eighth International Conference of American States, *Diario de Sesiones* (Lima, 1938), 87, 109.

Henceforward the defense of the Western Hemisphere became the joint responsibility of all the American republics.[48] However, the fact that the Declaration of Lima made much of common action was vitiated by the announcement that "the governments of the American republics *will act independently in their individual capacity,* recognizing fully their juridical equality as sovereign states." They were, therefore, bound to nothing more than to consult, a rather far cry from defensive alliances and mutual-security pacts.

Nor did the declaration "Pan Americanize" the Monroe Doctrine, as has been held by a number of authorities. Dr. Leo S. Rowe, director-general of the Pan American Union, declared that "the Conference transformed the Monroe Doctrine into a continental doctrine."[49] Professor C. G. Fenwick held that we took the Monroe Doctrine and converted it from a unilateral into a multilateral policy.[50] Our greatest authority on the Monroe Doctrine, however, Professor Dexter Perkins, is willing to concede only that the Lima declaration marked a step "toward common international action in the defence of the principles of 1823."[51]

The relation between the various consultative agreements and the Monroe Doctrine was well stated by Undersecretary of State Sumner Welles:

It would not be correct to say that the Monroe Doctrine had been replaced or superseded by the group of inter-American agreements that has grown up in recent years. . . . The Monroe Doctrine was promulgated, in the first place, as a unilateral declaration on the part of the United States. It still stands as such a declaration. It could still be invoked, if there were occasion, unilaterally, by the United States. . . . But what has happened is this. The purposes that it sought to accomplish have become the recognized concern of all the American nations and they have declared, multilaterally, their support of its objectives. . . . Thus we may naturally expect that in the future the unilateral character of the Doctrine will be pushed more and more into the background and its multilateral character emphasized. . . . What has taken place is not a change in policy but a change in emphasis. The emphasis is now on joint action rather than on single action.[52]

[48] Hull, *Memoirs,* I, 608.
[49] *Annals* of the American Academy of Political and Social Science (July 1939), 139.
[50] *Ibid.,* 119.
[51] Dexter Perkins, *Hands Off: A History of the Monroe Doctrine* (Boston, 1941), 355.
[52] Quoted in Robert A. Smith, *Your Foreign Policy* (New York, 1941), 200–201.

The Good Neighbor

The fact that the Declaration of Lima was not a formal convention, as was the Consultation Pact of Buenos Aires, was so noteworthy that it elicited comment from Mr. Hull. He emphasized the wisdom of incorporating agreements in declarations rather than in treaties "when the matters dealt with are of general character and of political nature."[53] The real reason, however, not mentioned by Mr. Hull, was the dilatoriness on the part of the Latin-American governments in ratifying treaties. For example, when the Lima conference convened, the Buenos Aires Consultation Pact had not been ratified by four countries: Argentina, Bolivia, Peru, and Uruguay. Because of the rapidly-gathering war clouds over Europe it was felt expedient to resort to a declaration, less binding than a treaty, in order to anticipate the expected crisis.

It is a debatable point whether the inter-American security system gains strength from the fact that more general agreement can be reached by simple conference resolution than by formal treaty. The objection to the treaty is, of course, the fear of limiting independence of action by the legal obligation of the formal contract. The resolution, on the other hand, is not binding—at least not legally. The adoption of the resolution procedure therefore implies the reserved right of any signatory to disregard the pledge at its own convenience and with impunity. Nevertheless the resort to resolution at Lima can be defended on the ground that it was the only means of establishing a broad—albeit a somewhat uncertain—basis for inter-American cooperation. Since it was, in 1938, a manifest impossibility to bind the Americas by a formal mutual-aid compact, the most promising alternative was to secure by resolution a pledge, supported by moral obligation, that *all of them* would consult when the peace or security of any one of them was threatened. This alternative was a concession to secure unanimity; it represented both the greatest common denominator and the measure of inter-American solidarity. Fortunately, subsequent developments fully justified the resolution approach.

Without in any way disparaging the Declaration of Lima and the provision for the consultative meetings of the foreign ministers, which evidently proved its worth during World War II, it is doubtful whether the declaration deserved the extravagant encomiums bestowed by some writers.[54] For could not the consultative meetings of Panama,

[53] U.S. Dept. of State, *Press Release*, Dec. 27, 1938.
[54] For example, C. G. Fenwick (*Annals*, 119) called it "a Magna Charta of American freedom," and R. A. Smith (*op. cit.*, 200) wrote, "It is hard to avoid superlatives when discussing the character of this agreement."

Havana, and Rio de Janeiro have been convened quite as readily by a straightforward interpretation of the Buenos Aires (1936) agreements? A Chilean objection that the Lima declaration added nothing to the Buenos Aires pacts was substantially correct. In this connection Chile opposed the practice of repeating obligations which had already been assumed under earlier treaty provisions. Her objections, however, did not prevent the Lima conference from taking other repetitious actions.

For example, the Declaration of American Principles and the Preamble to the Declaration of Lima were substantially a reiteration of the principles elaborated in the Declaration of Inter-American Solidarity at Buenos Aires. This reaffirmation of principles—nonintervention, the use of pacific measures, the illegality of the use of force, respect for international contracts, economic and cultural intercourse, and international cooperation—has been described as "one of the few negotiated and accepted definitions of what constitutes good behavior among nations,"[55] and as such was a challenge to the totalitarian states. Thus there was value in the reiteration.

Another illustration of reiteration was the unanimous endorsement by the Lima conference of another liberal-trade resolution sponsored by Mr. Hull. This resolution put the twenty-one American nations on record against restrictive trade devices. Similar resolutions had been unanimously approved at Montevideo and Buenos Aires, but were almost immediately violated. Unfortunately for Mr. Hull's liberal-trade program, which he regarded as the very foundation of the Good Neighbor policy and our principal contribution to the preservation of world peace, the Latin-American nations were moving almost in a body to barter practices, bilateralism, and exchange controls.

Still another repetitious action voted by the conference was a resolution declaring that the acquisition of territory by force shall not be valid or have legal effect. Nonrecognition of such acquisitions was declared to be "an obligation which cannot be avoided either unilaterally or collectively."[56]

Nazi-Fascist practices and activities were responsible for some additional resolutions voted by the Lima conference which must not be overlooked but which can be mentioned only briefly. To counter the attempts of the Axis to organize politically their nationals in Latin-

[55] Smith, 197.
[56] Eighth International Conference of American States, *Final Act* (Lima, 1938), No. XXVI, 45.

American countries, a resolution on "Foreign Minorities"[57] was adopted which declared that "residents who, according to domestic law are considered aliens, cannot claim collectively, the condition of minorities." Brazil, uneasy because of her large German population, was responsible for initiating this. Argentina and Uruguay, with large Italian populations, were also responsible for a resolution concerning the possible manipulation of minorities by their parent countries. This resolution, called "Political Activities of Foreigners,"[58] recommended that the governments of the American republics prohibit aliens from collectively exercising political rights conferred by the laws of their respective countries. This was intended to stop the Nazi practice of taking plebiscites of German nationals in foreign lands. A Cuban resolution, "Persecution for Racial or Religious Motives,"[59] declared that "in accordance with the fundamental principle of equality before the law, any persecution on account of racial or religious motives, which makes it impossible for a group of human beings to live decently, is contrary to the political and juridicial systems of America." Finally, a resolution entitled "American Standards on Immigration"[60] recommended that no distinction be made on the basis of nationality, creed, or race.

The acts of the Lima conference relating to the organization of peace can be quickly disposed of for the simple reason that little in this category was accomplished. After the agreements on the more pressing problems presented by the activities of the Axis nations, there was neither time nor disposition to take up the subject of the improvement and coordination of the inter-American peace instruments. Accordingly, most of the relevant projects were referred for further study. Drafts submitted by the United States and Mexico coordinating the extensive array of peace agreements, a proposal for a League of American Nations, and a report presented by the Committee of Experts on Codification of International Law dealing with a definition of "the aggressor" and the application of sanctions,[61] were referred to the International Conference of American Jurists for further study. As

---

[57] *Ibid.*, No. XXVII, 46–47.   [58] *Ibid.*, No. XXVIII, 47.
[59] *Ibid.*, No. XXXVI, 52–53.   [60] *Ibid.*, No. XLV, 63–64.
[61] The conference resolution "Definition of the Aggressor and Sanctions" (*Final Act*, No. XXIV, 43–44) declared: "Under the present status of international law and international relations in America, a special definition of aggression and the establishment of sanctions are not urgent since the pacific and juridical relations which exist between the countries of America do not warrant them."

for a proposed Inter-American Court of International Justice, the conference expressed sympathetic interest and recommended further study, but felt that "it is not possible to realize the establishment of this institution."[62]

Nor did the movement to codify American international law make any headway at Lima. The Committee on International Law studied various proposals suggested for codification, giving particular attention to the question of pecuniary claims, but this and all the other projects were referred back to the Committee of Experts for further study. It was thought inadvisable to risk the acrimonious debate which would inevitably occur should the controversial problems of expropriation of foreign property and pecuniary collections be injected into the discussions. After expending considerable time, patience, and appeasement to secure a solidary front, it was not the course of wisdom to rock the boat.

Accordingly, Mr. Hull was able to report on his return to the United States that at Lima "the American republics made it clear to all the world that they stand united to maintain and defend the peace of this hemisphere." And he added, "I return from the conference with the conviction that its results will be of real and permanent value . . . as time goes on."[63]

All too soon Mr. Hull's prediction was put to the test, for within nine months war broke out in Europe. How American solidarity measured up to this unprecedented crisis will be the subject of discussion in later chapters. First, however, we should take stock of the inter-American security system, as of September 1, 1939, noting particularly how it stood the test of the numerous controversies which perturbed the peaceful relations of the American nations during the decade preceding the outbreak of World War II.

[62] *Ibid.*, No. XXV ("The Inter-American Court of International Justice"), 44–45.

[63] U.S. Dept. of State, *Press Release*, Jan. 7, 1939.

VI The American Peace Structure on the Eve of World War II

The great increase in the sentiment of continental solidarity . . . is due to precisely two facts that took place eight years ago, that is, the enunciation of the Good Neighbor policy and the rise of Adolf Hitler to power, to absolute power, in Germany.

RICARDO ALFARO, 1941

The Inter-American Security Structure

BY SEPTEMBER 1, 1939, the inter-American security structure had attained rather grandiose and bewilderingly complex proportions. It comprised two poorly-balanced wings of unequal age and size: provisions for the organization of American peace, and provisions relating to overseas threats to American peace. It was not until 1936 that construction was started on the second wing; until that time the security concern of the American nations had been confined strictly to inter-American relations. Most of the work on the first wing had also been of rather recent date, for the great multilateral treaties, conventions, and protocols, which constituted the fundamental elements of the American peace system, dated only from 1923. The ramifications of the security organization can best be illustrated graphically by a topical outline.

I. Development of the inter-American security system to 1939.
    A. Development of peace procedures to 1923.
        1. Inter-American bilateral arbitration treaties.[1]

---

[1] All arbitration treaties and all arbitral clauses of other treaties which were signed between or among American nations before the close of 1910 and duly ratified are collected in William R. Manning (ed.), *Arbitration Treaties Among The American Nations To The Close Of The Year 1910* (New York, 1924).

2. Bilateral treaties of inquiry and conciliation. (The Bryan "cooling off" treaties fall in this category.)

3. Multilateral arbitration treaties.

    a) General Obligatory Arbitration Treaty, Mexico, 1902.

    Ratified by: the Dominican Republic, El Salvador, Guatemala, Mexico, Peru, and Uruguay. (NOTE: These and other ratifications indicated below are as of 1939.)

    b) Convention for the Arbitration of Pecuniary Claims, Buenos Aires, 1910.

    Originally negotiated at Mexico City in 1902; renewed at Rio de Janeiro in 1906 and at Buenos Aires in 1910.

    Ratified by: Brazil, Costa Rica, Dominican Republic, Ecuador, Guatemala, Honduras, Nicaragua, Panama, Paraguay, United States, and Uruguay. Bolivia adhered.

B. Evolution of the Pan American peace procedures, 1923–39.

1. Basic development, 1923–29.

    a) Treaty to Avoid or Prevent Conflicts Between the American States (Gondra treaty, 1923).

    Ratified by all the American countries except Argentina and Bolivia. Bolivia adhered.

    b) General Convention of Inter-American Conciliation, Washington, 1929.

    Not ratified by Argentina, Bolivia, Costa Rica, and Paraguay.

    c) General Treaty of Inter-American Arbitration, Washington, 1929.

    Not ratified by Argentina, Bolivia, Costa Rica, Paraguay, and Uruguay.

    d) Protocol of Progressive Arbitration, Washington, 1929.

    Ratified by: Cuba, Chile, Dominican Republic, Ecuador, El Salvador, Guatemala, Haiti, Honduras, Mexico, Nicaragua, and Venezuela.

2. Development of the security system, 1929–39.

    a) Additional procedures of pacific settlement.

        (1) Anti-War Treaty of Non-Aggression and Conciliation, 1933 (Saavedra Lamas treaty).

        Ratified by all countries except Paraguay and Costa Rica. The latter adhered.

        (2) Additional Protocol to the General Convention of Inter-American Conciliation, 1933.

        Ratified by: Chile, Dominican Republic, Ecuador, Guatemala, Haiti, Honduras, Mexico, Nicaragua, and the United States. Panama and Venezuela adhered.

        (3) Convention for the Maintenance, Preservation, and Re-establishment of Peace, 1936 (Consultation Pact).

Ratified by all countries except Argentina, Bolivia, Costa Rica, Paraguay, Peru, and Uruguay.

(4) Convention to Coordinate, Extend, and Assure the Fulfillment of the Existing Treaties Between the American States, 1936 (Coordinating Convention).

Ratified by all countries except Argentina, Bolivia, Costa Rica, Paraguay, Peru, Uruguay, and Venezuela.

(5) Inter-American Treaty on Good Offices and Mediation, 1936.

Not ratified by Argentina, Bolivia, Costa Rica, Paraguay, Peru, Uruguay, and Venezuela.

(6) Treaty on the Prevention of Controversies, 1936.

Not ratified by Argentina, Bolivia, Brazil, Costa Rica, Paraguay, Peru, Uruguay, and Venezuela.

b) Supplementary agreements, declarations, and resolutions (also a part of the security system).

(1) Declarations of American solidarity.

(*a*) Declaration of Principles of Inter-American Solidarity and Cooperation, 1936.

"Every Act (internal) susceptible of disturbing the peace of America affects each and every one of them, and justifies the initiation of the procedure of consultation" (Art. 2).

(*b*) Declaration of American Principles, 1938.

(*c*) Declaration of the Principles of the Solidarity of America, 1938 (Declaration of Lima).

"They reaffirm their continental solidarity and their purpose to collaborate in the maintenance of the principles upon which the said solidarity is based" (Art. 1).

(2) Inter-American agreements on nonintervention.

(*a*) Convention on Rights and Duties of States, 1933 (Art. 8).

Not ratified by Argentina, Bolivia, Haiti, Paraguay, Peru, Uruguay, and Venezuela.

(*b*) Additional Protocol Relative to Nonintervention, 1936.

Not ratified by Argentina, Bolivia, Costa Rica, Paraguay, Peru, and Uruguay.

(*c*) Declaration of Principles of Inter-American Solidarity and Cooperation, 1936 (Art. 3*b*).

(*d*) Declaration of American Principles, 1938 (Art. 1).

(3) Inter-American declarations relative to the nonrecognition of territory acquired by force.

(*a*) Recommendation of the First International Conference of American States, Washington, April 18, 1890.

(*b*) Resolution of the Sixth International Conference of American States, Havana, February 18, 1928.

(*c*) Declaration of August 3, 1932 (declaration signed in

Washington by the representatives of nineteen American republics).

(*d*) Declaration on Nonrecognition of the Acquisition of Territory by Force, 1938.

(4) Declaration on Improvement in the Procedure of Consultation, 1938.

Procedure of consultation applied to economic, cultural, and other questions.

C. Security against extracontinental threats to American peace.

1. Basic consultation agreements.

a) Consultation Pact, 1936.

b) Coordinating Convention, 1936.

"To take counsel together . . . when an emergency arises which affects their common interest in the maintenance of peace" (Art. 2).

c) Declaration of Lima, 1938.

Provision for the consultative meetings of the foreign ministers.

2. Supplementary declarations and resolutions relating to the political activities of non-American states.

a) Declaration on Foreign Minorities, 1938.

The economic factor. Were there economic components of the security structure which we have not yet noted? Although the several Pan American conferences, general and special, which convened before 1939 were greatly concerned with the promotion of trade relations and enacted a plethora of resolutions dealing with the subject, it cannot be recorded that any action having a security objective in mind was taken to bulwark the economies. "Foreign assistance" was a term unknown to that period. In fact, the equating of economic welfare with continental defense did not come until after the outbreak of World War II, for before that time the American countries manifested no fears concerning overseas aggression and no interest in organizing a common defense.

It is to be recalled that Honorio Pueyrredón declared at Havana in 1928 that Pan American unity was impossible without economic harmony. It is extremely doubtful, however that the Argentine understanding of "economic harmony" was equated with hemispheric defense. Nor was this the objective of the foreign economic policies of the New Deal, at least not in its earlier years.

The Roosevelt-Hull Administration came into power on the heels of Latin-American resentments against the Smoot-Hawley Tariff Act of 1930. It was a time of pent-up bitterness—a time when some of the countries, stung by our high tariffs, actually conferred with one another about forming a customs union for defensive action against us. It was Mr. Hull's hope that by negotiating reciprocal trade agreements our declining Latin-American trade could be reinvigorated. Under powers granted by the Congress in the Trade Agreements Act of 1934, agreements were negotiated with several of the countries, and although these agreements did exert some remedial influence, it must be conceded that they failed to break down the artificial trade barriers which clogged the channels of foreign trade. It seems that, owing to the pressures of the Great Depression, the acceptance and implementation of restrictive devices had been too considerable to allow for any return to the good old days of liberal, triangular trade. Nor were Latin-American resentments alleviated, for the United States market continued to be highly protectionist.

Most bitter of all was Argentina, whose beef was excluded by shadowy and evasive quarantine restrictions. In an attempt to appease the Plata nation, a Sanitary Convention was negotiated which was intended to moderate the restrictions on meat imports. However, despite all the pressure President Roosevelt was able to put on the Senate, the cattlemen's lobby proved to be the stronger and the treaty was never ratified. This illustrates the insuperable difficulties raised by American nationalistic interests in obstructing our Chief Executive in his sincere efforts to work out a truly liberal trade policy for this nation.

In 1934 there was also established by the Congress an Export-Import (Exim) Bank, provided with funds to encourage American foreign trade. Latin America was originally only an incidental beneficiary of the Bank's lending operations. It was not until after the outbreak of World War II that the Exim Bank was oriented toward strengthening the economies of the Latin-American republics as a means of assisting in the defense of the Western Hemisphere. In September 1940, President Roosevelt induced Congress to amend the Export-Import Bank Act not only to increase its lending power but to aid in the development of the resources, the stabilization of the economies, and the orderly marketing of the products of the countries of the hemisphere. Although the Bank had become frankly an instrument of public lending in support of foreign policy, its credits to Latin America during the period of neutrality were modest.

That the New Deal was prepared, as early as the Montevideo conference of 1933, to give grant economic assistance to Latin America can be inferred from an incident mentioned by Mr. Hull in his *Memoirs*. He says that while he was at Montevideo the President suggested that he offer to create a $5 million nonprofit-making semi-public engineering corporation, financed by the United States, to erect radio stations, beacons, and landing fields in South America to make night flying possible. Evidently the Latins were not yet conditioned for handouts from the United States, for Mr. Hull cabled the President that the reaction to the offer was unfavorable. According to the Secretary the Latins did not look with favor even on benefactions or accommodation loans or advances. "In other words," he said, "no dollar diplomacy."[2] It was not long, however, before this reluctance was overcome.

Application of Peace Procedures
to Inter-American Disputes (1929–39)

Since the inter-American security provisions relating to overseas aggressions had been so recently concluded prior to 1939, and therefore had not yet been put to test, a critical appraisement of this aspect of security must wait until after discussion, in succeeding chapters, of the implementation of American solidarity during World War II. But there is no reason to postpone an evaluation of the security features designed to preserve peace among the American republics, for by 1939, as the foregoing outline illustrates, it had grown to elaborate proportions. Moreover, during the decade of the 1930's there occurred in Latin America an exceptional number of critical international controversies which afforded fair and adequate tests of the efficacy of the agreed-upon peace procedures. Accordingly, we will now consider a number of these inter-Latin–American controversies, noting not the causes or merits of the disputes, but rather the nature and extent of recourse to peaceful and friendly settlement.

Mediation in the Chaco controversy. As has been noted,[3] the mediation of the Washington Commission of Neutrals (Colombia, Cuba, Mexico, United States, and Uruguay) resulted in cessation of the Chaco hostilities in 1929, but fighting broke out again in 1932. The president of the Council of the League of Nations, in reply to a Paraguayan appeal, telegraphed both countries, members of the

[2] Hull, *The Memoirs of Cordell Hull* (2 vols., New York, 1948), I, 332.

[3] See p. 109. For a survey of the Chaco mediation, see Gordon Ireland, *Boundaries, Possessions, and Conflicts in South America* (Cambridge, Mass., 1938), 72–95. For an excellent study of the Chaco War and the Buenos Aires Peace Conference, see David H. Zook, Jr., *Th Conduct of the Chaco War* (New York, 1960).

League, urging pacific procedures. In reply Paraguay agreed to arbitrate, but Bolivia hedged.[4] The mediatory efforts of the Washington Commission of Neutrals, and the proffer of good offices by Argentina, failed to halt the deterioration of the situation into a virtual state of war. Consequently the representatives of all the American republics, except the belligerents, signed at Washington on August 3, 1932, a declaration addressed to the governments of Bolivia and Paraguay. They were urged to resort to arbitration or some other peaceful procedure, and were put on notice that the American nations "will not recognize any territorial arrangement of this controversy which has not been obtained by peaceful means, nor the validity of territorial acquisitions which may be obtained through occupation or conquest by force of arms."[5]

While the conflict raged, the American neutrals, organized into two mediatory groups—the Washington Commission of Neutrals and the ABCP (Argentina, Brazil, Chile, and Peru)—continued their efforts to compose the dispute. The South American group had been organized by Saavedra Lamas ostensibly to support the work of the Washington neutrals, but as a matter of fact the Argentine Foreign Minister seemed to be more interested in exploiting the situation for the enhancement of Argentine prestige than in terminating the bloody conflict. On September 26, 1932, Argentina informed the Washington group that the other American republics had no right to use force or compulsion against Bolivia or Paraguay, and that their efforts should be limited to the use of good offices and moral influence.[6] In opposing collective intervention in the external affairs of other states, Saavedra Lamas successfully warded off a proposal of the Washington neutrals to implement the declaration of August 3, 1932, relating to nonrecognition of territorial acquisitions won by force.

---

[4] League of Nations, *Official Journal* (Sept. 1932), 1575–1586. The Covenant of the League of Nations was the only formal peace instrument binding upon both Bolivia and Paraguay. The Gondra treaty and the Washington conciliation and arbitration treaties were inapplicable because they were unratified by the disputants.

[5] Pan American Union, *Improvement and Coordination of Inter-American Peace Instruments* (5 vols., Washington, 1941–43), III (1941), 66–68. Although the resolution was immediately inspired by the recently-declared Stimson doctrine, its Pan American model was the resolution adopted by the Washington conference on April 18, 1890, which provided that "all cessions of territory made during the continuance of the treaty of arbitration shall be void if made under threats of war or in the presence of armed force."

[6] Ireland, 76.

On October 14, 1932, the Washington neutrals published telegraphic correspondence with the League of Nations to scotch rumors that the League was attempting to interfere with the negotiations. Shortly after this the League urged the belligerents to accept a plan proposed earlier by the neutrals. Both countries replied with conditional acceptance. On December 31 the Washington neutrals asked the ABCP what steps it was prepared to take to bring about peace. The four countries then came forward with various proposals, all of which were rejected. On May 4, 1933, the South American group announced that it had abandoned its peace efforts. At this juncture Paraguay formally declared a state of war with Bolivia.

On May 20, 1933, the League Council asserted its authority over the controversy, and proposed conditions of settlement. The Washington neutrals voted to suspend their activities and affirmed their support of the League's efforts. On July 19 a League commission, composed of representatives of Spain, France, Great Britain, Italy, and Mexico, was appointed to negotiate a cessation of hostilities and conduct a full inquiry into the dispute. The commission reached South America early in November.

Such was the situation in and concerning the Chaco when the Montevideo conference convened. The state of war which continued in defiance of all efforts to organize peace was a patent denial of American solidarity. It was a situation which the conference could not ignore if it hoped to preserve the security aspect of inter-American cooperation. This thought was voiced by Uruguayan President Gabriel Terra in his opening address to the Seventh International Conference of American States:

Bolivia and Paraguay have resorted to arms for the solution of a painful conflict. . . . We who have trained our spirit in the severe discipline of law, yearn for America a future of stable organization, based on respect for the juridical standards and on peaceful consecration of our solidarity. We have prided ourselves on being the continent of peace and arbitration, and it behooves the honor of all to regain our position before the world. . . . In my opinion, the Conference that I have the honor to inaugurate today, cannot leave unheard the clamor of American opinion that commands, that urges, that demands peace. I am confident that your appeal will move public opinion in both nations.

Gentlemen of the Conference, the noble juridical traditions of America cannot remain buried in the swamps of the Chaco; the noble covenants that united us in the past cannot be allowed to become mere declarations.[7]

[7] Seventh Int. Conf. of Am. States, *Plenary Sessions*, 20.

After debating the alternative procedures of attacking the Chaco question—either by cooperating with the League commission or by independently seeking a settlement—the conference decided in favor of cooperating with the commission. A special committee was appointed which, with the collaboratioᴜ of the League commission and President Terra, who had already initiated direct conversations with representatives of the belligerents, managed to secure agreement to a temporary armistice, effective from December 19, 1933, to January 7, 1934.

Just before its adjournment the conference, on December 24, turned over the responsibility of the Chaco negotiations to the League commission. The final plenary session, on December 26, was attended by members of the commission of the League of Nations and delegates plenipotentiary of Bolivia and Paraguay, all of whom, together with President Terra, were paid tributes in acknowledgment of their cooperative endeavors that had resulted in the truce. A resolution presented by Mr. Hull, and adopted at the closing session, reminded the belligerents of their obligations as members of the League of Nations and urged them "to accept the juridical processes for the solution of their differences as hitherto constantly recommended by the League of Nations Commission and consistently urged by the Chaco Subcommittee of this Conference presided over by his Excellency, President Terra of Uruguay."[8]

The hope that the League commission would be able to secure acceptance of a plan of arbitration, and thus extend the truce into a permanent peace, was soon destroyed. It was impossible to surmount the recalcitrance of the combatants, and fighting was renewed on January 7, 1934. The commission persisted, and on February 24, 1934, recommended to the belligerents its draft of a treaty of peace. When objections to the treaty were filed by both Bolivia and Paraguay, the commission, on May 12, issued an outspoken report on the war and urged an embargo on arms to both nations. The imposed embargo, in which the United States participated, was ineffectual because the immediate neighbors of the belligerents refused to cooperate.

After France and Britain had on September 19 denounced the Chaco War in the Council of the League, and declared that the League must act to stop it, the Council referred both the dispute and the arms-embargo question to a special session of the Assembly. On November 24, 1934, the Assembly adopted a report recommending a

---

[8] *Ibid.*, 126.

peaceful solution of the conflict by a conference at Buenos Aires and providing for a neutral commission of six (Argentina, Brazil, Chile, Peru, Uruguay, and the United States) to supervise demobilization. Bolivia accepted the League's peace plan, but Paraguay rejected it. The advisory committee of the Assembly then voted to recommend to all League members that the arms embargo be lifted from Bolivia and strengthened against Paraguay. On February 23, 1935, Paraguay announced that she would quit the League.

Ecuador, supported by Venezuela, advocated full application of League sanctions, but Uruguay announced that she would refuse to apply the arms embargo against Paraguay so long as neighboring countries did not apply it against Bolivia. Argentina and Chile also opposed sanctions and preferred to mediate the dispute outside the League. At their written request, supported and shared by Brazil and Peru, the committee of the Assembly, convoking by resolution a special meeting of the Assembly for May 20 to consider the question of further application of the Covenant, gave the South American countries until May 20 to end the war and thus render sanctions and the proposed Assembly meeting unnecessary. Brazil announced that she had not approved Argentina's move and would collaborate in the negotiations only on condition the United States participated. Argentina and Chile thereupon invited the United States to cooperate. The group of five countries thus constituted (Argentina, Brazil, Chile, Peru, and the United States) then invited Uruguay to join them at Buenos Aires in the Chaco Peace Conference.

The six American governments were not able to end the war by May 20, and the special Assembly of the League was held according to plan. Maxim Litvinov, presiding, urged settlement through mediation to keep the Covenant intact; but the Assembly decided to postpone the decision on whether or not to apply the Covenant until it was seen what the six American countries could accomplish. This was the end of League participation in the Chaco peace efforts.

On June 12 a protocol was signed at Buenos Aires providing for a cessation of hostilities and the adoption of a procedure of settlement. Since the present summary is concerned only with procedure, the terms of the plan are omitted. Hostilities ceased on June 14 and a truce agreement was ratified by both belligerents on June 21; by October, demobilization had been completed. But the disputants could not agree on a territorial settlement, and the establishment of an acceptable boundary was still unattained.

A peace conference, as provided by the protocol, met in Buenos

Aires on July 15. Composed of representatives of the two parties to the controversy and of the six mediatory nations (with the foreign minister of Argentina presiding), the Chaco Peace Conference remained in session for three full years—a period equal to the duration of the war. Eighteen different attempts to arbitrate the dispute were made, and sixty-five formulas for settlement were presented. On July 21, 1938, the Treaty of Peace, Friendship, and Boundaries was signed, and peace was once more restored between Bolivia and Paraguay; but paradoxically, the boundary issue remained unsettled. The treaty provided that the boundary line should be determined by the presidents of Argentina, Brazil, Chile, Peru, and Uruguay. The arbitral award of the South American presidents was announced on October 10, 1938. Following the natural frontiers as closely as possible, they gave nearly all of the Chaco to Paraguay—substantially the area that had been won by Paraguayan arms. Shades of pacts violated and pledges unredeemed, make way for the Declaration of August 3, 1932, pledging nonrecognition of territory acquired by force!

Not only was the Chaco War not prevented by either the inter-American peace procedures or by the League of Nations, but it is probably true that the termination of the war was not hastened by any of the mediatory efforts indicated. Indeed, the efforts of the peacemakers seem to have contributed to the delay of the peace. At any rate, the war came to an end only when one of the belligerents had won its objectives and the other was too exhausted to continue the struggle. To cap the sorry spectacle, the peace was concluded largely on the terms of the victor nation. Confidence in the inter-American security system descended to a new low.

The Leticia controversy. Another Latin-American territorial dispute —a heritage of inadequate boundary delineation by the former Spanish overlords—was that between Colombia and Peru concerning the "Leticia trapezium," a 4,000-square-mile enclave of almost impenetrable and undeveloped jungle land, extending between the Putumayo and Amazon Rivers near the point where the territories of Brazil, Colombia, and Peru conjoin on the Amazon about 2,500 miles from the Atlantic Ocean.

After a century of fruitless negotiation,[9] the long-standing boundary dispute between Colombia and Peru was believed settled by the Salomón-Lozano treaty, signed at Lima on March 24, 1922. This convention fixed the common boundary and declared (with unjustified opti-

---

[9] For the negotiations relating to the Loreto corridor, see Ireland, 185–196.

mism) that "all disputes which have arisen in the past with reference to the boundaries between Colombia and Peru are hereby finally and irrevocably settled" and that "the boundary line fixed by the present Treaty shall remain unaffected by any future dispute."[10] The Peruvian Dictator-President Augusto B. Leguía y Salcedo encountered opposition in his otherwise acquiescent Senate, and it was not until 1928 that the treaty was eventually ratified. Ratifications were exchanged in Bogotá on March 19, 1928, and two years later Colombia took possession of the territory awarded to it.

The Leticia trapezium, so called[11] from the little village of Leticia in the southeast corner of the quadrilateral on the Amazon, was a hot, dank jungle, about the size of Belgium, infested with fever and dangerous animals, and inhabited by about 500 white persons and 1,500 savage, head-hunting Indians. Altogether, the area was totally uninviting, but it did possess certain strategic and economic possibilities.

The negotiation and execution of the Salomón-Lozano treaty, so distasteful to Peruvian nationalistic sentiments, was a factor in forcing the downfall of President Leguía on August 24, 1930, just five days after the transfer of the disputed territory to Colombia. Local feeling in Peru's Department of Loreto, in which the Leticia territory previously had been incorporated, was resentful, and the people of the region threatened rebellion. Their threat was carried out when a band of 300 armed Peruvian citizens attacked and seized the little jungle village on September 1, 1932. This incident, trivial as it appeared, set in motion a train of events which brought two countries to the verge of war and sorely tested the inter-American peace commitments.

The new nationalistic president of Peru, General Luis Miguel Sánchez Cerro, at first disavowed the action at Leticia, and even declared that the movement was Communistic in origin.[12] Later, in a

[10] For text of the Salomón-Lozano treaty, see League of Nations, *Official Journal* (1933), 547–549.

[11] There is a romantic story concerning the way in which the village of Leticia got its name. A young Peruvian engineer had been commissioned by his government to construct a port on the Amazon. While working on the project, he became infatuated with the daughter of the British consul stationed at nearby Iquitos. The young officer bestowed her name upon his camp, which was later to become the village of Leticia.

[12] The author has been informed by a Peruvian source that "there are indications that these three hundred civilians were Apristas, in other words mortal foes of the Peruvian President, who, exploiting the nationalistic sentiment of the Department of Loreto, decided to invade Colombian territory to create seri-

sudden about-face, induced because of general popular support of the coup, Sánchez Cerro insisted that the patriotic aspirations of the local population should be respected, and proposed a revision of the Salomón-Lozano treaty. The Peruvians argued that since the treaty of 1922 had been forced on a reluctant nation by the coercive measures of Dictator Leguía, the whole question of boundaries should be reopened for discussion. In the meantime, Peruvian regular troops took over the occupation of Leticia. But Colombia stood on her rights as established by the ratified treaty, and dispatched troops to the Amazonian hot spot. An expedition of six vessels and 1,500 men sent up the Amazon arrived in Colombian-claimed waters early in February 1933.

Prior to the dispatch of the Colombian expedition, the Peruvian government invoked the formal procedures of inquiry and conciliation as provided by the Gondra treaty and the recently-concluded Washington conciliation convention. Both countries had ratified the treaties,[13] though neither had as yet deposited the ratifications of the conciliation convention. This technicality, however, need not have been a deterrent to invoking the pact had the two ratifying nations been really sincere in seeking a peaceful settlement.

On October 3, 1932, Peru appealed to the permanent diplomatic committee at Washington, composed of the ministers of Guatemala, Uruguay, and Venezuela, to aid in organizing an inquiry into the difficulty. Colombia rejected the proposed recourse to the Gondra treaty on the ground that the events in Leticia were strictly and exclusively of an internal nature, and that the matter had already been settled by the Salomón-Lozano treaty.[14] As for the Washington conciliation convention, Colombia contended that that treaty was not applicable to the dispute since neither party had deposited its ratification, a requirement stipulated by the treaty. Colombia informed Peru, however, that she was willing to discuss the boundary treaty, but only after Peru had withdrawn from Leticia—a condition which Peru rejected.

---

ous international complications for the Peruvian Government, and thus contribute to the rapid overthrow of the said President."

[13] The statement, contained in the *Report of the Council* of the League of Nations (March 18, 1933) that Peru had already deposited her ratification of the Washington conciliation convention (and accepted by Manley O. Hudson, *The Verdict of the League: Colombia and Peru at Leticia* [Boston, 1933], 7–8) was not correct. Peru did not deposit ratification until May 11, 1934. Colombia withheld deposit of ratification until June 21, 1938.

[14] The Gondra treaty excepted from investigation questions affecting constitutional provisions and questions already settled by other treaties. The Washington conciliation convention eliminated these exceptions.

Since Colombia ruled out both the Gondra treaty and the Washington conciliation convention, and since only Peru had ratified the Washington arbitration treaty,[15] none of the formal inter-American procedures of pacific settlement seemed to be available for composing the Leticia dispute. As in the Chaco conflict, the only recourses were *ad hoc* inter-American procedures, or the Covenant of the League of Nations and the Kellogg-Briand Anti-War Pact, for both disputants were adherents to these universal agreements.

Early in January 1933, Brazil offered to mediate, and proposed that temporary administration of the Loreto corridor be entrusted to her while the representatives of Colombia and Peru negotiated a settlement at Rio de Janeiro. The proposal was acceptable to Colombia, but, since Peru insisted on the restoration of her occupation in the event the negotiations failed, Brazil was forced to announce, on February 3, the failure of her mediatory efforts.[16]

The United States also intervened in the controversy. On January 23, Colombia appealed to the United States, and to the other signatories of the Pact of Paris, to intercede with Peru. Consequently, on January 25, Secretary Stimson, after consultation with representatives of other signatories of the War Renunciation Pact, addressed a strongly-worded note to the Peruvian government, urging it to abide by the pact and to accept the solution proposed by the Brazilian government. Mr. Stimson also reminded the Peruvians of the resolution voted at the Havana conference on February 20, 1928, condemning aggression, and of the declaration which Peru had signed, together with eighteen other American nations, on August 3, 1932, renouncing force as an instrument of national policy in the reciprocal relations of American countries.[17] On January 27 the Peruvian government replied, indicating that it had not forgotten the position it had taken and would abide by the various pacts and agreements mentioned by Mr. Stimson.[18] Nevertheless, Peru showed no disposition to withdraw from Leticia, where, with the approach of the Colombian expedition, an armed encounter impended. Notwithstanding this situation, the peace efforts of the American nations being exhausted, there now seemed to be a disposition to rely on the League of Nations. For the

[15] Peru ratified in 1930 but did not deposit ratification until 1934; Colombia ratified in 1937 and deposited ratification in 1938.

[16] John C. de Wilde, "South American Conflicts: The Chaco and Leticia," Foreign Policy Association, *Report,* IX, No. 6 (May 24, 1933), 67.

[17] U.S. Dept. of State, *Press Release,* Jan. 25, 1933.

[18] *Ibid.,* Jan. 31, 1933.

first time the U.S. State Department not only permitted intervention by the League in American affairs, it even solicited its cooperation.

On January 4, 1933, Colombia, following procedure called for in Article 15 of the Covenant of the League of Nations, gave formal notice to the Secretary-General that a dispute with Peru existed. On January 20 the Peruvian government, in response to a request by the president of the Council for information and to an injunction to both parties to observe their obligations to the Covenant, declared that while she regarded the Salomón-Lozano treaty of 1922 as still valid, she sought "to make it more elastic and to infuse new life into it" by rectification of the boundaries. The arbitrary transfer of the 17,000 inhabitants (a gross exaggeration) of the Loreto region "created an artificial situation and awakened irredentism."[19] After appointing a committee to study the matter, the Council adjourned.[20]

While the international peace machinery was functioning laboriously, military incidents were occurring in the contested area. On February 14 a Colombian gunboat on the Putumayo River was bombed by Peruvian planes, but without suffering damage. The next day the Colombians captured Tarapacá, a Peruvian village on the Putumayo. On the same day the two countries broke off diplomatic relations. On February 17, Colombia appealed to the League Council, asking that an extraordinary session be held "to effect a settlement of the dispute." When the Council met on February 21, the Peruvian representative refrained from attending on the ground that "South American legal doctrine has established that an international law exists for the [South American] Continent under which conflicts must be settled by American conciliation commissions or mediators."[21] Later, however, the Peruvians agreed to attend the Council sessions.

Within less than two weeks from the date of the Colombian appeal, the League Council had worked out a formula for a settlement whereby a League commission should take charge of the disputed territory while negotiations proceeded. Secretary Stimson endorsed the League proposal and urged both countries to accept.[22] Peru, however, insisted on unacceptable counterproposals. Following its failure to effect a

[19] League of Nations, *Official Journal* (1933), 567. "On January 24, 1934, the population of Leticia was 142 Colombians and 121 Peruvians, and on May 27, 1938, 253 in all, with 999 in the rest of the territory."—Ireland, 203.

[20] This committee, composed of Sean Lester (Irish Free State) as chairman, José Matos (Guatemala), and Salvador de Madariaga (Spain), had previously been set up to deal with the Chaco dispute.

[21] Hudson, 10–11.

[22] U.S. Dept. of State, *Press Release,* Feb. 27, 1933.

settlement, the Council proceeded to the next step as provided by Article 15 (par. 4) of the Covenant. On March 18 it adopted and published a report containing (1) a statement of the facts of the dispute, which were condemnatory of Peru; and (2) a recommendation that the Peruvian forces evacuate the trapezium, following which the two parties should negotiate all their existing problems.[23] The Peruvian delegate protested this "summary judgment" of the Council, and, following the unanimous adoption of the report by formal roll call, conspicuously arose and stalked from the room.

Following the precedent set in the recent Sino-Japanese dispute, the same session of the Council, on March 18, appointed an advisory committee to watch the situation and assist the Council in the performance of its duties under Article 4 (par. 4). The United States and Brazil were invited to collaborate.[24] Both countries accepted. Secretary Hull designated Mr. Hugh Wilson, minister to Switzerland, as United States representative without vote.[25]

It was sensational developments in Lima that terminated Peruvian recalcitrance and hastened a settlement of the controversy. On April 30, 1933, President Sánchez Cerro was assassinated. The attack came as no surprise, since he had created so many enemies by his ruthlessness that he was said to be already carrying no fewer than fourteen bullets in his body from would-be assassins. Congress met at once and elected as provisional president the Generalissimo of the Peruvian Army at the Leticia front, Óscar R. Benavides, a former president of Peru and an intimate friend of Dr. Alfonso López, the Colombian Liberal candidate for the presidency. The men had been colleagues as plenipotentiaries at the Court of St. James a few months before the Leticia incident erupted. Dr. López sent a telegram of congratulation to General Benavides, expressing hopes for a solution of the conflict. General Benavides' reply was an invitation to Dr. López to come to Lima for a conference with him. The conference took place in the historic House of Pizarro from May 15 to May 21. On May 27, Peru notified League authorities in Geneva that she was ready to accept earlier proposals and proceed to a final settlement. Thus it was a change in internal administration that brought about the complete reversal of Peru's position.

In accordance with League recommendations an administrative commission, composed of a citizen of the United States, a Brazilian, and a

---

[23] For text of the Council report of March 18, 1933, see Hudson, 17.–55.
[24] *Ibid.*, 58.   [25] U.S. Dept. of State, *Press Release*, March 20, 1933.

Spaniard, was appointed by the Council to take over the administration of Leticia and its corridor. Just twenty-nine days after the signing of the provisional agreement between Peru and Colombia, the commission arrived at Leticia and took over command of a detachment of Colombian troops to be used as an international police force. Within twenty-four hours the Peruvian forces had evacuated the area, leaving the League representatives in complete charge pending the outcome of the diplomatic negotiations to be held at Rio de Janeiro.

These negotiations were inaugurated under the mediatory auspices of Brazilian Foreign Minister Afranio de Mello Franco, who has been eloquently described as "a current of harmony transformed into a man." The conference lasted from October 1933 to May 1934; there were many dangerous moments indeed during the long discussions, but the patience and skill of Mello Franco were finally rewarded when a formula which he had proposed was accepted by both nations. On May 24, 1934, the Protocol of Peace, Friendship, and Cooperation was signed by the plenipotentiaries of Colombia and Peru, thus ending the Leticia incident.

According to the terms of the protocol the validity of the Salomón-Lozano treaty of 1922 was fully confirmed, and Peru recognized normal diplomatic negotiations as the only means of accomplishing any modification of the treaty more satisfactory to herself. It also provided for demilitarization of the Leticia area, free navigation of the Amazon and Putumayo, and a pledge of nonaggression. Ratifications of the treaty were exchanged on September 27, 1935.

The solution of the Leticia controversy was effected by a procedure identical with that proposed some months earlier by the Brazilian government, but with the exception that, during the Rio negotiations it was not Brazil, but a League of Nations commission that administered the territory. Therefore, credit for the settlement must be divided evenly between an American government acting in a mediatory capacity and the League of Nations. The procedure did not conform to anything already provided by the inter-American system, unless it be *ad hoc* mediation.

In accounting for the peaceful settlement of the Leticia controversy, the nature of the dispute itself must be taken into consideration. Peru's legal position was very vulnerable, to say the least. At no time did that nation deny the validity of the 1922 treaty, nor did it deny that the Leticia trapezium was Colombian territory; consequently by its own admission it had forcibly occupied the territory of a friendly neighboring power in order to secure treaty revision. In seeking to set aside a legal compact contracted by Dictator Leguía, Peru must have known how unacceptable to all American nations, to whom dictatorial regimes were a commonplace, this would be as a new principle of American international law.[26] Having no legal, and little moral, ground to stand on, it is small wonder that the Peruvian government took advantage of a change of administration to save face and beat a peaceful retreat. The Leticia peace settlement should not, therefore, be given exaggerated significance as an example of the devotion of the American nations to peaceful procedures for the settlement of international disputes.

The Ecuador-Peru boundary dispute. The century-and-a-quarter boundary dispute between Peru and Ecuador precipitated a number of crises in the relations between the two countries which afforded considerable opportunity to test the inter-American peace procedures. Unlike the Leticia dispute, in which the issues were relatively apparent and simple, the bases of disagreement between Peru and Ecuador over their boundary extending from the Andes to the Amazon were extremely complicated. Since it is not essential to our present purposes to recount the technical details of the respective claims of the two countries, these matters will be passed over briefly, as will be the various procedures resorted to prior to 1930 to effect a settlement, reserving for more detailed discussion those procedures dating from the time when the inter-American peace machinery had been sufficiently developed to be applicable to the controversy.[27]

The territory in dispute between Peru and Ecuador comprised some 120,000 square miles[28] of unexplored jungle lying behind the Andes between the Napo and Marañón Rivers. In the colonial period it had been organized into the provinces of Jaén and Maynas under the jurisdiction of the Audiencia of Quito, which in turn was a part of the Viceroyalty of Neuva Granada or Santa Fé. When Peruvian independence was proclaimed in 1821 the municipal councils of the two provinces assumed the right to declare themselves a part of the new Peruvian state. This was due perhaps to the fact that, since 1802, by virtue of a royal *cédula,* the provinces had been attached to the Viceroyalty

---

[26] The Chileans, for example, expressed concern about the Tacna-Arica settlement which had also been negotiated by President Leguía.

[27] Departing from the chronological limits of the present chapter, the post-1939 developments of the Ecuador-Peru dispute are included up to the date of its final settlement.

[28] This is in excess of the present area of Ecuador, which is about 105,000 square miles.

of Peru.[29] Since the boundary between Peru and Great Colombia (of which Ecuador was a component part) was indeterminate, the two states, in September 1829, signed a treaty which recognized the principle of colonial boundaries (*uti possidetis* of 1810) as the basis for fixing their territorial limits.

Before the boundary could be determined, as provided by the treaty of 1829, Great Colombia was dissolved (in 1830), Ecuador declared her independence, and Peru declined to be bound by the treaty. In 1832 a treaty was concluded between Peru and Ecuador which stipulated that "pending an agreement concerning the settlement of boundaries between the two states, the present ones shall be recognized and respected." If signing this treaty seemed to indicate that Ecuador acquiesced in Peruvian occupation of the provinces, this illusion was dispelled in 1841 when Ecuador announced that she stood on her rights under the treaty of 1829. The issue was joined.

Peru continued in occupation of the disputed territory. When, in 1857, Ecuador attempted to grant a concession in the region to some English creditors, this was frustrated by armed Peruvian intervention. In 1887, Ecuador again tried to cancel some of her foreign debts by land concessions in the disputed territories. This was the occasion for renewed negotiations between the two governments from which came a convention (signed at Quito, August 1, 1887) which provided for submitting the "boundary questions pending between the two nations" to the arbitral decision of the King of Spain. According to the Peruvians, the object of the arbitration was to settle the boundary problems, that is, "the tracing of a definite line of frontier," and not any question regarding sovereignty over Jaén and Maynas.[30]

Since the treaty provided that arbitration might be waived in favor of direct negotiations, the two countries again attempted to negotiate a settlement. These efforts, extending over a number of years, ended in failure. Then in 1904, as a result of Peruvian insistence, the case was submitted to the arbitral judgment of the King of Spain. Peru's reservation to the effect that the arbitration applied only to the adjudication of boundaries and not to the possession of the provinces, was sustained by the Spanish Council of State. In 1910 that high judicial

[29] It was the Ecuadorean contention that the transfer was only for ecclesiastical purposes.—Pastoriza Flores, *History of the Boundary Dispute between Ecuador and Peru* (New York, 1921), 35.

[30] *The Question of the Boundaries between Peru and Ecuador: Statement of the Peruvian Delegation* (Baltimore, 1937), 18.

body advised the King that, since "it has been established that the provinces of Jaén and Maynas . . . belong to Peru under whose sovereignty they were in 1832 when the state of Ecuador was established . . . the arbitration is limited to a determination of the size and boundaries of Jaén and the old province of Maynas, insofar as these boundaries affect the state of Ecuador."[31]

It was unfortunate that the report of the Council of State was not kept secret, for when it became known to the Ecuadorean government, it was regarded quite correctly as indicative of the nature of the pending arbitral award, which, Ecuador announced, would be rejected. This, coupled with hostile demonstrations in Ecuador against Peru, created a situation closely verging on war and influenced the King of Spain to withdraw from the arbitration and decline to make an award. The mediation of the governments of the Argentine Republic, Brazil, and the United States averted an armed conflict, but their efforts to secure Ecuadorean consent to submit the controversy to The Hague Tribunal ended in failure.

The next serious attempt to settle the dispute came in 1924, when the foreign ministers of Peru and Ecuador signed at Quito a protocol providing for a so-called "mixed formula," a combination of direct settlement and the fixing of zones for a restricted juridical arbitration. The protocol made provision for the two governments to send delegations to Washington to confer there on the question of boundaries; if this failed, they agreed to submit certain recognized zones to arbitral decisions by the President of the United States. However, it was not until 1933—nine years from the date of the protocol—that any definite move was made toward holding the conference in Washington, and indeed, it was not until September 30, 1936, that direct negotiation began. In a supplementary protocol signed at Lima, it was agreed that, in the event of the failure of the direct negotiations, President Roosevelt should arbitrate the dispute.[32]

The direct negotiations at Washington continued intermittently for thirteen months; but not only were the Peruvian and Ecuadorean delegations unable to agree on a general settlement, they were unable to agree upon even the zones to be submitted to President Roosevelt's arbitration. The controversy was still pending when, in the early months of 1941, there occurred clashes between the armed forces of Peru and Ecuador on the frontier. Once more the United States, Ar-

[31] *Résumé of the Historical Juridical Proceedings of the Boundary Question between Peru and Ecuador* (Washington, 1937), 11.
[32] Ireland, 227–229.

gentina, and Brazil offered their mediatory services. With the consent of Ecuador and Peru, the three mediators sent a commission of six military observers, who, together with military delegates of the two countries, met at Talara, Peru. There, on October 2, 1941, they signed an agreement providing for the cessation of border hostilities and the withdrawal of the troops of both countries from a demilitarized border zone. Thus matters stood when the Third Consultative Meeting of American Foreign Ministers convened at Rio de Janeiro in January 1942.

The Rio meeting was seized upon by the mediatory powers (Argentina, Brazil, Chile, and the United States) as the occasion to work out a compromise procedure for the settlement of the dispute which proved to be acceptable to both Peru and Ecuador. This agreement, the Protocol of Peace, Friendship and Boundaries, was signed at Rio on January 29, 1942, and on February 26, 1942, it was ratified by the two disputants. The protocol fixed eighteen definitive points through which the permanent boundary should be drawn. The final demarcation of the boundary was to be entrusted to technical experts of Peru and Ecuador, assisted by representatives of the four mediating powers. The area was to be demilitarized pending the final settlement. Peru pledged to Ecuador the same concessions enjoyed by Brazil and Colombia for navigation on the Amazon and its northern tributaries.[33]

In spite of the fact that the Rio protocol was ratified by a large majority of the Congress of Ecuador, the boundary settlement aroused bitter resentment in that country. The settlement added about 7,700 square miles in the Maynas Province to Peru, and it was felt that Ecuador had made too great a sacrifice· Because of this so-called "diplomatic defeat," Foreign Minister Julio Tabor Donoso was forced to resign. This being the atmosphere in Ecuador, progress toward a settlement stalled on the technical interpretations of the terms of the protocol. However, thanks to the persistence of Brazilian Foreign Minister Oswaldo Aranha, Peru and Ecuador finally agreed, on May 20, 1944, to give effect to the protocol signed at Rio in 1942. The two countries accepted the boundary for four sectors, as proposed by Aranha, and agreed to accept as the boundary for two remaining eastern sectors a line to be proposed by a neutral arbitrator, Captain Braz Díaz de Aquiar of Brazil, whose solution was to be offered after an actual inspection.[34]

[33] Pan American Union, *Bulletin*, LXXVI (May 1942), 241–244.
[34] *Ibid.*, LXXVIII (Oct. 1944), 590–591; *New York Times*, May 21, 1944.

February 16, 1945, was the date of the final settlement of the continent's oldest boundary dispute. At that time both Peru and Ecuador accepted the boundary proposed by the arbitrator for the two eastern sectors.[35] Henceforward the map-makers could dispense with the necessity of showing a large part of Ecuador as "territory in dispute." Incidentally, Ecuador was a heavy loser; of the territory claimed, it lost an area about equal to the present extent of the republic.

The final settlement of the Peru-Ecuador boundary dispute, like that of the Chaco and of Leticia, was effected, through the mediatory offices of a group of American nations, and without resort to the established procedures. Unlike the disputants in the Chaco and Leticia controversies, however, Ecuador and Peru did not want for common adherence to a number of inter-American peace pacts. Earlier than January 1, 1938, both countries had duly ratified the Gondra treaty, the Washington conciliation convention, the Washington arbitration treaty, and the Saavedra Lamas treaty of 1933. But these pacts were of no service in facilitating a settlement of the controversy; as in the Chaco and Leticia affairs, it was the inter-American mediatory efforts that gave abundant evidence of regional responsibility for continental peace.

There were other boundary disputes in America which also serve to test the efficacy of the inter-American pacts for the peaceful settlement of controversies.

The Guatemala-Honduras boundary dispute. This dispute originated in 1842, following the dissolution of the Federation of Central America. In 1845 a general treaty of friendship and alliance, signed by Guatemala and Honduras, provided for a mixed commission to determine the boundary and offer a solution of all disputed points by arbitration. The commission dissolved in 1847 without fixing the boundary.

The second attempt to agree on a boundary came in 1895 when a convention was signed which provided for a mixed technical commission to study all relevant documents and data and to propose a settlement to the two governments on the basis of its findings. There was considerable delay in appointing the commission; then, after brief and futile activity, it ceased to operate in 1910.

On August 1, 1914, another boundary convention was negotiated which repeated the terms of that of 1895. Because the boundary commission failed to make any progress, and because border conflicts were

[35] *New York Times,* Feb. 18, 1945.

threatening, the United States in 1917 invited the two governments to send special missions to a boundary conference at Washington. The conference began in 1918 and terminated in failure in 1921.[36]

In January 1930, at the insistence of the United States, there was a renewal of the Washington discussions, out of which came, on July 16, 1930, yet another treaty providing for arbitration of the boundary dispute. But the question of who was to act as arbitrator was a troublesome one. Guatemala insisted that the case fell under the jurisdiction of the International Central American Tribunal, created in 1923 by a pact which both Guatemala and Honduras had ratified. Honduras did not agree. The treaty accordingly provided a compromise. It created a special tribunal, organized in the same form prescribed by the convention of 1923 for the establishment of an International Central American Tribunal. This special tribunal, composed of a representative each of Guatemala and Honduras, and Chief Justice Hughes of the United States, was to decide whether it should function as the Central American Tribunal or as a special tribunal for the boundary question.[37]

On January 8, 1932, the special tribunal decided unanimously, as was expected, that since the International Central American Tribunal was not a permanent body, there was no Central American Court *in existence* to which the dispute could be submitted, as argued by Guatemala. Functioning, therefore, as a special tribunal, that body assumed jurisdiction and, on January 23, 1933, handed down its award, which amounted substantially to a division of the disputed territory between the two parties.[38] Following the arbitral award, a technical commission, with a United States officer as neutral member and chief, completed the actual demarcation of the line by September 1936.

By these procedures a protracted Central American boundary dispute was finally terminated. It is interesting that the long-delayed settlement was made possible only by resorting to a bit of obvious stage-play in order to avoid having to refer to an agreed-upon instrument for the peaceful solution of Central American controversies. It was a loss to the prestige of the Central American Court that it was denied credit for settling the century-old controversy.

The Honduras-Nicaragua boundary dispute. The attempts to settle

---

[36] The above summary is based on Gordon Ireland, *Boundaries, Possessions, and Conflicts in Central and North America and the Caribbean* (Cambridge, Mass., 1941), 86–90.

[37] *American Journal of International Law*, XXVI (1931), 326–327.

[38] F. C. Fisher, "The Arbitration of the Guatemalan-Honduran Boundary Dispute," *ibid.*, XXVII (July 1933), 403–427.

the boundary between Honduras and Nicaragua were less successful. The dissolution of the Federation of Central America also left indeterminate the boundary between Nicaragua and Honduras, and it was not until 1869 that the first serious effort was made to mark the line. In that year a mixed commission was appointed by the two countries to survey the whole line; however, the commission was unable to agree even on a starting point on the Atlantic side. In 1870, 1888, and 1889, boundary treaties were negotiated but failed of ratification. The treaty of 1894 was more successful. A mixed boundary commission created by this treaty was able to agree on a line extending from the Gulf of Fonseca eastward to a point about midway across the isthmus. But from that point—the Portillo de Teoticacinte—northeastward to the Atlantic the commission could not agree, and so, in 1904, it made a report and disbanded. Now, according to the terms of the treaty of 1894, the situation called for arbitration by either a member of the foreign diplomatic corps accredited to Guatemala, or any foreign or Central American public personage; or, if such a person should not be available, that the controverted point or points be submitted to the decision of the government of Spain.[39]

Departing from the exact provisions of the treaty, the two governments agreed to submit the dispute to the King of Spain. On December 23, 1906, Alfonso XIII handed down his award, which was generally favorable to Honduran claims. Although the decision was publicly accepted by President Zelaya of Nicaragua, no immediate steps were taken by either country to execute the award. This omission was unfortunate, for in 1912, Nicaragua announced that the Spanish arbitration was null and void because the contracting parties had violated the procedure for selecting an arbitrator as called for by the treaty of 1894. Nicaragua had, of course, been a party to this alleged "violation."

In 1913, Honduras requested the good offices of the United States in securing the execution of the award. The Nicaraguan response to mediatory proposals by the United States was a declared willingness to submit the whole matter to arbitral decision by President Woodrow Wilson. Although Honduras refused to consider another arbitration, that government did consent, in 1918, to amicable discussion at Washington under the auspices of the State Department. A proposal by the mediator, in September 1921, that the two governments agree to submit the validity of the Spanish award to the decision of the Chief

[39] Terms of the treaty of 1894 quoted in Ireland, *Boundaries, Possessions, and Conflicts in Central and North America and the Caribbean,* 133–134.

Justice of the United States was accepted by Nicaragua but rejected by Honduras. Ten years later, in 1931, an agreement negotiated by representatives of the two republics, which provided that the boundary was to be settled in accordance with the award by the King of Spain, was rejected by the Nicaraguan Congress on advice of President Moncada.[40]

A novel incident revived the boundary controversy in 1937. In September of that year Nicaragua issued a postage stamp bearing the map of the republic, and it showed a considerable part of southeastern Honduras as being "territory in dispute." Honduras took official notice of the stamp and declared it to be "an affront to her sovereignty." Nicaragua retorted that the map was official and refused to withdraw it from circulation. Thus was threatened "the War of the Postage Stamp."[41] Armed hostilities were prevented, however, by the mediation of Costa Rica, Venezuela, and the United States. At San José, Costa Rica, on December 10, 1937, the Pact of Reciprocal Agreements was signed by Nicaragua and Honduras. It contained a pledge to refrain from any resort to arms, and "to solve the present conflict by pacific means as established by International Law."[42] The pact made specific reference to the Honduran reservation to the General Treaty of Arbitration signed at Washington on January 5, 1929.[43] This meant that Honduras would oppose any effort to invoke the Washington treaty for the arbitration of the dispute.

Although the terms of the pact were fulfilled so far as abandoning forcible measures was concerned, no progress was made in adjudicating the boundary. This controversy between the two Central American republics was until 1960 the only significant unsettled boundary controversy between Latin-American nations.[44] A reminder of the continued existence of the dispute was Honduras' reservation attached to the Inter-American Treaty of Reciprocal Assistance, signed at Rio de Janeiro, September 2, 1947. The Honduran delegation declared that

[40] The above summary is based principally on *ibid.,* 128–144.

[41] *New York Times,* Sept. 12, 1937.

[42] U.S. Dept. of State, *Press Release,* Dec. 18, 1937, pp. 453–458.

[43] The reservation read: "The provisions thereof shall not be applicable to pending international questions or controversies or to those which may arise in the future relative to acts prior to the date on which the said Treaty goes into effect."

[44] Of course, boundary or territorial disputes are still existent between the United States and Mexico (the Chamizal), Guatemala and Great Britain (British Honduras), and Argentina and Great Britain (Falkland Islands).

in signing the treaty,[45] it did so with the reservation that the boundary between Honduras and Nicaragua had been definitely established: (1) from the Gulf of Fonseca to Portillo de Teoticacinte by the Joint Boundary Commission in 1901, and (2) from Portillo de Teoticacinte to the Atlantic by the arbitral award of the King of Spain on December 23, 1906. The ostensible purpose of the reservation was to ensure that any Nicaraguan attempt to occupy territory beyond the line of the award was an act of aggression. It was the view of the Hondurans that the Organization of American States, to comply with the letter and spirit of the Rio treaty, should require that any forces of Nicaragua that should venture to cross the frontier determined by the *laudo arbitral* of the King of Spain retire from Honduran territory.[46]

The Nicaraguan government undertook to checkmate the Honduran maneuver when, on November 12, 1948, it deposited its ratification of the Rio Treaty of Reciprocal Assistance. Referring to the reservation by Honduras, Nicaragua countered with its own reservation, to wit: the Nicaragua-Honduras boundary has *not* been determined from a point known as Portillo de Teoticacinte, to the Atlantic Ocean, because the award by the King of Spain was impugned and protested by Nicaragua as null and void. Consequently, the signature of the Rio treaty by Nicaragua cannot be regarded as acceptance of arbitral judgments whose validity has been impugned by Nicaragua. Whether the Nicaraguan government by its reservation made itself immune from designation as an aggressor under the terms of the Rio treaty remained a moot question.

Haiti versus the Dominican Republic. We consider finally a unique case, unique because it was the only controversy settled within the formal framework of the inter-American peace structure. This dispute, unlike the others considered, was not concerned with boundary or territorial claims. An old and vexatious boundary dispute between Haiti and the Dominican Republic was finally settled on February 27,

[45] ART. 9. "In addition to the acts which the Organ of Consultation may characterize as aggression, the following shall be considered as such:

b. Invasion, by the armed forces of a state, of the territory of an American State, through the trespassing of boundaries demarcated in accordance with a treaty, judicial decision, or arbitral award, or, in the absence of frontiers thus demarcated, invasion affecting a region which is under the effective jurisdiction of another State."

[46] "El Tratado Interamericano de Asistencia Reciproca y la Frontera de Honduras con Nicaragua," in *Ferrovia: Revista Continental Democrática, de Crítica y Combate e Informativa* (San Pedro Sula, Honduras, Jan. 1948), V, No. 13.

1935, when Presidents Vincent and Trujillo signed a protocol which resolved the remaining points of difference between the two countries.[47] But the settlement of the boundary line did not signify the termination of frontier clashes, a heritage of years of conflict between two markedly dissimilar nations forced to be neighbors on a very small island.

In October 1937 there was a frightful massacre by Dominican soldiers of Haitian laborers who had peacefully crossed the border in search of work. When the disturbances subsided, several thousand Haitians were dead,[48] victims of one of the most shameful bloodlettings in the modern history of the Americas.

The Haitian government immediately asked for an investigation, and when a month elapsed without receiving satisfaction, President Vincent on November 12, 1937, appealed to the presidents of the United States, Cuba, and Mexico, requesting their good offices and mediation. Consequently, beginning on December 2 a series of informal hearings and unofficial conversations took place in Washington, culminating in the suggestion that treaty agreements in force between the two countries be applied to the dispute. Fortunately, the two countries were mutual adherents to four inter-American pacts, having ratified the Gondra treaty, the Washington conciliation convention, the Washington arbitration treaty, and the Saavedra-Lamas antiwar treaty.

Accordingly, on December 14, 1937, Haiti invoked the Gondra treaty and the General Convention of Inter-American Conciliation, meanwhile designating her own representative to a commission of investigation and conciliation in accordance with the terms of the pacts. The next day the three Latin-American diplomatic representatives who were longest accredited to Washington—the minister of Guatemala, the ambassador of Peru, and the ambassador of Argentina—met as the permanent commission and forwarded to the Dominican Republic the Haitian request for settlement by applying the procedures of inquiry and conciliation. On December 18, President Trujillo accepted the invitation of the permanent commission and designated the Dominican representative to the commission of investigation and conciliation.

When the permanent commission was requested by the disputants on January 18, 1938, to exercise the conciliatory function, an option

[47] Ireland, *Boundaries, Possessions, and Conflicts in Central and North America and the Caribbean*, 66–67.

[48] The exact number of the victims was never divulged. Some estimates are as high as 12,000.

allowed by the General Conciliatory Convention, that body proceeded to invite the delegations of Haiti and the Dominican Republic to come to a direct understanding concerning the basis of conciliation. This was done, and an agreement was soon reached and signed in Washington on January 31, 1938. The terms required the Dominican Republic to pay an indemnity of $750,000 to Haiti, one-third in a lump sum, and the balance in five equal installments, beginning January 31, 1939; they also proposed measures for protecting nationals from the future occurrence of such incidents, and recommended that penalties be enforced on infracting persons.[49]

The case of Haiti versus the Dominican Republic is unique not only because this was the only settlement accomplished within the framework of the inter-American peace procedures but also because of the facility with which a settlement was reached. It proved that the peace machinery can operate when applied with sincerity and good faith. It is indeed a sad commentary that sincerity and good faith have been absent from the attempted settlement of so many inter-American disputes that its presence on this occasion should evoke special mention.

Technical deficiencies. It is to be noted that the Pan American peace structure in 1939, as applicable to purely American disputes, was seriously defective. Technical deficiencies revealed by the foregoing test cases will be discussed in the following order: (1) need to strengthen the compulsory character of recourse to pacific procedures, (2) need to expand the scope of these procedures, (3) need of defining "the aggressor" and providing sanctions, and (4) need of coordinating the duplicating and overlapping pacts.

First, it was easy to avoid recourse to the established pacific procedures because the instruments did not contain express and unconditional commitments to resort to them. To correct this defect the parties would have to bind themselves unequivocally to submit their disputes to the procedures of pacific settlement. Compulsory jurisdiction has always been the greatest stumbling block.

Recourse was also avoided because of the lack of a method or criterion for determining at what stage of the controversy the procedure would be appropriate. To remedy this defect a means would have to be found to determine whether a dispute existed which could not be settled by diplomatic means. Also, greater adherence to the

---

[49] "Settlement of the Dominican Republic–Haitian Controversy," *Pan American Union, Bulletin,* LXXII (March 1938), 288–304; U.S. Dept. of State, *Press Release,* March 19, 1938.

principle of compulsory reference was contingent on providing methods of initiating the procedure when the disputants failed to do so.

Second, if the inter-American peace mechanism was to be really effective, *all disputes*, regardless of their nature, should have been submitted to the procedures. The value of the peace pacts was severely weakened by the *exceptions* in the instruments; this was particularly true of the Washington arbitration treaty of 1929, probably the most important of the peace conventions.

The Pan American peace machine was further hampered by the *reservations* conditioning the adherence of the various states. Many of the Latin-American reservations excluded from compulsory reference disputes which were thought to be within the exclusive competence of the national courts; and, more important, they excepted questions arising under treaties already in existence. Such reservations removed a large number of disputes from the jurisdiction of the peace treaties. The United States was by no means guiltless of this practice; for example, the insistence of the Senate that it must approve the *compromis,* or agreement to arbitrate, under the Washington arbitration treaty destroyed its compulsory character. Thus, reservations must be carefully considered and analyzed when evaluating the effectiveness of a treaty.

Despite the exceptions and reservations noted, all of the Pan American peace treaties lacked *unanimous* ratification. This had long been recognized as an obstacle to the peace movement, and several measures have been taken to secure prompt ratification, but to no avail. To recapitulate, the ratification record for the five principal peace treaties was (1939) as follows: Gondra treaty, nineteen; Washington conciliation convention, seventeen; Washington arbitration treaty, sixteen; Saavedra Lamas treaty, nineteen; and Buenos Aires Consultation Pact of 1936, fifteen. It is to be noted that the United States had ratified every one of the peace pacts negotiated since 1923, albeit with some reservations; Argentina had ratified but one, the rather innocuous Saavedra Lamas pact. A difficulty in applying these pacts to controversies arose from the fact that the disputing nations frequently were not mutual ratifying parties to any of the peace treaties. Nonratification was a major obstacle to the successful functioning of the inter-American peace machine.

A third deficiency of the peace pacts was their failure to define "the aggressor" and to provide sanctions. The need of agreement on the *identification of an aggressor nation,* whether it be American or non-

American, has been recognized as necessary before sanctions can be applied. However, the Lima conference of 1938, in a "Resolution on Definition of the Aggressor and Sanctions," declared that, since there was no agreement on a definition of "aggressor," and since existing inter-American relations were peaceable, no need for a special definition existed. As for a threat from abroad, this, the conference held, could be dealt with on an *ad hoc* basis by using the established machinery for consultation.[50]

Resorting to force to secure the observance of obligations of peaceful settlement of international disputes is considered contrary to the spirit of Pan Americanism. Consequently the peace and security pacts made no provision, with one possible exception, for *sanctions,* unless public opinion, solidarity, and a sense of moral obligation can be so regarded. The exception noted was the Saavedra Lamas treaty (Art. 3), which provided that in case any state failed to comply with its obligations under the treaty, the contracting states, in addition to other efforts to maintain peace, "will exercise the political, juridical, or economic means authorized by international law." The interesting question regarding the nature and scope of these *authorized* means raises problems too complicated to be treated in the present discussion.

For the preservation of security against aggression from abroad, the American republics had developed by 1939 a cooperative approach to the problem of sanctions by resorting to the consultative procedure. There was no arrangement in the American system whereby, in the event of overseas attack, a constituted agency could summon the nations of the Western Hemisphere to take either economic or military action against the aggressor. Such cooperative defense measures emerging from the consultative meetings of the foreign ministers were to be entirely *ad hoc* in character.

The fourth technical deficiency of the inter-American peace structure was the existence of too many duplicating and overlapping pacts. The problem of simplifying and coordinating the numerous peace instruments had been given serious, but ineffectual, consideration ever since the Mexican delegation presented a Code of Peace to the Montevideo conference in 1933. A number of agencies had been delegated to coordinate the peace instruments, and several codes were drafted. However, the only action taken on this matter by the Lima conference was to refer it to the International Conference of American Jurists,

[50] Pan American Union, *Improvement and Coordination of Inter-American Peace Instruments,* I, 66–67, and Appendix C.

which was to report to the Ninth International Conference of American States.

This discussion of the technical deficiencies of the peace structure should not lend itself to any exaggerated conclusions when assessing responsibility for the halting, and sometimes ineffective, operation of the peace procedures. Effective implementation does not always follow the perfecting of the mechanism. Imponderable human factors, such as nationalism, can be expected to produce surprising developments. There is considerable truth in the cynical observation that the American states, including the United States, practiced lip service to arbitration more sedulously than any other group. In fact, they put it into practice extensively in painless instances where it interfered little with a state's having its own way.

An appraisement. On the basis of the record, what additional conclusions can be drawn from our test cases of inter-American security procedures? At first sight it would appear that the yield of positive and profitable applications of the agreed-upon multilateral peace procedures was so slight as to put the brand of failure and futility on the planting which had taken so many years of laborious effort. But before rendering judgment it may be advisable to take a broad view of the whole picture.

All of the test cases noted were inter-American disputes; the political situations in Europe and the Far East had not yet come to the point of being recognized as clear-cut threats to the peace and security of the Americas. These inter-American disputes were all, with but one exception (the Haiti–Dominican Republic crisis, in which the Gondra treaty was successfully invoked), territorial in nature. The roots of these controversies extended far back into the earliest days of the republics. Perhaps the very nature of the disputes, affecting as they did that most cherished national possession—territory—had something to do with nationalistic opposition to invoking agreed-upon peace procedures. It was necessary, therefore, in these instances to fall back on protracted mediation and negotiation leading eventually to temporary substitutes for the formal peace pacts.

Even though there was failure to implement most of these pacts, fabricating the peace structure was not all wasted effort. The fact of its very existence exerted strong moral pressure, for it held up to public view the obligation of the disputants to reconcile their actions, if not their formal commitments, with at least the *ad hoc* resort to peaceful settlement. There was present a pronounced sense of *collective* responsibility for the preservation of peace in the Western Hemisphere.

The outbreak of World War II posed for the American republics clear-cut threats to their peace and integrity. How did their security system measure up vis-à-vis this overseas threat?

VII Neutral America (1939–1941)

To be good neighbors is not enough. . . . Inter-Americanism demands more:
it makes it impossible for any of us to ignore the fate of our neighbors.

                                                 LUIS QUINTANILLA, 1943

IN VIEW OF THE PORTENTS of impending world conflict, the American republics were seriously remiss in not having devised cooperative defense plans by 1939. Urgent proddings by the United States,
as early as 1936, had been dismissed in Latin America as "crying
wolf" for selfish Yankee gains. In spite of sage counsel, the *Latinos*
decided against taking out war insurance, and so it was that not until
the holocaust had actually flared were they disposed to consider the
nature and extent of their cooperative security action. This, fortunately,
the American nations were able to do in a succession of consultative
meetings of their foreign ministers.

Thus it was that the consultation procedure agreed upon at Buenos
Aires and Lima paid off in rich dividends of inter-American security
action during the war. The encomiums pronounced by commentators
in 1936 and again in 1938 concerning the value of consultation seem
to have been fully justified by the record of inter-American security
cooperation during World War II. Moreover, the various declarations
of principles of American solidarity were proven by the common
measures taken during the course of the war to be more than pretentious verbiage. The war presented an exceptional opportunity for
testing the substance of inter-American solidarity as well as the
strength of the security structure, particularly in an extracontinental
crisis. In both respects the results were gratifying.

While paying tribute to the contributions of the consultation procedure to security during World War II, we should not fail to note
that the new Latin-American policy of the United States contributed
much to confirming the principles of inter-American solidarity. With
respect to the benefits of the Good Neighbor policy, it can be asserted

with confidence that if the situation which had prevailed for so many decades up to the year 1933 had existed in 1941, we would have confronted the war crisis with a New World divided and, in many quarters, animated by suspicions of the ulterior motives of the United States. In such muddy waters the agents of the totalitarian powers would have found good fishing. Happily, the waters of inter-American understanding and confidence were clear.

If it had been possible in the earliest days of the Roosevelt Administration to divine the trend of future events, it is doubtful whether it would have been necessary for it to alter its Latin-American policy in any important respect. During World War II the United States reaped the good harvest of an earlier wise planting.

The Panama Meeting of foreign ministers. When war broke out in Europe in September 1939, the United States and its sister American republics issued the usual neutrality proclamations. Since the nations of the Western Hemisphere had a real and common interest in avoiding involvement in the European conflict, it was felt that their interest could best be served by concerted action. Consequently, since an overseas situation had arisen disturbing to the peace of the Americas, it was in pursuance of the acts of Buenos Aires and Lima that there was an exchange of views among several of the governments, with Panama being asked by the United States to extend invitations to the ministers of foreign relations to enter into a consultation at Panama. The meeting convened on September 23 and continued in session until October 3. Its principal objectives were to keep the American republics out of war, and to consider the solution of economic difficulties that would arise as a result of the war.

In seeking to accomplish its first objective the meeting undertook, in the General Declaration of Neutrality, to clarify the rights and duties of the American republics in their capacity as neutrals. After declaring their unanimous intention not to become involved in the European conflict, they set forth certain standards of conduct which they felt obliged to observe if they expected their neutral status to be respected. However, any violation of their rights was to be vigorously protested, for, according to the Uruguayan delegate, "neutrality is not impassivity." In other words, the American nations hoped to avoid becoming involved in the war by maintaining a strictly neutral attitude—a naïve hope.

To study and formulate recommendations concerning new problems with respect to neutrality which would inevitably arise, the Pan American Union was authorized to appoint an Inter-American Neutrality Committee of seven experts in international law to sit at Rio de Janeiro for the duration of the war. The committee, composed of representatives of Argentina, Brazil, Chile, Costa Rica, Mexico, the United States, and Venezuela, held its first meeting in Rio on January 16, 1940. It formulated a series of recommendations concerning the problems of neutrality, "in the light of experience and changing circumstances," which were transmitted to the American governments through the Pan American Union. Those recommendations dealt with such subjects as internment, the entry of submarines into ports and territorial waters of American republics, the inviolability of postal correspondence, the treatment of vessels used as auxiliary transports to warships, and the treatment of crews of merchant vessels suspected of sabotage.[1] Ere the formal involvement of the American republics in the war, the undermining of the accepted rules of neutrality by both belligerents and nonbelligerents forced the committee into a position where it could not fulfill the purposes for which it was originally intended. Its efficacy, therefore, was highly debatable.

The most notable action of the First Meeting of Consultation of the Ministers of Foreign Affairs of the American Republics was the Declaration of Panama, which proclaimed a neutrality zone or safety belt around the Americas, averaging three hundred miles in width, to be kept free of belligerent activities. This hundredfold extension of the traditional three-mile limit, proposed by President Roosevelt himself,[2] was justified as a measure of continental self-protection based on an "inherent right" to have the waters of the American continents free from hostile acts committed by non-American belligerents. The American republics were seeking not only to prevent belligerent interference with inter-American sea-borne traffic but also to avoid war involvement which might result from such interference. The American governments agreed to endeavor, through joint representation to the belligerents, to secure compliance with the provisions of the Declaration of Panama.

As for its enforcement, the declaration merely provided that the American republics would consult when necessary to determine upon

---

[1] Charles G. Fenwick, "The Inter-American Neutrality Committee," *American Journal of International Law*, XXXV (1941), 12; Manuel S. Canyes, "The Inter-American Juridical Committee," Pan American Union, *Bulletin*, LXXVII (May 1943), 269; Harmodio Arias, Jr., "A Collective Neutrality Front for the Americas," *Inter-American Quarterly*, II (Jan. 1941), 59–67.

[2] Joseph Alsop and Robert Kintner, *American White Paper* (New York, 1940), 60–69.

measures; in the meantime they should be free to patrol the zone, individually and collectively, as they willed. As a matter of fact, patrolling devolved largely on the United States.

The keynote of the declaration was that, whatever the issues of the European conflict, the interests of the American nations dictated as distant a neutral aloofness as possible. Undersecretary of State Sumner Welles, writing at a later date, frankly admitted that at the time the declaration seemed to be both justified and desirable. The prevailing view at Panama, he said, was that the war in Europe would be won eventually by the forces of freedom without becoming universal, and that it was the legitimate right of the American republics as neutrals to make every effort to keep clear of the war. According to Welles, what we did not realize was that a war such as that which erupted in Europe in 1939 was destined to become world-wide, "a war between free men and the powers intent upon creating universal tyranny and oppression."[3]

Referring to the Declaration of Panama, Cordell Hull, writing also at a later date, commented that the hemisphere neutrality zone was the idea of the President, and was seconded by Welles. He himself was skeptical because it had no precedent in international law,[4] and could therefore be validly objected to by the belligerents; and in actual practice it would be difficult to enforce. But since the President wanted it, Hull said that he was willing to go along with him and see how it would work out.[5]

Among the acts of this First Meeting of Foreign Ministers the next in importance to the declaration was the Resolution on Economic Cooperation, which provided for the creation of an Inter-American Financial and Economic Advisory Committee consisting of twenty-one experts on economic problems, one from each of the American republics. This committee, to be installed in Washington, was to examine and attempt to find practical solutions to the economic problems with which the American nations were confronted as a result of the war. The work of the committee during the course of the war, as will be indicated shortly, proved to be both extensive and beneficial.

The Panama meeting produced a number of other resolutions, several of which related to continental security. Such a one was the Resolution on Transfer of Sovereignty of Geographic Regions of the

[3] Sumner Welles, *The Time for Decision* (New York, 1944), 212.

[4] A similar proposal had been made by Peru in 1914. See p. 78.

[5] Cordell Hull, *The Memoirs of Cordell Hull* (2 vols., New York, 1949), I, 690.

Americas Held by Non-American States. Because of the possibility that the war in Europe might result in the transfer of sovereignty of colonial possessions in America, the resolution provided that in such a contingency a meeting of foreign ministers should be called. Thus, a first step was taken to "Pan Americanize" the no-transfer principle of the Monroe Doctrine.

The acts of the Panama meeting, while revealing an awakened awareness of the necessities and virtues of security cooperation, also reflected the attitude of the American republics toward the war in its first phase, that is, the so-called "phony phase" of comparative calm from September 1939 to April 1940. There was a comfortable belief that the Anglo-French allies would win out eventually, thanks in part to the Maginot Line, and that America's problem was merely to ensure noninvolvement by preserving a scrupulous neutrality. Consequently, in order to keep the record clear, complaints were duly addressed to the belligerents on the numerous occasions when the neutrality zone was violated,[6] or when there were other infringements of neutrality rights.

During the first phase of the war the American republics, like the other neutrals, lived in a world of make-believe. Despite all the portents of calamity, the watchword was "business as usual." It is significant that military defense was not a subject on the agenda at Panama. Like Denmark, Norway, the Netherlands, Belgium, and Greece, the Pan American nations relied on a strict neutrality as their strongest shield of defense. It should be recorded, however, that the United States, by eliminating the arms-embargo provision from its Neutrality Act of 1937, gave evidence of an awakening consciousness of where its real interests lay. It should also be recorded that as early as January 1939 President Roosevelt had requested Congress for $300 million to provide at least three thousand more planes for the Army; in June Congress appropriated funds to permit the Army to embark on an air-expansion program to be completed in mid-1941. This was our first "hemisphere defense" air program.

Although it was crystal clear that this European war was different from any in the past, and that a German victory would adversely affect the rights and liberties of all states, even in the Western Hemisphere, the Pan American nations did not seem to recognize any difference between the war objectives of the Allies and the Axis powers. Accord-

---

[6] World Peace Foundation, *Documents on American Foreign Relations* (8 vols., Boston, 1939–46), II, 121–139, cited hereinafter as *Documents*.

ing to President Cárdenas of Mexico (September 17, 1939) the war was "an international conflict between ambitious, unscrupulous, and imperialistic interests." It was perhaps mere coincidence that this was also the Communist line.

A complete reorientation and reversal of fundamental attitudes and policy on the part of the American republics, including the United States, did not come until the *Blitzkrieg* of April and May 1940. Delusions concerning the real nature of the war in Europe were shattered abruptly by the news that Belgium, the Netherlands, and Luxembourg had been invaded and that an all-out assault on France was in the making. The efficacy of a perfect neutrality, such as had been observed by the Low Countries in Europe, was now revealed for what it was worth. The American countries were faced with the question: What shall we do, now that neutrality is an invitation to disaster? Obviously the goal of preserving neutrality and providing insulation against the effects of European war had to be shifted to actual defense of this hemisphere.

The Havana Meeting of foreign ministers. The United States took the lead in efforts to strengthen the economic and political defenses of the Western Hemisphere. At the urging of the President, Congress appropriated billions of dollars to make not only the United States and its possessions but *the entire hemisphere* impregnable. On June 17, 1940, the State Department warned that "the United States would not acquiesce in any attempt to transfer geographic regions of the Western Hemisphere from one non-American power to another non-American power." This warning was immediately endorsed by a Joint Congressional Resolution (June 18, 1940), which stated that in the event of such a transfer or any attempt to transfer, the United States would, "in addition to other measures, immediately consult with the other American Republics to determine upon the step which should be taken to safeguard their common interests."[7]

A few days later (June 23) our Minister to Uruguay announced that because of German pressure on the Uruguayan government, the United States was prepared to cooperate with the other American governments in curbing all activities arising from non-American sources that might imperil the political and economic freedom of the Americas. The preceding day President Roosevelt had announced that a cartel plan might be considered for the "economic defense" of the hemisphere. Since this "feeler" encountered so much opposition, how-

[7] *Documents*, II, 89–90.

ever, both in the United States and in Latin America, the plan was abandoned.

It had been resolved at Panama that there should be another meeting of the foreign ministers at Havana on October 1, 1940, but because of the urgency of the crisis it was agreed to advance the date to July 21, Secretary Hull taking the initiative in this.[8] The agenda of the meeting reflected a shifting emphasis from the simple preservation of neutrality to problems of hemisphere defense. The United States faced a difficult position, for the Latin Americans were not unaware that the existing forces of this country were inadequate to make any real defense of the southern portion of the continent.

The overwhelming of the Low Countries and France by the German legions and the threatened invasion of Britain raised the question of the fate of European colonies in this hemisphere. The threatened change of sovereignty to Germany posed a grave threat to the security of the American continent. By diplomatic and legislative action the United States had already reaffirmed its adherence to the no-transfer principle of the Monroe Doctrine, and at Panama it had been resolved that the transfer of sovereignty of colonial possessions in America would occasion a consultation of the foreign ministers. Thus the ground had been prepared for a common inter-American policy. Accordingly, the Havana meeting adopted a declaration known as the Act of Havana Concerning the Provisional Administration of European Colonies or Possessions in the Americas. It provided that when colonies in the Western Hemisphere were in danger of changing hands, the American nations might establish a regime of provisional administration with the understanding that the possessions would ultimately either be made independent or restored to their previous status. This provisional administration was to be entrusted to an emergency committee composed of one representative from each of the American republics. Most important, the act provided that "should the need for emergency action be so urgent that action by the Committee cannot be awaited, any of the American republics shall have the right to act in the manner which its own defense or that of the Continent requires." Territories or possessions which were objects of dispute between European powers and one or more of the American republics were omitted from the provisions of the act to quiet the concern of Argentina over the Falkland Islands, of Chile over Antarctica, and of Guatemala over a portion of British Honduras.

[8] Hull, *Memoirs*, I, 791–792.

The formal Convention on the Provisional Administration of European Colonies and Possessions in the Americas, which contained the essential features of the Act of Havana, was signed by the delegates. The convention called for establishing an Inter-American Commission for Territorial Administration, to be composed of representatives of each state that ratified the pact. The commission was authorized to establish a provisional administration and determine which states should exercise it. The convention, which was to go into effect when ratified by two-thirds of the American republics, became effective with the fourteenth ratification on January 8, 1942. Argentina, a notorious nonratifier of inter-American treaties, adhered because of her claims to the Falkland Islands. But as things turned out, it never became necessary to invoke either this convention or the Act of Havana.

Since force was to be the principal sanction of the Act of Havana—and necessarily had to be applied by the only power that possessed it—this act can be construed as a blanket authorization to the United States to occupy any European possession as a hemisphere danger spot. In other words the Latin-American nations were formally endorsing the United States' implementation of the no-transfer principle of the Monroe Doctrine. It would be difficult to present more convincing evidence of Latin America's new confidence in the integrity of the United States. The "Colossus of the North" was now embraced as champion of the security of the Americas.

Although the Act of Havana stole the limelight, the Second Meeting of the Ministers of Foreign Affairs adopted several other resolutions which dealt with political subjects. Of these the one most significant was Resolution XV, the Declaration of Reciprocal Assistance and Cooperation for the Defense of the Nations of the Americas, which announced that "any attempt on the part of a non-American state against the integrity or inviolability of the territory, the sovereignty or political independence of an American state shall be considered as an act of aggression against the states which sign this declaration." In the event of aggression by a non-American state the signatories pledged to consult in order to agree upon measures it might be advisable to take. Also, "all the signatory nations, or two or more of them, according to circumstances, shall proceed to negotiate the necessary complementary agreements so as to organize cooperation for defense and the assistance that they shall lend to each other in the event of aggression."

Resolution XV, proclaiming the "all for one, one for all" principle, has been described as "the strongest possible warning short of a defensive alliance, that the republics would unite for the purpose of defending the Western Hemisphere against an attack by an overseas power."[9] It is to be noted that the resolution contemplated aggression by non-American powers only, and consequently was *the first inter-American security instrument aimed specifically at such powers.*

That the Declaration of Reciprocal Assistance and Cooperation "confirmed the abandonment by the United States of its pretentions to act as the sole guardian of the Monroe Doctrine"[10] is open to question. The United States had never objected to other countries' adopting the principles of the Monroe Doctrine as their own. But it did object to any kind of international agreement which would limit its freedom of choice in the implementation of its own policy. The Declaration of Reciprocal Assistance and Cooperation did not limit that choice, for, if cooperative action failed, the United States would still be free to undertake whatever action it deemed necessary. The real importance of the declaration rested in the fact that its broad principles afforded a basis for the numerous agreements that were soon to be negotiated for reciprocal assistance in the event of an overseas aggression.

The Havana meeting also realized that foreign subversive activities constituted a grave menace to the stability and security of the American republics and should be combatted. Several resolutions sought to defend the Americas against techniques practiced by the Nazis in Europe which had contributed largely to the fall of Czechoslovakia, Poland, Denmark, Norway, Belgium, the Netherlands, and France— techniques which they had already begun to use in the Western Hemisphere as a first stage of total war against the American republics. Thus, the Havana ministers urged the governments of the American republics to prevent political activity by foreign diplomatic or consular agents; proposed that precautionary measures be taken in granting passports, and that rigorous vigilance be observed over the entry of nationals of non-American states; recommended effective police supervision of the activities of foreign extracontinental groups; and encouraged the adoption of measures to prevent and suppress any activities directed, assisted, or abetted by foreign governments, groups, or individuals. If the peace of any American state should be menaced by foreign subversive activities, the American governments should immediately consult on request of the affected state.[11] These resolu-

[9] John P. Humphrey, *The Inter-American System: A Canadian View* (Toronto, 1942), 181.

[10] *Ibid.*, 183.

[11] Second Meeting of the Ministers of Foreign Affairs of the American Re-

tions laid the foundation for later establishing the Emergency Advisory Committee for Political Defense.

To strengthen the procedures for the settlement of inter-American disputes, the Havana meeting adopted Resolution XIV: Peaceful Solution of Conflicts in the Western Hemisphere. It was a simple recommendation to the Governing Board of the Pan American Union to organize a committee of five representatives from the American republics, charged with the duty of constant vigilance to ensure that the states in dispute settle their controversy as soon as possible. This Inter-American Peace Committee, composed of representatives from Argentina, Brazil, Cuba, Mexico, and the United States, was duly installed on July 31, 1941, and then was immediately forgotten for a number of years. We shall note later its rediscovery and its emergence into a position of prime importance in the inter-American peace structure.

The actions at Havana on economic matters were no less important than the political ones. A resolution on economic and financial cooperation was adopted which substantially approved an economic program presented to the conference by Mr. Hull. Its principal features were the expansion of the functions of the Inter-American Financial and Economic Advisory Committee, the creation of facilities for the orderly marketing of accumulated surpluses, the development of commodity agreements, and adherence to the liberal principles of international trade.

At the very moment Mr. Hull was presenting his economic program to the conference, President Roosevelt was requesting Congress to increase the capital and lending power of the Export-Import Bank by $500 million to assist in "the stabilizing of the economies and the orderly marketing of the products of the Western Hemisphere." The promise of American dollars in seemingly unlimited quantities to relieve the economic distress of the Latin-American nations contributed more than anything else toward winning their support of our defensive efforts. Here truly was a case of dollars speaking louder than

---

publics, *Final Act* (Havana, July 21–30, 1940). Res. II: Norms Concerning Diplomatic and Consular Functions; Res. III: Coordination of Police and Judicial Measures for the Defense of Society and Institutions of each American State; Res. V: Precautionary Measures with Reference to the Issuance of Passports; Res. VI: Activities Directed from Abroad against Domestic Institutions; Res. VII: Diffusion of Doctrines Tending to Place in Jeopardy the Common Inter-American Democratic Ideal or to Threaten the Security and Neutrality of the American Republics.

words. Earlier reluctance of the Latins to become the beneficiaries of "dollar diplomacy" had been overcome.

The American republics, it is encouraging to report, complemented the acts and the spirit of the Panama and Havana meetings by undertaking a number of politico-military and economic defense measures. Although most of these were bilateral, they were based nevertheless in the declared principles of hemispheric solidarity. Obviously the United States was usually a party to these agreements.

Pre-Pearl Harbor politico-military cooperation. The Declaration of Panama (neutrality zone) carried the germ of a program of military cooperation. By its terms a *security* zone was to be patrolled, thus serving warning that the neutrality of the American nations was not to be passive. President Roosevelt had already, on September 5, 1939, ordered that a neutrality patrol be organized to report or track any belligerent air, surface, or underwater forces approaching the coasts of the United States or the West Indies. Apparently one purpose of the order was to emphasize the readiness of the United States Navy to defend the Western Hemisphere.

Since most of the states, parties to the declaration, had no means by which they could undertake to patrol their coastal waters, they were willing to put their facilities at the disposal of the United States. For example, agreements were entered into with Costa Rica and the Dominican Republic which opened the harbors, bays, and territorial waters of those republics to United States patrol vessels. Conversations with Panama led to the joint patrolling of the waters adjacent to the Canal.[12] Other countries entered into similar understandings. Although Brazil did not immediately participate in the naval patrol of the South Atlantic, it did agree shortly to open two Brazilian ports to American naval vessels.

Thus the United States Navy, with no more than token assistance from the Latin-American states, conducted a neutrality patrol in the Gulf of Mexico, the Caribbean, and the Atlantic as far out to sea as the circumstances dictated. By mid-October 1939, the Navy was operating a continuous patrol about two hundred miles offshore from Newfoundland to the Guianas.[13] Effectiveness of the patrol was limited by the relatively meager naval strength available. Nevertheless the Atlantic patrol was continued in varying forms through 1940; in 1941, with

[12] *Documents*, II, 208–216, and III, 134. *New York Times*, Jan. 17, 1940.
[13] Samuel Eliot Morison, *History of United States Naval Operations in World War II: The Battle of the Atlantic, September 1939–May 1943* (14 vols., Boston, 1947) I, 13–16.

the acquisition of British bases, it was extended to the mid-Atlantic.[14]

But not all of the naval defense agreements were negotiated with the United States as one of the contracting parties. Argentina, Brazil, and Uruguay had met on several occasions to discuss measures for the defense of the Plata estuary. From these meetings emerged the agreement of September 1939 which called for tripartite patrol operations along the eastern seacoast of South America, and an agreement between Argentina and Uruguay in December 1940 which established procedures for the joint defense of the Plata area in the event of attack.[15] In February 1941, representatives of Chile and Peru met to discuss appropriate measures for their joint defense of the lower western coast of South America.[16]

As had been anticipated by the skeptics, it cannot be recorded that the neutrality zone (Declaration of Panama) was a success, for as the war progressed, the American states gradually came to realize that the presupposed—or at least hoped for—cooperation of the belligerents in refraining from acts of war within the security belt was not forthcoming. Toward the end of 1939 and in the spring of 1940 several incidents occurred within the security zone, notably the one involving the German "pocket" battleship the *Graf von Spee*. Events revealed the apparent declaration of armed neutrality to be little more than verbiage—pretentious and hopeful, but devoid of substance. Fortunately, however, this was not the full measure of inter-American defense cooperation in the immediate pre-Pearl Harbor days, although it must be recorded that virtually all of the measures were initiated by the United States under bilateral arrangements with individual Latin-American nations.

Maintaining American neutrality and at the same time forestalling military attacks on the Western Hemisphere was the objective of United States strategic planning at the highest level. The product of this thinking was a plan known as "Rainbow,"[17] which allotted to the United States Army and Navy the primary task of defending the Western Hemisphere against attack from the Old World. When

[14] Hull, *Memoirs*, I, 690–692.

[15] Council of Foreign Relations, *United States in World Affairs* (New York and London, 1941), 367.

[16] *New York Times*, Feb. 2, 1941.

[17] For an account of the inception and development of the Rainbow plans, see Maurice Malloff and Edwin M. Snell, *Strategic Planning for Coalition Warfare, 1941–1942, United States Army in World War II* (Washington, 1953), 5–8.

accomplishment of that task had been assured, American forces might then engage in offensive operations. In pursuance of the plan the United States immediately took steps, after September 1939, to secure permission for American forces to use military-base facilities in the other Western Hemisphere nations. Progress was slow because of the fear of raising cries of "Yankee imperialism." Nor did the Army make any progress in finding ways and means of supplying Latin America with munitions. All this was changed, of course, when the spell of the "phony war" was broken in the spring of 1940. The United States had to move fast to secure assurances of military collaboration, for it looked then as if plans for hemisphere defense might soon have to be translated into practice.[18]

After the fall of France President Roosevelt decided that the United States must concentrate on mobilizing its manpower and economic strength for hemisphere defense. He felt particular concern about the vulnerability of the Brazilian "bulge." On May 16, 1940, the President directed his military advisers to prepare plans for developing closer military relations with Latin America. Thus, a proposal for conversations with Brazil broadened into a plan for conversations with the other Latin-American nations. It was decided that these discussions should be conducted on the military level between United States and Latin-American officers. All of the countries approached except Bolivia, Paraguay, and Panama approved the United States' proposal.

In June 1940, teams of United States Army and Navy officers departed for the respective Latin-American countries to engage in conversations designed to bring about closer military collaboration; that is, they were to construct a framework for hemispheric military cooperation. They were instructed to inquire how extensively the Latins were willing to cooperate in hemispheric defense and what assistance they could offer to the actual operations by United States forces. In essence, the negotiations were to seek fulfillment of one item of Rainbow 4 which read:

With respect to the Latin American Republics, universal assurance should be sought that each State will make available to the armed forces of the United States immediately as the necessity arises in carrying out our opera-

[18] Much of the discussion dealing with United States–Latin-American military cooperation during 1939–41 is based on Stetson Conn and Bryan Fairchild, *United States Army and World War II: The Framework of Hemisphere Defense* (Department of the Army, Office of the Chief of Military History [Washington, 1960]). This volume is the first of two volumes to be published in the subseries *Defense of the Western Hemisphere.*

tions for Hemisphere Defense or in behalf of any State, *the use of its available sea, air, and land bases* [italics mine].[19]

All of the nations approached, except Argentina, expressed general willingness to cooperate. All, except Argentina, agreed that the danger to the Western Hemisphere was great and very real. Before the end of October 1940, the Staff Conversations resulted in agreements which were generally honored after 1940 by all of the countries concerned. Thus by December 1940 the War Department was able to assure the State Department that the Staff Agreements had established satisfactory bases for cooperation of the respective armed forces.

By the terms of the Staff Agreements, each Latin-American nation, in return for pledges of United States defense assistance, stood ready:

1. To call on the United States for armed assistance in event of actual or threatened attack.
2. To report to the United States any non-American attack.
3. To explain, via radio, to the rest of the world, and especially to Latin America, the reason for its request of United States assistance.
4. To permit the transit of United States forces going to the aid of a neighbor.
5. To develop and maintain an effective and complete interchange of intelligence relating to continental security.
6. To develop and maintain an adequate and efficient secret service in order to keep under surveillance aliens and subversive groups.
7. To eliminate anti-United States propaganda in times of emergency.

Argentina rebuffed the overtures of the United States for military cooperation because she felt that she must dominate the defenses of the Plata region. Accordingly, when United States Army and Navy officers conferred separately with Paraguay and Uruguay during 1940, and particularly when the United States showed an interest in constructing naval and air bases in Uruguay, Argentina objected. The proud and ambitious Argentines refused to enter into the Staff Conversations unless the United States was willing to make a political agreement delineating their respective roles in hemisphere defense, coupled with political and military advantages to Argentina for its cooperation. Argentine arrogance had scaled the heights.[20]

The United States–Latin-American Staff Agreements and the consequent deployment of our forces throughout the hemisphere had no pre-World War II precedent. The commitment by the United States

[19] *Ibid.*, 176–177.
[20] *Ibid.*, 175–183.

to defend the whole Western Hemisphere was assuredly a new departure in United States policy, though it may be regarded as a natural outgrowth of American policy and practice under the Monroe Doctrine. Whatever the United States did for the hemisphere defense it did obviously to safeguard its own national security and interests. The seriousness of the Nazi threat was responsible for the United States' asking *for the first time in its history* to enter into close military relations with most of the other Western Hemisphere nations. Generally, the Latin-American nations had by now become sufficiently aware of the Nazi menace to be ready to collaborate with their powerful neighbor.

In mid-1940 alternative questions faced the War Department concerning a basic policy toward Latin America: Do we wish to embark seriously upon a program of raising the military efficiency of Latin-American forces to the point where they would be of material aid as allies in hemisphere defense? or Shall we limit our efforts to obtaining the indirect results which would follow a better mutual undertaking?

The decision was in favor of the second alternative, and the War Department adopted the basic policy, consistently followed after our entry into the war, that we did not expect to be able to use Latin-American forces as effective allies in the war, and that we would concentrate on those countries of the most immediate military importance to us. Thus, the United States government, from September 1940 on, charted a new course of much greater aid to Great Britain. This disrupted plans for a perimeter defense of the hemisphere as plotted in Rainbow 4, for after the crisis of the summer of 1940 President Roosevelt did not feel any acute concern about the possibility of a major Nazi attack on the Western Hemisphere.[21]

Since the war plans of the United States assumed that its forces would be required to defend the Latin-American area against major enemy attacks, it naturally followed that access to existing military-base facilities should be assured. Up to this time the United States had discreetly avoided acquiring new base sites in Latin America in order to avoid obvious insinuations.

One of the most important contributions of the pre-Pearl Harbor period to military cooperation between the American states was the beginning of the bases program, which was to prove so effective in combatting the submarine menace during the war. The Dominican Republic's opening of her ports and coastal waters to United States

21 *Ibid.*, 82–83.

patrol vessels was followed, in September 1940, by an Export-Import Bank loan of $5 million to be used for the development of harbors and air bases for joint use with the United States.[22] Interest in bases was heightened by the United States announcement, in September 1940, of the destroyer-base agreement with Great Britain whereby we acquired a chain of defense bases in British possessions extending northward from British Guiana. The United States immediately assured its Latin-American partners that it would share the new facilities with them.[23]

When the United States acquired a number of bases in the Caribbean area it naturally brought the question of Latin-American bases into open discussion. Following the disclosure that the United States was making arrangements for certain unspecified base areas in South America, and that it had already secured "courtesy use" of a number of South American airports, Uruguayan Minister of Foreign Affairs Guani announced that his government was considering a program whereby the United States might secure the use of Uruguayan bases. In his statement Sr. Guani provided a formula for such action which seemed to quell nationalistic protests against granting the bases. He said:

The resulting program has in view naval or air bases constructed in our case by Uruguayan authorities, directed, maintained and controlled by and placed only at the disposal of an American country in a pressing continental military defense necessity upon conditions established by the Government of this republic. . . . In an equal manner, Uruguay could make use of similar bases to be in determined spaces in other American states always considered necessary for collective defense.[24]

This clarification, followed by similar statements by Acting Secretary of State Sumner Welles, successfully allayed Latin-American fears that base agreements would entail actual transfer of sovereignty over the areas concerned and reassured them that the sites would be returned to national control at the end of the emergency. Although base agreements eventually came to be much more liberal to the United States than the terms allowed by Uruguay, an introduction to the fundamental idea of common bases had been accomplished.

On November 10, 1940, Uruguay announced that it had reached an agreement with the United States along the lines suggested in Sr.

[22] *New York Times*, Sept. 2, 1940.
[23] U.S. Dept. of State, *Bulletin*, III (Oct. 1, 1940), 186.
[24] *Documents*, III, 136.

Guani's statements. Uruguay, with financial assistance from the United States, would construct one or more air bases and naval stations to be utilized for the defense of the continent. The bases would "remain under Uruguayan sovereignty and would be manned by Uruguay, assisted by technical help from the United States." Any bases so construed would be made available to other nations of the Americas when necessary for their participation in the common defense.[25]

The earlier reticence of the other Latin-American nations to co-operate in the base proposals advanced by the United States was replaced shortly by an increasing willingness to participate, and several projects were soon under discussion. In September 1940, Costa Rica offered the United States base sites on Cocos Island, approximately four hundred miles west of the Panama Canal, for the establishment of air and naval bases to guard the Canal's western approaches. On October 14, press announcements noted that Chile and Brazil had agreed to lease defense sites to the United States, and in February 1941 Nicaragua invited the United States to establish coastal bases in her territory.[26]

In January 1941, Mexico announced that she was developing the La Paz area of Lower California into an air-naval base designed to assist in the defense of the western coastline of the continent, and on April 2 a joint announcement by Mexico and the United States revealed that a reciprocal air-transit agreement, which opened the air lanes and bases of either country to the military aircraft of the other, had been signed.[27] This practical measure opened an overland air route to United States planes passing from national bases to sites in the Canal Zone. Final agreement was not reached with Chile on terms for the construction of bases, but the Brazilian and Nicaraguan projects were begun, and by November 1941 the chain of ferry bases constructed along the Brazilian northern coast was playing an important part in supplying aircraft to Britain for her campaign in North Africa.[28]

The United States Army and Navy had agreed, since the initial Rainbow planning of 1939, that the most vital region to be defended in South America was the "bulge," or Natal, region of Brazil. Closer

---

[25] *New York Times*, Nov. 10, 1940.

[26] *Ibid.*, Sept. 6, Oct. 14, 1940; Feb. 2, 1941.

[27] *Ibid.*, Jan. 8, 1941; U.S. Dept. of State, *Transit of Military Aircraft, Agreement Between the United States and Mexico,* Treaty Series, No. 97 (Washington, 1941).

[28] "Next Door to Dakar," *Newsweek*, XVIII (Sept. 1, 1941).

to Africa than to the nearest of the Antilles, it was regarded as the one point of the hemisphere vulnerable to large-scale attack or invasion. Accordingly the United States military believed that the Brazilian bulge must be defended, for it was the pivotal point for hemisphere defense. As a preliminary to contractual base arrangements between the United States and Brazil, in June 1940 President Roosevelt authorized the Army to make arrangements with Pan American Airways to construct a chain of airfields leading from the United States to eastern Brazil, which could be militarily employed in an emergency. Brazil, however, was chary about allowing United States military personnel to take over the sites. Thus, despite the top priority of Natal on the list of desired bases, it took nearly three years of delicate and involved political and military negotiations to secure Brazilian permission to station United States Army forces in the area.[29] In the meantime the partially-developed airfields in Brazil were virtually unprotected, and instead of providing an American air-defense route to the Brazilian bulge, they offered a ready-made approach route to the Caribbean to Nazi air invasion from Africa.

A final strategic area in which the United States was accorded sites prior to the coming of the war to the Americas was in Panama. When the United States–Panamanian treaty of March 2, 1936, was signed, most of the restrictive privileges which the United States had retained in Panama since 1904 had been eliminated. In view of the importance of securing complete protection for its vital canal, however, the following arrangement was included in Article X of the new treaty:

In case of an international conflagration or the existence of any threat of aggression which would endanger the security of the Republic of Panama or the neutrality or security of the Panama Canal, the Governments of the United States of America and the Republic of Panama will take measures of prevention and defense as they may consider necessary for the protection of their common interest.[30]

On the basis of this agreement the United States, early in 1939, had already begun conversations with Panama concerning the enlargement of defense facilities in the canal area and had thus achieved a temporary working agreement by 1940. This embodied the use of a number of areas outside the Canal Zone for the installation of air bases, searchlights, and aircraft detectors. Although the implementation of this

[29] For details of the negotiations, see William L. Langer and S. Everett Gleason, *The Undeclared War* (New York, 1953), 518 ff.
[30] U.S. Dept. of State, Treaty Series, No. 945, p. 20.

agreement was interrupted briefly just before President Arias was ousted in October 1941, construction begun in 1940 on the major project at Rio Hato was nearing completion by the beginning of hostilities with the Axis powers.

The military importance of the barren Galápagos Islands, approximately eleven hundred miles to the west of Ecuador and the South American Pacific "bulge," had long been recognized, although the United States seems to have neglected opportunities to acquire them.[31] When the subject of United States bases in the Galápagos Islands was broached shortly after the outbreak of the war in Europe, public opinion in Ecuador raised a considerable barrier to the conclusion of an agreement. By May 1941, however, an agreement with Ecuador which provided for joint patrol action in cooperation with the United States Navy and for sending planes and instructors to Ecuador for flight training indicated progress in eventually achieving an arrangement.[32]

Although the American nations had been led to evaluate their armed strength in connection with the proposed patrol of the security zone, the intensity of the war after May 1940 created even greater concern over their military deficiencies. Rearmament programs were stepped up, and orders were placed in foreign countries for critical needs such as ships, planes, and tanks. The United States responded readily by a program designed to increase the armed strength of the other republics. The Pittman-Bloom proposal of 1939, which would have made arms available for purchase by the Latin-American states, was revived in a joint resolution and received President Roosevelt's signature in June 1940.[33]

In the fall of 1940 the Export-Import Bank, following Congressional action extending both its capital and its purposes, granted credits to Latin-American nations for arms purchases. Actually, before the "processing" of the applications of the Latin-American states had been completed these countries were included within the lend-lease framework and almost all of their "credits" for arms were therefore provided out of lend-lease appropriations. A special provision of the Lend-Lease Act, approved on March 21, 1941, made it applicable to the Latin-American nations as "governments . . . whose defense he

[31] Samuel F. Bemis, *The Latin American Policy of the United States* (New York, 1943), 381–382.

[32] *New York Times*, May 14, 1941.

[33] *Documents*, II, 173. For a discussion of the supply of arms to Latin America, see Conn and Fairchild, 207–238.

[the President] deems vital to the defense of the United States."[34] The act permitted the release of any type of weapon and thus ended the legal limitations on arms supply to the Latin-American nations. On March 3, 1941, the Joint Advisory Board recommended a gross allocation of $400 million for Army and Navy material to be supplied to the Latin-American nations within a three-year period. The first lend-lease agreement with a Latin-American state was signed August 2, 1941, with the Dominican Republic, and by the end of that year contracts had been made with six others.[35]

Despite the foregoing generous arrangements, in practice it was almost impossible for the United States to supply munitions in any quantity during 1940 and 1941. The simple truth of the matter is that prior claims of the United States itself and of Great Britain left almost nothing for our Latin neighbors, who refused to believe that the United States did not have unlimited supplies. It was not until late 1942 and 1943 that the United States could supply Latin America with an adequate number of modern arms. By that time the danger of Nazi invasion of the hemisphere had ended.

In addition to the bases projects and the rearmament program, the United States promoted prewar bilateral military cooperation by the interchange of military personnel and information, which included sending United States Army missions to the Latin-American nations; invitations to chiefs of their armed forces to visit and inspect installations and operations in the United States; and the opening of United States academies and service schools to students from Latin America.

The military-missions program was not a World War II innovation. A Congressional act of May 1926, amended in 1935, authorized the United States government to detail Army personnel to American nations requesting it. The provisions of the original act were enlarged and made more attractive by amendments in 1938 and 1939, and the details of the system had been fully developed and put into operation before Pearl Harbor.[36]

The importance of the inauguration of the military-missions program was emphasized by a survey made by the Navy Department in 1939. It was well known that during the early decades of the present century, Latin-American states had drawn heavily on Germany and Italy for their army and navy advisers. The 1939 survey showed that

[34] Documents, III, 713.
[35] Ibid., V, 364. Other agreements were with Haiti, Paraguay, Brazil, Nicaragua, Cuba, and Bolivia.
[36] Documents, I, 59.

although the practice was on the wane, those two nations still furnished most of the missions.

Just prior to the outbreak of World War II, fifteen Latin-American states received a total of twenty-nine military missions. Eleven of these were supplied by Italy, nine by the United States, four by Germany, three by France, and one by Spain and Chile.[37] These figures show that the Axis nations, until as late as March 1939, supplied more than half the military missions received by the Latin-American states. From a beginning of nine missions sent to six nations in 1939,[38] the United States during the next two years was able to add seven other nations to the list of its missions and, equally as important, to secure the dismissal of the Axis missions.[39]

A second type of exchange program opened United States training facilities in advanced and specialized services to selected personnel from the Latin-American nations. A Congressional act of July 14, 1941, opened the regular course of instruction at the United States Naval Academy to a quota "not exceeding twenty persons at a time from the American Republics." On October 18, a similar act opened aviation facilities of the various United States Air Force schools to Latin-American cadets. In addition, the various service schools such as the Infantry School at Fort Benning (Georgia), the Artillery School at Fort Sill (Oklahoma), and other facilities were opened to Latin-American personnel for refresher and training courses.[40]

A second method for providing practical training opportunities to Latin-American personnel was utilized by the United States Navy. Complete naval units of the Latin-American states were allowed to participate in maneuvers with United States fleet units, and individuals or crew units from the Latin-American naval services were assigned to sea duty on United States ships.[41] The third method of exchange—the visits of Latin-American military ranking officers—was important both as a good-will gesture from the United States and as a means of demonstrating the armed might and techniques of this country. The visit of the chief of staff of the Brazilian Army in July

[37] *Ibid.*, I, 68–69; U.S. Congress, House of Rep., Comm. on Appropriations, Navy Dept., *Appropriations Bill for 1940*, 76th Cong., 1st Sess. (March 27, 1939), 58. In 1939, Chile supplied Venezuela with a military mission.

[38] These missions were to Argentina, Brazil, Colombia, Guatemala, Haiti, and Peru.—*Documents,* I, 68–69.

[39] Nations added were Bolivia, Chile, Costa Rica, Ecuador, El Salvador, Nicaragua, and Venezuela.

[40] *New York Times,* Jan. 25, Feb. 1, April 8, Aug. 10, and Aug. 12, 1941.

[41] *Ibid.,* Feb. 4, Feb. 18, Oct. 5, 1941.

1939 was followed by many such tours in the United States. Probably the most notable visit occurred in May 1941, when the chiefs of naval staffs of eleven Latin-American republics spent several weeks inspecting naval installations from coast to coast. In October and November of 1941, military observers from Latin America were on hand to watch the United States First Army maneuvers in the Carolinas.[42]

Although the period from 1939 to 1941 was marked by significant multilateral measures for the political and military defense of the hemisphere, most of the effective action was through bilateral agreements with the United States. This obviously was because it was the only country financially and materially able to offer any appreciable assistance in an extensive military defense program. This was also true with respect to economic defense, although multilateral measures in this area were not without significance.

Pre-Pearl Harbor economic defense. Since the outbreak of the war in September 1939 was expected to occasion painful economic dislocation in all the American republics, this was an important topic on the program of the Panama meeting of the foreign ministers. The resolution which created the Inter-American Financial and Economic Advisory Committee declared that "today it is more desirable and necessary than ever to establish a close and sincere cooperation between the American Republics in order that they may protect their economic and financial structure, maintain their fiscal equilibrium, safeguard the stability of their currencies, promote and expand their industries, intensify their agriculture and develop their commerce."[43] The committee, which held its first meeting in Washington on November 15, 1939, gave attention to such problems as shipping, financing of surpluses, inter-American commodity agreements, and the promotion of industrial and agricultural enterprises. It acted as a central planning and executive agency to strengthen the inter-American economic front. The Havana meeting of 1940 extended and strengthened the functions of the committee.

One of the first projects taken up by the Financial and Economic Advisory Committee was that of an inter-American bank. A convention was signed by several of the countries, but it never received the requisite number of ratifications to become operative. The bank, generally speaking, was intended "to promote the fullest exploitation of

[42] U.S. Dept. of State, *Bulletin*, I (July 15, 1939), 47; *New York Times*, Nov. 3, 1941.
[43] Reunión de Consulta entre los Ministros de Relaciones Exteriores de las Republicas Americanas, *Acta Final* (Panama, 1939), 18.

the natural resources of the Americas, to intensify economic and financial relations among the American Republics, and to mobilize for the solution of economic problems the best thought and experience in the Americas."[44]

More successful was the committee's establishment, in June 1940, of the Inter-American Development Commission, to facilitate "the formation and financing, with mixed United States and Latin American capital, of such enterprises as will undertake the development of new lines of Latin American production for which a new or complementary market can be found in the United States or in other republics of the Western Hemisphere." According to Carlos Dávila, the Chilean statesman who was author of the motion which brought the commission into existence, the ultimate goal of the plan was to make the economies of the United States and Latin America complementary, and if need be, self-sufficient.[45] Specifically it was the purpose of the commission— a five-member body under the chairmanship of Coordinator of Inter-American Affairs, Nelson Rockefeller—to aid in "the establishment of enterprises for the exploration and exploitation of the mineral resources of Latin America, the cultivation and marketing of agricultural and forest products, and the establishment and development of industrial plants."[46]

In each of the American republics, affiliated National Development (*fomento*) Commissions were established, made up of citizens of the respective countries, representing finance, industry, agriculture, mining, transportation, and government. Thus private enterprise, represented by the national commissions and with the assistance of the national governments, was brought into the field of direct international collaboration. This was an innovation in practical international cooperation.[47]

The outbreak of the war and the closing of the European market created a serious situation for the Latin-American coffee industry. To meet this problem the Inter-American Financial and Economic Advisory Committee drafted a coffee-marketing agreement which was

[44] Pan American Union, *The Americas and the War* (Washington, 1942), 41.
[45] Carlos Dávila, *We of the Americas* (Chicago, 1949), 33.
[46] *The Americas and the War*, 42.
[47] Julian G. Zier, "First Conference of the Commissions of Inter-American Development," Pan American Union, *Bulletin*, LXXVIII (July 1944), 382–385; William Yale, "Certain New Instrumentalities for Economic Development in the South American Republics," U.S. Dept. of State, *Bulletin*, VI (Nov. 12, 1944), 571–576.

accepted by the United States and the coffee-producing countries of the continent. By the terms of the Inter-American Coffee Agreement, signed at Washington on November 28, 1940, the coffee market of the United States was divided and annual quotas were assigned to the fourteen producing American republics: Brazil, Colombia, Costa Rica, Cuba, the Dominican Republic, Ecuador, El Salvador, Guatemala, Haiti, Honduras, Mexico, Nicaragua, Peru, and Venezuela. The Inter-American Coffee Board was set up to administer the agreement, whose general purpose was to stabilize the coffee market in a manner equitable both to producers and consumers.[48]

The Inter-American Financial and Economic Advisory Committee also undertook the study of other commodities of which the American republics were important producers, notably cacao and cotton. Here the problem was more difficult to solve since their production of cacao and cotton, unlike coffee, did not dominate the situation. Since the interests of other producing areas had to be taken into consideration, protracted negotiations delayed the formulation of definite agreements.

The problem of shipping, which assumed serious proportions after the outbreak of hostilities, was also given consideration by the committee. As many of the foreign flagships, which normally carried more than half the ocean-borne trade of the Americas, were immobilized in their ports to avoid capture, the committee on April 26, 1941, recommended to the governments of the American republics that the foreign flagships in American ports be taken over by the respective American governments; that just and adequate compensation for such utilization be made; and that they declare their full right to the free navigation of these vessels under their own national flags.[49] When the British government agreed to respect the transfer of such vessels to the flags of the American republics, a plan proposed by the committee (August 28, 1941) for effecting the transfer and maintaining close cooperation among the maritime authorities of the respective American governments was put into effect. Later, the committee organized the Inter-American Maritime Technical Commission to assist in the more efficient use of all merchant vessels in the Latin-American service.[50] Although considerable success attended the efforts to put into use Axis ships immobilized in American ports, the efforts to coordinate the operations of the various merchant marines were less effective. The

[48] *Inter-American Financial and Economic Advisory Committee, Handbook of Its Organization and Activities, 1939–1943* (Washington, 1944), 50–58, 94–98.
[49] *Ibid.*, 58–59.   [50] *The Americas and the War*, 38–39.

Financial and Economic Advisory Committee also organized the Inter-American Maritime Conference, which met in Washington the latter part of 1940. The conference adopted a number of recommendations which served as guides to the committee in its subsequent consideration of shipping problems.[51]

Thus, during the pre-Pearl Harbor period, three important agencies were established on recommendation of the Inter-American Financial and Economic Advisory Committee and with its cooperation: the Inter-American Development Commission, the Inter-American Coffee Board, and the Inter-American Maritime Technical Commission. The first two agencies were autonomous and operated independently of the committee; the third was a dependency of the committee. All of them carried on work of positive utility to the economic and military defense of the hemisphere.

United States economic program. Supplementing these multilateral measures of economic defense was the far-reaching hemisphere economic program of cooperation and interdependence initiated by the United States. There is little doubt that these bilateral arrangements and activities were integral and essential features of the hemisphere defense structure.

On June 15, 1940, President Roosevelt addressed a note to his Secretaries of State, Commerce, Treasury, and Agriculture expressing his desire "to get in specific form from the several departments that are concerned with our economic relations with Latin America" their combined judgment concerning the action which this government should take. He enclosed a copy of a memorandum entitled "Hemispheric Economic Policy," prepared by Nelson A. Rockefeller. This memorandum was predicated on the necessity for the United States to protect its international position through the use of economic measures which would be "competitively effective against totalitarian techniques." At the same time it was pointed out that the security of the nation and its economic position in the hemisphere should be established in a frame of hemisphere economic cooperation.[52]

The program of the United States was foreshadowed by an act of Congress, in September 1940, amending the Export-Import Bank Act, to increase lending power of the Export-Import Bank from $200 million to $700 million, the increase being earmarked to assist in the development of the resources, the stabilization of the economies, and

[51] *Ibid.,* 39; U.S. Dept. of State, *Bulletin,* VIII (March 27, 1943), 262.

[52] U.S. Office of Inter-American Affairs, *History of the Office of the Coordinator of Inter-American Affairs* (Washington, 1947), 279–280.

the orderly marketing of the products of the countries of the Western Hemisphere.[53] A further amendment to this act provided that the Bank was to share responsibility for financing economic projects in Latin America with the subsidiaries of the Reconstruction Finance Corporation, i.e., the Metals Reserve Company, the Defense Plant Corporation, the Rubber Reserve Company, and the Defense Supplies Corporation. These subsidiary corporations had been organized in June 1940 to procure and finance the production of strategic materials in Latin America.

As of December 1941, the Exim Bank had loans or active undisbursed commitments in Latin America amounting to more than $300 million.[54] To provide our neighbors with dollar exchange needed for imports, the Bank was prepared to extend credits on a considerable scale. On the whole, however, the Latins did not find it necessary to draw extensively on credits granted by the Bank, for the rapid expansion of their exports to the United States made financial assistance for supplying dollar exchange much less necessary than had originally been expected.

Because of the defense-program needs of the United States, the Latin-American republics had no difficulty in disposing of most of their raw materials in the United States market. Indeed its needs for certain strategic materials were so great that we entered into agreements both to facilitate increased production and to purchase the entire exportable surplus, i.e., "preclusive contracts." By the end of 1941, the Metals Reserve Company had acquired a virtual monopoly over the strategic metal exports of Latin America.[55]

By Executive Order on August 16, 1940, a new agency was created to deal with inter-American affairs—the Office of the Coordinator of Inter-American Affairs, with Nelson Rockefeller named as the "Co-

[53] Public Law No. 792, 76th Cong., 2d Sess., approved Sept. 26, 1940.

[54] "Early in December, 1941, the president of the Bank revealed that its books showed disbursements and active commitments to Latin America aggregating $386,000,000, of which about $90,000,000 had been repaid and none was in default. In part, however, these loans antedated the outbreak of the European war."—John C. de Wilde, "Wartime Economic Cooperation in the Americas," Foreign Policy Association, *Report,* XVII (Feb. 15, 1942), 287.

[55] In 1940 the Metals Reserve Company negotiated a five-year contract with Bolivian tin producers, and in 1941, a contract for the entire tungsten output of Bolivia. A two-year contract with Brazil in 1941 provided for the purchase of her exportable surplus of ten important materials. A contract was negotiated with Argentina for her entire export of tungsten, and with Chile for additional copper.—United States Military Academy, *Raw Materials in War and Peace* (West Point, 1947), 94–95.

ordinator." The functions of this agency were primarily designed to meet an emergency need, but throughout its entire existence the Co-ordinator and his associates were as much interested in long-range projects looking toward improvement of conditions in the hemisphere as they were in those connected with the war effort. This was in line with Administration policy, for in June 1941 Assistant Secretary of State Adolf Berle frankly declared that the security of the United States had become inseparable from "the general safety, security, and *well being* of the Western Hemisphere." The United States stood ready, therefore, to assist the development of those countries. Said Mr. Berle, "This is the finance of cooperation and not the finance of money-lending."[56] Generally speaking, the pre-Pearl Harbor economic policies of the United States, whether based in self-interest or considerations of continental community, aided materially in keeping the economies of our hemisphere associates on an even keel when entering upon the stormy seas of belligerency.

Conclusion. In the interval between the First Meeting of American foreign ministers in 1939 and the Second in 1940, there was a complete reorientation and reversal of fundamental attitudes and policy by the republics. At the outset, thoroughly committed as were all the countries to the policy of neutrality, there seemed to be no occasion requiring the strengthening of the security structure. The Panama meeting of 1939, however, is to be credited with the formulation of policies and the setting up of programs, in at least two areas, which were to prove of value to the war effort: first, economic cooperation, including the establishment of the Inter-American Financial and Economic Advisory Committee; and second, the recommendation to the respective governments of political defense against "foreign doctrines that endanger the common inter-American democratic ideal."

The *Blitz* which overwhelmed France and the Low Countries served the useful purpose of arousing the American nations, including the United States, from their lethargic and complacent attitude. It was clear that old-fashioned neutrality was outmoded and that a more positive policy of hemispheric defense was needed. This changed approach was born of an awakening, albeit somewhat delayed, to the frightening reality of the Nazi threat to American security.

Many of the acts of the Havana meeting of 1940 reflected this awakened consciousness. For example, there was agreement on a com-

---

[56] Assistant Secretary of State Adolf Berle, Jr., "The Economic Interests of the United States in Inter-American Relations," U.S. Dept. of State, *Bulletin,* IV (June 28, 1941), 756, 761.

mon inter-American policy to deal with the contingency of a transfer of sovereignty of colonial possessions in America. There was the declaration that aggression against one American republic should be considered as aggression against all, and consequently the American republics should enter into agreement to ensure cooperation in defense. Also, the American governments expressed determination to take all necessary measures to combat fifth-column activities. In economic matters as well, the actions calling for cooperation reflected the necessity of mobilizing for economic defense.

It was through the negotiation of bilateral engagements between the United States and individual Latin-American countries that the most significant progress was made in the strengthening of hemisphere defense. These agreements covered a vast complex of subjects: bases; reciprocal air-transit; army missions; interchange of military personnel and information; procurement of strategic materials; and lend-lease. To the credit of American solidarity, great progress was made, before Pearl Harbor, in consolidating the defenses of the Americas. At least, a working basis was established for wartime security cooperation. Thus, when war came to the Americas the respective states were able to glide smoothly and naturally into their predetermined roles as cobelligerents.

VIII The War Comes to the Americas
(1941–1945)

We have met to perform our commitments of honor to sign and seal American solidarity. We have assembled to plan the common defense of our Hemisphere, to prepare an America that shall be ever stronger, more united, more invulnerable.

EZÉQUIEL PADILLA, 1942

WORLD WAR II posed a challenge to the validity of the numerous declarations and pledges of continental solidarity to which the American nations had subscribed. In their numerous conferences and meetings they had been long on pious pronouncements of adherence to common principles, but rather short on agreed procedures for defending those principles. Also, their formal security pledges did not go beyond the agreement to consult in the event of overseas aggression on any one of their membership. It remained to be seen, therefore, first, what was the degree of attachment of the American nations to the Havana "Declaration of Reciprocal Assistance and Cooperation," and second, how effective a common defense, beginning from scratch, could be erected by *ad hoc* procedures.

Pearl Harbor and the Rio Meeting. The immediate positive reaction of the American states to Japanese aggression on the United States was encouraging evidence that the political, military, and economic agreements that the nations of the hemisphere had entered into prior to and following the outbreak of war in Europe were not to be taken lightly. If the purpose of the Rome-Berlin-Tokyo Axis had been to assure the solidarity of most of Latin America with the United States, it could hardly have found a better way than by bringing war to the United States.

Profoundly shocked by the perfidy of the Japanese attack, and awakened to the terrible reality of the war and their own peril, most Latin Americans now saw the crisis in full light. This was particularly true of the Caribbean nations, for by December 12, all nine of these states (Costa Rica, Cuba, Dominican Republic, Guatemala, Haiti, Honduras, Nicaragua, Panama, and El Salvador) had declared war on Japan, Germany, and Italy. By December 31, Mexico, Colombia, and Venezuela had severed diplomatic relations with the Axis. Of the remaining Latin-American countries some affirmed their solidarity with the United States, others adopted a policy of benevolent neutrality toward the United States. These reactions to aggression against the United States, while emphasizing the considerable solidarity existent among the fellow American nations, nevertheless pointed up the need for common action. The entire complex of agreements on hemispheric solidarity in the face of outside aggression was now put to test.

Within two days after the attack on Pearl Harbor the Chilean government, invoking the Havana Declaration of Reciprocal Assistance and Cooperation that aggression against one American state shall be considered aggression against all, proposed the calling of a meeting of foreign ministers[1] "in order to consider the situation that has arisen and to adopt suitable measures required by the solidarity of our nations and the defense of the Hemisphere." The Pan American Union called the meeting, and the Ministers of Foreign Affairs of the American Republics met in the Brazilian capital January 15–28, 1942. The agenda fell under two headings: measures for the preservation of the sovereignty and territorial integrity of the American republics; and means to strengthen their economic solidarity.

The great issue of the Rio meeting was whether the American states should categorically resolve to sever forthwith their diplomatic relations with the Axis. This course was advocated by the United States and by the other nations that had already taken such action. Undersecretary of State Sumner Welles, head of the United States delegation, urged that "those republics engaged in war shall not be dealt a deadly thrust by the agents of the Axis ensconced upon the soil and enjoying the hospitality of others of the American republics."[2] Probably the most notable speech of the conference was that of Mexican Minister Ezéquiel Padilla, who supported with fiery eloquence a strong formula

[1] This was in response to prompting by the United States, for on December 9, 1941, the United States sent notes to the American republics expressing the desire to convene a meeting of the foreign ministers as soon as possible. —Cordell Hull, *The Memoirs of Cordell Hull* (2 vols., New York, 1949), II, 1143; Pan American Union, *Bulletin,* LXXVI (Jan. 1942), 39–40.

[2] U.S. Dept. of State, *Bulletin* (Jan. 17, 1942), 55–65.

for immediate rupture with the Axis by all the American nations still neutral.

It was evident from the outset that most of the delegations were willing to agree to a resolution categorically calling for a break in diplomatic relations with the Axis powers. The two that were not ready for a break were Argentina and Chile, whose delegations held out for a mild formula which would not commit their governments to an immediate rupture.

Of the two recalcitrants, the attitude of the Chileans was the more understandable, for they were really concerned with the problem of defending their long and vulnerable coastline against Japanese attack if they broke off relations. Before they would consent to make this move they demanded aid from the United States in strengthening their defenses.[3] On January 27, 1942, the United States was informed that Chile would not dare break relations with the Axis unless promised immediately thirty-six combat airplanes and sixty-three anti-aircraft guns. In fairness to Chile it is well to recall that in January 1942 the news from across the Pacific reported a discouraging succession of Japanese victories after the silencing of the United States fleet. In contrast to Chilean timidity, however, other Latin-American states, with equally vulnerable coastlines, did not hesitate to align themselves with the United States, even though her military fortunes were at low ebb. These certainly were not fair-weather friends. Their response was a remarkable demonstration of sincere attachment to the principle of continental solidarity.

The Argentine position was typically intransigent, for the refusal of the Buenos Aires government to sanction a resolution *requiring* a severance of diplomatic relations with the Axis was quite in character. From the very beginning of Pan Americanism (Washington, 1889–90) the republic of the pampas was seldom more than a nominal or lukewarm member of the inter-American association. The erection of the security structure had been marked at almost every step by Argentine indifference or outright opposition. On several occasions, in order to secure the Argentine assent required for obligatory unanimity, it had been necessary to water down and debilitate originally strong and potentially effective proposals. Moreover, it is a matter of record that of the several inter-American security treaties, only one—the

---

[3] David H. Popper, "The Rio de Janeiro Conference of 1942," Foreign Policy Association, *Report*, XVIII (April 15, 1942), 29.

Saavedra Lamas treaty—had been ratified by the Argentine government.

Of the numerous and complex factors which influenced Argentine attitude regarding inter-American cooperation, unquestionably a prominent one was jealousy and resentment of United States leadership. The Argentine government was eager in 1942 (as in the preceding years) to establish a bloc of Latin-American countries to serve as a counterweight to the influence of the United States. But to the traditional motivation of Argentine behavior must now be added a new factor: the pro-Nazi orientation of the Castillo government. Documentary evidence discovered in German archives thoroughly warranted the view of the U.S. Department of State that "the Castillo Government . . . pursued a policy of positive aid to the enemy."[4]

Since Argentina and Chile were opposed to a strong resolution calling for an immediate break in diplomatic relations with the Axis powers, an occasion was presented to Brazilian Foreign Minister Oswaldo Aranha to reconcile the conflicting points of view. Accordingly, on January 23, a watered-down resolution which merely "recommended" a break was unanimously approved. Thus, a strong resolution was sacrificed for the sake of formal unanimity. It should not be overlooked, however, that much of the strength of the inter-American movement depended upon the solidarity and the unity of action of *all* its component parts. Had the original strong resolution been approved by the nineteen countries which favored a rupture of relations, the contention might well have been made that Argentina and Chile had been excluded by the arbitrary action of the conference, whereas as a matter of fact the responsibility to act or not to act rested squarely upon them.

Although the resolution on the rupture of relations with the Axis commanded the spotlight, the Rio meeting was not without its significant achievements. In the category of "defense measures" there was created the Inter-American Defense Board, composed of military technicians to study and recommend the measures necessary for the defense of the hemisphere. The board, which was to sit in Washington, held its first meeting on March 30, 1942.

To improve defense against espionage, sabotage, and subversive propaganda by Axis agents, the Emergency Advisory Committee for Political Defense, composed of seven members, was established to study and coordinate measures against subversive activities. This com-

---

[4] U.S. Dept. of State, *Consultation Among the American Republics with Respect to the Argentine Situation*, Publication 2473 (Washington, 1946), 1, cited hereinafter as *Blue Book*.

mittee, designed to combat the activities of non-American elements that were "harmful to American security," took its permanent seat in Montevideo, under the chairmanship of Uruguayan Foreign Minister Alberto Guani.

As a corollary to the resolution on the severance of diplomatic relations, the Rio meeting recommended general rules for the severance of commercial and financial relations with the Axis. Full execution of these recommendations was expected to produce the complete economic isolation of the Axis from the Americas, and the paralysis of enemy activity in the New World.

Other actions of the Rio meeting included: (1) settlement of the long-standing and dangerous boundary dispute between Peru and Ecuador through the mediation of Argentina, Brazil, Chile, and the United States;[5] (2) conversion of the Inter-American Neutrality Committee into the Inter-American Juridical Committee, charged with the study of juridical problems relating to the war and the postwar settlement; (3) a resolution that an American state involved in war with a non-American state should not be considered a belligerent; and (4) proclaiming the Good Neighbor policy a norm of international law of the Americas. Such *pro forma* expressions of sentiment are not to be discounted, for they constituted the best basis for a durable Pan Americanism. The identification of the cooperative movement with the concepts of justice, equity, and humanitarianism has always been of the greatest value in sustaining hemispheric solidarity. The strength of the abstract has often been greater than that of the concrete.

Implementing the Rio agreements. By the end of the Rio de Janeiro Third Meeting of Consultation of Foreign Ministers, in January of 1942, ten states (United States, Costa Rica, Cuba, Dominican Republic, El Salvador, Guatemala, Haiti, Honduras, Nicaragua, and Panama) had declared war with Japan, Germany, and Italy, and all the remaining states except Argentina and Chile had severed relations with them. Mexico and Brazil followed with declarations of war in May and August 1942, respectively, and Bolivia and Colombia did so in 1943. Chile severed relations with the Axis powers in 1943, Argentina fol-

[5] This dispute had led to an undeclared war between the two countries in 1941. On January 14, Ecuador threatened to withdraw from the Rio de Janeiro conference unless it undertook to settle the boundary dispute. The protocol signed by Ecuador and Peru at Rio de Janeiro on January 29, 1942, was substantially a compromise settlement of conflicting claims to a large area lying partly on the Pacific Coast but mainly on the upper Amazon. The settlement, which gave Peru the larger part of the disputed area, provoked considerable discontent in Ecuador.—"Settlement of the Ecuador-Peru Boundary Dispute," Pan American Union, *Bulletin,* LXXVI (May 1942), 241–244.

lowed in 1944, and in 1945 the record was made unanimous with declarations of war by all the remaining states.[6]

The position of Argentina and Chile in not acting immediately on recommendations which they themselves had accepted at Rio was anomalous, to say the least. Acting President Ramón Castillo promptly declared that Argentina had no intention of severing relations with Germany and Italy. In fact, he informed the Germans that, rather than sever relations, he was determined, if necessary, "eventually to come out openly on the side of the Axis Powers."[7]

The intransigence of the Argentine and Chilean governments caused grave concern in Washington, for the United States wished to deny the Axis any diplomatic foothold in the hemisphere. Cordell Hull said that as long as he was in the Department he made it a point not to urge any American republic to declare war upon the Axis. The Department repeatedly stated, however, that all the republics should sever relations with them.[8]

On October 8, 1942, Acting Secretary of State Sumner Wells declared in a speech in Boston that Axis agents were still operating in Argentina and Chile and that as a result of their reports United States ships were being sunk by enemy submarines. Although this speech stirred up anti-United States sentiment in both Argentina and Chile, it was nevertheless true that the diplomatic immunity enjoyed in these two countries afforded the totalitarian allies means for espionage, sabotage, and subversion which they did not neglect. Eventually their Santiago embassies had to be closed when Chile broke off relations on January 29, 1943, exactly one year after the Rio meeting. According to Laurence Duggan, a former high official in the U.S. State Department, it was their democratic political institutions that enabled the people of Chile to push a reluctant government into action. The contrary was true of Argentina under the Castillo government, which felt no affinity for political democracy within either the country or the continent.[9]

Another year elapsed before Argentina finally severed diplomatic relations. The overthrow of Castillo by a military *coup d'état* in June 1943 meant no change in the pro-Nazi orientation of the Argentine rulers. The new Ramírez regime assured the Nazis of "their purpose not to break relations and of their need for military equipment to reinforce them in this position." Quoting further from the famous State

[6] Pan American Union, *Bulletin*, LXXIX (Sept. 1945), 528.
[7] *Blue Book*, 5.   [8] Hull, *Memoirs*, II, 1423.
[9] Laurence Duggan, *The Americas* (New York, 1949), 91.

Department *Blue Book* (p. 12), "Ramírez buttressed these requests by expressing the intention of his government to postpone any possible rupture at least until the fall, while seeking in the meantime to strengthen Argentina's position by drawing neighboring countries into a neutral bloc." That the Ramírez regime did not obtain military equipment from Germany was due not to any weakening of its desire to do so, but to the fortunes of war, for the Allied blockade prevented Germany from furnishing assistance.

Succumbing to pressure by the United States,[10] President Ramírez, on January 26, 1944, broke relations with the Axis, but he was either unwilling or unable to carry out enforcement measures necessary to make the nominal break real. Within a month Ramírez was ousted by a *coup* of the more rabid pro-Nazi elements in the Army, apparently because he had failed to consult them before rupturing diplomatic relations with the Axis, and because they feared he might follow up that action with a declaration of war. The succession of General Edelmiro Farrell to the presidency of Argentina and Juan Perón to the vice-presidency rendered the break meaningless, for although diplomatic relations with the Axis were not formally restored, the members of the Axis missions not only were not disturbed but were allowed ample opportunity to carry on their accustomed activities so injurious to inter-American solidarity and dangerous to the peace and security of Argentina's neighbors in South America. It was because of this fact that most of the American governments (except Chile, Paraguay, and Bolivia) denied recognition to General Farrell, although they did not recall their chiefs of mission from Buenos Aires.

It was truly anomalous that the pro-Nazi sentiment of the Argentine regime became stronger even while there was clear evidence of approaching Axis defeat. On June 10, 1944, immediately following the Allied invasion of Normandy, Colonel Juan Perón (the emerging strong man of the regime) declared that for Argentina there would be no difference between an Allied victory and an Axis victory, for in either event Argentina's future rested in military might and a totalitarian government.[11]

The problem now for the United States was not solely the facilities Argentina was affording Axis espionage and subversion, but also what to do about a regime that openly adhered to the totalitarian philosophy of government. Because the words and actions of the Argentine leaders challenged and contradicted most of the principles that the inter-

10 *Blue Book*, 6.   11 Washington *Post*, June 30, 1944.

American system stood for, it was no longer possible to delay an emphatic demonstration of solidarity. Accordingly the bloc of nonrecognizing powers, plus Great Britain, recalled their chiefs of mission "for consultation." Unhappily, beyond diplomatic quarantine, the members of the inter-American system soon realized the impossibility of imposing effective sanctions on their willful partner. The only resort was "moral" sanction, i.e., denouncing Argentina for violation of solemn inter-American obligations, for deserting the Allied cause, and for assisting the enemies of the sister American states. In this campaign President Roosevelt and Secretary Hull played leading roles. "The whole moral foundation and splendid structure of hemispheric cooperation had been undermined and seriously impaired by Argentina's desertion," said Mr. Hull.[12] In the end the resistance of the Argentine leaders was weakened by the military collapse of the Axis nations.

Popular appraisement of inter-American cooperation during World War II was gravely distorted because of Argentine intransigence. The defection of the republic of the Plata, the leading nation of Latin America, cast a shadow over the manifold demonstrations of solidarity on the part of the other republics. This was true not only on the diplomatic and political fronts, as has been demonstrated, but also on the military and economic fronts, as will now be noted.

Defensive military cooperation. During the excitement of the outbreak of war in the Western Hemisphere, the Latin-American states made certain emergency moves of military cooperation. A few examples will give a general picture of their nature. El Salvador, on December 8, 1941, authorized its president to permit the forces of any American nation to occupy part of its national territory or territorial waters while contributing to the defense of the continent, and on December 13, Venezuela announced that it was opening its ports without restriction to warships of the United States and of all other American nations at war. Uruguay also extended to the public ships of the American belligerents, and their noncontinental allies as well, the free use of her ports for purposes of defense.[13]

Long-range programs designed to meet the dangers and problems posed by the outbreak of the war in Europe had been the subjects of early planning. It is significant that the American states frequently referred to the Havana resolution of reciprocal assistance as provid-

---

[12] Hull, *Memoirs*, II, 1401.

[13] Pan American Union, *Bulletin*, LXXVI (April, June, Aug., 1942), 231. 331, 344. 352, 464.

ing legal authorization of their actions. For example, when an a[?] formalizing Brazilian-Cuban cooperation in the war was sign[...] August 1942, its relation to the Havana resolution was specifically stated.[14]

Much of the early defense planning was oriented to two possible sources of danger to the continent: (1) land invasion, either from Dakar in Africa against the Brazilian "bulge" or the Caribbean Islands, or from the west against the United States–Mexican coast or Panama, and (2) attacks by Axis submarines on shipping in the Atlantic, Gulf, Caribbean, and Pacific shipping lanes.

The material strength of the United States naturally assured its central position in defense planning. Consequently the system which evolved took chiefly the form of bilateral arrangements with this country, based on the pooling of existing resources in a manner most beneficial to the defense of the continent. From the beginning it had been United States policy to grant lend-lease aid to Latin America only in the form of military equipment and services, and these in restricted quantities for the purpose of hemisphere defense. The sole departures from this policy occurred in connection with the two active belligerents, Mexico and Brazil. Early in 1943, President Roosevelt authorized assistance to Brazil for training and equipping ground and air units for overseas services, and later this type of aid was given to Mexico for an aviation squadron. The wholehearted military cooperation of Brazil and Mexico qualified these two countries for special consideration in lend-lease aid. The allocations to these two countries accounted for more than 70 per cent of the $125 million worth of military equipment that the United States assigned to Latin America before June 1943.

Later, when by the spring of 1943 the war production of the United States had reached a level that permitted regular arms deliveries to Latin America, the strategic outlook had so changed that it was questionable whether the supply to those nations should be continued as originally planned. In fact, it became United States policy in 1944 to *reduce* lend-lease aid to Latin America to the greatest possible extent, except to those nations contributing directly to the war effort. A final tabulation of all lend-lease aid to Latin-American countries amounted to $500 million, and by 1948 they had repaid $70 million.[15]

Comprehensive pacts which entailed all phases of military cooper-

[14] *New York Times,* Aug. 28, 1942, p. 4.
[15] *Report to Congress on Lend-Lease Operations,* House Doc. No. 568, 80th Cong., 2d Sess. (Washington, 1941–51), 4–7.

ation, from joint operations by armed forces to the use of base sites, were concluded between the United States and the nations whose locations made them strategically important—Mexico, Cuba, Panama, and Brazil. Numerous other agreements calling for a less comprehensive degree of cooperation were signed with nations whose location served to bolster and reinforce the major defense areas. Agreements of this type, which resulted in the opening of base sites for use by the United States, were made with Peru, Ecuador, Colombia, Venezuela, and the Central American and Caribbean states. Ultimately the United States had bases in sixteen Latin-American states.

A pattern for the major bilateral defense pacts existed in the Joint United States–Canadian Defense Commission, which had been organized in 1940. It was first used as a model for the United States–Mexican defense pact. On January 12, 1942, the two governments announced that they had "found it expedient to establish a mixed defense commission to study the problems relating to the defense of the two countries and to propose to the respective governments the measures which should be adopted."[16] The commission, officially designated the Joint Mexican–United States Defense Commission, was composed of an Army and a Navy officer of high rank from each nation, with headquarters in Washington.[17] Under the specific provisions of United States–Mexican defense agreements each nation opened its territory and its facilities to military use by the other nation, and pledged its forces to mutual cooperation. The arrangement with Mexico, in addition to adding strength to West coast defenses, contributed to the effectiveness of submarine patrol in the Gulf of Mexico. For these patrol operations a substantial number of PT boats as well as other types of small vessels were obtained from the United States under lend-lease arrangements and were added to the Mexican Navy.

Cuba also contributed to the defense against submarine operations, both in the Gulf and in the Caribbean. In an agreement signed June 15, 1942, Cuba granted to the United States facilities for operations "against enemy underseas craft." The site chosen for this installation was on the extreme western tip of Cuba, a location which facilitated anti-submarine patrols over the entrance to the Gulf of Mexico.[18]

Two additional pacts, greatly extending the terms of the original United States–Cuba agreement, were negotiated later. On September 7, 1942, announcement was made of an accord which "coordinates

16 U.S. Dept. of State, *Bulletin,* VI (Jan. 17, 1942), 67.
17 Pan American Union, *Bulletin,* LXXVI (March 1942), 72.
18 Pan American Union, *Bulletin,* LXXVI (Sept. 1942), 539.

all the special military and naval measures which have been taken . . . and facilitates the taking of new measures . . . by the appropriate authorities of the respective armed forces . . . without the need for individual negotiation in each case."[19] This agreement, and an additional pact signed February 1, 1943,[20] brought Cuba into full cooperation with the United States under much the same conditions as those reached with Mexico.

A reciprocal defense arrangement between Cuba and Mexico, signed October 2, 1942, was intended to coordinate antisubmarine patrol activities in the zone between Cuba and the Mexican mainland. This agreement facilitated a close coordination of the efforts of the two countries and the United States in bringing submarine activities in the Gulf under control.[21] Here was an outstanding example of inter-Latin–American security cooperation.

In the Caribbean to the south and southeast of Cuba another and more elaborate defense chain—utilizing the Cuban bases as a northern terminus—was welded, extending southward to Panama, eastward to the new United States base on Trinidad, thence along the Antilles chain through Puerto Rico, the Dominican Republic, Haiti, and back to Cuba. The Dominican Republic, in 1941, made base rights near the Bay of Samaná available to the United States. A pact, signed April 6, 1942, with Haiti, allowed the United States to establish a naval patrol base in western Haiti to strengthen the vital Windward Passage between Cuba and Haiti.[22]

Since the key to the Caribbean defense system was the Panama Canal, the agreements with the Panamanian government were of the utmost importance. Panama's generous offer to the United States of full military cooperation on December 7, 1941, was expanded by May 18, 1942, into a full agreement on the terms of Panamanian cooperation. The amount of territory which Panama had granted the United States in the 1941 agreements was greatly increased, and the manner in which Panamanian naval units and armed forces would participate in the common defense was detailed. These agreements permitted the United States to occupy and utilize areas, totaling approximately 38,-000 acres, as gun emplacements, airplane detector stations, bomb ranges, and auxiliary airfields, the largest of these being the Rio Hato

[19] U.S. Dept. of State, *Bulletin,* VII (Sept. 12, 1942), 750.

[20] World Peace Foundation, *Documents on American Foreign Relations* (8 vols., Boston, 1939–46), V, 364.

[21] Pan American Union, *Bulletin,* LXXVI (Dec. 1942), 702.

[22] U.S. Dept. of State, *Bulletin,* VI (April 18, 1942), 353–355.

Air Base, eighty miles to the southwest of the Canal. By the end of the war more than 130 separate installations had been constructed and put into operation in Panamanian territory.[23]

Several minor agreements which provided additional operational bases in the Caribbean zone were concluded between the United States and the other Latin-American nations in the area. Air bases were constructed in Costa Rica; air and naval bases were built in Nicaragua; and in Venezuela civilian airfields were converted to military use with United States assistance. On January 15, 1942, a United States–Venezuelan Defense Agreement was negotiated. To aid in the defense of the oil-refining installations on the islands of Curaçao and Aruba, Venezuela allowed three battalions of United States troops to land on her territory at Barcelona, and American planes on patrol duty to protect the Canal were allowed to fly freely over Venezuelan territory. The training of Venezuelan replacements for the American oil-installations guard proceeded so slowly that the United States troops could not be withdrawn until 1943.[24]

Brazil's strategic location on the eastern South American coast gave her a vital role in the joint military operations undertaken during the war. An early and considerable contribution to the Allied cause had been Brazil's permission to the United States to use her territory for a ferry route to fly lend-lease planes to Europe. Even before her entry into the war, Brazil issued orders on May 28, 1942, to her coastal patrols to fire on any Axis submarine found in her waters. As early as March 1942 she had been forced to organize convoys, for the Nazis had sunk several neutral Brazilian ships. To these overt acts of hostility were added the sinister undercover activities of Axis spies and saboteurs.[25] By January 1942, considerable amounts of war material had begun to flow from the United States into Brazil, and joint United States–Brazilian air and naval bases, notably at Natal and Recife, were established on the vital east coast "bulge."[26] After concluding minor

[23] *Gaceta Oficial* (Panama, May 26, 1943); U.S. Dept. of State, *Bulletin*, VI (May 23, 1942), 448; "The Future of Our Bases to the South," *United States News*, XX (April 12, 1946), 24–25.

[24] *United States News*, XX (April 12, 1946), 24–25; New York *Herald Tribune*, March 19, 1942; David H. Popper, "Hemispheric Solidarity in the War Crisis," Foreign Policy Association, *Reports*, XVIII (May 15, 1942), 58–59; Stetson Conn and Byron Fairchild, *United States Army in World War II: The Western Hemisphere*, Department of the Army, Office of the Chief of Military History (Washington, 1960), 203–204.

[25] Pan American Union, *Bulletin*, LXXVII (Sept. 1943), 532.

[26] *New York Times*, June 30, 1942, p. 4.

agreements in March and May of 1942, Brazil and the United States consolidated and enlarged their numerous cooperative military measures under the supervision of the Joint Brazil–United States Defense Commission. This body was created in August 1942, coincident with Brazil's formal entry into the war.[27] From the commission came effective measures for the antisubmarine campaign, convoying ships in the South Atlantic, supplying Allied forces in Africa, and for utilizing Brazil's natural resources and industrial output to the limit. Brazil's agreements with the United States were complemented by pacts with Cuba and Uruguay which assumed the nature of formal wartime alliances.

The western approaches to the Panama Canal formed a final major defense area in which agreements leading to military cooperation were negotiated. To the northward the United States made arrangements for bases in Costa Rica, El Salvador, Guatemala, and Nicaragua.[28] Major installations constructed as a result of these agreements with the Central American states included bomber bases near Guatemala City and air bases and a naval patrol station at Corinto in Nicaragua.[29]

To the south and west of the Panama Canal another chain of bases was also arranged. Colombia allowed the construction of air and naval bases in her territory, and an air base was built at Talara in northern Peru. An artillery battery was installed at Talara on March 8, 1942, to protect the coastal oilfield. By August 1942 the Peruvian forces had completed their training and the United States transferred its guns and equipment to a new American air base, established near Talara, which permitted United States operations from Talara to Panama. Turning over to the Peruvians the protection of the oilfields was in pursuance of United States policy to encourage and aid the countries to do everything possible to guard installations vital to the war effort. In this connection the Army sent Brigadier General Sherman Miles, Chief of G-2, on an inspection tour to Panama and South America to survey installations and recommend how they could best be protected; of special concern were the oil refineries in Venezuela and Talara.[30]

The acquisition of strategic Ecuadorean base sites was a major ad-

[27] *Documents*, V, 226, 360.

[28] Agreements were made which resulted in the construction of an emergency military road along the route of the projected but unfinished Pan American Highway.—Pan American Union, *Bulletin*, LXXVII (Feb. 1943), 105, and (Aug. 1943), 462.

[29] "The Future of Our Bases to the South," *United States News*, XX (April 12, 1946), 24–25.

[30] Conn and Fairchild, 200–202.

dition to the defense perimeter. In March 1942, President Arroyo del Río announced that Ecuador was cooperating with the United States in the construction of a naval-air base at Santa Elena near the entrance of Guayaquil Harbor, and on September 8 he admitted that the United States "was occupying" bases in the Galápagos Islands.[31]

The extreme southern area of South America—Argentina and Chile —was not protected by the system of interlocking defense agreements, the presumed reasons for this gap having already been indicated. The only other countries not included in the American defense chain through base agreements were Paraguay, Bolivia, and Honduras. Paraguay had received United States assistance in improving certain air bases north of Asunción for use as potential bomber bases, but the situation never called for their military utilization.[32] Bolivia and Honduras apparently had never been asked to contribute base sites, but they did cooperate in other war measures with their sister states.

Although most of the inter-American military defense cooperation had taken the form, for obvious reasons, of bilateral arrangements with the United States, there were a few bilateral pacts between various Latin-American states. These added strength to the concept of mutual responsibility for continental defense. The activities of the Inter-American Defense Board reflected this cooperative spirit.

The Inter-American Defense Board. In accord with a resolution adopted by the Rio meeting of foreign ministers, the Inter-American Defense Board was created to study and recommend to the American governments the measures necessary for the defense of the continent.

Preliminary to a discussion of the war contributions of the Defense Board, it should be noted here that both the Army and the Navy Departments had vigorously opposed the creation of an additional defense commission, favoring instead revision or extension of the Staff Agreements of 1940. Chief of Staff George C. Marshall was a strong advocate of bilateral agreements as the best means of obtaining such

---

[31] *New York Times,* March 3, 1942, p. 9, and Sept. 9, 1942, p. 1; Pan American Union, *Bulletin,* LXXVI (Nov. 1942), 688. Former President Arroyo del Río told the writer that he himself had taken the initiative in offering the Galápagos base to the United States. This is confirmed by Laurence Duggan (*op. cit.,* 182), who writes: "Immediately after the attack on Pearl Harbor, the President of Ecuador, without waiting for a request, offered to allow the United States to build and use facilities on the Galápagos for the duration of hostilities. The people of Ecuador applauded this decision."

[32] Popper, "Hemispheric Solidarity in the War Crisis," 61.

cooperation as was not yet in effect. More specifically, Army objections to an Inter-American Defense Board were the following:

1. It would be too large and unwieldy for effective action.
2. Latin-American military matters required immediate action, and the establishment of the board would be too time-consuming.
3. It would be difficult to maintain secrecy.
4. The board would lack authority to carry out its adopted measures.
5. The board would absorb the kind of high-caliber men needed for more pressing duties.
6. The War Department feared that Latin Americans would try to use the board as a means of pressing their claims on the United States for munitions.

The State Department, on the other hand, wanted the Defense Board for political reasons, for it would provide a channel through which all the American republics, small and large, could voice their views and recommendations. The very existence of the Defense Board, said Sumner Welles, would serve to impress upon the nations of the inter-American community the unitary character of our defense problems. Welles persuaded the President and accordingly the subject was restored to the agenda of the Rio Consultative Meeting. As we momentarily pause to appraise the results of this decision it must be conceded that, although the Defense Board was not responsible for any significant contribution to the war effort, it did serve a valuable purpose as a symbol of inter-American solidarity and military cooperation. It was important that the nonactive belligerents should feel that they also were concerned with the military decisions of the war.[33]

The Defense Board, composed of army, naval, and air officers from each of the American states, held its inaugural session in Washington on March 30, 1942. On that occasion Secretary of War Stimson said: "The creation of this Board does not mark merely the beginning of joint hemisphere defense. It is a step in the fruition of that policy. . . . It is intended to effect the coordination of the measures of defense undertaken by the Americas."[34]

Although the addresses of Secretary Stimson, Secretary Knox, and General Marshall conveyed warm words of welcome, they did not fail to warn that the United States could not be expected to supply arms to

[33] Conn and Fairchild, 194–200.
[34] *Junta Inter-Americana de Defensa* (Washington, 1944), 26–27. Lt. Gen. S. D. Embrick (United States) was elected permanent chairman of the board.

Latin America beyond existing commitments for some time to come. Thereafter, during 1942 and 1943, the policy of the United States defense services was to avoid having the board deliberate any topic that could be satisfactorily adjusted through bilateral negotiations. Thus its work was limited to military matters of only peripheral significance in the conduct of the war.

When the board was organized, the Axis nations were at the peak of their power; consequently its attention was absorbed by matters of immediate defense. By May 20, 1942, barely two months after its inaugural session, it was able to offer the American governments a recommendation looking to the apprehension and subsequent elimination of clandestine telecommunication stations through the training and equipment of radio-detector personnel; another recommendation urged continuous intergovernmental exchange of information about aviation and other problems of continental defense; and a third called for simplification of legal procedure to facilitate the transit of military aircraft. These recommendations were approved and forwarded to the governments through the Pan American Union.[35]

As the tide of war turned in 1943, the board was able to undertake the study of measures designed to provide permanent security for the Americas. In general the wartime resolutions of the Defense Board may be classified under the following heads: communications security, aviation, naval protection of shipping, transportation, and miscellaneous.[36]

On March 5, 1943, nearly a year after its formation, the Defense Board received a report on the actions taken by the various governments on its recommendations. With respect to its first nine resolutions, of the thirteen reporting countries, three (Brazil, Colombia, and Guatemala) had taken action on all the resolutions. Chile and the Dominican Republic reported that they had acted on eight. All but two of the countries had taken action on four or more of the resolutions. These two, Mexico and Argentina, had acted on one each.[37] According to Col. Laurence Higgins, secretary-general of the board, its accomplishments, if at times imponderable, were nevertheless real and substantial.[38]

The contributions of the board were limited because of its purely advisory nature and because so many of the cooperative measures during the war were bilateral operations initiated by the United States and

[35] *The Inter-American Defense Board* (Washington, n.d.), 62.
[36] *Ibid.*, 13–16.
[37] *Minutes of the Plenary Sessions of the Inter-American Defense Board* (Washington, Jan. 1945). Minutes of the meeting of March 5, 1943.
[38] Pan American Union, *Bulletin,* LXXVII (July 1943), 402–403.

therefore beyond the scope of operations of the Defense Board/ ever, credit should be given to that agency for recommendation/ led to a well-ordered convoy system within the hemisphere, and ι‿ study of arms standardization. The projected program of arms standardization was incorporated in the proposed Inter-American Military Cooperative Act presented to the United States Congress in 1946 and again in 1947. Although Congress did not pass the proposed legislation, some of its features were later implemented.[39]

Mutual assistance. Through the build-up of a defense pattern for the hemisphere, the United States kept in operation the system of rearmament assistance through lend-lease aid and Export-Import Bank loans, programs which had been initiated before Pearl Harbor. As before, the purpose of this assistance was ostensibly to enable the various nations to equip and maintain armed forces sufficiently strong to carry out the requirements of actual defense against aggression. But in reality, next to the defense of vital installations, the purpose was to strengthen the control of the governments in power and thus diminish the likelihood of Axis-inspired revolutionary movements. Of course the policy was subjected to the criticism that United States lend-lease made revolutions more difficult and "froze" incumbent dictators in power. In partial answer to this charge, it is to be noted that apparently lend-lease or armaments to Latin-American governments neither discouraged revolutions nor decreased their number (to wit, Ecuador, El Salvador, Guatemala, and Venezuela, 1944 and 1945).

By the end of the war, lend-lease agreements had been made with all the Latin-American states except Argentina and Panama,[40] a total of $459,422,000 being expended during the period 1941–46. Of this amount, almost 75 per cent was given to Brazil for outfitting an expeditionary force; Mexico, Chile, and Peru received the next largest amounts.[41] Substantially all lend-lease aid[42] to Latin America consisted of fighting equipment such as guns, aircraft, military vehicles, and small naval craft, together with materials used in ordnance plants and

---

[39] *International Organization,* I (Feb. 1947), 159–160; Blair Bolles, "Washington Seeks Hemispheric Military Alliance," Foreign Policy Association, *Bulletin,* XXVI (June 13, 1947), 4.

[40] No lend-lease aid was extended to Panama because that country was furnished aid under special provisions for the protection of the Panama Canal Zone.

[41] U.S. Dept. of State, *Twenty-Third Report to Congress on Lend-Lease Operations.* Publication 2707 (Washington, 1946), 27.

[42] *Ibid., Thirteenth Report* (Nov. 30, 1943), 36–37.

other installations producing military equipment. No civilian supplies of any kind were furnished under lend-lease.

In return, tangible benefits accruing to the United States from lend-lease to Latin America included the following: (1) maintenance of antisubmarine patrols that protected our merchant ships carrying vital war materials; (2) permission to the United States to establish bases and the use of harbors and airports; (3) permission to fly military planes above their territories, and full cooperation in many other ways in our common war effort; and (4) permission from several of the countries for the FBI to send agents there as a part of the program to suppress Axis subversive activities. In addition, according to the *Fourteenth Report on Lend-Lease Operations*, "All Latin American countries having lend-lease agreements have complied with their basic commitments where cooperation in the war effort is concerned—they have rounded up Axis spies and saboteurs, impounded Axis funds, and have cut off all trade of benefit to the Axis."[43]

The program of exchanging military personnel and information, inaugurated before Pearl Harbor, was continued during the war years. The military-missions system was extended from a prewar total of thirteen receiving nations to all the Latin-American nations.[44] In addition numerous Latin-American armed forces dignitaries visited the United States to confer on special measures or to observe training facilities, training programs, and military demonstrations.

The original defense program of the American states had envisioned defense against all forms of attack; therefore much of the effort and planning proved to be unnecessary. Since no land invasion occurred, the measures designed to combat submarine operations were the only ones put to actual use. Brazil, Mexico, Cuba, Panama, Peru, and Uruguay joined the patrols against Axis sea raiders. Brazil, because of her location and her fairly large Navy, was the Latin-American state that contributed most to the antisubmarine campaign. In October 1944, she assumed the task of patrolling the entire western South Atlantic, an operation which previously had been carried out by combined Brazilian and United States forces.[45]

Offensive military cooperation. The Americas entered a new phase of military cooperation after the threat of actual invasion of the conti-

[43] *Ibid., Fourteenth Report* (Dec. 31, 1944), 51–52.

[44] The agreements with the individual countries providing for United States missions are found in U.S. Dept. of State, Exec. Agreements Ser.

[45] *New York Times,* Oct. 11, 1944, p. 6.

nent had been dissipated by Allied successes. This was joint participation in offensive combat operations overseas.

In the early days of the war, several of the American belligerents had expressed the desire to send forces overseas, but the United States discouraged such offers because of the administrative difficulties entailed. Toward the end of the war, however, realizing that joint operations overseas would strengthen the concept of solidarity, the United States agreed to assist in sending combat units from Brazil and Mexico to overseas theaters.

The Brazilian project proved to be fairly extensive. An expeditionary force of approximately division strength landed at Naples, Italy, on July 16, 1944. The unit, assigned to General Mark Clark's U.S. Fifth Army, went into combat in September and remained in action in northern Italy until the following April. The Brazilians acquitted themselves splendidly, and the anticipated "administrative difficulties" arising from differences in language, customs, and food presented no particular obstacle. Brazilian casualties totaled 2,112 men.[46] This participation in the Italian theater marked the first appearance of combat units from any Latin-American nation in an overseas campaign.

Mexico, in 1945, became the second Latin-American state to send troops overseas. On February 24, the Mexican government announced that the first units of its 201st Air Squadron were ready to leave for the Pacific theater. Placed with the United States forces commanded by General Douglas MacArthur, this unit first saw action in early June in the Philippines, and in August in the bombing of a port in Formosa.[47] Quite as important as the military contributions which Brazil and Mexico made at the battlefronts was the welding of a psychological bond between the United States and the other American republics. It dramatized in the most effective manner the fact that Latin-American cooperation in the war effort consisted not only of giving aid to the United States but of fighting in their own defense. It is necessary to note, however, the fact that among the populace of many of the Latin-American countries, there were elements that were unable to equate aid to the United States with their own national defense. For example, Mexico's participation was called "Señor Padilla's War," after their pro-United States foreign minister.

Defense against subversion. Even as the American republics reacted

---

[46] *Ibid.,* April 15, 1945, p. 1; Laurence Duggan, 96.
[47] *New York Times,* June 10, p. 4, June 13, p. 6, Aug. 11, 1945, p. 4.

offensively to the threats of Axis armed aggression, so likewise was there defensive reaction against political attack which assumed the forms of propaganda, espionage, sabotage, and other subversive activities. As an imperative practical necessity arising from Axis political aggression, the Emergency Advisory Committee for Political Defense was created by the Third Meeting of Consultation of the Ministers of Foreign Affairs. The Rio action was the culmination of a series of tentative measures which the American republics had slowly and reluctantly adopted in the two preceding meetings of their foreign ministers.

The first collective notice taken of subversive activities was the adoption of a resolution at Panama in 1939, calling for an exchange of views or a conference to facilitate the prevention or repression of unlawful activities undertaken by individuals "in favor of a belligerent state."[48] In another resolution, the Panama meeting had recommended that the governments "take the necessary measures to eradicate from the Americas the spread of doctrines that tend to place in jeopardy the common inter-American democratic ideal."

By the time the Second Meeting of Consultation of Foreign Ministers met in Havana in July 1940, the nature and dangers of Nazi subversion had become much more apparent to the peoples and governments of the American republics. Consequently the actions of that meeting were more specific. It recommended that the American republics exchange information covering subversive activities, and that each government apply all necessary measures to prevent and suppress activities by foreign governments—groups or individuals—tending to subvert democratic institutions or to foment disorder. The foreign ministers also agreed that measures should be taken to prevent political activities by foreign diplomatic or consular agents, that precautionary measures should be taken in granting passports, and that the entry of nationals of non-American states should be rigorously supervised.[49]

The Emergency Advisory Committee for Political Defense. When the foreign ministers met for their third consultative meeting at Rio de Janeiro in January 1942, they recommended the most comprehensive

[48] Res. VIII: Coordination of Police and Judicial Measures for the Maintenance of Neutrality. *Acta Final de la Reunión de Consulta entra los Ministros de Relaciones Exteriores de las Repúblicas Americanas en Panamá 1939* (Panama, 1939), 39–40.

[49] Res. II–VII, Pan American Union, *Report of the Second Meeting of the Ministers of Foreign Affairs of the American Republics, Habana, July 21–30, 1940* (Washington, 1940), 28–32.

measures yet undertaken to combat Axis subversive activities in the Americas. In pursuance of Resolution VIII, the Inter-American Conference of Police and Judicial Authorities was convened in Buenos Aires from May 27 to June 9, 1943, to coordinate measures aimed at "the elimination of activities inimical to the security of the American continent." The initiative for this conference had in fact been taken as early as August 1940, at the Havana meeting.[50] Although the 1943 conference was able to contribute a number of practical measures for handling subversion and sabotage, more effective work was accomplished by a specialized wartime agency, the Emergency Advisory Committee for Political Defense (CPD). This committee was comprised of seven members, named by the governments of Argentina, Brazil, Chile, Mexico, United States, Uruguay, and Venezuela. At its first meeting, held in Montevideo on April 15, 1942, Dr. Alberto Guani, minister of foreign affairs of Uruguay, was elected chairman. Thanks largely to the considerable ability and energy of Dr. Guani, the CPD soon emerged as one of the most active and valuable of the inter-American war agencies.

The CPD was an interesting experiment in the mechanics of intergovernmental cooperation, for its seven-man membership was a departure from the usual practice of all-inclusive membership on inter-American commissions. In theory the seven men represented no particular countries but the Americas as a whole. In practice, however, they "consulted" their own governments and were guided by their "advice."[51] Despite this the CPD functioned well and demonstrated the willingness of the American republics to cooperate with an advisory body, even though not directly represented on it.

The powers of the committee were to be purely advisory, and its recommendations, made through the Governing Board of the Pan American Union or directly to the various governments by means of liaison officers appointed by each state, were to be effectuated in whatever way each government should determine.

The CPD utilized four procedural instruments for implementing its

[50] Pan American Union, *Steps Taken by the Pan American Union in Fulfillment of the Resolution adopted at the Eighth International Conference of American States and the Three Meetings of the Ministers of Foreign Affairs of the American Republics,* Congress and Conference Ser., No. 44 (Washington, 1943), 56–57.

[51] Laurence Duggan, 94. For a discussion of the "representative principle" in limited membership entities, see Carl B. Spaeth and William Sanders, "The Emergency Advisory Committee for Political Defense," *American Journal of International Law,* XXXVIII (April 1944), 228–231.

work. The first was a system of liaison officers whose duties were to consult with their governments on the best means of applying the committee's recommendations, to inform the committee of all legislative and administrative measures adopted, and to submit to it proposals or projects for further study. A second instrument was the National Committee for Political Defense established in each country to coordinate the work of various governmental agencies concerned with national defense and the enforcement of the laws against subversion. A third instrument was the consultative visit by members of the committee to individual countries in the hemisphere to observe the measures taken by each government to combat subversion and to consult with the national authorities on more effective programs of political defense. The fourth instrument was the general and regional meetings held by American governments to decide upon ways to combat subversive activities on the international level. Such a meeting was held in September 1942, at Rivera, Uruguay, represented by Argentina, Bolivia, Brazil, Paraguay, and Uruguay, with two members of the CPD in attendance. The purpose of this regional meeting was to discuss the entry and exit of persons across national boundaries and the clandestine crossing of frontiers. The result was a strong recommendation on means of controlling and restricting the travel of subversives.[52]

During the war period, the CPD was responsible for twenty-nine resolutions recommending measures of political defense dealing with the following broad categories of subjects: (1) Control of Dangerous Aliens (registration, detention, and expulsion); (2) Prevention of the Abuse of Citizenship (control of grants to Axis nationals); (3) Transit across National Boundaries (entry and exit of persons and clandestine crossing); (4) Acts of Political Aggression (propaganda, espionage, and sabotage); and (5) Recognition of New Governments Established by Force (recognition of the government of Bolivia).

In accord with its decision that the public be made aware of information covering subversive groups and activities, the CPD on November 3, 1942, published copies of a memorandum which the United States had given to Chile on Nazi activities in that country. The Chilean people were so aroused by this revelation of the ramifications of the Nazi network that popular pressure forced the government to break relations with the Axis nations on January 20, 1943.[53]

[52] Emergency Advisory Committee for Political Defense, *Annual Report (First), Submitted to the Governments of the American Republics, July 1943* (Montevideo, 1943), 165–176, cited hereinafter as CPD, *Annual Report (First).*
[53] *Ibid.,* 85–104; Laurence Duggan, 93.

Encouraged by this success the committee published on January 22, 1943, a similar memorandum entitled "Axis Espionage Activities in Argentina," which revealed the German Embassy in Buenos Aires as a center of espionage affecting most of the nations of the hemisphere.[54] But proud Argentina, refusing to be "dictated to" by the Emergency Advisory Committee for Political Defense, continued, despite the irrefutable proof of the evidence, its policy of so-called "neutrality."

In view of the attitude of Argentina, the CPD was obliged, on several occasions, to remind that government of the principles agreed to by the American republics for the political defense of the hemisphere. On May 31, 1943, the committee, on the basis of a consultative visit to the Argentine republic in April 1943, informed that government that its "neutral" status made it impossible for the continent to present a united front against the Axis. A memorandum sent to Argentina on June 2, 1944—more than four months after its severance of relations with the Axis—noted that there had been no improvement over the previous situation.[55]

Because of the basic cleavage between the policy of Argentina and that of the other American republics, its membership in the CPD proved to be increasingly embarrassing. This culminated, first, on December 3, 1943, in the committee action to withhold confidential documents and reports from members whose governments had not broken diplomatic relations with, or declared war against, the Axis; and second, on September 6, 1944, a recommendation by the committee to the governments of the American republics that they terminate the unnatural situation of Argentine membership. Upon being informed of this action the Argentine government immediately withdrew its representative from the committee.[56] Peru was elected to fill the vacancy created by the Argentine withdrawal.

The Bolivian problem. Bolivia also gave the CPD special concern in its efforts to maintain "continental unity, the indispensable foundation for political defense." Since the Bolivian revolution of December 20, 1943, was believed to have been planned and backed by Axis diplomats in Argentina for the purpose of breaking down the anti-Axis front in South America, it was apparent that a political defense question of great importance had arisen. Circumstances had imposed on the committee a policy responsibility from which it did not shrink.

[54] CPD, *Annual Report (First)*, 105–129.
[55] CPD, *Second Annual Report, Submitted to the Governments of the American Republics, July 15, 1943–October 15, 1944* (Montevideo, 1944), 7–8.
[56] *Ibid.*, 9–10.

Meeting on Christmas Eve four days after the revolution, the committee adopted a resolution which recommended to the American governments that, for the duration of the war, they should not accord recognition to any new government established by force, without first exchanging information and consulting among themselves to determine the circumstances surrounding the revolution and to ascertain to their satisfaction that the new government adhered to the inter-American undertakings for the defense of the continent.

With the exception of Argentina, which recognized the Bolivian revolutionary regime on January 3, 1944, virtually all of the American republics expressed approval of the committee's recommendation—called the "Guani Doctrine," after its dynamic chairman. The United States, however, opposed a consultative meeting, not only because of the delay it would necessitate but also to obviate any discussion of the sovereign rights of individual republics. It suggested instead that pertinent information be exchanged through diplomatic channels. This suggestion was accepted and embodied in a second resolution approved by the CPD on January 5, which affirmed that the resolution of Decembe 24 was applicable to the Bolivian case and recommended that the governments move immediately to consult and exchange information through diplomatic channels.

Thus, after full exchange of information, which did reveal a connection between the Bolivian Junta and Nazi or pro-Nazi elements elsewhere, the United States and the other eighteen American republics announced, on January 28, their intention to withhold recognition. It would not be in the interest of the security of the hemisphere and the success of the Allied cause, they declared, to recognize the new regime. This was the criterion and the only criterion which they considered in passing upon the status of the Bolivian regime.

The Bolivian Junta protested to the CPD, charging that the committee had exceeded its authority. The pro-Nazi press of Buenos Aires likewise criticized the CPD and said that adherence to its recommendations would lead to abdication of sovereign prerogatives. Withholding recognition from a *de facto* government, they declared, constituted intervention in the internal affairs of another country. That there was some justice in this charge must be admitted.

In all matters relating to the security and defense of the hemisphere, however, we must look to the substance rather than the form. The inter-American system had as one of its purposes the defending of the sovereign republics of the hemisphere against aggression or intervention in their domestic affairs by influences originating outside the hemisphere and outside their individual frontiers. The Guani Doctrine, therefore, was put into effect when elements hostile to continental defense appeared to be involved.

Following the decision to withhold recognition, the provisional government of Bolivia carried out a number of decisive and affirmative acts in support of hemisphere security and the cause of the United Nations.[57] Also, changes within the regime itself appeared to go far toward reducing or eliminating the elements of danger which were apparent when the revolutionary Junta was first established. Early in May the American nations agreed to review the situation once more. Following exchange of information the respective states decided that the Bolivian regime deserved to be recognized. Accordingly, on June 23, all of the American governments, with the exception of Argentina and Uruguay, announced simultaneously with the United States the re-establishment of their relations with Bolivia. Recognition by Uruguay, which followed soon after, was briefly withheld to emphasize the fact that, although the consultations had been collective, recognition itself was an independent sovereign decision.

"The ability of the Committee to cope with this urgent and unique situation," declared two former American members of the CPD, "may, in retrospect, well stand as the high water mark of its functioning." Pan Americanism, they reflected, had progressed from the realm of aspirations, through the intermediary stage of an inorganic system of principles and techniques of international cooperation, to the point where full use can be made of emergency instrumentalities for joint political decision and action.[58]

The value of the efforts of the Committee for Political Defense is not to be measured solely by its many excellent recommendations or by the various types of controls which the American republics adopted pursuant thereto; rather its contribution to the war effort is attested by the very substantial success achieved in uncovering and stamping out Axis activities at a time when the hemisphere was threatened with aggression from both within and without. In this respect the United States offered tangible cooperation, for in order to encourage the detention of dangerous enemy aliens we agreed to "take them off the hands" of the Latin-American governments. During the war about one thousand aliens were deported to the United States and were held in custody.[59]

[57] *Ibid.*, 77–105.   [58] Spaeth and Sanders, 227–238.
[59] U.S. Dept. of State, *Bulletin* (Dec. 30, 1945), 1061.

The Inter-American Juridical Committee. Another specialized war agency was the Inter-American Juridical Committee. Organized in 1939 as the Inter-American Neutrality Committee, it became in 1942, by action of the Rio meeting of foreign ministers, the Inter-American Juridical Committee. The new committee continued to sit in the Brazilian capital, with the same membership assigned to Argentina, Brazil, Chile, Costa Rica, Mexico, United States, and Venezuela. Argentina and Costa Rica did not fulfill their obligations to appoint committee members.[60]

The inaugural session of the Juridical Committee was held in Rio de Janeiro on March 10, 1942. Except for the period from January 1943 to February 1944, when no meetings were held because the requisite quorum was lacking, the committee concerned itself with problems which fell in the following four categories: juridical problems arising out of World War II; postwar problems; development and coordination of the work of codification of international law; and the coordination of the resolutions of the meetings of ministers of foreign affairs.[61] These headings included both theoretical and practical problems—technical issues of law, questions of organization and administration, and recommendations inviting political judgment and moral idealism.

With respect to juridical matters created by the war, the committee made a number of studies which eventuated in recommendations for approval by the several governments. Because of the chilly reception of many of its recommendations, the Juridical Committee was forced to the conclusion that there were many subjects upon which it would be difficult to formulate rules without conflicting with positions already taken by the different governments. It should be recalled that the American republics, with reference to their war status, fell into three groups: belligerents, those that had suspended diplomatic relations, and those that had not ruptured relations. The difficulties attending the recommending of rules of procedure compatible with the difference in war status of the various republics can well be imagined.

Reserving for later discussion the work of the Juridical Committee on postwar planning, we turn next to its efforts to codify international

---

[60] On December 15, 1943, the Governing Board approved an amendment to the resolution of the Havana meeting of 1940 which required "the attendance of a minimum of five members of the Juridical Committee to enable it to carry on its work." The amendment lowered the quorum to four.

[61] Pan American Union, *Minutes of the Inter-American Juridical Committee* (Washington, Sept. 1942), I (March 20–July 3, 1942), 2.

law. Such elaborate provisions for codification had been made at the various inter-American conferences that at the time of the Rio meeting of 1942 there were six distinct codification agencies. Since these had been created without any idea of unity, the committee decided to confine itself to the single problem of coordinating the work of the existing agencies and not to venture into the field of codification itself.[62] The Juridical Committee, on October 19, 1944, recommended that a small committee of technical experts act as a central agency for coordinating the activities of other bodies.

At the Mexico City conference in 1945, this recommendation was endorsed by a resolution which ordered the Pan American Union to entrust to the Inter-American Juridical Committee the functions of a central agency for the codification of public international law. It must be recorded that this project was never completed.

Economic defense: multilateral. Fully as pronounced as those evidences of inter-American cooperation in the political and military realms are the economic. Indeed, since actual military participation in the war on the part of most of the Latin-American nations was neither feasible nor practicable, it remained for them to demonstrate an impressive and unprecedented solidarity in mobilizing their economic resources for the support of the common cause. If economic collaboration with the United States proved to be profitable to Latin Americans, this in no way negated their devotion to the requirements of hemispheric defense. Happily the bases for economic cooperation had already been laid prior to Pearl Harbor. The war effort, therefore, evoked a remarkably effective unfolding of these earlier initiatives.

The Inter-American Financial and Economic Advisory Committee (FEAC) continued to be the principal agency for economic cooperation on the multilateral plane. Resolutions adopted by the Rio de Janeiro meeting of foreign ministers and assigned to the committee for study and advisory action covered a wide range of economic subjects, a result of the new status of several of the American republics as belligerents. These additional tasks included production of strategic materials, maintenance of the internal economy of the American countries, strengthening of the Inter-American Development Commission, encouragement of capital investments in the American republics, mobilization of transportation facilities, and the severance of commercial and financial relations with the Axis. In addition, the FEAC was requested

---

[62] Charles G. Fenwick, "The Inter-American Juridical Committee," *American Journal of International Law,* XXXVII (1943), 24.

"to proceed to the study and preparation of recommendations on post-war economic problems." In view of its enlarged and altered duties the committee, in the summer of 1942, was reorganized into six sub-committees: Production, Markets, and Disposal of Surpluses; Finance and Credit; Transportation, Communication, and Tourism; Emergency Economic Controls; Postwar Problems; and Draft Coordination. The names of these subcommittees indicate the wide scope of the FEAC's activities.[63]

The American republics devised in the FEAC a collective economic weapon which demonstrated its effectiveness as a powerful instrument for mobilizing and developing the economic resources of the Americas in the cause of freedom. According to Secretary Hull, "The activities of the Committee constitute an indispensable supplement to the all out war effort of the United States, and should be supported [by the Congress] with the same realistic determination that characterizes our military contribution to the world-wide struggle against totalitarianism."[64]

A number of wartime specialized economic conferences were convened either with the assistance or under the auspices of the FEAC. The first of these was the Inter-American Conference on Systems of Economic and Financial Control, held in Washington from June 30 to July 10, 1942. In accord with a resolution adopted by the Rio meeting of foreign ministers, this conference of ministers of finance and representatives of the central banks was convened to determine the procedure for the uniform handling of bank credits, collections, contracts of lease, and consignments of merchandise involving real or juridical persons or nationals of a state which had committed an act of aggression against the American continent. The conference recommended measures to be adopted by each country for the elimination of Axis influence. In general these countermeasures of economic warfare, enacted by most of the American republics, were modeled after those taken by the United States.[65]

The Rio meeting was also responsible for a resolution requesting the Governing Board of the Pan American Union to convoke an Inter-

[63] Inter-American Financial and Economic Advisory Committee, Handbook of Its Organization and Activities, 1939–1943 (Washington, 1943), 20–22.

[64] U.S. Dept. of State, Bulletin, VIII (March 27, 1943), 263.

[65] Martin Domke, "Western Hemisphere Control Over Enemy Property," Pan American Union, Bulletin, LXXIX (Sept. 1945), 515; Manuel C. Gallagher, "Inter-American Conference on Systems of Economic and Financial Control," ibid., LXXVI (Sept. 1942), 481–488.

American Technical and Economic Conference to study present and postwar economic problems. The conference, originally scheduled to meet in Washington on September 6, 1944, was postponed several times, with the end result that it never met.

Another specialized economic conference of the war period was the Conference of Commissions of Inter-American Development, which met in New York, May 9–18, 1944. The Inter-American Development Commission (chairman, Nelson A. Rockefeller) and the twenty-one national committees affiliated with it met in conference to formulate a program for further development of the hemisphere's great resources in the postwar period, when materials, shipping, technical skill, and manpower would again be available for the usual types of productive enterprises. A total of forty-five resolutions and recommendations covered a wide field of planning for the future welfare of the American republics.[66]

Economic defense: bilateral. Despite the encouraging demonstrations of economic cooperation among the American countries undertaken on a multilateral basis, it is nevertheless a matter of record that far more was achieved through the bilateral engagements negotiated by the United States. These agreements obviously covered a wide range of subjects. Procurement agreements were entered into with the important producing countries.[67] For example, the Metals Reserve Company had contracts with several American republics to purchase their entire production of a number of strategic metals—copper from Chile and Mexico, tin and tungsten from Bolivia, manganese from Brazil and Cuba, antimony from Bolivia, Mexico, and Peru, zinc from Mexico, and chrome from Chile.[68] The Rubber Reserve Company entered into agreements with a number of countries, in addition to the prime producer, Brazil, for the development and purchase of raw rubber.

To aid those Latin-American countries that had commodities in surplus because of either lack of adequate markets or inadequate shipping facilities, the Commodities Credit Corporation, with credits supplied by the Export-Import Bank, contracted to purchase a substantial part of the crop and in some instances all of it: e.g., the bananas of

[66] Julian G. Zier, "First Conference of the Commission of Inter-American Development," Pan American Union, *Bulletin,* LXXVIII (July 1944), 382–385.

[67] See U.S. Dept. of State, Exec. Agreements Ser. These agreements were usually effected by an exchange of notes.

[68] Edgar B. Brossard, "The Effect of the War on Trade in the Americas," Pan American Union, *Bulletin,* LXXVI (Dec. 1942), 661–667, and LXXIX (May 1945), 283.

Central America, wool of Uruguay, wheat and corn of Argentina, cotton of Nicaragua, Haiti, and Peru, and the sugar of Cuba. The Defense Surplus Corporation and the Foreign Economic Administration were other United States agencies that contracted procurement agreements.[69]

The terms of these over-all procurement agreements varied widely, although they usually expressed the desire of the Latin-American government "to increase its contribution to hemispheric defense" and to implement the Rio resolution on strategic materials.[70] In some instances the local governments agreed to cancel import duties on equipment to be used in strategic production, and of export duties on certain commodities deriving from such production. Other requirements which might impede production were waived. The agreements and contracts also contained "labor clauses" which provided that contractors should be required to abide by all local laws for the benefit of labor. A proposal by the Board of Economic Warfare that compliance should be enforced by United States inspection was overruled by the State Department as interference in local affairs.[71]

At the Rio meeting of foreign ministers a resolution was adopted which pledged the American nations to cooperative measures for the maintenance of their internal economies. This obligation apparently rested on the United States, and indeed it was not shirked. At the Rio meeting the head of the American delegation, Undersecretary Sumner Welles said:

The Government of the United States is prepared to cooperate wholeheartedly with the other American republics in handling the problems arising out of these economic warfare measures. It stands prepared to render financial and technical assistance, where needed, to alleviate injury to the domestic economy of any of the American republics which results from the control and curbing of alien economic activities inimical to our common defense.

He declared that the United States was ready to enter into broad arrangements to acquire supplies of basic and strategic materials, and to cooperate with each of the other American republics in order to increase rapidly and efficiently their production for emergency needs.[72]

[69] *Ibid.*, 664–667.
[70] See "Procurement of Strategic Materials," *Agreement Between the United States of America and Colombia, March 29, 1943,* Dept. of State, Exec. Agreements Ser., No. 442 (Washington, 1945).
[71] Laurence Duggan, 98.
[72] U.S. Dept. of State, *Bulletin,* VI (Jan. 17, 1942), 61.

The policy of the United States which called for aiding the essential needs of the American republics was implemented primarily through the negotiation of general agreements for cooperation in a wide range of activities. Probably the most important of these was the agreement of April 30, 1943, between Mexico and the United States, providing for the creation of the Joint Mexican-American Commission for Economic Cooperation. This agreement was negotiated immediately following the meetings of Presidents Roosevelt and Ávila Camacho in Monterrey, Mexico, and Corpus Christi, Texas, in April 1943.[73]

The commission was formed in September 1943 to consider and make recommendations with regard to the most pressing economic problems calling for immediate joint action by the two countries. Certainly one of the most pressing problems was Mexico's unbalanced economy. On the one hand, Mexico was exporting a maximum amount of critical and strategic materials to the United States. On the other hand, because of the conversion of American industry to war production and because former overseas sources of supply to Mexico had been cut off, she was unable to obtain sufficient imports to maintain her national economy on an even keel. Incidentally, Mexico's problem was typical of most of Latin America. The commission recognized that Mexico's economic development along sound lines, and therefore her ability to meet her wartime economic responsibilities, depended on such amounts of material and equipment from the United States as could be made available without interfering with the war effort and the essential needs of other friendly nations.[74]

The commission, therefore, after a careful study of public and private projects, prepared a "Minimum 1944 Program," consisting of twenty projects at a cost of about $24 million. Practically all materials and equipment required by these projects were given clearance and made available by the United States.[75] In addition a "Long-Range Program on Industrial Development," consisting of some thirty-one projects, was also formulated and recommended by the commission. "The greater part of the required equipment for these projects," the commission reported in January 1945, "is now either in Mexico or in the process of being manufactured for delivery. Its purchase is being financed entirely by private enterprise, preponderantly Mexican, or, in

[73] "Mexican-American Commission for Economic Cooperation," Pan American Union, *Bulletin,* LXXIX (April 1945), 211–216.
[74] U.S. Dept. of State, *Bulletin,* IX (July 17, 1943), 45.
[75] Pan American Union, *Bulletin,* LXXVII (Dec. 1943), 676–681.

the case of public works, such as electric power, irrigation, and drainage, by the Mexican Government."[76]

In a letter to President Ávila Camacho, dated February 20, 1944, President Roosevelt expressed his satisfaction with the work of the Joint Mexican-American Commission for Economic Cooperation as follows:

In spite of the demands of war upon all the resources of the United States, it is a source of satisfaction to my Government that it has been able to carry out its pledge under the resolution of the Third Consultative Meeting of Foreign Ministers held at Rio de Janeiro in 1942 for the Maintenance of the Internal Economies of the American nations. Although in 1943 and 1944 the industry of the United States, through conversion and expansion, was primarily engaged in the production of war materials, it was nevertheless possible to make available and supply to Mexico for its consumption needs and the maintenance of its economy more products in those years than during any similar period of time in the trade between the two countries. . . . The Mexican-American Commission for Economic Cooperation has played an important role, not only in assisting in obtaining materials and equipment for Mexico's economic development, but also in focusing attention on the significance of this development, its problems, and its requirements for still greater expansion when peace comes.[77]

General agreements providing for cooperation in a wide range of activities were negotiated with a number of other countries also, including Brazil, Peru, Nicaragua, and Haiti. That with Brazil provided for "a program for the mobilization of the productive resources of Brazil" and for a line of credit of $100 million to be made available through the Export-Import Bank. In addition to its commitments to aid in the production of strategic materials, the United States also undertook to insure Brazil against a shipping shortage.[78]

Besides the general agreements there were innumerable contracts on more limited undertakings in specific fields, such as technical assistance and development aid in its many categories: agricultural, industrial, public works, etc. It was largely in support of the development (fo-

[76] Pan American Union, Bulletin, LXXIX (April 1945), 213–214.
[77] Ibid., 211.
[78] U.S. Dept. of State, Bulletin, VI (March 7, 1942), 282; George Soule, David Efron, and Norman T. Ness, Latin America in the Future World (New York, 1945), 250–251. For an enumeration of Brazil–United States wartime agreements, see Brazilian Government Trade Bureau, Brazil at War (New York, 1944), 7–12; also David H. Popper, "U.S.–Brazilian Economic Accords of March 3, 1942," Foreign Policy Association, Reports, XVII (March 1, 1942). 305.

mento) program that the Export-Import Bank authorized credits to most of the Latin-American republics. When the war came to an end, the amounts of credit still open often exceeded the amounts drawn by the individual countries.[79] This was because of the inevitable time lag in getting projects started, and also because of the inability of the United States to supply the needed materials and machines. When wartime restrictions were lifted, the unprecedented demand for such materials resulted in great increases in prices. Thus Latin America's dollar reserves and credits rapidly melted away.

As for technical assistance, it is a significant fact that the policy later embodied in "Point Four" did not originate in the famous message of President Truman on January 20, 1949, but in the wartime practices of the Institute of Inter-American Affairs, a subsidiary of the Office of the Coordinator of Inter-American Affairs. Created in March of 1942 "to aid and improve the health and welfare of the people of the Western Hemisphere in collaborating with their governments," the agency promoted technical programs and projects for health, sanitation, and food supply.[80]

The greater part of these operations, carried out under cooperative agreements with the other American republics, provided that agencies or units, called "Servicios," be set up within the appropriate ministries of the host country. The Servicio, which represented the institute and the local government, was a unique experiment in international cooperative ventures. The specific programs for health, sanitation, and food production were carried out by field parties of the institute, working in most cases through the *servicios*.[81] This unparalleled device evidently proved its worth, for it is still an important feature of our technical-assistance administration in Latin America. Moreover the worth of the program of technical assistance in Latin America, as developed by the Institute of Latin American Affairs, was amply demonstrated by the decision of the United States government to preserve the agency when the Office of the Coordinator of Inter-American Affairs was liquidated after the war.[82]

[79] For a chart showing Export-Import Bank loans to Latin America with the amounts drawn and credits still open, see *United States News*, XXI (July 26, 1946), 52.

[80] Government Printing Office, *History of the Office of the Coordinator of Inter-American Affairs* (Washington, 1947), 232–236.

[81] Institute of Inter-American Affairs, *The Program of the Institute of Inter-American Affairs* (Washington, 1949), 6–7.

[82] The Institute of Inter-American Affairs was reincorporated by Congress in 1947. See Brookings Institution, *The Administration of Foreign Affairs and*

THE UNITED STATES AND INTER-AMERICAN SECURITY

Taking the period of American neutrality after June 1940 and the war period together, the total amount of assistance, net of reciprocal assistance and repayments, to all Latin-American countries approached $600 million. Table 1 indicates the distribution of funds by program from July 1, 1940, through June 30, 1945.[83]

Table 1

Distribution of United States Assistance to Latin America by Program, July 1, 1940–June 30, 1945

Program	Millions of Dollars
Net foreign aid	593
Net grants utilized	423
Lend-Lease	365
Institute of Inter-American Affairs	50
Technical assistance	5
Reconstruction Finance Corporation	2
American Red Cross	. . .*
Net credits utilized	170
Export-Import Bank (including agent-bank loans)	105
Lend-lease current credits	62
Reconstruction Finance Corporation	2
Institute of Inter-American Affairs	. . .*

* Less than $500,000.

Conclusion. The foregoing is the record, in broad outline, of inter-American cooperation—diplomatic, political, military, and economic—during World War II. In the face of the greatest danger that had ever threatened the integrity and welfare of the American republics, their response to the necessities of cooperative security action was encouraging.

On the diplomatic and political fronts there was, with the exception of Argentina and Chile, instant and united action. Indeed, the recalcitrance of those South American republics, however unfortunate the fact, did not negate the more important fact that the other American states seriously endeavored to implement the principle of "all for one, one for all." In meetings of their foreign ministers and in numerous specialized conferences, measures for diplomatic and political action

Overseas Operations: Report Prepared for the Bureau of the Budget (Washington, 1951), 81.

[83] U.S. Dept. of Commerce, *Foreign Aid by the United States Government, 1940–1951* (Washington, 1952), 24.

were mapped out. Although many of the recommendations of the conferences and agencies were never executed, it is nevertheless a matter of record that the severance of ties, political and economic, with the Axis was about as complete and effective as the requirements dictated. So also were the measures enacted, pursuant to the recommendations of the CPD, to deal with acts of espionage and sabotage by Axis agents.

On the military front, also, were evidences of solidarity, though not nearly so convincing as those on the political and economic. Direct participation in the overseas theater was limited to the modest token contributions by Mexico and Brazil. Other countries were willing to send small contingents to the fighting fronts but were dissuaded by the United States because of problems of equipment, training, coordination, and transportation.

It was on the economic front that our Latin-American associates made their greatest and most significant contributions to the war effort. Suppliers of a number of strategically-indispensable raw materials for our war industry, the Latin-American producers cooperated earnestly and sympathetically with United States agencies in plans for stepping up production. There is no evidence that they exploited their production of essential raw materials or drove hard bargains with us. According to Assistant Secretary of State Will Clayton, at the Mexico City Conference in 1945, the procurement contracts "were made without undue bargaining . . . the prices were fair and every effort was made to extend production."[84] As a matter of fact it was United States policy that Latin-American producers and workers should benefit from our economic dependence.

That production was phenomenally increased is supported by the statistics. United States procurements from Latin America from July 1, 1940, to September 30, 1945, amounted to $2,520 million, a figure far in excess of any comparable period. Procurements, in millions of dollars, were in the following order: Cuba, 710; Chile, 671; Mexico, 343; Brazil, 205; Bolivia, 186; Argentina, 139, and Peru, 109. For example, in 1943 Mexico produced twice as much zinc as in 1937; Brazil and Cuba each produced more than twice as much manganese in 1943 as in 1937; Chile more than doubled its copper production over the same years, and the same was true of the sugar production of Cuba.[85]

An inevitable result of this great increase of our imports from Latin America, and of our inability to supply their demands for United States

[84] U.S. Dept. of State, *Bulletin,* XII (March 4, 1945), 334.
[85] United States Military Academy, *Raw Materials in War and Peace* (West Point, 1947), 110–111, 145–149.

goods during the war, was the build-up of huge dollar credits. A Brazilian complained that their position was comparable to that of Pizarro, who, when he asked the Incas for food, was served only gold. To add to this particular Brazilian's woes, when he was able eventually to spend his dollars in the American market he had to buy at inflated prices.

In appraising Latin America's economic cooperation in the war effort it is not amiss to refer to the fact that war procurement provided new income for their governments, greater profit to producers, and expanded employment at higher wages for labor. It proved to be most gratifying to hang economic cooperation and economic profit on the same peg. There is, however, another side. The programs for expansion often dislocated economic life. Labor was transferred from food production to that of minerals and nonedible products, resulting in food shortages. Also, this emphasis on the production of a few raw materials for export accentuated the gravity of the problem of finding markets under peacetime conditions. At best, however, references by noncombatant Latin Americans to their "sacrifices" fail to impress their war associates who contributed heavily to the casualty lists.

That so much of the cooperation in World War II was bilateral (United States vis-à-vis individual Latin-American countries) does not belie the fact that this occurred within the context of multilateral association. This derives from the unique nature of the inter-American system, composed as it is of one great power and twenty states varying greatly in the degree of their weakness and development. What is particularly remarkable about this association is the willingness of the great power to accept the other states as juridical equals. But in other respects they are not equals, and the inter-American system reflects this fact. In the organizing of defense against foreign aggression the United States must be a partner in all essential undertakings. Thus there are bilateral contracts based not only in particular reciprocal interests but also in hemispheric defense and continental solidarity.

An assessment of the inter-American security system after being put to the test of World War II yields the conclusion that in meeting its greatest crisis it demonstrated flexibility and adaptability. The agreed prewar obligation to consult in the event of an overseas aggression, coupled with the acknowledgment of a mutuality of defense interests, was the sum and substance of the formal security procedure. Although the over-all security structure was endowed with a plethora of procedures applicable to inter-American disputes, it had not reckoned with extracontinental attacks. This meant that the mounting problems of belligerency and nonbelligerency created by Axis violation of the peace and security of the Americas had to be met on an *ad hoc* basis. Step by step, as war developments required, the American nations by common agreement improvised policies and procedures.

Fortunately, these improvisations were generally sound, and proved to be effective, thanks to the recognition of a mutual-defense interest. This is not to say, however, that a more formalized system of security obligations and procedures would not have been of greater service in meeting the problems of World War II. At the least, much time could have been saved, not only in the making of policy but also in implementing vital war measures.

As a matter of fact, the war experiences of the American nations, collectively and individually, served the useful purpose of directing attention to the weaknesses and deficiencies of the inter-American security system, particularly to the problems of overseas aggression. Wartime experiences proved their value in stimulating demand for a postwar strengthening of the security structure. Indeed, there was no disposition to await the end of the war before attacking the problem, for there was a growing Latin-American demand that another inter-American conference or meeting be convened immediately to consider not only problems of the war in its final stages but also of their security system in the peace that was to follow.

IX   Integrating the Inter-American Security System into the United Nations

The subject itself was difficult—how to *save* legitimate regionalism (like Pan-Am.) and yet not destroy the essential over-all authority of the International Organization. . . . We have found an answer which satisfies practically everybody.

ARTHUR H. VANDENBERG, 1945

FOR SOME TIME BEFORE the end of the war there was increasing pressure on the United States by the other American governments for a meeting to discuss problems of the war and postwar period. The Latin Americans, greatly concerned that so much time had elapsed since the last meeting at Rio in 1942, feared that the United States was growing lukewarm in its support of hemispheric regionalism. In light of developments during the course of the war, they felt that there should be joint consideration without delay not only of the irritating problem of Argentina and the necessary means to strengthen the war effort in its final stage, but particularly of the postwar problems of security and economic cooperation. Such a conference, which eventually convened in Mexico City during February and March of 1945, crystallized views on the subject of inter-American regionalism, and so paved the way for the integration of the inter-American security system into the United Nations Organization at San Francisco.

The problem of Argentina. Undoubtedly the embarrassments created by the attitude of Argentina contributed to the delay in convening a conference. Applying a nonrecognition policy to the Farrell-Perón regime had proved to be ineffective, for the United States was not able to take the necessary supporting action. The British were strongly opposed to an economic embargo on the Plata nation, and frankly declared that it was not a case of disliking United States pork but rather of preferring Argentina beef. This impasse in United States–Argentine relations alarmed the Latin Americans, who in fact did not seem to be particularly concerned because of the fascist overtones of the Argentine government. A highly-regarded historian laments that Mr. Hull abandoned the Good Neighbor policy and reverted to "the United States dictate of other years."[1]

The situation was viewed as one confined essentially to the United States vis-à-vis Argentina. For example, when in October 1944, Argentina requested Mr. Hull, as chairman of the Governing Board of the Pan American Union, to convoke a meeting of foreign ministers to consider her situation, Brazil, Chile, and Peru told the U.S. State Department that they did not wish to take a stand for either Argentina or the United States.[2] The Chilean Foreign Minister protested that the voice of Argentina should not be drowned by the clamor of Pan American pronouncements from the United States. Solidarity was worth concessions to Argentina.

To a certain extent the earnest desire of the Latins to resolve the Argentine question, even at the cost of appeasement, was tied in with their greater concern for recognition of the autonomy of the inter-American system. The Dumbarton Oaks *Proposals for the Establishment of a General International Organization,* devised by the Great Powers and published on October 7, 1944, though making provision for regional arrangements as appropriate security agencies, declared unequivocally that "no enforcement action should be taken under regional arrangements or by regional agencies without the authorization of the Security Council." This meant that the inter-American security system was to lose its autonomy. Regional organization for security was to become a dependent instrument of a global body.

Since Latin-American opinion was definitely opposed to an "alien" veto of their security actions, they wanted to present a united front at the forthcoming United Nations Conference at San Francisco in order to impress the other countries with the unity of action in the Western Hemisphere. They would then be in a better position to point to the ability of the American nations to handle their own problems, and thereby add weight to their arguments for an autonomous regional arrangement within the universal organization. There is little question that the Latins preferred their own regional system over the proposed world organization, and that they would have been willing to sacrifice effectiveness in the world organization, if need be, to preserve what

[1] Francisco Cuevas Cancino, *Del Congreso de Panamá a la Conferencia de Caracas, 1826–1954* (2 vols., Caracas, 1955), II, 165.

[2] Laurence Duggan, *The Americas* (New York, 1949), 105–106.

they had. And why not? As members of the inter-American system they enjoyed privileges and rights which they undoubtedly would not have as members of a world organization that apparently recognized the inequality of nations. It must not be forgotten that in the inter-American system the Latin-American states enjoyed status and prerogative unique in the history of small states—Great Powers relations. Where else could one find a big power tied so effectively in its relations with small nations as in the regional arrangement of the Western Hemisphere?

Thus, not only was reconciliation with Argentina in order, but also there was need for inter-American consultation on measures to strengthen the hemisphere security system. Mr. Hull wrote later that he had opposed the idea of a consultative meeting at that time because, in view of the pending conference of the United Nations to establish a postwar organization, "it would be most unfortunate for the American Republics to enter that conference torn and rent by the Argentine question."[3]

After a delay of more than two months the Argentine request for a meeting of the foreign ministers was denied. On January 8, 1945, the Governing Board of the Pan American Union announced: "In view of the fact that the American nations cooperating in the war effort have agreed through diplomatic channels to hold a conference within the near future to study urgent war and postwar problems," the said conference would offer an opportunity to consider the request presented by Argentina.[4]

When the Argentine government learned of the decision to convene a conference of those American republics *collaborating in the war effort*—a device for excluding that non-cooperating nation—it informed the chairman of the Governing Board of the Pan American Union: "So long as Argentine rights continue to be disregarded and so long as the procedure of consultation continues to be altered, the Argentine Republic has decided to abstain from participating in meetings of the Pan American Union."[5] Although it remained to be seen what action would be taken on the Argentine problem by the forthcoming conference, it could be confidently predicted that it would be conciliatory and mild, given the earnest desire of the Latin-American states to restore relations with their sister republic, plus a definite re-

[3] Cordell Hull, *The Memoirs of Cordell Hull* (2 vols., New York, 1949), II, 1404, cited hereinafter as *Memoirs*.
[4] Pan American Union, *Bulletin*, LXXIX (March 1945), 153.
[5] *Ibid.*

versal of U.S. State Department policy following the retirement of Secretary Hull. Following the Stettinius-Rockefeller advent, a special mission was sent to Buenos Aires where it was agreed that, contingent on Argentine implementation of hemispheric defense commitments, and her acceptance of an invitation to re-enter the fold of American nations by endorsing the acts of the Mexico City conference, the United States would abandon its coercive attitude.[6] There is little doubt that the U.S. State Department was outmaneuvered in its handling of the Argentine question.

Postwar planning. When the American republics took their first steps in war planning, at the Rio meeting of 1942, they also initiated studies in postwar problems. These early initiatives included: first, a request that the Governing Board of the Pan American Union appoint an executive committee to function in the field of postwar problems; second, that the Inter-American Juridical Committee be entrusted with formulating specific recommendations relative to an international organization in the juridical and political fields and also in the field of international security; and third, that the Financial and Economic Advisory Committee undertake the study and formulation of recommendations on postwar economic organization.

As authorized, the chairman of the Governing Board, on February 25, 1942, appointed the Executive Committee on Postwar Problems which published, late in 1944, a report entitled *Pan American Postwar Organization,*[7] a report suggesting changes intended to strengthen the inter-American system. Included in the report was a draft treaty prepared by the Inter-American Juridical Committee which consolidated in one instrument the provisions of existing treaties and conventions relating to the pacific settlement of international disputes. The report also contemplated greater coordination between the Pan American Union and the various Pan American agencies that functioned in different countries. With respect to the emergency war agencies, it proposed that some be preserved after hostilities had ceased and that others be liquidated.

Of particular significance was the emphatic view expressed by the Executive Committee that inter-American questions should continue to be primarily the responsibility of the association of American states. While emphasizing their genuine interest in a world organization, and their intention to maintain close relations with this and other in-

---

[6] Sumner Welles, *Where are We Heading?* (New York, 1946), 206.

[7] Pan American Union, *Pan American Postwar Organization, Observations and Suggestions of the Executive Committee* (Washington, 1944).

ternational entities, the nations of the Western Hemisphere, according to the committee, adhered to the principle of regional-security arrangements. Finally, it was proposed that the best means of securing an expression of the collective views of the American republics on the subject of the relation of the inter-American system to a world organization would be through a meeting of their ministers of foreign affairs.

Turning next to the activities of the Inter-American Juridical Committee in postwar planning prior to the convening of the Mexico City conference, it is to be noted that this committee submitted two reports relating to postwar international organization: the first, issued on September 5, 1942, was *Preliminary Recommendation on Postwar Problems,* and the second, reported on June 5, 1944, bore the title *Recommendations for the Immediate Establishment of a Preliminary International Organization.*

The Preliminary Recommendation was, first, an analysis of factors which, in the opinion of the Juridical Committee, had contributed to the breakdown of international law and order and had resulted in two world wars; and second, a series of principles which the American states should follow in restoring law and order after World War II. In urging the necessity for a more effective international organization, the Juridical Committee conceded that the principle of universality of membership should be reconciled with the existence of regional groups operating autonomously in matters which do not concern the entire world community.[8]

Despite the reference in the draft to autonomous regionalism the Executive Committee of the Governing Board suspected that the Juridical Committee left much to be desired in its support of regional-security organization as opposed to global.[9] Accordingly, the Governing Board, to which the *Preliminary Recommendation* had been submitted, critically commented that the whole treatment was a very general one, with no particular consideration given to problems peculiar to the Americas. It proposed, therefore, that the Juridical Committee in its future studies give preferential consideration to "those matters

[8] Pan American Union, Inter-American Juridical Committee, *Preliminary Recommendations on Postwar Problems* (Washington, 1942), cited hereinafter as *Preliminary Recommendations.* See also Louise W. Holborn (ed.), *War and Peace Aims of the United States* (World Peace Foundation, Boston, 1945), 588–589.

[9] Dr. Charles G. Fenwick, United States member of the Juridical Committee, has assured the writer that it was the view of the committee that the inter-American system should be subordinated to the world organization.

that relate more specifically to the Republics of the American Continent, and especially to their position in and relationship to any international organization that may be created following the conclusion of the war."[10]

The second report of the Juridical Committee, dealing with postwar international organization, *Recommendations for the Immediate Establishment of a Preliminary International Organization,* also failed to relate the subject specifically to the inter-American situation.[11] Enough was said, however, to reveal that the committee was not particularly concerned with the formation of a stronger inter-American regional system. We are forced to the conclusion that, although the postwar studies of the Juridical Committee proved to be of value in drafting the Charter of the Organization of American States, the benefits from its services were negligible in meeting the problems attending integration into the United Nations.

Regionalism and general international organization. After the outbreak of World War II, when a successor to the discredited League of Nations was being discussed, considerable interest centered on the status of regional systems in the new general international organization. Many felt that, in the drafting of the Covenant of the League of Nations, it had been a mistake not to provide a more definite place for regionalism in the new world order. But, as we have noted, the inter-American system of 1919, because of its impotence, did not recommend itself to the framers of the League of Nations as a competent agency to be vested with the task of peace enforcement in the Western Hemisphere.

But how different had the inter-American system become in 1945! In the period between the two world wars hemispheric isolation had permitted the Pan American movement to develop in its own way, without being involved in the power politics of Europe. With the liquidation of American imperialism, the negotiation of Pan American pacts of peaceful settlement, United States renunciation of the right of intervention, and the development of the Good Neighbor policy, the inter-American system had acquired status and respect, not only in the Americas but in the rest of the world as well. It is not surprising, therefore, that in the discussions concerning a new world

[10] *Preliminary Recommendations,* 2; A. P. Whitaker, *Inter-American Affairs, 1942* (New York, 1943), 15, 180.

[11] Pan American Union, *Bulletin,* LXXVIII (Sept. 1944), 497–500; *Minutes of the Inter-American Juridical Committee, February 14–December 19, 1944* (Washington, 1946), 134–139.

organization there was insistence on retaining the system which had forged to the front as the world's principal successful international-security agency.

In a Memorial Day address on May 30, 1942, Mr. Sumner Welles, then Undersecretary of State, lauded the accomplishments of the inter-American system, saying that it constituted the only example in the world of a regional federation of free and independent peoples. "It lightens the darkness of our anarchic world. It should constitute a cornerstone in the world structure of the future."[12]

Discussions regarding a general international organization, and the relation of the inter-American system to it, received more purposeful stimulation by the publication of the Moscow Declaration on November 1, 1943, in which the governments of the United States, Great Britain, the Soviet Union, and China jointly declared that they "recognize the necessity of establishing at the earliest practicable date a general international organization, based on the principle of the sovereign equality of all peace-loving states, and open to membership by all such states, large and small, for the maintenance of international peace and security." Although the declaration contained no reference to regionalism,[13] and consequently gave no indication regarding its place in postwar world order, the response to the declaration throughout the Americas was overwhelmingly favorable. Since the United States, stalwart supporter of Pan Americanism, was one of the signatory powers to the Moscow Declaration, the Latin-American republics reasonably expected that the interests of the inter-American system would not be neglected.

In making his report on the results of the Moscow conference, however, Secretary Hull aroused some doubt about whether the continued development of a regional inter-American system was contemplated when, in expressing his enthusiasm for the proposed world organization, he said in a speech before Congress: "There will no longer be need for spheres of influence, for alliances, for balance of power, or any other of the special arrangements through which, in the unhappy

[12] "Address at Arlington National Amphitheatre, Arlington, Virginia," in *Vital Speeches of the Day* (City News Publishing Co., New York, 1942), VIII, No. 17, 514–516.

[13] "Nothing was said of regional security organizations in the declaration, and in the discussions at Moscow. I strongly argued against them."—Hull, *Memoirs,* II, 1647.

past, the nations strove to safeguard their security or to promote their interests."[14]

Although Mr. Hull did not intend that his remarks should include the inter-American system, at best his choice of words was poor. The inter-American system did most certainly rest upon "special arrangements" through which the member states strove to "safeguard their security" and "promote their interests." Latin-American diplomats in Washington immediately voiced their alarm over the prospective fate of the inter-American system. To allay their fears, Mr. Hull had to make an unconvincing public statement that what he had told Congress did not apply to the inter-American system.

In point of fact there was solid ground for Latin-American apprehension, for a struggle was going on in the U.S. State Department between those who emphasized the regional approach, led by Undersecretary of State Sumner Welles, and those who adhered to the global approach, headed by Secretary Hull, aided and abetted by Dr. Leo Pasvolsky. At the start Welles had the support of the President himself. According to Hull, Welles echoed the ideas of Roosevelt and Churchill on the subject of regionalism. Both the President and the Prime Minister were convinced that after the war the nations of certain geographical regions should organize to maintain peace in those areas. Insofar as there was to be an international organization it should do little more than coordinate the work of the regional organizations.[15]

Mr. Hull declared that he "could not go along with the regional feature." He felt very strongly that the trend of nations to rely on national and regional self-protective measures must be checked. While arguing for universal international organization, he conceded that he did not oppose regional or other special arrangements supplementary to the general organization so long as they did not infringe on the necessary superior powers in the general association of nations.

Naturally, then, the persistent refusal of the United States to meet with the other American states in a consultative meeting to consider such urgent problems as the Argentine question, the general international organization, and postwar economic readjustments in Latin America lent substance to general apprehension that emphasis in United States policy was being shifted from regional to universal organization. Latin-American fears about the future of the inter-Amer-

[14] *New York Times,* Nov. 19, 1943.
[15] *Memoirs,* II, 1640.

ican system were eloquent evidence of the preferred position which that regional arrangement had come to occupy in their esteem. There is little question that they wished to give this going concern priority over a prospective, untried, universal organization.

Hull felt himself bound by the Moscow Declaration to withhold discussion of the international organization with the smaller powers until after the Big Four—United States, Great Britain, Soviet Union, and China (immediately after her liberation France came in, making it the Big Five)—had agreed on a draft project. Therefore proposals from Latin America to consult on the subject fell on deaf ears, contributing to the unfair charge that Mr. Hull was disinterested.

Shortly after the announcement of the Moscow Declaration, Sumner Welles, who had recently resigned from the State Department, advocated in a speech before the Foreign Policy Association in New York on October 16, 1943, a plan for world organization that must have been very acceptable to the regionalists. Describing himself as a "convinced believer in the efficacy and in the need for the permanent continuance of the existing inter-American regional system," he proposed a world organization based upon regional arrangements, conforming in their general pattern to that evolved in this hemisphere and all of them coordinated under an executive council composed of four permanent members and representatives of each region. "In such an organization," he said, "each region would be primarily responsible for regional peace, and only in the event that a regional conflagration threatened the general peace, would wider action become necessary."[16]

Similar sentiments were expressed in Latin America. For example, Foreign Minister Ezéquiel Padilla of Mexico, in a speech on October 15, 1943, said he had in mind a league which would be "formed into regional sections," of which the Western Hemisphere would constitute one. Disputes would first be referred to regional agencies; if they were not settled there they would be referred to the central authority of the league.

Since it was generally taken for granted that the Pan American association of nations would be maintained, whether or not it was integrated into the general international organization, it was felt desirable to examine the possibilities of enabling the system to perform more effectively its role as guardian of the peace of the Western Hemisphere. This necessity was realized in various Latin-American chancelleries and in the U.S. Department of State as well, where, as has been noted,

[16] *Vital Speeches of the Day,* X (Nov. 1, 1943), 54.

considerable study was being devoted to the relationship between the inter-American system and the prospective general organization. These studies were hampered, however, by Hull's position that an exchange of views with the Latin-American countries should not take place until after the Big Four had agreed on a project for a general organization.

Eventually representatives of the Big Four met at Dumbarton Oaks in Washington on August 21, 1944, to draw up tentative plans for a world organization. The secrecy in which the conference deliberated perturbed the Latin Americans, concerned as they were over the preservation of the inter-American system. When their discontent became too vocal to be any longer disregarded, both Mr. Hull and Undersecretary Stettinius invited the Latin-American diplomats at Washington to private meetings at which they were given reports on the progress of the conference. However, nothing more was revealed to them privately than was being reported daily in the *New York Times* by its correspondent James Reston, who seemed to have access to a private pipeline to the conference.[17]

The conference dragged on for almost six weeks, and it was not until October 10 that the Dumbarton Oaks *Proposals* were presented to the world as the kind of international organization which the Big Four had agreed to sponsor. Section C, Chapter VIII, of the *Proposals* provided for regional arrangements as follows:

1. Nothing in the Charter should preclude the existence of regional arrangements or agencies for dealing with such matters relating to maintenance of international peace and security as are appropriate for regional action, provided such arrangements or agencies and their activities are consistent with the purposes and principles of the Organization. The Security Council should encourage settlement of local disputes through such regional arrangements or by such regional agencies, either on the initiative of the states concerned or by reference from the Security Council.
2. The Security Council should, where appropriate, utilize such arrangements or agencies for enforcement action under its authority, but no enforcement action should be taken under regional arrangements or by regional agencies without the authorization of the Security Council.
3. The Security Council should at all times be kept fully informed of activities undertaken or in contemplation under regional arrangements or by regional agencies for the maintenance of international peace and security.[18]

[17] For his reporting of the Dumbarton Oaks Conference, Mr. Reston was awarded a Pulitzer Prize.

[18] *Proposals for the Establishment of a General International Organization, Postwar Foreign Policy Preparation, 1939–1945, Department of State, Publica-*

At the Dumbarton Oaks Conference, the United States took the initiative in proposing that regional arrangements be integrated into the universal organization. The representatives of the other three powers agreed to support our position. At a Columbus Day reception for Latin-American diplomats, Mr. Stettinius sought to assure his guests that the United States delegation to the conference had done everything possible to preserve the inter-American system. He stated that the American delegates had kept constantly in mind inter-American relations and the contributions which all American nations cooperating together could make toward a peaceful and stable world order. Each proposal had been examined, he said, in light of the common interests of this hemisphere for peace, security, and friendly cooperation. Referring to the specific Dumbarton Oaks provision regarding regional arrangements, Mr. Stettinius declared his belief that the United Nations Security Council would encourage the settlement of local disputes through regional systems. He said, "We believe that the effect of this will be to enhance the position and responsibilities of the inter-American system."[19]

Despite the reassurances by Mr. Hull and Mr. Stettinius, the Latin Americans remained unconvinced that the Dumbarton Oaks *Proposals* accorded an acceptable status to the inter-American security system. They objected particularly to the provision that no enforcement actions could be taken by a regional agency without authorization by the Security Council. They saw in this the end of the inter-American system's autonomy. They also opposed accommodating hemispheric security actions to the will of a Security Council packed with the representatives of non-American powers. Another feature of the *Proposals* which aroused Latin-American criticism was the principle of unequal representation on the Security Council—with its five seats assigned permanently to the five principal powers. This was part of a pattern of Great Powers control, or "dictation," as some called it. The Mexico City newspaper *Excelsior* described the Dumbarton Oaks project as a disguise for the partition of the world among the Great Powers.[20]

But perhaps more pronounced than criticism of any particular feature of the *Proposals* was Latin-American resentment of the fact that four powers had arrogated to themselves the task of drafting in secret the project for a world organization. Under the circumstances, they

---

tion 3580 (Washington, 1949), 617, cited hereinafter as *Proposals*.

[19] *New York Times,* Oct. 13, 1944.

[20] *Excelsior,* Oct. 13, 1944.

argued, was it surprising that the *Proposals* were interlarded with in-
genious devices to ensure the formalization of Great Powers dominance? The criticism of the Dumbarton Oaks *Proposals* centered,
therefore, on two major points: one, the Great Powers were granted
too much authority and would dominate the organization; and two, the
inter-American system was not given the important role it should
enjoy.

The Latin-American nations, while deeply interested in the proposed
plan for a world organization, hoped to see it revised so as to embody
certain principles in which they were particularly interested. Believing that their purposes could be better achieved through concerted
action, they strongly urged that a consultative meeting of their foreign
ministers be called to consider the participation of the Americas in the
future world organization. Thus, these demands for a consultation
meeting were added to those concerning the Argentine question. If all
this did not provide enough pressure on the United States, there was
also their importuning of this government to confer without delay on
postwar economic problems.

Postwar economic cooperation. Although there were many problems
relating to the continued economic collaboration of the American republics during the final stages of the war which undoubtedly could be
profitable subjects of inter-American consultation, certainly it was not
because of them that the Latin-American states clamored for a consultative meeting. They wanted a conference to discuss their *postwar
economic problems,* particularly those of the transition period from
war to peace. They feared "the economic consequences of the peace."
As a Chilean official put it, "There loom two dramatic question marks
that beset the man who likes to think ahead: (1) what will be done
with the millions of men who will lose their employment upon the advent of peace, and (2) how will readjustment be made of raw materials upon termination of the requirements of war industries?"[21]

As the end of the war approached, reconversion to peacetime production and the return to peacetime economic relations presented serious
problems of readjustment. The excessive demand of war had induced
an expansion beyond all peacetime requirements, and also in order to
meet the problem of consumer-goods shortages, a considerable amount
of industrial expansion had occurred in many of the countries. Thus,
the end of the war would mean not only a drastic reduction and eventual termination of war-created demand for raw materials, but the

[21] *Chilean Gazette* (New York), July –Aug. 1943.

revival of foreign industrial competition as well. This realization emphasized necessity for a widespread reallocation of capital and labor resource within the national economies.

It was this concern with the effects of reconversion that prompted the Financial and Economic Advisory Committee, and the various governments and leaders of commerce and industry in Latin America, to anticipate their postwar economic positions and to formulate programs and policies respecting the problems they were likely to face. As far back as 1943 several of the countries had created postwar policy commissions.[22] Insofar as the planning depended on the support of foreign capital—and it was considerable—all eyes were turned to the United States.

In fact, Latin America believed that an inter-American conference could not meet too soon to attack postwar economic problems. Since the United States and the United States alone possessed the key to the solution of their problems, obviously a conference must be convened to wheedle concessions from this country.

Latin-American discontent. In view of the prolonged and increasing Latin-American demands on a reluctant United States for a conference to consider a number of problems close to their hearts, it would be idle to deny that some cracks had begun to make their appearance in the inter-American cooperative structure. Mounting criticism of the United States seemed to be the inevitable result of the changed character of the war; that is, as the sense of immediate crisis decreased, the bonds of unity loosened. With the end of the war approaching, there appeared to be both opportunity and justification for finding fault with the United States' handling of the Argentine problem, its trend to universalism at Dumbarton Oaks, and its apparent loss of interest in the consultative system.

Latent fears of the United States would not be downed. For example, Mexican Ambassador to Cuba José Rubén Romero, in a Pan American Day address on April 14, 1943, said:

Certainly we Latin Americans are not winning the war, possibly because it is far away and we have not suffered its deprivations, because it has not awakened our enthusiasm, our confidence, our faith, which every war requires. We see the United States advancing as a giant, fighting nobly for our ideals, but in the degree that the giant grows, its shadow falls on us, and we are frightened.[23]

[22] Foreign Policy Association, "Latin American Organizations for Postwar Planning," *Report,* XX (March 15, 1944), 12.
[23] *América* (Havana, April–May 1943), 5.

In the same vein was an indignant outburst in Ecuador following an unconfirmed report that the United States was seeking to procure permanent bases in the Galápagos Islands. The Quito newspaper *El Día* said that the Yankees should realize that the principal reason for Latin-American antipathy toward the United States in the past had been imperialism, dollar diplomacy, and the Big Stick, and if the recently-established good feeling was to last, then imperialism must be scrapped once and for all.[24] In Brazil, likewise, there was growing fear that the United States might wish to retain its military might there even after hostilities had ceased.

The frame of mind of many *Latinos* was reflected by an outstanding Peruvian intellectual who wrote, "To achieve a common inter-American front . . . the United States must demonstrate that it is concerned with the welfare of the common man in Latin America." Not only Luis Alberto Sánchez, but many others were asking: Will the policy of the United States be permanently broadened to carry forward, in this postwar period, economic relations between North and South America to help raise the standards of living of her southern neighbors? For the United States to assume this burden was regarded not only as an obligation but also as needed proof of our loyalty to the Good Neighbor policy. This being the criterion, it was well-nigh impossible for the United States to attain the status of the perfect Good Neighbor and thus earn a respite from Latin-American criticism and suspicion.

Despite the pressure exerted on the United States by the mounting tide of criticism, it did not consent to schedule a conference until it felt that the proper time had arrived. Eventually, by tying in the inter-American conference to plans for a general United Nations Conference to be held at San Francisco, and by confining the agenda largely to the subject of a United Nations organization and to wartime economic problems, it discovered a precedural device to exclude Argentina by limiting the conference to those American nations *that had cooperated* in the war effort and so earned the right to consider American problems arising out of the war, as well as the proposed United Nations Organization. Thus it was agreed in December 1944, that a conference would be held in Mexico City the following February to consider the collaboration and participation of America in the future world organization, measures to strengthen the inter-American system, and the economic solidarity of the continent.

The Mexico City Conference. The Inter-American Conference on

24 *El Día*, Dec. 9, 1943.

Problems of War and Peace convened in Mexico City on February 21 and continued in session until March 8, 1945. All the American nations (except Argentina) were represented. This was not one of the regular series of inter-American conferences, nor was it a consultative meeting of the foreign ministers. It was an extraordinary meeting, convened and organized in a manner somewhat different from that usually followed in convoking inter-American conferences. Thus the agenda, instead of being formulated by the Governing Board of the Pan American Union, was prepared by the Mexican government on the basis of consultations with the other invited governments. The four major categories of problems confronting the conference were: those related to the prosecution of the war; those concerning international organization; those related to postwar economic cooperation; and the Argentine question.

There were few "war" measures to be considered by the conference, for at that time World War II was in its final phase. Two resolutions which fell in this category were: (1) War Crimes (Resolution VI), which recommended that the American republics announce their adherence to the principle that persons guilty of war crimes should be tried and sentenced; and (2) Elimination of Centers of Subversive Influence (Resolution VII), which recommended that the governments intensify their efforts to eradicate the remaining centers of Axis subversive influence.[25]

If the problems of "war" did not seem to intrigue the delegates, most assuredly they were concerned with the problems of "peace" as they related to the proposed world-security organization. The establishment of a new universal organization emphasized the need for important changes in the inter-American system in order that it might function as a recognized regional arrangement within the larger framework of the world organization.

In an address to the Mexico City conference Secretary of State Edward R. Stettinius, Jr., said:

Let me remind you that the Dumbarton Oaks *Proposals* recognizes the value within the framework of a general organization, of regional arrangements for promoting peace and security. . . . The United States government believes that the stronger we can make the inter-American system in its own sphere of activity, the stronger the world organization will be.[26]

[25] Thomas C. Mann, "Elimination of Axis Influence in this Hemisphere; Measures adopted at the Mexico City Conference," in U.S. Dept of State, *Bulletin,* XII (May 20, 1945), 924–926.
[26] *Inter-American Conference on Problems of War and Peace, Mexico City,*

The Latin-American delegates, in considering the Dumbarton Oaks *Proposals,* wanted the United States to make a declaration favoring autonomous action for the inter-American system, but this Mr. Stettinius refused to do on the ground that he wanted to go to San Francisco and work for an efficient world organization without having his hands tied. The State Department feared that any commitments at this point to support Latin-American proposals at San Francisco would only help to confirm fears abroad of a Pan American bloc. Thus, in compliance with the wishes of the United States, the Mexico City conference made no positive declaration on regional arrangements, but it did adopt a resolution on the Dumbarton Oaks *Proposals* which was to be submitted to the San Francisco Conference. The resolution provided:

1. The world organization should strive toward the ideals of universality.
2. The section in the Dumbarton Oaks *Proposals* dealing with the principles and purposes of the world organization should be amplified and made more specific.
3. The powers of the General Assembly of the proposed world organization should be amplified and made more specific so that this organ could play a more effective part.
4. The jurisdiction and competence of the international court of justice should be extended.
5. An international agency specially charged with promoting intellectual and moral cooperation between nations should be created.
6. It would be "desirable" to solve "controversies and questions of an inter-American character, preferably in accordance with inter-American methods and procedures, in harmony with those of the general international organization."
7. An "adequate representation" in the world Security Council should be given to Latin America.[27]

Fifteen Latin-American countries submitted to the Mexico City conference "observations" on the Dumbarton Oaks *Proposals.* These were analyzed in a comprehensive report, and it was agreed that this report and the observations, in addition to the above resolution, should be transmitted to all nations invited to the United Nations Conference. The general tenor of the suggestions was well expressed by the president of the conference, Dr. Ezéquiel Padilla, in the following statement:

February 21–March 2, 1945: Report Submitted to the Governing Board of the Pan American Union by the Director General (Washington, 1945), 6.

[27] *Ibid.,* 64–65.

The small nations do not pretend to equal participation in a world of un-equal responsibility. What they do desire is that, in the hour in which injustice may strike at the doors of small nations, their voice may be heard; that they may appeal to the Universal Conscience, and that their complaints and protests against injustice shall not be shrouded in the silence and blind solidarity of the great powers.[28]

It is clear from their "observations"[29] that the Latin-American countries were strongly committed to their own system of regional association and felt that it should have priority in the settlement of hemispheric disputes. The adoption of the Act of Chapultepec strongly reinforced this position. This most notable action of the Mexico City conference declares that "every attack of a State against the integrity or the inviolability of the territory, or against the sovereignty or political independence of an American State, shall . . . be considered an act of aggression against the other states," and in case of an act of aggression "the States signatory to this Act will consult among themselves in order to agree upon measures" ranging from the recall of diplomatic envoys to the use of armed force to prevent aggression. Since the procedures contained in the act were to be effective only during World War II, it was recommended that, following the establishment of peace, a treaty should be negotiated formalizing these principles and procedures.[30]

Since the Act of Chapultepec contemplated the use of force to meet threats or acts of aggression from any source,[31] this immediately presented the question of the relation of this act to the charter of the proposed world organization. Section C, Chapter VIII (par. 2) of the Dumbarton Oaks *Proposals* specifically stated that "no enforcement action should be taken under regional arrangements or by regional agencies without the authorization of the Security Council." The Act

[28] *Ibid.*, 10.

[29] The above summary is based on the *Diario de la Conferencia Inter-Americana sobre Problemas de la Guerra y de la Paz* (Mexico, March 5, 1945).

[30] *Report of the Delegation of the United States of America to the Inter-American Conference on Problems of War and Peace, Mexico, February 21–March 8, 1945* (Washington, 1946), 72–75, cited hereinafter as *Report of the U.S. Delegation on Problems of War and Peace.*

[31] The act represented a radical departure from agreements previously adopted in that it applied to aggressor states within the continent as well as to states outside the hemisphere. Some of Argentina's neighbors, fearing aggressive intentions, wished to be guaranteed United States support. Also the act contained the first sanction in an inter-American agreement for the use of armed force if necessary.

of Chapultepec seemed to be incompatible with this provision. To reconcile this contradiction, a final paragraph was added, stating that the act constituted "a regional arrangement for dealing with such matters relating to the maintenance of international peace and security as are appropriate for regional action in this Hemisphere." A second clause, United States-inspired, provided that "the said arrangement, and the pertinent activities and procedures, shall be consistent with the purposes and principles of the general international organization, when established."

Did this mean that the use of force, sanctioned by the Act of Chapultepec, could be resorted to in this hemisphere without the approval of the Security Council? If so, the United States, in signing it, was guilty of repudiating the stand which it had taken on regional arrangements at Dumbarton Oaks. While endorsing the principles embodied in the act, the United States delegation maintained that it was subject to the international-security agreement of Dumbarton Oaks and Yalta. It will be recalled that the Dumbarton Oaks Conference failed to agree on the voting procedure to be followed in the Security Council. This matter was settled at the Yalta Conference of February 1945, when President Roosevelt, Premier Stalin, and Prime Minister Churchill agreed that no enforcement action was to be taken without the concurring vote of the five permanent members of the Security Council and the additional affirmative votes of at least two of the nonpermanent members. When the United States delegates said that the Act of Chapultepec was subject to the agreement reached at Dumbarton Oaks and at Yalta, they plainly meant that no action could be taken under the provisions of the act without the approval of the Security Council, and that this approval could be denied by the veto of one of the Great Powers. Thus the Act of Chapultepec and the Oaks provisions on regional arrangements were apparently in conflict, and the solution of this problem at the San Francisco Conference was awaited with interest and concern.

There was general recognition among the delegates at Mexico City that the intensification of the international relations of the American republics among themselves, with states in other parts of the world, and with the United Nations Organization required a broadening of the base and a strengthening of the whole structure of the regional system. Therefore the conference adopted a resolution entitled "Reorganization, Consolidation, and Strengthening of the Inter-American System."[32] Some of its provisions were to go into effect immediately,

---

[32] *Report of the U.S. Delegation on Problems of War and Peace*, 76–80.

but others were to await the adoption of a comprehensive charter on the inter-American system by the next general conference of American States, scheduled to be held at Bogotá in 1946. To this end the Governing Board of the Pan American Union was directed to prepare a project on the improvement and strengthening of the inter-American system.

Of the approved changes—which included annual meetings of the foreign ministers, quadrennial general conferences, annual elections of the chairman of the Governing Board who shall not be eligible for re-election, and limitation of the term of the director-general to ten years—probably the most significant was the enlarged functions and broader powers given to the Pan American Union and the Governing Board. The Governing Board was now to take action "on every matter that affects the effective functioning of the inter-American system and the solidarity and general welfare of the American Republics." The action by the Havana conference of 1928, which specifically denied political functions to the Union, was reversed. This reflected a significant change of attitude toward the role of the Union and its Governing Board in the inter-American system. No longer was there fear that the Colossus of the North would manipulate control of the Pan American Union to further its domination of the Americas. The resolution opened up new horizons for the Pan American Union.

Another significant action was the Declaration of Mexico,[33] which set forth certain fundamental principles which should govern interstate relations in the American community. In addition to basic principles, so often repeated, such as juridical equality of states, the pacific settlement of disputes, the outlawing of war, and nonintervention, the declaration emphasized the rights of the individual and the social obligations of the states. Furthermore, it declared that economic collaboration was essential both for the development of democracy and for the common prosperity of the American nations.

Thus, with respect to the fundamental problems of international organization, evoked from consideration of the Dumbarton Oaks *Proposals,* the Mexico City conference made substantial progress. There could be no doubt that the Latin-American membership desired to convert the inter-American system into a sufficiently strengthened and effective regional-arrangement that it would hold priority in the settlement of hemispheric disputes. But to the Latin Americans, important

[33] *Ibid.,* 80–81.

as were the problems of postwar security organization, equally important were those of postwar economic cooperation. In fact, the latter may have outweighed all other considerations.

In response to the concern expressed by various hemisphere countries regarding the manner, time, and degree of curtailment of procurement contracts for strategic materials, once war demand had begun to slacken, a resolution, Economic Adjustment of the Hemisphere During the Transition Period[34] was adopted, which provided in general for a "tapering off" process. That is, the American countries producing and acquiring strategic raw materials should enter into bilateral agreements for applying measures to minimize during the transition period the adverse consequences which might arise from the abrupt termination of procurement of such materials.

The resolution was adopted following the introduction of several proposed special measures to meet these problems, including gradual curtailment of purchases, stockpiling to take up excess surpluses, and a hemispheric trading corporation. A statement delivered by Assistant Secretary of State Will Clayton on February 27 clearly set forth the position of the United States on this matter. He assured the conference that the United States recognized a responsibility and proposed to meet it, consistent with its laws, public opinion, and a due regard for its economy. Thus, adequate notice of curtailment or termination of procurement contracts would be given. In addition, he held out hope that stockpiles of strategic materials might be maintained in the postwar period, permitting some current purchases. These were fine words which fortunately were not put to the test, for the anticipated termination of United States purchases did not take place. Latin-American raw materials were needed as much for economic recovery as they had been for military purposes. True, the contracts for materials having little peacetime use were terminated, but in the main those for the major products were continued. Hence there was no serious economic dislocation in Latin America caused by the change from a war to a peacetime economy during the early months following the cessation of hostilities. There was, however, real distress arising from inflation.

More fine words at the Mexico City conference were reserved for the Economic Charter of the Americas,[35] which contained a declaration of the fundamental economic aspirations of the peoples of America, and

[34] *Ibid.,* 92–94.
[35] *Ibid.,* 120–124.

the guiding principles for achieving these objectives. With respect to the objectives, the document specified the continued mobilization of economic resources until the achievement of total victory; an orderly transition of the economic life of the Americas from war to peacetime conditions; and a constructive basis for the sound economic development of the Americas. Guiding principles for achieving these objectives included: equality of access to raw materials and producers' goods needed for industrial and economic development; reducing barriers to international trade; eliminating the excesses of economic nationalism; just and equitable treatment for foreign enterprise and capital; promoting private enterprise; removing obstacles which retard or discourage economic growth and development; and international action to facilitate the distribution of production surpluses.

In the interest of long-range economic development, several of the Latin-American governments favored protection for their new war-created industries. They voiced the "infant industry" argument in support of high tariffs to meet the threat of heavy postwar competition from the industrial powers. The United States did not warm to this argument, favoring instead a lowering of tariff barriers. Eventually a weakened policy statement was adopted which provided only for finding "practical international formulae to reduce all barriers detrimental to trade between nations in accordance with the purpose of assuring all peoples of the world high levels of living and the sound development of their economies."[36] With respect to meeting Latin-American desires on the economic front, it must be recorded that the Mexico City conference was short on concrete programs but long on glowing generalities. Given the state of opinion in the United States and constitutional limitations, it is difficult to see how the American delegation at Mexico City could have acted otherwise.

As prearranged, when the other topics of the agenda had been disposed of, the problem of Argentina was taken up. Also prearranged was the solution. Thus, discussions of the matter were *pro forma,* and little difficulty attended the drafting and adoption of a resolution entitled "On the Communication Addressed by the Argentine Government to the Pan American Union."[37]

In this resolution the conference, after declaring that complete solidarity and a common policy among the American states were essential for the security and peace of the continent when threatened by aggression, deplored that Argentina had not found it possible to join with

[36] *Ibid.,* 122–123.   [37] *Ibid.,* 133–134.

the other American republics in Mexico City to consider the problems of war and peace. The hope was expressed that that notion would implement a policy of cooperative action with the other American states and thus achieve her incorporation into the United Nations. To this end the Final Act of the Mexico City conference was open to adherence by the Argentine nation.

This resolution, or "address," was transmitted to the wayward member by conference President Ezéquiel Padilla through the Pan American Union. On March 27 the Argentine government announced its adherence to the actions of the Mexico City conference, and declared a state of war against the Axis countries. It also announced the initiation of measures to prevent any activities by enemy aliens interfering with the war effort of the United Nations or threatening the security of the American nations. The members of the inter-American community, through their representatives on the Governing Board of the Pan American Union, decided unanimously that the measures taken by Argentina complied with the conditions, and so the Chargé d'Affaires of Argentina was allowed to sign the Final Act at Mexico City on April 4, 1945. On April 9 it was announced that the other twenty American republics, after consultation, had unanimously decided to resume diplomatic relations with Argentina.[38] And so ended the Argentine case. Or did it?

It soon became evident that Argentine compliance had been purely opportunistic. After that country had been readmitted, its military clique indicated no intention of doing more than was absolutely necessary. It was a mistake in judgment that the Mexico City resolution made no provision for any kind of follow-up procedure to check on the repentant's behavior. In view of evident backsliding, it was not long before the United States was forced once more to reverse its policy and return to unilateral threats against Argentina.

Despite the portents of dissension in the Mexico City conference, surprisingly an atmosphere of sweetness and light prevailed. There was remarkable unanimity, not only on the Argentine issue but also with respect to the strengthening of the inter-American system. And although Latin-American desires on economic matters were not satisfactorily met by the United States, nevertheless its promises warranted some optimism. It was on the issue of international-security organization, and particularly the future status of inter-American regionalism, that United States and Latin-American views conflicted; not that

---

[38] *Ibid.*, 38; Pan American Union, *Bulletin*, LXXIX (May 1945), 260–263.

the United States delegation was committed to the principle of universality, but it did not believe that, at this stage, the Oaks *Proposals* should be altered. To resolve this problem of clear conflict between the Act of Chapultepec and the regional-arrangements provision of the Dumbarton Oaks *Proposals* was the Mexico City challenge to San Francisco.

The San Francisco Conference. According to the Yalta Agreement, invitations to the pending United Nations Conference on International Organization were to be extended only to those states that had declared war on the Axis by March 1, 1945. There were (in addition to Argentina) six Latin-American countries that had not done so—Chile, Ecuador, Paraguay, Peru, Uruguay, and Venezuela. Early in 1945 the United States, acting on behalf of the sponsoring powers, informed these states that unless they complied with this requirement and so became members of the United Nations, they would not be eligible for invitations to the conference. There was almost immediate action; before the end of February the six countries had declared war, and on March 27 the seventh—Argentina—did likewise.

This action by the United States has been criticized[39] as being contradictory to earlier policy, for some of the six countries affected had been assured by this government that a severance of relations was sufficient; and a declaration of war was not required by the resolution of reciprocal assistance adopted at the Havana meeting of 1940. Moreover, not being members of the United Nations alliance had not prevented these countries from being invited to participate in other United Nations meetings. For example, in 1943 all but Argentina participated in the two conferences on food and agriculture, and relief and rehabilitation. Again, in 1944, all except Argentina were represented at the United Nations Monetary and Financial Conference (Bretton Woods). Nevertheless, there can be no denying that the requiring of declarations of war—a requirement for which the United States was not solely responsible—though it may have been harsh and inconsiderate of the sensibilities of cooperating nations, was effective in forcing a declaration of belligerency by Argentina, even though it was only *pro forma*. However, since the Argentine action came nearly four weeks after the March 1 deadline, that nation did not gain immediate admission to the San Francisco Conference, but had to wait upon Soviet approval.

The issue of admitting Argentina to the United Nations Conference was joined to that of plural membership for the Soviet Union in

[39] Laurence Duggan, 108.

the new organization. When the Latin Americans learned of the pledge President Roosevelt had given Stalin at the Yalta Conference for the admission of White Russia and Ukrainian Soviet Socialist Republics to membership, they insisted on tying the admission of Argentina to such a deal. Since the United States had assumed obligations to support not only President Roosevelt's Yalta commitment but also the Mexico City pledge to Argentina, Secretary of State Stettinius finally compromised, asking for the immediate seating of the delegates of White Russia and the Ukraine, and also Argentina.[40] Russia's strong objection to the seating of Argentina was finally overcome and the Stettinius proposal was approved. Former Secretary of State Cordell Hull recorded in his *Memoirs* that the United States had been outmaneuvered on the Argentine question and that he would have voted against admission.[41] President Truman was also reported as being opposed. However, in view of the earlier ill-considered pledges, it is difficult to see how Mr. Stettinius could have acted otherwise at San Francisco.

The intemperate opposition of Foreign Minister Molotov to Argentine admission, and the aspersions he cast on the so-called "Latin-American bloc" served very effectively to unite the Latin Americans against the Soviet Union. Equally effective was the occasion when Molotov shocked a committee meeting by deriding Mexico Foreign Minister Padilla as a puppet of the United States. The Latin Americans regarded this attack as an expression of contempt for the dignity and independence of the smaller nations, and thus as an insult to all of them. According to Senator Arthur H. Vandenberg, a leading member of the American delegation, "Molotov has done more in four days to solidify Pan America against Russia than anything that ever happened."[42] These incidents reinforced Latin-American determination that the Soviet Union should never be granted the right, through the exercise of the veto, to interfere in its intraregional affairs.

The interest and activities of the Latin-American states at the San Francisco Conference revolved about two kinds of issues: their relative position as small powers within the United Nations, and the position of their regional system in the world organization. It is the second problem which must engage our special attention. As for the first, a brief summary should suffice.

[40] Arthur H. Vandenberg, Jr. (ed.), *The Private Papers of Senator Vandenberg* (Boston, 1952), 178, cited hereinafter as *Private Papers*.

[41] Hull, *Memoirs,* II, 1722.

[42] Vandenberg, *Private Papers*, 179–182.

THE UNITED STATES AND INTER-AMERICAN SECURITY

The small-powers issue. The Latin-American nations took the typical small-nation attitude in asking for a clear definition of the principles and purposes of the world organization and for increased powers for the General Assembly. They sought acceptance of the concept of juridical equality, the cornerstone of the inter-American system. But the United Nations was not to be founded on this principle, for the five permanent Great Powers were to enjoy special privilege over the other members. In general the Latin Americans were unsuccessful in imposing a small power imprint on the basic principles of the United Nations. "The role of law," says a recent writer, "was given little emphasis, [and] the concept of absolute juridical equality was rejected."[43]

They were no more successful in their efforts to strengthen the role of the General Assembly in matters of peace and security. When it became evident that the Great Powers control of the Security Council could not be broken, it was only natural that the small powers should seek more authority for the General Assembly, for in that body they would have an equal voice with the powerful states. Although the General Assembly remained primarily a debating body, if it were allowed to discuss any question or matters within the scope of the organization, public opinion could be brought to bear upon the decisions of the Security Council. But efforts to have the jurisdiction of the General Assembly coordinated with, or superior to, that of the Security Council, thus enhancing the importance of the Assembly, were effectively blocked. The principal opposition came from the Soviet Union, which feared the potential effect that the "American bloc" might have in the world organization. This alone may have convinced Russia that she must retain full use of her veto power in the Security Council and oppose any great extension of the powers of the General Assembly. But however desirable it was to the Latin Americans to have the powers of the General Assembly enlarged, they were much more interested in the problem of integrating the inter-American security system into the United Nations, the problem to which we now turn.

How to integrate. There is little question that the Western Hemisphere delegates came to San Francisco determined to seek preservation of the inter-American system. They had aligned themselves, of course, with the other small states in the controversy over the veto power in the Security Council, but their real interest in the matter lay in the

[43] John A. Houston, *Latin America in the United Nations* (New York, 1956), 26.

effect that a veto would have over enforcement action taken by any regional-security agency such as the inter-American system. They were not opposing the veto as universalists but rather as regionalists.

In spite of their vital interest in the problem of integrating regional arrangements into the world organization, the Latin-American delegations were wise in letting the United States go to bat for them instead of trying to achieve their purposes alone. It was in "behind the scenes" conferences that the Latin Americans strove to convince the United States delegates, among whom there was substantial disagreement, for not all were willing to go so far as to advocate autonomous action for regional agencies. In fact it was U.S. State Department policy to oppose autonomous regionalism on the ground that it would promote inevitably the fragmentation of the universal organization. Dr. Leo Pasvolsky, architect of the State Department draft which proved to be the core of the Dumbarton Oaks *Proposals,* vigorously opposed the mere suggestion of regional autonomy.[44]

The principal discussions at the San Francisco Conference on regional arrangements took place in a subcommittee (Committee 4 of Commission III), of which Dr. Alberto Lleras, Colombian minister of foreign affairs, was chairman. Senator Vandenberg was the United States member. According to the Senator, the critical problem was to find a formula that would recognize the paramount authority of the world organization in all enforcement action and yet permit regional action independently in case of undue delay or ineffectiveness.[45]

A number of delegations submitted amendments to Section C, Chapter VIII, of the Dumbarton Oaks *Proposals,* the section dealing with regional arrangements.[46] Mr. H. V. Evatt, Australian minister for external affairs, proposed that instead of all five permanent mem-

[44] According to Harley Notter, Dr. Pasvolsky's chief aid, the *official American view* at San Francisco was that, while regional arrangements were permitted under the Charter, they should be effective only within the framework of the general international organization.—*Postwar Foreign Policy Preparation* (Washington, 1949), 127–138.

[45] Vandenberg, *Private Papers,* 198.

[46] For all amendments proposed by individual countries, see U.S. Dept. of State, *The United Nations Conference on International Organization, San Francisco, April 25 to June 26, 1945: Selected Documents* (Washington, 1946), 192–200, cited hereinafter as *Selected Documents.* Also, for the work of the committee dealing with regional arrangements, see Pan American Union, *The United Nations Conference on International Organization: Report by the Director General* (Washington, 1945), cited hereinafter as *Report to the Director General.*

bers of the Security Council having the right to veto action by regional agencies against aggression, the vote of only three should be required, since it was not desirable that a Great Power should be in a position to veto regional action within an area which it was not vitally concerned with. Furthermore, if the Security Council did not deal with the dispute, and did not refer it to the regional agency for solution, the regional agency should be free to take whatever action it liked.[47]

The majority of the Latin-American delegations took the position that the inter-American security system should be allowed to function independently of the Security Council. The delegations of Chile, Colombia, Costa Rica, Ecuador, and Peru submitted a joint draft amendment in which they specifically declared that the Pan American system should continue to function autonomously. The Security Council, however, would be permanently and fully informed concerning the activities of the regional system.[48]

Lest the impression be given that only the Latin-American nations were interested in the question of regional arrangements, we should note at this point some of the observations made on the subject by other nations. The Australian proposal has just been mentioned. France, having in mind her mutual-assistance treaty with Russia, declared that regional action should be permitted without the approval of the Security Council for measures taken to prevent renewed aggression by any of the present enemy states. Russia supported this proposal. Turkey proposed that all regional arrangements of a defensive nature should be permitted to take action without prior approval of the Security Council. Egypt wanted the Charter to include a clear definition of "regional arrangements" in order that the Pan Arab League could be recognized as such, but she argued that military alliances should not be considered as regional arrangements. Belgium, while justifying the veto power of the five permanent members of the Security Council on some matters, did not favor the veto with regard to regional action. In view of the fact that many countries, in addition to the twenty-one members of the inter-American system, were interested in regional

[47] The Australians were anxious not to be left unprotected. They wanted liberty of regional action if some one of the big powers vetoed action in the Council.—Vandenberg, *Private Papers*, 190.

[48] United Nations Conference, *Selected Documents*, 6, 21. For a fuller discussion of Latin-American participation in these matters, see Cuevas Cancino. II, 187–195.

arrangements, it is not surprising that the question dominated the discussion during the first three weeks of the conference when a real impasse developed.[49]

The Vandenberg formula. The regional problem became "the crux of the Conference." Mr. Nelson Rockefeller, reporting to one of the numerous United States delegation conferences held in the luxurious penthouse apartment of Secretary Stettinius atop the Fairmount Hotel, said that the South American republics were up in arms and had no intention of giving in.[50] It was at this critical juncture that Senator Vandenberg offered a compromise plan which reconciled the Australian proposal, the Latin-American viewpoint, and the position taken by the various countries having mutual-assistance pacts. It read as follows:

The right of self-defense is inherent in every nation-state. In the event of an attack against any one of a group of countries which have a tradition of mutual assistance, such as expressed in the principles and objectives of an arrangement such as the Act of Chapultepec, then states may take concerted action against an attack on any one of them. This right shall not, however, deny to the Security Council the right to take any action it deems necessary to maintain international peace and security.[51]

At Senator Vandenberg's urging, Secretary Stettinius called a meeting with the Latins and explained to them the proposed amendment, which clearly removed the threat that a veto in the Security Council could prevent regional action against aggression. When the Latin Americans were assured that the United States agreed to the calling of a Pan American conference at the earliest convenient date to conclude a regional-defense treaty, as envisaged by the Act of Chapultepec, and within the framework of the United Nations, they gave their unanimous approval.[52]

The Vandenberg formula, slightly modified in the subcommittee, became the famous Article 51 of the Charter. It provided:

Nothing in the present Charter shall impair the inherent right of individual or collective self-defense if an armed attack occurs against a member of the United Nations, until the Security Council has taken the measures necessary to maintain international peace and security. Measures taken by Members in the exercise of this right of self-defense shall be immediately reported to

---

[49] Pan American Union, *Report by the Director General*, 4–5.

[50] Vandenberg, *Private Papers*, 187.

[51] *Ibid.*, 188–189; *New York Times*, May 13, 1945.

[52] Vandenberg, *Private Papers*, 192–193.

the Security Council and shall not in any way affect the authority and re-sponsibility of the Security Council under the present Charter to take any such action as it deems necessary in order to maintain or restore international peace and security.

The chapter on regional arrangements in the Charter adhered sub-stantially to the general terms agreed upon at Dumbarton Oaks. The only modifications were those necessary to reconcile them with the sense of the new Article 51. The decision on regional arrangements seemed to please all concerned. Quite properly, Senator Vandenberg received a vote of thanks for his contribution to the settlement of the issue. "We have infinitely strengthened the world organization," said Senator Vandenberg, "by enlisting, within its over-all supervision, the dynamic resources of these regional affinities. We do not thus sub-tract from global unity on behalf of the world's peace and security; on the contrary, we weld these regional key-links into the global chain."[53]

The meaning of integration. Having recounted the steps leading to the integration of the inter-American security system into the United Nations, it is now in order to indicate briefly the nature, extent, and significance of the Charter provisions on this subject. Article 33 im-poses upon regional agencies or arrangements the primary responsi-bility to seek a pacific settlement of disputes among its members before they are referred to the Security Council. The Council is, in fact, ex-pected to encourage the solution of local disputes through regional arrangements, either on the initiative of the states concerned or by reference from the Council.

While it is true that the inter-American system could enjoy, under the foregoing provisions, considerable autonomy in the peaceful set-tlement of local disputes, its freedom of action is subject to certain limitations. Thus, not only must the Security Council be informed of any disputes which arise in this hemisphere, and of steps taken to settle them (Art. 54), but the Council can investigate those disputes to de-termine whether or not world peace is being threatened (Art. 34). Also, while every opportunity is to be given regional agencies to settle local disputes among their member nations, the Security Council re-tains the right to step in at any time to determine whether or not the regional machinery will be efficacious in settling the disputes, and to

[53] United Nations Information Organization, *Documents of the United Na-tions Conference on International Organization, San Francisco, 1945* (15 vols., London, New York, 1945), XI, 52.

make recommendations on the appropriate procedures or methods of adjustment (Art. 36).

In still another respect the jurisdiction of the inter-American system is abridged. A local dispute can be referred to the Security Council before any attempt is made to settle it in accordance with the procedures established by the regional agency. If, for example, Mexico were involved in a dispute with the United States, and felt that she could get a better deal if the dispute were brought to the attention of the Council instead of having it settled in accordance with the regional arrangement, the Council could be asked to investigate. Of course, the Security Council might then ask the United States and Mexico to settle their dispute through recourse to the procedures established by the inter-American system; but it could, on the other hand, recommend other appropriate procedures of adjustment or recommend such terms of settlement as it deemed appropriate.

Even with respect to the right of American nations to take collective measures of self-defense, as agreed in the Act of Chapultepec, the superior authority of the United Nations is recognized by Article 51, which provides that should any nation party to such a defense agreement be attacked, the other contracting states may carry out their obligations to join in its defense as an emergency measure until the Security Council has taken the measures necessary to maintain peace and security:

Measures taken by members in the exercise of this right of self-defense shall be immediately reported to the Security Council and shall not in any way affect the authority and responsibility of the Security Council . . . to take at any time such action as it deems necessary in order to maintain or restore international peace and security.

It remained for the future to disclose to what extent the exercise of the veto power by one of the permanent members would prevent action by the Security Council in the exercise of its superior authority over the inter-American system in the security realm. The veto power did not apparently extend to discussions in the Council or to the preliminary phase of peaceful settlement. Thus, if seven members of the Council voted to investigate any dispute in the Americas, neither the United States nor any other permanent member could block investigation by the exercise of its veto. However, any one of the Great Powers, even if a party to the dispute, could veto any action of the Security Council directed toward peaceful settlement. If the United States were a party to a dispute, say with Cuba, presumably it could not block investigation by the Council, but it could veto any enforcement action.

The discussion so far has pertained to the relationship between the inter-American system and the Security Council of the United Nations. It must be remembered, however, that the General Assembly can also discuss any question or problem relating to international peace and security, or discuss any problem within the scope of the world organization. While the General Assembly has no executive authority, it can make recommendations to the Security Council or to the members themselves on any problem or dispute taken up for consideration. The United States would not have the veto power in the General Assembly to block any recommendations made by that body since all nations have an equal vote in the Assembly. However, recommendations by the General Assembly must be approved by a two-thirds majority, difficult to obtain since the Latin-American nations would probably join with the United States in opposing any proposed recommendation that pertained to affairs in this hemisphere. The American nations have twenty-one votes in the General Assembly, and until recently that number was sufficient to defeat any motion requiring a two-thirds majority. Although action by the General Assembly is merely recommendatory and carries no obligatory force, it can be the means of mobilizing powerful world opinion.

The decision by the San Francisco Conference on the issue of regional arrangements raised a number of questions, and of these one of the most searching was: Will the inter-American security system continue to operate virtually independent of outside authority, and thus its so-called "integration" into the United Nations be merely *pro forma?* The answer to this question depended on future developments. If the inter-American system demonstrated its ability to settle local disputes and maintain peace and security in the Western Hemisphere, it undoubtedly would be cheerfully allowed by the United Nations to monopolize this area of responsibility. In this event its only obligation to the superior authority would be to keep the Security Council "fully informed of activities undertaken or in contemplation . . . for the maintenance of international peace and security."

In order to meet this added responsibility it was necessary for the American nations not only to strengthen the inter-American peace procedures but, more important, for them to develop a greater willingness than they had displayed in the past *to submit* to these procedures. Bumbling efforts to settle another Chaco War, for example, might prove fatal to their pretentions to autonomous action in the security field.

Too great reliance was not to be placed on the probability that the United States would exercise its veto in the Security Council to prevent the application of enforcement procedures in the Western Hemisphere. It could be expected that the United States would undoubtedly use the veto to check any measures by the United Nations deemed violations of the Monroe Doctrine or prejudicial to the solidarity of the American nations; on the other hand, however, the interest of this country in the preservation of hemisphere peace would probably induce it, when local efforts failed, to support intervention by the Security Council. The United States, a world power and therefore vitally interested in the maintenance of peace and security throughout the world, would, in all likelihood, refuse to subordinate this larger interest in favor of a regional organization which demonstrated its incapacity to settle disputes or preserve peace in its own area.

At the least, the "victory" of the Latin Americans at San Francisco imposed on them a very great obligation: *vindication* of their hemispheric security arrangement in its new role. How they measured up to the challenge will be the next subject of our inquiry.

X The Organization of American States (1945-1948)

It may be said that in the political field our Organization has now reached full maturity. . . . It has the means for settling pacifically disputes arising between the member nations, and it can also repel extra-continental aggression, through joint action, with all the force of its solidarity.

ALBERTO LLERAS, 1949

THE AMERICAN NATIONS had made it clear at Chapultepec, and underlined this decision at San Francisco, that they proposed to deal with purely American security questions through a stronger and more effective inter-American system. Thus, within two years the Inter-American Treaty of Reciprocal Assistance was negotiated at Rio de Janeiro, and shortly after, at Bogotá, additional improvements in the organizational set-up were effected. These developments were declared to be consonant with Article 51 of the United Nations Charter, and so represented further integration of the inter-American system into the world organization. Thus the end of the war afforded the awaited opportunity to create, from the patchwork of temporary expedients, a more cohesive security system.

The Rio de Janeiro Conference. It had been decided at the Mexico City conference that one of the first of the postwar actions would be to draft a treaty incorporating the principles and procedures of the Act of Chapultepec, for this notable document, which provided for reciprocal assistance, was a temporary wartime agreement and would lapse at the conclusion of the war.

Obviously, the drafting of such a treaty had to await the decision of the San Francisco Conference respecting enforcement action by regional arrangements. The acceptance of Article 51, which recognized the inherent right of individual or collective self-defense, was understood to make the Act of Chapultepec consistent with the United Nations Charter, and so a green light was given for the negotiation of a formal treaty based on the Act of Chapultepec. In addition, a pledge had been secured from Secretary Stettinius at San Francisco to support the early negotiation of such a treaty. He said, "The United States intends to negotiate in the near future a treaty with its American neighbors which will put the Act of Chapultepec on a permanent basis, in harmony with the World Charter."[1]

On August 29, 1945, the Governing Board of the Pan American Union decided that a conference to draft a mutual-assistance treaty would take place in Rio de Janeiro on October 20, 1945. However, on October 5 the U.S. State Department suggested a postponement of the conference. Why? Although no reason was given, it was well known that once more the United States and Argentina were at loggerheads. Surely, next to the United States itself, no country has exerted a greater influence on inter-American developments than Argentina, however negative the influence of the South American nation has been.

Although Argentina had declared war on Japan and Germany on March 27, 1945, her belligerence was purely *pro forma,* for she had not yet taken the steps necessary to fulfill the obligations assumed by her adherence to the acts of the Mexico City conference. These facts, coupled with the appointment of a new United States ambassador to Argentina, Spruille Braden, who openly attacked Perón, participated a new crisis in United States–Argentine relations. The crisis mounted when in February 1946 the U.S. State Department circulated the famous *Blue Book* which charged that the policies and actions of the recent regimes in Argentina had been aimed at undermining the inter-American system. Under the circumstances the United States raised the question "whether the military regime, or any Argentine government controlled by the same elements, can merit the confidence and trust which is expressed in a treaty of mutual assistance among the American republics."[2] To collaborate with Argentina in negotiating such a treaty would be a travesty.

Unfortunately, the attitude of the United States vis-à-vis the Argentine regime was not shared by Latin America. It was the same old story—the virtues of "unity," impossible without Argentina, were worth the sacrifice of democratic principles. The replies to the "consultation" initiated by the U.S. Department of State concerning the Argentine situation were most discouraging. Bolivia announced that

---

[1] U.S. Dept. of State, *Bulletin,* XII (June 3, 1945), 1009.
[2] *Blue Book,* 4.

she would maintain "cordial" relations with Perón. Brazil said that she also would continue "friendly" relations, and furthermore that a hemispheric mutual-assistance pact must include *all* the American states. Chile wanted to hear the Argentine side before signing a pact. Cuba regarded Argentina as a requisite member of a pact. Guatemala agreed with the United States that a pact should come *after* Argentina showed readiness to cooperate. Perón's government, in the view of Mexico, presented no threat to international peace and hemisphere solidarity. As for Peru, she believed that Perón's regime "deserved consideration" on the basis of free elections.[3]

Perón's election to the presidency of his country, despite the revelations in the *Blue Book,* placed the U.S. State Department in a very embarrassing position. A "softened" policy was presaged by the issuance, on April 8, 1946, of a memorandum on Argentina containing the following: "The military assistance commitments taken by the United States under the Act of Chapultepec will terminate with the expiration of the War Powers Act in this country. It is to the benefit of all the American republics that a treaty of mutual assistance by negotiated and signed at the earliest possible date."[4] On April 18 the Argentine government formally urged a restoration of Good Neighbor relations with the United States. It asserted its readiness to maintain "its traditional pacifist ideals and unequivocal democratic faith." It even conceded that its neutral position may have been incorrect, but insisted that the government had followed the popular will.[5]

Washington finally decided that, in view of the developing East-West tensions and Latin-American pressure, it would be better to include Perón's government in the hemisphere defense pact rather than have no treaty at all. Thus, on June 10, 1947, the State Department announced it was satisfied that Argentina had complied with the anti-Nazi provisions of the Act of Chapultepec and it was now willing to resume discussions regarding a defense pact. The announcement that "good relations" had been completed also carried the information that Assistant Secretary Spruille Braden—a too insistent advocate of the principle that the Good Neighbor policy is a two-way street—had been "permitted" to resign.[6] Under the leadership of U.S. Ambassador George S. Messersmith at Buenos Aires the forces of "business as usual" prevailed.

[3] *New York Times,* April 8, 1946.
[4] U.S. Dept. of State, *Bulletin,* XIV (April 21, 1946), 667.
[5] *New York Times,* April 18, 1846.
[6] *Ibid.,* June 10, 1947.

This was a victory for the Argentine dictator since he had in fact made no important concession. Although Perón and his military associates had no enthusiasm for the objectives of the forthcoming conference, they were unwilling to be left out. Accordingly, as a result of consultations initiated by Brazil, the Inter-American Conference for the Maintenance of Continental Peace and Security was convoked at Quitandinha near Petropolis, State of Rio de Janeiro, on August 15, 1947. The sole purpose of the conference was "the preparation of an inter-American treaty of reciprocal assistance to give permament form to the principles embodied in the Act of Chapultepec." The fact that the agenda was limited to this one subject, and that the several postponements afforded ample opportunity for preparation, augured well for an expeditious and successful conference. This indeed was the happy outcome.

The Inter-American Treaty of Reciprocal Assistance. Although most of the delegations were headed by the foreign ministers,[7] this was not a consultative meeting, but a special conference. All the republics participated except Nicaragua, which had not been invited because of a change of government "under abnormal circumstances." Toward the end of the conference, Ecuador lost its representation because of a *coup d'etat* which resulted in a new administration at Quito that was not immediately recognized by the other American republics. Of course the treaty negotiated by the conference was opened to the eventual signatures of the two absent members.

In broad terms, the Rio conference of 1947 was convened (1) to formalize in a pact of mutual assistance the obligation of continental solidarity in the face of aggression, and (2) to reconcile such a pact of collective self-defense with the obligations assumed under the United Nations Charter.

Since the Act of Chapultepec was accepted as a frame of reference, this meant, among other things, that the projected treaty would adhere to the principle that aggression *from any source* was violative of the sovereignty and security of all the American states and so imposed individual and collective security responsibilities.[8] Unfortunately the act did not provide effective sanctions; it merely enumerated the kinds of measures that could eventuate from consultation. Hence sanctions were not automatic but were entirely dependent on consultation. More-

---

[7] The exceptions were from Costa Rica, Cuba, and Honduras.

[8] Argentina proposed that the Americas act collectively to repel *only* outside aggression. After precipitating a near crisis in the conference this position was abandoned.—*New York Times,* Aug. 24, 1947.

over, the Act of Chapultepec was vague on the meaning of such vital terms as "attack" and "act of aggression." Nor was anything said in the act about voting procedure and the binding effect of the sanctions agreed upon. An examination and analysis of the principal provisions of the Inter-American Treaty of Reciprocal Assistance, signed at Rio de Janeiro on September 2, 1947, will reveal to what extent these deficiencies were corrected.[9]

Following the preliminary reference in the treaty to certain basic considerations and objectives of inter-American security cooperation and to a reaffirmation of the principles of pacific settlement, the obligations imposed by solidarity in the face of acts of aggression are set forth in clear and unmistakable terms. First, an *armed attack* by any state against an American state shall be considered an attack against all, and each one of the contracting states undertakes to assist in meeting the attack. Each one is privileged, immediately or prior to a consultative decision, to afford the aggressed member any assistance it may wish to extend. The nature of the assistance to be rendered collectively is to be determined by the regular organ of consultation of the inter-American system, i.e., a meeting of the ministers of foreign affairs, or in an emergency, by the Governing Board of the Pan American Union acting as a provisional organ. Delegating the consultative function to the Governing Board was an important and interesting enlargement of the role of the Pan American Union in security matters.

The measures that may be taken by the parties individually or collectively in case of armed attack are identical with those enumerated in the Act of Chapultepec. They include: recall of chiefs of diplomatic missions, breaking of diplomatic and/or consular relations, economic sanctions, and armed force.

The degree of obligation to assist the victim of armed aggression is conditioned by the locality of the attack. The Rio treaty indicates as the area of its incidence the Western Hemisphere and adjacent islands.[10] If an armed attack occurs within this region, the obligations already described obtain: that is, the contracting parties are obligated to assist

[9] For the text of the treaty, see U.S. Dept. of State, *Report of the Delegation of the United States of America, Inter-American Conference for the Maintenance of Continental Peace and Security, Quitandinha, Brazil, August 15–September 2, 1947,* Publication 3016 (Washington, 1948), 59–66, cited hereinafter as *Report of the U.S. Delegation;* see also U.S. Dept. of State, *Inter-American Treaty of Reciprocal Assistance,* Publication 3390 (Washington, 1949).

[10] *Report of the U.S. Delegation,* contains a map (p. 58) showing the region defined by Article 4 of the treaty.

in meeting the attack, the means depending, of course, on the decision of the organ of consultation. But with respect to armed attack outside the defined zone—which conceivably could be overseas possessions, positions held in varying degrees of sovereignty, and the naval or air forces of the American states—this calls for a different procedure. The organ of consultation will meet immediately in order to agree on the means to be employed to assist the victim of the attack. In this instance, prior consultation is obligatory before any individual state can offer assistance. A practical reason for this procedural variation is that the occurrence of armed incidents far removed from the Americas could lead to a misinterpretation of facts and consequent premature or ill-judged offers of assistance by other American states. To obviate such embarrassing incidents, a more deliberate prior consultation seemed advisable.[11] Moreover, this procedure represents a braking device to prevent the involvement of American nations in "extracontinental" conflict, even though an American member is included.

In the event of other forms of aggression that are not armed attack,[12] and other situations that might endanger the peace and security of America, the organ of consultation meets and agrees on the means to be taken. Likewise, in case of a conflict between two or more American states, the contracting states will meet in consultation to agree on necessary measures to re-establish peace. "The rejection of the pacifying action will be considered in the determination of the aggressor and in the application of the measures which the consultative meeting may agree upon."[13]

One of the most advanced and significant features of the Rio treaty is the provision for voting. The decisions of the organs of consultation shall be by a two-thirds vote of the states that have ratified the treaty. Such decisions, which presumably will impose sanctions of varying degrees of severity, will be binding upon all signatory states with the sole exception that no state shall be required to use armed force without self-consent.[14] This meant that each individual state, including the United States, committed itself to abide by the decisions of the majority

---

[11] Pan American Union, *Inter-American Conference for the Maintenance of Continental Peace and Security, Rio de Janeiro, August 15–September 2, 1947: Report on the Results of the Conference by the Director General* (Washington, 1947), 34–37.

[12] The Rio treaty did not improve on the Act of Chapultepec in defining "the aggressor." It circumvented the juridical problem by substituting a description of certain cases of aggression that may be considered typical.—*Ibid.*, 45.

[13] Art. 7.   [14] Art. 20.

in imposing different kinds of sanctions with the sole exception of armed force. Here truly was a historical innovation, for up to this time the tender sensibilities of national sovereignty never permitted a state to be bound in such matters by the decisions of other states. In particular this represented a distinct policy switch by the United States.

As a matter of fact the voting provisions of the treaty were identical with a compromise proposal submitted by the United States delegation on the eve of the Rio conference. Although the original position of the United States had been one of opposition to obligatory sanctions,[15] in view of the fact that a majority of the American republics, as revealed by preconference consultations, believed that collective measures should be obligatory on all parties, Secretary of State George C. Marshall announced a modification of the United States position. He proposed that those collective measures specifically mentioned in the Act of Chapultepec be obligatory on all contracting parties when agreed upon in consultation by a vote of two-thirds of the parties, with the sole exception that no state shall be required to furnish armed forces without self-consent.[16] Not only was this historic modification of United States policy, but the fact that most of the Latin-American republics expressed a willingness to accept the obligatory employment of force was equally significant.

The Rio treaty, as was also true of the Havana resolution on reciprocal assistance and cooperation (1940) and the Act of Chapultepec, undoubtedly covers Canada, not a member of the pact or the inter-American system. Since Canada is included within the geographical region defined by Article 4 of the treaty, and since it is included in the phrase "an American state," it is a beneficiary of the obligation imposed on the contracting parties to take positive action to assist in meeting an armed attack against any American state. Thus, not only the United States but the Latin-American countries as well have announced their intention to defend Canada from any attack by a non-American power, for they regard the defense of the hemisphere as indivisible.

Finally, it was necessary to coordinate the Rio Treaty of Reciprocal Assistance with the Charter of the United Nations. This was accomplished by having a number of references to the Charter appear in several of the articles of the treaty. First, in the Preamble, the American states "reiterate their will to remain united in an inter-American

[15] New York *Herald Tribune,* July 5, 1947.
[16] U.S. Dept. of State, *Bulletin,* XVII (Aug. 24, 1947), 367. The unanimity rule was favored by Argentina, the majority rule by Uruguay.

system consistent with the purposes and principles of the United Nations." Then, in Article 3, the obligation to assist the victim of aggression is declared to be "the exercise of the inherent right of individual or collective self-defense recognized by Article 51 of the Charter of the United Nations." These measures of self-defense, declares the treaty (Art. 3, par. 4), "may be taken until the Security Council of the United Nations has taken the measures necessary to maintain international peace and security." Complete information concerning activities undertaken in exercising the right of self-defense will be sent immediately to the Security Council (Art. 5). The most unequivocal of the articles (Art. 10) provides that "none of the provisions of this Treaty shall be construed as impairing the rights and obligations of the High Contracting Parties under the Charter of the United Nations." Finally, Article 15 establishes the Governing Board of the Pan American Union as the special liaison organ between the members of the Rio pact and the United Nations in all matters concerning this treaty.

In this manner integration was accomplished. This was the first treaty of collective self-defense to be concluded under Article 51 of the United Nations Charter. It was characterized by Senator Vandenberg, a member of the United States delegation, as "a supplement and not a substitute for the United Nations." The treaty was also described by the Senator as "sunlight in a dark world." It was destined to be accepted as the model for reconciling future treaties of defensive alliance with the obligations of United Nations membership, the first being the North Atlantic Treaty, signed on April 4, 1949.

Of course the Rio treaty was not without its critics. *Pravda*'s assertion that it was another step toward complete United States military subjugation of Latin America can be dismissed as being wholly in character. But the assertion of Mexican Foreign Minister Torres Bodet that politico-military defense was only half of the problem, the other half being mutual aid to raise living standards, gave food for thought. He declared that unless poverty, ignorance, and disease are opposed and overcome by the same unity of action as was projected against political foes, the American nations cannot say that they have gone to the heart of the problem.[17] Sumner Welles probably voiced the thoughts of many more when he wrote in his newspaper column that the new defense treaty would be of little value unless the American republics are politically stable and *economically* strong.[18] However,

[17] *New York Times,* Aug. 17, 1947.
[18] New York *Herald Tribune,* Sept. 9, 1947.

economic matters were not on the agenda of the Rio conference, and so were deferred to the pending Bogotá Ninth International Conference of American States.

Nevertheless, the Rio treaty added inestimable strength to the inter-American security structure. The agreed-upon procedures for handling acts and threats of aggression, both extra- and intra-continental, seemed to be as adequate as practical considerations would allow. Their efficacy could be known only when they were subjected to actual tests. This, in fact, was not slow in coming. The consideration of this must be delayed, however, pending our filling in the chronological gap from 1946 to 1948 with other relevant inter-American security developments.

Tasks assigned to the Juridical Committee. When the Mexico City conference approved the planning of a draft charter for the improvement and strengthening of the Pan American system, it was agreed that the charter should contain a "Declaration of the International Rights and Duties of Man," in order "to proclaim the adherence of the American republics to the principles established by international law for safeguarding the essential rights of man, and to declare their support of a system of international protection of these rights."[19] It was contemplated that the international protection of the essential rights of man would eliminate the misuse of diplomatic protection of citizens abroad. Accordingly the Juridical Committee was requested to prepare a draft declaration which was to be submitted, through the Pan American Union, to the American governments. Then, on the basis of comments offered by the governments, the committee was to prepare a final draft. Thus, the *Draft Declaration of the International Rights and Duties of Man and Accompanying Report* was formulated by the Juridical Committee and submitted on December 31, 1945.[20] This draft, somewhat revised as a result of the comments submitted by the respective governments, became the model for the American Declaration of the Rights of Man, adopted by the ninth conference at Bogotá in 1948.

Another task assigned the Juridical Committee by the Mexico City conference originated in a Guatemalan proposal to prevent the establishment of "anti-democratic regimes" in the Americas, as being dangerous to the solidarity, peace, and defense of the continent. It recom-

[19] *Report of the U.S. Delegation,* 108–109.
[20] Pan American Union, Inter-American Juridical Committee, *Draft Declaration of the International Rights and Duties of Man and Accompanying Report* (Washington, March 1947).

mended that the American republics refrain from recognizing or maintaining relations with such regimes, particularly those "that may originate from *coup d'etat* against governments of a legally established democratic structure."[21] Clearly this proposal was designed to supplement the Guani Doctrine, which was purely a war measure. It differed, however, in that it did not provide a system of collective nonrecognition, but merely that each government, in accordance with its own judgment, shall decide whether or not it would recognize a new government. Thus, this involved no change of the existent practice other than that the new government should be a democratic one.

The Juridical Committee, reporting on October 27, 1946, stated that it could not recommend the proposal to the American governments because the phrase "anti-democratic regimes" was too vague. And for one state to decide what constituted a democratic or antidemocratic regime in another would place in jeopardy the sacred principle of nonintervention. Moreover, the committee objected to withholding recognition from governments originating in a *coup d'etat,* for this would eliminate the substitution of governments by revolutionary action, and "might be unsuitable to the democratic future of America."[22] The Juridical Committee was well-advised in its opinion, for it realized how opposed were the Latin Americans to any procedure, however idealistic it might appear, which could serve as the entering wedge for the return of interventionism.

The Larreta proposal. Prior to the Juridical Committee's opinion on the Guatemalan project, there had come from Uruguay a proposal for nothing less than multilateral intervention in support of democratic principles and human rights. On November 22, 1945, Uruguayan Foreign Minister Eduardo Rodríguez Larreta, in notes to the American republics,[23] stated that the "parallelism between democracy and peace must constitute a strict rule of action in inter-American policy." Peace is safe, he said, only where democratic principles of government prevail. The basic rights of man are part of these principles. Hence, in case of their violation in any American republic, the other members of the community should take collective multilateral action to restore

[21] *Report of the U.S. Delegation,* 355.

[22] Pan American Union, Inter-American Juridical Committee, *Opinion of the Inter-American Juridical Committee on the Project Submitted by the Delegation of Guatemala, to the Inter-American Conference on Problems of War and Peace, Mexico, 1945* (Washington, 1946).

[23] "Inter-American Solidarity: Safeguarding the Democratic Ideal," in U.S. Dept. of State, *Bulletin,* XIII (Nov. 25, 1945), 864–866.

democracy. In an attempt to harmonize his proposal with nonintervention, Dr. Larreta declared that multilateral collective action, exercised with complete unselfishness by all the other republics of the continent and aimed at the mere re-establishment of essential rights, would not injure the government affected and would be for the benefit of all. "Nonintervention cannot be converted," he argued, "into a right to invoke one principle in order to be able to violate all other principles with immunity."

United States endorsement of the Larreta proposal was quick and unqualified. On November 27, Secretary of State James F. Byrnes announced agreement with the principle of opposing oppressive regimes among the American republics. "Violation of the elementary rights of man by a government of force and the nonfulfillment of obligations by such a government is a matter of common concern to all the republics," said the Secretary. "As such, it justifies collective multilateral action after full consultation among the republics in accordance with established procedures." Mr. Byrnes felt, as did the Uruguayan foreign minister, that the principle of nonintervention should not shield the notorious violation of the elementary rights of man.[24]

Although both Guatemala and Venezuela, in the flush of enthusiasm, having recently overthrown dictatorial regimes, applauded the Uruguayan initiative, the general Latin-American reaction could have been foretold. It was emphatic opposition to any compromise of the nonintervention principle. In addition to the United States, only five countries approved.[25] If the flouting of human rights by oppressive regimes was bad, intervention, whether unilateral or multilateral, was worse.

Before dismissing this subject, a brief explanation of the positions taken by Uruguay and the United States is in order. The little South American state, far in the lead of its Latin-American brethren in the purity of its democratic institutions, feared the ominous trend of developments within the borders of its powerful neighbor, Argentina, where the outlines of a fascist government were taking shape. Weak,

[24] "U.S. Adherence to Principle Opposing Oppressive Regimes Among American Republics," in U.S. Dept. of State, *Bulletin*, XIII (Dec. 2, 1945), 892.

[25] The U.S. State Department survey of Latin-American replies to the Uruguay intervention proposal revealed as favoring: Uruguay, United States, Panama, Guatemala, Costa Rica, and Nicaragua. Five qualified their objections, and the seven remaining were definitely opposed.—*New York Times*, Jan. 17, 1946.

unmilitarized Uruguay, concerned for her safety, was seeking the protection of a strong security system.[26] Conscious of her own record in democratic achievement, Uruguay could be almost certain that she would be immune to any such collective action against herself. Thus she risked nothing by promoting the principle of multilateral intervention against oppressive regimes. The Argentine government, evidently acknowledging that the shoe fitted, denounced Foreign Minister Larreta as a "puppet of the United States who stabbed Argentina in the back."[27]

The United States, on its part, was certainly less than circumspect in giving such unreserved endorsement of a procedure which could compromise the nonintervention principle. Many *Latinos* were already convinced that this country was seeking opportunity to escape the pledge which had come to be regarded as the keystone of the Pan American arch. Probably the real reason for United States approval of the Larreta proposal was unthinking dedication to idealism itself, that is, its belief that there is a "parallelism between democracy and peace." Even so, it is surprising that the State Department subscribed to the belief that democratic regimes could be instituted by multilateral intervention, and even more surprising that it was so naïve as to believe that the Latin Americans would accept multilateral intervention for *any* reason.

The problem of a prodemocratic policy. Despite the *Latinos'* emphatic rejection of the Larreta proposal, the United States did not abandon support of its integral idea, i.e., a positive, prodemocratic policy for the Americas. Merely mouthing words extolling the virtues of democracy was not enough. At the least, the United States would maintain aloof formality toward dictatorships and disreputable governments—no Marine landings, no White House visits, no favors, no decorations, no loans, no military equipment. This was the Braden policy for promoting democracy in Latin America.

Spruille Braden held, quite correctly, that United States influence, exerted or withheld, would continue to make and unmake hemisphere governments. Thus, he warned against intervention by inaction. He declared that the United States must distinguish between "legitimate" governments and those usurping powers from the people.[28] Secretary of State Byrnes was sold on the Braden idea, hence his unqualified approval of the Larreta proposal. President Truman himself declared

[26] *Christian Science Monitor,* Dec. 14, 1945.
[27] New York *Herald Tribune,* April 28, 1946.
[28] *Christian Science Monitor,* Feb. 14, 1946.

in Mexico City on March 4, 1947, that the United States would not be indifferent to happenings below the border when lawlessness threatened the existence of law upon which all nations depend. And at the Rio conference on September 2 the President said, "The attainment of world-wide respect for essential human rights is synonymous with the attainment of world peace."[29] Sr. Larreta could not have put it better.

It has already been noted that general Latin-American disapproval was one of the reasons responsible for the reversal of Braden's antidictatorship policy in Argentina. The United States was forced to forgo a positive policy in support of democracy and human rights. Whether sincerely or not, many Latins charged that the United States' opposition to Perón was inconsistent with its toleration of other Latin-American dictatorships.[30] Although it is true that the kind of attack the United States waged on Perón was withheld from Somoza of Nicaragua and Trujillo of the Dominican Republic, consideration has to be given to the fact that these dictators had been loyal in their observance of inter-American commitments.

In view of past and present Latin-American complaints that the United States has not chosen to distinguish between dictatorships and democracies in Latin America, it is well to recall the occasions just cited, when the Latin Americans themselves turned thumbs down on our efforts to implement a positive, although unwise, prodemocratic policy for the Americas.

Since Latin America registered an emphatic veto on proposals to employ collective intervention in support of democratic principles, we now turn our attention to nonrecognition as an alternative instrument. It was established at the Montevideo conference of 1933 that recognition was unconditional and could not be used as an instrument of policy. The Guani Doctrine, a departure from this policy, was by its own terms valid only for the duration of the war. Thus, when in May of 1947 Anastasio Somoza seized the Nicaraguan government by armed revolt and imprisoned President Leonardo Argüello, his hand-picked successor who had refused to be a rubber stamp, an occasion presented itself for using nonrecognition as an instrument in support of democratic procedures.

In February 1947 an "election" had taken place in Nicaragua in which the Somoza-backed Argüello was an easy winner, particularly

[29] U.S. Dept. of State, *Bulletin*, XVII (Sept. 14, 1947), 499.
[30] *Christian Science Monitor*, June 22, 1946.

since the opposition was prevented from participating in the electoral campaign. It was clearly a "stolen" election, and it put to the test the sincerity of Braden's antidictatorship declarations. Any question regarding recognition at this stage was clearly resolved by Somoza's act on May 27, 1947, in ousting Argüello on the pretext that he had plotted Somoza's "humiliation," i.e., his removal as chief of the National Guard. The Congress designated Benjamin Sacasa as provisional president, and he thereupon appointed Somoza Minister of War.[31]

The Somoza *coup* was studied by the various American governments to determine whether the Act of Chapultepec could be invoked against the resurgent dictator. Somoza expressed confidence that the change of government would be recognized "because all that occurred was within the letter of national laws."[32] However, the dictator proved to be over-confident, for the consultations resulted in a decision to abstain from relations with Nicaragua until after the elections, at which time the matter would be taken up for further review. In supporting nonrecognition, the Chileans said that the *coup* violated the democratic principles formulated in the Act of Chapultepec and the United Nations Charter. Guatemala also based her refusal to recognize on the "Chapultepec Conference doctrine concerning the preservation of democracy."[33] It is an interesting fact that, although Nicaragua had not been invited to the Rio conference because of a change of government "under abnormal circumstances," the Governing Board of the Pan American Union decided that Nicaragua should be allowed to attend the Bogotá conference despite nonrecognition. This decision was based on any American country's right to attend inter-American conferences despite nonrecognition by the other American states.[34] The practice adopted in the Somoza matter did not by any means establish precedent for the future. The consistent feature of the recognition policy of the American republics, including that of the United States, has been its inconsistency. This statement can be further supported by certain incidents occurring shortly after the Bogotá conference.

For example, in December 1948 the U.S. State Department voiced concern that several popularly-elected governments had been over-thrown by military forces in Latin America, and it expressed its desire to make every legitimate and useful effort to encourage democratic and constitutional procedures, these efforts to be consistent, of course,

[31] *New York Times,* May 27, 1947.
[32] *La Prensa* (New York), May 30, 1947.
[33] *Ibid.,* June 9, 10, 1947.
[34] *Ibid.,* March 9, 1947.

with inter-American commitments. It solicited comments from the other American republics on appropriate action that the inter-American organization might take to strengthen the democratic and constitutional framework of the continent.[35]

Clearly, this antidemocratic action—the use of force as an instrument of government rotation—was regarded as a blow at solidarity and raised the question of what was to be done about it. Consultation? The only effective action that could come from consultation would be to impose sanctions. This, as the Latin-American countries had clearly revealed by their attitude toward United States pressuring of Perón, they would not tolerate. Nor was nonrecognition an effectual approach to the problem, particularly in view of a resolution adopted at Bogotá which declared that "continuity of diplomatic relations among the American states is desirable," and therefore "the establishment and maintaining of diplomatic relations with a government does not imply any judgment upon the domestic policy of that government."

Because of the negative attitude resulting from the consultation solicited by the State Department, following the seizure of the Venezuelan government by the military on November 25, 1948, the United States recognized the military junta on January 21, 1949. It was clear that there was no general disposition in Latin America to favor the use of nonrecognition as an instrument of policy. The same attitude prevailed when a *coup d'etat* occurred in Panama in November 1949. Following the *coup,* Assistant Secretary of State Edward G. Miller announced that the United States would consult with the other American republics. Since some of the Latin-American governments had expressed the belief that the Bogotá resolution bound them to recognize new governments automatically, Secretary of State Dean Acheson formally announced a statement of United States policy on the matter:

When a freely elected government is overthrown and a new and perhaps militaristic government takes over, we do not need to recognize the new government automatically and immediately. We can wait and see if it really controls its territory and intends to live up to its international commitments. We can consult with other governments as we have so often done.[36]

The exchange of views resulted in a consensus favoring recognition of the government of the usurper Arias in Panama. On December 24 the United States granted recognition. Although there seemed to be a trend to consultation on the subject of recognition, there definitely was

[35] U.S. Dept. of State, *Bulletin,* XX (Jan. 2, 1949), 30.
[36] *Ibid.,* XXI (Dec. 12, 1949), 910–911.

no trend in support of nonrecognition as an instrument in defense of democratic practices and principles. Having noted these significant examples of pronounced Latin-American opposition to positive measures in support of the oft-declared democratic bases of inter-American solidarity, we turn next to the problem of maintaining adequate military cooperation following the end of World War II.

Proposed inter-American military cooperation. The problems of postwar inter-American military cooperation had engaged the attention of the Inter-American Defense Board for some time prior to the termination of hostilities. On March 14, 1944, the board recommended "maintenance of existing naval and air bases that are essential for the *permanent* security of the Hemisphere," and "planning and reviewing periodically an integrated system of bases to guarantee the security of the Hemisphere." On November 29, 1944, a report of the Committee on Postwar Military Problems of the American Continent listed the most important problems as follows: arms standardization, communications, utilization of manpower, industrial mobilization, military cooperation, and military geography.[37] Before the Defense Board got around to drafting resolutions on these subjects, certain actions of the Mexico City conference supplied additional stimulus.

It was the consensus of the delegations gathered in Mexico City that the advances in defensive military interaction made during the war should be preserved and extended. This idea was inherent in a proposal entitled "Inter-American Military Cooperation," submitted by the Uruguayan delegates, which declared: "The present world conflict has demonstrated that, if peace and security in the Western Hemisphere are to be maintained and world peace is to be aided and maintained, greater obligation will devolve upon the American Republics to coordinate and cooperate in the field of military activity."[38]

The conference adopted a resolution which recommended that the governments consider creating a permanent agency, formed of representatives of the General Staffs of the American republics, to propose measures for better military cooperation for the defense of the Western Hemisphere, and that, pending the establishment of this permanent body, the Inter-American Defense Board should continue to function.

[37] Inter-American Defense Board, *Minutes of the Plenary Sessions of the Inter-American Defense Board* (Washington, 1945), III, 959, cited hereinafter as *Minutes of the Plenary Sessions.*

[38] *Report of the Delegation of the United States of America to the Inter-American Conference on Problems of War and Peace, Mexico, February 21– March 8, 1945* (Washington, 1946).

In pursuance of this resolution, and also of the Act of Chapultepec, the Defense Board adopted several resolutions relating to military cooperation.[39] An enumeration and brief description follow:

1. Hemisphere Telecommunications (Res. XVII, June 12, 1945). The board urged that wartime improvements in hemisphere telecommunications be kept intact, that there be continued development and interconnection of civil and military telecommunications, a standardization of equipment and operating procedures, and a hemisphere-wide training program for personnel.

2. Standardization of Matériel (Res. XVIII, Oct. 9, 1945). Since the Act of Chapultepec and other inter-American agreements implied that the armed forces of several American republics should be prepared to participate in joint defense operations against a common enemy, the board was of the opinion that such operations would be facilitated by having all forces supplied with standard equipment. It therefore recommended that a permanent committee or agency be established to coordinate the standardization of war matériel and the means and methods of producing it.

3. Utilization of Manpower (Res. XX, Oct. 9, 1945). Recommended full and adequate use of human resources through measures such as compulsory military service, preliminary training, cadres, etc.

4. Standardization of the Organization and Training of the Armed Forces (Res. XXI, Oct. 23, 1945). Recommended that the tables of organization for the armed services of the United States be made available to the armed forces of the other American republics; that these standards be applied also to the air and naval forces; that there be uniform standards of training; that there be exchange of students among the academies of the armed forces; and that the use of military missions from American countries be continued and expanded.

5. Inter-American Military Cooperation (Res. XXII, Nov. 27, 1945). The board suggests the creation, as soon as possible, of a permanent military agency, to include representatives from every country, to call meetings of the General Staffs of the American republics, encourage the exchange of officers among the armed forces of these republics, strengthen and extend agreements for the use of bases and military establishments, and to study the production facilities of raw-material sources for strategic and critical materials.[40]

[39] *Minutes of the Plenary Sessions,* IV, pp. 1951–1968; Inter-American Defense Board, *Resolutions Forwarded to the Governments of the American Republics, May 9, 1946* (mimeograph).

[40] On May 31, 1946, the board elaborated on this resolution by proposing

It was in accord with these resolutions that the United States took steps to maintain or to strengthen the inter-American military defense structure bequeathed by the war. First there was the matter of the bases. Agreements had been negotiated by the United States with most of the Latin-American countries with the understanding that the bases would be returned to their original owners after the war. However, the unsettled state of world affairs which still faced the American nations at the end of the war caused the United States to enter into negotiations for the retention of certain key bases, notably in Ecuador, Brazil, and Panama. The War and Navy Departments, particularly eager to retain the bases, have been accused of attempting to take over the formulation of policy in this respect, and of making a botch of it.[41] At any rate, rumors that the United States was seeking long-term facilities in the Galápagos created violent public opposition in Ecuador. An agreement with Ecuador was finally concluded which provided that the bases had to be returned to Ecuadorean control, but that Ecuador stood prepared to extend their operational use to the United States if an emergency demanding such measures should arise. This settlement adhered to identical policy lines laid down by President-elect Grau San Martín of Cuba. [42]

In Brazil, instead of requesting permanent and exclusive use of the air-ferry bases, the United States proposed that they be jointly maintained and administered. Apparently President Getulio Vargas accepted this arrangement, but because of popular objection when it became known, he later disavowed it. Thus, from the experiences in Ecuador and Brazil, it did not appear that the United States was going to make much headway in negotiating the retention of wartime bases. What happened in Panama proved that this was, if possible, an underestimation.

At the end of the war the United States occupied 134 bases, areas, and sites in the Republic of Panama. These had been made available to the armed forces in defense of the Panama Canal by agreement of May 18, 1942. The agreement provided for the return of the sites one year after "the conclusion of peace." On September 4, 1946, in re-

---

the creation of an Inter-American Military Defense Council, to serve as a permanent military agency for the American republics. This became the core of Resolution XXLIV, adopted October 14, 1947, containing a draft treaty for the Bogotá conference.—*Minutes of the Plenary Session*, 2938.

[41] Laurence Duggan, *The Americas: The Search for Hemisphere Security* (New York, 1949), 91.

[42] *New York Times,* Sept. 3, 1944.

sponse to United States overtures, President Jiménez announced that Panama would negotiate for the defense sites only after all the bases then occupied had been released. It was the Panamanian contention that the war ended with the Japanese surrender, and therefore the 1942 agreement had lapsed. The United States held that the war would end only when a peace treaty had been signed, and accordingly until that time our rights were valid.[43]

On May 8, 1947, the United States announced that 98 of the sites had been returned to Panama, and that the majority of the remaining 36 comprised technical installations still in use and essential to safe air navigation in the zonal area. The United States proposed an agreement giving recognition to the fact that the requirements of modern warfare made necessary the use of certain areas outside the ten-mile Canal Zone.[44] By August the United States Army announced the abandonment of more sites, leaving only 18.[45] Eventually, after labored negotiations, an agreement was signed on December 10, 1947, providing for United States use of 13 sites, principally technical installations, for a period of five years. A fourteenth site at Rio Hato, an important military air base seventy miles west of Panama City, was to be leased by the United States for a period of ten years, renewal included. Under the terms of the accord the United States assumed authority and responsibility for all technical, military, and economic matters connected with the operation of the 14 defense sites.[46]

When the terms of the agreement became public there was violent protest. Students rioted and the minister of foreign affairs resigned. Thus, it was to be expected that the National Assembly would reject it, as it did on December 23, though hardly by unanimous vote. The National Assembly rejected the agreement because it alleged that it violated the principle of juridical equality of the contracting states and the spirit of inter-American defense. The rejection of the pact touched off wild rejoicing in the capital.[47] It is emotionally stimulating to the Latins to pluck a feather from the eagle's tail.

The State Department immediately announced that all sites outside the Zone would be evacuated as quickly as possible. In fact, barely

---

[43] *La Prensa* (New York), Oct. 27, 1946.

[44] U.S. Dept. of State, *Bulletin,* XVI (May 18, 1947), 1003.

[45] *New York Times,* Aug. 28, 1947.

[46] U.S. Dept. of State, *Bulletin,* XVII (Dec. 21, 1947), 1219.

[47] *New York Times,* Dec. 23, 1947. According to Sumner Welles, the Panamanians objected to the alienation of territory for longer periods than the existing emergency seemed to justify.—New York *Herald Tribune,* Dec. 30, 1947.

seven weeks later (Feb. 16), the United States was able to notify the Panamanian government that all troops had been withdrawn and that the May 1942 agreement was terminated.[48] The sites and the roads leading to them rapidly returned to jungle.

This precipitate action, born perhaps of irritation, left the Panamanians breathless and aghast. Perhaps they had only expected to contrive better terms. When the United States was informed by Panama, on January 14, 1948—during the withdrawal process—that it was ready to hear proposals for new discussion of base sites, it turned a deaf ear.[49] What prospects for an agreement in view of the weakness of the National Assembly under pressure of the students and other groups?

Communist insinuations that the United States was seeking to retain the bases as a preliminary step to imposing its hegemony over the whole region found some receptive recognition in latent fears and suspicions, and so reinforced opposition to renewal of base agreements. On the other hand, some of the actions by the United States itself may have been induced by this same propaganda charge. For example, when it was announced, on April 2, 1946, that the United States would give up all its wartime bases in Cuba, the Cuban ambassador declared that this would end the "malicious campaign" against the United States in his country.[50] Shortly thereafter, when the Rio de Janeiro naval base was turned over to Brazil, this was reported as an answer to the Brazilian Communist charge that the United States wished to use permanent military occupation to control local-market and economic facilities.[51] Again, when the Parnamarim Airbase, our largest in Brazil, was returned, the announcement that this practically ended the stationing of United States troops in that country was accompanied by the comment that this should put an end to Communist insinuations that the United States would never vacate the bases.[52] On April 15, 1947, the United States announced that all air bases built and manned by this country during the war had been returned to Brazil.[53] Bases and sites in the other Latin-American countries occupied by the United States during the war were also evacuated. This meant that in the event of another war it would be necessary to renegotiate base agreements.

[48] U.S. Dept. of State, *Bulletin,* XVI (March 7, 1947), 317–318.
[49] *New York Times,* Jan. 14, 1948.
[50] *La Prensa* (New York), April 2, 1946.
[51] *New York Times,* April 25, 1946.
[52] *Ibid.,* Oct. 6, 1946.
[53] *La Prensa* (New York), April 15, 1947.

In view of the recent negotiation of the Inter-American Treaty of Reciprocal Assistance, the Inter-American Defense Board deemed it "necessary to begin the planning of an integrated system of bases to insure the permanent security of the Western Hemisphere." Accordingly it recommended to the governments of the American states that they adopt the following measures of military cooperation: that planning be started immediately on an integrated system of bases; that an inter-American agreement be negotiated establishing the availability of the bases and facilities to all forces of the American states; and that the use and maintenance of such bases, derived from inter-American agreements, should not affect the sovereign rights of the countries in which the bases are located.[54] Although base agreements were thus "authorized" as being within the accepted framework of the inter-American security system, there were no further developments in this direction. In view of Latin-American opposition the United States was willing to let the matter rest. Another proposal for military cooperation, recommended by the Defense Board, will now be examined.

Arms standardization. It will be recalled that in October 1945 the Defense Board recommended that the governments of the American republics proceed immediately to the standardization of the organization and training of their armed forces. This recommendation appealed strongly to the military and political advisers of President Truman.

The upshot was that on May 6, 1946, the President delivered a message to Congress containing the text of a proposed bill entitled "The Inter-American Military Cooperation Act," which authorized a program of military collaboration with the other American states. "It is highly desirable," said the President, "to standardize military organization, training and equipment *as has been recommended by the Inter-American Defense Board."* He referred to "the Act of Chapultepec and other basic inter-American documents" as being the source of this proposed close collaboration of the American republics.[55] A powerful battery of support for the bill appeared before the Congressional committees, including Secretary of State Byrnes, General Eisenhower, and Admiral Nimitz. The House Foreign Affairs Committee was told that a main purpose of the program was to counter European military influence in Latin America. In response to the objection that the plan

[54] Res. XXV: *Reconsideration of Resolution XIV.—Minutes of the Plenary Sessions.* This resolution was an amendment of Res. XIV: Naval and Air Bases.

[55] U.S. Dept. of State, *Bulletin,* XIV (May 19, 1946), 859–860 [italics added]; U.S. Cong., H. Doc. 548, 79th Cong., 2d Sess.

would contribute to an arms race, Congress was assured, first, that new arms would be exchanged for old ones and, over all, there would be no arms increase, and second, that this government would approve no indiscriminate distribution of armaments.[56]

Despite strong Administration support the proposed bill failed to pass Congress during the 1946 session. Nevertheless, United States diplomatic representatives continued to negotiate with the Latin-American governments for the completion of military agreements with the expectation that the Eightieth Congress would approve the Truman proposal.[57] Accordingly, President Truman renewed his request in a second message to Congress in May 1947. He said that the plan would not place a useless burden of armaments on the Latin-American countries, nor would it place weapons in the hands of those who might use them contrary to peaceful and democratic principles.[58]

This time the bill was supported in committee hearings by Secretary of State Marshall, War Secretary Patterson, and Navy Secretary Forrestal, who urged that the act be passed "to prevent the Latin Americans from seeking weapons and training elsewhere." Assurances were given that there would be no armaments race, that the plan fitted the framework of the Act of Chapultepec and the United Nations Charter, and that great care would be taken to avoid setting up a "balance of power" among the Latin-American states.[59] The House Foreign Affairs Committee unanimously approved the bill, but with the proviso that aid should be withdrawn by the President if used *internally* by a dictator. Despite committee approval, however, Congress again did not pass the measure.[60] It was possible, nevertheless, to carry on to a limited degree the purpose of the defeated measure through the negotiation of military advisory-missions agreements. For example, such an agreement, negotiated with Brazil on August 15, 1948, provided for a detail of officers and men to advise the Brazilian government on the establishment and operation of a school similar to the United States War

---

[56] "Inter-American Military Cooperation," *Hearings* before the Committee on Foreign Affairs, H.R. 6326, 79th Cong., 2d Sess.; *New York Times,* May 7, 16, 29, 1946.

[57] Ernesto Galarza, "The Standardization of Armaments in the Western Hemisphere," *Inter-American Reports* (Washington, Oct. 1947), 6.

[58] U.S. Dept. of State, *Bulletin,* XVI (June 8, 1947), 1121–1124.

[59] *Hearings* before the Committee on Foreign Affairs, H.R. 3836; *Hearings* before the Committee on Foreign Relations, S.2153, 80th Cong., 1st Sess.

[60] New York *Herald Tribune,* July 18, 1947; *La Prensa* (New York), July 28, 1947.

College in Washington, for the instruction of senior officers of the Brazilian services.[61]

In rejecting President Truman's arms-standardization bill, Congress was perhaps not unmindful of the fears and criticism being voiced abroad.[62] The Latin-American press accused the United States of preparing to load them down with a costly armaments race, instead of practicing the true Good Neighbor policy of cooperating for the increase of production and trade.[63] This theme was widely voiced. If the United States really sought a friendly and strong Latin America, it should aid the countries in developing their resources and do everything possible to establish democracy. Many expressed fear that Truman's plan would put the hemisphere under United States domination. Its denunciation as "Yankee imperialism," as was to be expected, was so branded by Communist propaganda. Then there was the fear that the only effect of armaments would be to entrench the dictators and military caste. Instead of strengthening democracy, the United States would probably find that it was simply strengthening dictatorial government in Latin America. Nor did the Latin Americans have much faith in President Truman's assurance that weapons of war would not be placed "in the hands of any groups which may use them to oppose the peaceful and democratic principles to which the United States and the other American nations have so often subscribed." Literal adherence to this pledge might well block the flow of arms to most of the Latin countries. In view of the setbacks in connection with base agreements and arms standardization, the strengthening of inter-American military cooperation now became dependent on future developments, including the acts of the Ninth International Conference of American States, which opened in Bogotá on March 30, 1948.

The Bogotá Conference. Ten years earlier the eighth conference at Lima had selected Bogotá as the place and 1943 as the date of the next general conference of American states. Owing to the outbreak of World War II there were several postponements. Although the delays contributed to the accumulation of problems, they nevertheless afforded

[61] U.S. Dept. of State, *Bulletin,* XIX (Aug. 15, 1948), 211–212.

[62] *La Prensa* (New York), May 11, 13, 1946; *New York Times,* Nov. 20, 1946; Eduardo Santos, "Mis conferencias con el Presidente Roosevelt y los planas de organización militar inter-americana," *Revista de América* (Bogotá, April 1947), 10.

[63] It is an interesting fact that a number of the Latin-American states were buying United States surplus militarized and nonmilitarized combat matériel in quantity and at bargain prices.—U.S. Dept. of State, *Bulletin,* XXI (Aug. 1, 1949), 156; *New York Times,* Jan 15, 1949.

opportunity, which was well utilized, for careful planning, not only by the respective governments but particularly by the Governing Board of the Pan American Union and the specialized agencies. This intelligent preparation stood the conference in good stead when, following the destructive riots which occurred while the conference was in session in Bogotá, it was necessary to alter procedure in order to expedite the agenda.

The conference, in which delegations from all the American republics were represented, convened in the National Capitol in Bogotá on March 30, 1948. Its proceedings were in the early committee stage when, at noon on April 9, Sr. Jorge Eliécer Gaitán, leader of the Liberal Party, one of the two great traditional parties of Colombia, was assassinated. So outraged were the devoted followers of Gaitán that, holding the Conservative Administration responsible, a violent reaction set in immediately. Law and order disappeared and Bogotá was overrun by a mob which invaded the Capitol, headquarters of the conference, in search of Laureano Gómez, head of the Conservative Party, who as minister of foreign affairs was presiding over the conference. Fortunately the meetings were in midday recess, so the delegations and their staffs escaped injury. But the Capitol was so badly wrecked that no further meetings of the conference could be held there except for a few final sessions.

Although the uprising in its early stage appeared to have a local political character and was directed against the incumbent administration, it soon took on a more sinister aspect. Communist complicity in the tumultuous events, which resulted in a heavy loss of life and property, will be discussed later.[64] Suffice it to state at this point that international Communism had resorted to direct action in Bogotá to break up and discredit the great conference of American states. Since to adjourn or move elsewhere would be a recognition of Communist victory, the delegations decided stubbornly to remain in Bogotá. Accordingly, on April 14, under the presidency of Dr. Zuleta Angel, the new minister of foreign affairs of Colombia,[65] the sessions were resumed in temporary quarters, a secondary school in the suburbs of

[64] The material damages were estimated at $500 million, and loss of life as twelve hundred in Bogotá and three hundred in the rest of the country.— New York *Herald Tribune*, April 22, 24, 1948.

[65] Alberto Lleras, "Report on the Ninth International Conference of American States," *Annals* of the Organization of American States (Pan American Union, Washington, 1949), I, 8, cited hereinafter as "Report on Ninth Conference."

Bogotá. Following hasty repairs to the Capitol, the conference returned there for its final sessions.

Because of the disruption, it was agreed to forgo further committee meetings and decide most of the important problems, in first instance, by a steering committee, composed of the heads of the delegations. On the basis of these decisions the six working committees drafted the conclusions of the conference. Thanks to excellent preconference preparation this expedited procedure proved effective, and indeed ensured the success of the conference.

The principal objective of the Bogotá conference was to give effect to a resolution adopted at Mexico City concerning the reorganization and strengthening of the inter-American system. In accordance with this resolution, the Pan American Union had prepared for Bogotá an excellent draft entitled "Organic Pact of the Inter-American System," and the Inter-American Juridical Committee had also drafted a treaty on procedures of peaceful settlement. These projects proved to be the bases for the two greatest achievements of the Bogotá conference: the Charter of the Organization of American States, and the Treaty on Pacific Settlement, or "The Pact of Bogotá."

The Charter of the OAS. The organization of the inter-American system was the most important subject on the agenda of the conference, and the adoption of the Charter of the Organization of American States was its most significant achievement. This treaty consolidated in a single cohesive organization what had hitherto been a more or less informal union of nations. The attempt of the Havana conference of 1928 to put the Pan American Union on a treaty basis failed, not only because that treaty required unanimous ratification[66] but because the attempt was premature. By 1948 most of the obstacles had been removed, owing to the acceptance and *practice* of the cardinal precepts of inter-American association: sovereign equality, nonintervention, and consultation.

The pre-Charter inter-American system was, above all else, very flexible. It developed into the oldest and most successful of international regional organizations despite its uncertain and intangible basis. Since this flexibility was one of its greatest elements of strength, a natural question arises: Why put it on a treaty basis and produce a modified freeze? The answer is that whereas flexibility was an advantage during the difficult years of building up the organization, it no

[66] The Pan American Union treaty was eventually ratified by sixteen states. Those that never ratified were Argentina, Colombia, El Salvador, Honduras, and Paraguay.

CHART I

ORGANIZATION OF AMERICAN STATES

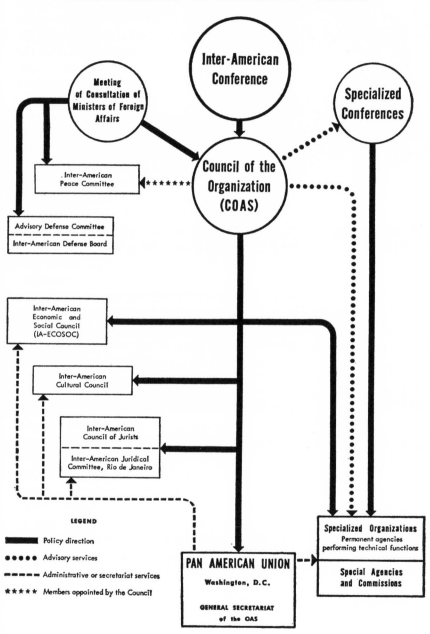

Inter-American Conference

Meeting of Consultation of Ministers of Foreign Affairs

Specialized Conferences

. Inter-American Peace Committee

Council of the Organization (COAS)

Advisory Defense Committee

Inter-American Defense Board

Inter-American Economic and Social Council (IA-ECOSOC)

Inter-American Cultural Council

Inter-American Council of Jurists

Inter-American Juridical Committee, Rio de Janeiro

Specialized Organizations Permanent agencies performing technical functions

Special Agencies and Commissions

PAN AMERICAN UNION
Washington, D.C.

GENERAL SECRETARIAT of the OAS

LEGEND

━━━ Policy direction

●●●●● Advisory services

━ ━ ━ Administrative or secretariat services

★★★★★ Members appointed by the Council

longer served a useful purpose after the inter-American system had attained such proportions and complexities that stabilization was essential. Closer coordination and a greater integration of the various elements of the system had become not only desirable but necessary.

While the Charter introduced changes into the inter-American system, it did not seek to throw out the old and replace it with something entirely new. To a large extent it meant the formalization, by treaty, of the inchoate organization and procedures of the existent inter-American system, based as it was in the congeries of resolutions and declarations. Thus, the Charter produced at Bogotá was not merely the work of the Ninth International Conference of American States, it was the cumulative result of fifty-eight years of Pan American endeavor.[67]

The Charter of the Organization of American States[68] is divided into three parts, Part I contains a reaffirmation of basic principles of inter-American solidarity and cooperation; Part II is concerned with the structural features of the organization; and Part III contains miscellaneous and protocolary articles.

Part I can best be described as laying the foundation, in principles and purposes, for the organization. It contains an enumeration of the fundamental rights and duties of states; the bases of economic, social, and cultural cooperation; the obligation of the American republics to settle their differences by peaceful means; and the obligation of reciprocal assistance by all states in the event of an aggression against any one of them.

Although it was unquestionably the intention of Resolution IX of the Mexico City conference that the Charter should be a self-contained general constitution covering all features of the inter-American system, it was agreed at Bogotá that, with respect to collective security, it would not be practicable to incorporate the entire Rio Inter-American Treaty of Reciprocal Assistance and a codified draft of all the treaties of peaceful settlement. This latter was to be the subject of a separate treaty on pacific settlement. It was agreed to incorporate in the Charter only fundamental provisions and certain general propositions relating to mutual assistance and peaceful settlement.

Since the unanimous ratification of the Charter by all the American

[67] William Manger, "The Charter of the Organization of American States," Pan American Union, *Bulletin*, LXXXII (July 1948), 362.

[68] Considerable discussion was necessary to reach agreement on the name of the organization. Such terms as "union," "association," "society," or "community" were discarded because it was thought that they carry the implication of a "superstate." For text of the Charter, see *Annals* (1949), I, 76–86.

states signifies their acceptance of its content, it may be of interest to learn that the obligations formally assumed by these nations include the following:

ARTICLE 5. The American States reaffirm the following principles:

(*d*) The solidarity of the American States and the high aims which are sought through it require the political organization of those States on the basis of the effective exercise of representative democracy. [This recalls the Larreta proposal, based on the principle that democracy and peace are parallel.]

(*h*) Social justice and social security are bases of lasting peace.

(*i*) Economic cooperation is essential to the common welfare and prosperity of peoples of the continent. [The member states, including the United States, agree to cooperate with one another to achieve just and decent living conditions for their entire populations.]

(*j*) The American States proclaim the fundamental rights of the individual without distinction as to race, nationality, creed or sex. [The United States lays itself open to embarrassing criticism.]

ARTICLE 15. No State or group of States has the right to intervene, directly or indirectly, for any reason whatever, in the internal or external affairs of any other state. The foregoing principle prohibits not only armed force but also any other form of interference or attempted threat against the personality of the State or against its political, economic, and cultural elements. [This carried nonintervention to its ultimate and impractical heights. It would be impossible for the United States to avoid violation, and consequently the inevitable charges of hypocrisy.]

ARTICLE 16. No State may use or encourage the use of coercive measures of an economic or political character in order to force the sovereign will of another State and obtain from it advantages of any kind. [Economic sanctions (boycott) are prohibited. As the United States delegation pointed out, this was already covered by Article 15, relating to the principle of nonintervention. At any rate, the inclusion of Article 16 emphasizes how broad is the scope of nonintervention.]

We turn now to Part II, the most important section of the Charter. It deals with the instrumentalities through which the OAS operates. We encounter a number of significant changes in the constitution of the inter-American system, but even here old basic features were retained. The seven organs of the Organization of American States, through which it accomplishes its purposes, are: the Inter-American Conference, Meeting of Consultation of Ministers of Foreign Affairs, Specialized Conferences, Council, Pan American Union, Specialized Organizations, and Dependent Technical Organs. A description of these organs, as provided in the Charter, follows:

I. INTER-AMERICAN CONFERENCE. This, the highest international assemblage of the hemisphere, is also the oldest, beginning with the First International Conference of American States, which met in Washington in 1889; the meeting in Bogotá was the ninth of this series. The Inter-American Conference is the supreme organ of the OAS, with authority to decide upon general matters of policy, to determine the structure and functioning of its components, and to consider all matters relating to friendly relations among the American states. All member states of the organization are represented and each has the right to one vote. This conference is supposed to meet every five years.

II. MEETING OF CONSULTATION OF MINISTERS OF FOREIGN AFFAIRS. Under the Charter the Meeting of Consultation considers problems of an urgent nature and, under the Rio treaty, serves as the organ of consultation. Any member state may request that a Meeting of Consultation be called. The Council decides whether a request should be granted. If an armed attack occurs within the region specified in the Rio treaty, the chairman of the Council must call a meeting of the foreign ministers immediately, and at the same time call a meeting of the Council itself, which is to serve provisionally as the organ of consultation. (By the time of the Bogotá conference there had been three meetings of the foreign ministers: Panama, 1939; Havana, 1940; and Rio de Janeiro, 1942.) To serve the organs of consultation in a military advisory capacity the Charter created the Advisory Defense Committee, composed of the highest military officers of the American nations, to meet simultaneously with the organ of consultation. This committee did not supplant the Inter-American Defense Board, which was continued by resolution and classified as a "specialized organization."

III. SPECIALIZED CONFERENCES. These special conferences meet to consider technical matters or to develop specific aspects of inter-American cooperation. Innumerable such conferences have met, their subjects ranging over the broad area of political, economic, social, and cultural matters. The Mexico City conference of 1945 and the Rio de Janeiro conference of 1947 fell in the category of special political conferences.

IV. COUNCIL OF THE ORGANIZATION. In this organ the Bogotá conference effected its most far-reaching alterations of the earlier organizational structure. In fact, a really new organ was created to take the place of the Governing Board of the Pan American Union. Originally the Governing Board, composed of diplomatic representatives accredited to Washington, watched over the Pan American Union in much the same manner that a board of directors attends the interests of a business concern. It was an integral part of the Pan American Union, created for the purpose of administering the institution with the aid of a director-general, in other words, a business manager of a sort.

Gradually the functions and powers of the Governing Board began to develop and it became much more than simply a board of directors. The culmination of this development began with the Mexico City conference authorizing the board to take action on political matters concerning the effective functioning of the inter-American system and was further implemented under the Rio de Janeiro Inter-American Treaty of Reciprocal Assistance, whereby the Governing Board was made the provisional organ of consultation in the event of armed attack or an act of aggression against an American state. Thus there was, prior to 1948, a definite trend toward making the Governing Board a more effective organ of the inter-American system .

The Charter of the OAS continued this tendency by converting the board into the Council and giving it enlarged powers which made it in a sense the permanent executive council of the organization. While the traditional relation of the Governing Board to the Pan American Union was preserved, the Council became the central and centralizing organ of the whole system. Thus, the technical agencies of the OAS, some of them more or less autonomous, are now under the Council. Although the organs of the Council have technical autonomy, they may not make decisions that carry them into the sphere of action reserved to the Council.

The Council of the OAS is unique among international bodies. It bears slight resemblance to the Security Council of the United Nations, for all states enjoy membership with equal vote, identical powers, and are subject to majority rule. The member states are privileged to be represented on the Council by either the diplomatic representative accredited to Washington or by a special representative bearing the rank of ambassador. A number of the countries, including the United States, have exercised the latter prerogative.[69] The chairmanship of the Council is for a term of one year and the incumbent cannot be immediately re-elected. This ensures a certain degree of rotation among the member states.

V. PAN AMERICAN UNION. Prior to 1948 the Pan American Union

---

[69] At the present time thirteen countries accredit special representatives to the OAS.

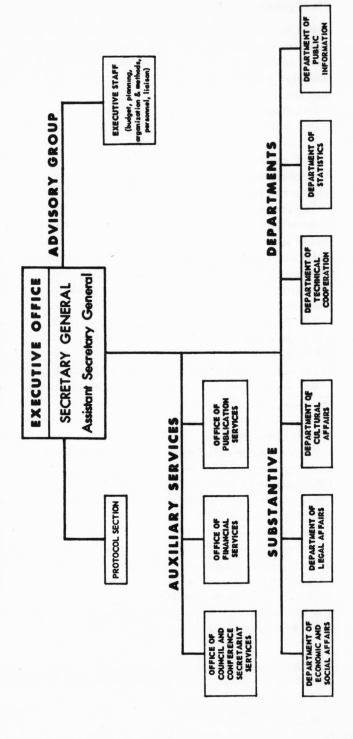

CHART II

PAN AMERICAN UNION
Permanent and Central Organ and General Secretariat of the OAS

EXECUTIVE OFFICE

SECRETARY GENERAL
Assistant Secretary General

ADVISORY GROUP

EXECUTIVE STAFF
(budget, planning, organization & methods, personnel, liaison)

PROTOCOL SECTION

AUXILIARY SERVICES

OFFICE OF COUNCIL AND CONFERENCE SECRETARIAT SERVICES

OFFICE OF FINANCIAL SERVICES

OFFICE OF PUBLICATION SERVICES

DEPARTMENTS

SUBSTANTIVE

DEPARTMENT OF ECONOMIC AND SOCIAL AFFAIRS

DEPARTMENT OF LEGAL AFFAIRS

DEPARTMENT OF CULTURAL AFFAIRS

DEPARTMENT OF TECHNICAL COOPERATION

DEPARTMENT OF STATISTICS

DEPARTMENT OF PUBLIC INFORMATION

served in a limited secretarial capacity. Under the Charter it has become the General Secretariat for the whole OAS. This means that it serves as the secretariat for the Inter-American Conference and the Meeting of Consultation, and for the Council and for all organs of the Council.

In addition to its enlarged secretarial functions, the Pan American Union continues to serve as an international bureau for the American republics in informational, advisory, and promotional activities in economic, cultural, social, legal, and technical matters. Although the Charter did not dictate the organization of the Pan American Union, leaving this to the Council, it nevertheless assumed that there would be departments of Economic and Social Affairs, Legal Affairs, and Cultural Affairs, by providing that the heads of these departments should serve as executive secretaries of the Inter-American Economic and Social Council, the Council of Jurists, and the Cultural Council. The work of the Union has been organized in six departments, the three already mentioned, and also Public Information, Technical Cooperation, and Statistics.

The former director-general of the Pan American Union became, under the Charter, the secretary-general of the OAS. He is elected by the Council for a ten-year term and may not be re-elected or succeeded by a person of the same nationality.

VI. SPECIALIZED ORGANIZATIONS. The specialized organizations are defined as those "established by multilateral agreements and having specific functions with respect to technical matters of common interest to the American States." Since they are very numerous, and since considerable advantage would result from some unified system of financing and reporting, the Council was requested to adopt the necessary measures looking toward the integration, and in some cases the elimination, of existing specialized organizations.

VII. DEPENDENT TECHNICAL ORGANS. The Charter provides three organs to serve the Council in a technical advisory capacity, as well as to render technical services to the respective governments: the Inter-American Economic and Social Council,[70] the Inter-American Council of Jurists, and the Inter-American Cultural Council. Com-

[70] The Mexico City conference (1945) created the Inter-American Economic and Social Council (IA-ECOSOC) to take over the activities of the Inter-American Financial and Economic Advisory Committee. It thus became the parent organization of the Inter-American Development Commission. On November 8, 1948, the Council approved a resolution through which it assumed the functions of the Development Commission as of December 31, 1948.

posed of a representative for each member government, these organs are responsible for promoting inter-American cooperation in their respective fields and of undertaking tasks requested by the Council or the conferences. As noted above, the directors of the respective departments in the Pan American Union serve these councils as executive secretaries. The Charter provided that the Inter-American Juridical Committee of Rio de Janeiro should become a permanent committee serving the Inter-American Council of Jurists.

Only two additional provisions of the Charter need claim our particular attention. First, the declaration (Art. 102) that "none of the provisions of this Charter shall be construed as impairing the rights and obligations of the Member States under the Charter of the United Nations" reminds us of the other provisions scattered throughout the instrument which reflect the determination of the American states that their regional arrangement should be completely integrated into the United Nations. Second, the Charter enters into force among the ratifying states when two-thirds of the signatory states shall have deposited their ratifications.[71] Pending that date, the Bogotá conference passed a resolution which put the organizational provisions of the Charter into immediate effect *provisionally,* and also specified that the new organs provided for in the Charter should be established on a provisional basis. It was believed that there was good reason for activating the organizational set-up at once, without waiting for the necessary fourteen ratifications, since the Charter was actually a reorganization of an existing system rather than a completely new organization.

The Pact of Bogotá. If the Charter of the OAS was the greatest single achievement of the Bogotá conference, its next most important contribution to the inter-American security system was the adoption of the Treaty on Pacific Settlement, designated as the "Pact of Bogotá." As has been amply demonstrated by the discussions of the preceding chapters, the hemispheric security structure did not want for instruments of peaceful settlement of every conceivable form and character. In fact, it was vulnerable to the charge of "overdevelopment." There was a long-recognized need to coordinate into one organized and unified instrument all the juridical measures to prevent war that were scattered in numerous treaties, conventions, pacts, and declarations.

Every major inter-American conference dating back to Montevideo in 1933 had had on its agenda the problems of coordinating and im-

---

[71] By the end of 1951 the Charter had received the necessary fourteen ratifications. It has since been ratified by all the states.

The Organization of American States

proving the existing inter-American treaties of peaceful settlement. The resultant steps are too numerous and complicated to be discussed here. Eventually, the Mexico City conference of 1945, regarding this as one of the major problems, requested the Juridical Committee to prepare a draft project for the Bogotá conference. Thus, a draft peace treaty prepared by the committee, and also a project submitted by the Governing Board of the Pan American Union, constituted the bases for discussions at Bogotá which revolved principally around the problem of obligatory resort to peaceful settlement. There were two conflicting views on the subject.

One view held for the obligatory reference of all disputes based on a claim of legal right to judicial or arbitral settlement, but reserved free choice of the means of seeking the solution of other controversies. Consultation was to be available to assist the parties in selecting a procedure when they could not agree upon one. The Governing Board strongly adhered to this "realistic" view. The other view, supported by the Juridical Committee, held that no dispute, whether legal or nonlegal, should be exempted from settlement, either by the disputants' acceptance of the results of good offices, mediation, inquiry, or conciliation, or by a binding award reached through judicial procedure or arbitration. Unfortunately, the second view prevailed in the drafting of the Pact of Bogotá.[72]

The treaty permits a number of alternatives for settling disputes: good offices, mediation, investigation, conciliation, judicial procedure, arbitration, and resort to the International Court of Justice. "The High Contracting Parties," says the pact, "recognize the obligation to settle international controversies by regional pacific procedures before referring them to the Security Council of the United Nations" and "bind themselves to use the procedures established in the present Treaty." It is intended to ensure that *every* dispute will be discussed and solved by some peaceful procedure, and that no state withdraws its disputes from consideration before peaceful settlement is reached. The treaty departed from all earlier pacts in providing that:

If one of the High Contracting Parties should fail to carry out the obligations imposed upon it by a decision of the International Court of Justice or by an arbitral award, the other party or parties concerned shall, before resorting to the Security Council of the United Nations, propose a Meeting of Consultation of Ministers of Foreign Affairs to agree upon appropriate measures to insure the fulfillment of the judicial decision or arbitral award.

[72] For text of the American Treaty on Pacific Settlement, see *Annals* (1949), I, 91–98.

Contrary to predictions, the treaty was signed by two-thirds of the governments, though seven of them, including the United States, signed with reservations. The United States objected particularly to Article VII, which reads:

The High Contracting Parties bind themselves not to make diplomatic representations in order to protect their nationals, or to refer a controversy to a court of international jurisdiction for that purpose, when the said nationals have had available the means to place their case before competent domestic courts of the respective state.

Why the conference adopted such a "bold" and impractical treaty baffles. Certainly in many of its "progressive" elements it ignored all the warnings of prior negotiations. According to Dr. Lleras, secretary-general of the OAS: "It does not represent progress on perfectly solid ground, and it is quite possible that several years will have to pass before the treaty enters into full effect throughout our continental community of nations."[73]

His prediction proved to be too optimistic, for it is now fairly certain that the pact will never receive unanimous ratification. Unlike the Charter and the Rio Treaty of Reciprocal Assistance, the Bogotá pact enters into effect only with respect to those states that ratify it. As soon as the Pact is ratified by two or more states, it supersedes, insofar as those states are concerned, the provisions of other treaties, conventions, and collective protocols for the pacific solution of controversies that have been in force since 1923. The ten states that have ratified are Costa Rica, Dominican Republic, El Salvador, Haiti, Honduras, Mexico, Nicaragua, Panama, and Uruguay.

Too "advanced" for 1948—and also for the present—the Bogotá pact represented an ideal which may find practical application some time in the future. According to Dr. Lleras: "It is certain to go down in the history of international law as part of institutional peace that is approaching, propelled by forces more powerful than any of those of an adverse nature that have been kept alive by uncompromising nationalism."[74]

It was expected that the inter-American security system would be formally and permanently founded on three great acts: the Charter of the OAS, the Rio de Janeiro Inter-American Treaty of Reciprocal Assistance, and the Inter-American Treaty on Pacific Settlement. So far as the pacific settlement of Inter-American controversies is con-

[73] Lleras, "Report on Ninth Conference," 44.
[74] Ibid.

cerned, the failure of the last-named treaty throws the organization back upon the numerous conflicting and inadequate instruments dating from the Gondra treaty of 1923. Surely it is in the area of peaceful procedures for the settlement of inter-American controversies that the regional-security system is at its weakest. Nor was the Bogotá conference any more successful in providing practical means for effective inter-American economic cooperation.

Economic agreement of Bogotá. Long before the Bogotá conference, inter-American security cooperation had ceased to be regarded as exclusively political and military. Increasingly in inter-American conferences, and particularly in those since the outbreak of World War II, economic defense measures had come to be regarded as essential features of hemisphere security. Indeed, in the years following the war, discussions on forms of economic cooperation had risen to first-place importance in the opinion of the Latin-American states. For example, at the Rio conference, convened for the sole purpose of drafting a treaty of reciprocal assistance, it was impossible to restrain delegates from delivering speeches on the necessity of economic cooperation. They strongly believed that programs to strengthen the economic structure, promote industry, develop agriculture, increase trade, and "achieve just and decent living conditions for their entire populations" were essential components of security cooperation. The Rio conference undoubtedly interpreted the views of most of the delegates when it adopted a resolution (Res. IX) which declared that economic security is indispensable for the progress of all the American peoples and is "the best guarantee of political security and of the success of their joint efforts for the maintenance of Continental peace." The resolution requested the Inter-American Economic and Social Council to prepare a draft agreement on inter-American economic cooperation to be submitted at Bogotá. Such a draft was prepared and was circulated among the twenty-one republics prior to the opening of the conference.

Economics threatened to eclipse politics and defense in the discussions. Many of the chairmen of the delegations put the main emphasis upon economic problems in their speeches. Despite the technicality that the Bogotá conference was to discuss only the basic *principles* upon which cooperation should rest, not any international economic or financial operation, or any immediate plan, most of the delegations seemed to think in terms of immediate and specific acts and projects.

The Latins wanted financial help to rescue them from their reliance on raw-materials exports and single crops. They wanted to build industries, develop their agricultural, mineral, and water resources, and raise their standard of living. Some reduced their demands to particulars: a financing corporation to make thirty-year loans at 1 per cent interest for development projects with $5 billion capital coming from the United States, and an inter-American bank with the United States supplying virtually all of the capital. Some even dreamed of a program of United States aid on the scale of the Marshall Plan for Europe. The failure of the United States to transmute to definite commitments the general promises of economic aid signed at Mexico City, plus the fact that the rising prices of United States goods were depleting the dollar reserves the Good Neighbors had accumulated during the war, added to the burden of their complaints. If hemisphere solidarity were to be gauged by economic cooperation only, then indeed there would be reason for apprehension, but certainly not so serious as to threaten the collapse of the inter-American system, as some alarmists prophesied.

It is highly important to note that immediately following the war (1945–48), the United States did not abandon its program of economic assistance to Latin America, as its critics would seem to imply, although it is true that Latin America received no more than 10 per cent of the $2 billion lent by the Exim Bank during the period. In addition to a number of remedial measures by this country to ease the return of Latin-American trade into more "normal" channels, the Export-Import Bank and the Institute of Inter-American Affairs were continuing to do business. The bank was making loans and, in March 1948, had $532 million in uncommitted funds available for "sound" projects. In the Congressional hopper was a recommendation for an increase of $500 million in lending authority, but this failed to gain Congressional approval.[75]

The program of technical assistance in the areas of education, health, sanitation, and agriculture also showed no abatement following the war. The Institute of Inter-American Affairs was the agency in charge of technical-assistance programs in Latin America. Upon the dissolution of the Office of the Coordinator of Inter-American Affairs in 1946, the Institute was placed under the direct control of the Department of State, and in 1947, the Institute and the Inter-American Educational Foundation (also an offshoot of the Coordinator's Office) were merged into a single federal corporation, known still as the In-

[75] William Adams Brown, Jr., and Redvers Opie, *American Foreign Assistance* (Brookings Institution, Washington, 1953), 414–415.

stitute of Inter-American Affairs. The purpose of the corporation was set forth in its charter:

To further the general welfare of, and to strengthen friendship and understanding among, the peoples of the American Republics through collaboration with other governments and governmental agencies of the American Republics in planning, initiating, assisting, financing, administering, and executing technical programs and projects, especially in the fields of public health, sanitation, agriculture, and education.[76]

Surely, in view of the foregoing, it can hardly be maintained that the United States had fallen down on its economic responsibilities to Latin America. Reduced to the simplest terms, it seems that this country was not giving economic assistance in the forms and amounts that the Latins thought their due. Although the United States was not unmindful of the needs of Latin America, its position at Bogotá was a difficult one, rendered no less so by its subscribing to idealistic Charter pledges of economic cooperation. As best they could, spokesmen for the United States presented the case for this country. Secretary of State Marshall urged the Latin-American nations to put their need of United States help second to the European Recovery Program.[77] Europe came first in Washington's planning, and he asked that they recognize the heavy burdens assumed by this country. While the United States was prepared to increase the scale of its economic assistance to Latin-American nations, they must recognize the availability of international private-investment capital, particularly if offered suitable safeguards. President William McChesney Martin, Jr., of the Export-Import Bank emphasized that the World Bank and the Export-Import Bank could act favorably only on sound projects, and stressed the fact that private capital must play a "major role" in the area's economic development. President John J. McCloy of the World Bank also stressed that "loans must be on a balanced and integrated basis," and "should be for sound, productive projects." The World Bank's mission, he said, was to blaze the trail for private international investment. Unfortunately, it was easier for the Latin Americans to build up arguments in support of "economic cooperation," as they understood it, than for the United

---

[76] Louis J. Halle, Jr., "Significance of the Institute of Inter-American Affairs in the Conduct of U.S. Foreign Policy," U.S. Dept. of State, *Bulletin,* XVIII (May 23, 1948), 660–661.

[77] *Latin America and the European Recovery Program, Preliminary Report of the House Select Committee on Foreign Aid,* H. Res. 296, 48th Cong., 2d Sess. (March 13, 1948).

States to counter with opposing arguments. The Latin Americans remained unconvinced. The sum total of the discussions was the innocuous Economic Agreement.[78]

The agreement negotiated at the Bogotá conference[79] was based in large part on the draft prepared by the Inter-American Economic and Social Council. This treaty sets forth in detail the rules to be observed regarding investments, business activity, transportation, and economic cooperation in general. It did little more than repeat the arguments and statements of principle already declared at Mexico City. Because of the insistence of the United States, the Economic Agreement contained provisions against unreasonable or discriminatory treatment of foreign private capital. This was a keenly-debated issue and probably was responsible for numerous reservations, and for eventual nonratification. The Latin Americans wanted foreign capital, but only on their own terms and without special privileges for protection by the country of its origin. This underlined their interest in intergovernmental, rather than private, financial assistance.

It would hardly serve a useful purpose to detail the content of the Economic Agreement. It suffered a worse fate than the Bogotá pact, for it never received more than three ratifications, not even that of the United States. Adhering to the legalistic fiction that the Bogotá agreement was to be merely a set of general rules and principles, whose details of practical application were to be worked out later, it was agreed that this task should devolve on a special economic conference to meet in the fall of 1948 in Buenos Aires. Among the subjects to be referred to this conference were: proposals for an Inter-American Bank, an Inter-American Development Corporation, an Inter-American Institute of Commerce, short-term commercial credit requirements, and commercial policy.[80]

Miscellaneous acts. Other actions of the Bogotá conference related more or less to the problems of inter-American security follow:

1. American Declaration of the Rights and Duties of Man (Res. **XXX**). This declaration, based on a draft prepared by the Juridical Committee, dealt with the rights and duties associated with the social and political activities of man. Although there was some support in the conference for the view that such a pact imposed an obligation on the states to protect human rights with some kind of international enforcement machinery,

[78] *New York Times,* April 2, 6, 17, 1948; *World Markets,* April 12, 1948.
[79] For text, see *Annals* (1949), I, 99–108.
[80] Res. VIII; *New York Times,* April 30, 1948.

the view which prevailed was satisfied with a simple declaration of principles and no provision of any kind for enforcement.

2. The Preservation and Defense of Democracy in America (Res. XXXII). This resolution, in condemnation of "international communism and any other totalitarian doctrine," was a consequence of the riotous events of April 9. The American republics declared their attachment to democratic principles and resolved to take measures to prevent the subversion of that way of life by alien systems which deny their very foundation.

3. Colonies and Occupied Territories in America and Creation of the American Committee on Dependent Territories (Res. XXXIII). This resolution declared that there should be no territories in the Americas in a status of dependency upon a non-American power. It therefore resolved to establish at Havana an American Commission on Dependent Territories, charged with the study of peaceful methods of terminating colonial possessions in America. The United States vigorously opposed, as did Brazil. However, the countries that had special interests, Argentina and Guatemala, were able to muster sufficient support to pass the resolution.

4. Representation of the United Nations at Inter-American Conferences (Res. XXXIX). It was agreed that the United Nations should be invited to be represented by its secretary-general, or by his alternate, at Inter-American Conferences and Meetings of Consultation of Ministers of Foreign Affairs.[81]

The work of the Bogotá conference was a tribute to the devotion of the Americas to the principles of continental solidarity. In spite of great disruptive factors the delegations stood their ground and succeeded in reorganizing and strengthening the inter-American system. What was accomplished at Bogotá went far in enabling the American nations to meet their responsibilities as an autonomous regional arrangement under the United Nations.

[81] On October 16, 1948, the General Assembly of the United Nations adopted a resolution inviting the secretary-general of the OAS to be present as an observer at the sessions of the Assembly.—United Nations, *Repertory of Practice of United Nations Organs* (New York, 1955), II, 446.

XI Developments in Inter-American Solidarity (1949–1960)

A major aspiration of all the countries of the Hemisphere is to strengthen and to put to practical use the inter-American system.

GALO PLAZA, 1954

THE BOGOTÁ CONFERENCE, with its record of qualified success, imposed largely by untoward circumstances, marked a turning point in the historical evolution of American regionalism. New forces and factors were destined to alter profoundly, during the ensuing decade, the bases and objectives of inter-American cooperation. The actual validity of declared principles of inter-American solidarity seemed to be called into question. Therefore, to establish a point of departure, it is in order to take stock of the continental-security arrangement at the half-century turn.

The inter-American security system at mid-century. In a lecture delivered at the Pan American Union on May 24, 1948, Alberto Lleras, secretary-general of the OAS, said: "The fact is that the Organization of American States is today, in spite of its shortcomings, the most perfect instrument of its kind that ever existed between sovereign nations. The Charter, in comparison with any analogous document of any era, is the most advanced that has been signed spontaneously, in complete unanimity, by the 21 states . . ."[1] Dr. Lleras is a man not given to exaggerated rhetoric, and what he said was substantially correct, for the Charter of the OAS largely confirmed the legal existence of a *de facto* system that had been functioning and developing for fifty-eight years. The Charter, together with the Rio de Janeiro Inter-American Treaty of Reciprocal Assistance and the Bogotá Inter-American Treaty of Pacific Settlement, completed the formal framework of an

[1] "The Bogotá Conference," Pan American Union, *Bulletin,* LXXXII (June 1948), 302.

international organization to govern the security activities of the nations of the Western Hemisphere.

It would be idle to hold that the inter-American peace structure, as of 1950, was free of serious deficiencies. Although the Charter and the Rio treaty measured up well to the requirements for advanced and effective instruments of a semi-autonomous regional-security arrangement, the Bogotá pact failed to fulfill its assigned role. We have already taken note of its weaknesses and the hopeless prospect of its eventual ratification. Accordingly, for the pacific settlement of inter-American disputes, it was still necessary to resort to the various procedures as provided by treaties, conventions, declarations, and resolutions enacted during the preceding quarter-century. Although these were as advanced and effective as any of the procedures of peaceful settlement found elsewhere in the world, they were, as has already been explained, deficient in many respects. Not only did they suffer from duplication and overlapping, but they were weakened by reservations, the lack of adequate ratification, and the failure to provide obligatory reference of disputes to peaceful procedures. Certainly there was need for more serious work on this particular feature of the security structure.

Flaws in the formal mechanism of the system fortunately did not offer any particular obstacle to the peaceful solution of numerous inter-American controversies that developed during the course of the decade, thereby demonstrating that the will to peace often surmounts "deficient" pacts. How the inter-American peace pacts measured up under test will be discussed later. At this point, we take note of the fact that serious doubts were entertained that the vaunted inter-American "solidarity"—the bedrock of the security structure—was as solid as it had been in the golden days of the "Good Neighbor." Indeed, so seriously had United States–Latin-American relations deteriorated by 1950 that there was a clamor both at home and abroad, for a *"return* to the Good Neighbor policy." This deterioration, which seemed to be intensifying, was largely an outgrowth of Latin-American economic discontent, and this disquieting trend is discussed in the following chapter, which deals with the economic factor in hemispheric solidarity. Undoubtedly this situation has been one of the principal influences on OAS developments since 1948. Another has been United States efforts to mobilize an anti-Communist front in the Americas, and this also has been reserved for discussion later. Our immediate attention is directed to pertinent political and military developments in inter-American security over the past decade.

Structural and functional developments: political and juridical. Following the Bogotá conference there have been a number of organizational and functional modifications of the security features of the OAS. Obviously, the first steps taken were those to give effect to certain acts of the Ninth International Conference of American States. As we saw in the preceding chapter, although the Charter of the OAS was to become operative when ratified by two-thirds of the signatory states, a resolution provided not only that existing organs should adopt the nomenclature and powers provided by the Charter but that the new organs should be established immediately on a provisional basis. Thus, following the Bogotá conference, and even after December 13, 1951—date of the formal ratification[2] of the Charter by the requisite number of states—little had to be done to bring the OAS into full conformity with the Charter provisions.

Immediately following the conference the Council proceeded to the implementation of the provisions of the Charter and other acts. On May 18, 1948, Alberto Lleras of Colombia, who had been elected director-general in 1947 to succeed Leo S. Rowe, was elected secretary-general for a term of ten years.[3] The great contribution of Dr. Lleras was that of wise guidance for the development of the OAS in its early formative years.

The Council, in discharge of its obligations, approved a body of regulations for the Pan American Union, and statutes for the Inter-American Economic and Social Council, the Inter-American Council of Jurists, and the Inter-American Cultural Council. Also, in accord with a resolution of the Bogotá conference, the Council assigned to its Committee on Inter-American Organizations the question of the discontinuance of those agencies that had outlived their usefulness, and the strengthening or merging of others, as seemed appropriate. Thus, the authorized committee ordered the dissolution of the Emergency Advisory Committee for Political Defense as being no longer necessary, despite a strong appeal by the Uruguayan government for its retention. That body, which had rendered important services during

---

[2] The Charter went into effect on December 13, 1951, date of deposit of the fourteenth ratification (by Colombia). The United States had ratified on June 17, but with a reservation designed to prevent any possibility of international action on civil rights that would bind its respective states.

[3] Dr. Lleras's successors were Dr. Carlos Dávila of Chile, from August 1, 1954, to October 19, 1955, and Dr. José Mora of Uruguay, who filled the unexpired term and was later elected to serve the next ten-year term, expiring in May 1968.

World War II, and which might well have been retained to combat Communist subversion in the Western Hemisphere, finally came to an end on December 10, 1948.[4] It should be mentioned, however, that the committee, having made a survey of the Inter-American Defense Board, recommended its continuance. This report was approved by the Council.[5] The Committee on Inter-American Organizations, noting that there were no fewer than six inter-American agencies concerned with the codification of American international law and that this function was now assigned by the Charter to the Inter-American Council of Jurists and the Inter-American Juridical Committee, recommended abolishing all these six agencies. The Council, on October 4, 1950, approved the report of the committee and declared the other inter-American codification agencies defunct.[6] To ensure that the representatives on the Council and the several organs of the OAS enjoy the privileges and immunities necessary for the performance of their duties, the Council prepared two draft agreements: (1) a multilateral agreement defining the privileges and immunities that should be conceded to the OAS by all the American states; and (2) a bilateral agreement between the OAS and the United States government. The multilateral agreement, opened for signature on May 15, 1949, has been ratified by only five governments.[7] Twelve states, including the United States, did not even sign. The bilateral agreement with the United States ran into legal technicalities which delayed its approval pending authorization by Congress. Finally, the agreement, whereby the members of the delegations to the OAS are accorded the privileges and immunities of diplomatic envoys, was signed by the OAS and the United States on July 22, 1952.

The preceding contributions of the Bogotá conference to the struc-

[4] Pan American Union, *Annals* of the Organization of American States, I (1949), 142, cited hereinafter as *Annals*.

[5] *Ibid.*, II (1950), 325–327.

[6] These were: the International Conference of American Jurists, the Committee of Experts for the Codification of International Law, the Permanent Committee of Rio de Janeiro for the Codification of Public International Law, the Permanent Committee of Montevideo for the Codification of Private International Law, the Permanent Committee of Havana on Comparative Legislation and Uniformity of Legislation, and the Permanent Committee of Jurists for the Unification of the Civil and Commercial Laws of America.—*Annals,* IV (1952), 7.

[7] For text, see Pan American Union, *Agreement on Privileges and Immunities of the Organization of American States,* Law and Treaty Ser., No. 31 (Washington, 1949).

tural and functional development of the inter-American security system were supplemented by the acts of subsequent conferences, notably, the Fourth Meeting of Consultation of Ministers of Foreign Affairs, held in Washington in 1951; the Fifth Meeting of Consultation of Ministers of Foreign Affairs, held in Santiago, Chile in 1959; and the Tenth Inter-American Conference, held in Caracas, Venezuela, in 1954. The work of the Washington meeting and the Caracas conference, concerned primarily with international Communism, and the Santiago meeting, concerned with interventionism in the Caribbean, will be discussed in later chapters.

The Inter-American Juridical Committee and Council of Jurists. The activities of the juridical organs of the OAS, although they operate for the most part on the periphery of the security sphere, require mention in any survey of security developments that took place after the Bogotá conference. As has been noted, the Inter-American Council of Jurists serves as an advisory body on juridical matters and promotes the development and codification of international law. It meets occasionally and only when convened by the Council of the OAS. There have been four meetings of the Council of Jurists: Rio de Janeiro, 1950; Buenos Aires, 1952; Mexico City, 1956; and Santiago, 1959. The Department of International Law of the Pan American Union is the secretariat of the Inter-American Council of Jurists.

The Inter-American Juridical Committee, as permanent committee of the Council of Jurists, meets in Rio de Janeiro and undertakes such studies and preparatory work as may be assigned to it. It has a membership of nine, representing Argentina, Brazil, Chile, Colombia, Dominican Republic, Mexico, Peru, United States, and Venezuela. Because of the difficulty of getting a quorum when the committee was in continuous session, it now meets only three consecutive months each year. Incidentally, the attendance has been excellent. Of the many subjects which have been studied by the Juridical Committee and the Council of Jurists over the past ten years, only a few, related more or less to security, are here selected for mention.

First, there was the problem of recognizing *de facto* governments. Because of the failure of the Juridical Committee to present a report on the subject, the Bogotá conference ordered the Council of Jurists to prepare a project for the tenth inter-American conference. The problem of recognition is a perennial one in inter-American relations, involving as it does an inherent conflict between two fundamental principles of international law: the sovereign right of a state to change its form of government, and the right of the international community to be assured that a particular government claiming to be the legal representative of the state is justly entitled to be accepted as such. The Council of Jurists, while aware of the abuse of the right of legation to obtain unjustified advantages under international law, was agreed that it was as yet premature to conclude a convention on the subject. Thus it has been allowed to rest.[8]

Second, the Bogotá conference forwarded to the Inter-American Juridical Committee for study a proposal of the Cuban delegation in the following terms: "The right of resistance is recognized in case of manifest acts of oppression or tyranny." The evident intention was to incorporate the right of revolution in the American Declaration of the Rights and Duties of Man. The committee pointed out in its report of June 14, 1950, that it was not possible in a legal order to reconcile the duty to obey the law with the right to resist its execution by revolution, and that it would be of little utility to formulate a project on the subject.[9]

Third, the Bogotá conference also ordered the Inter-American Juridical Committee to prepare a draft statute providing for the creation and functioning of an inter-American court to guarantee the rights of man. Since there was no assurance that the Bogotá declaration of rights would be respected and exercised in practice, it was felt that a draft agreement would be a means of making the declaration effective. However, the Juridical Committee and the Council of Jurists reported adversely, pointing out that the proposed court would involve radical changes in the constitutional systems of all the American republics. Despite the unfavorable reports of the juridical bodies, the tenth conference at Caracas, convinced of the merits of the proposal, sent it to the Council of the OAS for further study and for resubmission to the eleventh conference to meet at Quito.[10] In a meeting of the Council of the OAS Ambassador Julio A. Lacarte of Uruguay, on the occasion of the decennial of the American Declaration of the Rights and Duties of Man (May 28, 1958), called on the Quito conference to consider approval of both a convention on the protection of human rights and a statute for the inter-American court. He said, "The prevention of totalitarian intervention calls not only for restraining measures but also for the strengthening of the democratic system as one of the most effective

---

[8] *Annals*, V (1953), 151.   [9] *Ibid.*, II (1950), 288.
[10] *Ibid.*, III (1951), 35; VI (1954), 18–19.

means of forestalling such intervention."[11] Demands for effective instruments to protect human rights would not be downed.

Fourth, the Juridical Committee on September 15, 1958, approved a report—not signed by the United States—entitled "International Responsibility of the State." The report enumerated principles which had been accepted by a majority of the countries, including the following: "The state is not responsible for damages suffered by aliens through acts of God, among which are included acts of insurrection and civil war," and "The state is responsible for damages suffered by aliens when it is guilty of a denial of justice." The latter statement is largely negated by the following: "The state has fulfilled its international responsibility when the judicial authority passes down its decision, even though it declares the claim, action, or recourse brought by the alien to be inadmissible."[12] The Latin Americans are still campaigning for 100-per-cent U.S. endorsement of the Calvo Doctrine. They may eventually succeed.

Finally, of the various subjects studied by the juridical bodies, one of the most important because of its potential consequences was the "Continental Shelf and Marine Waters." A harbinger of what was to come was an article in the 1950 constitution of El Salvador, declaring that its national territory included adjacent seas to a distance of two hundred marine miles. The United States announced that it stood by the three-mile principle established by international law.[13] At the Second Meeting of the Council of Jurists (1952), the subject "System of Territorial Waters and Related Questions" was submitted to the Juridical Committee to draft a definitive report. At the Third Meeting of the Council of Jurists (Mexico City, 1956), a resolution entitled "Principles of Mexico on the Juridical Regime of the Sea" was adopted. This resolution, which endorsed "the enlargement of the zone of the sea traditionally called 'territorial water,' and rights to the continental shelf," was transmitted to the Inter-American Specialized Conference on the Continental Shelf and Marine Waters, which convened at Ciudad Trujillo during March 15–28, 1956. This conference met in accordance with a resolution adopted at the Caracas conference in 1954.

Of the several resolutions adopted at Ciudad Trujillo the one of

[11] Pan American Union, *Organization of American States, 1957–1958, Annual Report of the Secretary-General to the Council of the Organization* (Washington, 1958), 23, cited hereinafter as *Annual Report of the Secretary-General, 1957–1958.*

[12] *Ibid.,* 6–7.

[13] U.S. Dept. of State, *Bulletin,* XXIV (Jan. 1, 1951), 24.

particular significance was the "Resolution of Ciudad Trujillo," which submitted for the consideration of the American states the following conclusion: The sea-bed of the sea and the subsoil of the continental shelf belong to the adjacent coastal state. But as for the ownership of the living resources of the deep seas adjacent to the territorial waters there was disagreement. It was recommended that the American states continue negotiations.[14] The status of this problem is still about as open as its subject, the open sea.

Colonies and dependent territories. A subject which, at least to the satisfaction of a majority of the Latin-American nations, is intimately related to continental security is that of European colonies in this hemisphere. Inspired by the no-transfer resolutions of the Panama and Havana meetings of 1939 and 1940, the Bogotá conference adopted a resolution calling for the creation of the American Committee on Dependent Territories and recommended that it meet soon at Havana. A function of this committee was "to study the situation of the colonies, possessions, and occupied territories existing in America, and the problems related to such situation, whatever their nature, with a view to seeking pacific means of eliminating both colonialism and the occupation of American territory by extra-continental countries." The existence of dependent territories of non-American countries was declared to be a hazard to hemispheric peace and security because of the danger of extending extracontinental conflicts. Thus the liquidation of non-American possessions, it was maintained, would strengthen American security. Both the United States and Brazil refused to sign the draft resolution on the ground that an inter-American conference was not an appropriate forum for debating a question that affected the interests of countries outside the continent.

The American Committee on Dependent Territories met in Havana on March 15, 1949, with the following countries represented: Argentina, Colombia, Costa Rica, Cuba, Ecuador, El Salvador, Guatemala, Haiti, Honduras, Mexico, Panama, Paraguay, and Peru. The most interested parties were Argentina, which has for many years disputed British rights in the Falkland Islands, and Guatemala, which contested British possession of Belize (British Honduras).

In the course of committee discussions it was contended that the case of Puerto Rico fell within the committee's competence, even though the Bogotá resolution clearly stated that the function of the committee was to eliminate "colonialism and the occupation of American terri-

---

[14] *Annals,* V (1953). 168: IX (1957), 22–27, 70–71.

tories by *extra-continental* countries." Accordingly the governments were asked, through the medium of the OAS, whether the Bogotá resolution did authorize the study of any American territory under the effective jurisdiction of any American state. Approving the committee's competence were Costa Rica, Cuba, Ecuador, and Guatemala. Those against were: Bolivia, Brazil, Colombia, Dominican Republic, El Salvador, Haiti, Honduras, Mexico, Nicaragua, Panama, Paraguay, Peru, United States, and Venezuela. There is little doubt that the whole gratuitous procedure was designed to embarrass the United States. It had, however, a contrary effect, for it pointed up marked ignorance concerning the status and desires of the Puerto Rican people themselves. Governor Muñoz Marín has vigorously denied that the island commonwealth is a colony.

As must have been anticipated, the Havana meeting accomplished no more than the adoption of a resolution requesting the cooperation of non-American countries to the end that their American possessions might be established as independent states or placed under United Nations trusteeship. The resolution appealed to the European powers, which had "received abundant support and decisive cooperation from the American continent" in two world wars, to support the consolidation of the American security system "as an object of mutual interest."[15] To many Latin-American nations the problem of non-American colonies and possessions in the hemisphere is still an open question, for at both the Washington meeting of foreign ministers in 1951 and at the Tenth Inter-American Conference at Caracas in 1954 resolutions were adopted reaffirming principles regarding colonies in American territory. The eventual success of Latin America's efforts to liquidate colonialism in the hemisphere must not be discounted, for we have considerable evidence already of their ability to win issues by attrition.

The Inter-American Peace Committee. If the juridical organs concerned with the immediate preceding problem hovered on the outer fringe of the security concept, this certainly was not true of a new and most important addition to the inter-American security structure, the Inter-American Peace Committee. At the Second Meeting of Consultation of Ministers of Foreign Affairs held in Havana in 1940, the Governing Board of the Pan American Union was ordered by Resolution XIV to establish a committee consisting of five members. The committee was to keep constantly vigilant for any dispute that might arise

[15] *Ibid.,* I (1949), 389–392.

between states and to suggest means and methods for a pacific settlement as quickly as possible. In December 1940 the Governing Board decided that the "Committee for the Peaceful Solution of Conflicts" should have its seat in Washington and should be composed of the representatives of two North American countries—the United States and Mexico—two South American countries—Argentina and Brazil—and one Central American or Caribbean country—Cuba.[16] Beyond this no further action was taken, and even the fact of the paper existence of the committee was almost forgotten. Indeed, the organ seems to have escaped the attention of the framers of the Charter of the OAS, for it is not mentioned in that instrument. Credit for rescuing the Peace Committee from oblivion belongs to the government of the Dominican Republic, which, on September 23, 1947, sent a note to the Director-General of the Pan American Union requesting him to take the necessary steps to install the committee. On July 31, 1948, after such steps had been taken and the representatives of the five member countries composing the committee had been appointed, the organ was duly installed. The committee adopted the name "Inter-American Committee on Methods for the Peaceful Solution of Conflicts," and outlined its operational and procedural bases. In July 1949 the name was changed to "Inter-American Peace Committee."[17]

After its installation the Inter-American Peace Committee was called upon to act on three different occasions prior to 1952: in August 1948, when the Dominican Republic resorted to the committee in connection with a difference with the government of Cuba; in March 1949, when the government of Haiti resorted to it in connection with a difference with the Dominican Republic; and in August 1949, when the government of the United States brought to the attention of the committee the abnormal situation prevailing at that time in the Caribbean area.

Since a question had been raised by Chile regarding the juridical status of the Inter-American Peace Committee, in view of developments that had taken place since its creation in 1940, and particularly since the adopting of the Rio treaty and the Charter of the OAS, the Council of the OAS decided on January 3, 1951, that no problem existed with respect to the juridical status of the Peace Committee. It agreed that the functions of the committee did not duplicate those of any other inter-American peace instrument, and that it was in order for the next general conference, which was to meet in Caracas in 1954,

---

[16] *Ibid.,* IV (1952), 8.   [17] *Ibid.,* II (1950), 23.

to concern itself with the organization and bases of operations of the Inter-American Peace Committee.[18]

For the information and guidance of the Caracas conference the Inter-American Peace Committee submitted a report on its activities, including a draft resolution on its organization and operation. With respect to its activities, it had, since its installation in 1948, been requested to aid in resolving no fewer than six situations between American republics. A record of these performances will be found in the next chapter. Here we are concerned only with the formalizing of this addition to the inter-American peace structure. As was to be expected, the Caracas conference expressed its confidence in the Inter-American Peace Committee and resolved to continue that body. The Council of the OAS was requested to prepare statutes for the committee, based on the draft prepared by the committee and submitted to the conference.

In accordance with the Caracas resolution, the statutes for the Peace Committee were drafted and duly approved by the Council on May 9, 1956. At its meeting of August 6, 1956, Argentina, Brazil, Cuba, Mexico, and the United States were elected members with staggered terms. One member state of the committee was to be replaced each year by nomination of the Council of the OAS.[19] With respect to the competence of the committee, the statutes provided that (a) it should keep constant vigilance to ensure that states which were parties to any dispute or controversy solve it as quickly as possible, and to this end it should suggest means and steps conducive to a settlement; and (b) any American state directly concerned in a dispute or controversy with another American state might request the committee to take action, which it would do only with the prior consent of both parties. It is to be noted particularly that the committee had no authority to take the initiative in a controversy between states. It had to wait until both parties agreed to bring their dispute before it. Needless to say, this grave deficiency weakened the effectiveness of the organ.[20]

By these steps the Inter-American Peace Committee became a prime organ of the hemisphere peace system. Its status was further enhanced by action of the Santiago meeting of foreign ministers in August 1959, when the committee was called on to perform "watchdog" functions

---

[18] *Ibid.*, III (1951), 210.

[19] Replacements: El Salvador for Cuba (1957), Uruguay for Argentina (1958), Venezuela for Brazil (1959), Colombia for the United States (1960).

[20] For the statutes of the Inter-American Peace Committee, see *Annals,* VIII (1956), 194–196.

in the troublesome Caribbean pending the convening of the eleventh inter-American conference in Quito. The history of the Inter-American Peace Committee reminds that great oaks do grow from little acorns.

The Inter-American Defense Board. From the preceding post-Bogotá developments of political and juridical aspects of inter-American security, we turn now to the strengthening, during the past decade, of the military defenses of the Americas. This was accomplished both by multilateral action through the instrumentality of the Inter-American Defense Board, and through bilateral agreements with the United States. The work of the Inter-American Defense Board and the policies pursued by the United States in military cooperation with all other American republics were clearly based upon the political and legal commitments of the treaty of Rio de Janeiro, which established responsibility of every American republic to cooperate for the defense of the continent.

It will be recalled that the Bogotá conference decided that the Inter-American Defense Board should continue to act as the organ of preparation for collective self-defense against aggression, that is, "until the American governments decide by two-thirds majority to consider its labor terminated." The creation by the Charter of the OAS of the Advisory Defense Committee, composed of the highest military officers of the American states to advise the organ of consultation on call in exceptional circumstances, put the future of the Defense Board in doubt. This doubt was removed, however, when on October 18, 1950, the Council approved a resolution expressing satisfaction with the board and approving its continuance. Although the two-thirds-vote proviso of the Bogotá resolution seemed to indicate a temporary status, it proved in the end to give the Defense Board special privilege over other agencies, inasmuch as they can be dissolved by simple majority vote. As for the Advisory Defense Committee, it never developed beyond the paper stage, for it has never been convoked. It seems that the Defense Board, always available for advice in emergency situations, may well obviate any need for the Advisory Defense Committee.

The Defense Board, which has its seat in Washington, is composed of military representatives of the twenty-one republics, and they comprise the Council of Delegates. As host country the United States holds the permanent chairmanship. Several distinguished high officers of the armed services have held this position. There is a general officer to make studies and perform technical services. The three permanent committees of the staff are the Plans Committee, the Intelligence Committee, and the Logistics Committee.[21] The secretariat is headed by a United States officer.

The Council of Delegates is a sort of Inter-American military assembly where any subject bearing on hemisphere security can be discussed; each country has one vote on recommendations. In accordance with Resolution XXXIV of Bogotá, the mission of the Inter-American Defense Board "shall be to act as the organ of preparation and recommendation for the collective self-defense of the American Continent against aggression, and to carry out, in addition to the advisory functions within its competence, any similar functions ascribed to it by the Advisory Defense Committee."

The Defense Board has no legislative or treaty-making power. It is strictly nonpolitical. Nor has it armed forces under its direct control, for its mission is *defense planning* only. It provides a research organization and a forum where basic concepts and plans can be developed. Its recommendations go directly to the respective governments, and not via the Council as is the case of the other agencies. In fact the Pan American Union's only official connection with the Defense Board is to supply its required funds, which are included in the budget of the OAS.[22] The place of the Inter-American Defense Board in the inter-American security system is illustrated by Chart III; Chart IV illustrates its organization.

The *raison d'être* of the Defense Board, it bears repeating, is military planning for hemispheric security. Despite latter-day modifications in the defense plans of the United States and the associated free nations, there has been much added pressure put on the Inter-American Defense Board to reconcile the requirements of hemisphere defense to the concept of global strategy. In 1941 the United States was concerned over the possibility of attack via the southern continent. A decade later saw the situation greatly changed because of change in modern warfare. If the United States is to be attacked by present-day methods, the most probable course will be via the northern part of the hemisphere rather than the southern. Latin America can hardly be considered as one of the most likely combat areas. Nevertheless there remained the necessity for arrangements to ensure the military security of the Western Hemisphere. This fact was recognized by the fourth

[21] Council of Delegates, *Regulations for the Organization and Activities of the Inter-American Defense Board,* Appendix 1, Minutes, Sess. 202 (May 23, 1957).

[22] The assigned budget for the Defense Board for 1958/59 was $291,932.— *Annals,* X (1958), 46.

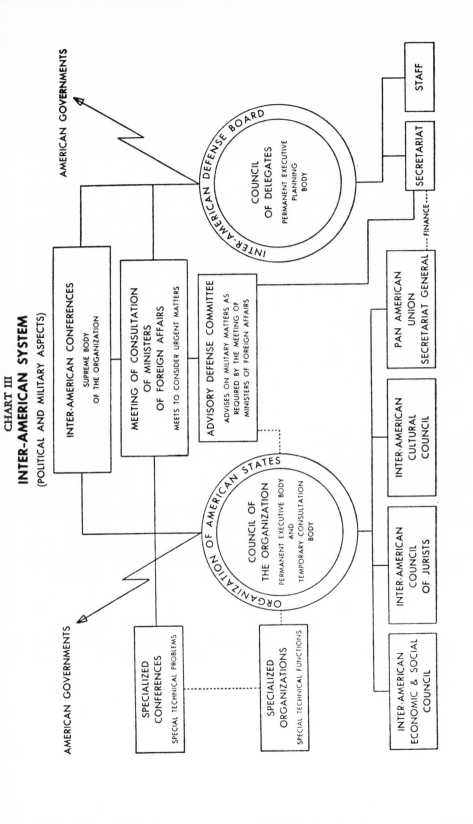

CHART III

INTER-AMERICAN SYSTEM

(POLITICAL AND MILITARY ASPECTS)

AMERICAN GOVERNMENTS

INTER-AMERICAN DEFENSE BOARD

COUNCIL OF DELEGATES

PERMANENT EXECUTIVE PLANNING BODY

SECRETARIAT

STAFF

FINANCE

INTER-AMERICAN CONFERENCES

SUPREME BODY OF THE ORGANIZATION

MEETING OF CONSULTATION OF MINISTERS OF FOREIGN AFFAIRS

MEETS TO CONSIDER URGENT MATTERS

ADVISORY DEFENSE COMMITTEE

ADVISES ON MILITARY MATTERS AS REQUIRED BY THE MEETING OF MINISTERS OF FOREIGN AFFAIRS

ORGANIZATION OF AMERICAN STATES

COUNCIL OF THE ORGANIZATION

PERMANENT EXECUTIVE BODY AND TEMPORARY CONSULTATION BODY

PAN AMERICAN UNION

SECRETARIAT GENERAL

INTER-AMERICAN CULTURAL COUNCIL

INTER-AMERICAN COUNCIL OF JURISTS

INTER-AMERICAN ECONOMIC & SOCIAL COUNCIL

AMERICAN GOVERNMENTS

SPECIALIZED CONFERENCES

SPECIAL TECHNICAL PROBLEMS

SPECIALIZED ORGANIZATIONS

SPECIAL TECHNICAL FUNCTIONS

CHART IV

INTER-AMERICAN DEFENSE BOARD

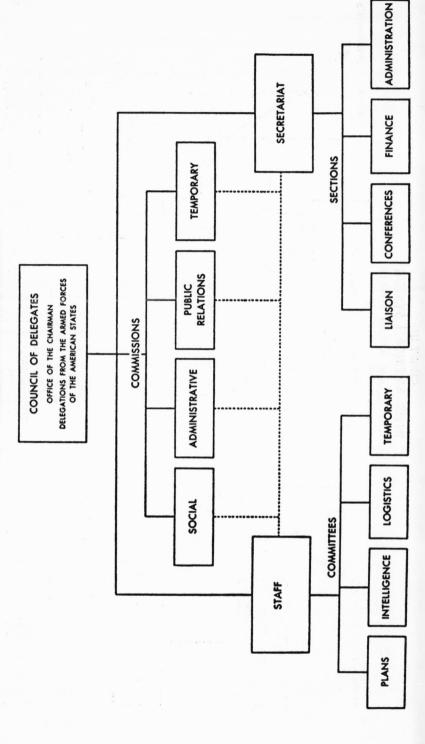

meeting of American foreign ministers, which convened in Washington shortly after the active intervention of Communist China in the Korean War. Considering the military problems of the hemisphere, the foreign ministers recommended that the American republics strengthen their armed forces and keep them in a state of readiness for the defense of the continent, and that they cooperate with each other in military matters in order to develop the collective strength necessary to combat aggression against any of them. The Inter-American Defense Board was specifically directed to carry forward its military plans for continental defense.[23]

The disturbed international situation and more particularly the pertinent decision taken at the Washington meeting greatly increased the role of the Inter-American Defense Board, both in scope and importance. The board intensified its efforts to develop a general hemisphere defense plan, and on November 15, 1951, it approved and forwarded to the respective governments the "General Military Plan for the Defense of the American Continent." Two annexes to the plan, entitled "Areas of Particular Strategic Importance—Charts and Intelligence and Counter-intelligence," were forthcoming in March and April of 1952. During the Washington meeting the Defense Board was available for military advice.[24]

The Defense Board has continued to work toward the coordination of common-defense measures and the establishment of the broadest possible bases for inter-American military cooperation. In July 1957 it approved a new military defense plan, said to be the first major revision since the adoption of the General Military Plan in 1951.[25] It seems that the board was making further accommodations in hemisphere defense plans in view of the clearer delineation of global defense. According to this concept the nations of the world are divided into two great areas: (1) "Primary Space," wherein the current struggle for power is taking place, which lies between the tenth and fortieth parallels north latitude and is occupied by nations whose territory could serve as areas of armed conflict in any war between the free world and the Communist nations; and (2) "Secondary Space," or that outside Primary Space. Latin America is classified as an area of Secondary Space. This fact the Latin-American military strategists are

[23] Pan American Union, *Proceedings* of the Fourth Meeting of Consultation of Foreign Affairs (Washington, 1951), Res. III.

[24] *Annals,* V (1953), 82–83.

[25] *Annual Report of the Secretary-General, 1957–1958,* 118–119; *New York Times,* July 19, 1957.

aware of and accept in their present planning. Thus, since a direct attack by Communist forces in South America is most unlikely, Latin America's chief contributions to the nations of the free world would be to maintain order and prevent subversive activities, defend vital military and economic installations, provide sea and air submarine patrols, keep communications open, and produce critical and strategic raw materials and other components of economic defense. Latin America's contributions do not, however, exclude uniformed military assistance, and for this reason there is ample latitude for military planning by the Defense Board. Incidentally, Latin America's assuming of these continental military responsibilities would free United States troops for service in the Primary Space area.[26] In view of the foregoing, the contention is here rejected that "as a purely military proposition the concept of collective planning and defense has little, if any, practical application."[27]

Among additional subjects which have occupied the Inter-American Defense Board in recent years are the following: measures for promoting the standardization of instruction and training of the armed forces of the American republics with a minimum cost-effect on the national economy of each country; the standardization of matériel within the American republics; a plan for organizing a coordinated system for exchange of appropriate information, with special attention to the question of public information; and a study of the possibility of convening a meeting of the highest military authorities of the American republics with a view to the future application of the General Military Plan. It was perhaps in pursuance of this idea that in April of 1957 delegations of defense ministers or high-ranking officers of eighteen Latin-American countries observed Marine amphibian and helicopter exercises, parachute drops, and air landings by two United States Army battalions in a Panama training exercise. The Defense Board is also interested in promoting regional-defense arrangements. Accordingly, in May 1957, there was in Buenos Aires a preparatory meeting for studying the "Bases of Organization of the South Atlantic Defense," with military representatives from Argentina, Brazil, Paraguay, and Uruguay participating. Closely related to the foregoing examples of multilateral defense cooperation initiated by the Inter-American Defense Board were the bilateral military agreements

[26] John E. Kieffer, "Defending the Western Hemisphere," Américas, VII (August 1955), 3–6.

[27] Edwin Lieuwen, *Arms and Politics in Latin America* (New York, 1960), 214.

Developments in American Solidarity

that the United States entered into with a number of the Latin-American republics.

United States Military Assistance Agreements. Like multilateral cooperation, United States military assistance also stemmed from the Rio treaty. Moreover, it was on the basis of plans devised by the Defense Board that the United States entered upon a variety of cooperative measures with its sister American nations.

The major problem of hemisphere defense is the military weakness of most of the Latin-American nations. What could and should the United States do in this important area to create stronger defensive forces? Since many of the Latin-American countries were willing to do their share of the defense job but were unable to because of this limitation, it was clearly a case of the United States helping them if it wished them to assume a greater share of the burden of continental defense. This was the obvious implication of Resolution III of the fourth meeting of foreign ministers, which convened in Washington. The United States was enabled to discharge this responsibility under the terms of a provision for assisting Latin America in the Mutual Security Act of 1951. Up to that date the Mutual Security Act had provided authority to supply only *important allies* with military assistance. And this did not include Latin America. The act of 1951 initially provided for $38,150,000 of direct military assistance to Latin America, to be used in those countries whose participation was judged by the President as indispensable. However, before providing assistance to any country, the United States had to enter into a bilateral military-assistance agreement with that country.

Soon the State and Defense Departments announced that negotiations for bilateral Military Assistance Agreements had been initiated with several of the Latin-American countries. On January 3, 1952, it was revealed that the initiation of conversations with Brazil marked the first of the bilateral negotiations under the military grant-aid program for Latin America authorized by the 1951 Mutual Security Act.[28]

To date, Military Assistance Agreements have been concluded with Brazil, Chile, Colombia, Cuba, Dominican Republic, Ecuador, Guatemala, Haiti, Honduras, Nicaragua, Peru, and Uruguay. The twelfth and last was signed with Guatemala on June 18, 1955. The failure of Mexico to sign up was a disappointment to Washington. The negotiations collapsed when, with an election pending, the neighbor republic refused to subscribe to terms governing the granting of military and

[28] U.S. Dept. of State, *Press Release,* Jan. 3, 1952, p. 50.

economic aid by this country. To Mexico these terms implied the possibility of her having to send troops outside the national territory. All sectors of Mexico joined in applauding President Miguel Alemán's rejection of the proposed agreement.[29] Since then Mexico has indicated no intention of concluding a military pact with the United States, and it is highly doubtful that any Mexican government would commit itself to send troops outside national territory. In several of the countries, notably Brazil, the Communists and leftists opposed bitterly any military alliance with the United States, alleging that it was a "Yankee maneuver" to force the sending of troops to Korea. President Carlos Ibañez del Campo of Chile deplored the pact with the United States, which had been contracted by a preceding regime, as "humiliating" to Chile, but he did not denounce it, since it was "the only means" of developing the republic's military power.[30]

The Military Assistance Agreements[31] are consistent with, and conform to, the inter-American instruments already in effect, such as the Inter-American Treaty of Reciprocal Assistance (the Rio treaty), the Inter-American Military Cooperation resolution approved at the Washington meeting of foreign ministers of 1951, and the continuous planning of the Inter-American Defense Board. The program is intended to help develop the capabilities of the countries concerned to join in performing missions important to the security of all the American republics. According to the provisions of the agreements, the United States undertakes to make available arms, equipment, materials, technical skills, and other military assistance "to promote the defense and maintain the peace of the Western Hemisphere." Each Latin-American government agrees to make effective use of the assistance received from the United States and to employ it solely for carrying out specific defense plans agreed upon by both governments. Also, each pledges "to facilitate the production and transfer to the Government of the United States of America for such period of time, in such quantities and upon such terms and conditions as may be agreed upon of raw and semiprocessed strategic materials required by the United States." The parties to the Military Assistance Agreements reaffirmed their determination "to give their full cooperation to the efforts to provide the United Nations with armed forces as contemplated by the Charter."

29 *New York Times,* Feb. 22–24, 1952.
30 *Christian Science Monitor,* April 27, 1952.
31 See U.S. Dept. of State, Treaties and other International Acts Ser. For text of the agreement with Ecuador, also see U.S. Dept. of State, *Bulletin,* XXVI (March 3, 1952), 336–338.

Although this declaration added nothing to the obligations already assumed by signatories of the United Nations Charter, it was erroneously and unfairly represented by opponents of the agreements as a solemn pledge to send Latin-American troops into overseas conflicts.

The grant of military aid. The United States has offered three types of military assistance to the Latin-American nations: (1) direct grants of equipment and other assistance to certain countries with whom we have contracted Military Assistance Agreements; (2) opportunities for purchasing United States weapons and equipment which they require for their own and for hemisphere defense; and (3) the establishment of U.S. Army, Navy, and Air Force missions to help train Latin-American armed forces.

The Mutual Security Act provides authority to supply arms and military equipment under three authorizations: grant assistance, sale for cash, and sale of limited amounts on three-year defense terms. The program of grant assistance must be directly related to the plans of the Inter-American Defense Board for collective defense; the assistance must be provided for military units already in being, though not at full strength; and the Latin-American governments must utilize the grants exclusively for the agreed-upon purpose. This, the so-called Moore Amendment of 1958, was intended to prevent the use of grant arms and equipment in civil strife. The United States cannot lend aid to dictators.

The first consolidated United States shipment of military equipment earmarked for Latin America under these agreements left New York on August 1, 1952, for Ecuador, Peru, and Colombia. The cargo included motor vehicles, weapons, ammunition, and spare parts for aircraft and naval vessels. Those nations that have signed the Military Assistance Agreements have continued to receive United States aid. For example, in July 1954, Honduras and Nicaragua were reported as getting "substantial shipments" of United States military supplies to supplement equipment sent earlier by plane in May under the standard mutual-aid agreements. Guatemala also, in December 1954, received a first United States armaments shipment "to modernize" her army under the military-assistance pact. More shipments, including fighter planes, were expected "eventually."[32] Beginning with the sum of $38,150,000 allocated by the Mutual Security Act of 1951 to help equip and train the armed forces of Latin America, the amount of grant aid was increased annually over the years until in 1959 military-assistance grants

[32] *New York Times,* July 5 and Dec. 16, 1954.

amounted to $67,058,000. By the end of fiscal 1959 the twelve countries in the program had received $317 million.[33]

We turn next to the second type of military assistance, that is, the sale of arms either for cash or on deferred terms. After the expiration of Lend-Lease, and until the expected adoption of the Arms Standardization Act, an "interim program" became the vehicle for the continued supply of military equipment immediately following World War II. This program, based on the Surplus Property Act, provided armaments to various Latin-American countries at about five to ten cents on the dollar.[34] However, after Congress failed to pass the Arms Standardization Act, despite strong urging by President Truman, authority under the Surplus Property Act expired, and with it the "interim program." This created a difficult situation, for it placed in jeopardy the future of United States military training missions in Latin America, whose success hinged on their using arms and equipment from this country. The drying up of the United States arms supply would inevitably result in Latin America's seeking other sources.

Fortunately, recourse to the Mutual Defense Assistance Act of 1949 relieved the situation, for this act allowed for the purchase of surplus weapons and equipment for cash. In 1951 Argentina, Brazil, and Chile each bought two light cruisers; Peru acquired three destroyer escorts, and Uruguay two; and Colombia bought a frigate. These and other sales of equipment were authorized from excess United States stocks at low prices, subject to assurances that the material would be devoted to hemisphere defense requirements. By the end of fiscal 1959 the Latin-American nations had obtained about $140 million of military equipment under the reimbursable aid provisions of the Mutual Defense Assistance Act. It was inevitable that this country would be accused of stimulating an arms race—and the Latin-American countries of buying beyond their means. The charge had little validity, however, since United States military-assistance grants and reimbursable aid averaged over the period 1951–59 only $65 million annually—this distributed among twenty nations. Altogether, United States military

[33] For military-assistance program shipments to Latin America, see House Committee on Foreign Affairs, "Staff Memorandum on Background Material in Mutual Security Program for Fiscal 1960," 86th Cong., 1st Sess. (Washington, 1959), 27.

[34] For direct sales of U.S. military surplus equipment to Latin-American countries, see U.S. Dept. of State, *Bulletin*, XXI (Sept. 26, 1949).

assistance has been modest, amounting to about 5 per cent of what Latin America spends to maintain its armed forces.[35]

On the subject of arms aid to Latin America the State Department and the Pentagon did not see eye to eye. The State Department would block or curtail the flow of arms on the theory that the possession of arms could cause wars rather than stop them. Highly sensitive to public opinion, both in this country and in Latin America, the Department feared that to arm Latin America would create hazards at least as serious as to leave it in its state of military ineffectiveness. To provide the republics with the capacity to conduct full-scale action would be, it held, to invite chaos. Furthermore, it was felt that new supplies of arms would be used by some governments against their own people. For many years the State Department has been keenly aware of the charge that United States arms bulwark Latin-American dictators.

Moreover, there has been, and still is, a rather general apprehension that heavy spending by Latin-American countries for armaments is detrimental to their economic development. This fear was expressed by the United Nations Economic Commission for Latin America when it met in Mexico City in 1951. And when in 1957 the Inter-American Defense Board revised the General Military Plan, it was reported that a significant feature of the new plan is recognition of the need for curbing armaments costs.[36] These apprehensions led to a draft resolution on arms limitation presented to the Council of the OAS on March 5, 1958, by Costa Rica, calling for a special committee to study the needs of inter-American defense with a view toward limiting arms and reducing military expenditures.[37] As might have been anticipated, the proposal met strong opposition, for it touched easily-offended national dignity and pride in their military establishments. One Council member was reported as declaring passionately that he did not believe the day would ever come when his country would be prepared to delegate to the United States the role of protector of Latin America.

The Pentagon, on the other hand, argued that arms supply to Latin America is an essential part of the price the United States must pay for the many advantages it seeks to gain through the Military Assistance Agreements. This country must provide at least the minimum of military equipment for hemisphere defense. Failing supply by the United States, there is no doubt that the Latin Americans would turn to other

[35] Lieuwen, 202, 216.
[36] *New York Times,* May 29, 1951; July 19, 1957.
[37] *Annals,* X (1958), 15–16.

quarters for their military equipment. Granted the risk that the armaments might be misapplied in internal strife, it is essential, nevertheless, that the United States continue to be a source of supply. Incidentally, it does not always follow that United States arms support dictatorships; there are examples of these very arms being turned against the dictators.

Nor is it true that Latin-American military expenditures are so heavy as to weigh on the national economies. In relation to the gross national production, expenditures are 2.9 per cent—next to the lowest for any region in the world—(South Asia spends 2 per cent). And, although the average is only from 15 to 20 per cent of the annual budgets for all the nations of Latin America, these expenditures for the military are not negative by any means.[38] The military services provide the very large number of illiterate recruits with schooling and training for the trades. They return to civilian life better prepared to enter upon productive careers. Moreover, there is need for the military as a stabilizing force and for prestige purposes. The army is the symbol of nationalism, almost the sole unifying element in a loosely-organized society. The military has not always usurped the role of decision and direction in serious situations, though this is in fact what is usually expected of it. There is a confident belief, often grievously abused, of course, that the army is above partisanship and therefore has a clearer conception of the national interest. It is interesting that in recent years the military in several of the countries, notably Argentina, Brazil, and Venezuela, has actively intervened politically to lend support to constitutionalism and democratic government. This is a new trend. Who knows where it may lead? Therefore, over and above considerations of hemisphere defense, if the United States is interested in stability, order, and democratic progress, it behooves this country to continue to give support through the military-assistance program to the professional military in Latin America; they are fair insurance against Communist *coups* in any of the governments.

As mentioned above, a third form of United States military assistance to Latin America is the establishment of missions to help train the armed forces. These Army, Navy, and Air Force missions are established at the request of the other American countries and are purely advisory. The over-all cost of these programs is small compared with our total commitments. Currently there are missions in eighteen countries. In addition to the on-the-ground training, since 1952 nine thou-

---

[38] These figures are from a reliable but confidential source.

sand young Latin-American officers have been trained in the United States. Theirs is called "specialized training."

As for United States bases in Latin America, the military planning over the past ten years has not called for the acquisition of new base sites. Greater dependence on the Latins themselves to man the defenses of the southern continent has obviated the need of more bases for the United States. In addition, the experiences following World War II in seeking to extend base rights in several of the countries may have demonstrated how futile it would be to enter into renewed negotiations. The United States has (at the present writing) but one base in Latin America, Guantánamo Naval Base in Cuba. Panama has pledged the use of the old site at Rio Hato for maneuvers. Finally, the United States has been given the right to establish missile tracking stations in the Dominican Republic and at Fernando de Noronha, an island off the hump of Brazil. Only two air centers are operative within the area, in the Canal Zone and Puerto Rico. The absence of occupied base sites need not be an impediment to hemisphere defense, for in an emergency the idea is for all United States and allied military forces in the Caribbean to work together, and if coordination is effected, the danger of a surprise attack would be reduced.

Tensions in the neighborhood. Although the responsibility of military planning and preparation for the defense of the Americas has been discharged with diligence and foresight on both the multilateral and bilateral planes, this alone cannot ensure effective implementation should an emergency arise. The effectiveness of inter-American defense cooperation can be expected to be equated with the degree of solidarity existent among the American nations. Tensions in United States–Latin-American relations, which have intensified since World War II and finally erupted in 1958 and 1959 in actual demonstrations of anti-Yankee hostility, must be regarded as serious weaknesses of the security system. This regional arrangement, as has been proclaimed so many times in inter-American treaties, declarations, and resolutions, is based on a mutuality of interests and common devotion to principles of civilized international behavior. It can be no more effective than the sincerity in which these common principles are held. Therefore the mounting jealousies, suspicions, resentments, and actual hostility toward the major member of the association must be examined in light of their relation to inter-American security.

Two incidents which shocked the American public into a belated realization of how greatly our relations with the Latin-American nations have deteriorated were the mob assaults on Vice-President Richard Nixon and the riots in Bolivia precipitated by an article in *Time* magazine.

On April 27, 1958, the Vice-President, accompanied by Mrs. Nixon, Assistant Secretary of State Roy R. Rubottom, Jr., and Samuel C. Waugh, president of the Export-Import Bank, left Washington for a good-will tour of South America. The principal purpose of the trip was to attend the inauguration of President Arturo Frondizi of Argentina at Buenos Aires. Mr. Nixon visited Uruguay, Argentina, Paraguay, Bolivia, Peru, Ecuador, Colombia, and Venezuela.[39]

The first country visited was Uruguay. The behavior of the students at Monteviedo was a harbinger of what was to come at later stops of the tour. The Student Federation, having made advance plans for a demonstration, greeted the Vice-President on his arrival with boos and shouts of "Nixon, go home!" Handbills were distributed denouncing American imperialism. Although Mr. Nixon was able later in debate to win over some student good-will, he left the country to the accompaniment of more shouts of "Nixon, go home!" and "Let's do business with the U.S.S.R.!"

The Vice-President's visits in Argentina and Paraguay were without hostile incident and happily this was also true in Bolivia, where there were negligible demonstrations born of a tense politico-economic situation which was undoubtedly exploited by the Communists. In answering students who accused the United States of imperialistic designs, Mr. Nixon called for "bold and imaginative" cooperation programs to cope with misery and ensure freedom. The fact that there were only mild demonstrations in Bolivia, a tinderbox of anti-Yankee feeling, encouraged the party to continue the tour despite forewarnings of inflamed dissatisfaction in Peru over United States restrictions and tariffs on certain basic products and materials exported by Peru. There was, however, nothing in the intelligence reports to indicate the probability of the real violence that was narrowly averted in Lima.[40]

Mr. Nixon arrived in the Peruvian capital on May 7. His stay included meetings with the Peruvian Senate, labor and agrarian leaders, mining and business representatives, and student groups. As usual, it

[39] For a summary account of the Nixon tour, gleaned from news reports, see Hispanic American Studies, *Hispanic American Report,* XI, No. 4 (Stanford University, April 1958).

[40] "Review of Recent Anti-American Demonstrations" (statement by Deputy Undersecretary Murphy before the Senate Foreign Relations Committee), U.S. Dept. of State, *Bulletin,* XXXVIII (June 9, 1958), 952–958.

was the students who manifested the most violent and well-planned hostility against the "most rabid proponent of Yankee imperialism." In view of Mr. Nixon's declared intention to put in an appearance at the University of San Marcos, despite a student resolution stating that they did not want him, a screaming mob of about two thousand blocked his entry into the University. It was reported that stones were thrown and that the Vice-President was spat on. From San Marcos Mr. Nixon and his party moved to the Catholic University, where his reception was almost as hostile. His efforts to debate with the students were interrupted by booing and shouting. The students seemed to be concerned about United States tariffs on lead and zinc and the alleged support of dictators. Their unwillingness to allow Mr. Nixon a reply drew from him the comment that "any institution of learning which denies freedom of expression cannot be considered great." As usual, the incidents were termed "Communist-inspired," but, granted that the Communists had been active in fomenting the demonstrations, it is also a fact that such demonstrations could not have been staged had there not been a climate that favored them.

The Vice-President's visits to Quito, Ecuador, and Bogotá, Colombia, were without incident. The next and final stop was Caracas, Venezuela. A spokesman for the State Department admitted to the Senate Foreign Relations Committee that "from the very start it had been anticipated that there might be more danger of disturbances in Venezuela than in any other place."[41] Although it was recognized that demonstrations might occur, the Vice-President rejected suggestions to cancel the visit; he did, however, agree to extraprecautionary measures. On the basis of assurances by the Venezuelan government of its security measures, violence in Caracas was not anticipated. The intensity of the demonstrations against Mr. Nixon and his party and the failure of the Venezuelan security forces to act effectively were not foreseen.

A screaming, spitting crowd greeted the Nixon party at the Caracas airport on the morning of May 13. When the motorcade entered Caracas and was held up in a noon-hour traffic jam, it seemed to be the signal for a mob to emerge from an intersection and attack the car in which the Vice-President and Mrs. Nixon were riding. The windows of the car were smashed with rocks and clubs, and the occupants were showered with spittle. It seemed that the rioters were intent on seizing

41 *Ibid.*, 957.

Mr. Nixon. Fortunately the two U.S. Secret Service agents riding inside the car were not forced to fire their drawn revolvers. Even after the Nixons were safely lodged in the American Embassy, hostile mobs roamed the streets until it was necessary for Venezuelan troops, tardily assembled, to use tear gas to break up the rioters.

President Eisenhower, alarmed for the safety of Mr. and Mrs. Nixon, ordered four companies of combat-ready Marines and paratroopers flown to Puerto Rico "as a precautionary measure," to be used only "if assistance were requested by the Venezuelan government." The reaction in Latin America generally to this precaution was highly educational. The mere fact of troops standing in readiness, on American soil, for the protection of a high governmental official was branded as tantamount to armed intervention itself. One would think, from the critical and hysterical clamor, that the United States had returned to "gunboat diplomacy." It was clear that, in the Latin view, United States renunciation of intervention also included its renunciation of the right to aid an ineffectual government in giving protection to the Vice-President of the United States. Fortunately, the Venezuelan authorities were able to restore order and to afford Mr. Nixon and his party sufficient protection to enable them to leave the country safely.

There were many reasons, peculiar to Venezuela, for the anti-Nixon demonstration. The political situation was unsettled, for only recently had the Pérez Jiménez dictatorship been overthrown, and the Communists and other political exiles had flooded back into the country. All joined voices in criticizing the United States, not only for support of the dictatorship but for giving asylum to the fallen tyrant. Also, there is no doubt that United States restrictions placed upon imports of Venezuelan oil were an important factor. Many would put the blame squarely on the Communists, but even Mr. Nixon, while recognizing Communist adroitness in exploiting discontent, pointed out the essential needs of United States economic assistance. President Eisenhower also plainly indicated that he thought the underlying causes of the strife in Venezuela were economic. Before we proceed to an examination of the various underlying causes of anti-American feeling in Latin America, one further instance of anti-United States mob demonstration is presented.

This incident occurred in Bolivia in March of 1959. A little background information will make the affair more comprehensible. Bolivia, like so many other Latin-American states released from dictatorships, is ruled by a "revolutionary" government. Since the revolution of 1952, the dominant party, the Nationalist Revolutionary Movement (MNR), has controlled the government ineffectively, and has tried to push an ambitious but unrealistic program of social and economic reform. Significant features of the revolutionary program are agrarian reform, nationalization of the tin mines, and the disappearance of the Army. The implementation of the program has brought the country to the brink of chaos. Production has declined on nearly every front. The absence of an army enhances the power of the miners, who regard themselves as the special beneficiaries of mine nationalization. The disorder in Bolivia is eloquent testimony to the need for a strong army to bulwark a government.

Since the United States cannot afford to abandon Bolivia to the debacle which would inevitably follow, the revolutionary government has been kept from foundering by a steady stream of American grant aid and economic assistance, and by a stabilization loan from the International Monetary Fund. One-third of the national budget is under joint Bolivian–United States supervision. The United States aid and assistance program to Bolivia is the largest in terms of per capita expenditures; from 1952 to December 1958, it poured $119 million into the desolate and distraught Andean country. Bolivia is truly "one of the most assisted countries in the world." Yet all this assistance has done little to solve its problems, and has not, moreover, ameliorated anti-United States resentment and hostility. It is unrealistic of course for the United States to expect friendship and admiration in exchange for economic assistance, but certainly it is entitled to expect something better than what the *Time* riots of March 2–4, 1959, seemed to imply.

The Latin-American edition of *Time* unwisely contained a facetious remark, attributed to a member of the American Embassy, that the only solution for Bolivia's travail was partition among her neighbors— a view, incidentally, which many responsible authorities share. This however, was nothing more than a typical *Time* "wisecrack," but the Bolivians were in no mood for a brand of humor that pricked the national pride. At any rate the issue of *Time* with the provocative article ignited an outburst of anti-United States demonstrations, born of shame and frustration. Significantly, banners prominently displayed read, "No more Yankee alms; relations with the U.S.S.R." There was much sound and fury, and both the Embassy at La Paz and the American Consulate at Cochabamba were stoned and required police guards for several days.

In assessing immediate responsibility for the riots, one informed

American observer holds that the Bolivian government, in order to stimulate more aid and loans from the United States, was responsible for the demonstrations. He says,

> The government gave its tacit blessing to the demonstrations by publicizing the *Time* insult. . . . Feelings of injured pride were widespread and the work of organizing into effective action was taken up by some strange bed-fellows: the Youth movement of the MNR, the Bolivian Workers' Union (COB), the Communists, and the rightest opposition Falange. The different organizations complemented one another instead of canceling each other out, and the result was havoc.[42]

An obvious but superfluous lesson of the anti-United States demonstrations at La Paz and Cochabamba was that massive aid is more likely to create resentment than friendship.

The Bolivian government, in expressing official regret for the incidents, conceded that the acts of violence went beyond "rightful" indignation because of the *Time* article, and "were the result of agitation by a small minority of extremists influenced by international Communism."[43] Once more the Communists were given too much credit for organizing demonstrations against the United States, for there were many other Yankeephobes ever ready to excite the deep-seated and latent feeling of hostility whenever provocative occasions afforded.

Causes of Latin-American hostility toward the United States. These shocking rifts in good neighborliness surprised and alarmed the United States public. The events of the Nixon tour, and later the riots in Bolivia, revealed a disquietude in the neighborhood which could not be ignored. Perhaps Latin-American friendship and devotion to the principles of continental solidarity had indeed been taken too much for granted. Many turned to the task of reassessing U.S. relations with the presumed good neighbors. The reaction was typical: wherein had the *United States* made mistakes? It was a season for soul searching.

There seems to be almost universal agreement that the principal mistakes have been in the economic area. Since this subject is discussed fully in the next chapter, we shall note here other reasons for Latin-American hostility toward the United States. As an aftermath of the Nixon demonstrations a subcommittee of the Senate Foreign Relations Committee was given a $150,000 appropriation for a study of inter-

[42] Richard W. Patch, *Bolivia: Decision or Debacle,* American Universities Field Staff (La Paz, Bolivia, April 18, 1959), 14–15.
[43] U.S. Dept. of State, *Bulletin,* XL (March 30, 1959), 436.

American relations. This committee confirmed and documented much that was already known about the weaknesses of Latin-American relations. It added little to what serious scholars of Latin-American studies have long known about Latin hostility toward the United States.[44]

The basic causes of this hostility in Latin America are psychological and cultural. With respect to the psychological factor, it has been plausibly suggested that the United States has been marked as a scapegoat upon which the Latins vent their hostility bred of a subconscious emotion arising from a feeling of inferiority or frustration. Conscious of the retarded development of their own countries, as contrasted with that of the powerful and progressive United States, they admire and envy this country. This envy of United States materialism leads to a dislike of the country for being so advanced. The more educated one is, the more he realizes the disparities between the United States and his own country; and the more frustrated this makes him, the more nationalistic he grows, for he must compensate for what he doesn't have. Thus, the Latins react against the power and the better conditions of the United States by saying, "Even though you are superior in some things, what we have is good, or even better in other respects." Politicians too, are eager to let the United States take the blame for their own failures. And, in many quarters the political and military power of the United States is contributing to a developing fear of the North American colossus. This fear, suspicion, and resentment provide a trigger for Communists to use in inciting hostile action against this country.

Anti-Yankeeism in Latin America also springs from basic differences in the cultures of the two peoples. There is general agreement that racial and cultural differences are an important, if not the most

[44] Studies prepared for the Senate Foreign Relations Committee under contract with private groups include the following: "Post-World War II Political Developments in Latin America," by the University of New Mexico; "Commodity Problems in Latin America," by the International Economic Consultants; "The Organization of American States," by Northwestern University; "U.S. Business and Labor in Latin America," by the University of Chicago; "U.S. and Latin American Politics Affecting Economic Relations," by the National Planning Association; and "Problems of Latin American Economic Development," by the University of Oregon. These reports are in Committee Print, 86th Cong., 1st and 2d Sess. (Washington, 1959–60).

For excellent studies dealing with Latin-American hostility toward the United States, see U.S. Dept. of State, *External Research Papers* (Brazil, No. 126, Feb. 24, 1956; Chile, No. 126.1, Aug. 28, 1956; Argentina, No. 126.2, May 27, 1957).

important, cause of misunderstanding. The contrasts in cultures, the different ways of doing things, the different attitudes of mind, set the people of Anglo America and Latin America far apart. There is little doubt that the directing of hostility against the United States is rendered easy by fundamental differences: racial, historic, religious. The Latins are no strangers to the antiforeign complex. The intellectuals in Latin America have traditionally been Yankee-haters. Their considerable influence extends widely across national boundaries. They regard themselves as defenders of the native Latin culture which is being threatened by the crass materialism of the despised Yankees. The Roman Catholic Church of Latin America has also shown evidence of being anti-United States. This attitude derives in part from a general belief that Protestantism is dominant in the United States and that morals are lax; witness the excessive divorce rate. The church also resents Protestant missionary-activities in a "reserved" Catholic area. It is to be noted, however, that the Catholic Church is united with the United States in its opposition to Communism.

Looking at the problem from another angle, we must note that the behavior of many officials and private individuals from the United States has also contributed to Latin-American criticism and hard feeling. The "Ugly American" of Southeast Asia can also be found in Latin America. It is probably true that many government officials, not only in the Point Four program but in the embassies as well, have not had the qualifications for representing the United States and have greatly irritated the Latin officials. It is also true that United States representation might be better performed if the heads of missions were career men, well-acquainted with the language, culture, and problems of the country and with the niceties of diplomatic intercourse. Incidentally, the fact that two of our most successful ambassadors to Latin-American countries—Josephus Daniels to Mexico, and Claude Bowers to Chile—did not during their long missions learn to speak Spanish was apparently an exception to the popular view that representatives must speak the language of the country. Nor was either of the two a professional diplomat.

It is here suggested that greater damage to good understanding between the Americas is chargeable to private individuals, businessmen, and tourists. Firms create bad feeling by making a difference in the pay scales between their own employees and the natives. Latins are also resentful of Yankees who come to do business but do not—or cannot—adapt themselves to native business practices and behavior; although permanent residents, they are often unable to integrate themselves in the lives of the Latin people. The behavior of North American tourists, as we well know, is not always a faithful facsimile of that of Anglo-Americans at home. This the Latin American does not know, for too often the worst comes out in the tourist. Psychiatrists point out that the actions of some North Americans abroad are caused by a certain anxiety over being in a strange land, where they do not speak the language and are not at home with the habits and customs of the people. The resultant frustration is manifested in behavior which is neither normal nor characteristic. The abnormal behavior of other individuals results from their being released of inhibitions which their positions at home exercise over them. In sum, the Latin's hostility or friendship for the United States depends largely on his impressions of the people whose behavior he observes, as well as on the accuracy of his information about the United States. It is only natural that any untoward actions or behavior of the powerful should be exaggerated.

Following both of his visits to Latin America, in 1953 and in 1958, Dr. Milton Eisenhower deplored our neighbors' misunderstanding of United States policies, programs, and capabilities. These misunderstandings, he said, "are pervasive, and are impediments to the development of more fruitful cooperation." Despite the good work of the United States Information Agency, the State Department, and mass media the problem of a misinformed Latin America remains. Dr. Eisenhower recommended that the OAS "place high on its program effective efforts to develop among the governments and people of the American republics that genuine understanding on which fruitful cooperation must be placed," and that "each one of the twenty-one governments be urged to assume a large measure of responsibility for promoting the relevant understanding within its own country."[45]

President Eisenhower's brother cited as an illustration of gross misconception based on distortion of facts the charge that the United States was supporting Latin-American dictators in face of a strong trend toward freedom and democratic government. Vice-President Nixon also reported that this was the accusation most frequently thrown at him in his encounters with Latin-American students. His answer was that the United States found all dictatorships "repugnant," but that it was necessary to maintain relations with an existent government lest this country be accused of interfering in the internal affairs of the Latin-American nations. The United States has to be most circum-

[45] "United States–Latin American Relations: Report to the President," U.S. Dept. of State, *Bulletin*, XL (Jan. 19, 1959), 91.

spect in avoiding the pitfalls of intervention. The repulse of its efforts, not ten years earlier, to discourage revolution and dictatorship by collective nonrecognition had not been forgotten. Also fresh in the memories of State Department officials was Latin-American resentment of Washington's efforts to accomplish the repudiation of Juan Perón. Now, following the overthrow of several dictatorships, the United States is accused of practicing nonintervention *too meticulously*. Adherence to the principles of American international law requires the continuance of official relations, even though the recognized government be a dictatorship, yet it must be conceded there is no requirement that these relations be cordial and that honors be accorded the dictator. In this respect the United States has erred, and Latin-American critics will not let us forget it. A protocol of proper behavior toward dictators was suggested by Mr. Nixon: the formal handshake but no embrace (*abrazo*). Finally, it must be confessed that Washington has worked with dictators because such governments caused fewer problems for United States enterprises in those countries.

Conclusion. The post-Bogotá developments in inter-American security cooperation began, in the Truman Administration, with vocal dissatisfaction throughout Latin America with United States policies, both political and economic—particularly economic. The Eisenhower Administration ended on the same note. Little progress was made in calming complaints and checking the spread of anti-Yankeeism, in spite of the outpouring of dollars for economic assistance and sincere efforts to convince the Latins that by no means had they been forgotten in the development of United States global policies.

Fortunately for inter-American security more satisfactory results attended the efforts, during the Truman-Eisenhower Administrations, to perfect the military defenses of the continent. In this area the Inter-American Defense Board was most cooperative in working out general defense plans. In accordance with these plans the United States was able to enter into military-assistance pacts with Latin-American nations. By these and other means, encouraging progress has been made in preparing the Americas for their military defense and cooperative support in the event of an overseas attack. The big question overshadowing these preparations is whether manifestations of hostility toward the United States in Latin America are indicative of a weakening of inter-American solidarity. Military plans and preparations are worthless without mutual determination to implement them.

The Latins must be brought to realize that the international power-balance has shifted, that a policy embodied solely in hemisphere defense is no longer adequate; other regions of the world have become vital to American security and must be shielded against dangerous aggressors. Nevertheless, within the new United States world strategy, Latin America is still our "inner fortress" and has not been forgotten amidst these global distractions.

XII Weakening Solidarity: The Economic Factor (1949–1960)

To allow the Hemisphere to become even poorer is to weaken the Western Cause. . . . Let nobody be deceived; it is impossible for people to join in the same effort, to fight the same battle, while their living standards are so unequal.

PRESIDENT JUSCELINO KUBITSCHEK, 1958

At MID-CENTURY the United States found itself, as we have seen, in the unenvied but not too unfamiliar position of being the object of Latin America's criticism and resentment. Dissatisfaction with an apparent trend of United States policies had been accumulating for several years, but when the advent of peace after World War II raised questions of social and economic adjustment, the conviction began to crystallize among the Latin neighbors that the rule of "all for one, one for all" should include economic cooperation as well as the political and military. Definitely from that time forward the problems of the economic aspects of inter-American cooperation and solidarity challenged the political for primacy in Pan American deliberations. Since inter-American economic cooperation means generally assistance by the United States, our discussion of the economic factor in continental solidarity and security must perforce be concerned largely with the role played by the United States.

Emergence of the economic factor. The refusal of the United States at Mexico City in 1945, at Rio de Janeiro in 1947, and at Bogotá in 1948, to commit itself to large-scale economic assistance, or indeed to offer any substantial tariff relief on vital Latin-American products, caused inter-American relations to operate under the cold clouds of disappointment and disillusionment. The self-conscious nationalism of the Latin-American countries had made them more eager than ever to develop their own industries and thus avoid the economic dislocations they suffered as a result of World War II. Strongly desiring assistance from the United States, they became increasingly critical of the fact that the United States had since the war allocated billions to other areas of the world, and relatively little (less than 2 per cent of the whole) to Latin America. A Latin-American journalist said, "We are the first orphans of the cold war." This feeling of "orphaned woe" sprang not so much from worsening economic misery (for in fact conditions were better than prewar) as from frustrated anticipation of huge amounts of United States grants and credits expected at war's end. It was Latin America's misfortune that Europe was picked by the United States as the prime defense front.

Leading United States advocates of the Latin-American case were not lacking. Former Ambassador Harry F. Guggenheim argued that, in the interest of a strong defensive alliance, we should eliminate tariff barriers where possible, increase the Export-Import Bank's capital, and put an end to the practice of sending ambassadors who think their mission is to make over Latin Americans into the U.S. political and social image.[1] Nelson Rockefeller, formerly Coordinator of Inter-American Affairs, blamed the Truman Administration for "failing to deal decisively with the Western Hemisphere problem." He charged that the United States was "ignoring, neglecting, and underestimating [its] fundamental ties with the other republics," and that "disunity and unrest in many parts of Latin America are far more widespread and serious than most people in the United States realize."[2]

Sumner Welles, perennial critic of the State Department's Latin-American policy, belabored the Truman-Acheson Administration for its "ineptness" in allowing Latin-American relations to descend to a new low. According to Welles, the "termination" of economic cooperation had contributed to inflation, commercial stagnation, and widespread depression. These in turn had paved the way for political and social upheavals such as had recently occurred not only in Bogotá but in several of the other republics. He said that there was no reason to expect any improvement in the hemisphere until there was a return to inter-American economic cooperation, and that presumably on a wartime scale. He cited a feeling among Latin Americans that the United States was always ready to use them for support when support was required, but was unwilling to offer cooperation when they needed help. Welles endorsed a "Marshall Plan for the Americas" as a return to the spirit of the Good Neighbor.[3]

Economic aspects of the Good Neighbor policy. The demand, so

[1] *Journal of Commerce* (New York), Dec. 11, 1950.

[2] *New York Times*, April 25, 1950; *Time*, May 5, 1950.

[3] New York *Herald Tribune*, Oct. 19, 23, 1948.

frequently voiced in both Anglo America and Latin America, that the
United States should *return* to the Good Neighbor policy raises a pertinent question. In what respects had the Truman-Acheson Administration abandoned this policy? The primary connotation of the policy,
as enunciated in 1933, was nonintervention. The Latin-American governments were actively fearful of United States interference in their
internal affairs. Its pledge of nonintervention, which was immediately implemented in practice, allayed those fears and laid the foundation for a Good Neighbor understanding among the peoples of the
Americas. By 1950 intervention ceased to be an issue in United
States–Latin-American relations, for despite occasional flare-ups such
as Spruille Braden's interference in the Argentine elections of 1946,
United States observance of its pledge could not be doubted. With
good reason Latin Americans were no longer seriously concerned with
political or military intervention by the United States in their internal
affairs. Thus, since the Truman Administration cannot be accused of
abandoning this cardinal tenet of the Good Neighbor policy, it must
have been some other facet of the policy that had been violated. Perhaps it was the economic?

It is merely to state a fact to say that the so-called "deterioration" of
United States–Latin-American relations resulted primarily from the
failure of the United States to continue economic aid to Latin America
on the wartime scale. In other words, inter-American relations were
such as might justify the cynic to declare that the measure of solidarity
was the rate and volume of the flow of United States assistance dollars
to Latin America. Apparently the economic aspects of the Good Neighbor policy had been neglected by President Truman.

What, in fact, were the economic aspects of the original policy?
Prior to the outbreak of World War II the United States did not give
direct economic aid to Latin America. The activities of the Export-
Import Bank and the operations of the Reciprocal Trade Agreements
Program benefited Latin America, it is true, but indirectly. The prime
objective of both was to aid and promote United States trade, a victim
of the Great Depression. It is an interesting and significant fact that,
for example, had "ideal" good neighborliness prevailed during the
days of the New Deal, President Roosevelt should have succeeded in
his efforts to secure Senate approval of the United States–Argentine
Sanitary Convention. However, Franklin Roosevelt, like Harry Truman and Dwight Eisenhower, had to reckon with American "interests"
that stood adamant in their demands for continued, and even greater,
tariff protection. Here is a national economic factor which has always

operated to limit "good neighborliness," even despite the strongest urging on the part of the President. A Good Neighbor policy satisfactory to the Latin Americans appears to be impossible so long as there is "economic nationalism" in the United States.

It was during World War II, as just mentioned, that the United States began to give direct economic assistance to Latin America. The net aid given to the American republics from July 1, 1940, to June 30, 1945, was: grants $423 million, and credits $170 million, making a total of $593 million. A pertinent question must be raised at this point: Was this direct and considerable economic assistance a facet of the Good Neighbor policy, or was it aid given to allies because of a war emergency? Perhaps it was a combination of the two, for there is little doubt that many of the assistance measures, notably the activities of the Institute of Inter-American Affairs, went beyond the more immediate requirements of wartime assistance. Stimulated by the war, the Good Neighbor policy took on a new meaning. It changed from a "be good" to a "do good" policy.[4] It was not a static policy confined to a given set of conditions, but rather it was elastic and evolving, adapting to changing conditions under the influence of "spiritual" motivaions, for after all, the core of the policy is a matter of spirit—the spiritual ingredients of good neighborliness.

After the war the United States did not by any means abandon assistance to Latin America. The continued operations of the Export-Import Bank and the Institute of Inter-American Affairs affirm this fact, though it must be admitted that aid no longer flowed so abundantly to Latin America. Reports of the Export-Import Bank revealed that from July 1945 to June 1948, credits totaled $213 million.[5] In 1948, the slackest year since the war's end, the total Bank loans amounted to only $138 million, 53.1 per cent of this amount going to Latin America. During the six-year period ending in June of 1951, according to the Mutual Security Program's second and third reports, Exim Bank loans aggregated $315 million net. Brazil, Mexico, Chile, Argentina, and Colombia were the major recipients. At the close of 1948 the Bank had $916 million waiting for loan outlets. But, according to *Business Week* (Feb. 19, 1949), potential borrowers tended to see the stigma of imperialism on every investment dollar, for the Bank insisted on reliable technicians as insurance that loans would be wisely spent. The biggest obstacle to increased loans was the

[4] Donald M. Dozer, *Are We Good Neighbors?* (Gainesville, Fla., 1959), 112–113.
[5] *Christian Science Monitor,* Nov. 5, 1949.

lack of foreign technical skill, for countless Latin-American loan applications were turned down because United States control at the technical level was refused. Evidently considerable sums were available for "sound" investments, as defined by the Bank, but sensitive nationalism rejected needed aid with "strings attached.'

Technical cooperation with Latin America, under the auspices of the Institute of Inter-American Affairs, continued after the end of the war, though with a reduced budget. Thus, from a wartime peak of $10 million contributed by the United States to technical cooperative projects, the annual contribution shrank to $5 million in 1949. Interestingly, Latin-American contributions to the program constantly increased to the point where they exceeded United States grants by more than 60 per cent.[6] Since 1947 the Latin-American governments have borne this larger part of the expense of the technical-assistance program, in some instances running to three or four times as much as the United States' share. Viewing the technical cooperation as a logical extension of the Good Neighbor policy and not as another "giveaway" plan, Congress responded favorably to President Truman's request that a five-year extension of the Institute be approved so that it could enter into basic long-term projects with the Latin-American republics. At that time (1949) the Institute was active in sixteen of the Latin-American countries and was conducting twenty-five work programs in education, agriculture, health, and sanitation.[7]

The United States was also supporting a program of cooperation in Latin America provided by its Department of Agriculture. This program, with fifteen countries, was in its tenth year in 1949. It was aimed at increasing agricultural efficiency and improving living standards. More than three hundred research and demonstration projects were in operation in 1950.[8] The Aftosa Commission's extensive and expensive campaign to stamp out the dread foot-and-mouth disease in Mexico was also a Department of Agriculture project.

The net aid given to the Latin-American republics from July 1, 1945, to June 30, 1951, was: grants $139 million, and credits $298 million, making a total of $437 million, in comparison to the war-

[6] U.S. Dept. of State, *Bulletin,* XXII (Feb. 13, 1950). For a chart showing comparative contributions by the United States and other American republics, 1943–50, see *Notícias,* V (March 29, 1949), 8.

[7] *Christian Science Monitor,* Sept. 17, 1949.

[8] Simon G. Hanson, *Economic Development in Latin America* (Washington, 1951), 527.

period aid totaling $593 million. A breakdown of the economic assistance is given in Table 2.[9]

Table 2

Total Amount of United States Assistance, Net of Reciprocal Assistance and Repayments, to Latin America, July 1, 1945–June 30, 1951

Program	Millions of Dollars
Net foreign aid	437
Net grants utilized	139
Lend-Lease	5
Institute of Inter-American Affairs	38
Foot-and-mouth disease eradication	83
Technical assistance	15
Reconstruction Finance Corporation	X[1]
Less: Credit agreement offsets to grants	2
Net credits utilized	298
Export-Import Bank	315
Lend-Lease current credits	28Y[2]
Surplus property (including merchant ships)	10
Reconstruction Finance Corporation	X[1]
Credit agreement offsets to grants	1
Institute of Inter-American Affairs	Z[3]

[1] Less than $500,000.
[2] Net return of aid to U.S. Government.
[3] Net return of aid of less than $500,000.
Source: Data supplied by the International Cooperation Administration, Office of Statistics and Reports (Washington, June 1959).

Nor did Latin America fail to reap some benefit from the Marshall Plan, for the Economic Cooperation Act of 1948 authorized the purchase of Latin-American products necessary for European recovery. Although these purchases did not attain the proportions anticipated, and so were termed "a consolation prize," nevertheless ECA offshore procurement authorizations were not without benefit to Latin-American producers, particularly in a few favored countries. From April 1948 to June 1951, the purchases amounted to $759 million; from April 1948 to March 1959, the offshore procurement in Latin America under ECA and successor agencies amounted to $1,422 million.[10] Over and

[9] U.S. Dept. of Commerce, *Foreign Aid by the United States Government, 1940–1951* (Washington, 1952), 24.
[10] Data supplied to the author by International Cooperation Administration, Office of Statistics and Reports (June 3, 1959).

above the foregoing benefits, Latin America's greatest advantage reaped from the Marshall Plan was the restoration of European markets for her products. Here was assistance, albeit indirect, of inestimable value to her economy.

Further evidence in support of the fact that the United States did not forget Latin America's needs in the years immediately following World War II can be found in the following figures: the Stabilization Fund granted over $100 million to Mexico and Brazil; surplus property originally costing $145 million was disposed of for $36.4 million in the same area; and loans by the World Bank (operating largely with United States funds) to Mexico, Chile, and Brazil amounted to $125 million. In addition, United States imports from Latin America reached $2,168 million in 1947, and $2,352 million in 1948, as opposed to a yearly average of $553 million from 1936 to 1940. Exports to Latin America from this country amounted to $3,858 million in 1947 as opposed to $3,166 million in 1941.[11] Finally, total United States private investments in Latin America amounted to $4,009 million in 1946, and $5,698 million in 1950. Direct private investments were $3,005 million in 1946, and $4,445 million in 1950.[12] A somewhat disproportionate amount of the total direct private investment was in the extractive industries, particularly petroleum.

It should be clear from the foregoing facts and figures that the Truman Administration had not by any means abandoned the Good Neighbor policy. Nevertheless the fact remained that there was great discontent and resentment among the *Latinos*. The aid which they received from the United States was paltry compared with the dollar value of aid to European and Asiatic nations, some of them former wartime enemies. Need we wonder that they resented being "taken for granted?" Our "good neighbors" questioned whether it paid to be such good friends of a nation that was so free with handouts elsewhere, while forcing from them in the meantime the purchase of raw materials at bargain prices.

A good friend of the United States, Ezéquiel Padilla, former foreign minister of Mexico, lamented that the spirit of Pan American cooperation had been frittered away since World War II. Only a bold new United States initiative, he said, could restore good hemisphere relations.[13]

[11]U.S. Dept. of Commerce, *Foreign Commerce Weekly*, April 13, 1959.

[12] U.S. Dept. of Commerce, Office of Business Economics, *U.S. Investments in the Latin American Economy* (Washington, 1957), III; *Christian Science Monitor*, Nov. 5, 1949.

[13] *New York Times*, May 20, 1953.

Brazilian writer Hernane Tavares de Sá warned that the Bogotá uprising should convince the United States that the situation in Latin America was steadily deteriorating. He cautioned that the southern sector of the hemisphere was no longer the "secure flank" that the United States must have to challenge the rising tide of Communism on the other side of the Atlantic.[14]

United States reaction to economic pleas. Unfortunately for the needed strengthening of hemisphere solidarity, the United States never launched "a bold new initiative" such as was suggested by Dr. Padilla. The fact of deteriorating relations was noted, but its seriousness was underestimated, as evidenced by the kind of remedial measures attempted. These proved to be mere palliatives, for the deterioration of relations never abated, not even after a Republican administration took over the reins in Washington in 1953. In fact, the identical criticisms aimed at Truman and Acheson were redirected at Eisenhower and Dulles. Evidently the government and the people of the United States failed to realize that Latin America is a continent in a terrific hurry, that a great nationalistic revolution is in the making, and that there is an impatient and heedless desire for prosperity and social reform. A perceptive observer has said, "They won't believe us when we say that the development of agriculture is more important to South America right now than industrialization. . . . Let's face it: they're dead set to industrialize, and we've got to help them do it or lose every friend we've got down there."[15] This is a fact of tremendous significance, and we turn now to the official reactions to Latin America's economic pleas.

Secretary of State Dean Acheson, on September 19, 1949, outlined three major objectives of the Department's Latin-American policy: security of the United States and the hemisphere; encouragement of democratic representative institutions; and positive cooperation in the economic field. With reference to the third, he said that the official policy on loans was not to extend them for projects when private capital was available. Public funds were to be only "supplementary" to private-capital efforts. To increase the flow of private capital he advocated treaties which would give reasonable assurances to investors while protecting the integrity of the countries. The Secretary declared that the most rapid progress would come to those nations that "help themselves vigorously."[16]

---

[14] New York *Herald Tribune,* April 21, 1948.
[15] *Journal of Commerce* (New York), April 13, 16, 1953.
[16] *Christian Science Monitor,* Sept. 19, 1949.

Assistant Secretary of State for Inter-American Affairs E. G. Miller was positively hard-boiled in his rejection of the concept of United States "obligation" to Latin America. He emphasized two general misconceptions which he encountered in the "obligation" theory: (1) the United States, because of its size and prosperity, is responsible for solving Latin America's problems; and (2) because the United States is meeting particular emergencies (in Europe) it is obligated to cooperate on a similar scale in other areas even though conditions are quite different. Mr. Miller noted, both here and abroad, an obsession that the United States is *under obligation* to help other nations. "We are under no such obligation," he declared. But according to Mr. Miller, meeting emergencies in the Eastern Hemisphere has not prevented this country from continuing cooperation with the countries of the Western Hemisphere.[17] Earlier, the Assistant Secretary had declared that no important change in policy toward Latin America was being considered. This meant, particularly, that Latin Americans should look to private capital and not the United States government for aid in economic development.

The encouragement of private investments. Although private capital was continuing to flow into Latin America in respectable volume,[18] it was felt that amounts more commensurate with the needs of the Latin-American economy could be promoted by creating a more suitable climate of investment. To this end, assurances to investors against loss by expropriation, currency inconvertibility, and other hazards of foreign operations were needed. Both the State Department and Congress took a hand in the matter. The former sought to establish "rules of the game" for the investment of capital by private interests through the negotiation of "new style" bilateral treaties of friendship, commerce, and navigation.[19] The first such treaty negotiated with a Latin-American nation was the Treaty of Friendship, Commerce, and Economic Development, signed with Uruguay on November 23, 1949. This treaty, which was intended to serve as a model for pacts with other Latin-American nations, guaranteed just compensation in the event of expropriation, free introduction and

[17] U.S. Dept. of State, *Bulletin,* XXII (April 3, 1950), 522.

[18]According to the *Federal Reserve Bulletin* (May 1953), United States investments in Latin America had been climbing steadily by about 8 per cent since World War II.

[19] The United States had treaties of friendship and commerce in force with only seven of the Latin-American republics: Argentina (1853), Bolivia (1858), Colombia (1846), Costa Rica (1851), Paraguay (1859), El Salvador (1926), and Honduras (1927).

withdrawal of capital, the liberalizing of exchange control, free introduction of executive and technical personnel by United States firms, equality of treatment of property and personnel, and other guarantees designed to promote private investment and economic development.[20] Similar treaties were signed with Colombia on April 26, 1951; Haiti, March 3, 1955; and Nicaragua, January 21, 1956. Only the Nicaraguan treaty ever entered into force, thus proving that the Latin-American governments were not interested in this effort to "reassure" private investors.[21]

More success attended the Congressional initiative. When the Investment Guaranty Program was created by the Economic Cooperation Act of 1948, the legislative authority provided that guarantees of convertibility could be issued only in those countries participating in the Marshall Plan which had agreed with the United States to institute the Guaranty Program. The legislation was later expanded in philosophy and in geographic scope so that Latin America was included and guarantees against expropriation were added to the Guaranty Program.

The Mutual Security Act of 1951 conveyed authority to extend guarantees to *new* United States investors in any of the Mutual Security program countries upon the concluding of guarantee agreements between the United States and the country involved. A number of such agreements were entered into. The one with Haiti (April 2, 1953) was the first signed with an American republic. This agreement made possible Mutual Security Act guarantees protecting new American investors in that country against currency inconvertibility and loss by expropriation. Other American nations that belatedly and unenthusiastically signed similar investment-guarantee agreements were: Bolivia (Sept. 23, 1955), Colombia (Nov. 18, 1955, convertibility only), Costa Rica (Feb. 25, 1955), Cuba (Nov. 29, 1957), Ecuador (March 29, 1955), Guatemala (March 23, 1955), Honduras (June 10, 1955), Nicaragua (April 14, 1959, convertibility, expropriation, and war risk),

---

[20] For full text of the treaty, see U.S. Dept. of State, *Bulletin,* XXIII (Sept. 25, 1950), 502–509.

[21] The history of the "new style" Friendship, Commerce and Navigation Treaties is as follows: (1) Uruguay, signed, Nov. 23, 1949, disposition: Senate advice and consent achieved, but it has not been approved by Uruguay; (2) Colombia, signed, April 26, 1951, disposition: on failure of Colombian Congress to ratify, was withdrawn from the U.S. Senate on June 30, 1953; (3) Haiti, signed, March 3, 1955, disposition: submitted to U.S. Senate, June 22, 1955, but withdrawn on Aug. 8, 1957; Nicaragua, signed Jan. 21, 1956; disposition: entered into force on May 24, 1958.—U.S. Dept. of State, Office of the Legal Advisor, to the author (June 4, 1959).

Paraguay (May 4, 1956), and Peru (March 16, 1955, convertibility only).[22] Significantly, Brazil and Mexico excused themselves.

The first MSA-guaranteed investment contract in Latin America was signed in Guatemala, wherein a United States firm, the Farmer Logging Company (Oregon) was guaranteed that, should it not be able to convert its receipts into dollars through regular foreign-exchange channels, the United States government would provide dollar exchange up to a limit of $70,000. In the event of expropriation the firm was to have protection up to a maximum of $177,000.[23] As of June 30, 1958, $12,163,000 represented the total amount of investment guarantees in only three countries of Latin America (Bolivia, Guatemala, and Peru): $8,591,000 for convertibility, and $3,572,000 for expropriation.[24]

Other suggestions designed to encourage foreign private-investment in Latin America, but too numerous to detail here, include: reducing taxes on business income from subsidiaries or branches, deferring of the tax on branch income until it is withdrawn from the country where it is earned, and negotiating tax treaties under which income taxes waived for an initial limited period by the foreign government as an incentive to new business can be credited against the United States income tax. Such a treaty has been negotiated with Honduras.

Obviously it is impossible to determine the amount of direct influence investors' insurance and other forms of reassurance have had on American private investments in Latin America. It is argued rather convincingly that these investors' guarantees are quite beside the point, for private capital is not scared off by risk when the speculative prospects are substantial. Whatever may have been the influence of investment guarantees, the incontrovertible fact is that the dollars of private Yankee investors have continued to flow into Latin America in ever increasing quantity. This is illustrated by Table 3.

Despite the substantial flow of United States private capital into Latin America there has been no abatement of either Latin-American worry about foreign private-investments, or their insistence on the grant of more credit by public lending agencies (the United States government). The extremists—the Yankeephobes and the Communists—do not cease to brand American investments as the instruments

---

[22] Information furnished by the International Cooperation Administration, Investment Guaranties Staff (June 4, 1959).

[23] *Journal of Commerce*, Aug. 29, 1956; *Visión*, July 8, 1955.

[24] International Cooperation Administration, *Operations Report* (June 30, 1958), 60.

Table 3

Value of United States Direct Investments in Latin America, by Industry, 1936–58

(in Millions of Dollars)

Year	Total	Mining and Smelting	Petroleum	Manufac- turing	Public Utilities	Trade and Dis- tribution	Other Industries*
1936	$2,803	$ 708	$ 453	$ 191	$ 936	$100	$415
1943	2,721	405	601	322	871	140	382
1946	3,045	506	697	399	920	72	452
1947	3,716	425	1,059	595	846	209	582
1948	4,205	439	1,327	678	854	265	742
1949	4,590	595	1,467	667	1,035	212	715
1950	4,735	628	1,408	780	1,042	242	635
1951	5,176	736	1,408	992	1,044	303	693
1952	5,738	871	1,577	1,166	1,076	344	726
1953	6,034	999	1,684	1,149	1,093	354	755
1954	6,256	1,003	1,688	1,248	1,120	402	795
1955	6,233	1,024	1,561	1,372	1,008	442	826
1956	7,459	$1,096	$2,232	$1,543	$1,210	$504	$875
1957	8,325†						
1958	$8,730†						

* Including agriculture.
† Revised (*Survey of Current Business*, Aug. 1959, 29).
Source: Based on *Survey of Current Business* and compiled for the author by U.S. Dept. of Commerce, Office of Business Economics (June 1959).

of imperialism which impose a colonial status on Latin America. The foreign investor is a voracious and heartless vampire who sucks the lifeblood of the weak and helpless nations. Exploitation of the national resources, material and human, are the stock in trade of the foreign investor. It is surprising how many otherwise rational individuals subscribe to this preposterous doctrine.

Even the more moderate of the Latin-American critics complain of the influence of foreign business in their countries: the rapid exhaustion of their nonrenewable resources, the "siphoning out" of exorbitant profits, and the uneven economic development of the country. These moderates frequently voice the plausible argument that foreign private-capital has no interest at all in developing domestic industries in the smaller, poorer, and more backward countries because they present inadequate markets for the products of home industry. Not only is there little or no incentive for private capital to go to work to expand the domestic economies of low-income countries, but the flow of these funds to expand raw-material supplies for export is dependent upon confident expectation of a steady and sizable expansion of demand. Thus, "for foreign private capital to be mobilized in a given region, it is necessary either that the foreign demand for native products offer decent prospects or that the region itself have created a good-sized internal market."[25] The inescapable conclusion drawn from these hard economic facts is that countries in the greatest need of economic assistance are the least attractive to the private investor.

As has been noted so many times, the United States government has insisted that Latin America must look, first and foremost, to private capital as a source for development loans. Indeed, the Latins are familiar, from the frequent telling, with the story of the United States' own economic development with the aid of foreign private-loans. Why is it, they are asked, that Latin America cannot do the same thing now? Dr. Alberto Lleras, former secretary-general of the OAS and later president of Colombia, gives us an answer to this question.

Dr. Lleras calls attention to the vastly different position and role of the United States government in relation to private enterprise during the last century, as contrasted with that of Latin-American governments today in the economic lives of those nations. The winning of the West, he says, was an oustanding feat of individualism, less regulated than Times Square in New York City at five o'clock in the afternoon. Government was nothing more than a promoter, a stimulator, of private enterprise. But as for Latin America today, the state seems to wish to absorb everything and leave no field for the development of individual initiative. "When the North American investors contemplate all the enterprises and industries in which the state is directly interested in Latin America, they are apt to define the political administration predominating south of the Rio Grande as socialist or collectivist." While it is true, acknowledges Dr. Lleras, that private North American capital has very bright prospects in Latin America, this is not enough to foster the development of the Latin-American countries. "The economic backwardness of many of them cannot be remedied except through constant use of official credit, and the consequent intervention of the State to encourage certain undertakings of public

[25] Jorge Mejía-Palacio, "Why an Economic Conference?" *Américas,* IX (July 1957), 6.

interest that private capital, either national or foreign, is not in a position to promote."[26]

Supplementing Dr. Lleras's argument, it is to be noted that Latin-American impatience with United States insistence on private investment derives in considerable degree from the fact that foreign private-investors prefer the beachhead type of investment, to which they have lately added the branch plant and distribution types. They largely tend to neglect investments in social capital and basic industry designed to serve other domestic interests, though the growth of cities and commerce makes deficiencies in social capital and basic industry acute. The foreign private-investor generally prefers resources which can be transported to the metropolitan economy or which are suitable for branch plants for partial processing and distribution of products of home industry. This constantly promotes an imbalance in the underdeveloped economy which can be corrected only by public loans or some similar source.

Divergent points of view on economic cooperation. An economic conference had been in prospect since the adjournment of the Bogotá meeting in 1948. It will be recalled that the Ninth International Conference of American States drafted the Economic Agreement of Bogotá, a statement of general principles, and recommended that at an early date a special inter-American economic conference be convened in Buenos Aires to attack the vital issues of economic cooperation. Since the United States government was lukewarm on the subject of a conference, believing that more could be accomplished through bilateral negotiations, it continually interposed objections to the early meeting of the conference, and a series of postponements resulted. The inevitable recriminations brought about this rejoinder from Assistant Secretary Miller at the extraordinary session of the Inter-American Economic and Social Council (April 10, 1950):

There has been some tendency to attribute many of the economic ills of the hemisphere to the delay in holding the Conference . . . and to blame the United States because the Conference has not yet been held, but it is an incontrovertible fact that the huge complicated problem of economic development does not lend itself to solution through the mere holding of conferences nor the passing of resolutions.

[26] Alberto Lleras, "Report on the Ninth International Conference of American States," Pan American Union, *Annals* of the OAS, I (1949), 57–61. Carter Goodrich ("Economic History and Economic Development," in Eastin Nelson

Although the Mutual Security Act (approved Oct. 10, 1951) gathered together, with the exception of the Export-Import Bank, the various programs dealing with economic, military, and technical assistance, it was significant fact that for the Latin-American republics the act included only technical and military assistance. This lack of authorization for economic assistance to Latin America had been foreshadowed at the recent meeting of the ministers of foreign affairs held in Washington from March 26 to April 7, 1951.

The United States, following its involvement in the Korean War, hoped to persuade the Latin-American governments to participate more fully in the defensive mobilization of the free world through effective development and allocation of Western Hemisphere resources. But the Latin-American governments did not, on the whole, share the sense of urgency that impelled this country. Their main concern apparently was that the cooperation desired by the United States should take place under terms as advantageous as possible to themselves. What the Latin Americans feared was that the United States, with its preeminent interest in developing and procuring raw materials, would become increasingly negligent of other activities likely to benefit their countries more directly. Thus they made strenuous efforts to secure explicit recognition of the importance of continuing economic development even during a period of rearmament. Aside from their concern with economic development, they wanted to avoid repeating their disillusioning financial experience of World War II. They wanted firm guarantees, if possible, not only that the pace of economic development would be stepped up but also that their needs for essential imports would be met, and that the momentarily favorable price relation between their exports and imports would be maintained. The United States obviously could not buy such a bill of goods, and so the Washington meeting was not able to provide answers to such basic questions of inter-American economics. Its actions in the field of "Emergency Economic Cooperation" took the form of declarations of economic principles. Certainly the Washington meeting failed to stimulate any great advance in long-range economic development.

Technical assistance. The State Department was hopeful, however, that a vigorous implementation of President Truman's program of extending United States know-how to underdeveloped areas (Point Four Program) would contribute much to the desired ends. The Inter-

[ed.], *Economic Growth* [Austin, Tex., 1960] p. 4) comments on the uses of subsidy in the promotion of U.S. development.

American Economic and Social Council (IA-ECOSOC) also held high hopes for the President's "new and bold policy," and in evidence of its belief that Latin America would be the principal beneficiary, declared (Jan. 21, 1949): "Among these areas [underdeveloped], suffering all the deficiencies which President Truman pointed out in his speech, the majority of the countries of the Western Hemisphere stand uppermost."[27]

Technical assistance, regarded as "the most direct expression of the Good Neighbor policy," and the least expensive of the aid programs, received hearty Congressional approval. Not only were there increased allotments to Latin America, to be administered by the Institute of Inter-American Affairs as agent for the Technical Cooperation Administration, but there were also small contributions to the technical-assistance program of the OAS. This program was started in 1951, and for the four years 1951–54 the United States pledged the sum of $1 million per annum. Beginning in 1955, the commitment was increased to $1,500,000 yearly.[28]

Under the terms of the Mutual Security Act of 1951, the Technical Cooperation Administration was to negotiate general agreements with individual countries defining the basic terms of cooperation. Accordingly, Point Four General Agreements were signed with every Latin · American country except Argentina by June 1953. The basic programs of health, sanitation, food supply, and education continued as before. However, since 1951, the projects have been extended to include such fields as housing, transportation, communications, development of natural resources, social welfare, civil aviation, industrial and managerial techniques, public administration, and other activities for economic expansion. For example, the general agreement signed with Mexico on July 9, 1951, provided for such technical cooperation projects as mining, fisheries, geological investigations, rubber development, and various programs of student exchange. A joint United States–Mexican *servicio* had, during the preceding nine years, succeeded in developing a comprehensive health and water-supply pro-

---

[27] *Annals,* I (1949), 243.
[28] The United States has always stipulated, however, that its actual contribution in any given year would not exceed 70 per cent of the total contributions from all member states. Since some of the other states have not contributed their full pledges in certain years, actual contributions by the United States have not been as large as the sums pledged. Its cumulative obligations to 1959 have amounted to $8,520,000; actual expenditures to that date have been $7,592,000.

gram. In June 1957, Argentina became the twentieth and last Latin-American country to sign a technical-assistance agreement with the United States.

Although the program of United States technical aid to Latin America has not escaped considerable criticism, in this country as well as in Latin America, it is nevertheless a fair assumption that it has been a helpful one. In Ecuador, for example, healthy development over the period 1950–60 has been due in no small measure to the various technical-assistance projects. One would be naïve indeed, however, to believe that Point Four is the key solution to Latin America's economic problems.

The contributions of the United States to technical assistance for Latin America are graphically illustrated by Tables 4 and 5:

Table 4

United States Programs in Latin America, 1943–60
Technical Cooperation and Closely Related Activities

Fiscal Year	Obligations (in Millions)	Agency
1943	8.8	IIAA[1]
1944	13.3	"
1945	10.6	"
1946	7.4	"
1947	6.7	"
1948	7.4	"
1949	4.0	"
1950	4.6	"
1951	5.8	"
1952*	20.3**	TCA[2]
1953	18.5	"
1954	24.3	FOA[3]
1955	27.3	"
1956	28.0	ICA[4]
1957	29.7	"
1958	29.8	"
1959	34.3	"
1960	45.2†	"

* Beginning of world-wide program.
** Inclues OAS from fiscal year 1952 to date.
† Request to Congress.
[1] Institute of Inter-American Affairs, incorporated March 1942 under the Office of the Coordinator of Inter-American Affairs, which latter office was created by Executive Order in August 1940. Obligations indicated by the Institute of Inter-American Affairs for the period shown (1943–51) do not include the currently undeterminable portion of the total of $15.7 millions as many have been obligated for technical assist-

Weakening Solidarity

Table 5

United Nations Expanded Program for Technical Assistance for Latin America, 1950–59

Fiscal Year	Thousands of Dollars
1950–51	$1,181
1951–52	4,911
1952–53	4,616
1953–54	3,921
1954–55	5,482
1955–56	7,298
1956–57	7,136
1957–58	6,698
1958–59	$5,561

NOTE.—United States annual grant to the United Nations is $15,500,000.
Source: International Cooperation Administration, *Operations Reports.*

In spite of these contributions for technical assistance, Latin-American demands for economic "relief" continued without abatement to the end of the Truman Administration and into that of President Eisenhower. Smoldering resentment against United States trade-restrictive actions was well illustrated by an editorial in one of Peru's leading newspapers, *La Prensa.* The editorial cited the United States' dispute with Bolivia over tin prices, with Chile over copper, and Peru's own protest at the proposed high tariff on tuna fish. It concluded, "with all that, it is gross fraud to talk of Pan Americanism."[29]

Old problems and new administration. The Eisenhower-Dulles Administration inherited gravely deteriorated United States–Latin-American relations, resulting from an upsurge of aggressive nationalism and a conviction that whatever the United States was doing in Latin America was not enough. The very foundations of inter-American solidarity seemed to be crumbling. Thus, one of the more persistent

ance by the Interdepartmental Committee on Scientific and Cultural Cooperation (scc) during its official existence from May 1938 to October 1950, much of which assistance is considered to have been of wartime nature.

[2] Technical Cooperation Administration (under the Department of State), established by Public Law 535, June 1950.

[3] Foreign Operations Administration, established under the government's Reorganization Plan No. 7, effective April 1953.

[4] International Cooperation Administration, created by Executive Order 10610 of May 9, 1955 (effective June 30, 1955).

Source: International Cooperation Administration, *Operations Reports.*

[29] *New York Times,* June 17, 1952.

foreign-policy problems of the new administration was to halt the steady erosion of United States prestige in Latin America.

In an early foreign-policy statement before the Senate Foreign Relations Committee, Secretary of State Dulles said, "I have a feeling that conditions in Latin America are somewhat comparable to [those in] China in the mid-30s when the Communist movement was getting started; they were beginning to develop hatred of the United States and the British, but we didn't do anything adequate about it." Mr. Dulles asserted that he attached "utmost importance" to rebuilding and reinforcing the spirit of cooperation in the Americas, and he insisted that the United States should never take it for granted that such solidarity was going to go on "automatically." Little wonder that Latin America was heartened by his insistence on ending the policy of indifference. "Dulles hits the bullseye," commented Bogotá's *El Tiempo*.[30]

Protestations of deep friendship for Latin America have been the stock in trade of incoming administrations in Washington, and the Eisenhower Administration was no exception. It was going to take considerably more than speeches to repair the damage, real and imagined, to the Good Neighbor policy. In evidence of the fact that he was seriously concerned, President Eisenhower in early April of 1953 asked his brother, Dr. Milton S. Eisenhower, to serve as special ambassador to the republics of South America, for the purpose of considering what "changes might be desirable in United States policies and programs in order to contribute to the meaningful unity we all desire." Dr. Eisenhower left Washington on June 23 and returned on July 29, 1953. In those thirty-six days he discussed with the presidents and ministers of the ten republics of the continent, the problems of economic, military, political, and cultural relations. On November 18, 1953, he made his report to the President.[31]

Dr. Milton Eisenhower's report. After referring first to the importance of Latin America and the United States to each other (an impressive recital of United States–Latin-American economic, military, political, and cultural interdependencies), Dr. Eisenhower recounted what he had discovered on his trip. He found tragic misunderstanding of the United States—especially misunderstanding of its economic capacity. The *Latinos,* he said, see the assistance programs in Europe, the Middle East, and the Far East, and conclude that U.S. financial capacity is unlimited. Moreover, failing to understand the reasons for

---

[30] *Christian Science Monitor,* Feb. 7, 1953.

[31] Milton S. Eisenhower, "United States–Latin American Relations: Report to the President," U.S. Dept. of State, *Bulletin,* XXIX (Nov. 23, 1953), 695.

generous assistance to other areas, they conclude that the denial of equal assistance to them means that the United States considers other areas of the world more important to its future than the countries of Latin America.

Dr. Eisenhower also became convinced that "economic cooperation is without question the key to better relations between the United States and the nations to the South." Everything else, he said, must take secondary place. He called attention to the various needs: agricultural production, transportation, power and fuel, industries, and *capital.* "It is difficult to exaggerate," he said, "the need of South America for capital to promote sound economic development."

Such capital, so far as the United States is concerned, he said, must be "attracted" rather than "induced." A primary requisite for Latin America is "a genuine belief in the value to the community of private competitive enterprise and private profit." Confidence in the value of the local currency must also be restored, and this can be accomplished only by sound budgetary, fiscal, and credit policies. The report emphasized the need of "conditions of political and economic stability and fair and equitable treatment" in order to attract United States investors. But unhappily, he pointed out, the need for foreign capital in great volume was being accompanied throughout most of Latin America by a rising tide of nationalism, which "leads to laws and practices which prevent the entrance of foreign capital essential to development." According to Dr. Eisenhower, "ultra-nationalism is being fostered by Communist agitators."

Thus, in the view of Milton Eisenhower, there is much that Latin Americans themselves can and must do to ameliorate their economic ills. As for the United States, the following are some of his recommendations:

1. That the United States adopt and adhere to stable trade policies with Latin America, with a minimum of mechanisms permitting the imposition of increased tariffs or quotas.

This was his principal recommendation. Everywhere in Latin America Dr. Eisenhower found officials concerned about the tariff policies and apprehensive about restrictions, existent or prospective, on United States imports of petroleum, lead, zinc, fish, wool, and various agricultural products.

2. That the United States adopt a long-range basic-material price-support policy providing for its stockpiling certain of their imperishable materials when prices are dropping.

3. That the United States carefully examine whether or not it would be expedient to amend present tax laws to remove existing obstacles to private investment abroad.
4. That "substantial" public loans, by the World Bank and the Export-Import Bank, be provided for sound economic development projects for which private financing is not available.
5. That the technical-cooperation program in Latin America be expanded.

Dr. Eisenhower alluded not only to the success of the program and to the fact that it was making friends for the United States but he pointed out also that in most countries the local contributions were three times or more the amount of United States' contribution.

6. That the United States should, in very unusual circumstances, make grants of food from our surplus stocks to Latin-American countries.

In addition to the foregoing recommendations Dr. Eisenhower emphasized that the task of developing understanding between Anglo Americans and Latin Americans was a mutual one. The United States should expand programs of intellectual and cultural cooperation—including scholarships, binational centers and language institutes, libraries, and exchange of students. On the other hand, the Latin-American governments and peoples need to comprehend what the United States is doing in other parts of the world and what this "distant" continental-defense program means to them. Latin America complains that the United States "takes them for granted." Perhaps the Latin Americans themselves take their favored economic relations with the United States for granted and consider that they have been neglected merely because commitments in other areas of the world have led the United States to embark on emergency-type programs. Indeed, reported Dr. Eisenhower, there appeared to be great need of a better recognition on the part of Latin-American countries of their stake in what is virtually a joint enterprise.

In view of the prominence of the author, the Eisenhower report attracted considerable attention, as indeed it merited, for its recommendations were sound, albeit rather conservative and only slightly in advance of the established governmental policy of more "substantial" loans and a relaxation of tariff restrictions. To state that his recommendations were inadequately implemented is merely to record a fact. In his message to the Congress on January 7, 1954, President Eisenhower said: "Military assistance must be continued. Technical assistance must be maintained. Economic assistance can be reduced."

The Caracas Conference. After the release of Dr. Eisenhower's report, the Latin Americans were expectant of important developments in the forthcoming Caracas general conference. They were particularly eager to obtain a clearer notion of the United States' intentions with regard to such questions as capital investment and stabilization of the prices of their export products. But Washington had determined months earlier to give the conference a narrow focus and to use it primarily to mobilize inter-American sentiment against the growing Communist danger in Guatemala.

The Tenth Inter-American Conference was in session at Caracas, Venezuela, from March 1 to March 28, 1954. Reserving for discussion at another place the more important deliberations of the conference on the Communist issue, we record here the sad fact that the United States delegation gave little encouragement to the numerous economic proposals submitted by their Latin-American compatriots. A number of the proposals relating to foreign trade reflected a demand for preferential treatment of their export products by the United States through tariff concessions or a guarantee of "remuneration prices." The Latins failed to realize the strength of the opposition within the United States government to the type of measures most of them had in mind. Since it had already been agreed that there should be a meeting of the ministers of finance, it was convenient to postpone consideration of a number of specific economic problems and projects.

The Rio and Buenos Aires Economic Conferences. Since it was not politic for the United States to force further postponement of multilateral economic discussions, a meeting of the ministers of finance had been approved. It met at Rio de Janeiro (Quitandinha) from November 22 to December 2, 1954. It appeared that the problems which had been sidetracked at the Washington meeting of foreign ministers and the Caracas conference were going to receive a full airing.

In opening the conference, Brazil's President João Café Filho urged the delegates not to let posterity judge inter-American efforts at economic cooperation as "too little and too late."[32] Brazil's Minister of Interior expressed the opinion that economic defense should be placed before military defense. For the United States, Secretary of the Treasury Humphrey offered more substantial and speedier loans. He noted that the Export-Import Bank had been given increased lending authority and had opened a new line of credit, enabling United States exporters to offer medium-term credit on production equipment. However, Mr.

[32] *New York Times,* Nov. 23, 1954.

Humphrey's assurances of easier public loans did not alter his government's policy of relying primarily on private investments. CIO President Walter Reuther asserted that Secretary Humphrey acted "like a banker" and not like a man well informed about the problems of Latin America. According to Reuther, "The United States should provide economic assistance of the same magnitude as in the military field, and direct a movement to assure fair prices for Latin American raw materials."[33]

The fundamental problem was that the Latins wanted guaranteed minimum prices so that they could sell their products at "fair" prices. Naturally the United States was chary about going beyond a certain point in that direction. Likewise, the perennial proposal for creating an inter-American financial institution was countered by the assurance that the Export-Import Bank's lending capacity was now virtually unlimited for all practical purposes and that it was in position to approve sound loan applications that could not be handled by the World Bank.

It is not possible to record that the Rio Economic Conference, despite its forty-eight resolutions, made much progress in solving the impasse existent between the United States and its Latin-American neighbors. It was agreed to hold the next special inter-American economic conference in Buenos Aires in 1956, and a resolution was approved calling for the preparation of the draft text of a general economic agreement to be substituted for that of Bogotá, which had failed to receive more than three ratifications. This draft text was to be submitted to the Buenos Aires conference.

The "Economic Conference of the OAS," scheduled to meet in 1956, finally convened in Buenos Aires on August 15, 1957. The Latins went to Buenos Aires determined that the United States should give them better and more stabilized prices for their raw materials, extend more generous amounts of credit for the industrialization of the continent, contribute to a new international bank devoted exclusively to the economic development of Latin America, and take a more benevolent attitude toward their plan for a common Latin-American market.

Although the conference approved forty resolutions and an economic declaration, it was the same old story: Latin-American hopes were blasted by unmistakable evidence that United States policy had not changed. Shortly before the conference (June 18, 1957) Mr. Dulles had said, "In the case of the Americas, . . . they are now in the

[33] *Ibid.*, Dec. 26, 1954.

main able to meet their increased demands through private loans and Export-Import Bank loans."[34] Secretary of the Treasury Robert B. Anderson, in his speech at the opening session, said, "As far as we can see ahead we believe that the adequacy of capital to meet the needs of sound development is not a question of additional institutions but the fuller utilization of those in being." He also made it clear that the United States opposed the establishment of international price-stabilization machinery.

The most widely-discussed topic at the Buenos Aires conference was the draft "General Economic Agreement," a modification of the ill-fated Bogotá Economic Agreement. Unhappily it was impossible to reach a consensus on the substantial points that should be incorporated in such a document, the general purpose of which was to establish common standards of inter-American economic relations. The United States vetoed key articles dealing with measures to prevent excessive fluctuations both in markets and in terms of trade of basic export products of the Latin-American nations. In view of the impasse it was decided to refer the Economic Agreement to the Council of the OAS for further study, and to adopt instead the Economic Declaration of Buenos Aires, an affirmation of the general principles of economic relations. This declaration, beyond voicing good intentions to promote trade and better economic relations, contained nothing so novel or significant as to evoke the fulsome praise of Deputy Undersecretary C. Douglas Dillon as being "without precedent" in inter-American affairs.[35]

As for the Latins' demands for larger and easier credit through the agency of an inter-American bank or loan fund, the United States' position was, as indicated by Secretary Anderson, that the existing institutions were adequate to finance sound projects. President Samuel C. Waugh of the Export-Import Bank, who was present at the conference, later said, "I think we sold them [the Latin republics] on the fact that there are enough dollars available for development loans from our bank and the World Bank, within their capacity to absorb in terms of repayment capacity, and in terms of availability of management skills." It is a standing claim of the Exim Bank that there has not been a *sound* economic-development project that has been turned down.[36]

---

[34] House Committee on Appropriations, *Hearings* on Mutual Security Appropriations for 1958, 85th Cong., 1st Sess., 132.

[35] *New York Times*, Sept. 4, 1957. For draft, see Economic Conference, *Final Act*, 27–28.

[36] *Journal of Commerce*, Aug. 27, 1957; *New York Times*, Sept. 17, 1957.

There was, however, another side of this problem—the Latin-American side. The apparent adequacy of Exim funds to meet Latin America's loan requests was the result of hard-boiled bankers' insistence on financing only "sound" projects. Numerous worthy projects were rejected because they could not qualify under the high standards set by the Bank. Another Latin-American complaint was that the loan negotiations were interminable because of the Bank's insistence on many technical and often humiliating details. A not unusual Latin-American reaction was, "Just because they are lending us their lousy money, they think they can tell us how to run our country."[37] Also, the high price of American products was discouraging loans; by law loans have to be used to purchase United States-manufactured equipment. Since equipment and machinery of identical or even superior quality can be bought at considerably lower prices in Europe and Japan, there has developed a disinclination to negotiate new United States credits or even to use up the outstanding credits. It is not that the Good Neighbors don't want United States loans, but rather that they want to be free to spend where and how they please. This they hoped to accomplish through an inter-American development bank or loan fund.

Consequence of economic impasse. The failure of the United States and its Latin-American friends to work out a mutually agreeable program of "economic defense" sowed a harvest of hatred which it was the fate of Vice-President Nixon to reap. It is unquestionable that Latin-American hostility for the United States, as manifested by the anti-Nixon demonstrations during his good-will tour in the spring of 1958, derived in large part from bitter resentment for acts, or omissions, by this government in the area of economic relations. In reviewing these anti-United States demonstrations while appearing before the Senate Foreign Relations Committee on May 19, 1958, Deputy Undersecretary of State Robert Murphy referred to: (1) Uruguayan resentment of United States economic policies, particularly the countervailing duty on wool tops; (2) Peru's long-standing dissatisfaction over United States restrictions and tariffs on certain basic agricultural commodities exported by Peru, and more recently, the bitter criticism aroused because of threatened restrictions on lead, zinc, and copper, and also because of the report of the United States Tariff Commission on lead and zinc; and (3) Venezuelan criticism of the United States' voluntary restrictions on petroleum imports, an "inflammable" issue.[38]

[37] *New York Times Magazine,* May 25, 1958, p. 75.
[38] U.S. Dept. of State, *Bulletin,* XXXVIII (June 9, 1958), 952–958. To off-

Weakening Solidarity

The hostile demonstrations directed against Vice-President Nixon point up two interesting observations, first, that the single greatest contributor to Latin-American resentment against the United States is the restrictive-trade practices, and second, that Latin America is prone to embrace collectively the grievances of individual sister states. Nations not particularly affected by these tariff restrictions appear to be as resentful as if they were. Thus, while only Mexico and Peru are directly concerned with the lead-zinc tariff, all the Latin-American countries are critical of these import restrictions.

The following figures illustrate the importance of allowing competitive Latin-American products to enter the United States market: Venezuela's 1957 imports from the United States totaled $998 million. In the same year Venezuelan petroleum exported to the United States amounted to $902 million. This points up the truth of the economic principle that one must buy if he wishes to sell. The move by the United States to curb lead and zinc imports was criticized in a *New York Times* editorial as follows: "To protect a minor industry, and save the jobs of a relatively few thousand men, the United States is seriously damaging the economies of a number of friendly countries and has created a great deal of hard feeling." A Mexican spokesman is quoted as saying, "Such a step by President Eisenhower makes a mockery of the Good Neighbor policy," and in Peru the move was branded "economic aggression against our country."[39]

Shortly after the ill-fated Nixon tour of South America, Dr. Milton Eisenhower was commissioned by the President to make another fact-finding trip, this time to Central America. The report on this trip was in the nature of an addendum to that of 1953. The present discussion will be confined to its economic aspects.[40]

Dr. Eisenhower reported that he reaffirmed essentially all that he had said in the earlier report, but now he felt he should add a note of urgency to his general recommendation that the United States and Latin America re-examine their attitudes and policies toward one another. The misunderstandings which had been given special attention in the earlier report had not abated, but indeed seemed "to be even more serious than they were in 1953."

In the United States, he believed, the problem stemmed from a lack

set the lead and zinc import quotas, the United States in October 1958 promised to give priority to Peru in extending financial aid to her development plans.

[39] *New York Times,* Sept. 25, 1958.

[40] For full text of the report, see U.S. Dept. of State, *Bulletin,* XL (Jan. 19, 1959).

of knowledge. "Our people generally do not truly comprehend the problems and aspirations of our neighbors, and thus we sometimes take actions which are detrimental to the good relationships we wish to foster." And in Latin America there are misunderstandings of United States policies, programs, and attitudes. More particularly, the belief persists that the economic capacity of the country is unlimited, and since it is doing so much for other areas of the world, it is sheer perversity or discrimination to refuse to do more for Latin America. The fact that this is not true is beside the point, says Dr. Eisenhower, but "should warn us that new and dramatic action to overcome it is now imperative."

The report also refers to another serious misconception—that the United States sometimes fixes prices, to the detriment of Latin America. Everywhere the complaint was voiced, "We must sell to you at prices you are willing to pay, and we must buy from you at prices you dictate." That the United States does not fix prices, that raw-commodity and industrial prices are determined in the competitive markets of the world, was again, said Dr. Eisenhower, in one sense beside the point. The important thing is that the erroneous belief is widely held and causes bitterness and resentment.

With respect to particular economic recommendations contained in the report there is no need to comment, except to note that Milton Eisenhower was finally won over to the idea of an inter-American development institution. He declared his concurrence in the recently-announced willingness of his government to consider in principle the establishment of an inter-American bank. He therefore urged that the United States proceed as rapidly as possible with leaders of the Latin-American republics in creating such a bank. As for the several existent lending institutions, Dr. Eisenhower urged that they "take a more positive approach in using credit as an effective means of forwarding American foreign policy; this clearly involves helping Latin America achieve its sound economic goals and thus serving the best interests of the United States itself."

Economic meetings and committees. The economic problems of Latin America have not failed of solution because of a lack of international conferences and committees dedicated to the subject. At the Meeting of the Chiefs of State of the American Republics, held in Panama City, Panama, in July of 1956, President Eisenhower proposed that each of the presidents appoint a special representative to a committee to prepare concrete recommendations for making the OAS "a more effective instrument of inter-American cooperation in economic, social, financial, and technical fields, including the problem of the peaceful use of atomic energy."

The proposal was well received and accordingly the presidents of the American republics named representatives to the Inter-American Committee of Presidential Representatives. This committee, under the chairmanship of Dr. Milton Eisenhower, met on several occasions, and on May 25, 1957, issued a final report containing a number of recommendations in terms of activities which the OAS should undertake or augment, and which the committee believed to be of sufficient importance to warrant the necessary investments for carrying them out. In the economic and financial field the committee recommended: (1) strengthening and broadening the activities of the OAS in agriculture, including expansion of the work of the Inter-American Institute of Agricultural Sciences; (2) expanding services to member states on industrialization and industrial statistics; (3) further study by the OAS of the problem relating to the financing of economic and social development in the hemisphere, including the creation of an inter-American technical agency to assist in the study of "bankable" projects for economic development; (4) eliminating tax obstacles and other impediments to the movement of private capital; and (5) periodic meetings of high-level governmental experts.[41]

Certainly there was nothing startling in the above recommendations. A fair inference to draw from them is that the problems of economic cooperation were very complicated and required much further study. In public health, education, technical cooperation, social security, and the peaceful uses of atomic energy the committee was able to make more specific recommendations, indicating that these were paths less difficult to travel than the economic.

A number of recent developments concerned with the problems of inter-American economic cooperation were initiated in a communication addressed by President Juscelino Kubitschek of Brazil to President Eisenhower, dated May 28, 1958, immediately after the anti-Nixon demonstrations. "The hour has come," he said, "for us to undertake jointly a thorough review of the policy of mutual understanding in this hemisphere." There followed an exchange of correspondence between the two presidents, in the course of which the Brazilian President set forth his proposal for "Operation Pan America," the "battle against the festering sore of underdevelopment." A report on this ex-

---

[41] U.S. Dept. of State, *Bulletin*, XXXVI (June 24, 1957), 1014–1016; "Inter-American Committee of Presidential Representatives," *Annals* of the OAS, IX (1957), 167–178.

change was channeled to all the American chiefs of state, and, in a broadcast to the Brazilian nation (June 20, 1958), President Kubitschek said, "There are also ethical and political aspects to underdevelopment. . . . To allow the Hemisphere to become ever poorer is to weaken the Western Cause."[42] He called for an inter-American conference at the highest political level to seek solutions for the "disease of underdevelopment." The idea gained momentum as various Latin-American governments gave their support to the proposal to take stock of practical Pan Americanism.

In August 1958, when Secretary of State Dulles made a visit to Brazil, he discussed with President Kubitschek the proposal for a high-level meeting to consider the whole matter of economic underdevelopment. They agreed not only to adopt a six-point memorandum listing economic problems that required study but to "suggest to the other American republics that their Foreign Ministers should meet at regular intervals within the framework of the Organization of American States, to consult on mutual problems."

In accord with these agreements, an Informal Meeting of the Foreign Ministers occurred in Washington during September 23–24, 1958. Although the ostensible purpose of the meeting was to reaffirm inter-American solidarity in view of the recent manifestations of anti-United States hostility, it should come as no surprise that Latin delegates took advantage of the presentation of a Brazilian *Aide Memoire*,[43] outlining in great detail "Operation Pan America," to point up economic discontent as the basic reason for the weakened solidarity that they had come to reaffirm. The United States was warned that if it did not help to ease Latin America's economic troubles it would weaken their faith in democratic capitalism. Foreign Minister Víctor Andrade of Bolivia declared, for example, that if practical solutions are not found for the complicated economic problems of Latin America it is quite possible that the people will abandon hope of improving them through the inter-American system. Uruguayan Foreign Minister Oscar Secco Ellauri agreed with Andrade, saying that not only the masses but the privileged classes as well would lose faith in democratic principles and in the inter-American system if early solutions are not

[42] "Operation Pan America," *Américas*, XI (Jan. 1959), 2; *New York Times*, June 21, 22, 1958.

[43] For text of the *Aide Memoire*, see Council of the OAS, *Special Committee to Study the Formulation of New Measures for Economic Cooperation. First Meeting, Washington, D.C., Nov. 17–Dec. 12, 1958* (Washington, 1959), I, 33–41.

found for the basic economic problems. These views were echoed by other delegates. Peruvian Foreign Minister Raúl Porras Barrenechea was more specific in placing blame on the United States. He deplored the recent action of this country in placing quotas on the imports of lead and zinc. "In Peru," he said, "the people and the press are puzzled by our presence in this conference, after learning of the decision by the United States. This measure means that in Peru there are thrown into the streets 12 thousand workers, and $20 million in annual income is lost."[44]

In a communique of this meeting, it was the consensus of the foreign ministers that, "in keeping with the aspirations and needs of the peoples of America expressed on numerous occasions, action to promote the greatest economic development of the continent must be intensified." They therefore recommended that

special attention be given to working out additional measures of economic cooperation, taking as the point of departure the six topics proposed by the government of Brazil in its memorandum of August 9, 1958. . . . For this purpose and to facilitate other informal talks, the Ministers are of the opinion that the Council of the Organization of American States should set up a Special Committee of the Council on which the governments of the twenty-one American republics would be represented.[45]

The Council immediately, on September 24, appointed a special committee (known as the "Committee of Twenty-one") to study, as preparation for the eleventh inter-American conference to be held in Quito, the formulation of new measures of economic cooperation. The Council decided that the first meeting of the Committee of Twenty-one should convene in Washington on November 17. Also, one of the specific proposals of the Informal Meeting of the Foreign Ministers was that there should be established an inter-American development institution and that the Inter-American Economic and Social Council should convene as soon as possible a "specialized committee" of governmental representatives to draft the articles of agreement for such a bank. Drafting the charter of an inter-American bank was now in order, for the United States had formally announced on August 12, 1958, that it was "prepared to consider the establishment of an inter-American regional development institution which would receive support from all of its member countries."[46]

[44] *Visión,* Oct. 10, 1958, pp. 14–15.
[45] U.S. Dept. of State, *Bulletin,* XXXIX (Oct. 13, 1958), 575. For text of the communique, see Council of the OAS, *Special Committee,* 42–45.
[46] U.S. Dept. of State, *Bulletin,* XXXIX (Sept. 1, 1958), 347.

The Specialized Committee for Negotiating and Drafting the Instrument of Organization of an Inter-American Financial Institution, created by the IA-ECOSOC, began its work on January 8, 1959, at the Pan American Union in Washington. The closing session was held on April 8, 1959, when the Agreement Establishing the Inter-American Development Bank was opened for signature.[47]

The charter of the Inter-American Development Bank declares its purpose to be "to contribute to the acceleration of the process of economic development of the member countries, individually and collectively." It provides for a capitalization of $1 billion, of which the United States will put up $450 million, Argentina and Brazil $113 million each, Mexico $72 million, Venezuela $60 million, and smaller amounts for the remaining nations, each nation putting up 50 per cent of its share the first year, and the remainder when further funds are needed. The agreement was to become effective when the charter should be ratified by the nations whose allotted subscriptions represent 85 per cent of the authorized capital stock. On December 30, 1959, eighteen countries representing 87 per cent of the capital had ratified and the institution was brought into existence.

The Inter-American Development Bank is designed to serve the needs of the Latin-American republics on a sound financial basis. Unlike the United States lending agencies, it does not tie the borrower to buying within the hemisphere. Although the bulk of the Bank's funds will finance hard loans, the charter provides for a $150 million Special Operations Fund to finance projects not necessarily self-liquidating. The Bank, located in Washington,[48] with a Board of Directors and National Governors, maintains an office to help the republics in planning development, assigning priorities, and preparing loan projects. When urging Congress to enact promptly legislation enabling the United States to join with the other members of the OAS in establishing the Bank, President Eisenhower referred to the "desirability of an institution which will specialize in the needs of Latin America, which will be supported in large part by Latin-American resources, and which will give the Latin-American members a major responsibility in determining priorities and authorizing loans."[49]

[47] Pan American Union, *Agreement Establishing the Inter-American Development Bank*. Treaty Ser. No. 14 (Washington, 1959).

[48] Venezuela was keenly disappointed that the Bank was not located in Caracas.

[49] U.S. Dept. of State, *Bulletin*, XL (June 8, 1959), 849–850. For a good description of the Bank, see *Américas*, II (June 4, 1959), 2, 32.

United States acquiescence in Latin America's demand for an inter-American bank represented the reversal of a long-time policy. Ever since 1939 the unalterable position taken by this government was that such a bank would not be in the national interest. Latins were constantly reminded that existent lending agencies, United States and international, were adequate for their needs. Why, then, this recent policy reversal? It is difficult to escape the conclusion that, in the interest of good neighborliness and solidarity, and to make amends for any possible responsibility for the anti-Nixon demonstrations, the United States bowed once more to Latin-American pressure. This was one of a series of efforts by the United States to check the tide of "deteriorating" relations which had weakened the security structure.

In the meantime, while the Specialized Committee was working on an agreement for an inter-American bank, the Committee of Twenty-one was studying the formulation of new measures for economic cooperation. Its first meeting took place in Washington from November 17 to December 12, 1958. This meeting, taking the Brazilian plan known as "Operation Pan America" as a frame of reference, was devoted to a general airing of the points of view of the respective governments on the economic matters under study. The general discussions were followed by the appointment of a working group to draft concrete formulas and specific proposals. When the working group had completed its conclusions and recommendations it reported back to the full Committee of Twenty-one, which held its second meeting in Buenos Aires from April 27 to May 8, 1959.

The Buenos Aires meeting produced no fewer than thirty-five draft resolutions, covering almost every conceivable subject connected with inter-American economic cooperation. Probably the most significant was Resolution II, which proposed that a country under severe economic crisis call for a consultation of the foreign ministers, since, it declared, "the principles of solidarity that inspire Pan American cooperation in the political field and in that of mutual security necessarily include the economic field." This resolution was approved by the Council of the OAS on July 8, 1959. Thus, economic threats from any source, internal or external, are now on the same plane as those of a political or military nature. Generally, the other resolutions were directed to the respective governments, recommending desirable action in the interest of mutual economic benefit. Since these were purely recommendatory and were couched in broad terms, they presented no particular embarrassment to the United States.[50] Realizing the desir-

[50] Premier Fidel Castro of Cuba, a visitor to Buenos Aires, startled the Spe-

ability of translating its purposes "into practical and effective measures and achievements," the Special Committee formally requested the IA-ECOSOC to prepare drafts of inter-American agreements on the subjects referred to it, for eventual consideration by the Quito conference.

The pressure of Communist orientation in Cuba and the threat of Castro-like revolutions in other parts of Latin America made it clear to President Eisenhower that the United States should immediately intensify its efforts to aid the peoples of the Americas in achieving the material progress they so greatly desired. Accordingly the President, on July 11, 1960, pledged United States cooperation in promoting a program of social progress and economic growth in the Americas, providing for improvement in conditions of rural life through better use of agricultural land, better housing and community facilities, and improvement in education. The President recommended—and the Congress, in August 1960, authorized—an appropriation of $500 million to establish a special inter-American social-development fund. This program of social improvements was not intended as a substitute for the economic-development projects financed by the Exim Bank and the Development Loan Fund.

A meeting at Bogotá, September 5–13, 1960, of the economic representatives of the American republics (Committee of Twenty-one) afforded the United States opportunity for frank consultations "on measures to advance the political, economic, and social welfare of the peoples of the Americas." The deliberations of the meeting culminated in the Act of Bogotá, a statement of measures for social improvement and economic development within the framework of Operation Pan America.[51]

We note a revealing acknowledgment by the Committee of Twenty-one, at its meeting in Buenos Aires, that there had been "substantial progress in the economic growth of Latin America during the past decade."[52] Indeed, between the years 1950 and 1957 there was a 4.5 per cent average annual rate of growth in the gross national product, a rate substantially greater than that for the United States and other areas of the free world. And there is good reason to expect that this

---

cial Committee by proposing a $30 billion Marshall Plan for Latin America over a ten-year period.

[51] U.S. Dept. of State, *Bulletin,* XLIII (Oct. 3, 1960), 537–540; (Dec. 5, 1960), 853–855.

[52] Special Committee to Study the Formulation of New Measures for Economic Cooperation, *Draft Resolution* (second meeting, Buenos Aires, April 1959), Res. I, 1.

rate will be not only maintained but accelerated. However, if we speak of increasing the *per capita* income, as distinguished from the national income, that is another story, for we must reckon with the population explosion which is taking place in Latin America. In 1920 Latin America had 91 million inhabitants; in 1956 she had 187 million. If the current trend continues to the end of the century, Latin America will have almost 600 million people. In view of these figures, the prospects for achieving any substantial increase in the per capita income are not encouraging.[53]

The increasing flow of United States funds. Although the United States has consistently opposed grant (i.e., gift) assistance to Latin America, this type of aid has not been ruled out when emergency situations seem to require it. Economic assistance in the form of outright grants has been given to Bolivia, Guatemala, and Haiti. With respect to Guatemala, considerable grants in various forms were given to help the new anti-Communist government of President Carlos Castillo Armas stabilize and strengthen the nation's economic position. The United States was particularly concerned that the restoration of popular government in this Central American republic be attended by a return to economic stability. Since 1956, grants to Guatemala have greatly lessened. As for Bolivia and Haiti, the simple fact is that United States grants are necessary to save those distraught countries from economic collapse and political chaos. At the end of 1956 the total emergency economic aid to the three countries was approximately $65 million.[54] In 1957 and 1958, Bolivia was given $38,282,000 out of a total grant to Latin America of $44,965,000.[55] It is an interesting fact that, on a per capita basis, Bolivia has been the recipient of the largest grant economic aid given to any country in the world. From 1954 through 1958 the United States gave $101.1 million in outright gifts, part of which was used to balance the otherwise hopeless budget. Despite this, the country was recently described as being in "a state of chaos which must be seen to be believed."[56]

On January 13, 1958, Assistant Secretary of State Roy R. Rubottom reported that in the preceding two years: (*a*) the Exim Bank had

[53] Population Reference Bureau, Inc., "Latin America, the 'Fountain of Youth' Overflows," *Population Bulletin* (Washington, August 1958), XIV, No. 5.

[54] U.S. Dept. of State, *Bulletin*, XXXIV (April 20, 1956), 318.

[55] International Cooperation Administration, Office of Statistics and Reports, *Operations Report, Oct. 10, 1958*, 29.

[56] Richard W. Patch, *Bolivia: Decision or Debacle,* American Universities Field Staff (La Paz, Bolivia, April 18, 1959).

issued loan authorizations totaling $659 million; (*b*) the United States' share of the jointly-operated United States Technical Assistance Program reached $68 million; (*c*) the United States contributed an additional $11.7 million to the UN and OAS technical-assistance programs; (*d*) $80 million was granted as special aid; and (*e*) under Public Law 480 (Surplus Commodities Disposal) the United States had made available $221 million.[57] To illustrate the application of Public Law 480 to Latin America, on June 12, 1959, an agreement was entered into with Argentina for the sale, in pesos, of $33 million worth of edible oil and rice under provisions of Title I, Public Law 480 (The Agriculture-Trade Development and Assistance Act).

On February 28, 1959, the State Department provided the delegates of the Committee of Twenty-one with a very revealing statement concerning the increasing flow of United States funds into development projects. The statement referred to the following:

1. Authorization by the Congress of an increase of $2 billion in the lending authority of the Exim Bank, which conducts close to one-half of its total operations in Latin America.

2. Increased resources of the recently-created Development Loan Fund. Congress was asked to make a supplementary $225 million for fiscal year 1959 and $700 million for fiscal year 1960.

3. President Eisenhower's request of February 12, 1959, for Congressional authority to increase the contribution to the International Monetary Fund by $1,375 million. This will facilitate increased quotas for Latin America to ease balance-of-payments difficulties. In 1958 the IMF disbursed to Latin America $118 million.

4. President Eisenhower's request of February 12, 1959, for Congressional authority to increase by $3,175 million to the contingent liability of the United States to facilitate the doubling of the lending facilities of the International Bank for Reconstruction and Development (World Bank). A substantial proportion of this increase may be expected to be utilized in Latin America.[58] In 1958 the IBRD disbursed to Latin American countries $72.9 million.

The status of United States economic assistance to Latin America, according to recent figures, is shown in Table 6:

[57] U.S. Dept. of State, *Press Release,* Jan. 13, 1958. With respect to Public Law 480, the United States' dumping of farm products has injured the normal export markets of several of the Latin-American nations.

[58] U.S. Dept. of State, *Press Release,* March 10, 1959.

Table 6

United States Assistance to Latin America, Calendar Year 1958

Grants	
Military-assistance grants	$ 67,058,000
Other grant aid*	111,776,000
Total	$178,834,000
Loans	
Exim Bank (credits utilized)	$569,980,000
Development Loan Fund (credits utilized)	300,000
Mutual security and related loans	10,619,000
Loans to foreign governments under Agricultural Trade Development and Assistance Act	26,219,000
Loans to private enterprises under Agricultural Trade Development and Assistance Act	1,889,000
Total	$609,007,000

* Includes economic- and technical-assistance appropriations, Atoms for Peace, famine and other urgent extraordinary relief, multilateral technical assistance, agriculture commodities through private agencies, and inter-American and related highways.
Source: *Foreign Grants and Credits by the United States Government*, U.S. Dept. of Commerce, Office of Business Economics (May 1959).

Concluding observations. The foregoing lends support to the argument that the United States government never abandoned the Good Neighbor policy nor did it "neglect" Latin America or forgo a hemispheric policy in favor of a global one. After World War II several forms of economic assistance were continued, and over the years the amounts have been substantially increased. Despite these gestures Latin-American insistence on greater economic assistance became more and more pressing. Were it not for the exceptional size of United States grants and other forms of economic and defense assistance to free countries in other parts of the world, we submit that the nature and very respectable proportions of United States aid to Latin America would probably have stimulated more satisfaction and less criticism. But whether, in view of the aid to other nations, the Good Neighbors' insistence on better treatment is arguable, is quite beside the point. The stark fact is that they resent what they consider neglect and the down-grading of their importance to this country.

Thus, in view of the alarming deterioration of relations and dangerous undermining of the inter-American security structure, the United States has been forced to pay greater heed to her neighbors' com plaints. As has been noted, the Eisenhower Administration made serious efforts, particularly in its last two years, to convince the Latins that the United States does not take hemispheric solidarity for granted and that it is really concerned about their welfare. It remains to be seen however, whether these good neighborly actions, and those promised by the Kennedy Administration, will serve to abate the widespread hostility.

Repeated warnings by Latin Americans—some of them high governmental officials—that inter-American solidarity will crumble without more substantial "economic cooperation" are most disquieting. Without disparaging in any way the sincerity and seriousness of demands for increased economic assistance as an obligation of good neighborliness, it hardly seems compatible with the realities of national defense and self-interest to make this a requisite of security cooperation. It is inconceivable that, for the lack of greater economic and financial support, the Latin republics would cut the cords with which they induced the United States to bind itself.

This would indeed raise grave questions concerning the sincerity of the numerous declarations of attachment to common democratic principles as the basis of inter-American solidarity. In 1941, when the economic conditions of Latin America were *considerably worse* than they are today, there was little hesitation to proclaim inter-American solidarity in the face of a totalitarian threat from abroad. But today it is heard in many quarters that Latin America will "sit out the next one."

This unfinished story has no predictable end. Only the future will reveal whether our hemisphere neighbors will be content to cooperate for the long pull in President Kennedy's Alliance for Progress, or whether, impatient for the better life, they choose the easy and quick Castro way. However, forces tending to ameliorate Latin-American poverty are under way and they are gaining momentum. The economic growth rate in Mexico, for example, has been substantially higher during the postwar period than that of the United States or the industrialized countries of Western Europe. It is the belief of most economists studying problems of development that Mexico is not isolated, but is rather the prototype of a continent which has "achieved takeoff into sustained growth." Is it too much to hope that the satisfaction deriving from a sense of real achievement in Latin America may begin shortly to neutralize the invidious element in the Latin feeling of economic insecurity?

XIII Caribbean Turbulence (1949–1960)

It is no longer thinkable that a problem arising between two or more American States should be foreign to our essentially common political solidarity.

GUILLERMO SEVILLA SACASA, 1949

SINCE THE PERFECTING of the peace apparatus of the American republics at Rio de Janeiro in 1947 and at Bogotá in 1948, there has been no paucity of international incidents to put the security commitments to test. These controversies were strictly inter-American affairs, confined almost exclusively to the Caribbean area. Because of the weakness of the countries involved it was possible in most instances to induce or pressure their acceptance of peaceful settlement. For this reason it does not necessarily follow that the security procedures would be equally effective in controversies between stronger Latin-American states. Nevertheless, the lessons learned and experiences gained from applying the Rio treaty and other procedures to these minor controversies should serve at least two useful purposes. (1) They establish precedents in the "methodology" of applying the pacts, and so should obviate delay or confusion in any really serious future controversy. (2) The numerous instances of successful recourse to the pacts, even though the incidents have often been trivial, create a "climate" of public expectation that *all* controversies, no matter what the status of the contestants, must be submitted to the same procedures. Moreover, it is a matter of simple fact that a small brush fire, if neglected, can result in a great conflagration. It is for these reasons, therefore, that we examine the application of security commitments to inter-American controversies.

Caribbean interventionism. Since the controversies of the post-Bogotá years which were responsible for the invoking of the Rio treaty or recourse to the Inter-American Peace Committee arose from the constant interference by Caribbean and Central American governments in the affairs of their neighbors, it should be helpful to present here a little background information on this practice.

Latin-American interventionism in the Caribbean is an old and monotonous story. It began with the independence of the several states, particularly those of Central America. Bound together in a single Spanish American colonial subdivision called the Audiencia of Guatemala, the five provinces seceded from Spain, and, following a brief connection with Mexico, formed a federal union in 1824. The union broke up in 1838, but during its life political parties were formed that called themselves "Liberals" and "Conservatives." Following the liquidation of federalism, according to an authority on the history of the Central American states, "they faced also the constant threat of intervention by neighboring state governments which were in the hands of the opposite party, for the solidarity created by mutual action in federal affairs led the Conservatives and Liberals in each state to assist their former brothers in arms in other states even after all formal political connection had been broken."[1] This party solidarity was strengthened by the ambition of a large Liberal section to re-establish the federal union, and by the Conservatives' opposition to this plan. The habit of interventionism had been formed, and it outlasted the disintegration of the great historic political parties. Each state had too much interest in internal developments in neighboring states to remain indifferent to revolution or other political changes going on there. If it lagged, this interest was stimulated by the prodding and intriguing of political exiles.

Although Cuba, Haiti, and the Dominican Republic do not share with Central America the same kind of historical background for interventionism, most assuredly all of the republics share equally the experience of civil war and tyranny as intermittent phases of their political evolution. Consequently they share in a constant flow of political exiles who, while enjoying territorial asylum, direct their efforts toward the overthrow of the governments of their own countries. An investigating committee of the Council of the OAS reported in 1950:

The nationals of a given country not only try to fight against the government of their homeland, but also tend to congregate with those of other countries who have similar purposes. Many of those exiles are sincere and idealistic individuals who, being deprived of democratic guarantees in their native lands, inevitably strive to return to political life. Others are adven-

[1] Dana G. Munro, *The Five Republics of Central America* (New York, 1918), 32.

turers, professional revolutionaries, and mercenaries whose primary objective appears to be the promotion of illegal traffic in arms and revolutionary expeditions against countries with which they have no ties whatever.[2]

It is common knowledge that all too frequently the government of the state granting asylum wantonly shirks its obligation to prevent the organizing of revolutionary expeditions. In fact, not infrequently it actually contributes to the planning, organizing, and recruiting. All this, of course, is a flagrant violation of the Convention on the Duties and Rights of States in the Event of Civil Strife, signed at the sixth conference at Havana in 1928. That convention, which had been ratified by all of the Central American and Caribbean states prior to January 1, 1949, specifically obligated the contracting parties, in the event of civil strife in any one of the states: (1) to prevent all inhabitants of their territory, natives as well as aliens, from assembling and leaving the territory for the purpose of initiating or fomenting civil strife; (2) to disarm and intern rebel forces crossing the national frontiers; (3) to prohibit traffic in arms to the rebels of a recognized government; and (4) to prevent within their territorial jurisdiction the equipping, arming, or adapting for belligerent purposes any ship intended to operate in the interest of a rebellion. Certainly interventionism flourished in the Caribbean not for want of an explicit convention pledging the obligations of states in the event of civil strife but because it was a way of life of the area. For these states, nonintervention is for the United States but not for them. The issue to be discussed in the following pages was whether the OAS should permit several of its members to assume the right to overthrow the governments of other republics.

The Dominican Republic and Cuba, 1948. It has been noted above[3] that the Inter-American Peace Committee, rescued from oblivion by request of the Dominican government, was duly installed on July 31, 1948. The committee was comprised of representatives of Argentina, Brazil, Cuba, Mexico, and the United States. On August 13, 1948, the Peace Committee was requested by the Dominican government to lend its services in helping to resolve a situation that had arisen with Cuba.

The dispute between the two countries stemmed from activities on Cuban territory apparently directed against the government of Dictator Rafael Trujillo, one of the strong men of the Americas, who had

---

[2] Pan American Union, *Aplicaciones del Tratado Interamericano de Asistencia Reciproca, 1948–1958* (Washington, 1959), 110, cited hereinafter as *Aplicaciones del Tratado.*

[3] See pp. 326–328.

seized the presidency of the Dominican Republic in 1930. His harsh rule was responsible for many political exiles whose most convenient vantage points for revolutionary plotting were Haiti and Cuba. Cuban President Grau San Martín, a leftist, obviously viewed Trujillo with disfavor, and therefore did not scrupulously enjoin revolutionary preparations on Cuban soil. The tenacity and harsh effectiveness with which the self-styled "Benefactor of the Dominican People" clung to absolute authority for so many years made him the chief target of antidictatorship campaigns. Adept at counterattack, Trujillo prepared his campaign well, and, deciding that it would best serve his purposes, asked for the installation of the Inter-American Peace Committee; this accomplished, he submitted to it the controversy with Cuba.

The Peace Committee undertook immediately a painstaking investigation of the situation. After hearing the views of both parties, and after considering pertinent documents submitted by the Dominican government, the committee handed down on September 9 a recommendation that direct negotiations be initiated through official channels, with a view to settling the dispute in a manner satisfactory to both disputants.[4] The good offices of the Inter-American Peace Committee produced fruitful results, for evidently the airing of their difficulties before the committee paved the way for amicable negotiations between Cuba and the Dominican Republic. The Cuban government arrested the leaders of an expedition being organized against Trujillo, and seized the ships and planes which had been assembled. This happy result, reported the Peace Committee, was "motivated by the highest feeling of American fraternity, and by the spirit of unshakable solidarity characteristic of inter-American relations."[5] Unfortunately the accolade was undeserved, for shortly both parties were back again before the bar of American public opinion—but not, however, before two Central American states had put the Rio de Janeiro Treaty of Reciprocal Assistance to its first test.

Costa Rica and Nicaragua, 1948. On December 3, 1948, when Costa Rica deposited the fourteenth instrument of ratification (and thereby the required two-thirds), the Rio treaty entered into full effect among

[4] Pan American Union, *Annals* of the OAS, II (1950), 24–25; *Second Report of the Inter-American Peace Committee Submitted to the Tenth Inter-American Conference* (Washington, 1954), 5–6, cited hereinafter as *Second Report of the Inter-American Peace Committee.*

[5] Pan American Union, *Bulletin,* LXXXII (Oct. 1948), 591.

393

the ratifying states.[6] Eight days later, on December 11, the treaty met its first test when it was invoked by the Costa Rican government.

On the night of December 11, Argentine Ambassador Enrique V. Corominas, chairman of the Council of the OAS, was called on by the Costa Rican ambassador, who delivered a note stating that on the night of December 10 "Costa Rican territory had been invaded by an armed force proceeding from Nicaragua." It was estimated that it numbered about 800 men. The Costa Rican note declared:

This action is the climax of preparations that have been openly under way for some time in the Republic of Nicaragua, apparently by a group of Costa Ricans associated with the previous administration, whose purpose is to overthrow the present Costa Rican government. A considerable number of nationals of other countries have taken part in the subversive movement.

In view of this situation Costa Rica invoked the Rio treaty and urged a meeting of the Council so that it might be informed of the situation and act as Provisional Organ of Consultation. The Council met the next day (Sunday, December 12) to consider the Costa Rican charges and request.[7]

The members of the Council, from the very outset, were fully cognizant of the historic importance of their task: first, the steps they were about to take in implementing the Rio treaty would become precedents for future action; and second, since the eyes of a critical and skeptical world were on the OAS, it must not fail to discharge its responsibilities as a regional-security arrangement.

At its first session the Council authorized the chairman to seek additional information, and to call another meeting for the following Tuesday to discuss the new information and to decide whether to hold a Meeting of Consultation of Ministers of Foreign Affairs.[8] At the second session on Tuesday, December 14, the Council, having decided

[6] Ratifications had been deposited by the following countries: Dominican Republic, Nov. 21, 1947; United States, Dec. 30, 1947; Panama, Jan. 12, 1948; Colombia, Feb. 3, 1948; Honduras, Feb. 5, 1948; El Salvador, March 15, 1948; Brazil, March 25, 1948; Haiti, March 25, 1948; Paraguay, July 28, 1948; Uruguay, Sept. 28, 1948; Venezuela, Oct. 4, 1948; Nicaragua, Nov. 12, 1948; Mexico, Nov. 23, 1948; and Costa Rica, Dec. 3, 1948. Cuba, which ratified on Dec. 9, 1948, qualified for membership on the Provisional Organ of Consultation. Chile ratified on February 9, 1949. The ratifications of Argentina, Bolivia, Guatemala, and Peru came later.

[7] "How the Treaty Works," *Américas*, I (March 1949), 9–11, 47.

[8] For a detailed account of all steps attending the incident, see *Aplicaciones del Tratado*, 19–57.

that it could function as a Provisional Organ of Consultation only when a meeting of the foreign ministers had been called, proceeded by unanimous vote of all the states that had ratified the Rio treaty (thirteen, excluding Nicaragua and Costa Rica) to call a Meeting of Consultation, the seat and date to be set later. Thereupon the Council turned itself into a Provisional Organ of Consultation. Its first act was to appoint a Committee of Information to conduct an on-the-spot investigation. This committee, composed of four members of the Council—Luís Quintanilla of Mexico, José María Bello of Brazil, Silvio Villegas of Colombia, and Paul Daniels of the United States—flew to the trouble spot aboard an airplane put at the disposal of the committee by the United States government. From December 18 to December 23 the committee conducted an inquiry in both Costa Rica and Nicaragua. It soon became apparent that neither country had any intention of declaring war, and that all concerned were most anxious to settle the difficulty. The crossing of the Costa Rican border by no more than 200 men (rather than the estimated 800) did not develop into a serious threat to that government, but there was evidence that both governments had been remiss in failing to discourage revolutionary groups aiming to overthrow both governments: the liberal Costa Rican government of "Pepe" Figueres, and the Nicaraguan dictatorship of "Tacho" Somoza.

On December 24 the Committee of Information presented its report to the Provisional Organ of Consultation. This was speedy action, for it had been only ten days since the appointment of the committee. The findings of the committee were the following. (1) There was no doubt that a revolutionary movement against Costa Rica had been organized in Nicaraguan territory, and equally certain was the neglect of the Nicaraguan government to prevent these activities. (2) Precautionary measures by the Nicaraguan government were not taken until after December 10. (3) The armed forces of Nicaragua did not participate in the crossing of the Costa Rican frontier, nor had there been any contact between the troops of the two countries. (4) The Costa Rican government had given material and moral support to the Caribbean Legion which had been organized by expatriates and adventurers to overthrow certain governments, including the regime of Somoza in Nicaragua.

As a result of the report, the Council approved a resolution calling upon both governments to eliminate those conditions which had led to the dispute, to give the Provisional Organ of Consultation full assurance that they would thenceforth abstain from hostile acts against each other, and to observe faithfully the principles and rules of non-intervention. Special committees of the Provisional Organ of Consultation, acting in conjunction with representatives of the two countries, collaborated in drafting the Pact of Amity (*Pacto de Amistad*), which was signed in Washington on February 21, 1949.

According to the pact, the recent events would not destroy the fraternal amity existing between the two peoples, and the respective governments pledged themselves to prevent their repetition through faithful observance of inter-American principles and compacts. They mutually pledged that the American Treaty of Pacific Settlement would be invoked in disputes arising between them, even before it was formally ratified and in full force. The pact also specified that an agreement should be reached between the two parties concerning the fulfillment of their obligations under the Havana Convention on the Duties and Rights of States in the Event of Civil Strife.[9]

With the signing of the Pact of Amity between Costa Rica and Nicaragua, the Provisional Organ of Consultation brought the incident to an end, and so it was unnecessary for the foreign ministers to meet as an organ of consultation. The outcome of the affair left all concerned well pleased. The general view was that the OAS has satisfactorily discharged its responsibilities as a regional-security arrangement.

The Dominican Republic and Haiti, 1949. The tensions of the Costa Rican-Nicaragua incident had hardly relaxed when, on February 15, 1949, the Republic of Haiti filed a complaint with the Council of the OAS against its neighbor, the Dominican Republic. The Haitian charge was that one Astrel Roland, a former Army colonel and military attaché of the Haitian Embassy in Washington, and chargé at Quito, had plotted a conspiracy to overthrow the constitutional government of Haiti, and that these activities were being conducted with the knowledge and approval of the Dominican government. The Haitian representative to the Council asked in the meeting of February 16 that the provisions of the Rio treaty be invoked. After the response of the Dominican representative, in which he asserted that the Rio treaty did not apply since it contemplated a *de facto* situation, the Council, evidently in agreement, decided to suspend further consideration until a subsequent meeting.

---

[9] Pan American Union, *Pacto de Amistad entre los Gobiernos de las Repúblicas de Costa Rica y Nicaragua, 21 de Febrero de 1949.* Law and Treaty Ser., No. 30 (Washington, 1949). The treaty entered into full effect on July 15, 1949.

When the Council learned later that the two governments were ready to arrive at a friendly settlement, on February 25 it published a resolution declaring that, since the two countries might arrive at a friendly settlement through recourse to peaceful procedures, it would refrain from convoking the organ of consultation. Pursuant to this understanding the Haitian government on March 21 addressed a note to the Inter-American Peace Committee, informing it of the situation and requesting its help. While the functions of the Peace Committee were limited to offering suggestions, its procedures were much less formal than those set forth in the Rio treaty, and thus afforded a useful approach for settling the dispute.

The Peace Committee met on March 24, 1949, to take cognizance of the Haitian request for its services, and to report this to the Dominican government. After several meetings with the representatives of both parties, the committee, with the consent of both governments, decided to send a delegation to the Dominican Republic and Haiti. The delegation, composed of the Council representatives of Mexico, Argentina, and the United States, on May 29 went to Haiti and the Dominican Republic to study the question. There they interviewed the presidents and other high officials of the two countries. They returned to Washington one week later and immediately turned over to the Peace Committee the text of a joint declaration which had been approved by the foreign ministers of the two republics. This agreement was formally incorporated in a declaration signed on June 9, 1949, by members of the committee and representatives of Haiti and the Dominican Republic. The two governments, after protesting "good neighbor sentiments based on the lofty principles of nonintervention, mutual respect, and American solidarity," solemnly declared that they would not "tolerate in their respective territories the activities of any individuals, groups, or parties, national or foreign, that have as their object the disturbance of the domestic peace of either of the two neighboring Republics or of any other friendly nation." They further declared that in any future difference between the two states they would resort to direct negotiation and the procedures of peaceful settlement.[10] These were familiar words, the oft-repeated pledges, as frequently violated.

The situation in the Caribbean, 1949. Although the inter-American machinery for peaceful settlement had again apparently proved its usefulness, it was a disquieting fact that within the Caribbean area there remained obvious seeds of future controversies. The situation

[10] *Aplicaciones del Tratado,* 57–63; *Annals,* I (1949), 325–326; II (1950), 23–24; *Second Report of the Inter-American Peace Committee,* 6–7.

was so disturbing to the United States that on its initiative the Inter-American Peace Committee met in Washington on August 3, 1949, to determine whether it could propose a constructive approach to the problem. Here was a situation remarkably parallel to the one which was to lead to the Fifth Consultative Meeting of Foreign Ministers at Santiago, Chile, almost ten years later to the day. Thus, the decade began and ended on the same tone of Caribbean interventionism.

The occasion for the United States' call for a meeting of the Inter-American Peace Committee was a series of headlines concerning the so-called "Caribbean Legion" and other activities aimed at the overthrow of dictatorial regimes in Honduras, Nicaragua, Venezuela, and the Dominican Republic. Guatemala's President Juan José Arévalo headed the Committee for Caribbean Liberation which, in the spring of 1948, had helped José Figueres to overthrow a usurper Costa Rican government. In the affair, as was their wont, neighboring countries intervened: Nicaragua and Honduras in support of the faltering Picado government, and Guatemala and the "Legionnaires" in support of the revolutionaries.[11]

Concerning the elusive Legion, which specialized in aiding the overthrow of dictators, the Investigating Committee of the Provisional Organ of Consultation reported in 1950:

Even if the so-called "Legion of the Caribbean" does not exist as a concrete military organization bearing that particular name, nevertheless there is in existence a collection of elements constituting a subversive force, less organized and systematized than the hypothetical Legion, but more dangerous and more apt to create serious warlike situations.[12]

The Investigating Committee added that side by side with men of sincerity, battling for their ideals and political rights, were mercenaries and adventurers acting for selfish purposes.

At its first meeting the Inter-American Peace Committee, despite the fact that the Argentine and Mexican representatives doubted its juridicial competence "to deal with situations of a general nature," decided to request from all American governments information and suggestions pertinent to the situation. Costa Rica, Cuba, the Dominican Republic, Guatemala, Haiti, the United States, and Venezuela responded. Boiled down, their suggestions urged the solution of problems at the diplomatic level. The failure of all the South American countries, except Venezuela, to reply must have indicated a significant

[11] *Time* (Latin America edition), Oct. 4, 1948; New York *Herald Tribune*, Oct. 5, 1948.
[12] *Aplicaciones del Tratado*, 120–121.

disinterest in the matter. Perhaps the very fact that the initiative had been taken by the United States, which strongly implied that the Latin-American countries could not keep their houses in order, was not appreciated. Most of the governments that did respond to the request did so with reaffirmation of their attachment to peaceful principles. The United States memorandum, submitted August 18, 1949, by its representative Ambassador Paul C. Daniels, deserves our attention.[13]

The memorandum noted that since 1945, citizens of one or another of the countries of the Caribbean area had engaged in preparations for, or participated in, movements to accomplish by intimidation or armed invasion changes in the governments of the area. While the effectiveness of inter-American peace procedures had been successfully demonstrated on three recent occasions, new situations had developed and tensions had not lessened. The situation demanded that methods be found for getting at, and eliminating if possible, the causes of friction and discord. Thereupon the memo pointed out the steps that had been taken by the United States itself in cases of illegal activities carried on within its jurisdiction. Numerous cases were cited resulting in fines, imprisonments, suspension of passports, dissuasion of American participation in political enterprises, and the impounding of fighting equipment. In conclusion, the memorandum called attention to the numerous inter-American agreements on nonintervention, and specifically to the 1928 Convention on the Duties and Rights of States in the Event of Civil Strife. The memo urged that this convention be studied to find out whether it needed clarification or strengthening.

After carefully considering the problems presented by the memorandum, the Inter-American Peace Committee formulated a series of conclusions that were approved at its meeting on September 14, 1949. Since the committee believed that its competence was limited to the reaffirmation of certain standards and principles basic to American peace and solidarity, it could do little more than urge the faithful observance of treaties, conventions, and declarations pledging nonintervention and enumerating the obligations of states in the event of civil strife. With reference to the problem of dictatorship versus democracy—the basic cause of the Caribbean turmoil—the committee merely pointed out that a common denominator of American political life is adherence to the principles and exercise of democracy, and that the member states are pledged by solemn agreements to effectively exercise representative democracy. The Peace Committee seemed to

[13] *Annals,* I (1949), 393–398.

feel that keeping the ideal or "trade name" of peaceful settlement dusted off would be enough to discourage armed plots.

This was the feeble outcome of the meeting of the Peace Committee. The governments were to be vigilant, as they were disposed, to prevent conspiracies against neighboring regimes. The United States should have known when it requested the meeting that effective measures which did not compromise the nonintervention principle were nonexistent. This certainly had been the recent experience of this government when it proposed antidictatorship and prodemocratic measures.[14] Nothing short of some form of collective action by the American states could bring order to the Caribbean.

Immediately after the meeting of the Inter-American Peace Committee, Secretary of State Acheson denounced the Caribbean plots and counterplots as "repugnant to the entire fabric of the inter-American system." Since aggression or plotting against any nation in the hemisphere is of concern to the United States, the Secretary pledged that his country would use its "strongest efforts, in keeping with our international commitments . . . to defend the peace of the hemisphere."[15] Later, in a Columbus Day speech, President Truman called on the OAS to lead a move for "representative democracy" in all the American republics. This evidently was a reference to the rash of military dictatorships which so alarmed the United States. These efforts to mobilize opinion, public and governmental, failed insofar as they were intended to deter further plots and interventions in the Caribbean.

The controversies of 1950. On January 3, 1950, an American government once again invoked the Rio treaty.[16] This time it was Haiti that asked that the organ of consultation of the OAS be immediately summoned because of "a situation that threatened the peace of the Continent." At the meeting of the Council on January 6, the Haitian Ambassador was given an opportunity to present the charges of his government.

The Dominican government was accused of a series of flagrant acts of intervention affecting the territorial inviolability, the sovereignty, and the political independence of the Republic of Haiti. Specifically, the Dominican government was charged with violating the terms of the joint declaration of June 9, 1949, which was supposed to terminate the controversy created by the subversive activities of former Colonel Astrel Roland. Not only Roland but other Haitian nationals had been

---

[14] See pp. 291–292.
[15] U.S. Dept. of State, *Bulletin,* XXI (Sept. 26, 1949), 463.
[16] *Aplicaciones del Tratado,* 67–132.

allowed to continue their plotting, including an alleged plan to assassinate Haiti's president. In addition to these subversive activities there had been frequent instances of violations of Haitian territory by Dominican planes and soldiers. As evidence of Dominican intention to invade its island neighbor, the Haitian government pointed to the recent action by the Dominican Congress granting Trujillo full powers to declare war upon any Caribbean state that might give asylum to the enemies of his government. The Haitian Ambassador did not hesitate to mention that Secretary of State Dean Acheson had deplored this action by the Dominican Congress.

In his response the Dominican Ambassador not only categorically denied the charges, he countercharged. Alluding to the Caribbean Legion, and implicating not only Haiti but Cuba and Guatemala as well, he repeated a long-standing Dominican charge that these and other countries in the Caribbean area harbored or fostered plots against the Trujillo regime. Since the "Benefactor of the Dominican People" felt that words by diplomats in Washington might not be enough to prevent outlaw aggression, he had been forced to request his Congress to grant full powers to exercise the right of self-defense against any fresh assault on the Dominican nation. Therefore, according to the Dominican version, President Trujillo's war-powers request was the result rather than the cause of the "profound state of emergency." Also, Trujillo offered to abandon a two-year $20 million armaments program, contingent upon effective assurances that his government would not be attacked. Finally, since the Dominican Republic had tried, but without success, to bring the problem to the Inter-American Peace Committee, it readily acquiesced in the request to invoke the Inter-American Treaty of Reciprocal Assistance.[17] Convinced of the seriousness of the situation because of the charges and countercharges, the Council voted on January 6, 1950, to apply the treaty of Rio, to constitute itself a Provisional Organ of Consultation, and to convoke a meeting of the foreign ministers.

Those countries represented in the Council that had ratified the Rio treaty constituted the Provisional Organ of Consultation, which immediately appointed an Investigating Committee to conduct an on-the-spot investigation in the four countries involved: Haiti, the Dominican Republic, Cuba, and Guatemala. The countries represented on the committee were Bolivia, Colombia, Ecuador, the United States, and Uruguay. In response to requests, the governments of the four Carib-

[17] *New York Times*, Jan. 1, 20, 1950.

bean republics welcomed visits by the committee. The Investigating Committee, on January 22, 1950, began a tour for the purpose of interviewing certain officials and private citizens of Haiti, the Dominican Republic, Cuba, and Guatemala; it also visited Mexico. The committee returned to Washington on February 15, and an extensive report giving a detailed account of the mission was submitted to the Provisional Organ of Consultation on March 13.

The report named names and cited incidents. The evidence which it had collected left little doubt that there was substance both to the charges and countercharges. In short, the committee found that the Dominican Republic, Cuba, and Guatemala were all involved in the subversive developments in the Caribbean region; Haiti alone was not found to have violated her responsibilities.

On April 8 the Provisional Organ of Consultation approved five resolutions as follows:

1. To request the Dominican Republic to take immediate measures to prevent its officials from aiding and abetting subversive and seditious movements against other governments; to point out to both the Haitian and Dominican governments the need of adherence to the Havana convention of 1928 relative to civil strife; and to request both governments to avoid the continuation of hostile propaganda directed against each other.
2. To request the governments of Cuba and Guatemala to adopt adequate measures to prevent the use of their territories for the organizing and dispatching of military elements against the security of other countries, and to prevent illegal traffic in arms.
3. To appoint a committee of five to take note of the manner in which Resolutions 1 and 2 were being carried out and, if necessary, to facilitate compliance.
4. To reaffirm the principles of representative democracy, and to declare that these principles in no way authorize any government or group of governments to violate international commitments relative to the principle of nonintervention.
5. To recommend to the Council of the OAS that it undertake the study of the following matters:
   (a) due respect to the sovereignty of states and the effective exercise of representative democracy;
   (b) the strengthening and perfecting of the 1928 Havana Convention on the Duties and Rights of States in the Event of Civil Strife;
   (c) the regimen of political asylees, exiles, and refugees.

Given the obstacle of nonintervention, the recommendations of the Provisional Organ of Consultation were about as much as could be expected, that is, very little. Once more, we wearily note, the guilty parties were admonished to observe their solemn commitments. Apparently, sanctions were unthinkable. The appointment of a "watchdog" committee to take note of whether they complied with the admonishments of the organ of consultation had some virtue, for the knowledge that they were being watched probably would put a brake on states. The subjects which had been recommended to the Council for study rested at the very heart of the Caribbean turmoil, but in this instance study was quite unnecessary, for the malady was well known. What was needed was a cure, something the studies could not provide.

The "watchdog" committee, which took the name Special Committee for the Caribbean, was to report within three months after April 8, and again when its work had been completed. The committee submitted its first report on June 30, 1950, and expressed gratification that it had received no reports indicating disregard for the resolutions adopted by the Provisional Organ of Consultation.[18] In its second report, dated October 31, 1950, the committee declared that relations between the various governments in the Caribbean were continuing to improve. The committee submitted its final report on May 14, 1951.[19] With the restoration of diplomatic relations between Haiti and the Dominican Republic and a friendly meeting between the presidents of the two republics near the common boundary on February 19, 1951, and with a steady improvement of relations between the governments of Cuba, the Dominican Republic, Guatemala, and Haiti, the Special Committee for the Caribbean considered its work ended. There is little doubt that this special committee served a useful purpose in inducing a certain respect on the part of the Caribbean republics for their obligations. It was to be regretted, therefore, that the committee disbanded. Perhaps the failure to check further flare-ups in the Caribbean was due to the absence of a watchdog.

Although the Rio treaty was invoked in the Guatemalan situation of 1954, this whole matter will be discussed later in connection with the problem of international Communism. The next occasion when a Caribbean controversy evoked a convocation of the organ of consultation occurred in 1955.

Costa Rica and Nicaragua, 1955. The personal feud between Presidents Somoza of Nicaragua and Figueres of Costa Rica was threatening once more to revive Caribbean turmoil. The antagonism between the two men, however, was more than personal—it also had a political basis. Figueres was one of the outstanding liberals of Latin America.

[18] *Annals,* II (1950), 406–411.
[19] *Ibid.,* III (1951), 338–339.

A man truly dedicated to democracy and socio-economic reform, he did not necessarily confine his enthusiasm to his own country. His aggressive campaigns in seeking these admirable goals had aroused the bitter opposition of the dictatorial triumvirate: Venezuela's Pérez Jiménez, Dominican Republic's Trujillo, and Nicaragua's Somoza. Somoza accused Figueres of fomenting plots against him, even including his assassination.

A succession of acts by the Nicaraguan government were alarming to Costa Rica and had convinced Figueres of Somoza's aggressive intentions. These acts included: the closing of the San Juan River to navigation by Costa Rican merchant vessels; defamatory campaigns by the Nicaraguan press and radio; military maneuvers by Nicaraguan forces, and the concentration of motorized troops on the common border with Costa Rica; Nicaragua's acquisition of a disturbing amount of armaments, particularly of airplanes; and, more serious in the Costa Rican view, the granting of facilities in Nicaragua to the enemies of the Costa Rican government for the organizing of plots against the peace and security of that nation.[20]

On April 21, 1954, Costa Rica appealed to the Council of the OAS, requesting it to convoke a Commission of Investigation and Conciliation, as provided by the American Treaty on Pacific Settlement (Pact of Bogotá), to investigate the situation with Nicaragua. It will be recalled that the Pact of Bogotá was fully recognized by the Pact of Amity, signed by the two countries on February 21, 1949. No action was taken by the Council, however, when it appeared that the matter could be handled by direct negotiation between the two countries.[21]

Since months elapsed without bringing the controversy to an end, and since the situation was becoming worse, the Costa Rican government, on January 8, 1955, proposed to the Council that a Meeting of Consultation of Ministers of Foreign Affairs be convoked in accordance with Article 6 of the Rio Treaty of Reciprocal Assistance. Before the Council arrived at a decision on the request, Costa Rica, on January 11, reported the alarming news that an actual invasion of its territory was in progress "by military forces proceeding from abroad, which have already occupied various points in the north boundary zone, among them the important town of Villa Quesada."[22] In an extraordinary session on the same day, the Council convoked the organ of consultation (without specifying place or date) and resolved to constitute

[20] *Aplicaciones del Tratado,* 145–201.
[21] *Annals,* VI (1954), 169.
[22] *Aplicaciones del Tratado,* 148.

itself and to act provisionally as a consultative organ. The next step was to appoint an on-the-spot Investigating Committee to find the pertinent facts and report them to the Council. The Council also requested the other American governments to take the necessary measures to prevent the use of their territories for any military action against the government of another state.[23]

Costa Rica and Nicaragua having agreed to cooperate with the Investigating Committee and to refrain from any act that might aggravate the situation, the committee left for those countries on January 12, 1955. While it was en route a new element entered the picture: Costa Rica reported that several towns, including the capital, had been bombed and strafed by aircraft coming from the north. Having no air force of its own, Costa Rica urgently solicited assistance.

In response the Council decided to establish an air patrol, under supervision of the Investigating Committee, to make peaceful observations over the affected region. Immediately after this decision the governments of Ecuador, Mexico, the United States, and Uruguay made planes available. The use of peaceful observation flights was a new development in inter-American peace procedures. The Investigating Committee, in its interim reports to the Council, confirmed that planes coming undoubtedly from Nicaragua had machine-gunned and bombed several places in Costa Rica, and that arms were entering the country from across the northern frontier.

Since it was reported that the air strength of the revolutionary group had been reinforced and that it was engaged in strafing operations, and since the Costa Rican government had no combat aircraft with which to meet the threat, the Council was forced to consider the fact that Costa Rica had asked the United States to sell it four P-51's. Although the United States had the legal right to sell the planes to Costa Rica, it preferred to defer to the decision of the Council. That body, on January 16, voted unanimously to approve the sale. Accordingly, the four P-51's arrived in Costa Rica on January 17 and were turned over to the government. It is a matter of interest that, though the planes were being sold to Costa Rica at a token price according to the standards specified by the Mutual Security Act of 1954, later, because of price and other reasons, the Costa Rican government chose to return the planes to the United States.[24] The three-plane air force of the revolutionaries, being subjected to aerial surveillance, returned to a Nicaraguan base and there surrendered to Nicaraguan authorities.

[23] *Ibid.*, 151.
[24] U.S. Dept. of State, *Bulletin,* XXXII (Jan. 31, 1955), 181.

President Somoza closed the common border as a gesture of "unalterable attitude of nonintervention in the internal revolutionary movement." He emphatically denied that he had inspired the invasion but made no effort to conceal his contempt for President Figueres and his hopes for the Costa Rican President's overthrow. Somoza denounced the United States' sale of planes to Costa Rica as "madness"—and asked to be supplied with an identical shipment.

On January 25 about 250 rebels recrossed the border into Nicaragua, were disarmed, and interned, among them the leaders of the movement. The invasion of Costa Rica had failed and the Investigating Committee, after many interviews with officials and individuals of all categories in both countries, returned to Washington to make its final report, which was the usual milk-toast type. The Ecuadorean member of the committee, Ambassador José R. Chiriboga, objected. He saw no reason to avoid specific mention of Nicaragua as aggressor, for the facts were clear. He felt that there should be an early meeting of the ministers of foreign affairs to consider the possibility of establishing a permanent inter-American police force and to investigate the improvement of the system of control of traffic in arms and ammunition.[25] Obviously a police force was too drastic for consideration.

On February 24, 1955, the Council, acting as the Provisional Organ of Consultation, approved several resolutions designed to put into effect the recommendations of the Investigating Committee and thus bring the Costa Rica-Nicaragua affair to a successful conclusion. Specific and significant features of the recommendations were the following: (1) that the two governments sign the bilateral agreement mentioned in Article IV of the Pact of Amity of 1949, concerning the best manner of putting into practice the provisions of the Convention on the Duties and Rights of States in the Event of Civil Strife; (2) that there be established a special committee of the Council, acting provisionally as an organ of consultation, to cooperate with Costa Rica and Nicaragua in preparing the bilateral agreement; and (3) that the special committee maintain the services of the military observers.[26]

It is a matter of record that all these recommendations were eventually fulfilled. On January 9, 1956, Costa Rica and Nicaragua signed two bilateral agreements. One of them implemented the 1949 Costa Rica—Nicaragua Pact of Amity by binding the two countries to specific means for reducing possibility of future hostilities. In addition to

[25] *Aplicaciones del Tratado,* 173.
[26] *Ibid.,* 177–182. When the Investigating Committee returned to Washington, it left five military observers on duty in the area for the next two weeks.

surveillance of the common frontier by two committees composed of officers from the armed forces of each country, the agreement put into effect many provisions of the Convention on Territorial Asylum, adopted at the Caracas conference in 1954. The second agreement defined the competence of the Committee of Investigation and Conciliation as provided by the American Treaty on Pacific Settlement. The parties agreed to give the members of the Committee of Investigation and Conciliation free access to all parts of both countries, and to set up safeguards for them.[27]

The signing of the two agreements apparently terminated the issue between the two Central American countries. The Council, feeling that OAS action had restored Costa Rica to the sense of security to which she was entitled, voted on January 18, 1956, to cancel the convocation of a meeting of ministers of foreign affairs.[28] The way the OAS had risen to this emergency was encouraging, but particularly satisfying was the way the U.S. State Department had handled this delicate matter. It was widely charged by Latins that the United States, in its support of democracy, would do anything to combat Communism but nothing against dictators. Thus, if Figueres and his regime were allowed to be driven out by right-wing Costa Ricans aided by the Nicaraguan dictator, the repercussions would be most damaging to hemispheric solidarity. All this was prevented by the vigorous role played by the State Department in getting action and in providing fighter planes. Incidentally, this was most disappointing to Somoza, since he. like Trujillo, had usually cooperated with the United States .

The peace machinery not utilized. For the record, we note two instances, in 1953 and 1955, in which requests for the services of the Inter-American Peace Committee, and for invoking the Inter-American Treaty of Reciprocal Assistance were unsuccessful. On November 18, 1953, the Colombian government requested the services of the committee in finding a procedure conducive to settling the dispute between Colombia and Peru over the long-continued asylum of Víctor Raúl Haya de la Torre in the Colombian Embassy in Lima. The Peace Committee immediately sent a copy of the Colombian note to the government of Peru and offered its good services in settling the dispute. Peru declined them. Therefore, since the committee had failed to secure the consent of both parties, it had to retire, but in doing so it informed the Colombian government on January 21, 1954, that after a careful study of the case it believed that bilateral negotiation would

[27] *Annals,* VIII (1956), 183–187.
[28] *Ibid.,* 190.

prove efficacious in the present circumstance.[29] It is a matter of interest that Colombia and Peru did in fact break the stalemate by direct negotiation. It is also a matter of note that this was the last resort to the Peace Committee until 1959. Rescued from oblivion, it seemed to be returning to oblivion.

An abortive attempt to invoke the Rio treaty occurred in connection with the Peru-Ecuador boundary flare-up in 1955. Ever since the signing of the Rio de Janeiro Protocol of Peace, Friendship and Boundaries in 1942, which forced Ecuador to relinquish a large part of disputed boundary territory to Peru, the little nation astraddle the equator was very touchy and lived in fear of further Peruvian aggression.

On September 8, 1955, Ambassador Chiriboga of Ecuador submitted a note to the Council of the OAS invoking the Rio treaty and requesting that the Council convoke a Meeting of Consultation of the Ministers of Foreign Affairs. The charge was that the government of Peru was endangering the territorial integrity, sovereignty, and independence of Ecuador. Heavy concentration of Peruvian forces had been noted on the border, and vessels of the Peruvian Navy were stationed near the Ecuadorean coastline. Said Dr. Chiriboga, "My government is convinced that at any moment Peru intends to launch an invasion of Ecuador, and thereby violate her national sovereignty and integrity."[30]

At a special meeting of the Council, held on the same day, it was noted that Ecuador had already submitted the matter to the governments of Argentina, Brazil, Chile, and the United States—the four guarantor states of the Rio protocol of 1942. The Council was informed that at that moment representatives of the guarantor states were meeting in Rio de Janeiro and planned to launch an on-the-spot investigation of the charges. Because of this development the Council decided to defer to the guarantor states. Thus the Rio treaty was not applied to the controversy and Ecuador withdrew its request.[31]

With respect to the action of the guarantor states, an investigating committee, composed of the military attachés of the four states who were stationed in Lima and Quito, was created. After aerial reconnaissance and other investigations the guarantors' committee reported that nothing out of the ordinary had been observed. Nevertheless they proposed steps for reducing the tension and ensuring tranquility between Ecuador and Peru.[32]

[29] *Second Report of the Inter-American Peace Committee*, 41.
[30] *Annals*, VII (1955), 290.
[31] *Aplicaciones del Tratado*, 205–213.
[32] *Annals*, VII (1955), 290–292.

Unfortunately the hoped-for tranquility did not develop. Ecuador's dissatisfaction with the Rio protocol of 1942 culminated in the announcement, in September 1960, that it would no longer be bound by the agreement. The refusal of the guarantor nations to recognize the validity of this unilateral abrogation led to Ecuador's violent denunciation of the sponsor powers, particularly the United States. Its embassy at Quito and several consulates and cultural centers were the targets of mob demonstrators, who voiced hatred of the "Yanqui" and friendship for Russia. Even President José María Velasco Ibarra lent his voice to the anti-United States and pro-Soviet chant of the mob. The friendship of Ecuador, a country which had been one of the prime beneficiaries of United States economic assistance, seemed to lack both substance and conviction. Why do many people, when affronted by the United States, hasten to declare their friendship for the Soviet Union?

Honduras versus Nicaragua, 1957. Another flare-up in Central America which required that the Rio Treaty of Reciprocal Assistance be applied occurred in 1957. This developed out of a long-standing boundary dispute between Nicaragua and Honduras. In an early attempt to settle the question, an arbitral award was handed down by the King of Spain on December 23, 1906. The award, in support of Honduran claims, was not accepted by the Nicaraguan government, and therefore it did not recognize the territorial right of Honduras to the region. Until 1957 both Honduras and Nicaragua exercised control over various areas in the territory in question.

The dispute between the two countries was revived in early 1957 when Honduras established a new province which included some of the territory claimed by Nicaragua. Although the area was nothing but jungle borderland, the rival claims to it were sharpened by the belief that it contained oil deposits. At any rate, on May 1, 1957, Honduras addressed a note to the Council of the OAS invoking the Rio treaty because of Nicaragua's "having invaded Honduran territory with military forces by crossing the boundary line of the Coco or Segovia River, established by the King of Spain in his arbitral award of December 23, 1906."[33]

After hearing statements by the representatives of Honduras and Nicaragua, the Council decided to meet again on May 3. However, Nicaraguan allegations that Honduran troops had fired on and killed Nicaraguan soldiers necessitated a special session of the Council on May 2. Nicaragua had also invoked the Rio treaty, denouncing Honduras as an "aggressor state." In view of the existent situation, the

[33] *Aplicaciones del Tratado,* 219–292; *Annals,* IX (1957), 264–270.

Council voted unanimously to take cognizance of the charges of the two states. The customary procedure was followed: (1) the organ of consultation, in accordance with the provisions of the Rio treaty, was convoked, the seat and date of meeting to be fixed later; (2) the Council constituted itself Provisional Organ of Consultation; (3) the chairman of the Council was authorized to appoint a committee to investigate and report the pertinent facts; (4) the governments of Honduras and Nicaragua were requested to provide full cooperation to facilitate the work of the committee, and were asked to refrain from any acts that might aggravate the situation; and (5) the Security Council of the United Nations was informed of the text of the resolution and of all activities relating to the matter. By this time the procedures to be followed in applying the Rio Treaty of Reciprocal Assistance had become well formalized.

The Investigating Committee, composed of the representatives of Argentina, Bolivia, Mexico, Panama, and the United States, together with military experts assigned by the governments of the countries represented on the committee, left Washington on May 3, arriving at Tegucigalpa, Honduras, the following day. Hurried conversations with the high officials of the two governments at their respective capitals resulted in a cease-fire agreement which went into effect on May 5. To help work out the technical and military aspects of troop withdrawal, the Investigating Committee, on May 6, set up a Committee of Military Advisers. Both governments agreed to plans for withdrawing troops and this became effective on May 10. The Investigating Committee, its task completed, returned to Washington, and at the meeting of May 16 it submitted its report to the Council with conclusions and recommendations.

The substance of the committee's report was that, owing to the complexities of the situation and in light of the facts observed, it had not been possible to determine responsibility for the aggression. The territory in which the hostile contacts had occurred had long been claimed by both countries and they had exercised control over various parts of it. The committee did not feel that it was competent to judge the legal facets of the controversy. It did, however, make certain recommendations.

On May 17 the delegations of Argentina, Bolivia, Mexico, Panama, and the United States presented a draft resolution based in large part on the Investigating Committee's recommendations, which had been approved by the Council. It called for the termination of the Investigating Committee and for the creation of "an *ad hoc* committee composed of five members, to collaborate with the governments of Honduras and Nicaragua in complying with the recommendations of the Council." This committee was charged with assuming all unfinished business of the Investigating Committee.[34]

The rest of the draft resolution, approved by the Council on May 24, included the following: to keep in effect the respective plans for troop withdrawal; to recommend to the parties that they endeavor to find, within thirty days, an acceptable procedure for the final solution of the conflict; and to remind both Honduras and Nicaragua that they are ratifying states of the American Treaty on Pacific Settlement, which pledges recourse at all times to pacific procedures.

On May 17, 1957, the Council appointed the *Ad Hoc* Committee, made up of the representatives of Argentina, Bolivia, Mexico, Panama, and the United States. The governments of Honduras and Nicaragua approved this committee's proposal to set up a joint military committee to ensure compliance with the cease-fire agreement and the plans for troop withdrawal. On June 28 the committee reported to the Council that both parties had consented to submit to the United Nations International Court of Justice their dispute concerning the validity of the arbitral award by the King of Spain in 1906. The formal agreement was signed at the Pan American Union on July 21, 1957. The decision of the court was to be final; there was to be no appeal, and it was to be carried out at once. If one of the parties should fail to comply, the other could call a meeting of the foreign ministers to adopt measures to enforce it. This was the first case involving a boundary in the Americas to be submitted to the World Court. Pending a settlement by the court, the two parties were requested to maintain the *status quo*. Meanwhile, the joint military committee was to continue to patrol the border and deal with any differences that might arise.[35] Thus ended the fifth successful application of the Rio treaty to an inter-American controversy. The members of the OAS were justifiably proud of the swift and effective manner in which a serious situation had been met. On November 18, 1960, the International Court of Justice rendered its judgment. It found that "the award made by the King of Spain on 23 December 1906 is valid and binding and that Nicaragua is under an obligation to give effect to it."[36]

Turmoil returns to the Caribbean, 1959. The last year of the twelve-

[34] Pan American Union, *Annual Report of the Secretary-General, 1956–1957* (Washington, 1957), 8–9.

[35] *Annals,* IX (1957), 268.

[36] International Court of Justice, *Reports, 1960,* 217.

year period under review presented a situation of turbulence in the Caribbean remarkably similar to that of the first years. Interventionism once more was rampant, and the basic issue was the same: democracy versus dictatorship. The success of Fidel Castro in overthrowing the Batista tyranny in Cuba was the catalyst of a series of events leading eventually to a Fifth Consultative Meeting of the Foreign Ministers at Santiago, Chile.

The victory of Castro spawned its imitators. There is no doubt that the Castro overthrow of the Batista dictatorship created a profound impression throughout the Caribbean and fired other rebels' hopes, whether democratically-inclined or not. There flocked to Havana sincere exiles from Haiti, the Dominican Republic, and Nicaragua, as well as freebooters and adventurers. Although they did not come by express invitation, it was nevertheless true that Cuba's new hero had voiced the necessity and inevitability of terminating dictatorships in Latin America. He was urging a crusade and was not overly circumspect in avoiding the involvement of his government with other governments. Nor was he reticent about expressing his contempt for the Organization of American States: "I do not have faith in the OAS. This organization does not resolve anything. It only has intervened in some small wars but has not lent any service to the peoples of America."[37]

Behind the Caribbean turbulence is the fact that all of Latin America today is in a state of revolution. It is not only a revolution of democratic aspirations but, more prominently, of rising hopes for attaining the better things of life. There seem to be two schools of thought concerning the problem of the remaining dictatorships. One group apparently supports conspiracy, subversion, and invasion. A second group, more moderate, seeks to support liberal independence forces within each country so that revolution may be native in origin. The first group, inspired by the success of the Castro revolution, mounted invasions with haphazard zeal.

The first of these invasions was the *opéra bouffe* Panama affair. On April 25 some 80 invaders, presumably from Cuba, landed in Panama and "occupied" Nombre de Dios, a town of 1,000 people twenty miles northeast of Colón and fifty miles north of Panama City. Reportedly, one of the band said on landing, "Fidel sent us."

The Panama government, with a thoroughly ineffectual National Guard, was thrown into a panic and immediately appealed to the Council of the OAS for support in "resisting foreign invasion." It charged that two or three more boatloads were being assembled in

[37] *Christian Science Monitor,* Feb. 21, 1959.

Cuba to increase "to about 400 the number of Cubans attempting to invade Panama." The Isthmian government also charged that Panamanian revolutionaries were hiring Cubans through a headquarters established in Havana.

In an emergency session on April 28 the Council unanimously voted, with Cuba joining, to apply the procedures of the Rio treaty to the situation. The Council constituted itself a Provisional Organ of Consultation and sent an Investigating Committee to Panama. Air and naval patrols, supplied by the United States, Colombia, Ecuador, Costa Rica, and Guatemala, were established to detect any approach of additional sea-borne contingents. Although none were detected, here was the first instance under the Rio treaty in which armed assistance was given the victim of aggression, in spite of the fact that the aggressor was not named.[38]

Why the invasion? One of the party said that they had come to Panama on being told that the country was being ruled by a dictatorship. Their leader, César Vega, a former Havana night-club owner with a reputation as a revolutionist, declared that the expedition had been launched with the idea of liberating an oppressed people and that he had hoped their landing would touch off an uprising. Said Vega, "We seriously thought that the present Panamanian government was not a popular one." While perhaps not the most popular, the De la Guardia government was not, according to Latin-American standards, a dictatorship. There evidently was a tie-in between this expedition and the adventures of Roberto Arias, exiled scion of a wealthy and politically powerful family in Panama. A few days earlier Arias had slipped ashore from a yacht, eluded troops for six days, and finally took refuge in the Brazilian Embassy in Panama City. President Adolfo de la Guardia accused Arias of being the mastermind behind the planned revolt.[39]

Fidel Castro denied vigorously that Cuba had any part in the attempted revolution in Panama. Greatly embarrassed, Cuba's government, in seeking to dissociate itself from the Panama landings, joined with the other American states in voting to help Panama. Also it announced that any violation of Cuba's proclaimed policy of nonintervention in the affairs of other countries would be brought before her military courts. Therefore, without hope of reinforcements, the bedraggled band of invaders, immobilized at Nombre de Dios, sur-

[38] New York Times, April 29, 1959.
[39] Christian Science Monitor, April 29, 1959; May 4, 1959.

rendered on May 1 to the Panamian government under the eyes of the Investigating Committee. On May 4 the patrol operations ended and calm prevailed. Once more prompt action by the OAS was instrumental in resolving a problem apparently trivial but nevertheless with a serious potential.

A month to the day after the calming of the Panamanian situation, the OAS had another "invasion" problem dumped in its lap. This time the aggrieved party was Nicaragua. On June 3, 1959, Nicaragua reported that its territory had been invaded by armed forces coming from another country with the purpose of overthrowing its government and that further invasions threatened. The Nicaraguan Ambassador to the OAS requested that the Rio treaty be invoked with the view of maintaining peace and security in the area. A special meeting of the Council was held on June 4 to consider the request.

On June 1 it had been reported that an invasion of Nicaragua was under way from Costa Rica by some 400 exiles, intellectuals, students, and refugee Army officers, who were entering Nicaragua by planes in several "air waves." The invasion coincided with a general strike called to protest the dictatorial rule of President Luís A. Somoza, who was carrying on the tradition of his assassinated father Anastasio. The leader of the air-borne invasion was an exiled Nicaraguan physician, considered a liberal. The Nicaraguan Ambassador told the Council that the invading planes were filled with rebels of various nationalities and that unless the Council acted, Nicaragua might attack or pursue Costa Rican ships or aircraft suspected of sending reinforcements to the invaders. Attention was called to the fact that only the day before the Costa Rican Congress had passed a resolution expressing solidarity with the Nicaraguan revolutionaries. The Ambassador urged the Council to take action to avert a "bloodbath" in Central America.

The Costa Rican representative to the Council emphasized his government's determination to halt any aid to the rebels. Also he alluded to the fact that the Costa Rican government had expressed its regret that aircraft of Costa Rica registry had been made available to the revolutionaries. He held, and was supported by the representatives of Cuba and Venezuela, that the Rio treaty was inapplicable to the situation, for since the revolutionaries were Nicaraguan, this was not a "foreign" invasion but an internal affair.

This contention was strongly rebutted by Ambassador John C. Dreier, the United States representative, who held that the nationality of the persons entering Nicaragua was not the determining factor. He said, "The fact that the invading force had come from abroad, had been armed abroad, and was being supported by airplane flights from abroad was sufficient to remove all doubt that action of the OAS was justified and was in fact called for under the Treaty of Rio de Janeiro."[40]

Although many of the members were reluctant to aid a dictatorship, Ambassador Dreier's argument that the principle of nonintervention was at stake carried the day. The vote, on June 4, which invoked the Treaty of Reciprocal Assistance, was seventeen in favor, two against. Cuba and Venezuela voted against, and Bolivia was absent. Nicaragua, as the party involved, could not vote. Eleven votes were necessary for approval. The Council, as the Provisional Organ of Consultation, appointed a Special Committee to gather additional information.[41]

The committee found that, in addition to the first two attacks on Nicaragua, at least three armed expeditions had been organized with a view to entering that country. It also had information of a force of men flown to Honduras to invade Nicaragua from its northern frontier. Even in August, near the time of the Santiago meeting of foreign ministers, there were two minor "invasions" of Nicaragua. The whole situation remained unsettled.[42]

At its meetings of July 2 and 6, the Council was informed that the Caribbean situation had deteriorated further. The powder keg of the Caribbean—the antagonism between Castro of Cuba and Trujillo of the Dominican Republic—began to threaten an explosion. The long-time hatred of Castro for Trujillo, because of Trujillo's support of Batista during the Castro rebellion, was now accentuated by Trujillo's granting asylum to the fallen Cuban dictator. The Dominican government, evidently taking note of OAS aid to Panama and Nicaragua, made an appeal to the Council for action under the Rio treaty. The Cuban and Venezuelan governments were accused of participating in the preparations for two recent "invasions" of the Dominican Republic. It was charged that 56 men from Cuba had landed at Constanza by plane on June 14. On June 20 an additional 140 men disembarked from two yachts on the north coast. The evident purpose was to start and promote civil war in the Dominican Republic. The Dominican representative also held that large contingents were at that moment in training in Cuba with the intention of initiating new invasions.

The representatives of Cuba and Venezuela, as would be expected, registered emphatic denials. Indeed, they made charges of threatened

[40] U.S. Dept. of State, *Bulletin*, XLI (July 6, 1959), 30–31.
[41] *Ibid.*
[42] *Ibid.*, XLI (July 27, 1959), 136; *Christian Science Monitor*, Aug. 15, 1959.

attack and subversive propaganda against their own governments by the Trujillo regime. When the Dominican representative saw that he was not going to receive adequate support from the other Latin-American republics, he withdrew his request for action under the Rio treaty. The situation had developed to the point where a Latin-American state, because of the nature of its government, was apparently not covered by the protective shield of the Rio treaty. This was an understandable, but unfortunate and dangerous, development. In the view of the United States government, a mutual assessment of the Caribbean situation, particularly the problems of democracy versus dictatorship, was needed.

The Santiago Meeting of Foreign Ministers. At the Council meeting of July 10, Ambassador Dreier proposed a meeting of the OAS foreign ministers. It was time, he said, to examine the Caribbean situation on a broad front without reference to any particular country. Basic principles of inter-American association, if left unsolved, would be jeopardized. First, if the principle of nonintervention was permitted to be violated in the present situation, it would be violated increasingly in the future. As a result the very foundation of the American security structure would crumble. Second, the principle of collective security set forth in the Rio treaty and the Charter of the OAS applies equally to all members and must at all times be supported and made effective if the inter-American relationship is to endure. Third, and finally, the principle of representative democracy, shared by the American republics in their protestations of solidarity, is a benefit that every people must win for itself. Revolutions against authoritarian rule do not necessarily result in perfect democracy. "It therefore seems to us," said Ambassador Dreier, "that democratic progress which all of us seek requires among other factors a strict compliance with those very principles of nonintervention and collective security to which I have referred."[43]

The governments of Brazil, Chile, and Peru joined with the United States in proposing a resolution calling for an early meeting of foreign ministers. On July 13 the Council voted unanimously to call the Fifth Meeting of Consultation of Ministers of Foreign Affairs, to convene at Santiago, Chile, on August 12, 1959.

At the risk of oversimplification we reduce the primary issue at Santiago to the following alternatives: whether the remaining Latin-American dictatorships—in the Dominican Republic, Paraguay, and Nicaragua—should be eliminated by some form of international ac-

[43] U.S. Dept. of State, *Bulletin,* XLI (July 27, 1959), 137–138.

tion, or whether dictatorships are shielded by the sacrosanct principle of nonintervention, despite the numerous inter-American commitments in support of human rights and representative democracy. Secretary of State Christian Herter, recently returned from Geneva, and now meeting in an inter-American conference for the first time, was apparently trapped by the dilemma of supporting the principle of nonintervention, and at the same time by this very act, seeming to block the elimination of dictators. In other words the problem was how to get to "the side of the angels" without crossing that sensitive line known as "intervention"; how to combat persistent charges that the United States supports dictatorships and neglects Latin-American democracies.

On his arrival in Santiago on August 11, Mr. Herter said, "Human dignity and national independence can only endure and flourish when our international relations are guided by a system of law and order." If this seemed to indicate that the Secretary was determined to stand foursquare on the principle of nonintervention, the indication was confirmed when he addressed the opening session of the meeting. He told his fellow delegates that nonintervention is the foundation stone of hemisphere relations and to weaken the principle in an effort to promote democracy would be self-defeating. The turbulence and tensions which result from such interventionist actions, he said, provide "just the opportunity that International Communists are always seeking."[44]

The delegates of Cuba and Venezuela, whose governments were engaged in a vendetta with Dominican President Trujillo, did not believe that the principle of nonintervention should block the way to the overthrow of dictators. They argued that, since the Charter of the OAS proclaims "the consolidation on this continent, within the framework of democratic institutions, of a system of individual liberty and social justice," the violation of this ideal by any dictatorship must be corrected by collective action. This is defense of the democratic principle.

Cuba's Foreign Minister Raúl Roa argued that those who insisted on strict nonintervention were merely trying to save Trujillo's skin. Roa's charge that the Dominican government was organizing a foreign legion of mercenaries to invade Cuba set off a wild exchange of insults and threats between the chief delegates of the two countries.

While the foreign ministers were in conference in Santiago—and

[44] *Christian Science Monitor,* Aug. 24, 1959; *Time,* Aug. 24, 1959; U.S. Dept. of State, *Bulletin,* XLI (Aug. 31, 1959), 299.

as if to underline the problem confronting them—there occurred two more "invasions" in the Caribbean area. Premier Castro charged that former Dictator Fulgencio Batista, aided and abetted by Trujillo, had launched an invasion effort from the Dominican Republic against Cuba. Haiti also reported the landing of some 30 rebels from Cuba. The Dominican Republic announced that it would come to the aid of Haiti if necessary. Inquiry into these charges was undertaken by the Inter-American Peace Committee.

The tensions of the Santiago meeting were sensationalized by the Latin-American press and exploited by the Communists, who played on the dilemma of the United States' desire not to use force. Parades and rallies were organized by the Reds and other Yankeephobes, screaming charges that United States imperialism was "dealing blows to the liberation movement in the rest of the Latin-American nations." From Havana came the report that Fidel Castro had branded the Santiago meeting as a farce and said that it was seeking to destroy the Cuban revolutionary government. The bearded hero was evidently serving notice that nonintervention did not apply to himself.

A potent majority of the twenty-one foreign ministers, agreeing with Secretary Herter that intervention, no matter what the motives for it, was loaded with perils, voted in favor of a strong reaffirmation of the principle of nonintervention. Between the choice of compromising the principle of nonintervention or tolerating dictatorships the latter was the lesser evil. The dangers of collective action against dictatorial regimes had been well stated by Alberto Lleras: "A group of democratic nations may destroy an anti-democratic government by coercion and intervention. But who is going to guarantee that a coalition of anti-democratic governments will not proceed in this identical form against a pure and democratic regime?"[45] Democracy cannot be imposed from without; the only possible cure for dictatorships must come from within. However, as Mr. Herter suggested, there is much that other states can do to help develop a favorable climate in states where representative democracy and respect for human rights are denied. He proposed the "establishment of an Organization of American States Commission to chart a course that the OAS could follow in evoking the maximum cooperation for the effective achievement of democratic principles." The Secretary of State, in agreement with the general view that economic underdevelopment was a basic cause of unrest, reaffirmed the determination of the United States to lend economic assistance to our Latin neighbors.

[45] *New York Times,* Aug. 24, 1959.

The results of the fifth meeting of the foreign ministers were incorporated in the Declaration of Santiago, issued on August 18. The declaration condemned dictators; reasserted the principle of nonintervention; approved democratic systems; stated that democracy cannot be forced on a country but must come as a natural growth from within; and delegated to the Inter-American Peace Committee watchdog supervision of Caribbean peace until it should report to the eleventh inter-American conference scheduled to meet at Quito, Ecuador, in February 1960.

The function of the Peace Committee was to investigate and report quickly on trouble in any area of the hemisphere. It could examine methods and procedures "to prevent whatever activities provoke cases of intervention or aggression." Further, it might examine "the relationship between violations of human rights or lack of exercise of representative democracy on the one hand, and political tensions affecting continental peace on the other."[46] The committee was given the power to investigate trouble on the spot and without the requirement that both the accuser and the accused must agree to the investigation. It could make investigations either at the request of a victim of aggression or on its own initiative. However, this function was not so radical as might appear, for the committee had to obtain consent of the country it wanted to investigate if it wished to make an on-the-spot check. In the event an aggressor refused consent to an inquiry, a meeting of the foreign ministers could be called to throw the floodlight of publicity on the refusal. Of course, the Peace Committee could make its investigation from the outside and its publicized report might be expected to focus public opinion on the trouble-maker.

Considering the difficulties of the problem it faced, the Santiago meeting acquitted itself quite well. Skeptics had predicted failure, given the road-block presented by the principle of nonintervention. However, although the principle was reaffirmed in strong terms, those who advocated strong measures against dictators found some solace in the vigorous Declaration of Santiago condemnation of undemocratic regimes:[47]

[46] For the texts of the Declaration of Santiago de Chile and the Resolution on the Inter-American Peace Committee, see U.S. Dept. of State, *Bulletin,* XLI (Sept. 7, 1959), 342–344. See also, Pan American Union, *Fifth Meeting of Consultation of Ministers of Foreign Affairs, Final Act* (Washington, 1960).

[47] Former Foreign Minister Eduardo Rodríquez Larreta of Uruguay has recently declared that the trend in Latin America is to endorse his original proposal for collective intervention in support of democratic principles.—"El derecho a la intervención colectiva," *Combate* (Costa Rica), II, No. 7 (July–Aug. 1959), 23–26.

It is advisable to announce in a general way a few principles and attributes of the democratic system in this hemisphere so as to permit national and international public opinion to gauge the degree to which political regimes and governments conform to that system, thus helping to eradicate forms of dictatorship, despotism, or tyranny without weakening respect for the right of poples freely to choose their own form of government.

The OAS condemns Trujillo. As has been noted, one of the functions assigned the Inter-American Peace Committee was to investigate cases of flagrant violation of human rights which affected continental peace. When the excesses of the Trujillo dictatorship in the Dominican Republic exceeded the norm of cynical disregard of human and civil liberties, a complaint was submitted on February 7, 1960, by the government of Venezuela to the OAS Council that denial of human rights in the Dominican Republic threatened the already precarious peace in the Caribbean. The Council referred the matter to the Peace Committee.

When the Peace Committee asked to be allowed to visit the Dominican Republic for an on-the-spot inquiry, it was refused permission by Trujillo. Nevertheless, the committee interviewed refugees, former Dominican officials, and others. The Venezuelan Ambassador to the OAS presented an impressive documentation of violations of human rights and also of continuous Dominican interferences in the affairs of the neighboring countries, particularly Venezuela, even to the extent of helping plots to overthrow the government of President Rómulo Betancourt.

On June 8 the Peace Committee made public a report which accused the Dominican Republic of "flagrant and widespread violations of human rights," including "the denial of free assembly and of free speech, arbitrary arrests, cruel and inhuman treatment of political prisoners, and the use of intimidation and terror as political weapons." In the view of the committee these violations aggravated tension in the Caribbean area. It advised that steps be taken by the Dominican Republic to remedy these conditions.

The Peace Committee's uncompromising indictment of the Trujillo regime, an action without precedent in the history of the OAS, was intended as a prelude to diplomatic isolation until such time as human rights should be restored in the island republic. Trujillo naturally protested this "intervention in the internal affairs of the Dominican Republic," but surprisingly the Cuban government joined in the attack on the report of the Peace Committee. No doubt this was because Cuba feared that intervention by the OAS in the Dominican Republic would open the door to intervention against herself.

Soon Dictator Trujillo was accused of an even more serious offense, that of personally plotting the nearly successful assassination attempt, on June 24, 1960, of Venezuela's President Betancourt. When it became plain that Trujillo was back of the murder plot, the OAS found the case persuasive enough to vote for a consultative meeting of the foreign ministers to meet at San José, Costa Rica, on August 16, 1960. Shortly before the meeting Trujillo manipulated a considerable revamping of the government to simulate the return of democracy to the island republic.

When it voted for a consultative meeting, the Council of the OAS appointed a committee to investigate the charges of aggression and intervention brought by Venezuela against the Dominican Republic. The findings of the investigating committee seemed to prove beyond much doubt that Trujillo had indeed engaged in grave acts against the sovereignty of Venezuela. Thus the San José meeting of foreign ministers, the sixth meeting of consultation, had to decide on a course of action against Trujillo. This was another application of the Rio treaty.

Most of the Latin-American delegations favored strong condemnation of the Dominican government and the imposing of sanctions so severe as to ensure the overthrow of the dictator and his regime. Of course, this would be multilateral intervention, but there seemed to be agreement that when one of the twenty-one American states itself violates the sacred nonintervention code—as the Dominican Republic had—then the OAS must radically intervene. But there was no disposition to sanction intervention for the protection of human rights so grievously violated by the Trujillo government.

The United States, on the other hand, wished to ensure that the Dominican Republic, after Trujillo, would be safe for democracy and human rights. Accordingly, Secretary Herter proposed that in lieu of imposing sanctions there be free elections under the supervision of an international commission "to establish such additional safeguards as would be necessary to assure observance of the principles of the Declaration of Santiago." It was Mr. Herter's belief that "the transition of a representative democracy can . . . best be achieved by resorting to orderly and peaceful processes."[48]

The United States proposal—branded as "soft on Trujillo"—was rejected by the meeting. Since it was clear that the Latins were determined to punish Trujillo, Mr. Herter decided to join them, hoping thereby to win their support in the forthcoming consultations on the Cuban problem.

[48] U.S. Dept. of State, *Bulletin,* XLIII (Sept. 5, 1960), 357.

On August 20, the sixth meeting, by a vote of nineteen—the Dominican Republic and Venezuela abstaining—adopted a resolution condemning the government of the Dominican Republic for acts of aggression and intervention against Venezuela. The resolution provided for two sanctions by all member states: the suspension of diplomatic relations with the Dominican Republic, and the immediate cessation of trade in arms and implements of war of every kind. The desirability of extending the suspension of trade was to be studied.[49]

The adoption of the San José resolution was a momentous decision, both by the Latins and by the United States. For the first time the Latin-American members of the OAS qualified absolute nonintervention; they apparently decided to be noninterventionist only toward those members who practice nonintervention. However, the principle of nonintervention would continue to shield dictators who confine their tyranny to their own subjects. The United States, on its part, hoping to convince the Good Neighbors that it disapproved as much of dictatorships of the right as of the left, supported the resolution even at the risk of creating chaos in the Dominican Republic.

Trujillo reacted violently to the OAS action. His charge that the United States had sold him out in return for Latin-American support against Castro was substantially correct. The Dominican radio vied with that of Castro's Cuba in the intensity of its vilification of the United States. On occasion Trujillo hinted at an accommodation with the Soviet Union.

Although the sanctions of suspension of diplomatic relations and arms embargo were imposed on the Dominican Republic, the overthrow of Trujillo was not accomplished, for the dictatorship was too well entrenched in the island republic. Certainly the assignment to the Dominican Republic of 322,000 tons of the canceled Cuban sugar quota did not contribute to the weakening of Trujillo. President Eisenhower's plea for Congressional authorization to withhold this extra sugar allotment was ignored. Thus the United States found itself in the embarrassing position of aiding a dictator whom it was committed to overthrow. In the end it was neither the United States nor the OAS but assassins' bullets that terminated one of Latin America's most ruthless tyrannies.

Conclusion. The dreary and repetitious recital of inter-American controversies in the Carribbean since the ratification of the Rio treaty points up a number of significant observations. First, the record seems to prove that whenever the Inter-American Treaty of Reciprocal As-

[49] *Ibid.,* 358.

sistance was invoked and applied to situations threatening to the peace, the pacific procedures of the OAS have been able to resolve the problems. Our conclusion, therefore, is that the incidents did not reveal any serious deficiencies of the Rio treaty unless it be that the organs of consultation cannot be convoked and the on-the-spot inquiry cannot take place without the consent of the parties to the dispute. To circumvent this obstacle, which incidentally was raised only once—by Trujillo—in any of the Caribbean controversies, the Santiago meeting gave the Inter-American Peace Committee power to initiate inquiries independently.

Second, it would be a serious mistake to conclude that, because the peace procedures were successfully applied to controversies between little states of the Caribbean area, they would be equally effective in conflicts between larger and stronger states of Latin America. However, it is a fair assumption that because of the precedents established and the general acceptance of collective responsibility for hemisphere peace and security, even the largest states would be under strong constraint to abide by the established procedures.

Third, it is a significant fact that, without Trujillo, most of the controversies which have been discussed in the preceding pages probably would not have taken place, *provided*, however, that an earlier passing of Trujillo had not been followed by political chaos and the eventual establishment of another form of dictatorship—perhaps a Communist-oriented government like that of Cuba. The uneasy tenure of the Trujillo succession in the Dominican Republic today following the assassination of the old Dictator merely delays the inevitable showdown. Thus the big question is: after Trujillo, the Somoza dynasty, Stroessner, and their ilk, what? It cannot be taken for granted that, as idealistic revolutionaries naïvely imagine, democracy will blossom from the ruins of fallen dictatorships. The political evolution of Latin America proves the contrary. Has Fidel Castro forgotten that Sergeant Fulgencio Batista himself emerged in Cuba on the crest of an antidictatorship tidal wave?

Finally, in the last years of the Eisenhower Administration, the State Department showed signs of abandoning the trend-defying and essentially non-American policy of supporting dictators. Concurring in declarations adopted by the Santiago and San José meetings of foreign ministers, this government began to employ the tactic advocated by Vice-President Nixon, Dr. Milton Eisenhower, and others: generous support of democracies and cold formality for dictators. While desiring to avoid specific condemnation or boycott of any particular country, the United States made it clear by forthright statement, action, and agreement that it had abandoned support of Latin-American dictators.

It would be a mistake to regard this reversal of policy as being motivated exclusively by an expectation of the early triumph of Latin-American democracy. No one, least of all the policy-makers of the State Department, entertains the delusion that in the Caribbean republics, democracy is just around the corner. Since sentimentality has no place in the planning of national security, the State Department undoubtedly is reckoning on the very uncertain advent of democracy in the area and is prepared to make further "tactical changes of policy," as political exigencies require.

As an addendum to the foregoing it can be stated with considerable assurance that international Communism had very little to do with the Caribbean turmoil discussed above. It cannot be doubted that in some instance the Communists added their bit to roiling the waters, but generally the issues and the participants were unaffected by Red influences. This is not true, however, of continental-security issues raised by international Communism. How the OAS has measured up to this mounting threat represents a recent and contemporary development of inter-American security cooperation. It is the subject of the following chapter.

XIV The OAS and International Communism

> We oppose Communism as we have opposed all dictatorships whether they be with or against the United States.
>
> JOSÉ FIGUERES, 1959

HOWEVER IMPORTANT is the inter-American regional arrangement for the preservation of peace among the member republics themselves, it is of even greater importance, at least in the view of the United States, as a defensive shield against overseas aggression. Since, shortly after the end of World War II, it became increasingly clear that overseas attack would probably come from but one source, that is, Soviet Russia, the inter-American security structure has been perfected and strengthened with this potential aggressor in view. More than overt military aggression must be reckoned with, however, for, by insidious and subversive undermining American governments can be toppled by the agents of international Communism without the firing of a shot. How the OAS and its member nations have reacted to the deadly threat of aggressive, imperialistic Soviet Communism will now be examined, for it may weigh heavily in the eventual outcome of the ideological conflict.

Communism in Latin America. It is hardly necessary for our present purposes to present a lengthy, documented discussion of Communist activities in Latin America. As background for a discussion of cooperative inter-American reaction to the threat of international Communism, only a few selected facts, observations, and conclusions are necessary.[1]

Apparently most of Latin America is fertile soil for the propagation

[1] For a detailed discussion, see Robert J. Alexander, *Communism in Latin America* (New Brunswick, N.J., 1957); see also Frank R. Brandenburg, "Communism and Security in Latin America," *Yale Review,* XLVI (Spring, 1957), 413–424.

of Communism. Exploitation of the masses has been commonplace, whether by foreign capital or native landowners and politicians. In contrast to the stark reality of ignorance, poverty, and degradation in make-believe democracies, the glittering promises of Communism are most persuasive. Since Latin America is in the throes of a great political, social, and economic revolution, the Latins, like the inhabitants of other backward areas throughout the world, are impatient for change, which they feel could hardly leave them any worse off, whatever the outcome.

Such success as the Communists have had in Latin America since World War II has been due largely to their ability to exploit this revolutionary trend. Particularly it has served their purposes well to stimulate inherent nationalistic resentments against foreign capital, resulting in rabid anti-imperialism and hostility toward the United States. The attempt of the Communists to use the rising tide of socio-economic revolution as a means of bringing themselves to power has not succeeded, but they are successful in heightening internal dissensions, setting class against class, and encouraging hatred for the United States.

In 1960 it was estimated that hard-core Communist Party membership in Latin America did not exceed 250,000. The distribution is very uneven among the several countries varying from a few dozen Communists in some of the Central American republics to around 50,000 to 80,000 in Argentina and Brazil, respectively. Cuba and Mexico rate between 25,000 and 50,000, respectively. As is well recognized, mere numbers do not necessarily indicate their influence. In 1960 the Communist Party was legal in nine Latin-American republics: Argentina, Bolivia, Chile, Colombia, Cuba, Ecuador, Mexico, Uruguay, and Venezuela. Despite legal prohibitions elsewhere, the Communists participate in elections, sometimes by open declarations, sometimes by identifying themselves with popular groups.[2] The maintenance of diplomatic relations with the U.S.S.R. has been an on-and-off affair for several of the countries. The not infrequent rupture or straining of official relations usually results from the subversive activities of Soviet agents enjoying diplomatic immunity. In 1960 only Argentina, Cuba, Mexico, and Uruguay exchanged diplomatic representatives with the Soviet Union. In addition to these four countries, Bolivia, Brazil, and

[2] Frank R. Brandenburg, "Political Parties and Elections," in Harold E. Davis (ed.), *Government and Politics in Latin America* (New York, 1958), 198–199. In April 1960, the Dominican Republic lifted the ban on the Communist Party.

Colombia maintained official relations with some of the Soviet satellites. Cuba was the first and only American state to recognize Communist China.

A fact which must be underlined is that the Latin-American Communists are not their own masters but must follow the twisting Moscow line. A well-informed scholar writes, "The Latin American Communists are not only totalitarians, they are totalitarians whose first
loyalty is to the Soviet Union, whose first duty is to serve the Soviet
Union."[3] They are part of the international Communist movement and
receive aid and direction from it. This explains how many of the Latin-
American Communist groups, though small in membership and of
limited resources, have substantial amounts to spend on propaganda
and election campaigns. The money probably comes from the
Comintern.

Latin-American Communists also play the same sinister role as do
those elsewere. This role involves both aspects of international Communism: subscribing to the ideology of the party line, and subversive
intervention in the internal affairs of other peoples and states. The
Latin Communists change their tactics with the changing international
situation, but their strategy is always in line with the Comintern
strategy of world domination.[4]

Latin-American reaction to the wiles and intrigues of Communism
has been greatly misunderstood and depreciated in the United States.
All too frequently the Latin is regarded as the willing and gullible
buyer of Communist propaganda. Those who subscribe to this view
are woefully uninformed, not only of the intensive campaigns the
Communists have been waging for several years but, more important,
how effectively the Latin-American governments have struck back.
Most of the countries, as has been noted, have outlawed the Communist Party and have adopted drastic legislation against all anti-
democratic elements who spread foreign ideologies aimed at overthrowing governments.

Latin-American awareness of the Communist threat can also be
found in their consistent opposition in the United Nations to the
Soviet Union. In questions relating to the "cold war" and to the
conflict between Soviet imperialism and the free world, the Latin-

[3] Alexander, 44.
[4] Communist tactics are well described by a former Peruvian Communist,
Eudocio Ravines, *The Yenan Way* (New York, 1951). See also Víctor Alba,
La América Latina y los congresos del partido comunista ruso (San José, Costa
Rica, 1959).

American republics have usually taken positions consistent with their democratic ideology and anti-communistic way of life. The United States has had no greater asset than the normally faithful support of the great majority of these states. Until recently the balance of power in the General Assembly was such that this support was usually sufficient to carry the day on issues related to the cold war. Their support made possible the adoption of the key resolution on Korea.[5] The frequent allegations by the Soviet that the Latin-Americans "subserviently acquiesced" in the wishes of the United States have been fiercely challenged by the Latins as misrepresenting their true feelings.

The Americas react to the threat. Was the Rio de Janeiro Treaty of Reciprocal Assistance aimed at the Soviet Union? The Soviet Union was not regarded as a threat when this treaty was originally proposed at the Mexico City conference of 1945. It was agreed that, immediately after a peace treaty was concluded, the signatory states of the Act of Chapultepec should conclude a treaty giving permanent force and validity to the principles stated in the act. There is no evidence that fear of the U.S.S.R. was a factor responsible for the Act of Chapultepec itself. The principal reason for the resolution on "reciprocal assistance and American solidarity," better known as the Act of Chapultepec, was the desire to strengthen the inter-American security system before the United Nations Conference convened at San Francisco.

The first anti-Russian reaction among the Latin Americans was manifested at San Francisco where, quite independently of the regional problem, Mr. Molotov proceeded deliberately, and gratuitously, to offend the twenty states by classifying them arbitrarily as satellites of the United States. In a very short time it became all too apparent that the crushing of the Nazis and Fascists had not liberated mankind from totalitarian darkness; the menacing clouds of Soviet Communism began to overshadow the free world. The magnitude of their postwar victories and their ultimate goal of world domination was clear for all to see. Thus, the Pan American treaty of reciprocal assistance to be negotiated, which did not have originally a specific anti-Soviet objective, eventually became the answer of the Americas to the Communist threat.

As has been pointed out in another connection in a preceding chapter, the convening of the conference to negotiate the treaty was postponed several times because of the strained relations between the

[5] John A. Houston, *Latin America in the United Nations* (New York, 1956), 105, 290.

United States and Argentina. Eventually the United States, concerned over the critical status of the cold war and realizing the necessity for an effective pact of mutual assistance to supply the gap left by the Act of Chapultepec, made its peace with Argentina and agreed to the meeting of a conference at Rio de Janeiro in August 1947.

At Rio, President Truman referred to the common danger and the need for cooperation in solving it. He said:

The postwar era has brought us bitter disappointment and deep concern. ... We find that a number of nations are still subjected to a type of foreign domination which we fought to overcome . . . I need not tell you how important it is to our success that we have your understanding, support, and counsel.[6]

Neither President Truman nor others who were in agreement with him mentioned the Soviet Union by name. It was not necessary, for the problem at hand was ostensibly (and in this all agreed) to negotiate a security agreement against aggression from any source. Some Latins, however, saw the pact not only as an undertaking against Russia but as an unfortunate subserving of themselves to the United States. For example, said a critic in presenting a "South American View":

The policy of the United States is no longer Pan American but rather ecumenical, and the ideological struggle which Yankee capitalism is now undertaking against Russia may possibly compromise us in the future. . . . We Latin Americans do not want to let ourselves be docily led to such a position that we cannot avoid being burned in the coals of a future conflagration. We demand our right to peace, to prosper, and to grow.[7]

Several months before the Bogotá ninth conference of March 1948, Ellis O. Briggs, a high official of the Department of State, speaking of Soviet ideology, said with uncanny prescience, "That belief [that man exists for the benefit of the state] is being challenged today, and the echoes of the challenge will be heard at the Bogotá Conference."[8] At the opening session of the conference, and before the Bogotá riots occurred,[9] Secretary of State Marshall referred to "the determined and open opposition of the Soviet Union to world recovery and peace," and emphasized the need for the United States to understand and

[6] U.S. Dept. of State, *Bulletin,* XVII (Sept. 14, 1947), 498, 500.

[7] Mariano Picón-Salas, "Imperialismo y buena vecindad," *Cuadernos Americanos,* XXXV (Sept.–Oct. 1947), 68.

[8] U.S. Dept. of State, *Bulletin,* XVI (April 27, 1947), 769.

[9] See p. 301.

cooperate with the other nations of the Americas in meeting the new totalitarian threat.[10] Also before the uprising, some of the Latin-American delegations wanted a collective condemnation of international Communism, but others expressed the fear that a measure of that nature would indirectly make the Bogotá conference seem to be political in character. The tragic events of April 9, however, and the alleged Communist involvement in the riots, dissolved all opposition, and the result was unanimous approval of a resounding anti-Communist hemisphere resolution.

This resolution, entitled "The Preservation and Defense of Democracy in America,"[11] declared that "by its anti-democratic nature and its interventionist tendency, the political activity of international Communism or any other totalitarian doctrine is incompatible with the concept of American freedom." It condemned the action of international Communism in suppressing political and civil rights and liberties and urged measures to keep its agents from tampering with the true will of the peoples of America. It was suggested that the respective governments exchange information concerning Communist activities and measures for controlling them. The Bogotá conference was significant for a number of things, but certainly one of the most important was the acute awareness of the presence of Communist danger and the need of collective defense. The Korean situation soon came as a test.

Korea and the Washington Meeting. When the Korean War broke out, the Latin Americans lined up behind the United States. In the Security Council of the United Nations, the two Latin-American members—Cuba and Ecuador—supported the resolution of June 25, 1950, which called for the withdrawal of the North Korean forces to the thirty-eighth parallel. Failure of the Reds to comply led to a second resolution, introduced on June 27 by the United States, which recommended that "members of the United Nations furnish such assistance to the Republic of Korea as may be necessary to repel armed attack and to restore international peace and security in the area." Since Yugoslavia voted against this crucial resolution, and both India and Egypt abstained, the votes of Cuba and Ecuador were indispensable to achieve the necessary seven-member majority. In view of the significant de-

[10] U.S. Dept. of State, *Bulletin*, XVIII (April 11, 1948), 470.

[11] The defense of democracy was a topic on the agenda, a carry-over from the Mexico City conference, but it was aimed only at native dictatorships. It was altered to include the condemnation of international Communism.—Pan American Union, *Annals* of the OAS, I (1949), 70.

cision taken by the Security Council, the Council of the OAS met in a special session on June 28 and adopted a resolution declaring its firm adherence to the decisions of the competent organs of the United Nations and solemnly reaffirmed the pledges of continental solidarity.[12]

When the Soviet representative returned to the Security Council and used the veto to block any further UN action regarding Korea, the two Latin-American representatives were scathing in their denunciation of Soviet duplicity and dictatorial spirit. Since the veto checked further action by the Security Council, the problems of Korea were shifted to the General Assembly, which convened in September 1950. In the debates in that body the Latin-American delegations usually followed the United States' lead. Following the intervention of the Chinese Communist forces in Korea in November 1950, when the United States proposed a resolution which found Communist China guilty of aggression and called on the Peking government to withdraw its troops from Korea, there was absolutely no Latin-American dissent. Later, when in May 1951 the United States introduced a resolution recommending that all United Nations members apply an embargo on shipments of strategic materials to China, again the Latin-American delegations were in hearty agreement.[13]

Were these actions of the representatives of the American republics in the United Nations born solely of a sense of individual responsibility as members of the world organization? Or were they also induced by a feeling of continental solidarity and mutual interest with one of their own members? Clearly the OAS resolution of June 28, 1950, had already given an affirmative answer to both questions, for it not only declared adherence to United Nations obligations but also reaffirmed the pledges of continental solidarity.

To what extent did the Latin-American states, all pledged to the United Nations Charter, immediately respond to UN appeals for military support in Korea? According to an official UN listing, up to November 18, 1950, Latin America offered the following for the war in Korea: *Argentina,* canned and frozen meat (under negotiation); *Bolivia,* 30 officers (acceptance deferred); *Brazil,* $2,720,000 (acceptance deferred); *Chile,* strategic materials (no specific offer received); *Colombia,* general economic assistance (no specific order received) and a frigate (accepted); *Costa Rica,* sea and air bases (accepted) and

[12] *La Prensa* (New York), June 3, 1950; *Annals,* II (1950), 222.
[13] Houston, 120–128.

volunteers (acceptance deferred); *Cuba,* 2,000 tons of sugar (accepted) and 10,000 gallons of alcohol and human plasma (pending); *Ecuador,* medical substances (no specific order received) and 220,000 pounds of rice (accepted); *El Salvador,* volunteers (deferred) and economic assistance (no specific offer received); *Mexico,* $348,000 worth of beans, chickpeas, and so forth (accepted); *Nicaragua,* foodstuffs and raw materials (no specific offer); *Panama,* "contingent" volunteers, training bases, use of merchant marine, free use of highways (all under negotiation); *Paraguay,* $10,000 in medical supplies (under negotiation); *Uruguay,* $2 million (accepted but not yet deposited) and 70,000 blankets (accepted); *Venezuela,* $100,000 in medical supplies (accepted).[14]

The Colombian frigate *Almirante Padilla,* which joined Task Force 95 in Korean waters, was Latin America's first armed contribution to the United Nations war against the Communist aggressor. In May 1951 a Colombian infantry battalion of 1,080 men left for Korea, with the Colombian government paying all the expenses. Several of the countries made offers of small contingents but were discouraged by the stock United States reply (determined by the Pentagon) that the United States would welcome help provided it be in contingents of not less than 1,000 each, and with the country concerned providing the shipping and sustenance for its forces in the field for sixty days.[15] By a high-pressure campaign in press, radio, and public meetings, Cuban Communists defeated the island's plan to send a battalion to Korea. "No cannon fodder for Yanqui imperialists!" was the cry. A newspaper poll showed 70.2 per cent of the people of Cuba opposed to contributing troops. This was typical of the popular attitude throughout Latin America. The opposition was stronger in Mexico, and even Brazil—the only other Latin-American nation in World War II with troops abroad—indicated that she would render aid consistent with her resources but would not send troops.[16]

On December 20, 1950, the United States presented to the Council of the OAS a request that a Meeting of Consultation of Ministers of Foreign Affairs be held "to consider problems of an urgent nature and of common interest to the American States." Since the aggressive policy of international Communism had brought about an emergency situation in which the entire free world was threatened, the United States declared its desire "to consult its fellow members in the Organization

[14] *New York Times,* Nov. 19, 1950.
[15] Washington *Post,* Sept. 2, 1950.
[16] Washington *Star,* Aug. 6, 1950.

of American States with respect to the world situation which we all face and on the coordination of the common effort required to meet it." Accordingly on January 3, 1951, the Council voted to convoke the Fourth Meeting of Consultation of Ministers of Foreign Affairs, and designated March 26, 1951, as the opening date. Among the subjects included on the agenda for the meeting in Washington, as approved by the Council, were political and military cooperation for the defense of the Americas; cooperation to strengthen the internal security of the American republics; and emergency economic cooperation.[17]

All the governments of the American republics were represented at the fourth meeting, held in Washington from March 26 to April 7, 1951. This, the first such meeting following the adoption of the Charter of the OAS in 1948, resulted in the adoption of thirty-nine resolutions,[18] briefly summarized in the following paragraphs.

The most important actions were taken under Topic I, "Political and Military Cooperation." First was the resolution known as the "Declaration of Washington," which announced the firm determination of the American republics to remain steadfastly united in the existing emergency, or in the face of any aggression or threat against any one of them. They reaffirmed their faith in the principles set forth in the Charter of the Organization of American States and other inter-American agreements, and declared their conviction that strengthening the action of the United Nations is the most effective way to maintain the peace, security, and well-being of the peoples of the world under the rule of law, justice, and international cooperation. The Declaration of Washington was a pledge of unity against international Communism. Not only did it reaffirm continental solidarity but it registered firm support of UN decisions in the Korean crisis.

A second resolution, entitled "Preparation for the Defense of the American Republics and Support of the Action of the United Nations," declared the necessity for positive support by the American republics in achieving the collective defense of the continent through the OAS, and for cooperation within the UN to prevent and suppress aggression in other parts of the world. It recommended that each of the American republics examine its resources and determine what it could contribute

[17] Pan American Union, *Proceedings* of the Fourth Meeting of Consultation of the Ministers of Foreign Affairs (Washington, 1951), 2–3, cited hereinafter as *Proceedings*. As a demonstration of her support of the meeting and its purpose, Argentina had proposed Buenos Aires as the place of meeting.—*New York Times*, Dec. 21, 1950.

[18] For the discussions and actions of the fourth meeting, see *Proceedings*.

to the defense of the continent and to the United Nations' collective-security efforts. The republics were particularly urged to give attention to developing and maintaining armed units that could be made promptly available both for continental defense and for service as United Nations units.

The only controversy during the meeting arose in connection with the subject of the second resolution. While there was no disagreement concerning the necessity for perfecting the defenses of the Americas, grave doubts were expressed that it was a proper function of a regional agency to concern itself with organizing support for UN action in another part of the world. It was a question of whether such action should be undertaken only in the United Nations when the aggression does not directly affect the regional system, or whether some action should also be taken within that system in support of the United Nations. Argentine Foreign Minister Hipólito J. Paz, who had raised the question, said that the draft resolution treated of "a matter solely within the province of the United Nations" and that what they were proposing had already been accomplished by the UN resolution entitled "Uniting for Peace." Despite his disagreement on the subject of OAS jurisdiction and competence, the Argentine minister declared his intention to vote for the draft resolution "for the sake and the benefit of inter-American solidarity."[19]

The view of those who saw no incompatibility of jurisdictions raised by the resolution, was well stated by Foreign Minister Neftalé Ponce of Ecuador: "It is our opinion that on as serious a point as the maintenance of peace there must be collaboration between the part and the whole, between the region and the world."[20] The debate led to a unanimous conclusion, described by Dr. Alberto Lleras as

the most categorical joint declaration ever made in time of peace by the American nations, whose strongest bond has been the principle of abolishing the use of force in international relations . . . If the other American nations were not thoroughly convinced that the United States will not go to war without a provocation impossible to avoid or ignore, that document would not have been signed. . . . Never have the Latin American countries given the United States a greater vote of confidence.[21]

Resolution III, entitled "Inter-American Military Cooperation," set forth positive measures to be undertaken by the American republics. It recommended that, in conformance with the Rio Treaty of Reciprocal

[19] *Ibid.*, 190–192.   [20] *Ibid.*, 193.
[21] *Américas*, III (May 1951), 30–31.

Assistance, the American republics orient their military preparations in such a way as to give increased emphasis to the principle of collective defense. This called for maintaining armed forces that could be promptly available for the defense of the continent, and for cooperation among the American republics in military matters. The Inter-American Defense Board was charged with preparing military plans for common defense, to be submitted to the governments for their consideration and decision. As we have already noted, the Defense Board's planning has been basic for the military security of the continent. Under Topic II, "Strengthening of Internal Security," a resolution bearing the same title emphasized the need for each country to examine its respective laws and regulations to assure that subversive activities of Communist agents be adequately prevented and punished. The Pan American Union was requested to make technical studies to facilitate the execution of this resolution.[22]

The third topic of the program, "Emergency Economic Cooperation," brought forth the majority of the resolutions adopted by the Washington meeting. This was in evidence of the considerable concern of the Latin-American governments with the economic factor in inter-American security cooperation (discussed in a preceding chapter). After President Truman, in the opening address to the meeting, had urged the Latin-American nations to "establish the principle of sharing our burdens fairly," the Brazilian Foreign Minister, in his formal reply, declared that while all were ready to bear their part of the sacrifices, any repetition of the economic experiences of World War II would ruin them. He urged that a formula be worked out for mutual economic cooperation which would last beyond the emergency and would provide for future reconstruction. He added, "By stimulation of industrial development through technical and financial assistance, the standards of living of the inhabitants of the various parts of the Western Hemisphere could be elevated, creating an atmosphere favorable for work and for the welfare of all."[23]

Thus the tone was set for economic discussions which went far beyond what the United States had contemplated. Seventeen resolutions

---

[22] In accordance with this assignment, the Department of International Law of the Pan American Union concluded in 1953 a detailed *Report* covering the following subjects: (1) Definition, Prevention, and Punishment of Sabotage and Espionage; (2) General Measures for the Protection of Human Rights and American Democratic Institutions; and (3) Measures to Prevent the Abuse of Freedom of Transit within the Hemisphere.

[23] *Proceedings*, 131, 136.

of an economic character were approved by the foreign ministers. There were broad policy declarations, as well as specific recommendations, on the production and distribution of products in short supply and on measures to facilitate carrying out programs of economic development. To the Inter-American Economic and Social Council was entrusted the further study of proposing solutions for continuing economic problems and for formulating specific recommendations to be sent to the respective governments. The United States, through Assistant Secretary of State for Economic Affairs Willard L. Thorp, recognized that the economic development of the underdeveloped regions of the free world "cannot be made a casualty of the defense program," and pledged various kinds of economic assistance "subject to necessary limitations and priorities."[24]

In evaluating the acts of the Washington consultative meeting, it should be recalled that the United States, in asking for the meeting in view of the emergency situation created by the aggressive policies of international Communism, wished "to consult its fellow members in the Organization of American States with respect to the world situation which we all face and on the coordination of the common effort required to meet it." Did the resolutions of the Washington meeting measure up to this objective? Unquestionably yes, for, short of formal pledges of military cooperation, about as much was accomplished as could be expected. In addition to the recommendations for military, political, and economic preparations to oppose Communist imperialistic aggression, the principal contribution of the meeting was the demonstration of moral solidarity among the American nations on the ideological issue.

There were, of course, some dissenting voices, particularly among Latin-American intellectuals. Luis Cardoza y Aragón, writing in *Cuadernos Americanos* (Mexico), regarded the Washington meeting as a step toward war, not peace. He said, "Our countries were put on the road to destruction and death. Our republics have been put at the service of imperialism." Jesús Silva Herzog, an outstanding Mexican intellectual and liberal, declared that the meeting was of very doubtful benefit to Latin America. There will be armies and armaments, he said, to oppress more tyranically. The poor and the hungry will go to fight in far off lands for things they never have enjoyed "in defense of the American way of life." Not untypical of the view of many more Latin-American "liberals-intellectuals," Sr. Silva Herzog concludes,

---

[24] U.S. Dept. of State, *Bulletin*, XXIV (April 30, 1951), 697.

"The Soviet Union is not, nor can it be, the ideal of those who defend and love liberty of thought, belief, and work; but neither can it be the United States . . . which is becoming (with respect to internal and external political methods) more like the Soviet Union." The fact that "universities of North America subject their professors to humiliating questionnaires and oblige them to sign degrading declarations" puts the United States in the same class with Communist tyrannies.[25] Narciso Bassols charged that Latin America had been beguiled by Washington to accompany it on its bellicose adventures headed for world conquest. The acts of the Washington meeting supported the United States policy of "continental militarization."[26] To Latin-American liberals, wrote J. Álvarez del Vayo, the meeting was a very serious threat; in fact, the proposed security front was "an act of homicide."[27]

It is the opinion of the writer, however, that more typical of majority Latin-American opinion were the views of Nemesio García Naranjo, which appeared in *Hoy* (Mexico) on March 31, 1951:

Experience tells us that this is not the time to oppose the United States. . . . The most rudimentary instincts of self-preservation advise us not to rebel at this meeting when the Colossus of the North confronts one of the greatest crises of its history. Furthermore, let us not forget that at this critical time the United States is right and girds itself with the standard of western culture.[28]

Communist threat in Guatemala. Although Communism was introduced into Guatemala shortly after World War I, General Jorge Ubico, the long-time dictator, was able to put an end to their activities by 1935. No effort to restore the Communist Party of Guatemala was successful until after the overthrow of Ubico in 1944. During the presidency of Juan José Arévalo (1945–51) the Communists moved into Guatemala, for the new liberal regime, professing its democratic ideals, opened the doors wide—too wide—to the enemies of democracy. For the next ten years the Communists, though small in numbers, were able to play on the political ignorance of the liberals and capitalize on the unrest, the hopes, and the social changes wrought by "the revolution."[29]

[25] "La Reunión de Cancilleres," *Cuadernos Americanos*, LVII (May–June, 1951), 55–84.
[26] "Veinte Ratones y un Gato o La Conferencia de Washington," *Revista de Guatemala*, II (July, Aug., Sept. 1951), 5–18.
[27] "Regimenting the Americas," *The Nation* (April 7, 1951), 315–317.
[28] "Los aplausos de la galería," *Hoy*, March 31, 1951, pp. 14–15.
[29] For Communism in Guatemala, see Alexander, *Communism in Latin*

The 1944 revolution provided the Communists with a unique opportunity which they cleverly exploited, for, though they contributed little or nothing to the socio-economic upheaval, they were able to identify the revolution almost completely with themselves. This was because they entered wholeheartedly, apparently, into the support of the revolutionary program, which included social legislation, agrarian reform, economic development, the encouragement of labor and peasant movements, and the integration of the Indian into the general life of the nation. And since the revolution was strongly nationalistic, it was most compatible with the objectives of international Communism to encourage opposition to foreign capital—i.e., the United Fruit Company and Yankee imperialism. Thus, since the Communists were the champions of Guatemalan nationalism and socio-economic betterment of the masses, and since they carefully concealed ulterior motives, it can be understood why anti-Communists came to be regarded as enemies of the revolution.

Although theoretically under legal ban, the Communists made considerable headway during the Arévalo Administration in gaining control over organized labor and becoming entrenched in the government. The President, though aware of what was taking place, was apparently more interested in avoiding trouble than in having a showdown with the Reds. Perhaps Arévalo was so dependent on the masses that he could not have challenged the Communist leaders even had he wished. It was not until 1952 that the Communist Party of Guatemala was registered as a legal political organization. By that time the Communists had achieved great influence both in labor and governmental circles. During the administration of President Jacobo Arbenz (1951–54) the Communists made such rapid gains in influence as to arouse the most serious apprehension of the United States and other members of the hemisphere community. Since it was charged in June 1954 that the government of Guatemala had fallen into the control of the international Communist movement, it will be well to indicate here how

America, Chap. XVI; Daniel James, *Red Design for the Americas: Guatemalan Prelude* (New York, 1954); Ronald M. Schneider, *Communism in Guatemala, 1944–1954* (New York, 1959). Schneider's study is based on Communist documents confiscated after the fall of the Arbenz regime. Publications of the State Department on the subject include: *A Case History of Communist Penetration: Guatemala,* Dept. of State Publication 6465, Inter-American Ser., No. 52 (1957); *Intervention of International Communism in Guatemala,* Dept. of State Publication 5556, Inter-American Ser., No. 48 (1954); *Penetration of the Political Institutions of Guatemala by the International Communist Movement* (Washington, 1954).

and with what success the Reds had infiltrated the Guatemalan government.

The control of labor, the key to Communist success, came first. Then followed infiltration of, and influence over, the revolutionary parties. The Reds had the greatest voice in shaping, at the end of 1952, the National Democratic Front (FDN), composed of the Communists, the three other leftist government parties, the labor and peasant confederations, and presided over by the President himself. This body, which was dominated by the Communists, supplanted the Cabinet and became the highest political and decision-making authority. According to a recent authoritative work on Communism in Guatemala, "it is no wonder that the Communists were able to exert an influence over the national and international policies of Guatemala far out of proportion to their numbers."[30]

There were only a few thousand Communists in Guatemala, but their tactic was to capture key posts and dictate official policy. The principal government agencies in agriculture, social security, propaganda and public information, education, and labor were in the direct hands of the Communist Party. The labor organizations of the country were entirely dominated by the Communist-controlled unions affiliated with the Communist labor federation for Latin America, the CTAL. Thus, in sum, they ran the labor unions, wrote the government's propaganda for the press and radio, administered the government's hospitals and social-security system, supervised teacher training and textbook preparation, sponsored and then directed the application of the agrarian-reform law, and finally, as police officials, under Communist direction, terrorized the anti-Communists.[31]

The spectacular success of international Communism in establishing its ascendancy over the Guatemalan government was made possible by the indulgent attitude of President Jacobo Arbenz. Whether Arbenz was a Communist or not made little difference, for he was unflagging in his support and loyalty to his Communist friends. Because they had worked hardest in his behalf, both in his electoral campaign and for his administrative program, Arbenz came to look upon the Red leaders as his most reliable adherents. Later, in exile in Prague, the former President said, "Through their activities the Partido Guatemalteco de Trabajadores [the Communist Party] was always distinguished by the intransigent defense of every action of the Government

[30] Schneider, 219.
[31] John E. Peurifoy, "The Communist Conspiracy in Guatemala," U.S. Dept. of State, *Bulletin*, XXXI (Nov. 8, 1954), 692.

which was in benefit of the working classes." Little wonder, then, that President Arbenz turned over to them the implementation of major social and economic programs and followed their lead in shaping the international policy of his government.[32]

Ambassador John E. Peurifoy reported that shortly after he presented his credentials he had a six-hour conversation with President Arbenz and got nowhere in his efforts to point out the dangers of Communist infiltration. Many notorious Reds Arbenz denied to be Communists, and if they were, he said, they were not dangerous. In any case, according to the President, Guatemala's difficulties were due to the malpractices of United States business. As for the individuals alleged to be Communists, they would continue to enjoy the full advantages accorded all Guatemalans since they were valuable allies in the fight for social reform. If their rights were interfered with, Guatemala could no longer be called a democracy. The President thought and talked like a Communist, said Peurifoy.[33]

Arbenz denied that the U.S.S.R. had designs on Guatemalan sovereignty. He ridiculed the idea of intervention by international Communism. Nevertheless, in spite of his denials, Communism in Guatemala was not solely a domestic affair; it played a definite and significant role in the plans of Moscow. The Reds in Guatemala were working for Soviet aims under consistent and disciplined Soviet control. According to Ambassador Peurifoy, a majority of the Guatemalan Communist leaders had made one trip or more to the Soviet Union and satellite countries for training and instruction. The fact of Soviet direction was never clearer than when the Communist Party of Guatemala accepted the dictum, brought back from Moscow by Communist Party Secretary-General José Manuel Fortuny Arana that "agrarian reform was not an approved policy for semi-colonial countries such as Guatemala." The policy of using the party as a brake on popular aspirations was intended to foster discontent rather than find a solution for it.[34] The fundamental task set for the Guatemalan Communists was to fight Yankee imperialism. Tactically, they directed their chief attention to the United Fruit Company and its International Railways of Central America. The Unifruitco, the largest United States economic enterprise in the country, was a natural target for the anti-imperialist, nationalistic propaganda that the Communists found so effective.

It was with good reason, therefore, that the United States held that

[32] Schneider, 188, 193.
[33] U.S. Dept. of State, *Bulletin*, XXXI (Sept. 6, 1954), 334.
[34] Schneider, 60.

the extensive Communist penetration of Guatemala called for action. Its own security and the safety of the other nations of the Americas were in jeopardy, for the agents of international Communism, using Guatemala as a base, were seeking to penetrate and subvert the neighboring Central American states. There was a flow of propaganda material and trained agitators into El Salvador, Honduras, and Nicaragua. They attempted political assassinations and strikes, such as a general strike in Honduras which was planned, instigated, and directed from Guatemala.

Given the unquestioned tie-up between Guatemalan and Soviet Communism, the developments in the Central American republic represented a challenge to the principles of the Monroe Doctrine. According to this historic foreign policy, any attempt by a non-American state to extend its political system to any portion of the hemisphere would endanger the peace and safety of the United States, and could not be viewed with indifference. The intervention of international Communism in Guatemala certainly would extend the Soviet political system to this continent, greatly endangering its peace and security. However, by its nonintervention pledges the United States had forsworn unilateral action such as had been practiced in the old days. As for collective inter-American action, neither the Rio treaty nor the other pacts seemed to fit the peculiar problem presented by Guatemala. It was a situation which seemed to call for a consultation meeting of the foreign ministers, but fortunately this was not necessary, for the matter was referred to the forthcoming tenth inter-American conference.

The Caracas Conference. The Tenth Inter-American Conference met in Caracas, Venezuela, from March 1 to March 28, 1954. All the American republics participated with the exception of Costa Rica, which boycotted the conference in protest against the jailing of political prisoners by the Venezuelan dictator. But provision was made whereby Costa Rica might adhere to the Final Act. The conference adopted 117 resolutions and 3 conventions covering the whole range of inter-American relations—juridical, political, economic, social, and cultural. The actions of the conference on subjects other than the problem of international Communism have been discussed in preceding chapters.

When the agenda for the tenth inter-American conference was being prepared, the United States, with the Guatemalan situation in mind, suggested on October 6, 1953, that the topic "Intervention of International Communism in the American Republics" be included. On November 11 the topic was put to a vote by the Council of the OAS and was approved with but one dissent—Guatemala.[35] Rather than withdraw from the OAS or boycott the Caracas conference, the Arbenz government decided, at a meeting of the National Democratic Front, to attend and use the conference as a forum from which to attack the United States. To exploit the opportunity to the fullest advantage, an able and fiery orator, Guillermo Toriello, was recalled from his post as ambassador to Washington and was appointed foreign minister and chief delegate to the conference. It is of significance that the line Toriello was to follow at Caracas was determined by the Communist-dominated FDN (National Democratic Front).[36]

The delegates of the United States and those of most of the Latin-American republics convened in Caracas with markedly divergent preoccupations: the United States wanted strong action on Communism and the Latins wanted massive economic assistance. Not sharing the United States' anxiety regarding the threat of international Communism in the Americas, their concern at Caracas was the United States' economic policy toward Latin America. Harmonizing these two concerns was Mr. Dulles' problem. Over and above the Latins' apparent apathy on the Communist issue, the United States faced the delicate problem of seeking collective action without disturbing the hornets' nest of noninterventionism. It was hard to see how a resolution on the subject of the intervention of international Communism in the hemisphere could go beyond the categorical declarations of the Meeting of Consultation of Ministers of Foreign Affairs in Washington in 1951. Secretary Dulles succeeded in resolving the dilemma.

On March 4, 1954, at an early session of the Caracas conference, Mr. Dulles warned that there is not "a single country in this hemisphere which has not been penetrated by the apparatus of international Communism, acting under orders from Moscow." He added, "I believe it is time to make clear with finality that we see that alien despotism is hostile to our ideals, that we unitedly deny it the right to prey upon our hemisphere, and that if it does not heed our warning and keep away we shall deal with it as a situation that might endanger the peace of America." Mr. Dulles emphasized that his suggestion did not involve interference in the internal affairs of any republic, for there is ample room in the Americas for natural differences of political institutions, but there is no place here for political institutions which serve alien masters.[37] The Secretary did not mention Guatemala by name; it

[35] *Annals*, V (1953), 293–300.   [36] Schneider, 296.
[37] U.S. Dept. of State, *Bulletin*, XXX (March 15, 1954), 380.

was clear enough to all that he had that Central American republic in mind.

A draft resolution presented by the United States declared that the domination or control of the political institutions of an American state by the international Communist movement constituted a threat to the sovereignty and independence of the American states, endangered the peace, and called for the adoption of appropriate action in accordance with existing treaties. Thus the establishment of Communist political control over any American state was to be regarded as foreign intervention and a threat to the peace of the Americas, and would call for decisive collective action. Presumably the treaty to be invoked in such a situation was the Rio de Janeiro Treaty of Reciprocal Assistance, which provides that in case of an aggression which is not an armed attack, a meeting of consultation shall be called immediately to agree on measures to be taken for the common defense and the peace and security of the continent.

Though the proposal did not name Guatemala as a case in point, Foreign Minister Toriello accepted the implication and accused the United States of leading a campaign to overthrow his government and of attempting to return to the policy of the big stick and dollar diplomacy. He charged that the reactionaries were using the "negative flag" of anti-Communism to disguise their real purpose of opposing the people's progress. He expressed hope for the hemisphere's final liberation from the United States and declared that Pan Americanism had no meaning unless it tackled the real problem of misery, poverty, and social backwardness. A delegate was quoted as saying that Toriello "said many things some of the rest of us would like to say if we dared." The spectacle of little Guatemala twitching Uncle Sam's beard aroused no little amusement and titillation among the Latins.[38]

Mr. Dulles could not ignore the abusive attack. He replied:

We deplore the fact that this inter-American meeting should be used as a platform for efforts which seek to defame other American States and to exploit every possible difference with a view to disrupting the harmony of our gathering. Guatemala's position with respect to international Communism will be put to the test when this agenda item is taken up.[39]

Owing to the insistence of Secretary Dulles, vigorously supported by the delegates of Cuba, the Dominican Republic, and Peru, the subject of the Communist menace was given priority for conference dis-

[38] *Noticias*, X (March 9, 1954), 5–6.
[39] U.S. Dept. of State, *Bulletin*, XXX (March 22, 1954), 419.

cussion. Guatemala, supported by Argentina, opposed. Mr. Dulles made an impressive speech for the United States proposal. Recalling the dictum of the Monroe Doctrine, which opposes the extension of the European political system to any portion of the American continents, he said:

Those sentiments have long since ceased to be unilateral. They have become the accepted principle of this hemisphere. That is why it seems to us, we would be false to our past unless we again proclaimed that the extension to this hemisphere of alien despotism would be a danger to us all, which we unitedly oppose.

The new declaration which he proposed was designed to deal with the present danger of Trojan horse aggression carried on by internal conspirators at the behest of a foreign power.[40]

The most spirited debate of the conference took place in connection with the resolution on Communist infiltration. The United States did not find unconditional support for its proposal except from Nicaragua, the Dominican Republic, El Salvador, Peru, and Venezuela, *all under dictatorships*. Panama and Uruguay tried unsuccessfully to add to the resolution a condemnation of racial discrimination, respect for human rights, and support of higher standards of living. Several speakers who endorsed the United States project appealed for a more effective fight against the social and economic conditions that breed Communism. Next to Guatemala, Argentina and Mexico offered the strongest opposition to the resolution on the ground that it weakened the principle of nonintervention. To these countries, apparently, there is no evil greater than intervention.[41]

Mr. Dulles made some impression on the delegates when he said, "The slogan of nonintervention can plausibly be invoked and twisted to give immunity to what is in reality flagrant intervention." The debate made it clear that the Latin-American states put above every other consideration the right of each to govern itself in its own way, without interference from outside. If this comes from international Communism, they condemn it. But they also condemn any improper intervention by their own members on this pretext. Mr. Dulles sought to eliminate the fears of some delegates by adding the following statement to the resolution:

This declaration of foreign policy made by the American republics in relation to dangers originating outside this hemisphere is designed to protect

[40] *Ibid.*, 422–423.
[41] *Noticias*, X (March 9, 1954), 5–6; *New York Times*, March 10, 1954.

and not to impair the inalienable right of each American state freely to choose its own form of government and economic system and to live its own social and cultural life.

This was the essence of another resolution adopted by the conference, the Declaration of Caracas.[42]

In the end the draft resolution proposed by the United States, altered only by the addition of the Dulles statement, was approved by seventeen of the twenty republics represented at the Caracas conference; Guatemala cast a dissenting vote and Argentina and Mexico abstained from voting. Narciso Bassols, an open supporter of Communism and a foreign-affairs adviser to President Ruíz Cortines, was back of Mexico's opposition to the United States' anti-Communist resolution. Later, following the conference, Argentina formally and Mexico tacitly declared their adherence to the Caracas resolution. Costa Rica, the absent member, announced in April 1954 that it would adhere, at which time its President Figueres said, "I hope this resolution is only a step towards a general anti-totalitarian policy in this hemisphere." Thus by action of the Caracas conference the principles of the Monroe Doctrine became the common policy of the American republics. The Pan Americanization of the famous policy of President Monroe was now accomplished.

Many of those who voted in favor of the anti-Communism resolution admitted later their displeasure at having been pressured by the United States. Uruguay stated, "We contributed our approval without enthusiasm, without optimism, without joy, and without feeling that we were contributing to the adoption of a constructive measure." The approval of the anti-Communist resolution was called "a Pyrrhic victory" for the United States.[43] Robert Alexander shares this view: "Not only did Dulles use the full weight of the United States government to induce the Conference to take a position uncongenial to the majority of the Latin American countries, he did it in a manner likely to lose friends and alienate the peoples of the southern part of the hemisphere." Mr. Dulles was concerned apparently only with seeing that the anti-Communist resolution was adopted and seemed indifferent both to the Latins' fears of Yankee intervention and to the concentration of their interest on entirely different problems. Dr. Alexander, overlooking the requisite of diplomatic protocol, illogically criticizes

[42] U.S. Dept. of State, *Bulletin*, XXX (March 22, 1954), 423–425.
[43] *New York Times*, March 11–16, 1954; *Hoy* (Mexico), March 27, 1954, pp. 31–33.

the Secretary of State for refraining while in Caracas—the capital of one of Latin America's most notorious dictatorships—from condemning militarism and dictatorship.[44]

The Communists achieved their goal of using the Caracas conference as a propaganda platform. The Arbenz regime gained a sympathetic hearing from Latin-American nationalists, leftists, and intellectuals, who bore a deep resentment for the United States. According to *Humanismo,* the Mexican review of culture:

There can be no doubt that after the Caracas Conference the most popular name recalled by the people of America [the name most strongly etched in the memory of Americans] was the brilliant Guatemalan Foreign Minister Guillermo Torriello Garrido. . . . He interprets the music we like to hear and he attacks the things we disapprove. . . . He saved his country and covered himself with glory.[45]

Any substance in this effusion was soon shattered by further developments in Guatemala.

The overthrow of Communism in Guatemala. The Caracas resolution precipitated a war of nerves in and around Guatemala. The opponents of the Arbenz regime had achieved a fair degree of unity: (1) abroad, the high command of the Anti-Communist Liberating Front had established headquarters in Honduras under the leadership of Lt. Col. Carlos Castillo Armas, an Army officer who had led an unsuccessful revolt in 1950; and (2) within Guatemala, the National Anti-Communist Front was attempting to unite the various opposition groups. On the grounds that it had detected a plot, the secret police instituted a reign of terror: there were mass arrests, constitutional guarantees were suppressed, opposition leaders were killed, and other brutal tactics normally employed by Communism to consolidate its power were used. On April 9, Archbishop Mariano Rossel Arellano published a pastoral letter calling the attention of all Catholics to the presence of Communism in Guatemala and demanding that the people "rise as a single man against this enemy of God and country."[46]

On the occasion of a May Day celebration President Arbenz, in a highly nationalistic speech, condemned the United States' effort to intimidate Guatemala at Caracas, and announced most emphatically

[44] Alexander, 400–401.

[45] "Guatemala en Caracas," *Humanismo* III (March, April, May 1954), 11–16.

[46] *Time* (Latin America edition), April 26, 1954; U.S. Dept. of State, *Bulletin,* XXXI (Aug. 16, 1954), 236.

his rejection of a recent diplomatic note demanding fair compensation for the United Fruit Company's expropriated banana lands. The U.S. government was accused by the labor leader, Víctor Manuel Gutiérrez Garbin, of condemning Guatemala to the voracity of the Unifruitco and other United States monopolies.

Tensions between Guatemala and her three neighbors, El Salvador, Nicaragua, and Honduras, mounted when a Swedish cargo ship arrived late in May at the Atlantic port of Puerto Barrios with a nineteen-hundred-ton cargo of arms and ammunition, purchased by the Guatemalan government in Czechoslovakia and shipped from Stettin, Poland. The United States, alarmed because of the source of the shipment and fearing it would be used in a Communist aggression against Guatemala's Central American neighbors, immediately proceeded to send emergency-arms shipments to Honduras and Nicaragua. Washington defended this move on the ground that the arms sale to Guatemala was a direct challenge to the anti-Communist resolution adopted at Caracas. The Arbenz government, on the other hand, defended its right to buy wherever it could, particularly since the United States refused to sell it arms. Costa Rica declared that the size of the Communist arms shipment to Guatemala was clearly excessive and cautioned the rest of Central America to beware.[47]

Not only did Guatemala's purchase alarm her neighbors but it also alerted the Guatemalan Army to the Communist danger, for according to recurring rumors the arms were to be used to equip a people's militia. On June 5, 1954, Army officers demanded that the government remove known Communists from all official posts. Arbenz refused, saying that this would not be democratic. Later, when the showdown came and Arbenz announced his intention to turn to the "armed populace," he was dumbfounded when told by his Army Chief, Colonel Carlos Enrique Díaz, that the other officers had not allowed him to comply with Arbenz' order to equip the civilians.[48]

On June 18, Castillo Armas struck across the Honduras-Guatemala frontier at three different points. His "Liberation Army" numbered only a few hundred men, but he counted on an internal uprising. The rebels penetrated only about twenty miles, and very few casualties were suffered by either side. It is alleged that some of the equipment used by Castillo Armas was drawn from the supply which the United States had given to the Honduran government under the terms of a

[47] *Visión*, May 4, 1954; *New York Times*, May 25, 1954.
[48] Schneider, 312.

recently-concluded military-assistance pact. If the United States was guilty of giving indirect aid to the rebels, through the cooperation of Honduras, this aid proved to be unnecessary, for Arbenz was unable to mount any effective defense because of the defection of the Army.

Long before the Castillo Armas attack, the Army leaders were opposed to arming the populace because they viewed the virtual civil war as a Communist disruption of the nation. In their view Arbenz had forfeited his claim to their support and his regime was not worth destruction, sacrifice, and bloodshed. Therefore on June 27 representatives of the officer corps met with President Arbenz and demanded his resignation. Despite the strenuous efforts of the Communist leaders to organize a popular defense, Arbenz resigned and gave the command to Colonel Díaz. Immediate collapse of the Communist government followed. Hundreds of its former adherents sought asylum in friendly embassies, later to be given safe conduct out of the country. Arbenz himself went first to Mexico and then to Europe behind the Iron Curtain. Colonel Díaz governed for but a day, then he was replaced by an officers' junta headed by Col. Elfego Monzón. After several days of negotiations in El Salvador between Monzón and Castillo Armas, a new junta was formed, with Armas as the leading figure. As of July 19, 1954, twenty-three countries including the United States had recognized Castillo Armas. In September 1954 the other junta members resigned and Castillo Armas became president. It is necessary now to turn back to the beginning of the Guatemalan affair and record UN and OAS involvements in the issue.

The issue before the UN and the OAS. The Arbenz government reacted to the Castillo Armas invasion by appealing to both the OAS and the UN. On June 19 Dr. Alfredo Chocano, the Guatemalan Chargé d'Affaires in Washington, delivered a note to the chairman of the Inter-American Peace Committee, Luis Quintanilla of Mexico, stating that he was appealing to the committee "to avert a violation of the peace of the American Continent." He cited acts which, in the opinion of his government, constituted violations both of the principle of nonintervention and of the sovereignty of Guatemala. The note ended with a request that the Peace Committee be convoked immediately on an emergency basis.

Chairman Quintanilla acted promptly and the committee met on the same day. Since Honduras and Nicaragua were specifically mentioned in the Guatemalan note as the instigators of the acts denounced, copies of the Guatemalan communication were given to the ambassadors of those two countries. It was decided that a subcommittee of the committee should be sent to Guatemala immediately. However, on the next day, June 20, Chairman Quintanilla was informed by the Chargé of Guatemala that his government was requesting the Peace Committee to suspend its trip in view of the fact that the case had been submitted to the Security Council of the United Nations *on the same day* as to the Peace Committee, and that the Security Council had already taken cognizance of the Guatemalan complaint of aggression. The committee thereupon, on June 21, suspended consideration of the case.

However, the Peace Committee met two days later to hear the requests of the Honduran and Nicaraguan ambassadors that a special subcommittee be designated to go to Guatemala, Honduras, and Nicaragua to obtain all the facts "necessary to define responsibilities in a conflict in which continental peace is being disturbed." When asked whether it would consent to having a subcommittee dispatched for information, the Guatemalan government replied that it "cannot consent to having this matter brought before that body before the decision of the Security Council is fully carried out." In a note to the Inter-American Peace Committee on June 25 the Chargé d' Affaires of Guatemala was downright insulting, asserting that in a matter of aggression the committee enjoyed no competence. Interestingly enough, however, late the next day (June 26) the Peace Committee was informed by the Guatemalan Chargé that, since the Security Council had postponed consideration of the case pending a report from the Inter-American Peace Committee, Guatemala would be pleased to place at the disposal of the Subcommittee of Information all the facilities within its power.[49]

The interesting and significant episode of the attempted referral of the Guatemalan case to the United Nations Security Council calls for special mention, for it was the first time that the relation between the regional-security arrangement and the world organization had been put to the test. The issue, according to Ambassador Lodge, was whether the formula agreed to at San Francisco, reconciling universality and regionalism, was to be given reality or was to be ignored. In this instance Guatemala, the plaintiff, sought to avert any regional action and to restrict consideration of the case to the United Nations. On June 19, Guatemala protested to the Security Council that an open aggression had been perpetrated by Honduras and Nicaragua, and requested an emergency meeting of the Council. Ambassador Lodge, president of

[49] "Report of the Inter-American Peace Committee on the Controversy between Guatemala, Honduras, and Nicaragua," *Annals*, VI (1954), 239–245.

the Security Council, appeared at first to be in no hurry, but yielding to strong pressure, he called a meeting for Sunday, June 20. At this meeting, not only Lodge but the representatives of the two Latin-American members of the Security Council—Brazil and Colombia—called attention to the availability of inter-American peace machinery to handle the case. This appeared to be precisely the kind of problem which should in the first instance be dealt with by an appropriate agency of the Organization of American States. That the requests to to the OAS and the UN were simultaneous strengthened this view.

In clear opposition to the understanding at San Francisco concerning the meaning of Article 51 of the UN Charter, why did Guatemala take the case to the United Nations and ask for the withdrawal of the Inter-American Peace Committee? According to Secretary Dulles, the Foreign Minister of Guatemala connived with the Foreign Minister of the Soviet Union "in open correspondence and ill-conceived privacy" to refer the matter to the UN.[50] The Arbenz government, in an effort to disrupt the inter-American system and because it enjoyed the full support of the U.S.S.R. in the Security Council, tried to bring the matter before that body.

In an emergency meeting of the Security Council, held on Sunday, June 20, the United States presented a draft resolution asking that the Guatemalan complaint be transferred to the OAS. It was defeated by a Soviet veto, which drew from Lodge the warning that the U.S.S.R. should "stay out of this hemisphere."[51] The final action of this meeting was the adoption of a French resolution which called for "the immediate termination of any action likely to cause bloodshed," and all members of the United Nations were admonished to abstain from giving assistance to any such action. Guatemala expressed the hope that the resolution would cause member states (i.e., Honduras and Nicaragua) to close their frontiers. This was an idle hope, for, as hostilities mounted, the Guatemalan delegate to the UN, in a letter to the secretary-general, announced that the resolution of the Security Council had not been complied with and so, with the support of the U.S.S.R., asked for another meeting of the Council.[52] Thus on June 25 there was a second meeting of the Security Council to consider the Guatemalan request. It occasioned another hot exchange between Ambassador Lodge and the Russian representative. Lodge took the position that the United States and the other American republics were bound by

[50] U.S. Dept. of State, *Bulletin*, XXXI (July 12, 1954), 44.
[51] *Ibid.* (July 5, 1954), 28.   [52] Houston, 108.

Article 20 of the Charter of the OAS, which provides: "All international disputes that may arise between American states shall be submitted to the peaceful procedures set forth in this Chapter, before being referred to the Security Council of the United Nations." Said Lodge, "If we adopt the agenda, we in effect give one state, in this case Guatemala, a veto on the Organization of American States." The Soviet representative based his case largely on Article 24 of the Charter, which conferred "on the Security Council primary responsibility for the maintenance of international peace and security." He also accused Ambassador Lodge of employing delaying tactics in order to give the aggressors time to accomplish their purpose in Guatemala. A motion for United Nations discussion of the Guatemalan case was defeated five to four, with Britain and France abstaining. In view of the fact that the Inter-American Peace Committee had set in motion steps to get at the facts, the Security Council decided not to resume consideration of the Guatemalan issue at that time. Guatemala announced that a visit by the Peace Committee would be acceptable. This was the end of United Nations involvement in the issue. No clear-cut decision had been arrived at concerning the conflict of interpretations of the Charter provisions on regional arrangements. At least it was fortunate that the appeal of Guatemala was not sustained in the Security Council, for that would have amounted to repudiation of the Vandenberg formula agreed to at San Francisco. The referral of the issue to the OAS was proper procedure, and so there was no basis for the fears expressed by some that this action weakened the primacy of the United Nations over regional arrangements.[53]

The withdrawal of the United Nations left the Guatemalan affair to the procedures provided by the Organization of American States. On June 26, the United States and nine Latin-American countries (Brazil, Costa Rica, Cuba, Dominican Republic, Haiti, Honduras, Nicaragua, Panama, and Peru) addressed a joint note to the chairman of the Council of the OAS, asking that a Meeting of Consultation of the Ministers of Foreign Affairs be convoked to consider the situation created by the intervention of international Communism in Guatemala. The Council, on June 28, 1954, convoked a Meeting of Consultation of the Ministers of Foreign Affairs, to meet at Rio de Janeiro on July 7, 1954. Since the consultation was to consider all aspects of the danger to the peace and security of the continent resulting from the

[53] *Ibid.*, 109; *New York Times*, July 4, 1954; U.S. Dept. of State, *Bulletin*, XXXI (July 5, 1954), 30; United Nations, *Repertory of Practice of United Nations Organs* (New York, 1955), II, 449–454.

penetration of the political institutions of Guatemala by the international Communist movement, this action was clearly in accordance with the anti-Communism resolution adopted at Caracas. Because of the collapse of the Arbenz government the proposed consultative meeting was never held.[54] Politico-military developments in Guatemala also made unnecessary any further contributions by the Inter-American Peace Committee.

When the Arbenz government turned once more, on June 26, to the Inter-American Peace Committee, that body decided to constitute itself a Subcommittee of Information and go to Guatemala, Honduras, and Nicaragua to get the facts concerning the alleged invasion of Guatemala. Despite the resignation of Arbenz and a completely changed political situation in Guatemala, the subcommittee started its trip on June 29 but did not go farther than Mexico City because the new government in Guatemala advised against the trip. On July 2 the subcommittee was informed by Guatemala, Honduras, and Nicaragua that the controversy between them, which was the occasion for the committee's trip in the first place, had ceased to exist. A copy of the *Final Report* of the Peace Committee was sent to the secretary-general of the United Nations, for transmittal to the Security Council.[55]

The aftermath in Guatemala. The Guatemalan affair unloosed a veritable hornets' nest of criticism of the United States. Always receptive to reports that seem to support fears of United States intervention, many of the Latins seized on the events in Guatemala and the role played by this country. There was slight disposition to take note of the issue of international Communist intervention,[56] but the fact of the powerful United States maneuvering the overthrow of the government of little Guatemala was a stark reality apparent to all. Here truly was an illustration of Latin America's concern over intervention outweighing any possible realization and fears of Communist aggression. It is only a statement of fact to assert that the overthrow of the Arbenz regime created no enthusiasm in Latin America, but much criticism of the United States.

Latin-American newpapers, many of them normally sympathetic to the United States and far from leftist, joined the criticism of students, intellectuals, and labor leaders in Brazil, Cuba, Bolivia, Ecuador, and

---

[54] *Annals*, VI (1954), 159–162.   [55] *Ibid.*, 241–245.

[56] In like manner when several of the Latin-American governments felt obliged, in 1953, to blast British action in suppressing Communism in Guiana as "vicious colonial imperialism," not a word was said about the Communist threat there.

Mexico. The national legislatures of Argentina and Uruguay condemned the "aggression against Guatemala." Former President Lázaro Cárdenas of Mexico, always leftist, sent a sympathetic note to the Arbenz government. Some of Latin America's most violent anti-United States demonstrations took place in Chile in protest of "United States intervention." There were editorials terming the alleged action "an insult to the Continent," and the Chilean Chamber of Deputies sent messages to all the Latin-American Congresses, inviting them to express jointly their repudiation of the United States' "armed intervention in Guatemala."[57]

Unquestionably, United States prestige was hurt by these reactions. The hemisphere, indeed the world, believed that obviously the United States was directly responsible for the rebellion on moral grounds, that is, that the invasion by the Guatemalan exiles would not have been possible without at least the tacit approval of Washington. There is little evidence that the United States took an active part in producing the "invasion." But there is evidence that the governments of Honduras and Nicaragua, with United States arms, did give some help to the invading forces. Ambassador Peurifoy, testifying before a Congressional committee, declared that his role had been "strictly that of a diplomatic observer" and that the first and only active role he played in the events of June 1954 was to lend his good offices in negotiating a truce between the forces of Col. Castillo Armas and the military junta that was established in Guatemala after the resignation of President Arbenz.[58] The ousted President of Guatemala, in exile in Mexico, blamed his downfall on his "independence of North American imperialism," which he said was gradually subjugating Latin America. Latin-American liberals generally refused to recognize the true problem at issue in Guatemala.[59]

It is interesting that later, when the truth of the United States' charges against the Arbenz regime were verified, much of the criticism abated.[60] This all tended to prove that, among the Latins, there was great disinterest and misinformation on the subject of the Communist threat. Notably, the Mexican government underwent a dis-

[57] *Visión*, July 16, 1954; *New York Times*, June 23, 24, 27, 1954.

[58] U.S. Dept. of State, *Bulletin*, XXXI (Nov. 8, 1954), 690.

[59] Juan Bosch, "Trujillo: Problema de América," *Combate*, I, No. 5 (March–April 1959), 9.

[60] Francisco D. Espinosa F., "Pruebas incontrovertibles de la barbarie Comunista de Arbenz en Guatemala," *Hoy* (Mexico), Sept. 9, 1954, pp. 32, 66. In August 1954 the United States issued a "White Paper" to alert all Latin-American governments to the threat of international Communism.

tinct official change of thinking about the Communist problem in Guatemala. In an address to the Mexican Congress on September 1, 1954, President Ruíz Cortines declared his unequivocal rejection of "any attempt of international Communism to interfere in our hemisphere." This declaration received loud and long applause in the Congress.[61] Thus after all the returns were in, we find that the United States was justified not only in its fears but also in the course of action it followed. We cannot but wonder, however, what would have been the outcome of the Rio meeting of consultation had it been held. We can be fairly certain that, even had some kind of collective action against the Arbenz government been voted, it would have been over strong opposition injurious to inter-American unity. It was fortunate that the meeting was not held.

Communist activities heightened. Following the Guatemalan affair of 1954 there was no decline of Communist activity or a lessening of its threat. Quite to the contrary, the setback in Guatemala, particularly since it came so close to success, apparently caused the Kremlin to step up its activities in Latin America, and consequently the Communist conspiracy became an even greater danger to hemisphere security.

A new Soviet tactic was a trade drive in Latin America. On January 16, 1956, it was revealed that Premier Nikolai A. Bulganin, in reply to questions put by the magazine *Visión,* spoke of the possibility of increased trade and technical assistance between the U.S.S.R. and Latin America. The prospect of Soviet competition in the Latin-American market was disturbing to the United States and the other American republics. What worried Washington diplomats most was that trade deals would open the door for deeper Soviet political and propaganda penetration. At the time, only three republics—Mexico, Argentina, and Uruguay—had Soviet embassies, while a few other nations had diplomatic relations with Soviet satellites. If the U.S.S.R. succeeded in negotiating long-term trade relations with the Latin-American nations, official diplomatic ties would probably follow. These in turn would bring in a surge of Communist espionage, subversion, anti-United States agitation, and a weakening of inter-American solidarity.

Following the Bulganin statement there were many reports of trade deals—real and prospective—all pointing to a stepping-up of Russian economic activity in the hemisphere. It seemed that the Soviet Union had found a way to breach the barrier erected around the Americas by the "Pan Americanized" Monroe Doctrine. It was part of the new Rus-

---

[61] *Time* (Latin America edition), Sept. 13, 1954.

sian tactic to concentrate on the one-crop republics as the prime targets, for large purchases of basic products would put these countries in a position of dependence on the Soviet Union.

Some of the Latin-American countries even expressed interest in fuller trade relations with the U.S.S.R., Communist China, and other Red countries when there was a drastic drop in prices for Latin-American exports and the United States refused to enter into price-stabilization agreements. Russia also offered assistance in major development projects and those forms of "technical assistance" which would afford opportunity for penetration by Soviet agents.[62]

Although the over-all extent of the Russian trade drive in Latin America was minor, the potential threat was very great, for if Moscow wanted to give top priority to Latin America, it could make a big impact there. In 1959, however, the trade of the U.S.S.R. and its satellites accounted for only 2 per cent of Latin America's foreign trade, the United States' share being 47 per cent and that of Western Europe 28 per cent. Most of the Soviet-bloc trade was with Argentina, Brazil, Cuba, and Uruguay. By the end of 1960 Cuba had drifted almost completely into the Communist trade orbit.

The Soviet Union has been spending large sums for the traveling expenses of Latin-American Communists and others to visit Moscow and the Iron Curtain countries for training and indoctrination. Prominent among these are labor leaders and professors, for the infiltration of labor unions and teachers' organizations enjoys high priority in Communist strategy. By the end of 1960 the propaganda activities of Communist China in Latin America closely paralleled those of the Soviet Union.

In spite of the foregoing, the Communists in Latin America are not numerous, and by themselves they would present no immediate threat to the governments of either Latin America or the United States. They are in no position to gain power through legal means, but, as a well-organized minority directed and supported by foreign powers, the Communists present a constant danger. They have adopted the "gradual approach" of leaguing with the non-Communist left and catering to nationalistic aspirations. As in Guatemala, and in Cuba, they infiltrate intellectual circles, student groups, labor, and public-opinion media. Masquerading as supernationalists, they penetrate behind the scenes where they can work more effectively in the interest of an inter-

[62] *Visión*, Jan. 27, 1956; *New York Times*, Jan. 31, 1956, and Dec. 27, 1957; Philip B. Taylor, *Hemispheric Security Reconsidered*. Middle American Research Records (Tulane University, New Orleans, 1957), II, No. 5, 103.

national conspiracy. Their prime objective is to exploit the Latins' latent anti-United States attitude and thus create disunity among the American republics, as became grievously apparent in Cuba.

The Cuban situation. The regime of Fidel Castro in Cuba, because of its Communist orientation and calculated efforts to infiltrate its brand of revolution into other Latin-American states, put a strain on American solidarity probably unmatched by any situation in the past. Winning the Latins to a united hemisphere policy on the Cuban problem has been a slow and difficult task because of their sympathy with Castro's proclaimed revolutionary objectives. However, the stepped-up aggressiveness of the Sino-Soviet bloc in Latin America and the extent to which it manipulated the Cuban revolution as its own instrument were such a stark challenge to inter-American security that even the most blind, prejudiced, and hesitant of the Good Neighbors were forced to concede eventually that there was indeed justification for the Yankees' anxiety.

Fidel Castro's overthrow of Fulgencio Batista's harsh dictatorship had been hailed with delight not only in Cuba but throughout Latin America. Castro became the idol of the masses, who longed for fundamental social and economic reform. He was the symbol of the new nationalistic movements of "workers and peasants" that were breaking the shackles of serfdom imposed by cynical dictators supported by alien capitalistic imperialists. Obviously the *Latinos* were reluctant to accept any modification of this original image of Fidel as freedom's crusader. Not the excesses of revolutionary reprisals or the wholesale expropriation of private property, not the suppression of civil rights or the indefinite postponement of constitutional government—nothing, seemingly, dimmed the luster of Cuba's savior. So strong was the popular predilection for Fidel Castro that any criticism of his program was branded as imperialistic resistance to needed revolutionary reform.

Thus the United States, though confronted by successive expropriations of private investments, and the Cuban government's systematic and provocative campaign of slander and hostile propaganda, neither dared to act unilaterally because of its nonintervention commitments, nor could it count on the neighbors' support in multilateral OAS action. There seemed to be no alternative to the humiliating policy of "turning the other cheek," which in fact was highly regarded and commended in the various Latin-American capitals. The State Department had to content itself with paper protests, as for example, the memorandum of June 29, 1960, to the Inter-American Peace Committee entitled "Provocative Actions by the Cuban Government," which described Cuba's systematic campaign of "distortions, half-truths, and outright falsehoods" against the United States. Significantly, the memo did not mention the confiscations of properties, nor did it call for action by the Peace Committee or by the OAS. It was merely a formal list of Castro's excesses for the record.[63]

Inevitably Latin America's patience with the Cuban Premier wore thin, not only because of developing ideological differences such as marked breaks with leading liberals like Figueres and Betancourt but because of Castro's calculated undermining of the inter-American security structure. Shortly after he came to power, Castro declared Cuba's neutrality in the cold war, and disavowed the obligations of the Rio treaty. This was followed by an unmistakable orientation of Cuban policy away from the traditional support of the OAS—now branded in Havana as "a ministry of colonies" of the United States— and toward more intimate relations with the Communist bloc. This trend led, as a result of Cuba's alleged effort to free herself of economic dependence on the United States, to the negotiation of a Soviet-Cuban Commercial Agreement on February 13, 1960. By the terms of the pact the Soviet Union extended a twelve-year credit of $100 million to Cuba at 2.5 per cent and pledged to buy over the next five years five million tons of Cuban sugar at the world price, one-fifth to be paid in dollars, and the other four-fifths in barter arrangements. On June 26, 1960, Castro frankly declared that his government would regard anti-Communist agitation and activities in Cuba as counter-revolutionary. Apparently Castro's pro-Communist inclinations were long-standing.

The drift of the Cuban regime into the arms of the Communists provoked a highly significant statement by the Executive Board of the International Confederation of Free Trade Unions (Brussels, July 1, 1960), addressed to all affiliated organizations, including the Inter-American Regional Organization (ORIT). The circular declared:

When the Cuban revolutionary movement overthrew the dictatorship of Batista, it was generally hoped that the new regime would restore democracy and secure all those political and personal rights which are part and parcel of democracy. The Cuban regime has failed to do so. It has frankly stated that it has no intention to submit to free elections. It has prevented the functioning of a democratic party system by banning any critical opinion as counter-revolutionary, but it has given the Communists free rein. It has in fact abolished freedom of the press by suppressing independent newspapers.

[63] U.S. Dept. of State, *Bulletin*, XLIII (July 18, 1960), 79–88.

Personal freedoms have also been curtailed, by the suspension of habeas corpus.

In the trade union field particularly democratic rights have been smothered. . . . The regime has taken over and succeeded in removing all anti-Communists from leading positions in the trade union movement and in subjecting it to its complete control.[64]

Because of the unfriendly and dangerous course of Cuban policy, President Eisenhower, on July 6, 1960, canceled all United States imports of Cuban sugar under the existent quota, which provided a premium considerably above the world price. The Cubans screamed that this was an act of "economic aggression" condemned by inter-American agreements. Former President Lázaro Cárdenas of Mexico was quick to accuse the United States of waging an economic war against Cuba. He asked, "Will the official commitment contracted by all American countries against economic aggression be respected?" Two prominent leaders of the Mexican Congress, apparently speaking for Cárdenas, defended the Cuban revolution and demanded that the Mexican government manifest its hostility to the United States economic reprisals.[65] These views were representative of an all-too-prevalent pro-Castro attitude throughout Latin America. The time had not yet arrived for the Latins to consent to cooperative OAS action.

With respect to the charge of "economic aggression," it is indeed true that Article 15 of the Charter of the OAS provides that "no state or group of states" may intervene in the internal or external affairs of any other state, and this includes, under Article 16, the use of "coercive measures of an economic or political character." Also economic pressures which threaten the peace of America evidently come within the meaning of the term "aggression" as construed in Article 6 of the Rio treaty, and warrant a consultative meeting of the foreign ministers. It is extremely doubtful, however, that cutting the sugar quota was an act of economic aggression, for it was a justifiable measure of self-protection by the United States to insure a needed sugar supply. Furthermore, under the sugar agreement the United States was under no obligation to purchase raw sugar from Cuba, nor was Cuba obliged to sell to it.

The Communist bloc hastened to the aid of beleaguered Cuba. When the island republic's normal oil supply from Venezuela was cut off— following Castro's confiscation of British and American oil refineries

[64] Inter-American Regional Organization of Labor, *Inter-American Labor Bulletin,* XI, No. 8 (Aug. 1960), 1.

[65] *Christian Science Monitor,* July 20, 1960.

because of their refusal to process Soviet oil—the U.S.S.R. rushed Black Sea tankers to Cuba's aid. Likewise, when Cuba's sugar quota was cut by President Eisenhower, Communist China negotiated a five-year trade pact, signed July 25, providing for the annual purchase of 500,000 tons of Cuban sugar to be paid for almost entirely in Chinese goods. By the end of 1960 most of Cuba's sugar production had been contracted for by the Communist bloc on a barter basis. Economic ties with the West approached the vanishing point. All United States sugar purchases from Cuba had been canceled and a general embargo on trade had been imposed.

Apparently the feature of the Cuban revolution that most appealed to Moscow was that it was a near-perfect model for other revolutions in Latin America. It differed from the usual Latin-American political upheaval in that instead of excluding the collaboration of local Communists, it opened its arms to international Communism and copied many of its practices. Because of these differences Premier Krushchev embraced it for export to the other countries of the Western Hemisphere. This objective of Soviet policy became clearer and clearer as the Russian Premier moved from propaganda, to economic support, and then to threatened military support of Cuba's revolutionary regime.

In a startling move to claim Cuba as a Communist protectorate, Nikita Khrushchev, on July 9, 1960, declared that any attack on Cuba would bring about instant retaliation against the United States by Soviet intercontinental missiles. The Monroe Doctrine, he said, is dead, and should be buried "so that it should not poison the air by its decay."

The death of the Monroe Doctrine was sharply disputed by President Eisenhower, who immediately issued a warning that "the United States will not be deterred from its responsibilities by the threats Mr. Krushchev is making. Nor will the United States, in conformity with its treaty obligations, permit the establishment of a regime dominated by international Communism in the Western Hemisphere."[66] The Latin-American press generally was in agreement that a joint policy of the nations of the Americas had been threatened. Said *El Mercurio* of Santiago, Chile, "Khrushchev's threats are not only against the United States but against all countries in Latin America. They must be answered by all countries acting as one." *O Jornal* of Rio de Janeiro said, "Brazil will comply with her commitments to defend Pan American solidarity and the Monroe Doctrine."[67]

[66] U.S. Dept. of State, *Bulletin*, XLIII (Aug. 1, 1960), 170–171.
[67] *Time*, July 25, 1960, p. 34.

Since the Cuban situation had degenerated to a point threatening to the peace of the Americas, there obviously was need for consultation by the American republics. However, because of the Cuban government's disdain of the OAS as a "tool of the United States imperialism," it preferred to bring its charges of economic aggression against the United States to the United Nations Security Council. But the Latin Americans were in no mood to allow the OAS to be bypassed. Once more, as in the Guatemalan situation of 1954, the integrity of the inter-American security system was at stake. On July 19 the two Latin-American members of the Security Council, Argentina and Ecuador, succeeded by a vote of nine to zero (the U.S.S.R. and Poland abstained) in having a resolution adopted whereby the UN should withhold consideration of the question pending a report by the OAS. The Russian delegate, Mr. Arkady A. Sobolev, seeking to inflame Latin America against the United States, told the Council that the Soviet Union would not remain indifferent if an armed intervention was undertaken against Cuba, but "using its armed might will assist Cuba if Cuba asks for assistance." He said, "Do not touch Cuba. Leave Cuba alone. This is our policy toward the Latin American countries and toward Cuba," that is, an unsolicited blanket of Soviet "protection" to an entire continent.

Not only did Ambassador Lodge reject the Soviet intervention as inadmissible interference in inter-American affairs, but the Ecuadorean president of the Security Council, Dr. José A. Correa, said: "The Latin American countries will struggle for nonintervention against any attempt to violate it—I repeat, against any attempt. . . . We have achieved maturity and we do not accept any sort of guidance. We do not believe in having happiness imposed upon us."[68] However, Cuba's government-inspired *Cadena Oriental de Radio* (Havana, July 19, 1960) saw no reason why Russia "should deprive itself of the chance of doing on the United States borders what the United States is doing on the Soviet borders."

Undoubtedly the missile-brandishing by Khrushchev backfired, for now most of the Latins realized that the real issue was Communist intrusion in the Western Hemisphere, not merely a dispute between "Yankee" imperialists and Cuban revolutionaries. The Latins, though not fond of the United States, had less taste for the bully whom Fidel Castro had invited into the community. Apparently the time had arrived for OAS action.

[68] *Christian Science Monitor*, July 20, 1960.

The OAS Council voted to convene a meeting of the foreign ministers on August 16 at San José, Costa Rica, to deal with the threat of Communist penetration in Cuba. This meeting was to follow immediately another consultation (also at San José) to hear Venezuela's charges against Trujillo. As has been noted in the preceding chapter, the United States had joined reluctantly in the condemnation of the Dominican dictator because of its desire to win Latin-American support on the Cuban issue in the forthcoming meeting.

Specifically the Seventh Meeting of Consultation of the Ministers of Foreign Affairs was convened to consider the threat of extracontinental intervention in hemisphere affairs. It seemed that it was the purpose of the Soviet Union and Communist China to exploit the Cuban situation in order to sow distrust and fear and break the bonds of inter-American solidarity.

At San José, Secretary of State Christian A. Herter asked the meeting to distinguish between the basic issues which threatened hemisphere peace and security, and those of a bilateral character between Cuba and the United States. As for the latter he merely suggested that a fact-finding committee be appointed. But with respect to the former he warned that "the installation of a Communist regime in any American Republic would automatically involve the loss of the country's independence." It would become an operational base for infiltration, subversion, and interference in the internal affairs of the Americas. Mr. Herter wanted to make it clear that international Communism was invading the Western Hemisphere through Cuba, and he hoped to get the foreign ministers gathered at San José to join in a specific denunciation of Sino-Soviet Communist intervention, and of Cuba for inviting it.[69]

Several of the Latin-American delegations, taking a pronounced pro-Cuban position, suggested a mild resolution deploring outside intervention but not mentioning either the U.S.S.R. or Cuba. Finally the opposition to a firm resolution crumbled, for the Latins realized that their continued failure to support the United States would endanger the inter-American system. Since the delegates were prepared to condemn Communism, but not Cuba, a compromise Declaration of San José was adopted on August 28 by a vote of nineteen to zero. (The Dominican Republic did not participate in the seventh meeting, and Cuba withdrew before the vote was taken.) By a vote of nineteen to one the meeting rejected, on the same date, a Cuban resolution call-

[69] U.S. Dept. of State, *Bulletin*, XLIII (Sept. 12, 1960), 395–407.

ing on the United States to refrain from aggressive acts against the Castro government.[70]

The Declaration of San José (1) condemned intervention by an extracontinental power in the affairs of the American republics and declared that the acceptance by any American state of such intervention jeopardized American solidarity and security; (2) rejected the attempts of the Sino-Soviet powers to exploit the political, economic, and social situation in any American state as threatening to hemisphere unity and security; (3) declared that no American state may intervene for the purpose of imposing upon another American state its ideologies or political, economic, or social principles; and (4) proclaimed that all members of the OAS are under obligation to conduct themselves in accordance with the principles stated in the Declaration of Santiago and to comply with the provisions of the Charter of the OAS.[71]

The resolution contained no direct mention of Cuba, but the implication was obvious, and in fact precipitated a Cuban walkout. In the words of Secretary Herter, "The action taken by the foreign ministers in the case of Cuba expressed their conviction that the Soviet Union should not export its doctrine or otherwise intervene in the Western Hemisphere through the gateway of Cuba."[72]

As for the bilateral dispute between the United States and Cuba— as the Latins preferred to call the issue—an Ad Hoc Good Offices Committee was created by the seventh meeting to "facilitate, by clarifying the facts and extending its good offices, the settlement of controversies between American governments." The reluctance of the meeting to condemn the antidemocratic developments in Cuba was evident. It was also clear that the Latins regarded Cuban violations of the rights —personal and property—of United States citizens as matters of no serious concern to themselves. On the contrary, they would not be disposed to view kindly any highly improbable move by the United States to protect its citizens in Cuba. The world's greatest power was apparently immobilized by the ban on intervention. Or was it Nikita Khrushchev's missile-brandishing which imposed restraint on the United States?

---

[70] *Christian Science Monitor*, Aug. 29, 1960. Efforts of the Cuban government to induce the UN to consider alleged plans of United States aggression and acts of intervention against the Republic of Cuba were likewise rejected.

[71] Pan American Union, *Final Act: Seventh Meeting of Consultation of Ministers of Foreign Affairs, San José, Costa Rica, August 22–29, 1960* (Washington, 1960), 4–5, cited hereinafter as *Seventh Meeting of Consultation*.

[72] U.S. Dept. of State, *Bulletin*, XLIII (Sept. 19, 1960), 437.

The Declaration of San José, however, did not impose restraint on Premier Castro. Quite the reverse was true, for there was an intensification of Cuba's campaign to export its special type of revolution to other Latin-American countries. From many of the hemisphere capitals came reports of Cuban embassies spreading inflammatory propaganda. Tons of Communist literature enjoyed the immunity of Cuban diplomatic pouches. In Venezuela President Betancourt had to order out troops to crush revolutionaries trying to impose "Cuban methods." In Costa Rica, Guatemala, and Nicaragua, revolts which broke out in November 1960 were branded by the presidents of those countries as Castro-inspired. Guatemala protested to the OAS and, along with Nicaragua, sent pleas to Washington requesting a naval patrol in the Caribbean to thwart any Cuban invasion. The United States promptly dispatched the necessary task force, and for a few days it patrolled the waters separating Cuba from the Central American republics. Although developments seemed to prove that the patrol had been unnecessary, the incident was significant because the United States acted without awaiting the deliberations of its Latin-American associates. Some critics contended that this was a type of action which should have been multilateral.

The Cuban situation at the end of the Eisenhower Administration was threatening in the extreme. The United States finally joined six of the Latin-American governments—the Dominican Republic, Guatemala, Haiti, Nicaragua, Paraguay, and Peru—in breaking relations with Cuba. However, despite the rupture of political and economic relations, the Castro regime continued to survive. There can be little doubt that this was due to Sino-Soviet assistance and that the future of Castroism will be largely dependent on the nature and extent of the support of the Communist powers. In view of the heavy Soviet rearmament of Cuba and the island republic's absorption into the Communist bloc, the time is rapidly approaching when the United States, and also the OAS, will have to decide whether the Monroe Doctrine has been violated and whether it is worth defending.

Conclusion. The problem of combatting Communism in Latin America, from the point of view of the United States, is that of winning and keeping the loyalty of the people for the democratic way of life and of fortifying them in their rejection of Communism. This requires of the United States both economic and democratic support. Arguments to the effect that democratic freedom and liberty mean little to people living in poverty and ignorance carry conviction. Thus the United States cannot expect the Latins to go along with it in giving priority to the dangers of Communist aggression until after they have been freed of native dictatorship and misrule, and after they have been assisted to higher standards of living. The Seventh Meeting of Consultation (San José, Costa Rica, August 1960) emphatically declared:

> The obligation of economic cooperation among the American states is essential to the strengthening of hemisphere solidarity and the reinforcement of the inter-American system in the face of threats of intervention that might affect it politically or economically.[73]

In this connection, "Pepe" Figueres of Costa Rica has said that there are two principal Latin-American complaints against the United States: one economic and one political. The economic complaint is directed against its opposition to schemes to stabilize the international commodity market and the other proposals to improve trade relations. The political complaint arises from the belief that under the pretense of nonintervention the United States has not given encouragement to the prodemocratic movement in Latin America, and that this country has even appeared to be on the side of the dictators.[74] Its apparent support of military dictators has enraged the democratic elements of Latin America more than anything else. Both Milton Eisenhower and Vice-President Nixon reported that this was the accusation most often voiced against the United States.

Many Latins caution that the United States cannot lead their nations to freedom if its hysteria about the Reds prevents it from distinguishing between progress and reaction. There is a feeling in Latin America that the United States, dedicated to the *status quo*, prefers to support native dictators, meanwhile branding the opposition of the democratic left as "Communistic." The liberal Costa Rica journal *Combate* criticizes the so-called "professional anti-Communists," to whom it seems the only problem in Latin America is Communism. These brand as "Communists" all who agitate for a substantial improvement in the condition of the people by economic reform or by liquidating hated privileges.[75]

Sr. Figueres calls on the United States for democratic leadership. "The United States has been very hesitant," he says, "to assume this moral leadership, and we are encouraging it to assume it." Like President Betancourt of Venezuela and other liberal-democratic leaders in

[73] *Seventh Meeting of Consultation*, 6.
[74] *Christian Science Monitor*, June 3, 1959.
[75] *Combate*, I (March–April 1959), 1, 9.

Latin America, Dr. Figueres feels that United States policy toward Latin-American dictators has supplied propaganda fuel for the Communists. He frankly tells the United States:

You're behind in upholding the true democratic creed. You're not fighting with an idea. The Communists are trying to infiltrate with an ideology . . . whereas the United States' representatives do not seem to be aware that they have a better weapon, which is freedom. And they are not wielding it. There is no effort made to make the United States appear as the champion of individual freedom.[76]

Unfortunately, the problem of democracy as contrasted with dictatorship, and its relation to the threat of international Communism, is not so simple as it appears to many of the Latin liberals. They are sublimely heedless of the sad fact that democracy is no immediate practical alternative and cannot be until certain democratic requirements are met by their respective nations. The masses of Latin America are just emerging from a feudal past and lack the bases of democracy: experience in self-government, deep respect for the law, a literate electorate, organized political parties, and respect for civil rights. Thus the liquidation of a dictatorship does not necessarily ensure the succession of a stable and popular government. Witness Castro's Cuba. And after Trujillo, what? It is entirely possible that situations even more inviting to Communist subversion and intrigue could develop, for there is no reason to believe that the alternating cycle of dictatorship and "popular" government in Latin America will cease in the foreseeable future.[77] This being the outlook, the first objective should be to give all aid possible, economic and moral, to create the conditions of effective democracy, but it should never be forgotten, either by the United States or by the Latins themselves, that democracy develops from within.

Any evaluation of the oas in answer to the charge that it has not faced up to the crises created by the Cuban situation and the intervention of international Communism must take into account that the Organization of American States, like the United Nations, is no more than the instrument of the governments that comprise it. It acts only when the member governments so desire, and it does only what they decide it shall do. There is no serious mechanistic defect in the oas. It can

[76] *Christian Science Monitor*, May 29, 1959; José Figueres "La Revolución en Latinoamérica," Suplemento de *Combate* (May 1959), 3–8.

[77] See J. Lloyd Mecham, "Latin American Constitutions: Nominal and Real," *Journal of Politics*, XXI (May 1959), 258–276.

operate as expeditiously and effectively as its members will it to operate.

Two political impediments have inhibited the governments from throwing the OAS machinery into high gear against Cuba: the pro-Castro sentiment in Latin America and the problem of intervention. Since no government in Latin America that seeks to be responsive to the popular will can stay in office without the support of the leftist-oriented masses, and since it is these left-wing groups that are pro-Castro, it is easy to see why governments have been reluctant to support anti-Castro international action. As for the other political impediment —the nonintervention principle—so emphatically has it been the first rule-of-conduct in inter-American affairs that it has imposed a rigorous veto on any action by the OAS which could be interpreted as interfering in the affairs of Cuba.

Not until these political impediments have been surmounted will the OAS be able to act in the Cuban crisis. When a majority of the governments shall have concluded that the intervention of the U.S.S.R. and Communist China in Cuba and the intervention of Cuba in the other Latin-American countries are realities, then cooperative action will no longer be avoidable.

XV Conclusion

The OAS past is ennobled by ideals of peace, union, and friendship among
our peoples. Its present is an international order that respects the juridical
equality, sovereignty, and territorial integrity of nations united to face any
threat and to seek peaceful solutions to controversies. Its future is a challenge to the men of today, to our ability to respond to the heroic mission
of America.

JOSÉ A. MORA, 1956

THE ORGANIZATION OF AMERICAN STATES is the oldest, the largest, the best integrated, and in many respects the most successful
of the regional arrangements attached to the United Nations. Unlike
other regional arrangements in the UN, the OAS did not come into
being recently and overnight; its evolution parallels that of the American nations themselves since the winning of their independence. Hence
the strength of the inter-American system is to be found in a long historical experience which has peculiarly fitted it to the hemisphere where
it has developed.

Evolving Pan Americanism. The Western Hemisphere idea of a
community of neighbors sharing common interests and ideals had dis-
parate and independent beginnings in Anglo America and Latin America. In the United States Thomas Jefferson was one of the first to call
attention to the identity of hemispheric interest and the need of excluding all European influence from the Americas. Henry Clay became
the greatest propagandist of the idea and advocated, in opposing European tyranny, an "American system" of which the United States would
be the center and in which all of Latin America would act with it. A
belated convert to the Western Hemisphere idea, Secretary of State
John Quincy Adams, joined President Monroe in making it the basis of
national policy in 1823. Although the Monroe Doctrine was originally
defined as a unilateral policy of the United States and therefore not an
appropriate subject for inter-American action, this does not negate the

fact that the mantle of United States protection was cast over Spanish America because of "a community of interests." This idea was entertained by President Adams when he accepted an invitation for the United States to take part in the first international conference of American states, the Congress of Panama, in 1826. Although fate decreed that the United States' representatives were not to participate in the deliberations at Panama, President Adams had made clear the moral presence of this country at that meeting.

It is important to remember that Simón Bolívar's conception of inter-American cooperation differed in two important respects from the American system of John Quincy Adams. The Liberator would have restricted his amphyctionic union to the newly-created Spanish American states, and he would have had them contract formal alliances for their mutual protection. President Adams, while favoring an American system which embraced all the Americas, balked at permanent political entanglements with the new states and wanted no part in their war against Spain. In short, inter-American cooperation, from the United States' point of view, was to be nonpolitical and, of course, nonmilitary.

During the period of the so-called "old" Pan Americanism, Bolivarian security cooperation among the Latins was attempted but without success. There were several efforts to create federations or alliances for mutual defense, all of which ended in failure. The Bolivarian concept of cooperation and union was rejected because there was a pronounced indisposition on the part of the Latin-American states to ratify commitments for mutual defense, particularly since they could see no existent danger. As for agreements to settle controversies among the Latin American nations themselves, a number of bilateral treaties of arbitration and conciliation were in existence. Despite the fact that it produced no concrete results, the "old" Pan Americanism was an important phase in the historical development of the inter-American system, primarily because it inculcated the idea and cultivated the habit of inter-American conference. It prepared the way for the second phase of cooperation: the "new" Pan Americanism.

The inauguration of Anglo- and Latin-American cooperation in 1889 in what became known as the "Pan American movement" was established on the sensible basis of feasible and practical measures for advancing and protecting common interests. This meant that the subjects of cooperative action were generally limited to those that lent themselves most readily to mutual agreement in the economic, social, and cultural realms. The difficult and contentious political problems were to be avoided, for experience, both in the United States and in Latin America, had proved that the American nations at the end of the nineteenth century were not prepared to jeopardize national sovereignty by entering into commitments which afforded uncertain security. It took time to allow for the further development of continental solidarity necessary to induce a more favorable attitude toward effective security cooperation.

After World War I, in spite of the warnings of experience, the American nations seemed to be completely oblivious of the desirability of providing for common defense against overseas aggression. The defeat of Germany, the creation of the League of Nations, and particularly the unchallenged might of the United States, evidently dispelled all prospect of external threat. So nothing was done to cope with such a contingency until European war clouds began gathering in the late 1930's. Dating from 1923, however, when the Treaty to Avoid or Prevent Conflicts Between the American States (Gondra treaty) was negotiated, the first effective step was taken in laying the foundation for a security structure dedicated to the peaceful solution of controversies among the American nations themselves. Significant additions to the structure prior to World War II were: General Convention of Inter-American Conciliation, 1929; General Treaty of Inter-American Arbitration, 1929; Anti-War Treaty of Non-Aggression and Conciliation (Saavedra Lamas pact, 1933); and Convention on Maintenance, Preservation and Re-establishment of Peace (Conciliation Convention, 1936). Although these pacts were far short of being 100 per cent effective in preventing inter-American conflicts, notably the Chaco War, they did represent significant and valuable progress in the willingness of American nations to submit to certain restrictions on national sovereignty in the interest of peace.

The progress made by the American republics in building an impressive peace structure in this short span of less than two decades proved that a sound foundation of inter-American solidarity had been laid during the period 1889–1923 by the careful selection and control of the subjects of cooperative action. Public opinion in the Americas, North and South, had been conditioned for the eventual negotiation of security pacts. The last roadblock was removed in 1933, when intervention was proscribed in inter-American relations. It is no exaggeration to state that the keystone in the arch of the inter-American system is the principle of nonintervention. The Latins, on their part, eventually manifested confidence and trust in the United States, and even came to cherish their regional association of nations as a prized possession. The United States, on its part, discovered that a policy of good neighborliness paid rich dividends in reciprocal cooperation, particularly in erecting a security barrier against overseas aggression.

The cooperative action of the American republics in World War II, both multilateral and bilateral, principally with the United States, left little to be desired. Owing largely to the consultation agreements of Buenos Aires and Lima, the American states were able to confront the war situations, whether as neutrals or as belligerents, in consultative meetings of their foreign ministers. Barring the fact that most were not actual military participants in the war, generally through no fault of their own, and barring the exceptional defection of pro-Nazi Argentina, it would be difficult to cite examples of Latin-American neglect to fulfill the responsibilities of hemisphere defense. Inter-American cooperation in World War II, much of it on a more or less *ad hoc* basis, proved beyond question the strength of American solidarity, and the value of the inter-American security system.

It is ironical that the inter-American system, which had measured up so well to the challenge of World War II, almost proved to be a casualty of the victory. In planning a postwar world organization, the Great Powers wished to relegate regional arrangements to subordinate and dependent status. The issue of universalism versus regionalism was joined at the San Francisco United Nations Conference and developed into a dangerous stalemate. This was a great crisis in the history of the inter-American system. Tacit acknowledgment of regional autonomy was eventually won, thanks largely to a united and passionate campaign conducted by the Latin-American delegations. Here is significant evidence of the prized status that the inter-American security system had come to occupy in the esteem of the Latin neighbors.

Realization by the American states of their obligation to make good their claims for the inter-American system as an autonomous regional-security agency within the United Nations was a specific reason for the formalizing and strengthening of the Organization of American States. Key pacts which accomplished this objective were: the Inter-American Treaty of Reciprocal Assistance (the Rio treaty, 1947), the Charter of the Organization of American States (1948), and the American Treaty of Pacific Settlement (Pact of Bogotá, 1948). While all these pacts affirmed that the OAS was a regional agency within the United Nations and that the inter-American system was consistent with the purposes and principles of the United Nations, both the Charter of the OAS and the Pact of Bogotá provided that regional procedures should first be invoked in international controversies of a regional nature before turning to the United Nations. The Rio treaty, referring to Article 51 of the Charter of the United Nations, provided that measures of self-defense can be taken *prior* to action by the Security Council of the United Nations. It was a clear understanding at San Francisco that the United Nations would withhold its intervention while a controversy was in process of settlement by regional procedures. In 1954 and in 1960 the UN deferred to OAS priority in the Guatemalan and Cuban crises. The obligation, under Article 54 of the Charter of the UN, to keep the Security Council fully informed of regional-security action has been faithfully observed by the OAS. The channel of communication is the respective secretariats of the Organization of American States and the United Nations. An effort by the Soviet Union to have the Security Council endorse the OAS report on the Sixth Meeting of Consultation was rejected because it might imply UN control of OAS action.

Since 1948, when the inter-American system was reorganized, consolidated, and perfected at the Bogotá conference, it has been necessary to further perfect the peace procedures in order to meet new situations, particularly those created by the insidious activities of international Communism and the breakdown of order in the Caribbean. The American republics formally declared at the Caracas conference in 1954 that when any American government fell under the domination and control of the international Communist movement this would be tantamount to extending to this hemisphere the political system of an extracontinental power. The significance of the Declaration of Caracas is that the Latin-American republics had virtually joined the United States in support of the Monroe Doctrine.[1]

At the end of 1960 the inter-American security commitments to meet overseas threats were numerous and extensive and, barring unforeseen developments and granting the will to implement, provided an adequate base for the mounting of common defense when emergencies arise. Not only have extensive political defense lines been established, but military ones as well. One would be foolish to declare their adequacy, but he would be equally foolish to deny the fact of earnest planning and comprehensive preparations. Nor need it be conceded, as presumed by certain critics, that the action of the United States in supplying armaments to several of the Latin-American countries has been ill-advised. Since the Latin governments are not yet prepared to

[1] This idea is shared by Jesús María Yepes, a leading authority on Pan Americanism (*Del Congreso de Panamá a la Conferencia de Caracas 1826– 1954* [Caracas, 1955], II, 237–238).

abandon armaments, they assuredly will turn to other sources if the United States ceases to supply their needs.

It has also been necessary to perfect the procedures of peaceful settlement applicable to controversies among the Latin-American nations themselves. A state of turmoil in the Caribbean, created by the active practice of interventionism on the part of a number of the Caribbean and Central American states, revealed weaknesses in the existent peace instruments, however numerous and complex they undoubtedly were.

The most important addition to the inter-American security system, as reorganized and perfected at the Bogotá conference in 1948, was the Inter-American Peace Committee, created in 1940 but not installed until 1948. This five-nation group was originally set up to help governments compose their differences by providing a neutral meeting ground and by suggesting to the disputants measures and steps conducive to settlement. The committee lacked the power to intervene directly in the settlement unless the parties concerned agreed for it to do so. However, the Fifth Meeting of Consultation (1959) assigned to the Peace Committee the additional duty of studying the causes of international tensions in the Carribbean and also removed the requirement of prior consent of both parties. The eleventh inter-American conference, scheduled to meet in Quito, was to decide whether these new powers should be permanent.

The "liberating expeditions" of political exiles, organized on the soil of neighboring countries and aided and abetted by the local governments, were patent violations of the 1928 Convention on Duties and Rights of States in the Event of Civil Strife. In an effort to stop these evasions of that convention, in 1957 there was opened for signature a protocol to the convention, which provided a more specific enumeration of the obligations of states not to interfere with each others' internal affairs. Interestingly, however, ratification of the protocol by four of the Caribbean republics seems to have imposed no perceptible restraint on their actions.[2]

The Rio de Janeiro Treaty of Reciprocal Assistance was put to test by Caribbean controversies on eight different occasions. In every instance the disputes were apparently settled, the Council of the OAS acting as the provisional organ of consulation. Only once (the sixth

---

[2] By the end of 1960 the protocol had been ratified by Costa Rica, Cuba, Haiti, and the Dominican Republic.

meeting at San José, Costa Rica, in August 1960) was it necessary for the foreign ministers to meet. That the settlement of most of these controversies did not usually prove to be permanent was probably due to the fact that the Rio treaty did not provide sanctions to enforce the settlements.

The peace machinery of the OAS is far from a streamlined model of efficiency. According to U.S. Ambassador John C. Dreier, "It is far easier to apply the brakes than to step on the gas." Even the Rio treaty, although cumbersome, has the means, says Dreier,

to take effective action against a government that threatens the peace and security of the continent. The question is first of all one of deciding to move. And this brings us back to the observation that the OAS will act only when the governments so decide. In the Cuban crisis this will be when a majority of governments conclude that the intervention of the Soviet Union and Communist China in Cuba, and the intervention of Cuba in other Latin American countries, have become sufficiently serious to make such action no longer avoidable. That time may well be at hand, and the way through the juridical maze will then be found.[3]

United States predominance. A fact which has not been ignored throughout this study is the exceptional position the United States occupies in the OAS. Although nominally a regional arrangement of twenty-one juridically equal and sovereign states, the Organization of American States is actually an association of one Great Power with twenty small weak member nations in which evidences of United States predominance are readily apparent. For example, not only are the OAS headquarters located in Washington, but the United States is a member of all permanent committees and most of the special committees of the OAS Council. Most important, the United States pays two-thirds of the annual budget of the OAS, and, in addition to the burden of continental defense, it bears most of the financial responsibilities for the support of economic, social, and cultural activities.

Because of its overwhelming power it is difficult for the United States to be a working partner in the OAS without becoming dominant. Generally, this country, in its efforts to avoid the criticism of dominance, has been exemplary in the modesty of its conduct at the meetings of the OAS. Unfortunately, these unnatural self-imposed restraints on its own leadership have not made it less difficult for Latin-American political leaders to assert themselves or seize leadership opportunities

[3] John C. Dreier, "The OAS and the Cuban Crisis," *SAIS Review,* V (Winter, 1961), 8.

because of fear of displeasing the United States. This situation will not change until the Latin-American countries increase their own capabilities to work with their North American partner on more equal terms. In the meantime there seems to be no alternative to having the United States assert vigorous leadership.

Inter-American solidarity. An appraisement of the inter-American security system must take account not only of the strength and weakness of the security mechanism itself but, more important, of the will, spirit, and unity of purpose which control the operation of the machinery. All else fails if the member partners weaken in their sense of solidarity, for a keen realization of unity is an absolute requisite of effective regional coaction.

The elements making for both union and division among the American peoples are many. One can understand the inter-American security system better if he is clearly aware of both the binding and disuniting factors. Community of language, race, religion, and culture, often important factors in historic regional associations, are, of course, absent in the inter-American system. Anglo Americans and Latin Americans not only speak different languages but they also stem from radically different cultural backgrounds. There is more harmonious and compatible cultural understanding between the United States and Western Europe by far than with Latin America. The terms "alien" and "foreigner," with all they connote, stand as a barrier between the peoples of the two Americas. Praiseworthy cultural-relations programs have helped to improve understanding, but they cannot be expected to eradicate the deep-seated, seemingly inherent, hostility toward foreigners. Much of this prejudice is existent in the United States, but it is more pronounced among the Latins, for they have been the victims, real or imagined, of North American interventionism and economic imperialism. Latin-American nationalistic resentments of the uncouth Yankee are highly impregnated with envy of the marvelous progress and achievements of the Colossus of the North, and also with futility and indignant shame because of their dependence on the United States. They seem to be in the vortex of American power and can do nothing about it. They are not their own masters.

Since it is not in language, race, or culture, it has been suggested that perhaps the source of the unity of the American republics comes from the fact that they all inhabit a common vast geographical area, separated from the rest of the world by broad oceans. Geographical location cannot of itself create regional unity, but there is no denying that it is an important factor in the development of regional association; the very term "region" attests this point. But, given the region—the Western Hemisphere in this instance—what is it that has been responsible for the world's best example of a regional security arrangement?

History, a prime factor in the molding of nationalities, has been important in the development of our regional system. The fact that the American republics were born in popular revolt against a foreign sovereign produced a consciousness of community of origin. Latin America's adoption of national constitutions influenced by that of the United States, and the establishment of democratic governments, at least in name, contributed to a sense of community of political institutions and objectives. Sprung from similar origins as European colonies, and embarking on independent careers under the republican form of government, the United States and the Latin-American nations possessed a common tradition of belonging to "the New World." They shared the Western Hemisphere idea. The converging lines of the historical development of the United States and of Latin America provided many examples to prove that the American republics shared a common destiny.

It has been well said that Pan Americanism has been made possible because of our geographic isolation, our similar political institutions, and our common conception of human rights. Many hold that the cooperation of the American republics is a natural consequence of the fact that they form a state system modeled on similar lines and based on common democratic principles. But there are many who disparage the importance of this alleged community of political institutions and ideals as a source of unity, for despite superficial constitutional similarities between the two Americas, in the actual functioning of political institutions they are as far apart as the poles. Although most of the Latin-American peoples have demonstrated that a century and a half has not been long enough to convert their democratic ideals into stable institutions, one cannot ignore the fact that these ideals have never been abandoned. No Latin-American dictator would dare to condemn democracy; one and all pay it lip service. Note the affirmation of principle contained in the Charter of the Organization of American States (Chap. 5, Art. 5, *d*): "The solidarity of the American States and the high aims which are sought through it require the political organization of those States on the basis of the effective exercise of representative democracy." In confirming this principle a spokesman for the State Department has declared, "Our concern for the development and strengthening of the inter-American system cannot be separated from our concern for the maintenance and development of democratic ideals and practices in all the American republics."[4]

Thus, even though the Latins falter in establishing permanent, stable, and truly popular, representative, republican governments, they are at one with the United States in striving toward the same objective. There may be a difference between the Americas in progress but not in purpose. The peoples of both are motivated by deep underlying spiritual forces: they desire independence, peace, democracy, and rising economic, educational, and social levels. It was natural, therefore, for the American republics to capitalize on their geographical location by joining in a security arrangement based on the oft-declared principles of inter-American solidarity which have been incorporated in international treaties and declarations and are a part of the basic law of the continent. The fundamental principles which govern inter-American juridical relations, and constitute the essence of their international order, are the following: (1) the juridical equality of states and respect for their personality, sovereignty, and independence; (2) respect for, and faithful observance of, treaties; (3) no recourse to the use of force except for self-defense; (4) settlement of controversies of an international character by peaceful procedures; (5) nonrecognition of special advantages or territory acquired by force; (6) no intervention by one state in the internal or external affairs of another state; and (7) continental responsibility for the maintenance of peace. The idea of collective responsibility for peace in the hemisphere is an old one and is shared by all.

Continental solidarity, based on these shared beliefs of the American republics, has in recent years been threatened by an alarming increase of anti-United States feeling in Latin America. Since the security structure is based on inter-American solidarity, obviously an appraisement must take into account the nature of this hostile sentiment and suggest what should be done about it.

Threatened solidarity. The responsible causes and the nature of anti-United States sentiment in Latin America have been discussed at some length in preceding chapters. However, at the risk of oversimplification here, we note again that since the end of World War II there has been mounting discontent with United States policies: political and economic. In the political area there is a belief that the United States has not bulwarked democratic efforts in Latin America as it should. Preoccupied with the cold war, this country has tried to main-

[4] Ellis O. Briggs, U.S. Dept. of State, *Bulletin,* XVI (April 27, 1947), 769.

tain order and stability in the Latin-American states, even though this meant in many instances its support of dictators. Hence the charge that this country is antirevolutionary. The United States now finds itself in an embarrassing position, for many of the dictators with whom it was once in evident cordial relations have been overthrown by successful popular revolts. The new regimes feel that they owe no thanks to the United States; on the contrary, this country is blamed for the crimes of the dictators. Thus it is that successful popular revolutions have added to anti-United States sentiment. This raises an interesting question: How can the United States maintain relations with Latin-American administrations without identifying itself as a supporter of those regimes?

In view of its seeming unconcern about accepting Latin-American dictators, the zeal of this country in mobilizing continental defense against the Communist dictatorship struck many Latin liberals as grotesquely inconsistent. They were unable to accept illusory Communist dictatorships as being more dangerous to them than the existent ruthless native dictatorships.

Quite true, the State Department erred in being over-cordial and even benevolent to certain tyrants, but its policy toward them was defensible on at least two counts: first, the Department did not dare risk being accused of violating the nonintervention principle by opposing them; and second, the dictators were usually cooperative in organizing continental defense against the Communist threat. But later, when revolutionary action toppled dictators in rapid succession, and so-called "popular governments" became the considerable majority among the Latin-American states, it became necessary for the State Department to adjust to the new political order. That it was too slow in making these adjustments is possibly a valid criticism.

It is of significance that in its final months the Eisenhower-Herter Administration went all out in reversing the earlier policies toward dictators. Not only did the United States join its OAS associates in sharply condemning Trujillo's extramural activities, but it strongly advocated collective intervention in cases of flagrant violations of human rights in the Dominican Republic. It remains to be seen whether the new antidictatorship policy of the State Department will strengthen the OAS, or whether, because of the uncertainties of Latin America's political future, it will contribute to a weakening of the united front essential to hemisphere safety.

During the recent manifestations of hostility, Latin America's reaction to United States economic policy has probably been more violent and threatening to inter-American solidarity than has its political resentments. Indeed, this country has been put on notice by leading Latin-American statesmen, and others, that without economic cooperation there can be no Pan Americanism. Dating from World War II, and particularly since the Bogotá conference of 1948, economic cooperation has been elevated to prime status as a basic principle of the inter-American system. The Charter of the OAS affirms, "Economic cooperation is essential to the common welfare and prosperity of the peoples of the continent," and this idea has been reaffirmed in several subsequent inter-American declarations. For example, a resolution of the Washington meeting of foreign ministers (1951) declared that "the economic development of underdeveloped countries should be considered as an essential factor in the total concept of Hemisphere defense," and a resolution of the Caracas conference of 1954 held that "the countries members of the Organization of American States should have, as one of the basic objectives of continental solidarity, a close coordination of their economies with a sense of unity."

The problem of inter-American economic cooperation is put in its proper perspective when we note that among the Latin-American nations almost all of the foreign investment-capital comes from the United States and that most of the inter-American trade is with the United States. Thus the term "inter-American economic cooperation" is equivalent to "United States–Latin-American economic cooperation." The burden of the Latin-American complaint is that on at least two scores the United States has not been "cooperative." First, it is charged with ignoring the economic truth that if it wishes to enable them to buy the products of its industry and resist the enticements of extracontinental competition, it must provide a favorable market for their own raw materials. The Latin Americans' keenest resentments of recent years stem from what they regard as the unfair and unneighborly burdens which United States tariffs impose on the import of many of their key products. Also they have been inveighing against the widely fluctuating prices for their products in the United States market, and have been demanding some kind of price stabilization.

Second, the United States has aroused Latin-American complaint because of its alleged failure to make good on the adequate economic assistance apparently pledged by the Charter and other inter-American instruments. That the Good Neighbors in the OAS regard U.S. economic assistance as an obligation there can be little doubt. How else can one explain complaints and criticism, even in the highest echelons of government, that the inter-American defense system stands or falls on this economic cooperation? Not only is the United States apparently obligated to give assistance, but it must be assistance "adequate" for meeting Latin America's fundamental critical needs, for example, in housing, education and health programs, food supply, and communications. The commitments involving long-term undertakings with no immediate profits, have been consistently refused by the United States lending agencies as not being "sound" projects. It is argued that because of the orientation of the Latin-American economy toward the United States, and because of the United States' dependence on Latin America, this interdependence makes their social and economic problems quite as much a concern of this country as of theirs.

Thus the United States, which, since the end of World War II, has been most generous by ordinary standards in financing various assistance programs, is criticized as not having done enough when its aid is equated in terms of the multibillions appropriated for Europe and Asia. The Latin Americans' expectation of United States assistance rests simply in their belief that as the oldest, the most faithful, and the most indispensable allies of this country, they are certainly entitled to equal if not preferential treatment.

Remedies, tried and proposed. In view of these criticisms of United States policy, so injurious to inter-American solidarity, what can be done? The situation calls for rational understanding, tolerance, and mutual concessions between Anglo America and Latin America. First, with respect to Latin America, the nations of that region must understand that the primary responsibility is on themselves to work out their own increasingly complex problems for which there are no short-term solutions. The answers must be found largely in their own resources, industry, and genius. They must use their own resources wisely to provide increased standards of living for their people, for no amount of United States assistance would suffice. They must increase their economic productivity not only with the aid of foreign investment-capital and improved techniques of production, but also through intelligent governmental participation and the industry of their own people.

The Latins should dismiss any thought that they enjoy a right to be aided by the United States, which most assuredly is under no such obligation. The United States gives aid because of an obligation to itself, for it views the problem of aid in terms of national self-interest. It would make for better understanding on the part of the people of the United States if the Latins abandoned their importunate insistence on economic assistance and tried to know more about the actual facts

Conclusion

of United States domestic politics and the national economy. If they can be made aware of the internal economic and social forces in this country, they will come to realize that the making of economic policy is not the free prerogative of the President, the State Department, or even of the Congress. Perhaps even the ultranationalists of Latin America might then concede that United States policy can also be defended on nationalistic grounds. After all, nationalism is not a one-sided proposition. They should also be brought to realize the magnitude of the burden which the United States has assumed in the defense of the free world, remembering that its wealth is not illimitable.

There can be no doubt that Latin Americans cherish the inter-American system. They fought for it tenaciously at San Francisco, and have been apprehensive whenever there were indications that United States policy was tending to universalism at the expense of regionalism. One of Latin America's greatest statesmen, Dr. Alberto Lleras, now President of Colombia, has frankly declared that the inter-American organization, while producing regional benefits for all, is of much greater value to the Latin-American republics than to the United States. He has written:

These nations have enjoyed, and will continue to enjoy, the inestimable advantages of being neighbors to one of the greatest empires in all history without suffering the fear of imperialism or the threat of violence; they bask in an international order based on law which preserves their independence and guarantees their security more fully with each passing day.[5]

It is no contradiction of the foregoing comments on Latin-American devotion to the inter-American system to add here that the concept lacks popular support in Latin America. In fact, there are many who subscribe to the Fidel Castro charge that the OAS is in fact a colonial secretariat of the United States. On the one hand, Latin-American governments, controlled by the ruling classes, have been fairly consistent in their support of the inter-American system, but on the other hand the masses either have been uninterested or regard the OAS as a tool of United States imperialism which supports the *status quo* in Latin America. It is fairly safe to predict that in the long run the future of the OAS will depend on the extent to which Latin-American governments can free themselves of the mass pressures of anti-United States hostility. Perhaps the greatest problem facing the OAS is that of selling

[5] Pan American Union, *Bulletin*, LXXXII (June 1948), 303.

itself to Latin Americans and freeing itself of the false stigma of being under United States domination.

Every country of the Western Hemisphere, if realistic, must know that any weakness of the United States that invites aggression, political or military, also exposes each one of them to aggression, whether as a preliminary target, an incidental target, or the target of a mopping-up operation. No country in the hemisphere is likely to preserve its independence if the independence of the United States is lost; and the independence of the United States would certainly be jeopardized if other American nations were subjugated by an overseas power.

In view of their acknowledged reliance on a strong OAS, the Latin members surely are wise enough to know that it is not in their own interests to condone anti-United States demonstrations. They need to make every effort to curb unreasonable and irrational emotional and nationalistic outbursts which might induce the United States to reappraise its aid policies, widening thereby a breach so sought by the U.S.S.R. Raúl Haya de la Torre, famous Peruvian Aprista leader and once a Yankeephobe, has confessed that United States power is not as dangerous to Latin America as is the latter's "habitual complex of inferiority." He holds that the United States and Latin America are in need of each other and should live united "without domination, exploitation, or injustices."[6]

Important as it is that the people of Latin America realize and appreciate the magnitude of this country's effort and sacrifice in treasure and blood in the far-flung fields of the East-West conflict, it is equally important that the people of the United States become more fully aware of the importance to them of Latin America and of the necessity of giving adequate attention to the needs and aspirations of their sister republics. It is well said that the United States cannot win the cold war in Latin America but it can lose it there.

According to Vice-President Nixon, "There is no area of the world with which we are more closely associated—there is no area of the world which is more important as far as the United States is concerned—than these, our closest neighbors of the American hemisphere." Then Mr. Nixon cautions, "We must never take our friends for granted. We do not take our friends for granted in Latin America. We don't think that we ever have, but some of them have gotten the impression that we did."[7] It is highly important to avoid even the appearance of neglect, for this can be harmful to inter-American relations. For

---

[6] *La Prensa* (New York), Sept. 21, 1946.

[7] U.S. Dept. of State, *Bulletin,*XXXVIII (June 9, 1958), 951.

this reason the Eisenhower Administration acted in its last years to strengthen economic cooperation with Latin America. Not only was there a steady increase in the appropriations for assistance programs, but with respect to the import of certain raw materials, negotiations were initiated to meet Latin America's demands for an adequate market at fair prices in terms of production costs. And, after years of resistance, the United States finally acquiesced in the founding of an Inter-American Development Bank, whose purpose is "to contribute to the acceleration of the process of economic development of the member countries, individually and collectively." Because of this and other recent developments, culminating in the Kennedy Alliance for Progress, there is reason to hope that the economic barrier to better understanding between the Americas may begin to dissolve.

It also would be conducive to better understanding if the people of the United States and their government did not hold the Latins to such strict standards of conduct and obligation as allies. They should realize that Latin America's interests are not world-wide, and so should be moderate in their requests for its support on international questions. For many Latins, a defensive regional arrangement has meaning only if it is confined to problems of continental defense. They object to being forced to support the extracontinental role of the United States; they charge that this country has transformed the system from a regional-defense arrangement to an instrument of world policy. Says one of these critics, "As long as the United States followed an isolationist policy, the advantages for the Latin American countries of a joint defense treaty with the United States would have outweighed the disadvantages. Today, its benefits are not evident."[8] Thus, not only should the United States restrain its use of the OAS as an instrument of policy but it also should be moderate in requests for Latin-American support in the UN. On the other hand, it should support Latin-American interests in international questions whenever possible.

We of the United States are prone to assume that since the members of the OAS are solemnly pledged to resist the common enemy, international Communism, and since we regard this threat as greater than all else, this problem should have priority over all else. Consequently we are disappointed and even scandalized when we learn that the Latins do not accept our assessment of the Communist danger. Not only do they regard their own dictators as rating more immediate attention, but they regard interventionism itself as a greater evil than Communism.

[8] Jorge Castañeda, "Pan Americanism and Regionalism: A Mexican View," *International Organization*, X (Aug. 1956), 386.

It serves no useful purpose to question the devotion of our associates to the necessities of the anti-Communist crusade; the situation calls instead for tolerant understanding. It is obvious that the issues of the cold war cannot be viewed in the same light by the United States as by its OAS allies. The disparities of power, wealth, and economic development, as well as those of social and democratic achievement, mean that in the event of disaster the United States would lose so much more. Thus it has more to fight for. The Latins, on the other hand, are asked to fight not so much for democratic freedoms and economic well-being as for the promise of these treasures in an uncertain future. We should not forget, therefore, that there are greater concerns to the Latin than international Communism, and for these reasons he becomes quite weary of our preoccupation with this alleged bogey. This does not signify necessarily a disinclination to associate with the United States in the fight against international Communism, but it does point up the necessity of its giving them aid for the solution of their internal problems. This the United States must accept as part of the anti-Communist campaign. Like it or not, it really has little choice in the matter.

It is most disconcerting, nevertheless, that so many of the Latins apparently take the position that the objective of their association with the United States in the cold war is to help this country. Therefore they expect reward for their assistance. The fact that the very existence of free nations is threatened, and thus that all are cooperating in a common struggle for survival, seems to be overlooked. Whether the *Latinos* do not understand the issues of the ideological conflict, or whether they are merely unconcerned, their attitude presents a definite challenge to the State Department and the propaganda genius of the United States Information Agency.

An equivalent challenge is presented by the rising tide of "anti-Americanism" in Latin America. Too much dependence has been placed on "dollar diplomacy" as a means of meeting this—and other problems—in Latin America. We of the United States seem to be obsessed by the belief that the mere expansion of economic assistance will remedy all ills and recover the friendship of the hemisphere neighbors. We delude ourselves in assessing the influence of the almighty dollar.

The objective of Washington diplomacy need not necessarily be that of winning friends; more important, it should seek to command respect, for leadership is dependent on respect, not friendship. The United States has evidently failed to win the respect which its power and world position demand. Moreover, it should never be forgotten that power is lost by default—that retention is dependent on its exercise. There is great need for virile imagination in formulating a new positive and aggressive Latin-American policy. To its preoccupation with presumed obligations toward the underdeveloped nations, should not the United States also add some consideration of its rights and privileges in international society? If it does not, the day may come when it will be forced to abandon the so-called Good Neighbor policy as a luxury it can no longer afford.

What of the future? Have United Nations and world developments since 1945 contributed in any way to a weakening of the regional view and a strengthening of the universalist view? Are we more disposed today, as contrasted to pre-1945, to entrust the solution of hemisphere problems to the world organization? Are there any indications pointing in this direction from either the United States or from Latin America? A categorical answer to all these questions is an emphatic NO! The simple truth of the matter is that, so far as the Organization of American States is concerned, regionalism is as strong today as ever. Not only has there been no indication of any desire to entrust the peace of the Americas to United Nations supervision, but the OAS has met with fair success the various tests which challenged its pretensions as the protector of Western Hemisphere peace.

The machinery of inter-American security has been perfected to the limits permitted by contemporary practical considerations and presents no real obstacle to organizing defense against foreign aggression and to the peaceful solution of inter-American controversies. Hence the future of the OAS will be influenced not by possible defects in the mechanism itself but by the strength of continental solidarity. The same sentiments of unity which bind individual nations in meeting great national emergencies must also unite the nations of the Americas.

Does the status of inter-American solidarity augur well for the future? Never have American governments been more aware of a community of interests. This is stated advisedly, in spite of Latin-American criticism of United States policies. Most Latins in positions of authority support the OAS, and they would be as reluctant today to see it weakened as they were at San Francisco in 1945. Emotional outbursts to the effect that there can be no Pan Americanism without increased economic cooperation are by no means a threat to secede. Any movement to weaken or liquidate the inter-American system is unthinkable. It is the Latin view that the United States, not they, has raised these doubts.

It has been difficult for these republics to understand the global

THE UNITED STATES AND INTER-AMERICAN SECURITY

orientation of United States policy. They have incorrectly inferred that because the United States abandoned isolationism and entered into commitments around the world, this has altered its view with respect to the inter-American system. Does "world orientation" mean side-tracking regional policy? Global and hemispheric policies are not incompatible, and regionalism remains a cardinal principle of U.S. foreign policy. The great popular, and governmental, reaction in the United States to the anti-Yankee demonstrations and Cuban developments proves the high position Latin America occupies in United States policy; it also proves that we of the United States fully realize we share with our neighbors equal need of a continental-security arrangement.

For a considered evaluation of the inter-American security system, we quote from a speech delivered by Secretary of State John Foster Dulles in Rio de Janeiro on August 6, 1958:

As I have participated in meetings of other regional security organizations, I have frequently cited to them our OAS as having many advanced characteristics which ought to be followed. And indeed, they have been followed. We can be proud of the leadership which the American Republics have given in promoting international order on a regional basis.[9]

[9] U.S. Dept. of State, Public Services Division, Ser. S., No. 69.

Bibliographical Note

The Columbus Memorial Library, Pan American Union, Washington, D.C., provides a convenient and well-organized concentration of extensive and diverse materials on the subject of inter-American security cooperation. Here is assembled the documentation of the conferences and the activities of the OAS, and its precursors, with a degree of completeness not to be found elsewhere. Much of this material has been published, of course, by the Pan American Union and is available in various libraries.

A valuable *Bibliografía de las Conferencias Interamericanas* was published by the Pan American Union in 1954. It contains a listing not only of the official documents of the conferences and meetings from 1889 to 1951 but also of books, articles, and other materials relating to the conferences. The *Indice por materias de los diversos instrumentos interamericanos, suscritos o aprobados en las conferencias panamericanas principales de 1889 a 1951* (1953) is a subject index to the conventions and resolutions of the American conferences. Equally valuable as a bibliographical aid is the monthly issue of the Pan American Union: *List of books accessioned and periodical articles indexed in the Columbus Memorial Library*. This index to the periodical literature of Latin America covers a wide selection of periodicals and is a handy guide to Latin-American opinion on the subject of inter-American cooperation.

A listing of special publications of the Pan American Union, pertinent to security cooperation, includes the following: *Improvement and Coordination of Inter-American Peace Instruments*, 5 vols. (1944); *Report on the Activities of the Organization of American States, 1948–1953* (1953); *Manual of Inter-American Relations* (1956); *Inter-American Treaties and Conventions* (1957); *Aplicaciones del Tratado Interamericano de Asistencia Recíproca, 1948–1958* (1959); and *Bilateral Treaty Developments in Latin America*, 3 vols. (1938–55). Since 1933, in compliance with a resolution adopted by the Seventh Inter-American Conference of American States, the Pan American Union has issued semiannually (more or less), a *Status of the Pan American Treaties and Conventions*, showing the ratification record of the respective American republics.

The annual reports of the Director-General of the Pan American Union, and his successor the Secretary-General of the OAS, contain much useful information. These originally appeared in the *Bulletin* of the Pan American Union, later in the *Annals* of the Organization of American States, and, since 1955, in separate publications. The *Bulletin* of the Pan American Union, a monthly periodical containing articles, documents, and official records and notices, was published during the years 1893–1948. In 1949 the Pan American Union initiated the publication of the *Annals* of the Organization of American States, an official quarterly which records the documents of the Inter-American conferences, the meetings of consultation, the Council, and the other agencies of the organization. The series was terminated in 1958. Also in 1949 appeared *Américas,* a monthly magazine on inter-American affairs.

Second only to the Pan American Union as a source of materials relating to the inter-American security system is the United States Department of State, which publishes, in a regular series and in special issues, materials on general and specific subjects connected with United States foreign relations. The *Monthly Catalog of United States Government Publications* (cumulative annually) is a guide to these materials. Also a cumulative list of Department of State publications for the period October 1, 1929, to January 1, 1950, has been published; and, since then, cumulative lists of current publications have been issued semiannually by the Department.

Foremost among the Department of State regular publications is the *Foreign Relations of the United States,* an annual volume of state papers, and the *Bulletin,* a weekly publication containing basic official information on developments in American foreign relations. A special series—Treaty and Executive Agreement Series—contains the texts of promulgated treaties and agreements. Until the end of 1947, treaties and executive agreements were published in separate series. The reports of United States delegations to inter-American conferences are published in the International Organization and Conference Series, known prior to 1948 as the Conference Series. Illustrative of the numerous significant special publications of the Department of State are: J. Reuben Clark, *Memorandum on the Monroe Doctrine* (1930); *Consultation Among the American Republics With Respect to the Argentine Situation* (1946); and *A Case History of Communist Penetration; Guatemala* (1957).

Other departments and agencies of the United States government are also sources of publications and materials relevant to inter-American security cooperation. Since this cooperation has expanded so prominently in the economic area, particularly since the inauguration of the United States' foreign-assistance program, the reports, statistics, and other official documents of the participating agencies have become important contributions to the bibliography of inter-American cooperation. Illustrative of this kind of material are the reports of the foreign-lending agencies (Export-Import Bank and Development Loan Fund) and the foreign-assistance agencies

487

Bibliographical Note

(Mutual Security Administration, Foreign Operations Administration, and International Cooperation Administration). A helpful introduction to the United States' technical-assistance program in Latin America is the *History of the Office of the Coordinator of Inter-American Affairs* (Office of Inter-American Affairs, 1947). The *Foreign Commerce Weekly,* published by the Department of Commerce, the *Treasury Bulletin,* a monthly, and the *Federal Reserve Bulletin,* a monthly, contain valuable information on the problems of the United States' economic relations with Latin America. Congressional documents also deal with the various aspects of inter-American cooperation. Particularly valuable are the *Hearings* of the House and Senate committees on the foreign-aid program, anti-Americanism in Latin America, and other problems of United States–Latin-American relations.

Official Latin-American publications on, or relating to, inter-American security cooperation are meager. The foreign offices of the respective countries publish nothing comparable to the State Department's *Bulletin* and *Foreign Relations* unless it be their annual reports, usually called *Memorias,* which often contain selected correspondence and documents dealing with some contemporary foreign problems. They publish a number of occasional and special numbers dealing with subjects of international concern, notably boundary and other territorial controversies. For example, the documentary material relating to the controversies between Ecuador and Peru, Honduras and Nicaragua, and Bolivia and Paraguay (the Chaco War) are quite ample. Most of the governments also publish reports of their delegations to inter-American conferences. However, because of classified and unpublished diplomatic correspondence, it is difficult to penetrate into the chancelleries to discover motivations for policy decisions and diplomatic maneuvers.

An unofficial documentary source is the series of volumes on the inter-American conferences published by the Carnegie Endowment for International Peace. These comprise, J. B. Scott (ed.), *The International Conferences of American States, 1889–1928* (1931), *First Supplement for 1933–1940* (1940), *Primer Suplemento, 1938–1942* (1943), and *Segundo Suplemento, 1945–1954* (1956). These volumes contain a collection of the conventions, recommendations, resolutions, reports, and motions adopted by the first ten Inter-American conferences and the first four consultative meetings of the foreign ministers.

An exhaustive list of secondary works (books, articles, pamphlets) on the inter-American system would be staggering. There are, however, no general surveys of the inter-American system worthy of special mention. I merely list, therefore, those works that, despite their inadequacies, rise above the general level of publications in this category. These are: Francisco Cuevas Cancino, *Del Congreso de Panamá a la Conferencia de Caracas, 1826–1954,* 2 vols. (1955); Luis Hernández-Solís, *El Panamericanismo, Una Moderna Interpretación* (1944); John P. Humphrey, *The Inter-American System: A Canadian View* (1942); Alejandro Magnet, *Origines y*

Antecedentes del Panamericanismo (1945); Eugéne Pépin, *Le Panameri-canisme* (1938); José Sansón-Terán, *El Interamericanismo en Marcha: de Bolívar y Monroe al Rooseveltianismo* (1949); and Jesús María Yepes, *Del Congreso de Panamá a la Conferencia de Caracas, 1826–1954,* 2 vols. (1955). The works by Yepes and Cuevas Cancino were winners of the first and second prizes, respectively, offered by the Venezuelan government in honor of the meeting of the Tenth Inter-American Conference of American States at Caracas. Since the authors were bound to relate the influence of Simón Bolívar to the Pan American movement there is a distinct lack of balance in their treatment of the subject. Of the works mentioned, that by Humphrey, though much out of date, has probably the greatest merit.

There are many helpful studies and discussions relating to aspects of the inter-American cooperative movement. A few of these titles follow: M. Margaret Ball, *The Problems of Inter-American Organization* (1944); Stetson Conn and Byron Fairchild, *The Framework of Hemisphere Defense* (1960); Donald M. Dozer, *Are We Good Neighbors?* (1959); Laurence Duggan, *The Americas: The Search for Hemisphere Security* (1949); Alberto Guani, *La Solidaridad Internacional en America* (1942); John A. Houston, *Latin America in the United Nations* (1956); Gordon Ireland, *Boundaries, Possessions, and Conflicts in South America* (1938); also his *Boundaries, Possessions, and Conflicts in Central and North America and the Caribbean* (1941); Luis Iterralde Chinel, *De Ginebra a la Defensa Continental* (1945); Warren H. Kelchner, *Latin American Relations with the League of Nations* (1929); J. B. Lockey, *Pan Americanism: Its Beginnings* (1920); Helio Lobo, *O Panamericanismo e o Brasil* (1939); T. F. McGann, *Argentina, the United States, and the Inter-American System, 1880–1914* (1957); P. A. Martin, *Latin America and the War* (1925); Hermann Meyer-Lindenberg, *El Procedimiento Interamericano para Consolidar la Paz* (1941); Luis Quintanilla, *A Latin American Speaks* (1943); also his *Pan Americanism and Democracy* (1952); Aureliano Rodríguez Larreta, *Orientación de la Política Internacional en America Latina,* 2 vols. (1938); Enrique Ruíz-Guiñazú, *La Politica Argentina y el Futuro de América* (1944); and A. P. Whitaker, *The Western Hemisphere Idea: Its Rise and Decline* (1954).

For a balanced view of the inter-American security system, due attention must be given to the critical opinion of Latin-American intellectuals which finds expression in a large outpouring of books and articles. Typical of works whose exaggerations affront the intelligence of the informed reader is Genaro Carnero Checa, *El águila rampante; el imperialismo yanqui sobre América Latina* (1956). Slightly more restrained are Jorge Castañeda, *Mexico y el orden internacional* (1956), and Ezéquiel Ramírez Novoa, *La farsa del panamericanismo y la unidad indoamericana* (1955).

The only newspaper index is that of the *New York Times.* However, *Noticias, Weekly Digest of Hemisphere Reports,* (1945——), issued by the

Bibliographical Note

Council of Inter-American Cooperation in affiliation with the National Foreign Trade Council, can also serve, on a limited scale, as an index to Latin-American reports, principally trade and financial, in a wide selection of newspapers and periodicals. *Hispanic American Report,* published by Hispanic American Studies of Stanford University, is a monthly report on developments in Spain, Portugal, and Latin America, based largely on current newspaper accounts. Finally, one of the most valuable bibliographical tools is the *Handbook of Latin American Studies,* an annual publication, since 1936, prepared originally by the Committee on Latin American Studies of the American Council of Learned Societies, and since 1948, by the Hispanic Foundation of the Library of Congress. The purpose of the *Handbook* is to furnish a cumulative and permanent body of reference materials (primary and secondary; books, articles, and pamphlets) in the fields of Latin-American social sciences and humanities. Each volume records, in the International Relations section, a year's harvest of selected published works relating to the inter-American regional arrangement.

Index

495

Index

Peru-Ecuador dispute, 168–169; claims of, to Antarctica, 187; defense measures of, 192; no defense-sites agreement with, 197; invokes Havana declaration, 210; at Rio Meeting, 211–212; breaks relations with Axis, 214; foreign policy of, 214; not in defense chain, 222; Nazi activities in, 230; U.S. procurements from, 243; pressured to declare war, 268; supports Argentina, 280; on juridical status of Peace Committee, 327; signs Military Assistance Agreement, 335; opposition in, to Military Assistance Agreement, 336; buys cruisers, 338; Communist Party in, 425; aids Korea, 430; anti-Americanism in, 452

China: on meaning of Article XXI, 91

China (Communist): recognized by Cuba, 426; purchases Cuban sugar, 458

Chiriboga, José Ricardo: urges police force, 405; invokes Rio treaty, 407

Churchill, Winston: on the Council of Europe, 13

Clark, J. Reuben: proposes declaration on mediation, 117

Clay, Henry: views on continental unity, 34–35; instructs delegates, 36–37; and the "American system," 466

Clay, J. Randolph: report on Lima Conference, 41; report on Santiago Conference, 43

Clayton, Will: on procurement contracts, 243; on economic policy of U.S., 265

Cleveland, Grover: and the conference project, 51

Colombia: negotiates treaties of confederation, 30–31; in Panama Congress, 38; at Lima Conference (1864), 44; at Washington Conference (1889), 55; original member of League, 88; peace proposal by, 105; member Washington Commission of Neutrals, 154; and Leticia question, 159–166; breaks relations, 210; declares war, 213; bases in, 221; signs Military Assistance Agreement, 335; buys frigate, 338; investment guarantee by, 361; dispute with Peru, 406; Communist

Party in, 425; recognizes Soviet satellites, 426; aids Korea, 430; in Korean War, 431

colonialism: Havana Meeting on, 325–326

Colonies and Occupied Territories in America (resolution): 317

Combate (Costa Rica): on U.S. anti-Communism, 463

Commercial Bureau of American Republics: created, 57; drafts conference agenda, 58–59; reorganized, 62

Committee for the Peaceful Solution of Conflicts: precursor of Peace Committee, 327

Committee of Experts on Codification of International Law: report by, 147–148

Committee of Twenty-one: appointed, 381; meets at Buenos Aires, 383–384; State Department statement to, 386

Committee on Inter-American Organizations: recommendations by, 320

Commodities Credit Corporation: 237

Communism: and Bogotá riots, 301; Bogotá resolution on, 317; in Brazil, 336; and anti-U.S. riots, 346; Catholic Church opposition to, 348; and Caribbean turmoil, 423; in Latin America, 424–427; condemned at Bogotá, 429; in Guatemala, 436–440; and Caracas Conference, 440–445; in Guatemala, 445–447; adopts new tactics, 453–455; "gradual approach" of, 454; in Cuba, 455–462 *passim*; downgraded by Latins, 481–482

Communists. *See* Communism

conciliation: bilateral treaties of, 74; at Washington Conference (1928), 106–107; in the Saavedra Lamas treaty, 119; applied to Haiti-Dominican dispute, 175–176

Conference of American States on Conciliation and Arbitration (Washington): acts, 106–109

Conference of Commissions of Inter-American Development: 337

consultation: value of, 181; in Caribbean controversies, 398–423 *passim*

Consultation Pact: analyzed, 129–130; embraces Monroe Doctrine,

Inter-American Neutrality Committee: activities of, 183; changed to Juridical Committee, 213; becomes Juridical Committee, 234

Inter-American Peace Committee: created, 190; added to security structure, 326–329; first investigation by, 391–392; investigates Haiti-Dominican Republic case, 396; special meeting of (1949), 397–399; unsuccessful resort to, 406; studies Cuban charges, 417; functions of, enlarged, 418; indicts Trujillo, 419; considers the Guatemala problem, 447–451; U.S. memorandum to, 455–456; added to peace structure, 471

Inter-American Reciprocal Assistance Treaty. *See* Rio treaty

inter-American security system: strengthened by crisis, 9–10; appraised (1914), 73–76; in 1917, 87; and League of Nations, 87–94 *passim*; relation of codification to, 121; resolution procedure in, 145; an appraisal (1939), 179–180; pre-Pearl Harbor political and military defense, 182–202 *passim*; pre-Pearl Harbor economic defense, 202–205; appraised in World War II, 242–248; prized by Latin America, 247–248; acquires status, 251–252; lauded by Sumner Welles, 252; integration of, into UN, 270–274; relation to the UN, 274–277; Latins obligated to vindicate, 276–277; as of 1950, 318–319; value of, to Latins, 479–480

—structure of: components of, in 1939, 149; topical outline of (1939), 149–152; economic components of, 152– 153; technical deficiences of, 176–179; project to strengthen, 249; strengthened by Mexico Conference, 264–265; strengthened at Bogotá, 302; organization of, 302–310; weakness of, 312–313; the economic component, 313–316 *passim*; structural and functional developments, 320–322; Peace Committee aded to, 326–327; component parts of, 468; perfected, 470–471

—operation of: early tests of, 109–111; put to test, 154–180; tested by Chaco War, 155–159; tested by Le-

ticia controversy, 159–166 *passim*; and by Ecuador-Peru boundary dispute, 166–170; and by Guatemala-Honduras boundary dispute, 170–171; and by Honduras-Nicaragua dispute, 171–174; and by Haiti–Dominican Republic dispute, 174–176; and by Caribbean turbulence, 391–423 *passim*; appraised in light of Caribbean tests, 421–422

inter-American solidarity: in World War I, 81–87 *passim*; Cantilo on, 140–141; affirmed by Declaration of Lima, 142; denied by Chaco War, 156; in World War II, 181, 209, 242–245; deterioration of, 319, 359; and anti-U.S. hostility, 341; economic factor weakens, 352–353; crumbling, 369; reaffirmed, 380; reinforced by Washington Meeting, 432–435 *passim*; foundation of, laid, 468; appraised, 472–475; recent threats to, 475–478; remedies for, 478–483; in the future, 483–484

Inter-American Specialized Conference on Continental Shelf and Marine Waters: at Ciudad Trujillo, 324–325

Inter-American Technical and Economic Conference: 237

Inter-American Treaty on Good Offices and Mediation (1936): ratifications of, 151

International Bank for Reconstruction and Development. *See* World Bank

International Bureau of American Republics: created, 62; activties enlarged, 68; reorganized, 72

International Central American Tribunal: created, 94; recourse to, avoided, 171

International Commission of Jurists: created by Rio Conference, 68; made permanent, 120–121

international Communism. *See* Communism

International Confederation of Free Trade Unions: on Cuban revolution, 456–457

International Conference of American Jurists: drafts referred to, 147

International Court of Justice: settles Honduras-Nicaragua case, 410

International High Commission: created by Financial Conference, 79

Index

Index

Index

Index

Index